Modelling, Simulation and Design Optimization

Modelling, Simulation and Design Optimization

Edited by Garrett Taylor

Clanrye International
www.clanryeinternational.com

Clanrye International,
750 Third Avenue, 9th Floor,
New York, NY 10017, USA

ISBN: 978-1-63240-653-8

Cataloging-in-Publication Data

Modelling, simulation and design optimization / edited by Garrett Taylor.
p. cm.
Includes bibliographical references and index.
ISBN 978-1-63240-653-8
1. Simulation methods. 2. Models and modelmaking. 3. Systems engineering.
4. Engineering design. 5. Engineering mathematics. I. Taylor, Garrett.
TA343 .M63 2018
620.004 4--dc23

For information on all Clanrye International publications
visit our website at www.clanryeinternational.com

CLANRYE INTERNATIONAL

Contents

Preface

This book on modelling, simulation and design optimization deals with the latest technologies used in the creation, visualization and analysis of a design. Computer software and computer systems are used for designing concepts and 2D and 3D models of the same are created for refinement and improvement. Dimensions and processes may be visualized through digital drafting techniques as well as raster graphics. It is a method that is used in a variety of industries ranging from aerospace and automotive engineering to molecular biology. The book is appropriate for students seeking detailed information in this area as well as for experts. It is an essential guide for both academicians and those who wish to pursue this discipline further.

The researches compiled throughout the book are authentic and of high quality, combining several disciplines and from very diverse regions from around the world. Drawing on the contributions of many researchers from diverse countries, the book's objective is to provide the readers with the latest achievements in the area of research. This book will surely be a source of knowledge to all interested and researching the field.

In the end, I would like to express my deep sense of gratitude to all the authors for meeting the set deadlines in completing and submitting their research chapters. I would also like to thank the publisher for the support offered to us throughout the course of the book. Finally, I extend my sincere thanks to my family for being a constant source of inspiration and encouragement.

Editor

Topology and generalized shape optimization: Why stress constraints are so important?

P.Duysinx[1a], L. Van Miegroet[1], E. Lemaire[1], O. Brüls[1], and M. Bruyneel[2]

[1] LTAS - Department of Aerospace and Mechanics, Institute of Mechanics and Civil Engineering, Université de Liège, 4000 Liege, Belgium
[2] Samtech S.A, Liege Science Park. 4031 Angleur, Belgium

Abstract –The paper continues along the work initiated by the authors in taking into account stress constraints in topology optimization of continuum structures. Revisiting some of their last developments in this field, the authors point out the importance of considering stress constraints as soon as the preliminary design phase, that is, to include stress constraints in the topology optimization problem in order to get the most appropriate structural layout. Numerical applications that can be solved using these new developments make possible to exhibit interesting results related to the specific nature of strength based structural layout for maximum strength compared to maximum stiffness. This particular character of stress design is clearly demonstrated in two kinds of situations: once several load cases are considered and when unequal stress limits in tension and compression are involved.

Key words: Topology optimization, stress constraints, compliant design

1 Introduction

Since Bendsøe and Kikuchi [3] have initiated a huge research domain with the so-called topology optimization, literature review (see for instance Bendsøe and Sigmund [4]) shows that the number of works considering stress constraints (see for instance Ref. [8,16, 21, 23]) is rather limited compared to the large number of studies that are based on stiffness problems. More recently a similar observation can be made when considering the recent field of generalized shape optimization using level set methods with pioneer works by Allaire et al. [1], Belytschko et al. [2], Wang and Wang [26]. Following the tracks of topology optimization, this new approach has mainly been focusing on compliance minimization problems than on stress constraints problems. Recently local stress constraints have been included as design restrictions by Van Miegroet and Duysinx [25]. The latter work shows it is possible to solve also the strength problem using a level set description of the geometry and an X-FEM solution for tackling non conforming meshes to the moving boundaries. However this kind of study remains rather seldom.

The 'compliance type' formulation has produced quite interesting results in many problems because controlling the energy and the displacements under the loads is generally good for deflection control and because, for one load case, the compliance minimization leads to a fully stressed design nearly everywhere in the structure (see for instance Rozvany and Birker [18], Rozvany [19, 20]). However there are theoretical results that clearly show that the strongest and the stiffest structural layout can be quite different. For example Rozvany and Birker [18] demonstrated that, for trusses, topology optimization can lead to different results when there are several load cases, different stress limits in tension and compression, or when there are several materials involved.

Therefore, the goal of the paper is to point out the importance of considering stress constraints as soon as the preliminary design phase, that is, to include stress constraints in the topology optimization problem in order to get the most appropriate structural lay-out. Revisiting some contributions of the authors [8, 9, 10], this paper aims at illustrating the key role of stress constraints in the framework of topology optimization of continuum structures. The developments of Ref. [9] and [10] have extended the work initiated in Ref. [8] to treat:

Integrated stress criteria (i.e. global) relaxed stress constraints that aggregate the stress constraints in each finite element in order to be able to circumvent the large scale character of the local stress constraints [9]. Integrated stress criterions are usual way to consider stress constraints in some work. However this study will show that optimal results obtained do not always have the same character as locally stress constrained designs but, because of the looser control of the stress level get closer to compliance minimization and to stiffness design.

Stress criteria that are able to tackle non equal stress limits in tension and compression [10]. Whereas the von Mises criterion is very usual to predict very precisely failure for ductile materials and metals, von Mises criterion is unable to predict real-life designs when the structure is made of materials with unequal stress limits like concrete or composite materials. One can also remember that thin structural members, like cables or thin sheets, are not able to sustain high compressive loads because of buckling. An indirect procedure to take into account this buckling constraint in the preliminary design phase consists in restricting the compressive loads by reducing the stress limit in compression. From a practical point of view these different behaviors in tension and compression result in quite specific designs.

Numerical applications that can be solved using these new developments make possible to point out interesting results related to the different nature of structural lay out for maximum strength compared to maximum stiffness. This one is

[a] Corresponding author: P.Duysinx@ulg.ac.be

clearly demonstrated in two kinds of particular situations: once several load cases are considered and when unequal stress limits in tension and compression are involved.

2 Problem formulation

2.1 Maximum stiffness and strength problem formulation

In the following we consider two kinds of problems. The first one is the classic compliance minimization problem subject to a volume constraint. If the equilibrium equation after discretization by finite element writes K qk = fk where K is the stiffness matrix, fk and qk are respectively the load vector and the generalized displacement vector of the load case number 'k', the minimum compliance problem can be formulated as the following min-max problem:

$$\begin{aligned} &\min_{0\le\rho(x)\le 1} \quad \max_{k} f_k^T q_k \\ &s.t. \quad V=\int_\Omega \rho(x)\, dx \le \bar{V} \end{aligned} \tag{1}$$

$\rho(x)$ is the material density at point x. Compliance minimization problem gives rise to the stiffest structural design for the given load case measured in energy norm.

The second problem considered is the problem of maximum strength. In the following the maximum strength problem is the stress constrained optimization problem. In this study strength problem will be formulated as the following: finding the structural topology design that supports the applied loads using a minimum amount of material while avoiding the material failure everywhere in the structure.

$$\begin{aligned} &\min_{0\le\rho(x)\le 1} \quad \int_\Omega \rho(x)\, dx \\ &s.t. \quad \|\sigma^{eq}(\rho(x),x)\|\le T \quad if\ \rho(x)>0 \end{aligned} \tag{2}$$

where $\|\sigma^{eq}(\rho(x),x)\|$ is an equivalent stress criterion which predicts the failure of the material at point x while T is the stress limit. Usually Von Mises criterion is considered, but we can also use other criteria in order to take into account different stress limits in tension and compression. Please note also that, in this study, a pure elastic regime is assumed, so that the criterion predicts the end of the elastic behavior everywhere in the material (and in the microstructure).

2.2 Topology optimization problem

Generalized shape optimization of structures without any a priori on the structural topology can be achieved by formulating the problem as an optimal material distribution on a given design domain (see Bendsøe and Sigmund [4]). As the optimal material distribution problem is generally solved numerically using a finite element discretization approach, the design domain is divided into finite elements and a density variable is attached to each element. The optimal material distribution problem could be solved as a discrete valued problem, but this approach is very complicated because of its highly combinatorial nature. Here this highly combinatorial formulation is avoided by considering an alternative formulation in which we allow the density parameter running continuously from void to solid via all intermediate densities, so that composite materials of intermediate densities are included in the design. The continuous formulation presents the advantage to allow using sensitivity analysis and mathematical programming algorithms to solve the problem in an efficient way. Unfortunately the discretized problem is ill-posed and its numerical solutions are mesh-dependent. To overcome the difficulty, we use here a restriction method of the design space based on a bound over the perimeter [13], a low-pass filtering scheme [22], or a combination of both.

The modelling of the intermediate density properties is based on the power-law model (also called SIMP model [4]). If the script * denotes the effective properties of the porous material and the index 0 is relative to the solid material properties, the effective Young's modulus E^* is given in term of the density ρ by:

$$E^* = \rho^p E^0 \tag{3}$$

The factor p is introduced to penalize the intermediate densities in order to end up with 'black and white' designs. Moreover to consider stress constraints in continuous topology optimization, one also needs the definition of a relevant stress measure in the porous composites. Following the approach developed in Duysinx and Bendsøe [8] we consider an overall stress measure that controls the stress state in the microstructure. For the SIMP model of stiffness, a careful study [8] showed that a power-law model with the same power p is a consistent model for the micro-stresses σ_{ij} :

$$\sigma_{ij} = \sigma^*_{ij} / \rho^p \tag{4}$$

Therefore if the failure is predicted by a quadratic failure criterion $\|\sigma^{eq}\|$ like von Mises equivalent criterion, the first failure in the microstructure of the porous composites is predicted by the following criterion in terms of effective stresses:

$$\|\sigma^{eq}(\rho)\| = {}^*\sigma^{eq} / \rho^p \le T \tag{5}$$

3 Stress constraints in topology optimization

3.1 Stress singularity phenomenon

At first it is interesting to remind the reader with a very important difficulty that arises when dealing with stress constraints in topology optimization. As it has been shown for instance in Kirsch [14] and in Cheng and Jiang [6], topology optimization with stress constraints is subject to the so-called 'singularity phenomenon'. At short the paradox comes from the fact that the optimization procedure is often unable to remove or to add some vanishing members without violating the stress constraints although one would end up with a perfectly feasible design if they were removed or added. From a mathematical point of view, the classical gradient based math programming algorithms, which rely on the Karush-Kuhn-Tucker optimality conditions, are unable to reach some optimum configurations because of the degeneracy of the design space. In order to turn around the difficulty, one has to use a perturbation technique of the stress constraints, generally known as the relaxation technique (Cheng and Guo [7]) that results in a relaxation of the stress limits in the low-density regions. In this paper we use the following relaxed formulation of the overall stress criterion (see Ref. [8]):

$$\frac{1}{T}\frac{{}^{*}\sigma^{eq}}{\rho^{p}}-\frac{\varepsilon}{\rho}+\varepsilon\leq 1 \qquad (6)$$

This relaxed formulation of the stress constraints is considered in the numerical solution of the topology optimization problem with stress constraints. The solution procedure requires solving of a sequence of perturbed problems with decreasing values of the parameter ε.

3.2 Integrated global stress criterion

In Duysinx and Bendsøe [8] the stress is treated as a local constraint, i.e. for every finite element. This formulation offers a full control of the stress state, but it also dramatically increases the size of the optimization problem and thus the computation time of the solution. Here we propose an alternative approach based on an integrated version of the □-relaxed failure criterion. The global stress constraint (i.e. integrated constraint) simplifies the computational complexity of the optimization problem at the expense of a weaker control of the local stress state. A key issue is to take into account the 'singularity phenomenon' of the stress constraints. So an original aspect is to include simultaneously the □-relaxation technique that alleviates the singularity phenomenon and the use of effective stress criteria into the global stress constraint.

We propose to consider two global measures of the relaxed distributed stress criterion. The first global constraint is the '*q-norm*' of the relaxed stress criterion (6); the second one is the '*q-mean*' of the relaxed stress criterion (7).

$$\left[\sum_{e=1}^{N}\left(\max\left\{0,\frac{1}{T}\frac{({}^{*}\sigma^{eq})_{e}}{\rho_{e}^{p}}-\frac{\varepsilon}{\rho_{e}}+\varepsilon\right\}\right)^{q}\right]^{1/q}\leq 1 \quad (7)$$

$$\left[\frac{1}{N}\sum_{e=1}^{N}\left(\max\left\{0,\frac{1}{T}\frac{({}^{*}\sigma^{eq})_{e}}{\rho_{e}^{p}}-\frac{\varepsilon}{\rho_{e}}+\varepsilon\right\}\right)^{q}\right]^{1/q}\leq 1 \quad (8)$$

To prevent negative valued relaxed criteria from contributing to the norms, one must consider the maximum value of the relaxed stress criterion and zero. Negative values of the relaxed criterion appear only for low stressed elements and thus can be truncated without influencing the global constraint. Furthermore, the function remains continuous up to derivative '*q-1*', so that the constraint remains sufficiently smooth. A major advantage of '*q-norm*' and '*q-mean*' functions comes from the fact that they make possible to set bounds of the maximum value of the relaxed criterion by upper or by lower values. The '*q-norm*' is an upper bound of the maximum value of the criterion while the '*q-mean*' is a lower bound of the maximum local value of the criterion. In addition this gap closes to 0 when '*q*' value is going to infinity. So sharp bounding needs to take high values of '*q*' parameter. However in practice, we take $q=4$ because it allows controlling weakly the maximum value of the stress criterion while avoiding ill-conditioned optimization problems.

3.3 Different stress limits in tension and compression

As in most of metallic structural problems, stress constrained topology optimization is usually based on the quadratic von Mises criterion, which predicts the end of elastic behavior. However Von Mises is inappropriate to predict different behaviors in tension and compression. For this kind of behavior, one requires particular failure criteria that are able to cope with unequal stress limits as in studies related to composite materials or concrete and rocks. Based on the work of Laschet [15] and Boresi et al. [5] that reviewed different criteria that are able to cater with unequal compressive and tensile stress limits, we have selected two criteria generally used in prediction of plastic design of adhesive materials: Rhagava [17] and Ishai [12] criteria. Both are quadratic criteria which predict a different behavior in tension and compression through the dependency of the criterion upon the first invariant of the stresses. Let's remind the reader with the definition of the first stress invariant $J_1=\sigma_{ii}$ and the second deviator stress invariant $J_{2D}=0.5s_{ij}s_{ij}$. The second deviator stress tensor is directly related to the distortional shear stress τ_0 and to the equivalent von Mises stress σ_{VM}: $3J_{2D}=\tau_0^2=\sigma_{VM}^2$. The presence of the second invariant is obvious because the two criteria have to recover the von Mises criterion when the stress limits are equal. The first invariant is related to the hydrostatic pressure $J_1=3\sigma_h$ and its presence in the criterion is essential since it introduces the dependence upon the sign of the stress state and hence the different behaviors in tension and compression.

The Rhagava [17] and Ishai [12] stress criteria and the related equivalent stress can be written as:

$$\sigma_{RAG}^{eq}=\frac{J_1(s-1)+\sqrt{J_1^2(s-1)^2+12J_{2D}s}}{2s}\leq T$$
$$\sigma_{ISH}^{eq}=\frac{(s+1)\sqrt{3J_{2D}}+(s-1)J_1}{2s}\leq T \qquad (9)$$

In which we have used the following notations: T and C are the stress limits (in absolute value) respectively in tension and compression, while '*s*' is the ratio between the stress limits in compression and in tension: $s=C/T$.

As it is demonstrated in Laschet [15], the Raghava criterion can also be viewed as a particular case of Tsai-Wu criterion of orthotropic materials when one assumes that the stress limits along the 3 orthotropy directions are the same. The Ishai criterion belongs to the Drucker-Prager plasticity criterion family that is of a general use for chalk, rocs and soils materials. The two criteria can be compared in Fig. 1 and 2 where their failure envelopes are plotted in the space (σ_h , τ_0) of the hydrostatic pressure and of the distortional shear stress. At first the failure surface of the Raghava approach is a parabolic curve whereas the Ishai criterion is a hyperbolic one. But from the figures, one also notices that the two theories predict the failure for different maximum hydrostatic pressures and for different pure distortional shear stresses. The pure hydrostatic stress limit predicted by the Ishai theory is twice the Raghava's one. We remind the reader that this hydrostatic failure stress is infinite in von Mises theory. Failure under a pure shear stress state is also different in the two theories. The pure distortional shear stress limit for Raghava's theory is always greater than Ishai's one because $\sqrt{s}\geq 2s/(s+1)$

4 Implementation and sensitivity analysis

The implementation of topology optimization including stress constraints has been realized in computer code coupling a finite element analysis code, its sensitivity analysis and an optimization solver based on the *sequential convex programming approach*. The finite element code has 4-node and 9-node plane stress finite elements. The optimization is based here on the CONLIN solver by Fleury [13]. This architecture is now classical. However because of the large number of stress constraints to consider, there is a general interest in describing the guidelines of the implementation of the sensitivity analysis of stress criteria. Here the work is detailed for the Ishai and Raghava criteria that generalize von Mises criterion (s=1).

The equilibrium equation after discretization by finite element writes $\boldsymbol{K}\,\boldsymbol{q}=\boldsymbol{f}$ where $\boldsymbol{K}$ is the stiffness matrix, $\boldsymbol{q}$ is the generalized displacement vector and $\boldsymbol{f}$ is the load vector. In a vector form the macroscopic stress in the finite element is given by $\boldsymbol{\sigma}=\boldsymbol{T}\,\boldsymbol{q}$ where $\boldsymbol{T}$ is the stress matrix of the element. The two first invariants of the stress in the finite element that are required to calculate the equivalent stress criteria can also be written in matrix form:

$$J_1^* = 3\sigma_h^* = w^T\sigma = Wq$$
$$J_{2D}^* = 1/3\,\left(\sigma_{VM}^*\right)^2 = 1/3\,q^T V q \tag{10}$$

As the stress matrix depends linearly upon the stiffness properties, one can also write $T=\rho^p\,T^0$ where $\boldsymbol{T^0}$ is the stress matrix of an element of relative density of 1. In the same way the influence of density can be put in evidence in matrices $\boldsymbol{W}$ and $\boldsymbol{V}$: $V=\rho^{2p}V^0$ and $W=\rho^p W^0$ where matrices the $\boldsymbol{V^0}$ and $\boldsymbol{W^0}$ are respectively the von Mises stress matrix and the hydrostatic stress matrix of the solid element.

Therefore one can evaluate easily the effective failure criteria based on Ishai and Raghava theories with the following expressions:

$$\|\sigma_{ISH}^{eq}\| = {}^*\sigma_{ISH}^{eq}/\rho^p = \frac{s-1}{2s}W^0 q + \frac{s+1}{2s}\sqrt{q^T V^0 q} \tag{11}$$

$$\|\sigma_{RAG}^{eq}\| = {}^*\sigma_{RAG}^{eq}/\rho^p = \frac{(s-1)W^0 q + \sqrt{(s-1)^2 (W^0 q)^2 + 4 s q^T V^0 q}}{2s} \tag{12}$$

Sensitivity analysis can also be implemented efficiently for Ishai and Raghava criteria as it can be done for Von Mises theory. As only the guidelines of the implementation are presented we give only the main results of the derivation calculus.

For Ishai equivalent stress, we get:

$$\frac{\partial\|\sigma_{ISH}^{eq}\|}{\partial\rho_i} = \left\{\frac{s-1}{2s}W^0 + \frac{s+1}{2s}\frac{1}{\sqrt{q^T V^0 q}}V^0 q\right\}^T \frac{\partial q}{\partial \rho_i} \tag{13}$$

Raghava criterion is a bit more difficult. After some calculus the derivative of the averaged stress criterion can be written as:

$$\frac{\partial\|\sigma_{RAG}^{eq}\|}{\partial\rho_i} = \left\{\frac{s-1}{2s}\frac{\|\sigma_{RAG}^{eq}\|}{\sqrt{(s-1)^2 (W^0 q)^2 + 4 s\, q^T V^0 q}}W^0 + \frac{2}{\sqrt{(s-1)^2 (W^0 q)^2 + 4 s\, q^T V^0 q}}V^0 q\right\}^T \frac{\partial q}{\partial \rho_i} \tag{14}$$

In a direct approach of the sensitivity analysis one would evaluate all the derivatives of the generalized displacements $\partial q/\partial\rho_i$, which could be a major work in topology optimization. However the number of active stress constraints is generally smaller than the number of design variables and the adjoined method is generally preferred because only one additional load case is required per active constraint. In this case the adjoined load vector is the vector that is put between curly braces.

One will also notice that a strategy to delete stress constraints that are likely not to be active during the optimization iteration is very useful to reduce as much as possible to dimension of the optimization problem. Stress constraints are simply evaluated and we save the sensitivity analysis.

5 Numerical applications

5.1 Two-bar truss problem

The first application is the classic two-bar truss problem. Despite its simplicity the two-bar truss problem is an interesting example to illustrate the difficulties of stress constraints in topology optimization. Indeed even if the lay-out of the solution is the obvious two-bar truss for equal stress constraints and the von Mises stress criterion (see Fig. 3 top), one have to be able to overcome the problem of the singular stress paradox. The part of the design domain that is enclosed inside the two bars remains highly strained and thus highly stressed while all its material vanishes. Without the relaxation technique it is impossible to remove totally this part.

In the framework of unequal stress limits the second point of interest is to be able to check the analytical solution for this problem. The analytical solution has been exhibited by Rozvany [19] while discussing shortcoming of Michell's truss theory. When adopting a tensile stress limit is 3 times higher than the compressive stress limit, the solution is still a two bar truss, but the two bars make an angle of 30° and 60° degrees respectively with the foundation wall. Ishai equivalent stress is adopted to take into account the different stress limits effect. The optimized material distribution is presented in Fig.3 (lbottom). The numerical result totally matches the theoretical prediction, which validates the method. It also shows immediately that stress constraints can modify at least the optimal solution of topology optimization, at least in terms of shape.

5.2 Three-bar truss problem

The 3-bar truss problem is very well suited to illustrate the specific character of maximum strength versus stiffness design when considering several load cases in topology optimization. The geometry of the problem is given in Figure 4. The sizes and material data of the benchmark are normalized: L=1m, W=2.5m, E=100N/m², ν=0.3. Three load cases (with different magnitudes and orientations) are applied at the center of the free edge. The design domain is meshed with 50 x 20 finite elements. This means that for local stress constraints one has to deal with 3 x 1000 restrictions. The volume bound is set to 25% of the design domain area.

At first, the minimum compliance design (minimum of the maximum of the compliance for the three load cases) is studied (Figure 5a). The optimal topology is clearly a 2-bar truss. Compliances for the 3 load cases are equal to 73.3 Nm. A posteriori computation of the stress level in the two-bar truss solution shows that the stress level is quite high. The maximum value of the local von Mises criterion varies from 228 N/m² to 571 N/m² per load case. In a second optimization run one investigates the strength problem and one considers local von Mises stress constraints with a stress limit of 150 N/m² and one obtains the topology of Figure 5b, which is a 3-bar truss. The compliances of the minimum stress design solution are a bit bigger than minimum compliance solution (91.2 Nm, 45.6 Nm and 45.0 Nm for load cases 1, 2 and 3). This means that the compliance design (a two-bar truss) with nearly the same volume is overstressed by nearly a factor 1.5 compared to the maximum strength design. This also shows that the three-bar truss is not a local optimum but clearly an alternative design to the two –bar truss with a different topology. This also points out that compliance designs and minimum stress designs can lead to different topology solutions when there are several load cases.

One can further compare the local stress constraint formulation and the alternative approaches based on global restrictions (‘*q-mean*’ and ‘*q-norm*’ with q=4) with optimization runs presented in Figures 6. One has the solution when minimizing the volume of material with a (heuristic) bound of 92 N/m² over *the ‘q-mean’* of relaxed von Mises stresses (Figure 6a). The area of the optimal design solution is 0.56 m². In Figure 6b, the bound over ‘*q-norm*’ is set to 500 N/m² and the optimal area is 0.62 m². Topology results, which are 2-bar truss designs in both cases, look more like the compliance design and not like the local stress constrained design. This suggests that once we lose the control over the local stress state, we get closer to a global criterion like the minimum compliance design. However considering the stress constraints even in a “globalized way” is favorable to reduce the maximum local stress values compared to the compliance design. For ‘*q-mean*’ one has the following maximum von Mises stresses: 237 N/m², 215 N/m², and 207 N/m² for the first, second and third load cases. For the ‘*q-norm*’ on has a maximum von Mises stresses of 230 N/m², 235 N/m², and 231 N/m² respectively for the three load cases. One advantage of the stress constraint global approach is to allow saving one or two orders of magnitude in the optimizer solution time compared to the local stress approach, but we lose the very specific character of the stress constrained design.

Finally one can exploit the example to appreciate the effect of unequal stress limits in tension and compression and Ishai criterion. Figure 7 shows the optimum material distribution for unequal stress limits with Ishai criterion (T=150 N/m² and C=450 N/m² in Fig 7left and T=450 N/m² and C=150 N/m² in Fig.7 right). Both optimal lay-out configurations are once again two-bar trusses but their geometry is different in order to make use of the better strength respectively in tension or in compression. When the material is very resistant to compressive stresses, middle and left bars merge. Conversely when material is very good in tension, the optimal structure looks like a cable structure. This shows that real characteristics of the problem, here the unequal properties in tension and compression, may strongly influence topology results.

5.3 Four-bar truss problem

The third example stems from an application initially suggested by Swan and Kosaka [24] to demonstrate that ultimate strength optimization can lead to substantially different results from a minimum elastic compliance design. In the present study the same example is revisited in the framework of first failure stress constraints and elastic behavior. The design domain is a square (L= 1m) clamped in its four corners. A unit load is applied downwards in the center of the square domain. Using a normalized material (E=100N/m² and ν=0.3) one bounds at first the von Mises equivalent stress to T=C=10 N/m² (see Fig 8-left). The same optimal topologies could be obtained for minimum compliance as for minimum volume subject to stress constraints. It is cross-like structure that withstands the load in tension (upper members) and compression (lower members). Now if one uses a material that has a better strength limit in compression than in tension (T=6 N/m², C=24 N/m²), the optimal structure (Fig 8-center) is an arch that works only in compression. Conversely if the material works better in tension than in compression (T=24 N/m², C=6 N/m²) one gets a structure (Fig. 8-right) working exclusively in tension like cables in suspension bridges. We have also to remark that the results for unequal stress limits have been made with the Ishai criterion, but the same results can be obtained with the Raghava criterion since they give exactly the same strength for members under a one dimensional stress state as here.

6 Conclusion and perspectives

Based on some developments of topology optimization of continuum structures including stress constraints, this work has provided several illustrative examples of the conjuncture that structural lay-out may be different for maximum stiffness and strength as soon as we have several load cases (even in metallic materials) and / or when we have a different behavior in tension and compression. The conclusion of the work leads to stress that designers have to pay attention to the relevant constraint for their problems as soon as the preliminary design phase and to include them early in the design process.

The specific character of structural lay-outs when including stress constraints encourages the authors to develop further research work in order to cope efficiently with local constraints in many design problems such MEMS design, material microstructure tailoring, etc. Stress constraints states also several challenges for research such developing solution algorithms able to handle more efficiently optimization problems with fast growing size rising up to one million of design variables and several hundred thousand of constraints.

Acknowledgments

Part of this research has been realized under research project ARC 03/08-298 'Modeling, Multiphysics Simulation and Optimization of Coupled Problems - Application to Micro ElectroMechanical Systems' supported by the Communauté Française de Belgique. The authors want to thank Professor C. Fleury for making the CONLIN software available.

References

1. G. Allaire F. Jouve, A.M. Toader, Structural optimization using sensitivity analysis and a level-set method. *Journal of Computational Physics.* **194**, 363-393 (2004).
2. T. Belytschko, S. Xiao, C. Parimi, Topology optimization with implicit functions and regularization. *Int. J. Num. Meth. in Engng,* **57**, 1177-1196 (2003).
3. M.P. Bendsøe, N. Kikuchi, Generating Optimal Topologies in Structural Design Using a Homogenization Method. *Computer Methods in Applied Mechanics and Engineering,* **71**, 197-224 (1988).
4. M.P. Bendsøe, O. Sigmund, *Topology optimization: theory, methods, and applications.* (Springer Verlag 2003).
5. A.P. Boresi, R.T. Schmidt, O.M. Sidebottom, *Advanced Mechanics of Materials*. (5th Edition. John Wiley and Sons, New York 1993).
6. G.D. Cheng, Z. Jiang, *Difficulties in truss topology optimization with stress constraints. Eng. Optim.*, **20**, 129-148 (1992).
7. G.D. Cheng, X. Guo, *ε-relaxed approach in structural topology optimization. Struct. Opt.,* **13**, 258-266 (1997).
8. Duysinx P. and M.P. Bendsøe. (1998). Topology optimization of continuum structures with local stress constraints. In: Int. J. Num. Meth. Engng., 43, 1453-1478.
9. P. Duysinx, O. Sigmund. *New developments in handling stress constraints in optimal material distribution. In*: proceedings of 7th Symposium on Multidisciplinary Analysis and Optimization A1AA-98-4906, 1501-1509 (1998).
10. P. Duysinx, *Topology optimization with different stress limit in tension and compression, In*: Proceedings of the Third World Congress of Structural and Multidisciplinary Optimization WCSMO3, Buffalo (NY-USA 1999).
11. C. Fleury, *Mathematical programming methods for constrained optimization: dual methods. In*: volume 150 of Progresses in Astronautics and Aeronautics (M.P. Kamat ed.) 183-208, AIAA (1993).
12. S. Geli, G. Dolex, O. Ishai, *An effective stress/strain concept in the mechanical characterization of the structural adhesive bonding*. Int. J. of Adhesion & Adhesives, **1981**, 135-140 (1981).
13. R.B. Haber, C.S. Jog, M.P. Bendsøe, *A new approach to variable-topology shape design using a constraint on perimeter.* Struct. Opt., **11**, 1-12 (1996).
14. U. Kirsch, *On singular topologies in optimum structural design*. Struct. Opt. **2**, 133-142 (1990).
15. G. Laschet, *Prédiction par eléments finis du comportement non linéaire et de la résistance d'assemblage multimatériaux collés*. Ph.D. thesis. University of Liège (in French, 1991).
16. J.T. Pereira, E.A. Fancello, C.S. Barcellos, *Topology optimization of continuum structures with material failure constraints.* Structural Multidisciplinary Optimization **26**, 50-66 (2004).
17. R. Raghava, R.M. Caddel, G.S. Yeh, *the macroscopic yield behaviour of polymers.* Journal of Material Sciences, **8**, 225-232 (1973).
18. G.I.N. Rozvany, T. Birker, *On singular topologies in exact layout optimization*. Struct. Opt., **8**, 228-235 (1994).
19. G.I.N. Rozvany, *Some shortcomings in Michell's truss theory*. Struct. Opt., **12**, 244-250 (1996).
20. G.I.N Rozvany, *Exact analytical solutions for some popular benchmark problems in topology optimization.* Struct. Opt., **15**, 42-48 (1998).
21. P.Y. Shim, S. Manoocheri. *Generating optimal configurations in structural design using simulated annealing.* International Journal for Numerical Methods in Engineering. **40**, 1053-1069 (1997).
22. O. Sigmund. *On the design of compliant mechanisms using topology optimization*, Mechanics of Machines and Structures, **25**, 493-526 (1997).
23. M. Stolpe, K. Svanberg. *On the trajectory of the e-relaxation approach for stress-constrained truss topology optimization.* Structural Multidisciplinary Optimization **21**, 140-151 (2001).
24. C.C. Swan, I. Kosaka, *Voigt-reuss topology optimization for structures with nonlinear material behaviors*. International Journal for Numerical Methods in Engineering, **40**, 3785-3814 (1997).
25. L. Van Miegroet P. Duysinx. *Stress concentration minimization of 2D filets using X-FEM and level set description.* Structural Multidisciplinary Optimization, **33**, 425-438 (2007).
26. M. Wang, X. Wang, D. Guo. *A Level Set method structural topology optimization*. Comp. Methods in Appl. Mech Engng, **191**:227-246 (2003).

2

Multi-Body Simulation and Multi-Objective Optimization Applied to Vehicle Dynamics

Fabiano Maggio[1,a]

[1] EnginSoft S.p.A., Via Giambellino 7, 35129, Padova, Italy

Abstract – This paper describes a demo application, where modeFRONTIER, a commercial software for design optimization, is coupled with a parametric 2D Multi-Body model of a touring motorcycle. The optimizer is asked to identify the characteristics of the front suspension (telelever scheme) that deliver more safety, more stability, and more riding comfort for a braking maneuver in straight running. All objectives are described through 4 scalar indexes, extracted from the braking kinematics.

As expected, results highlight that trade-off relationships connect the objectives. Only 13, among the 1900 tested configurations, are able to simultaneously improve the 4 indexes. Moreover, no design in this selection assures a decisive improvement of the stability. In order to accomplish this priority requirement, the best design is chosen accepting a slight reduction of stability.

Key words: Motorcycle Optimization, Braking Maneuver, Telelever, Multi-Objective Optimization, Design Optimization

1 Introduction

Dynamical performances of two wheeled vehicles largely depend on the response of each component. Among all components, tires and suspensions are the most important sub-systems, because their role is to modulate any force going from the road to the chassis [1, 2, 3, 4]. Therefore, a deep knowledge of such parts can be the turning key to develop better and safer motorcycles.

Multi-Body Simulation is the most suitable approach to perform vehicle dynamics investigation [5, 6, 7]. By creating parametric models, different configurations can be quickly evaluated, even at the earliest stage of the entire development process. From a business perspective, this means that wrong gateways can be dropped long before they lead to costly and useless real prototypes.

These benefits can be further increased by coupling the Multi-Body Simulation software with modeFRONTIER, which automatically plans and drives sets of simulations in order to perform complex tasks such as Design of Experiment, Parameter Sensitivity Analysis, and Multi-Objective Optimization.

This paper describes a demo application, where modeFRONTIER is asked to identify the parameters of a motorcycle front suspension to deliver more safety, more stability, and more riding comfort for a braking maneuver in straight running. Although the research is targeted to a very specific case, the proposed methodology can be straightforwardly extended to any user-defined running condition. Potentially, it is possible to build a single modeFRONTIER project to optimize different vehicle parts for various maneuvers.

As expected, results highlight that trade-off relationships connect the objectives, hence full optimization is almost impossible. Only 13, among the 1900 tested configurations, are able to simultaneously improve the 4 scalar indexes that have been previously defined to measure the objectives. Moreover, no design in this selection promises a decisive improvement of the stability. In order to meet these primary requirements, the best design is chosen accepting a slight reduction of stability. The decision task has been totally supported by the Multi Criteria Decision Making tool implemented in modeFRONTIER.

2 The 2D Motorcycle Model

The Motorcycle is a complex multi-body system and special efforts are necessary to reliably simulate the overall dynamics. The broad range of literature available on this topic covers all simulation fields, such as time domain behavior [6, 7], optimal maneuver [8, 9], steady trim [10], frequency response [11], modal properties [5, 14, 15], tire dynamics [12], and so on. Since this research aims at highlighting the benefits of implementing an optimizer into the simulation chain, a detailed and validated model is not available. Model features have been implemented following state-of-art guidelines [13] to ensure sufficient result reliability.

As a simple test case, the vehicle behavior at braking during straight line motion is considered. In general, lateral dynamics plays an important role and a detailed 3D model would be recommended to perform thorough investigation. However, a 2D model includes enough features to study the influence of the front suspension on the braking distance, keeping the simulation complexity at reasonable level. Indirect considerations on stability and vehicle comfort can be made in any event by examining the variation of some in-plane quantities [4, 14].

The motorcycle model used in this research consists of 7 rigid bodies, such as chassis (which includes the rider), rear wheel, swinging arm, front wheel and three bodies for the front suspension with telelever scheme. Bodies are connected using proper joints to obtain the exact number of in-plane degrees of freedom.

[a] Corresponding author: f.maggio@enginsoft.it

2.1 Front Suspension

A special description is required for the fully parametric front suspension geometry (Fig.1).

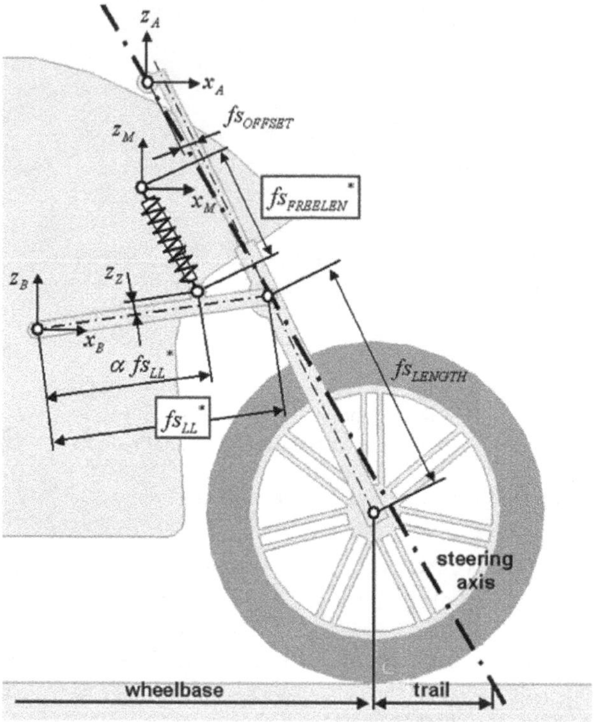

Fig. 1. Front Suspension layout and geometrical parameters (inputs for the optimization problem)

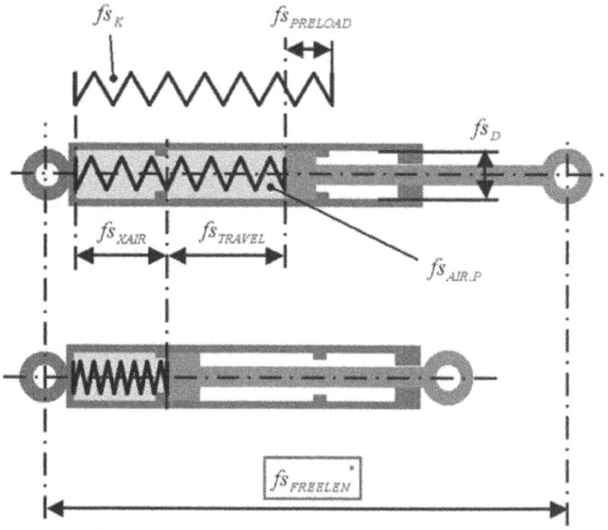

Fig. 2 Parameters for the Spring-Damper assembly (further inputs for the optimization problem)

Parameters allow to change the position of "A", "B", and "M" pins with respect to the chassis. Also, front fork offset, lower fork length, and the main link characteristics are adjustable. Suspension geometry directly affects important vehicle dimensions such as wheelbase, mechanical trail, and center of gravity height. Wheelbase and center of mass position play a fundamental role in determining the vehicle braking response. Since this research only aims at studying the suspension effects on the braking response, some tricks are used to make the above quantities almost independent from the general parameter assignment.

The spring-damper assembly (Fig. 2) is also included in the parameterization. The overall force is obtained by combining the action of a linear spring and a pressurized air piston. The working travel is governed by two high stiff end-stroke pads. Initial preload is obtained by assigning a non-zero air pressure and by imposing a partial compression of the spring. The linear damper has different coefficients for the elongation and compression phases. The free length of the assembly is calculated in order to keep the center of mass height constant when performing the static assembly.

2.2 Tire

Tires are modeled to accurately describe the generation of the longitudinal force. In accordance with Pacejka's formula [16], the longitudinal force S is a non-linear function of the longitudinal slip and a linear function of the vertical load. The D_x coefficient controls the maximum force that the tire can generate (adherence factor), whereas the others govern the shape of the force function. Maximum occurs for low slip ratio, whereas high slip leads to tire saturation and smaller forces. The tire model implemented here does not take into account any delay between slip and force raising.

Effective rolling radius:

$$r_e = r - \delta \tag{1}$$

Longitudinal slip:

$$\kappa = (V - \omega r_e)/V \tag{2}$$

Vertical load:

$$N = k_r\, \delta_r + c_r \dot{\delta}_r \tag{3}$$

Longitudinal force:

$$\begin{aligned} \psi &= C_x \arctan\{B_x\kappa - E_x[B_x\kappa - \arctan(B_x\kappa)]\} \\ S &= N D_x \sin(\psi) \end{aligned} \tag{4}$$

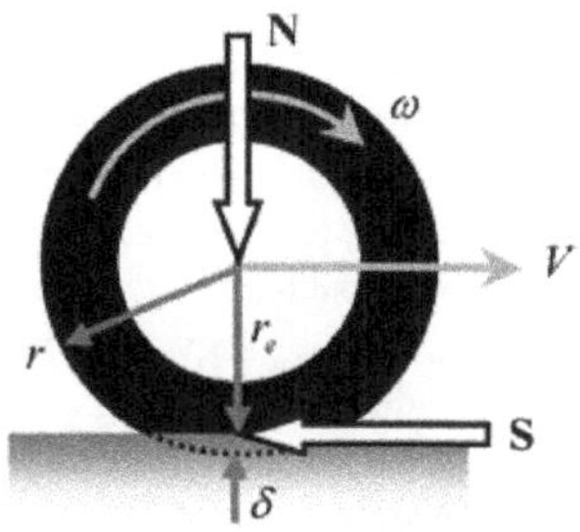

Fig. 3. Tire model

2.3 Braking Control

The simulation reproduces a typical emergency situation where the front brake is activated to stop the motorcycle from straight running at 130 km/h. The front brake simply reduces the angular speed of the front wheel, increasing the longitudinal slip that modulates the longitudinal braking force. During the entire maneuver, the vertical load is transferred from rear to front tire, proportionally to the deceleration [4]. This means that the front tire becomes capable of generating a greater braking force.

Braking dynamics are governed by two practical limits. In case of good adherence, the front braking force can become high enough to cause the lift of the rear wheel (stoppie condition). On the contrary, with small values of the D_x coefficient, the front tire reaches its saturation point and the front wheel locks.

The planned optimization makes sense if a control system (Fig. 4) instantaneously calculates the braking torque that leads to the maximum braking force, with no rear wheel lift. This will fully exploit the motorcycle's braking capabilities. If any suspension update (design generation) affects these capabilities, the simulation will be able to capture such effect.

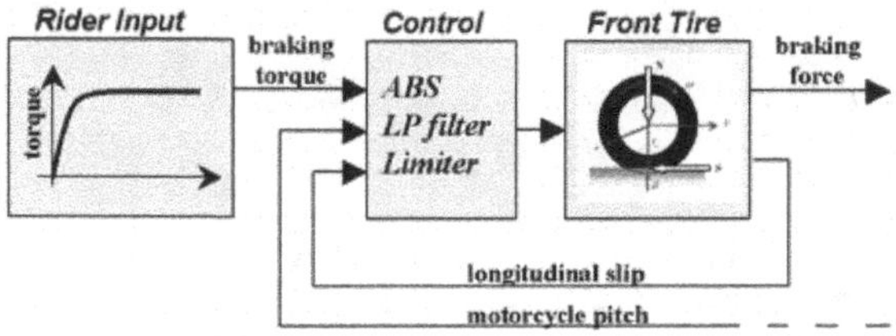

Fig. 4. Braking control

3 Optimization Problem and Objectives

The suspension characteristics influence both the way the braking force is generated (transient phase) and its value in steady condition (constant deceleration phase). It is expected that by changing the suspension parameters, it will be possible to obtain a higher force at a shorter interval, and hence a reduction of the total stopping distance. This is the most important objective for the optimization problem.

During the braking maneuver, both the wheelbase and the trail tend to get shorter, usually causing a reduction of the lateral vehicle stability [13, 14]. These phenomena can be limited by choosing an opportune suspension layout. Therefore, two objectives corresponding to trail and wheelbase shortenings are defined.

Table 1. Objectives and their priority

Quantity	Field	Pr	Baseline	Objective
trail variation	stability	2	-7.4 mm	increase
wheelbase variation	stability	3	-5.1 mm	increase
stopping distance	safety	1	81.7 m	decrease
pitch angle variation	comfort	4	3.7 deg	decrease

A further consequence of any braking action is the pitching forward of the motorcycle. This is not necessarily a problem, but excessive pitching might disturb the rider. For this reason, we ask the optimizer to identify designs that also limit the pitching.

All of the optimization objectives are listed in Table 1, which includes also the performances given by the baseline motorcycle (i.e. initial design).

4 Software Implementation

The parametric motorcycle model has been developed using commercial multi-body software. Geometrical properties for the initial design have been indirectly measured from digital pictures, whereas inertial properties have been estimated. Control routines have been written in FORTRAN code and then linked to the main model. VISUAL BASIC modules have also been written to automatically export time domain results at the end of each simulation.

The workflow is fully defined in the modeFRONTIER environment, which controls any task and, most importantly, drives the optimization using its internal algorithms. The optimization philosophy is to explore the design domain (14 dimensional space) looking for the configurations that improve the system behavior in accordance with the 4 objectives. First, a DOE population with 112 designs is generated to map how the 4 objectives depend on the 14 input variables. Then, the Multi-Objective Genetic Algorithm of modeFRONTIER generates populations of new designs, using the information gained from previous runs.

To test each configuration and extract the corresponding outputs, modeFRONTIER executes internal operations and launches external applications. The sequence of the main tasks is given in Table 2.

Table 2. Process integration tasks

Action	Linked resource
generation of input variable set	modeFRONTIER DOE or MOGA algorithms
assembly of motorcycle model	static multi-body simulation
calculation of intermediate variables	external spreadsheet
braking simulation	time domain multi-body simulation
calculation of scalar indexes that describe the 4 objectives	external spreadsheet

The entire project has tested the behavior of 1904 different suspensions (17 MOGA generations). Each design took about 2.5 minutes, hence total CPU time was 80 hours.

5 Optimization Results

modeFRONTIER stores input variables, derived variables and output variables in a design table, whose rows reflect the tested configurations. Such a table is then processed to extract key information about the optimization scenario.

Main statistical relationships between variables (input-input, input-output, and output-output) may be investigated by plotting the correlation matrix. The example proposed in Fig. 5 has been created to check for possible links between the 4 optimization objectives. The bottom-left section of the matrix shows the correlation factors, which provide a statistical measure of the linear association between objectives. Null, or small correlation indexes mean that there is no clear trend between the variables, whereas value +1 or close to +1 (or -1) indicate good direct (or inverse) correlation.

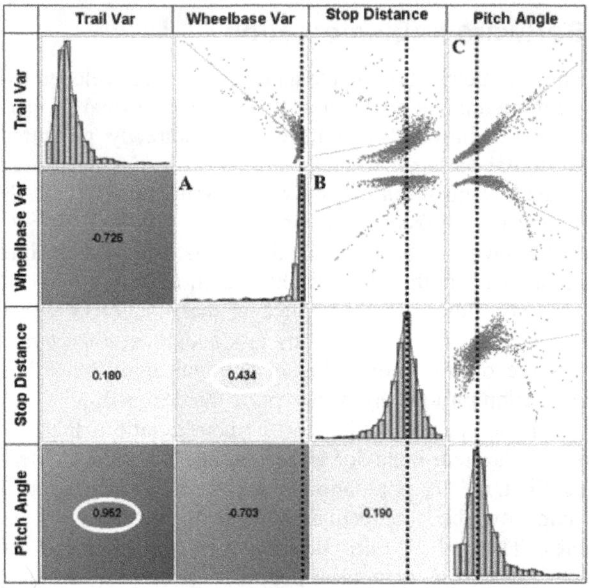

Fig. 5. Correlation matrix for the objectives

There are clear negative correlations between trail variation and wheelbase variation, as well as between pitch angle and wheelbase variation. Statistically, this means that when the wheelbase shortening is small, both trail shortening and pitch angle tend to be more pronounced.

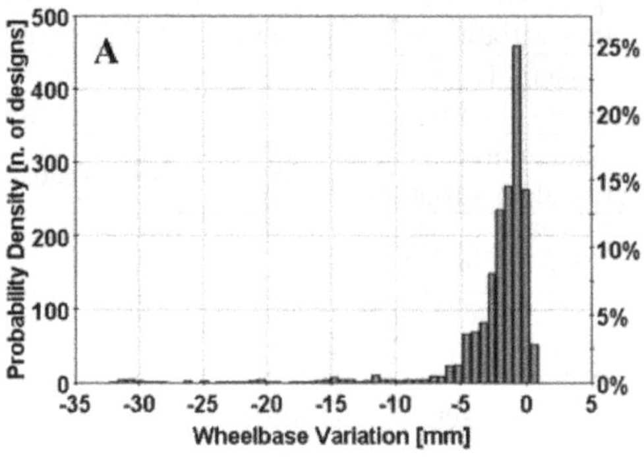

Fig. 6. Probability Density Function for the wheelbase reduction objective

Diagonal cells illustrate the Probability Density Function Chart for each objective. They allow the identification of trends that may not be obvious. For example, the wheelbase variation distribution is strongly asymmetric, with higher probability density on the right side of the total range, from -65.0 mm to +0.8 mm. Since the optimizer was asked to limit the wheelbase shortening, the result is very satisfactory: more than 95% of motorcycles exhibit a wheelbase reduction between -5.0 mm and 0.0 mm (Fig. 6). Other objectives are characterized by wider distributions, with less strong trends.

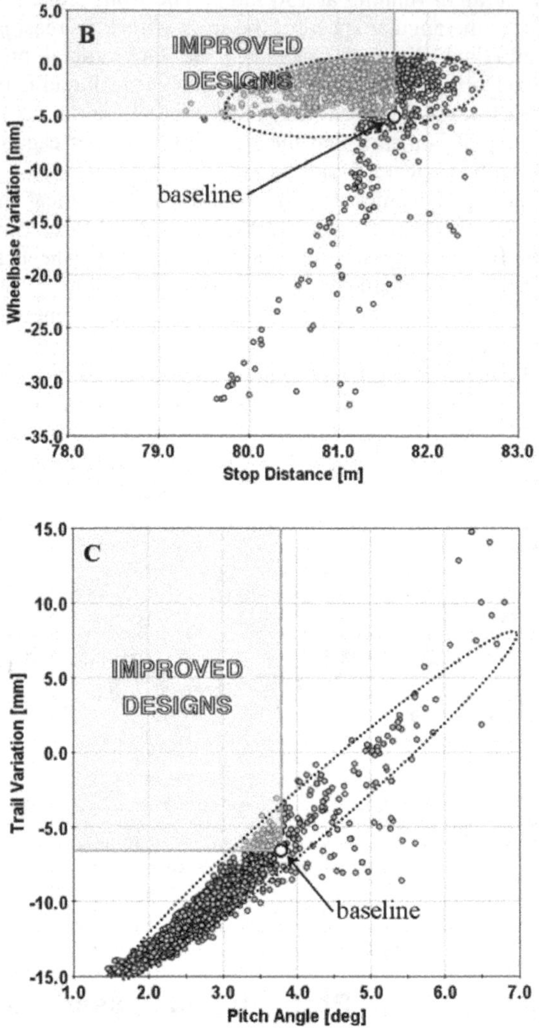

Fig. 7. Design evaluation

The upper-right section of the correlation matrix contains scatter charts, which represent the design distribution on 2D Cartesian graphs having X & Y axes in accordance with row & column of the matrix. Two of these charts are highlighted and zoomed in Fig. 7, for a better understanding.

The upper plot shows the connection between stopping distance and wheelbase. Design spots lie in a wide cloud, thus confirming a low correlation level (0.434). Trail variation and pitch angle, in contrast, are strongly correlated (0.952) as proved by the bottom plot, where design spots substantially lie on a narrow inclined area.

Besides examining object correlations, it is essential to analyze the relationships between objectives and input parameters. modeFRONTIER provides specific tools to rate the importance of each parameter, which is the first step towards a simplification of the problem.

As an example, Fig. 8 shows the t-Student chart for the stopping distance objective. The input parameters are listed from left to right, according to their effect on the chosen objective. The strongest (inverse) effect is given by the parameter which defines the position of the attaching point of the spring-damper assembly on the lower link of the suspension (see Fig. 1). In order to reduce the stopping distance, such point should be placed as forward as possible.

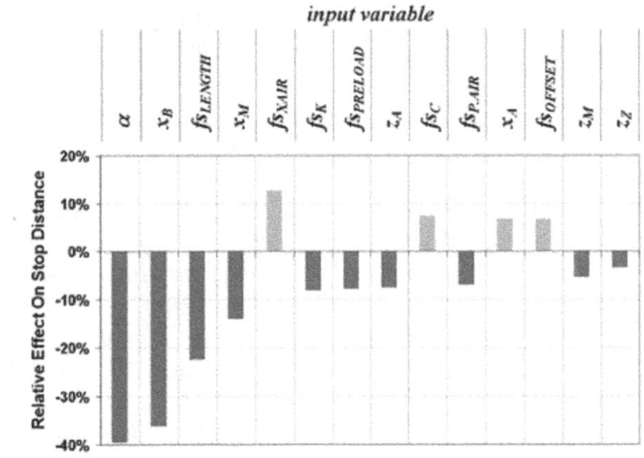

Fig. 8. Student chart: Effects of design parameters on stopping distance (see Fig. 1 and Fig. 2 for labels)

6 Selecting the Best Design

In order to understand how effective the optimization has been, it is necessary to compare the designs, focusing on objective values. Fig. 9 shows a parallel chart, where a graphical filter is used to hide all designs that do not meet one or more optimization goals. Considering simultaneously the 4 optimization criteria, the 13 visible designs of Fig. 9 are better than the baseline model. This selection is rather small (0.68 % of total), meaning that the baseline motorcycle was already well designed for the objectives we have chosen.

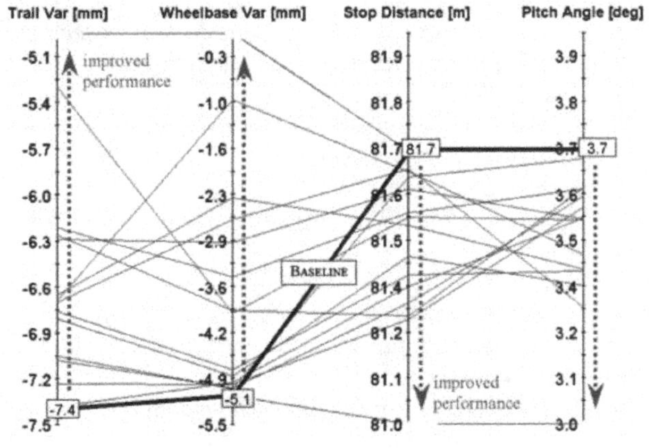

Fig. 9. Parallel chart to identify the best design

Theoretically the best design - among all - belongs to this sub-set. However, it can be observed that the only noticeable improvement concerns the wheelbase variation (from -5.1 mm to -0.9 mm). The gains for the other objectives, including the reduction of the stopping distance, are rather poor. To be fair, none of the 13 selected configurations improves the braking behavior sufficiently to justify a review of the baseline design.

Although at first glance it appears that the optimization failed, this may be a precipitate conclusion. In most cases, trade-off relationships exist between the objectives meaning that a slight loss in secondary ones opens a new scenario where the priority goal can be reached. modeFRONTIER includes a Multi Criteria Decision Making tool that uses pre-defined priorities to drive the choice in similar situations.

By applying such tool to the full design table, two "best" candidate designs have been selected; their performances are summarized in Table 3.

Table 3 Performances of best candidate designs

QUANTITY	BASELINE	DES. 566		DES. 792	
trail var	–7.4 mm	–1.1	– 85%	-15.2	+105%
wheelbase var	–5.1 mm	–31.6	+519%	-3.8	–25%
stopping dist	81.7 m	79.6	–2.5%	79.4	–2.8%
pitch angle var	3.7 deg	5.2	+40%	1.8	–51%

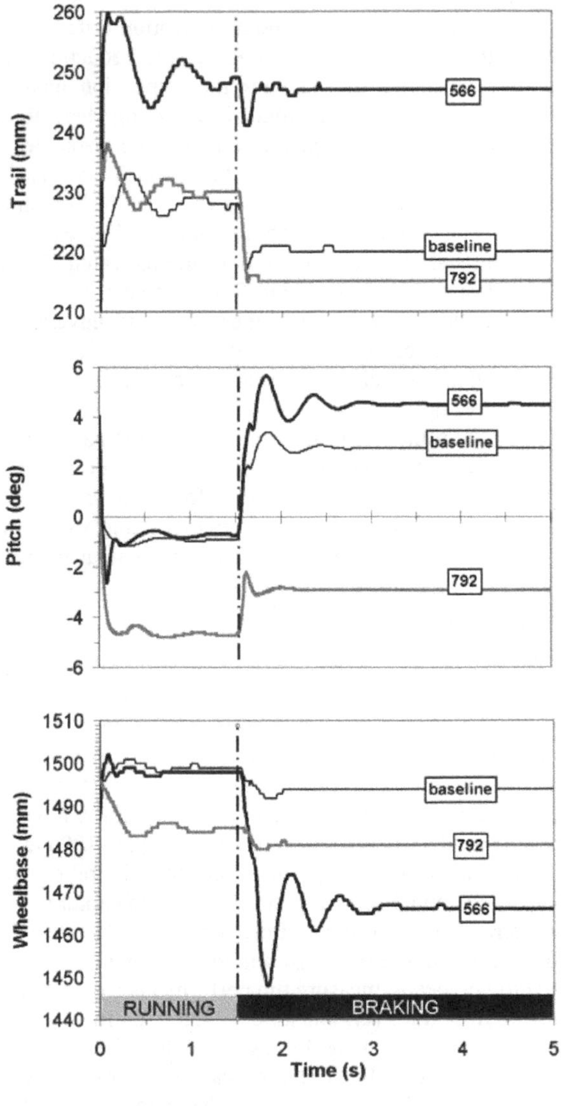

Fig. 10 Comparison between baseline and both optimized designs

Both solutions provide a significant reduction of the stopping distance which is an important step forward in terms of safety. Such positive results can only be reached provided that, in braking condition, either the shortening of the wheelbase (des. 566) or the shortening of the mechanical trail (des. 792) gets more pronounced with respect to the corresponding shortening measured on the baseline motorcycle. The first selected configuration (des. 566) also causes a slight increase in pitching motion.

To make a definitive choice, it is useful to compare both optimized motorcycles with the baseline model.

The Fig. 10 clearly shows that design 566 does not differ too much from the starting vehicle, except for the trail that is initially longer. However, the suspension of this design is too soft and too low which causes undesired effects, such as front diving, wheelbase shortening, and lasting oscillations. Design 792, however, is quite different from the baseline motorcycle, e.g. the initial wheelbase is about 15 mm shorter and the chassis is inclined 4.7 deg forward. Suspension characteristics now appear adequate to prevent oscillations and excessive diving.

Finally and according to the optimization criteria, design 792 is the best choice. Presumably, the reduction of the stopping distance is not linked to the suspension update, but to the shorter wheelbase. Indeed, assuming that the ABS fixes the longitudinal slip, the braking force becomes proportional to the vertical load on the front tire, which is inversely proportional to the motorcycle length. To complete the research, both overall stability and handling capabilities should be investigated using a more sophisticated 3D model.

The design 792 saves about 2.3 m in stopping distance, which might be crucial in emergency maneuvers. Other objectives are less important, although improvements have been obtained as well, confirming the efficiency of the Multi-Objective optimizer.

Apart from the suggested application, this paper presents an innovative methodology for the design approach. modeFRONTIER provides capabilities for automatic and fast investigation of the various alternatives and offers smart tools to extract key information from the generated data.

7 Conclusions

This work has demonstrated the effectiveness of multi-objective optimization techniques in improving vehicle dynamics. The main parameters of a motorcycle front suspension have been tuned to shorten the braking distance, increasing, at the same time, the stability and the comfort. Despite these objectives are opposed each other, it has been possible to identify a good solution among the 1900 tested.

The quality of the optimization strongly relies on the multi-body model accuracy, which needs to capture (at least) the correct trends in the vehicle response. The second crucial step is the definition of suitable scalar indexes, which have to univocally measure the performances of the vehicle, starting from time-variable kinematical quantities.

The proposed methodology, which relies on modeFRONTIER capabilities, can be easily generalized and applied to any vehicle type, whose behavior is reproducible through parametric multi-body simulation.

References

1. V. Cossalter, R. Lot, F. Maggio, *The influence of tire properties on the stability of a motorcycle in straight running and in curve*, SAE Paper 001-014, 2002.
2. E.J.H. De Vries and H.B. Pacejka, *The effect of tire modeling on the stability analysis of a motorcycle*, *In* proc. 4th International symposium on Advanced Vehicle Control (1998).
3. R. Lot, *A motorcycle tire model for dynamic simulations: theoretical and experimental aspects*, proc. 3rd International Tribology Conference, (2002).
4. V. Cossalter R. Lot, F. Maggio, *On the stability of motorcycle during braking*, SAE Paper 2004-32-0018, 2004.
5. R.S. Sharp, *The stability and control of motorcycles*, Journal of Mechanical Engineering Science, **13**, 316-329 (1971).
6. V. Cossalter, R. Lot, *A motorcycle multi-body model for real time simulations based on the natural coordinates approach*, Vehicle System Dynamics, **37**, 423-448 (2002).
7. V. Cossalter, R. Lot, F. Maggio, *A multibody code for motorcycle handling and stability analysis with validation and examples of application*, SAE Paper, 2003-32-0035, 2003.
8. F. Biral, M. Da Lio, *Modeling drivers with the optimal maneuver method*, *In* proc. of 7th ATA International Conference & Exhibition, (2001).
9. F. Biral, M. Da Lio, F. Maggio, *How gearbox ratios influence lap time and driving style - an analysis based on time-optimal maneuvers*, SAE Paper 2003-32-0056, 2003.
10. D. Bortoluzzi, R. Lot, and N. Ruffo, *Motorcycle steady turning: the significance of geometry and inertia*, *In* proc. of 7th ATA International Conference & Exhibition, (2001).
11. M. Da Lio, V. Cossalter, D. Bortoluzzi, F. Biral, *Experimental and theoretical study of motorcycle transfer functions for handling evaluation*, Vehicle System Dynamics, **39** , 1-25 (2003).
12. R. Lot, *A motorcycle tire model for dynamic simulations: theoretical and experimental aspects*, 3rd International Tribology Conference, (2002).
13. V. Cossalter, *Motorcycle Dynamics,* 2006, ISBN 978-1-4303-0861-4
14. D.J.N. Limebeer, R.S. Sharp, S. Evangelou, *The stability of motorcycles under acceleration and braking*, Journal of Mechanical Engineering Science, **215**, 1095-1110 (2001).
15. V. Cossalter., R. Lot, F. Maggio, *The modal analysis of a motorcycle in straight running and on a curve*, Meccanica, **39**, 1-16 (2004).
16. H.B. Pacejka, E. Bakker, *The magic formula tire model*, Vehicle System Dynamics **21**, 1-18 (1992).

3

Finite element modelling of shot peening process- A progress overview

Y. H. Yang, M. Wan, W.H. Zhang[1]

The Key Laboratory of Contemporary Design & Integrated Manufacturing Technology, Ministry of Education, Northwestern Polytechnical University, P.O. Box 552, 710072 Xi'An, Shaanxi, China

Abstract –It is very significant to investigate the shot peening mechanism in ensuring a good resistance to fatigue and stress corrosion. This paper reviews the recent advancements in shot peening process. Emphasis is put on the application of numerical simulation techniques and finite element method in residual stress prediction during shot peening process. Different methods related to shot peening modelling and prediction of plastic deformation and surface integrity are reviewed. Some key issues such as algorithms and simulation procedures are discussed.

Key words: Shot peening; Finite element method; Compressive residual stress; Plastic deformations

1 Introduction

In order to achieve the final shape in metal forming, some structural panels must be formed by shot peening, which is a surface cold-working process usually employed to improve the fatigue strength of metallic part or members. Such a process is accomplished by bombarding the surface of the members with small spherical shots made of hardened materials at high velocities. As a result of collision of a shot with the surface of a component, an indentation is created which is surrounded by a plastic region followed by an elastic zone. Subsequently, the recovery of elastic zone will produces a large compressive residual stress on the surface. This compressive residual stress field is highly effective in preventing premature failure under conditions of cyclic loading. Therefore, it is very useful to be able to predict the pattern and magnitude of the residual stress distribution near the surface after shot peening. For this reason, many research efforts have been focused on this issue.

2 State of the art

It is well recognized that the result of shot peening depends strongly upon the shot parameters such as shot size, density, shape, impact velocity, hardness etc., the target parameters such as initial yield stress, work hardening characteristics, hardness, strain-rate dependence etc. and the process parameters such as mass flow rate, air pressure, angle of attack, peening time etc. If the related parameters are not well chosen (e.g., large shot, over peening, high velocities, etc.), superficial defects such as overlaps, scales, micro-cracks and surface roughness imperfections may occur [1-4]. As a result, the strength of the treated part may be significantly decreased [5,6]. To ensure a better resistance to fatigue and stress corrosion, the quantitative relationships between these parameters and residual stress characteristics must be established.

Numerous experimental studies have been attempted to evaluate the residual stress distribution, fatigue life and the influence of shot, target and process parameters [7-9]. The evaluation, however, is both time-consuming and cost-expensive. Besides, because the research is based on the specific designed target, it would not allow a careful examination of the effect of the parameters on the residual stress pattern.

To study the shot peening process quantitatively, a theoretical shot peening model was firstly proposed by Guechichi et al. [10] based on the simplified method of elastic plastic calculations of Zarka and Casier [11]. Guechichi's model was further improved by Khabou et al. [12] and Fathallah et al. [13]. The above works [10,12,13] have the advantage taking into account the majority of controlling process parameters have been taken into account. Based on a new model of spherical cavity expansion, Al-Obaid [14] developed a number of theoretical expressions for the process parameters to study the residual stress distribution in the target. Kobayashi et al. [15] investigated the mechanism of compressive residual stress in shot peening by performing static compression tests and dynamic impact tests using a single steel ball against a flat steel plate. Besides, other authors [16–18] have developed simple theoretical schemes to analyze the shot peening process. Those analytical approaches principally lead to determine the residual stresses and the plastic deformations induced in the first affected layers of the shot peened part.

With the appearances of powerful finite element software such as ABAQUS, ANSYS and NASTRAN, attention was focused on numerical simulation of shot peening process [19-38]. Such a simulation method provides a cheap and easy way to study the dynamic impact of a shot with high velocity, the double non-linearity of the problem due to the contact of two bodies and the elastic–plastic behaviour of the target, etc.

Hardy et al. [19] used the FE method to solve the contact problem of a rigid sphere indenting an elastic–perfect plastic half-space for the first time. The first numerical analysis of shot peening using the commercial FE code was carried out by Edberg et al. [20], who simulated a single shot impacting visco-plastic and elasto-plastic materials but the parameters used in their study do not represent realistic peening parameters. The numerical simulation procedures of single and multiple shot impacts on a target have been developed by Al-Hassani et al. [21], Deslaef and Rouhaud [25,26]. Al-

[1] Corresponding author: zhangwh@nwpu.edu.cn

Hassani et al. [21] examined single shot impact with an incident angle whereas Deslaef et al. [25,26] examined the effect of rigid and deformable shot by comparing with experimental measurements. Both works, however, showed some differences.

To improve the modelling accuracy, dynamic analysis of single and multiple shot impacts have been conducted by many researchers [33-38]. Johnson [33] initially developed a dynamic model of a single shot using a pseudo-dynamic approach. In this approach, only the inertial properties of the shot were considered. As a result, a relationship between the depth of the plastic zone and the shot parameters, such as radius, mass and velocity, was obtained. This relationship was later validated by Clausen [34] and Iida [35]. Edberg et al. [36] conducted dynamic three-dimensional finite element analysis of a single shot impinging viscoplastic and elastoplastic materials with multi-linear isotropic strain-hardening and a strain rate scale factor. Meguid et al. [37,38] presented a systematic study of shot peening process based on dynamic FE analysis accounting for the effect of some shot and target parameters. In Ref. [37], Meguid et al. developed a three-dimensional finite element dynamic model of single and twin shot impacts using rigid spherical shots and metallic targets. The examined results of the effects of shot velocity, size and shape and target characteristics on residual stress distribution indicated that the effects of shot parameters were more important than the strain-hardening rate of the target. In another work [38], results revealed that multiple shot impacts result in a more uniform residual stress and plastic strain distribution and that the separation distance between shots significantly influences the residual stress field.

It is worth noting that although above works [19-38] provide a powerful method for establishing quantitative relationships between shot and target parameters and residual stress characteristics, FE methods could not still simulate a stream of discrete shots impacting on a target. Recently, discrete element (DE) method has been adopted to simulate shot peening process by Han et al. [39-41]. In their work, a DE representation of shot was adopted and different contact interaction laws for shot–target collision were extensively studied with special attention given to the proper selection of the parameter values involved. Besides, the modelling of the residual stresses on crack propagation and on the stress relief during load service was also performed [42-45].

3. Methodology

3.1 Mechanics of shot peening process [27]

If the impact between two solids is completely elastic, the potential energy is totally transformed into returned kinetic energy. Whereas, if the contact is elastic-plastic, the potential energy is only partially transformed. If there are internal degrees of freedom such as temperature, vibrations, deformations etc., a part of the stream kinetic energy and internal energy can be transformed each other. Let us consider a shot with mass, m, impacting a semi-finite body at a velocity, V_i, under an angle of impingement, α, and returning at a velocity, V_i, under an angle, α' (see Fig. 1). The impact can be characterized by a coefficient, e_r, called the coefficient of restitution, which is calculated as the ratio of by the normal projection of the return velocity to the normal projection of the stream velocity.

$$e_r = \frac{V_r \sin\alpha'}{V_i \sin\alpha} \tag{1}$$

Experimentally, it is shown that e_r depends on the conditions of the contact between the shot and the treated material, and the shot/material hardness ratio. It equals 1 for an elastic contact, 0 for a plastic contact and between 0 and 1 in the case of elastic-plastic contact.

During the shot peening process, the movement of the shot can be a sliding, an in depth penetration, a spin or a combination of these motions. In order to simplify the problem, the movement of the shot particles is supposed to be an in-depth penetration and the surface sliding was supposed to be negligible. Consequently, the energy restored in the plasticized first outer layers by the static indentation is equal to that restored by the dynamic impact.

In the case of normal impact, the difference between the initial and the restored kinetic energies is given by the following expression:

$$\Delta W_{(\alpha=90^\circ)} = mV_i^2(1-e_r^{\,2})/2 \tag{2}$$

with

$$\Delta W_{(\alpha=90^\circ)} = W_p + W_d \tag{3}$$

where W_p and W_d are the energy needed to plastify the shot peened surface layers and the dissipated energy during the impact (by vibrations, superficial heating, etc.), respectively.

The energy transmitted by plastic deformation to the treated material can be expressed as:

$$W_p = K\Delta W = mV_i^2(1-e_r^{\,2})K/2 \tag{4}$$

where K is an efficiency coefficient defined as the ratio of energy transmitted to the treated material to the supplied total initial energy. Generally, it is about 0.8–0.9 for mechanical impacts [33].

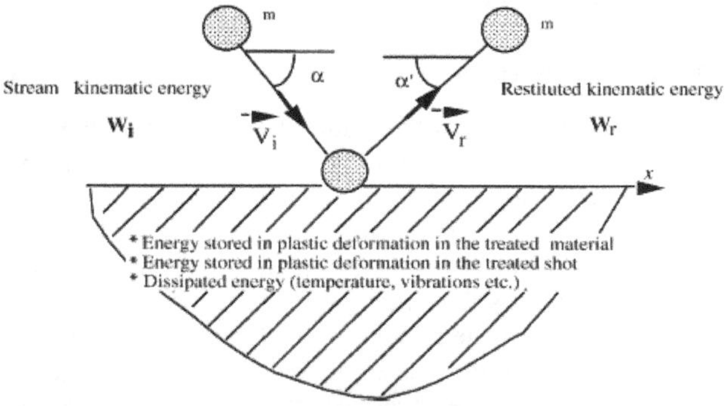

Fig. 1. Energy transmitted during contact shot/material [27]

3.2 Two-dimensional axisymmetric model [23]

Based on software ADINA 7.1, Schiffner et al. [23] used a dynamic two-dimensional (2D) axisymmetric finite element model to simulate the perpendicular impact of a single elastic sphere on an elastic-plastic workpiece, as shown in Fig. 2. The shot is defined as the target and the workpiece is defined as the contactor which is opposite to perception. The governing equations for the shot and the workpiece which are coupled by the contact conditions between the shot and workpiece are:

for the shot

$$\begin{aligned} &\underline{\underline{M}}_s \ddot{\underline{d}}_s + \underline{\underline{K}}_s \underline{d}_s = \underline{R}_s \\ &\underline{d}_s(t=0) = 0 \\ &\dot{\underline{d}}_s(t=0) = v_0 \end{aligned} \tag{5}$$

for the workpiece

$$\begin{aligned} &\underline{\underline{M}}_w \ddot{\underline{d}}_w + \underline{\underline{K}}_w \underline{d}_s = \underline{R}_w \\ &\underline{d}_w(t=0) = 0 \\ &\dot{\underline{d}}_w(t=0) = 0 \end{aligned} \tag{6}$$

Note that damping has been neglected in Eqs. (1) and (2). Implicit time integration method is used to solve the above governing equations. Due to the high expected strains, high order axisymmetric elements must be used in this method.

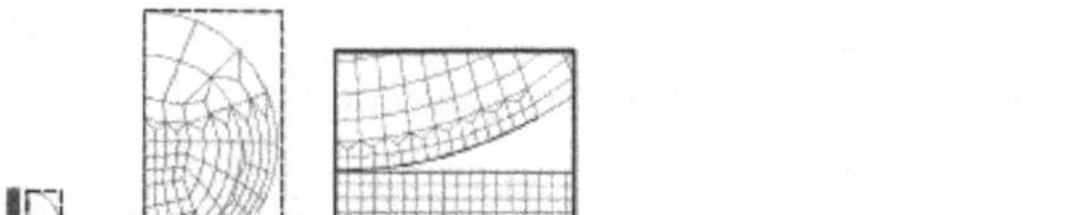

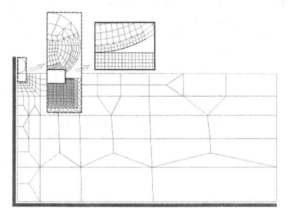

Fig. 2. Discretization of the axisymmetric FE model [23]

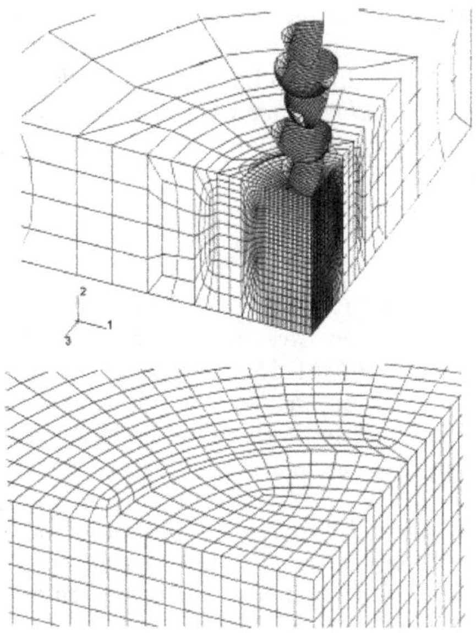

Fig. 3. 3D finite element model for the determination of residual stresses due to the multiple impact of shots [22]

3.3 3D FE method [22]

Using ABAQUS Explicit Code, Guagliano [22] used a 3D finite element, as shown in Fig. 3, to calculate the residual stress field induced by multiple impacts on an elasto-plastic body. The relationship between Almen intensity and residual stress field is considered. The Almen intensity is defined as

$$h = \frac{3Ml^2}{2Ebh^3} \tag{7}$$

where l is the reference distance for measuring Almen intensity. b is the strip width. h is the strip thickness. Note that the effect of the transverse curvature is not considered in this model.

3.4 3D FE method for dynamic model [28, 37]

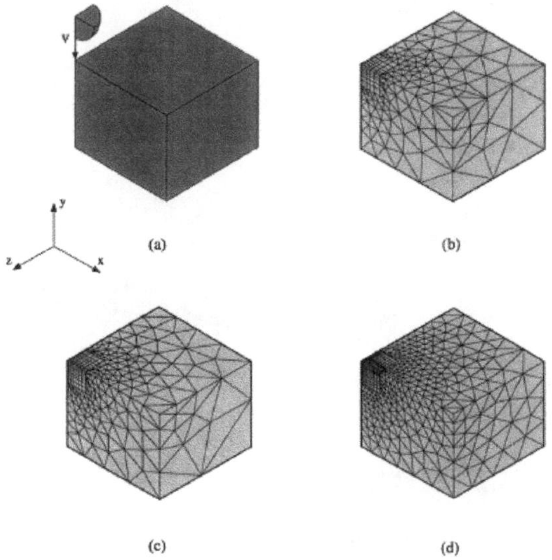

Fig. 4. Geometry and discretized models used in the single-shot model: (a) one-quarter of geometry, and (b-d) three discretized geometries of target with different mesh densities. [37]

Based on commercial finite element code ANSYS 5.3, two models are considered to study the effect of shots impinging a metallic target at normal incidence. The first is concerned with a single shot and the second with twin shots. Due to the symmetry, only a quarter of the single shot model was discretized, as depicted in Fig. 4a. Both eight-noded brick and four-noded tetrahedral finite elements were used to discretize the target. Convergence tests were conducted using the meshes depicted in Fig. 4b-Fig.4d. Contact elements were used to model the shot/target interface. The three dimensional contact elements adopt a contact node-target segment approach in conjunction with the penalty function method. The contact nodes were created on the top surface of the peened target around the common normal. The target segments were generated only on the lower half of the shot surface (Fig. 4), since it was anticipated that the contact would take place only in that area. The elastic Coulomb law was used.

3.5 Prediction models of stress, deformation and surface integrity [27]

Frija et al. [27] numerically studied the simulation method of the shot peening process by using energy equivalence between the dynamic impact and a static indentation of a peening shot in the treated surface. Their model is able to evaluate the residual stress, the plastic deformation profiles and the surface damage.

In their model, the shot is supposed to be a rigid sphere. The mechanical behaviour of the subjected material is assumed to be elastic-plastic coupled with damage, using an integrated form of the Lemaitre and Chaboche model. The shot peening loading is simulated by a static indentation, obtained by an energy equivalence with the dynamic impact. The whole simulation procedure is shown in Fig. 5.

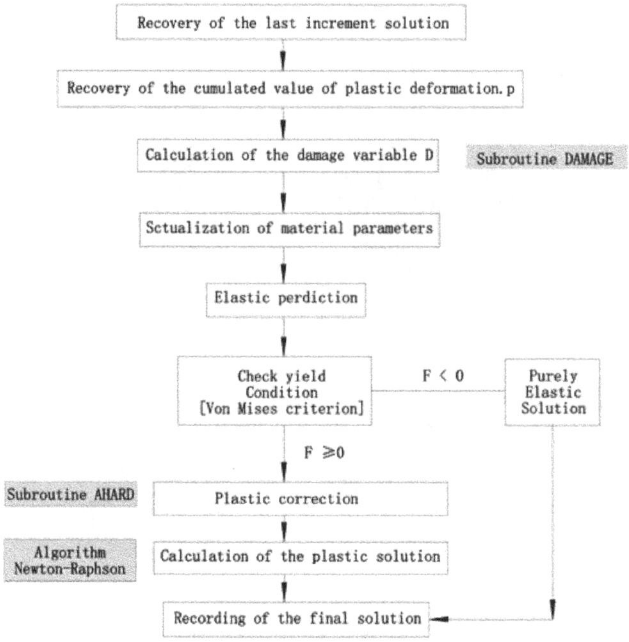

Fig. 5 Flowchart of the calculation [28]

4. Conclusion

The criterion to reasonably select the parameters for controlling the shot peening process is of great value for metal sheet forming. The advances of computing techniques make it possible to perform shot peening operations in a comprehensive simulation environment. Before actual operations, one can simulate the critical machining characteristics such as residual stress, plastic deformation firstly. Controlling parameters optimization and selection procedures are then carried out to ensure the process quality. In this paper, the existing numerical techniques are presented to model the shot peening process. These models provide general information about the relations between the process performance and the process parameters. They are the basis to simulate the actual cases and to optimal select the parameters for improving the process performance.

References

1. R. Fathallah, H. Sidhom, C. Braham, L. Castex, *Effect of surface properties on high cycle fatigue behaviour of shot peened ductile steel.* Mater. Sci. Technol. **19**, 1050–1056 (2003)
2. B. Gentil, M. Desvignes, L. Castex, *Analyse des surfaces grenaillées: fissuration, rugosité et contraintes résiduelles Shot peened surface analysis: cracks, roughness and residual stresses.* Mater. Technol. **75**, 493–497 (1987)
3. M. Desvignes, *Influence du grenaillage de précontrainte sur la tenue en service de l'acier 35CD4*, Thèse de Doctorat de l'ENSAM, (1987)
4. R. Ahmed, *Etude de la creation des fissures en surface de lacier 35CD4lors du grenaillage de precontrainte, memoire de DEA mecanique appliquee a la construction.* ENSAM, Paris (1987)
5. L. Wagner, *Mechanical surface treatments on titanium, aluminum and magnesium alloys*. Mater. Sci. Eng. A **263**, 210–216 (1999)
6. N. Sidhom, A. Laamouri, R. Fathallah, C. Braham, H.P. Lieurade, *Fatigue strength improvement of 5083 H11 Al-alloy T-welded joints by shot peening: experimental characterization and predictive approach.* Int. J. Fatigue **27**, 729–745 (2005)
7. S. Kyriacou, *Shot Peening Mechanics: A Theoretical Study*. 6th ed., ICSP, 505–516 (1996)
8. S.A. Meguid, *Mechanics of shot peening*. Ph.D. Thesis, UMIST, UK (1975)
9. Y.F. Al-Obaid, *A rudimentary analysis of improving fatigue life of metals by shot peening*. J. Appl. Mech. **57**, 307–312 (1990)
10. H. Guechichi, L. Castex, J. Frelat, G. Inglebert, *Predicting residual stresses due to shot peening*. In: A. Meguid, Editor, Impact Surface Treatment, Elsevier Applied Science Publishers, 11–22 (1986)
11. J. Zarka, J. Casier, *Mechanics Today*, Pergamon Press, Nemat-Nasser, 6 (1979)
12. M.T. Khabou, L. Castex, G. Inglebert, *Effect of material behaviour law on the theoretical shot peening results.* Eur. J. Mech. A/Solids 9, 537–549 (1989)
13. R. Fathallah, G. Inglebert, L. Castex, *Prediction of plastic deformation and residual stresses induced by shot peening in metallic parts.* Mater. Sci. Technol. **14**, 631–639 (1998)
14. Y.F. Al-Obaid, *Shot peening mechanics: experimental and theoretical analysis.* Mech. Mater. **19**, 251–260 (1995)
15. M. Kobayashi, T. Matsui, Y. Murakami, *Mechanics of creation of compressive residual stress by shot peening.* Int. J. Fatigue **20**, 351–357 (1998)
16. S.T.S. Al-Hassani, *Mechanical aspects of residual stress development in shot Peening.* In: Proceedings of the First International Conference on Shot Peening, 583–602 (1981)
17. H. Wohlfahrt, *The influence of peening conditions on the resulting distribution of residual stress.* In: Proceedings of the Second International Conference on Shot peening, Chicago, USA, 316–331 (1984)
18. S. Kyriacou, *Shot peening mechanics, a theorical study.* In: Proceedings of the Sixth International Conference on Shot Peening, ICSP6, (1996)

19. C. Hardy, C.N. Baronet, G.V. Tordion, *The elasto-plastic indentation of a half-space by a rigid sphere.* Int. J. Numer Methods Eng. **3**, 451–462 (1971)
20. J. Edberg, L. Lindgren, K. Mori, *Shot peening simulated by two different finite element formulations.* In: Shen S, Dawson E, editors.Simulation of materials processing: theory, methods and applications–NUMIFORM95, 425–430 (1995)
21. S.T.S. Al-Hassani, K. Kormi, D.C. Webb, *Numerical simulation of multiple shot impact.* In: Proceedings of the 7th international conference on shot peening, Warsaw, Poland, 217–227 (1999)
22. M. Guagliano, *Relating Almen intensity to residual stresses induced by shot peening: a numerical approach.* J. Mater. Proc. Technol. **110**, 277–286 (2001)
23. K. Schiffner, C.D. Helling, *Simulation of residual stresses by shot peening.* Comput Struct **72**, 329–340 (1999)
24. S. Baragetti, *Three-dimensional finite element procedures for shot peening residual stress field prediction.* Int. J. Comput Appl. Technol **14**, 51–63 (2001)
25. D. Deslaef, E. Rouhaud, S. Rasouli-Yazdi, *3D finite element models of shot peening processes.* Mat. Sci. Forum **347-349**, 241–246 (2000)
26. E. Rouhaud, D. Deslaef, *Influence of shots' material on shot peening, a finite element model.* Mat. Sci. Forum **404-407**, 153–158 (2002)
27. M. Frija, T. Hassine, R. Fathallah, C. Bouraoui, A. Dogui, *Finite element modelling of shot peening process: Prediction of the compressive residual stresses, the plastic deformations and the surface integrity.* Mater. Sci. Technol. A **426(1-2)**, 173–180 (2006)
28. S.A. Meguid, G. Shagal, J.C. Stranart, *Finite element modelling of shot-peening residual stresses.* J. Mater. Proc. Technol. **92-93**, 401–404 (1999)
29. A. Levers, A. Prior, *Finite element analysis of shot peening.* J. Mater. Proc. Technol. **80-81**, 304–308 (1998)
30. M. Meo, R. Vignjevic, *Finite element analysis of residual stress induced by shot peening process.* Adv. Engin. Soft. **34(9)**, 569–575 (2003)
31. G.H. Majzoobi, R. Azizi, N.A. Alavi, *A three-dimensional simulation of shot peening process using multiple shot impacts.* J. Mater. Proc. Technol. **164-165**, 1226–1234 (2005)
32. T. Hong, J.Y. Ooi, B. Shaw, *A numerical simulation to relate the shot peening parameters to the induced residual stresses.* Eng. Failure Anal. **15(8)**, 1097–1110 (2008)
33. W. Johnson, *Impact Strength of Materials*. Arnold, London, (1972)
34. R. Clausen, *Ermittlung von Einflussgressen beim Kugelstrahlen durch Einzelkornversuche.* In: Proceedings of the First International Conference on Shot Peening, 279–285 (1981)
35. K. Iida, *Dent and affected layer produced by shot peening.* Second International Conference on Shot Peening, Chicago, USA, 217–227 (1984)
36. J. Edberg, L. Lindgren, K. Mori, *Shot peening simulated by two different finite element formulations.* In: Shen, Dawson (Eds.), Simulation of Materials Processing: Theory, Methods and Applications, Balkema, Rotterdam, 425–430 (1995)
37. S.A. Meguid, G. Shagal, J.C. Stranart, J. Daly, *Three-dimensional dynamic finite element analysis of shot-peening induced residualstresses.* Finite Elem Anal Des **31**, 179–191 (1999)
38. S.A. Meguid, G. Shagal, J.C. Stranart, *3D FE analysis of peening of strain-rate sensitive materials using multiple impingement model.* Int. J. Impact Eng. **27**, 119–134 (2002)
39. K. Han, D. Peric, A.J.L. Crook, D.R.J. Owen, *A combined finite/discrete element simulation of shot peening processes. Part I: Studies on 2D interaction laws.* Eng. Comput **17**, 593–619 (2000)
40. K. Han, D. Peric, D.R.J. Owen, J. Yu, *A combined finite/discrete element simulation of shot peening processes. Part II: 3D interaction laws.* Eng. Comput. **17**, 680–702 (2000)
41. K. Han, D.R.J. Owen, D. Peric, *Combined finite/discrete element and explicit/implicit simulation of peen forming process.* Eng. Comput. **19**, 92–118 (2002)
42. S. Shen, *Assessment, Development and Validation of Computational Fracture Mechanics Methodologies and Tools for Shot-peened Materials Used in Rotorcraft Principal Structural Elements* [S.I.], (2004)
43. I. Lillamand, *Cyclic modelling of the mechanical state produced by shotpeening.* Fatigue Fract. Eng. Mater. Struct. **24**, 93–104 (2001)
44. H. Guechichi,, L. Castex, *Fatigue limits prediction of surface treated materials.* J. Mater. Proc. Technol. **172**, 381–387 (2006)
45. A.S. Franchim, C.V. De, D.N. Travessa, M.N. De, *Analytical modelling for residual stresses produced by shot peening.* Mater. Des., (In Press) Accepted Manuscript. (2008)

4

Bending and dynamic analyses of sandwich panels considering the size effect of sandwich core

Ke-peng Qiu, Wei-hong Zhang[a], Ji-hong Zhu

The Key Laboratory of Contemporary Design & Integrated Manufacturing Technology, Northwestern Polytechnical University, 710072, Xi'an, Shaanxi, China

Abstract – In this paper, the bending and dynamic responses of sandwich panels with the size variation of different sandwich cores and the homogenized cores are analyzed numerically, including the hexagonal and rectangular cores, the square and rhombic cores and the circle and X-shape corrugated cores. In dependence on the ratio of the span dimensions to thickness, the laminate plate theory is also adopted for the static and dynamic analysis of sandwich panels with the homogenized cores. The computational results demonstrate the influencing rule of size variation of unit cells in the sandwich core on the bending and dynamic response of sandwich panels.

Key words: Sandwich panel, Bending response, Dynamic analysis, Homogenization method, Size effect

1 Introduction

A typical sandwich panel is composed of the upper and lower skins and a lightweight core. Common patterns of sandwich cores, e.g. foam, truss, honeycombs and corrugated cores [1-4] are shown in Fig.1. Different detailed structural forms are involved such as the foam cores with the open or close cells, different truss configurations, honeycomb cores and the corrugated core with different shapes. Moreover, attractive properties like high specific stiffness and strength, high impact energy absorption, sound damping, electromagnetic wave absorption, thermal insulation and non combustibility [5-7] can be obtained. Therefore, sandwich panels are extensively used in the aerospace, building, automobile, package, and shipbuilding industries.

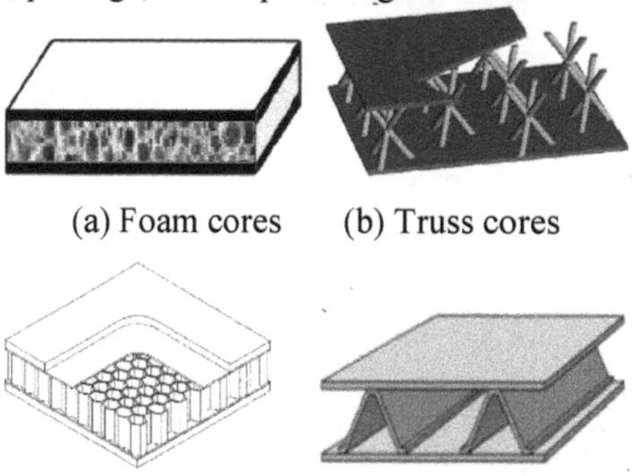

(a) Foam cores (b) Truss cores

(c) Honeycomb cores (d) Corrugated cores

Fig. 1. Sandwich panels with the different cores

Most studies on the sandwich panel presently focus on the following two aspects. Firstly, various kinds of methods involved in the homogenization method, the analytical method and the experimental method are pursued to obtain the effective properties of sandwich panels with the different cores. Buannic et al. [8] computed the effective properties of sandwich panel with the corrugated core with the homogenization method and derived the equivalent Kirchhoff-Love and Reissner-Mindlin homogeneous plate. Meraghni et al. [9] developed three approaches of finite element analysis, analytical study and experimental tests to determine the mechanical properties of the honeycomb and tubular cores for sandwich panels. Xu and Qiao [10] applied the multi-pass homogenization technique to solve the equivalent stiffness of the sandwich with the skin effect. Hohe and Becker [11] used a strain energy-based representative volume element procedure for the determination of the effective properties of two-dimensional cellular sandwich cores with arbitrary cell topology and geometry. Xue and Hutchinson [12] proposed a valid constitutive model for quasi-static deformation of three kinds of metallic sandwich cores. Secondly, structural responses of sandwich panels including the bending, impact, vibration and bulking responses are evaluated. Romanoff and Varsta [13] evaluated the bending response of web-core sandwich plates by transforming an originally discrete core into an equivalent homogenous continuum with the effect of thick-face-plates considered. The equivalent stiffness properties of the plate are determined by analytical formulations. Glenn and Hyer [14] developed a theory to predict the out-of-plane deflections of sandwich plates. Paik et al. [15] investigated the strength characteristics of aluminum sandwich panels with aluminum honeycomb core. Koissin et al. [16] addressed the elastic response of sandwich panels to local static and dynamic loading. Meo et al. [17] made an experimental investigation and a numerical simulation on the impact damage over a range of sandwich panels. They revealed the load distribution in damaged sandwich structures and studied the failure mechanisms of such a structure in the presence of impact damage. Pokharel and Mahendran [18] investigated local buckling behavior of sandwich panels using experimental and finite element analysis. Frostig and

[a] Corresponding author: zhangwh@nwpu.edu.cn

Thomsen [19] presented free vibration analysis of sandwich panels with a flexible core based on the high-order sandwich panel theory. Chang et al. [20] presented a closed-form solution based on the Mindlin-Reissner plate theory to describe the behavior of corrugated-core sandwich plate bending with various boundary conditions.

The above-presented researchers and many others have carried out plenty of outstanding and in-depth studies on the sandwich panel. However, few attentions are paid on the size effect on the mechanical properties of the few of the sandwich cores. Tekoglu and Onck [21] pointed out that mechanical properties of cellular materials depend strongly on the specimen size to the cell size ratio. The size effect was addressed by Onck et al. [22] for the in-plane elastic constants of hexagonal honeycombs based on the finite element modeling and experimental tests. Recently, Dai and Zhang [23] studied size effects of the 2D basic cell of sandwich beams in a systematic way and demonstrated the importance of size effect theoretically and numerically. Therefore, it's necessary to further explore the size effect of 3D sandwich core in analyzing the mechanical response of sandwich panel. In this paper, by varying the size of the unit cells composing sandwich cores, the bending and dynamic responses of the sandwich panel are evaluated and compared by using the analytical and numerical methods on the basis of homogenization method.

The rest of this paper is organized as follows: in Section 2, the homogenization method and classical laminate plate theory are introduced simply. In Section 3, the bending responses of sandwich panels with the different size honeycomb and corrugated cores are computed numerically. And also, the laminate plate theory and the finite element method are adopted to analyze their bending responses based on the effective sandwich cores predicted by the 3D homogenization method. In Section 4, we also analyze numerically and theoretically the dynamic responses of sandwich panels with the different size honeycomb cores and the homogenized cores. In Section 5, conclusions are drawn and further works are pointed out.

2 Basic formulation

2.1 Homogenization method

The homogenization method is based on a two-scale asymptotic expansion of material behaviors with periodic unit cells. The overall properties of an elastic body can be described by considering two different scales: the macroscopic or global level x, and the microscopic or local level y. The global level x is related to the local level y by $y = x/\varepsilon$, where ε is a very small positive number. Using a double-scale asymptotic expansion, the displacement field can be written as:

$$u^{\varepsilon} = u^{0}(x,y) + \varepsilon^{1}u^{1}(x,y) + \varepsilon^{2}u^{2}(x,y) + \cdots \quad (1)$$

Introducing Eq.(1) into the virtual displacement equation of the general elasticity problem and equating the terms with the same power of ε, after a series of derivation, it yields,

$$E^{H}_{ijkl}(x) = \frac{1}{|Y|}\int_{Y}\left(E_{ijkl} - E_{ijpm}\frac{\partial \chi^{kl}_{p}}{\partial y_{m}}\right)\mathrm{d}Y \quad (2)$$

where E^{H}_{ijkl} represents the equivalent homogenized elastic modulus. $|Y|$ denotes the volume of the unit cell. χ^{kl} is a Y-periodic admissible displacement field associated with load case kl, which can be obtained from the following integral equation over the unit cell with periodic boundary conditions.

$$\int_{Y} E_{ijpq}\frac{\partial \chi^{kl}_{p}}{\partial y_{q}}\frac{\partial v_{i}}{\partial y_{j}}dY = \int_{Y} E_{ijkl}\frac{\partial v_{i}}{\partial y_{j}}dY \quad \forall v \in Y \quad (3)$$

where v is set to be a admissible arbitrary displacement field. Numerically, χ^{kl} is computed over the unit cell by the FE analysis in which the corresponding loads are obtained as the discontinuity of elastic material properties along the interfaces between distinct constitutive phases. The detailed concepts and derivation are seen in Ref. [24, 25].

2.2 Laminate plate theory

A sandwich panel can be considered as a multi-layered plate when the sandwich core is homogenized by using the homogenization method. Therefore, the laminate plate theory [26, 27] can be used to analyze its bending response. According to the assumption of the laminate plate theory that the lines perpendicular to the surface of the laminate remain straight and perpendicular to the deformed surface as well. The functional forms of the displacements for the laminate plate are:

$$\begin{aligned} u(x,y,z) &= u_0(x,y) + z\overline{\alpha}(x,y) \\ v(x,y,z) &= v_0(x,y) + z\overline{\beta}(x,y) \\ w(x,y,z) &= w_0(x,y) \end{aligned} \quad (4)$$

where u_0, v_0 and w_0 are the displacements of the mid-plane (that is, the *x-y* plane in Fig. 2 below) of the laminate plate on *x*, *y* and *z* direction respectively. The second terms in the first two equations are related to the rotations of the lineal element. In classical plate theory,

$$\overline{\alpha} = -\frac{\partial w}{\partial x}, \quad \overline{\beta} = -\frac{\partial w}{\partial y} \quad (5)$$

The equilibrium equations for the three dimensional elasticity can be written as follows:

$$\begin{aligned} &\frac{\partial \sigma_x}{\partial x} + \frac{\partial \sigma_{yx}}{\partial y} + \frac{\partial \sigma_{zx}}{\partial z} + F_x = 0 \\ &\frac{\partial \sigma_{xy}}{\partial x} + \frac{\partial \sigma_{y}}{\partial y} + \frac{\partial \sigma_{zy}}{\partial z} + F_y = 0 \\ &\frac{\partial \sigma_{xz}}{\partial x} + \frac{\partial \sigma_{yz}}{\partial y} + \frac{\partial \sigma_{z}}{\partial z} + F_z = 0 \end{aligned} \quad (6)$$

In classical laminate plate theory, we define and use stress resultants (N), stress couples (M), and shear resultants (Q) for the overall plate.

$$\begin{Bmatrix} N_x \\ N_y \\ N_{xy} \\ Q_x \\ Q_y \end{Bmatrix} = \int_{-h/2}^{+h/2} \begin{Bmatrix} \sigma_x \\ \sigma_y \\ \sigma_{xy} \\ \sigma_{xz} \\ \sigma_{yz} \end{Bmatrix} dz, \begin{Bmatrix} M_x \\ M_y \\ M_{xy} \end{Bmatrix} = \int_{-h/2}^{+h/2} \begin{Bmatrix} \sigma_x \\ \sigma_y \\ \sigma_{xy} \end{Bmatrix} zdz \qquad (7)$$

Then the body force items (F_x , F_y , F_z) are neglected. It is further assumed that the plate is composed of a laminated composite material that is mid-plane symmetric. From Eq.(6) and Eq.(7) through integrating term by term across each layer, the plate equilibrium equations for the bending of the plate can be expressed as

$$\frac{\partial M_x}{\partial x} + \frac{\partial M_{xy}}{\partial y} - Q_x = 0 \qquad (8)$$

$$\frac{\partial M_{xy}}{\partial x} + \frac{\partial M_y}{\partial y} - Q_y = 0 \qquad (9)$$

$$\frac{\partial Q_x}{\partial x} + \frac{\partial Q_y}{\partial y} + P(x,y) = 0 \qquad (10)$$

Eq.(8) and Eq.(9) can be substituted into Eq.(10), which generates

$$\frac{\partial^2 M_x}{\partial x^2} + 2\frac{\partial^2 M_{xy}}{\partial x \partial y} + \frac{\partial^2 M_y}{\partial y^2} = -P(x,y) \qquad (11)$$

From the following equation:

$$\begin{bmatrix} N \\ M \end{bmatrix} = \begin{bmatrix} A & B \\ B & D \end{bmatrix} \begin{bmatrix} \varepsilon \\ k \end{bmatrix} \qquad (12)$$

and according to Eq.(4) and Eq.(5) and the relations among displacements, strains and stresses of the laminate plate, we obtain:

$$\begin{aligned} M_x &= D_{11}k_x + D_{12}k_y \\ M_y &= D_{12}k_x + D_{22}k_y \\ M_{xy} &= 2D_{66}k_{xy} \end{aligned} \qquad (13)$$

where

$$\begin{aligned} k_x &= \frac{\partial \overline{\alpha}}{\partial x} = -\frac{\partial^2 w}{\partial x^2} \\ k_y &= \frac{\partial \overline{\beta}}{\partial y} = -\frac{\partial^2 w}{\partial y^2} \\ k_{xy} &= \frac{1}{2}\left(\frac{\partial \overline{\alpha}}{\partial x} + \frac{\partial \overline{\beta}}{\partial y}\right) = -\frac{\partial^2 w}{\partial x \partial y} \end{aligned} \qquad (14)$$

$$D_{ij} = \frac{1}{3}\sum_{k=1}^{N}\left(Q_{ij}\right)_k \left[h_k^3 - h_{k-1}^3\right] \qquad (15)$$

Here the principal material directions (1, 2, 3) coincide with the x-y-z coordinate system. The Q_{ij} quantities are the stiffness matrix quantities that have the following simple forms by ignoring the fine accuracy.

$$\begin{aligned} Q_{11} &= E_{11}/(1-\nu_{12}\nu_{21}) \\ Q_{22} &= E_{22}/(1-\nu_{12}\nu_{21}) \\ Q_{12} &= Q_{21} = \nu_{21}E_{11}/(1-\nu_{12}\nu_{21}) = \nu_{12}E_{22}/(1-\nu_{12}\nu_{21}) \\ Q_{66} &= G_{12} \end{aligned} \qquad (16)$$

Substitute Eq.(13) and Eq.(14) into Eq.(11), which results in:

$$D_{11}\frac{\partial^4 w}{\partial x^4} + 2(D_{12} + 2D_{66})\frac{\partial^4 w}{\partial x^2 \partial y^2} + D_{22}\frac{\partial^4 w}{\partial y^4} = P(x,y) \qquad (17)$$

According to Eq.(17), the bending response of a sandwich panel, except transverse shear deformation and coupling terms subjected to a lateral distributed load $P(x, y)$, can be obtained by the Levy and Navier solution.

3 Bending responses of sandwich panels

3.1 Sandwich panels with the honeycomb cores

3.1.1 Hexagonal and rectangular cores

Sandwich panels with the hexagonal and rectangular honeycomb cores, as shown in Fig.2, are simply supported on the left and right side. The line load P=100N/m is imposed on the center of the plate. The sandwich panel has the dimensions assigned as: width a=0.8865m, length b=1.5354m, thickness $h_u = h_l = 0.0125$m, $h_c = 0.0375$m (u-upper skin, l-lower skin, c-core), and the material properties: $E_u=E_l=2.0$GPa, $E_c=0.91$GPa. These two honeycomb cores have the same volume fraction 26.53%.

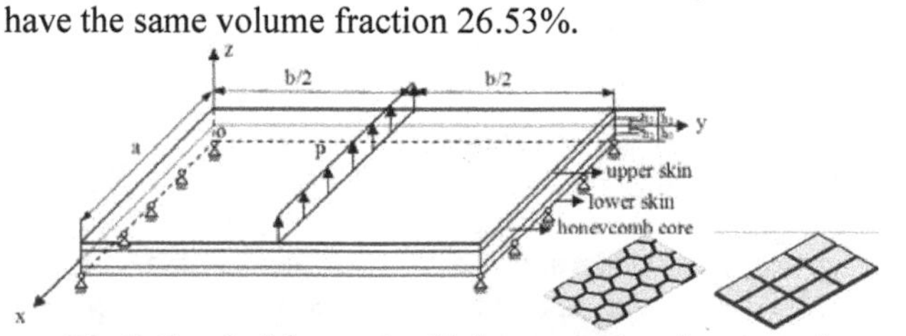

Fig.2. Sandwich panel with hexagonal and rectangular cores

The effective material properties of hexagonal honeycomb core are obtained by the 3D homogenization method.

E_x^H=3.118352E+07, E_y^H=3.116449E+07, E_z^H=2.414286E+08

G_{xy}^H=8.770264E+06, G_{yz}^H=5.272060E+07, G_{xz}^H=5.273506E+07

ν_{xy}^H=7.818590E-01, ν_{xz}^H=3.874876E-02, ν_{yz}^H=3.872511E-02 (18)

The effective material properties of rectangular honeycomb core are

$$E_x^H = 1.714326E+08,\ E_y^H = 1.029486E+08,\ E_z^H = 2.414286E+08$$
$$G_{xy}^H = 1.425520E+06,\ G_{yz}^H = 3.840819E+07,\ G_{xz}^H = 6.499972E+07$$
$$v_{xy}^H = 2.119053E-02,\ v_{xz}^H = 2.130228E-01,\ v_{yz}^H = 1.279243E-01 \quad (19)$$

According to the boundary conditions on those edges: w(x, 0)=0, w(x, b)=0, and My(x, 0)=0, My(x, b)=0, Levy assumed the following solution form of Eq.(17): a single infinite half range sine series:

$$w(x,y) = \sum_{n=1}^{\infty} \phi_n(x) \sin\frac{n\pi x}{b} \quad (20)$$

The load $P(x,y)$ is also expanded in terms of a half range sine series. Then, by substituting Eq.(20) into Eq.(17), the equation concerning $\phi_n(x)$ is obtained. Its solution is composed of the particular solution $\phi_{n_P}(x)$ and the homogenous solution $\phi_{n_H}(x)$ that has three different forms depending on the relative plate stiffness in various directions.
The total potential energy is:

$$U = \int_0^a w(x, b/2) P(x, b/2) dx \quad (21)$$

Via the calculation, the Levy solution converges when the expansion number n equals to 5. The maximum displacement module is 2.94×10-4m, and the total potential energy is 2.44×10-2N·m for the hexagonal core. The maximum displacement module is 2.622×10-4m, and the total potential energy is 2.41×10-2N·m for the rectangular core. The deformation of sandwich panels is shown in Fig.3.

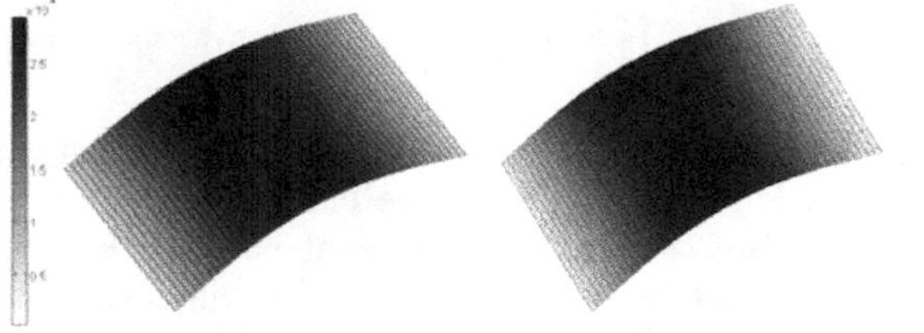

(a) Hexagonal cores (b) Rectangular cores
Fig.3. Levy solution of sandwich panel with homogenized cores

The bending response of the sandwich panel made of three-layered homogeneous media is obtained via the finite element software SAMCEF®. The maximum displacement module is 2.57×10-4m, and the total potential energy is 2.139×10-2N·m for the hexagonal core. The maximum displacement module is 2.499×10-4m, and the total potential energy is 2.0885×10-2N·m for the rectangular core. The detailed deformation is shown in Fig.4.

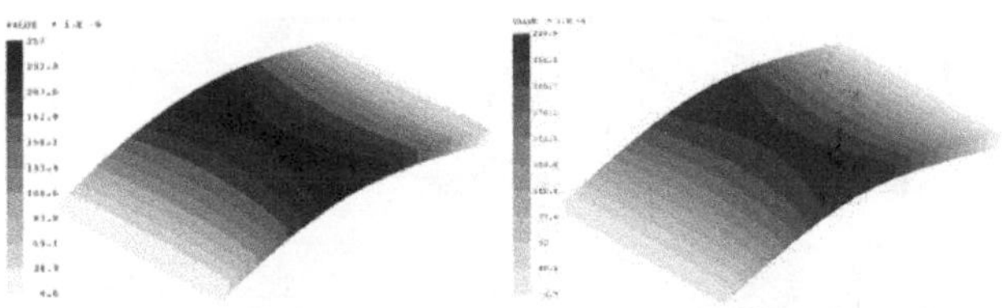

(a) (b)
Fig.4. FE solution of sandwich panel with the homogenized (a) hexagonal and (b) rectangular cores

Table 1. Bending deflections of sandwich panels with different size hexagonal cores

Number of unit cells	Different size cores	Bending responses of sandwich panels	Bending values of sandwich panels	
			Total potential energy	Total potential energy
1×1=1	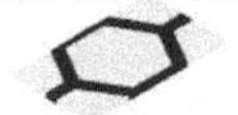		4.24E-2	6.19E-4
2×2=4	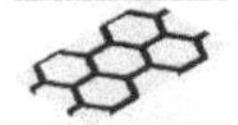		2.51E-2	3.37E-4
3×3=9	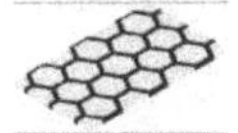		2.26E-2	2.66E-4
4×4=16	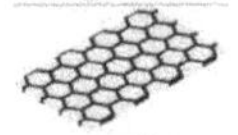		2.18E-2	2.67E-4
6×6=36	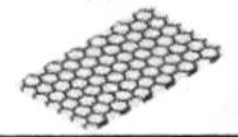		2.14E-2	2.58E-4

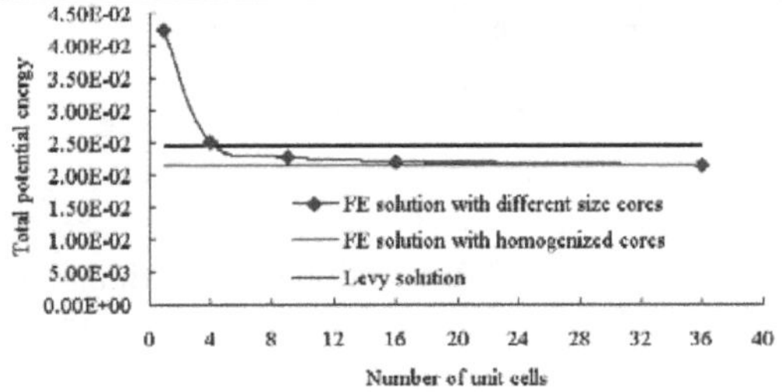

(a)

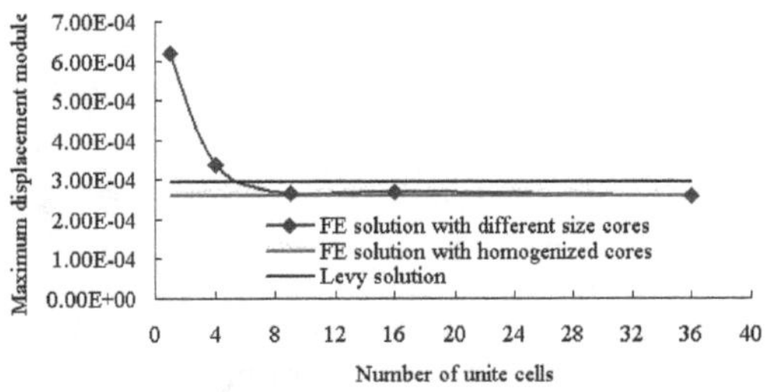

(b)

Fig.5 (a) Total potential energy and (b) Maximum displacement module of sandwich panel with the hexagonal core

Table 2. Bending deflections of sandwich panels with different size rectangular cores

Number of unit cells	Different size cores	Bending responses of sandwich panels	Bending values of sandwich panels	
			Total potential energy	Total potential energy

1×1=1	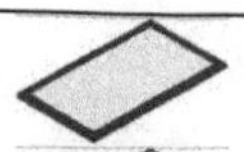		4.26E-2	6.87E-4
2×2=4			2.26E-2	2.61E-4
3×3=9	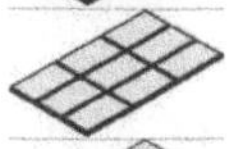		2.21E-2	2.59E-4
4×4=16			2.11E-2	2.50E-4
6×6=36	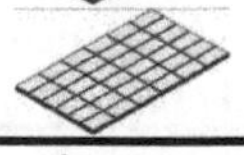		2.09E-2	2.49E-4

The finite element models of sandwich panels with the different size hexagonal and rectangular cores are built and their bending responses are analyzed as shown in Table 1, 2 and Fig 5, 6.

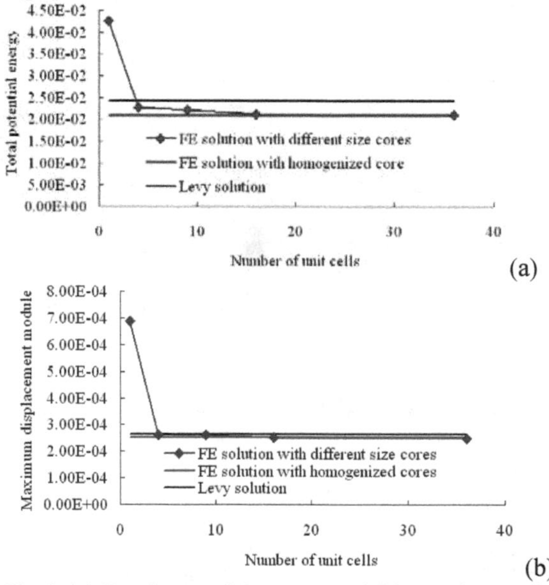

Fig.6. (a) Total potential energy and (b) Maximum displacement module of sandwich panel with the rectangular core

3.1.2 Square and rhombic cores

Consider sandwich panels with the square and rhombic honeycomb cores as shown in Fig.7. All the four edges are simply supported. The uniform surface loading $q=100N/m^2$ is applied on the upper surface. The sandwich panel has the dimensions assigned as: $a=1.1m$, $h_u=h_l=0.0125m$, $h_c=0.0375m$ (u-upper skin, l-lower skin, c-core), and the material properties: $E_u=E_l=2.0GPa$, $E_c=0.91GPa$. These two honeycomb cores have the same volume fraction 17.35%.

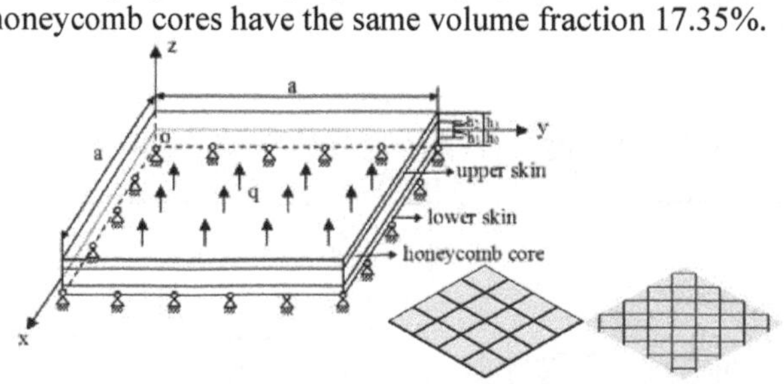

Fig.7. Sandwich panel with square and rhombic cores

The effecitive properties of the square honeycomb core are obtained by the homogenization method.

$$E_x^H=8.769525E+07,\ E_y^H=8.769525E+07,\ E_z^H=1.579339E+08$$
$$G_{xy}^H=4.154834E+05,\ G_{yz}^H=3.270143E+07,\ G_{xz}^H=3.270143E+07$$
$$v_{xy}^H=-6.337963E-03,\ v_{xz}^H=1.665797E-01,\ v_{yz}^H=1.665797E-01 \quad (22)$$

The effecitive properties of the square honeycomb core are:

$$E_x^H=2.142905E+06,\ E_y^H=2.149689E+06,\ E_z^H=1.579339E+08$$
$$G_{xy}^H=4.454896E+07,\ G_{yz}^H=3.305019E+07,\ G_{xz}^H=3.295121E+07$$
$$v_{xy}^H=9.740973E-01,\ v_{xz}^H=4.070510E-03,\ v_{yz}^H=4.083396E-03 \quad (23)$$

According to the boundary conditions on the four edges, in the Navier approach we can simply expand the deflection, w(x, y) and the applied uniform loading, q(x, y), into a doubly infinite half range sine series.

$$w(x,y)=\sum_{m=1}^{\infty}\sum_{n=1}^{\infty}\frac{a^4 q_{mn}}{D\pi^4}\sin\frac{m\pi x}{a}\sin\frac{n\pi y}{a} \quad (24)$$

$$q(x,y)=\sum_{m=1}^{\infty}\sum_{n=1}^{\infty}q_{mn}\sin\frac{m\pi x}{a}\sin\frac{n\pi y}{a} \quad (25)$$

where

$$q_{mn}=\frac{16q}{mn\pi^2},\qquad m,n=1,3,5,\ldots \quad (26)$$

$$D=D_{11}\left(\frac{m}{a}\right)^4+2\left(D_{12}+2D_{66}\right)\left(\frac{mn}{a^2}\right)^2+D_{22}\left(\frac{n}{a}\right)^4 \quad (27)$$

The total potential energy is:

$$U=\iint_A w(x,y)q(x,y)dxdy \quad (28)$$

Via the calculation, the Navier solution converges when the expansion number n is 7. The maximum displacement module is 1.687×10^{-5}m, and the total potential energy is 1.4×10^{-3}N·m for the square core. The maximum displacement module is 1.682×10^{-5}m, and the total potential energy is 1.4×10^{-3}N·m for the rhombic core. The deformation of sandwich panels for the detail is shown in Fig.8.

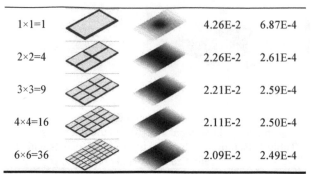

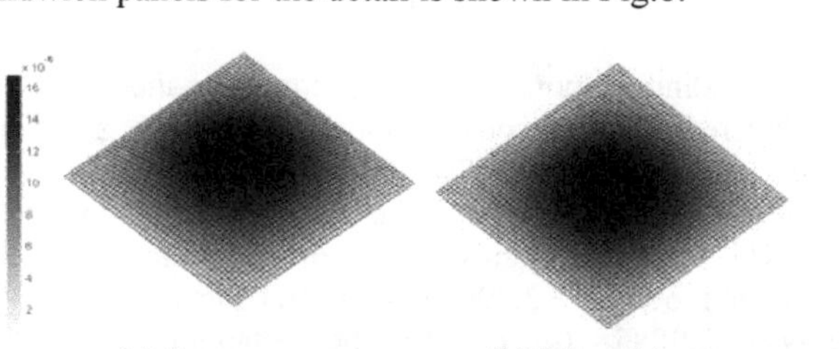

(a) Square cores (b) Rhombic cores

Fig.8. Navier solutions of sandwich panels with homogenized cores

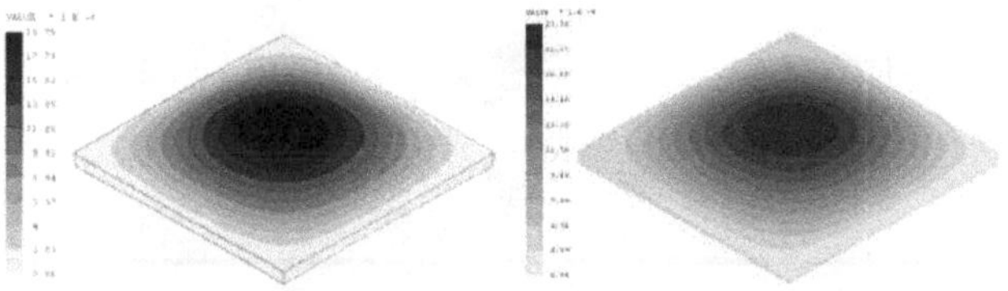

(a) Square cores (b) Rhombic cores

Fig.9. FE solutions of sandwich panels with homogenized cores

Likewise, the finite element models of sandwich panels with the different size square and rhombic cores are built and their bending responses are analyzed as shown in Table 3, 4 and Fig.10, 11.

Similar to the previous analysis, for this kind of sandwich panel made of three-layered homogeneous media, the maximum displacement module is 1.975×10^{-5}m, and the total potential energy is 9.868×10^{-4}N·m for the square core. The maximum displacement module is 2.352×10^{-5}m, and the total potential energy is 1.246839×10^{-3}N·m for the rhombic core. The deformation is shown in Fig.9.

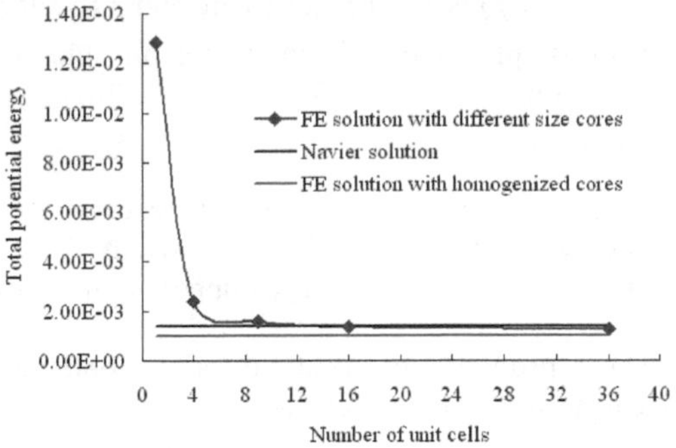

(a)

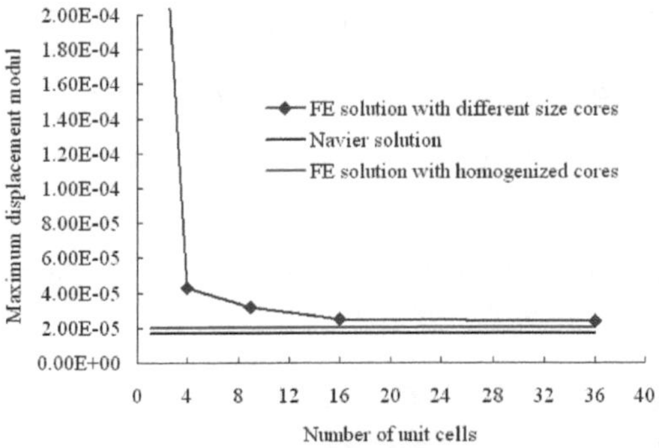

(b)

Fig.10. (a) Total potential energy and (b) Maximum displacement module of sandwich panel with the square core

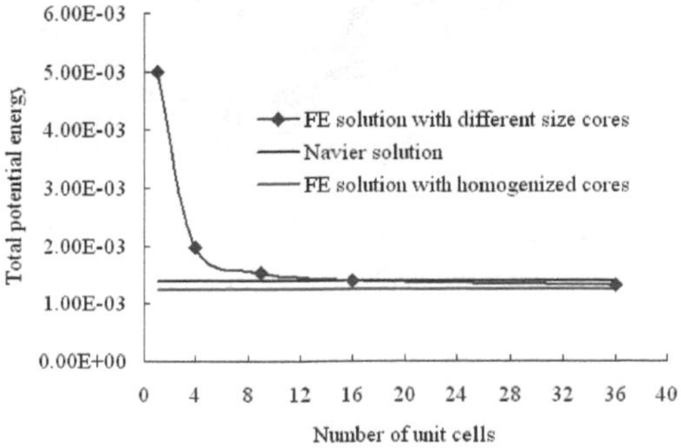

(a)

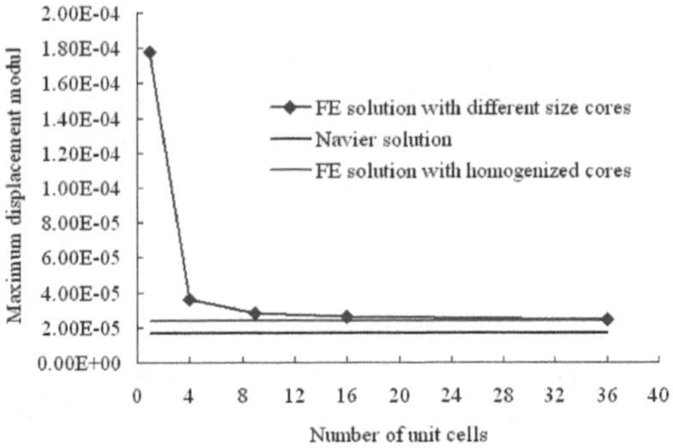

(b)

Fig.11. (a) Total potential energy and (b) Maximum displacement module of sandwich panel with the rhombic core

Table 3. Bending deflections of sandwich panel with different size square cores

Number of unit cells	Different size cores	Bending responses of sandwich panels	Bending values of sandwich panels	
			Total potential energy	Maximum displacement module
1×1=1	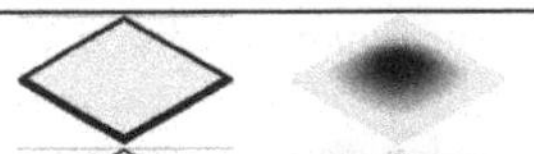		1.28E-2	3.93E-4
2×2=4			2.40E-3	0.43E-4
3×3=9	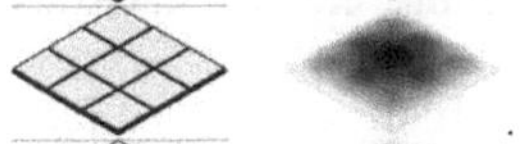		1.58E-3	0.32E-4
4×4=16	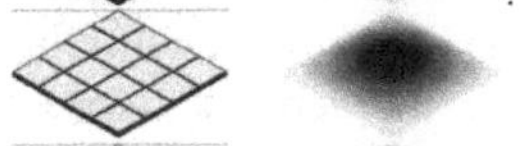		1.37E-3	0.25E-4
6×6=36	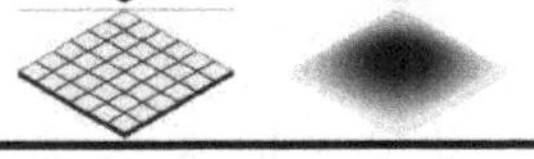		1.28E-3	0.24E-4

Table 4. Bending deflections of sandwich panel with different size rhombic cores

Number of unit cells	Different size cores	Bending responses of sandwich panels	Bending values of sandwich panels	
			Total potential energy	Maximum displacement module
1×1=1	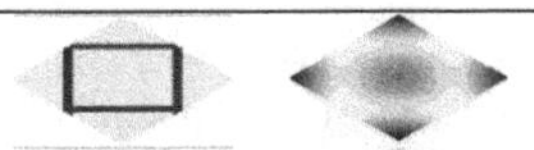		5.0E-3	1.78E-4
2×2=4	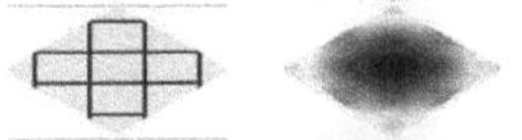		1.98E-3	0.36E-4
3×3=9			1.53E-3	0.28E-4
4×4=16	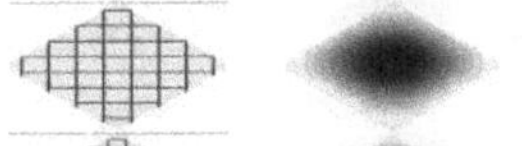		1.40E-3	0.26E-4
6×6=36	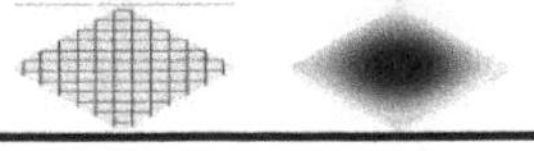		1.31E-3	0.25E-4

3.1.3 Discussion

According to the figures and tables in the above two examples, it is found that bending response of sandwich panel tends to a limit case with the decreasing size of honeycomb core. This limit case is approximately the bending response of sandwich panel with homogenized cores with the same boundary conditions. At the same time, we also find that the coincidence between Levy solution and FE solution with homogenized hexagonal cores is worse than that between Navier solution and FE solution with homogenized square cores. The reason lies in the fact that the ratio of the span dimensions to thickness ($\alpha = a/(h_u + h_c + h_l)$) is 14.184 for the hexagonal core and 17.6 for the square core. According to the basic assumption of the laminate plate theory, the classical lamination theory is only valid for thin laminates with small displacement in the transverse direction [26]. Therefore, when the ratio α increases, the theoretical solution is closer to the finite element solution equally well with the homogenized core.

Moreover, the bending deflection of sandwich panel with the rectangular cores is smaller than the hexagonal cores under the boundary condition of three points bending when the number of core unit cells rises or with the homogenized core. Comparing their effective elastic constants, we can find that the elastic moduli E_y^H and G_{xz}^H of the rectangular core are bigger than the hexagonal core, which play the leading role in the three points bending. In another example, the bending deflection of sandwich panel with the square cores is smaller than the rhombic cores with the four simply-supported edges by the finite element analysis. Similarly comparing their effective elastic constants, we can see that the effective elastic moduli in x and y directions of the square core are bigger than the rhombic core, but the effective shear moduli in y-z and x-z planes are close.

From these two cases, we can see that the configuration of unit cells in sandwich cores affects the bending performance of sandwich panels although they have the same volume fraction.

3.2 Sandwich panels with the corrugated cores

Table 5. Bending deflections of sandwich structures with different size circle cores

Number of unit cells	Different size cores	Bending responses of sandwich structures	Bending values of sandwich structures	
			Total potential energy	Maximum displacement module
1×6=6			1.26E2	8.64E-2
2×12=24			7.12E1	4.82E-2
3×18=54			6.45E1	4.36E-2
4×24=96			5.94E1	4.01E-2
5×30=150			5.35E1	3.6E-2
6×36=216			5.17E1	3.07E-2

In this section, the bending responses of sandwich panels with corrugated cores are analyzed with different sizes. Two forms of the cores i.e. the circle-core and the X-core are involved here. The boundary condition of three points bending is the same as Fig.2. The material properties of two sandwich panels are assigned as: E_u=E_l=2.0GPa for upper and lower skins, E_c=0.91GPa for cores. The difference between the two sandwich panels lies in that the simply supported sides are parallel to the extended direction of the unit cell for the circle-core, and vertical to the extended direction of the unit cell for the X-core. Here, only finite element solutions with the different size cores and homogenized cores are obtained. The levy method isn't adopted because the ratio of the span dimensions to thickness of sandwich panels ($\alpha = W/(h_u + h_c + h_l)$) is 1.9 for circle core and 2.857 for X-core. The laminate plate theory is no more applicable by the validation of examples in section 3.1.

3.2.1 Circle-core

For the sandwich structure with the circle core, the dimensions are set to be: length L=2.4m, width W=0.8m, thickness h_u=h_l=0.01m, h_c=0.40m (u-upper skin, l-lower skin, c-core).

The effecitive properties of the circle core are obtained by the homogenization method as follows.

$$E_x^H = 4.388174E{+}05,\ E_y^H = 4.461644E{+}05,\ E_z^H = 6.961283E{+}07$$
$$G_{xy}^H = 5.557200E{+}05,\ G_{yz}^H = 1.132639E{+}07,\ G_{xz}^H = 1.132639E{+}07$$
$$v_{xy}^H = 8.938214E{-}01,\ v_{xz}^H = 1.891106E{-}03,\ v_{yz}^H = 1.922768E{-}03 \quad (29)$$

Bending deflections of sandwich structure with the homogenized core is shown in Fig.12.

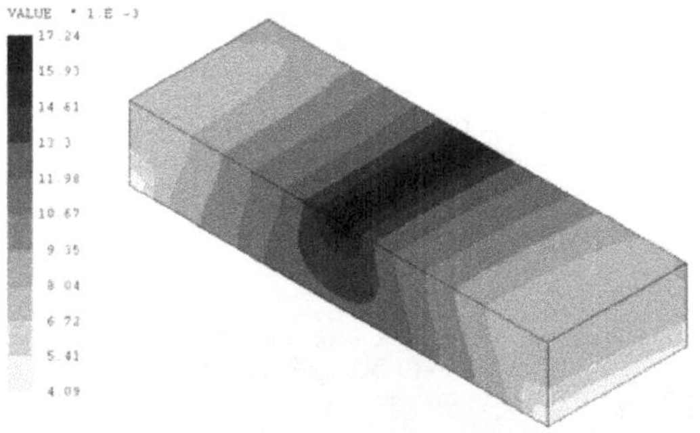

Fig.12. Finite element solution of sandwich structure with the homogenized core

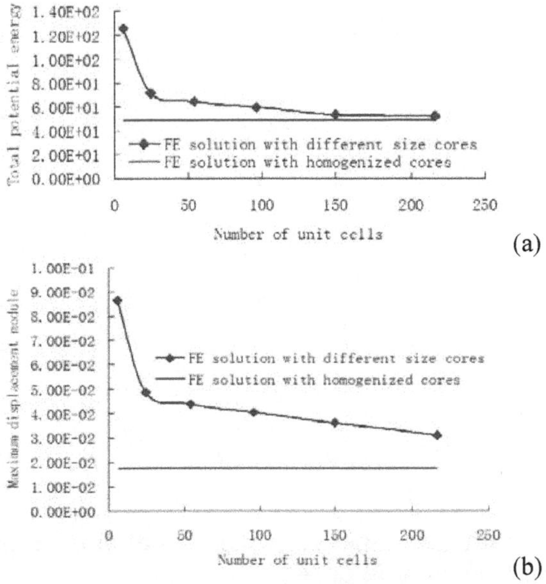

Fig.13. (a) Total potential energy and (b) Maximum displacement module of sandwich structure with the circle core

In Fig.13, it shows the values of the potential energy and the maximum displacement versus the number of the unit cells that have been used in the sandwich core.

3.2.2 X-core

For the sandwich structure with the X-core, the dimensions are: length L=2.0m, width W=1.2m, thickness $h_u=h_l=0.01$m, $h_c=0.4$m (u-upper skin, l-lower skin, c-core).

The effecitive properties of the X-core are obtained by the homogenization method.

$$E_x^H=3.927310E+04,\ E_y^H=1.666816E+05,\ E_z^H=5.940933E+07$$
$$G_{xy}^H=2.988478E+06,\ G_{yz}^H=1.542861E+07,\ G_{xz}^H=8.097270E+06$$
$$v_{xy}^H=4.839506E-01,\ v_{xz}^H=1.983178E-04,\ v_{yz}^H=8.416942E-04 \quad (30)$$

The bending deformation of sandwich structure with the homogenized core is seen as Fig.14. And the values of the potential energy and the maximum displacement versus the number of the unit cells that have been used in the sandwich core are plotted as shown in Fig.15.

Table 6. Bending deflections of sandwich structures with different size X-cores

Number of unit cells	Different size cores	Bending responses of sandwich structures	Bending values of sandwich structures	
			Total potential energy	Maximum displacement module
1×4=4	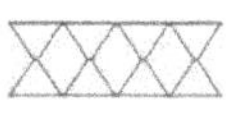		6.23E-3	8.92E-5
2×8=16			3.40E-3	3.59E-5
3×12=36			3.17E-3	3.02E-5
4×16=64	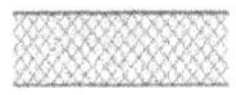		3.13E-3	2.94E-5
6×24=144			3.12E-3	2.91E-5

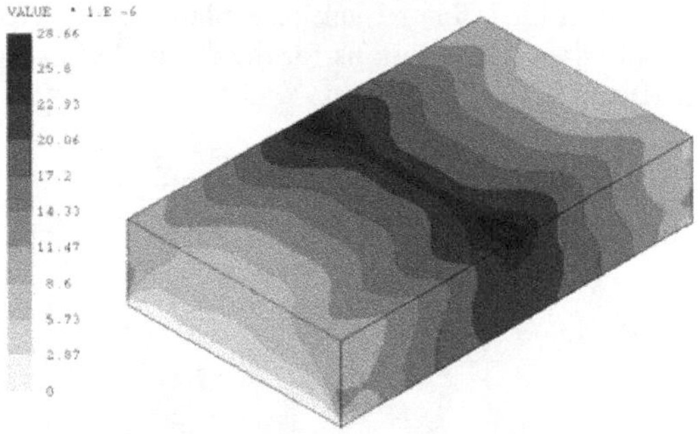

Fig.14. FE solution of sandwich structure with the homogenized core

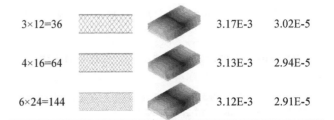

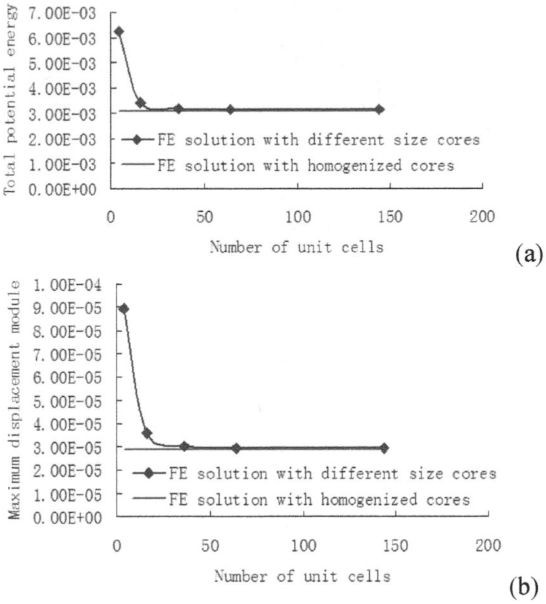

Fig.15. (a) Total potential energy and (b) Maximum displacement module of sandwich panel with the X-core

As known from Table 5, Table 6 and Fig.12, Fig.13, Fig.14 and Fig.15, the bending responses of sandwich structures with both circle cores and X-cores similarly converge to those obtained with homogenized cores when the sizes of honeycomb cores decrease. But the latter is faster and closer. There are two reasons. On the one hand, the latter ratio α of span dimensions to thickness is bigger. On the other hand, the simply supported sides are vertical to the extended direction of the unit cell for the X-core so that they are more homogeneous than circle cores under action of the transverse line load.

Therefore, for both the honeycomb core and the corrugated core, the bending response of sandwich panel has the common regularity with the size effect that the overall bending stiffness gradually increases along with ratio of the specimen size to the cell size. The conclusion is also verified by Ref. [21].

4 Dynamic analysis of sandwich panels

4.1 Dynamic analysis of laminate plate including transverse shear deformation

As given in [26], for the laminate plate simply supported on all four edges, the solutions for the flexural vibration may be written as

$$w(x,y,t)=\sum_{m=1}^{\infty}\sum_{n=1}^{\infty}C_{mn}\sin\frac{m\pi x}{a}\sin\frac{n\pi y}{b}e^{i\omega t} \quad (31)$$

$$\bar{\alpha}(x,y,t)=\sum_{m=1}^{\infty}\sum_{n=1}^{\infty}A_{mn}\cos\frac{m\pi x}{a}\sin\frac{n\pi y}{b}e^{i\omega t} \quad (32)$$

$$\bar{\beta}(x,y,t)=\sum_{m=1}^{\infty}\sum_{n=1}^{\infty}B_{mn}\sin\frac{m\pi x}{a}\cos\frac{n\pi y}{b}e^{i\omega t} \quad (33)$$

The governing differential equations including the transverse shear deformation and neglecting the rotatory inertia terms are following

$$D_{11}\frac{\partial^2\bar{\alpha}}{\partial x^2}+D_{66}\frac{\partial^2\bar{\alpha}}{\partial y^2}+(D_{12}+D_{66})\frac{\partial^2\bar{\beta}}{\partial x\partial y}-2A_{55}\left(\bar{\alpha}+\frac{\partial w}{\partial x}\right)=0 \quad (34)$$

$$(D_{12}+D_{66})\frac{\partial^2\bar{\alpha}}{\partial x\partial y}+D_{66}\frac{\partial^2\bar{\beta}}{\partial x^2}+D_{22}\frac{\partial^2\bar{\beta}}{\partial y^2}-2A_{44}\left(\bar{\beta}+\frac{\partial w}{\partial y}\right)=0 \quad (35)$$

$$2A_{55}\left(\frac{\partial\bar{\alpha}}{\partial x}+\frac{\partial^2 w}{\partial x^2}\right)+2A_{44}\left(\frac{\partial\bar{\beta}}{\partial y}+\frac{\partial^2 w}{\partial y^2}\right)=\rho h\frac{\partial^2 w}{\partial t^2} \quad (36)$$

where h is the thickness of laminate plate and

$$\rho=\frac{1}{h}\sum_{k=1}^{N}\rho_k(h_k-h_{k-1}) \quad (37)$$

$$A_{ij}=\frac{5}{4}\sum_{k=1}^{N}(\bar{Q}_{ij})_k\left[h_k-h_{k-1}-\frac{4}{3}(h_k^3-h_{k-1}^3)\frac{1}{h^2}\right] \quad i,j=4,5 \quad (38)$$

Substituting the solutions (Eq.(31)-Eq.(33)) into the governing equations (Eq.(34)-Eq.(36)) results in a set of homogeneous equations as follows

$$\begin{bmatrix} L_{11} & L_{12} & L_{13} \\ L_{12} & L_{22} & L_{23} \\ L_{13} & L_{23} & L'_{33} \end{bmatrix}\begin{Bmatrix} A_{mn} \\ B_{mn} \\ C_{mn} \end{Bmatrix}=\begin{Bmatrix} 0 \\ 0 \\ 0 \end{Bmatrix} \quad (39)$$

where $L'_{33}=L_{33}-\rho h\omega_{mn}^2$.

The square of the remaining natural frequency can be obtained by solving the above homogeneous equations.

$$\omega_{mn}^2=\frac{(L_{11}L_{22}-L_{12}^2)L_{33}+2L_{12}L_{23}L_{13}-L_{22}L_{13}^2-L_{11}L_{23}^2}{\rho h(L_{11}L_{22}-L_{12}^2)} \quad (40)$$

where, m and n are the number of x and y axial half-waves respectively. If $\lambda_m=m\pi/a$ and $\lambda_n=n\pi/b$,

$$L_{11}=D_{11}\lambda_m^2+D_{66}\lambda_n^2+2A_{55} \quad (41)$$

$$L_{12}=(D_{12}+D_{66})\lambda_m\lambda_n \quad (42)$$

$$L_{13}=2A_{55}\lambda_m \quad (43)$$

$$L_{22}=D_{66}\lambda_m^2+D_{22}\lambda_n^2+2A_{44} \quad (44)$$

$$L_{23}=2A_{44}\lambda_n \quad (45)$$

$$L_{33}=2A_{55}\lambda_m^2+2A_{44}\lambda_n^2 \quad (46)$$

4.2 Sandwich panel with hexagonal and rectangular honeycomb cores

Sandwich panels with the hexagonal and rectangular honeycomb cores, as shown in Fig.2, are simply supported on the four bottom edges. The dimensions of the sandwich panel are following as: width a=0.8865m, length b=1.5354m, thickness h_u=h_l=0.01m, h_c=0.03m (u-upper skin, l-lower skin, and c-core). The elastic moduli of the upper and lower skins are 210GPa. The density is 7800kg/m^3. For the core, the elastic modulus is 75GPa and the density is 2700 kg/m^3 (solid or black part). In order to calculate the effective elastic constants of sandwich core, we assume that the void or white part is a very weak material: the elastic modulus is 0.00001GPa and density is 0.00001kg/m^3.

The effective material properties of hexagonal honeycomb core are obtained by the 3D homogenization method.

E_x^H=2.570071E+09, E_y^H=2.568502E+09, E_z^H=1.989796E+10

G_{xy}^H=7.228240E+08, G_{yz}^H=4.345104E+09, G_{xz}^H=4.346297E+09

v_{xy}^H=7.818590E-01, v_{xz}^H=3.874876E-02, v_{yz}^H=3.872511E-02

(47)

The effective material properties of rectangular honeycomb core are

E_x^H=1.412906E+10, E_y^H=8.484773E+09, E_z^H=1.989796E+10

G_{xy}^H=1.174879E+08, G_{yz}^H=3.165510E+09, G_{xz}^H=5.357120E+09

v_{xy}^H=2.119053E-02, v_{xz}^H=2.130228E-01, v_{yz}^H=1.279243E-01

(48)

And the effective density of hexagonal honeycomb core is following,

$$\rho_c=\left((S_T-S_{void})\times 2700+S_{void}\times 0.00001\right)/S_T=716.3265 \quad (49)$$

where S_T is the area of whole core in the *x-y* plane and S_{void} is the area of void part.

$$S_T=4\times 0.7677\times 0.4432=1.3611 \quad (50)$$

$$S_{void} = 8 \times 0.5 \times (0.2193 + 0.4387) \times 0.3799 = 0.9847 \quad (51)$$

Because these two honeycomb cores are identical with the volume fraction, the effective density of rectangular honeycomb core is also 716.3265. The average of the mass density across the thickness for sandwich panel is:

$$\rho = \frac{1}{h}\sum_{k=1}^{N}\rho_k(h_k - h_{k-1}) = \frac{1}{0.05}(7800 \times 0.02 + 716.3265 \times 0.03) = 3549.796 \quad (52)$$

According to Eq.(40), the natural frequencies of sandwich panel with the homogenized hexagonal and rectangular cores are obtained in Table 7.

Table 7. Natural frequencies with different m and n

m, n	m=1 n=1	m=1 n=2	m=1 n=3	m=2 n=1	m=2 n=2
for the hexagonal core	272.75	474.17	803.55	868.13	1061.99
for the rectangular core	273.55	474.42	803.88	873.4	1065.4

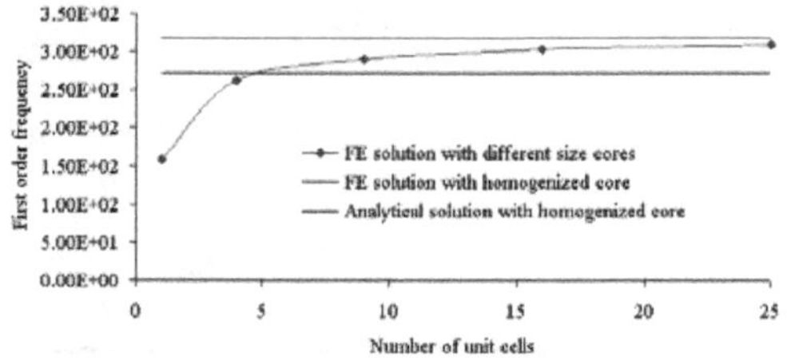

(a)

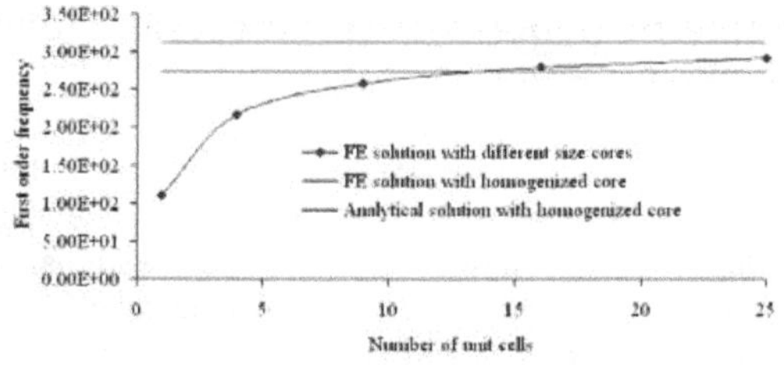

(b)

Fig.16. Frequency variation of the first order vibration with different size (a) hexagonal and (b) rectangular cores

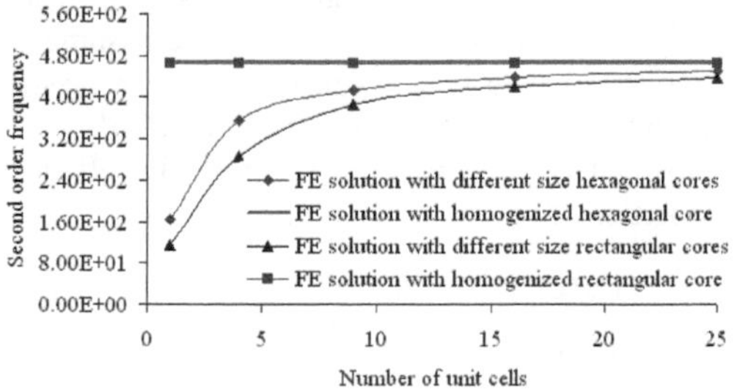

Fig.17. Frequency variation of the second order vibration with different size hexagonal and rectangular cores

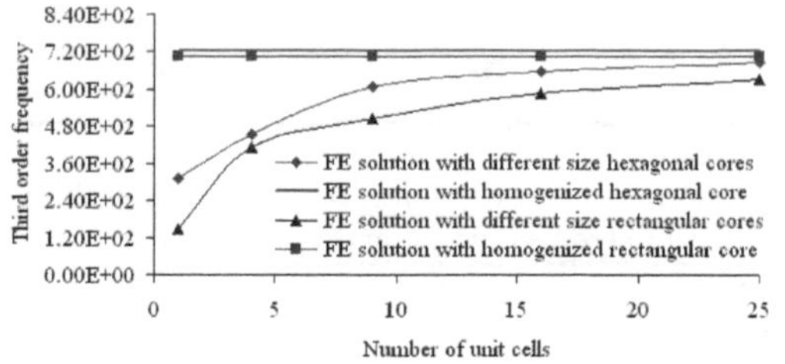

Fig.18. Frequency variation of the third order vibration with different size hexagonal and rectangular cores

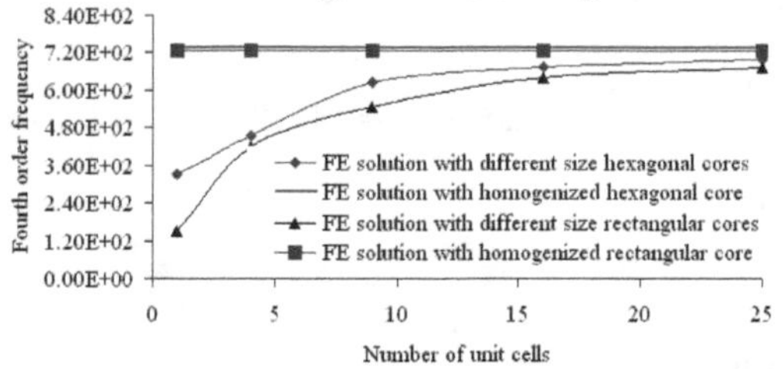

Fig.19. Frequency variation of the fourth order vibration with different size hexagonal and rectangular cores

The finite element models of sandwich panels with the different size hexagonal and rectangular cores and their homogenized cores are built and their eigen-frequencies and the five order vibration modes are calculated as shown in Table 8 to Table 12 and Fig.16 to Fig.20.

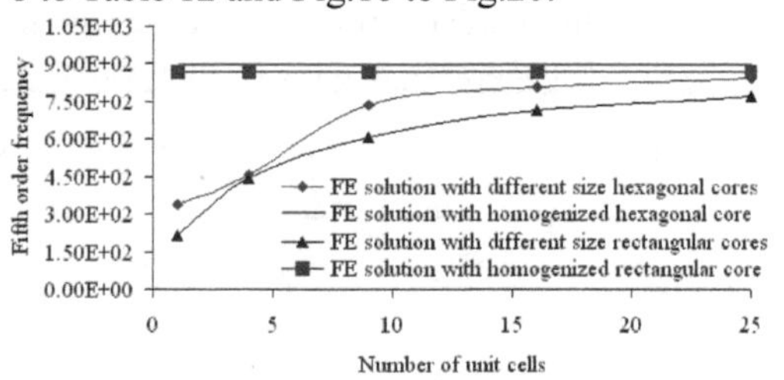

Fig.20. Frequency variation of the fifth order vibration with different size hexagonal and rectangular cores

Table 8. The first order vibration response with the different size hexagonal and rectangular cores

Number of unit cell	1×1	2×2	3×3	4×4	5×5
Different sizes cores	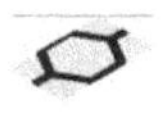	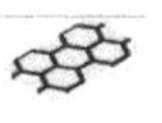	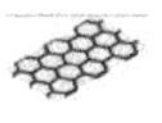	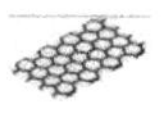	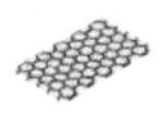
Frequency	1.59E+2	2.62E+2	2.91E+2	3.03E+2	3.09E+2
Mode of sandwich panel	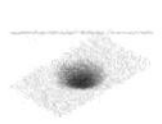			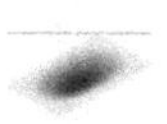	
Different sizes cores	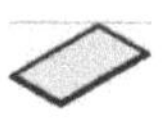				
Frequency	1.10E+2	2.17E+2	2.57E+2	2.80E+2	2.92E+2

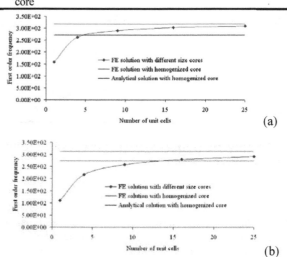

Mode of sandwich panel	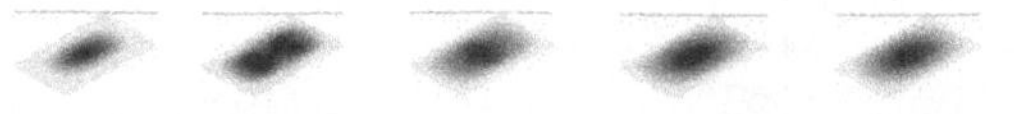				

Table 9. The second order vibration response with the different size hexagonal and rectangular cores

Number of unit cell	1×1	2×2	3×3	4×4	5×5
Different sizes cores	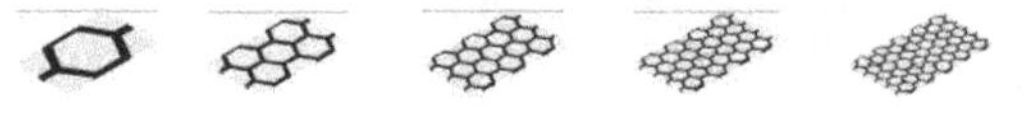				
Frequency	1.64E+2	3.55E+2	4.14E+2	4.37E+2	4.49E+2
Mode of sandwich panel					
Different sizes cores	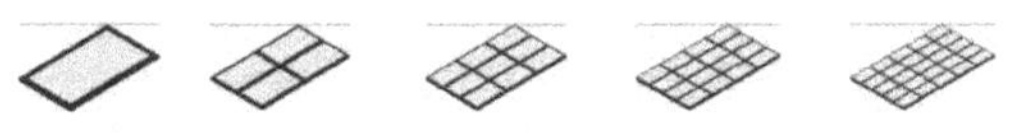				
Frequency	1.14E+2	2.85E+2	3.87E+2	4.20E+2	4.38E+2
Mode of sandwich panel					

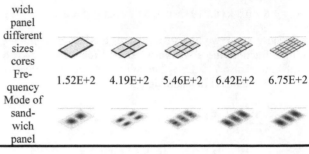

Table 10. The third order vibration response with the different size hexagonal and rectangular cores

Number of unit cell	1×1	2×2	3×3	4×4	5×5
different sizes cores	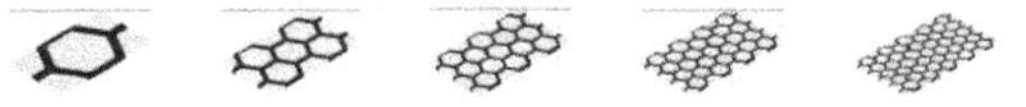				
Frequency	3.12E+2	4.53E+2	6.06E+2	6.58E+2	6.83E+2
Mode of sandwich panel					
different sizes cores					
Frequency	1.48E+2	4.14E+2	5.05E+2	5.87E+2	6.32E+2
Mode of sandwich panel					

Table 11. The fourth order vibration response with the different size hexagonal cores

Number of unit cell	1×1	2×2	3×3	4×4	5×5
different sizes cores	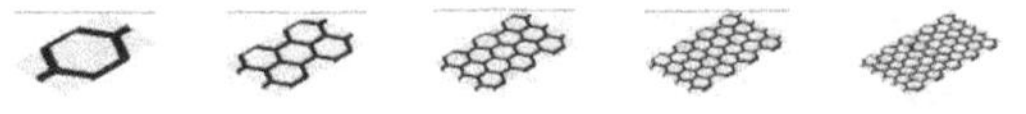				
Frequency	3.30E+2	4.53E+2	6.25E+2	6.74E+2	6.99E+2
Mode of sandwich panel					
different sizes cores	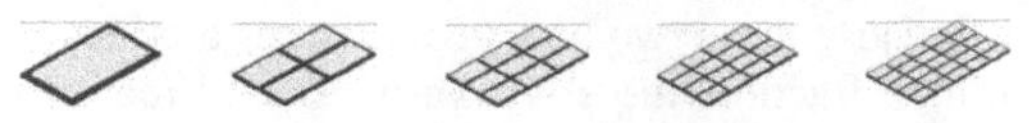				
Frequency	1.52E+2	4.19E+2	5.46E+2	6.42E+2	6.75E+2
Mode of sandwich panel					

Table 12. The fifth order vibration response with the different size hexagonal and rectangular cores

Number of unit cell	1×1	2×2	3×3	4×4	5×5
different sizes cores	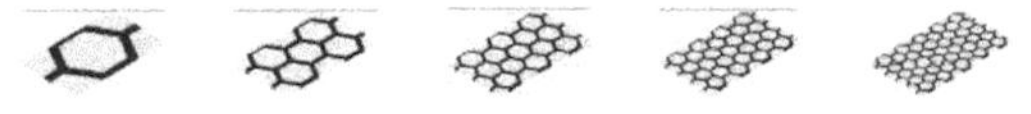				
Frequency	3.38E+2	4.53E+2	7.34E+2	8.06E+2	8.42E+2
Mode of sandwich panel					
different sizes cores	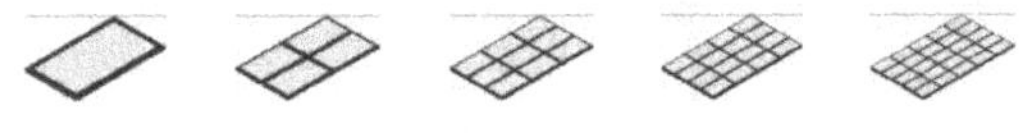				
Frequency	2.15E+2	4.42E+2	6.07E+2	7.13E+2	7.70E+2
Mode of sandwich panel					

4.3 Sandwich panel with square and rhombic honeycomb cores

Consider a sandwich panel with the square and rhombic honeycomb core as shown in Fig.7. All the four edges are simply supported. The dimensions of the sandwich panel are assigned as: a=1.1m, h_u=h_l=0.01m, h_c=0.03m (u-upper skin, l-lower skin, and c-core). Similar to the hexagonal core in the section 6.2.1, the elastic moduli of the upper and lower skins are 210GPa. The density is 7800kg/m3. For the core, the elastic modulus is 75GPa and the density is 2700 kg/m^3 (solid or black part). In the same way, we assume that the void or white part is a very weak material: the elastic modulus is 0.00001GPa and density is 0.00001kg/m^3.

With the 3D homogenization method, the effective material properties of square honeycomb core are

$$E_x^H=7.227631E+09,\ E_y^H=7.227631E+09,\ E_z^H=1.301653E+10$$
$$G_{xy}^H=3.424314E+07,\ G_{yz}^H=2.695173E+09,\ G_{xz}^H=2.695173E+09$$
$$v_{xy}^H=-6.337963E-03,\ v_{xz}^H=1.665797E-01,\ v_{yz}^H=1.665797E-01 \quad (53)$$

The effective material properties of rhombic honeycomb core are

$$E_x^H=1.766130\text{E}+08,\ E_y^H=1.771721\text{E}+08,\ E_z^H=1.301653\text{E}+10$$
$$G_{xy}^H=3.671618\text{E}+09,\ G_{yz}^H=2.723917\text{E}+09,\ G_{xz}^H=2.715759\text{E}+09$$
$$v_{xy}^H=9.740973\text{E}-01,\ v_{xz}^H=4.070510\text{E}-03,\ v_{yz}^H=4.083396\text{E}-03 \quad (54)$$

And the effective density of two honeycomb cores is same and computed as following,

$$\rho_c = ((1.1^2 - 1^2) * 2700 + 1^2 * 0.00001 / 1.12 = 468.595 \quad (55)$$

The average of the mass density across the thickness for sandwich panel:

$$\rho = \frac{1}{h}\sum_{k=1}^{N} \rho_k (h_k - h_{k-1}) \quad (56)$$
$$= \frac{1}{0.05}(7800 \times 0.02 + 468.595 \times 0.03) = 3401.157$$

According to Eq.(40), the natural frequencies of sandwich panel with the homogenized square and rhombic cores are obtained in Table 13.

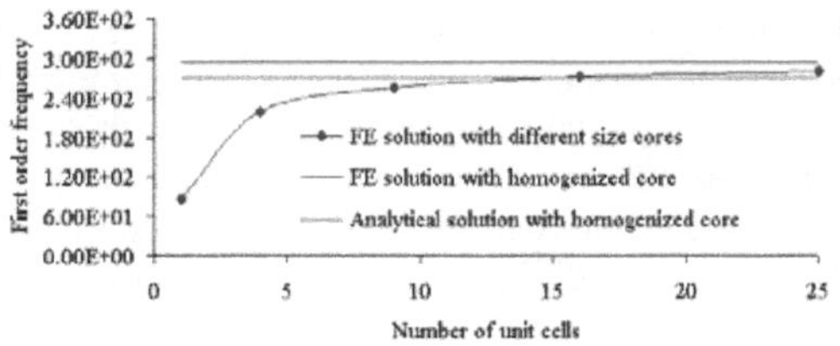

(a)

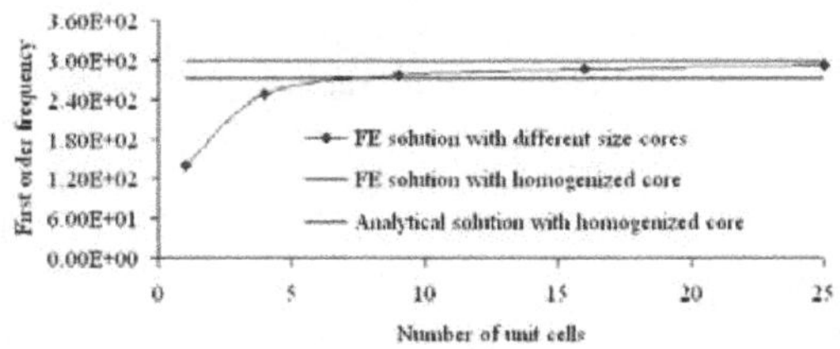

(b)

Fig.21. Frequency variation of the first order vibration with different size (a) square and (b) rhombic cores

Table 13. Natural frequencies with different values of m and n

m, n	m=1 n=1	m=1 n=2	m=1 n=3	m=2 n=1	m=2 n=2
for the square core	271.29	669.17	1308.9	669.17	1055.2
for the rhombic core	271.56	668.61	1306.1	668.61	1056.2

The finite element models of sandwich panels with the different size square and rhombic cores and the homogenized cores are built and their five order eigen-frequencies and vibration modes are calculated as shown in Table 14 to Table 18 and Fig.21 to Fig.25.

Table 14. The first order vibration response with the different size square and rhombic cores

Number of unit cell	1×1	2×2	3×3	4×4	5×5
different sizes cores	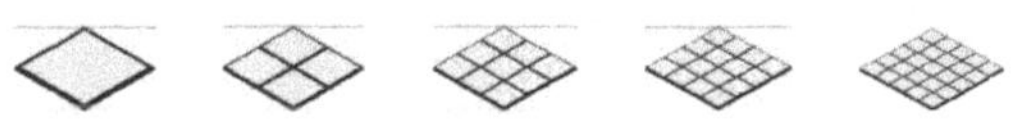				
Frequency	8.62E+1	2.18E+2	2.55E+2	2.72E+2	2.81E+2
Mode of sandwich panel					
different sizes cores	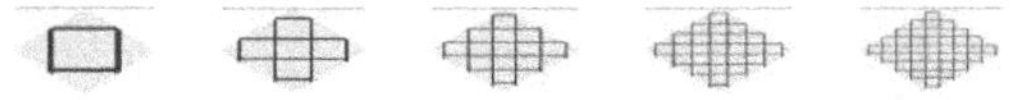				
Frequency	1.41E+2	2.47E+2	2.77E+2	2.86E+2	2.91E+2
Mode of sandwich panel	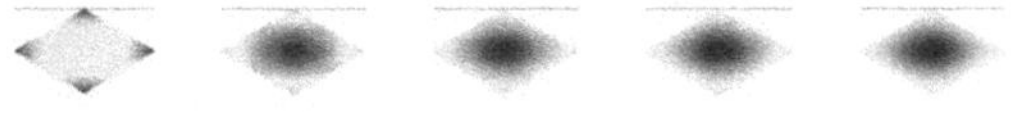				

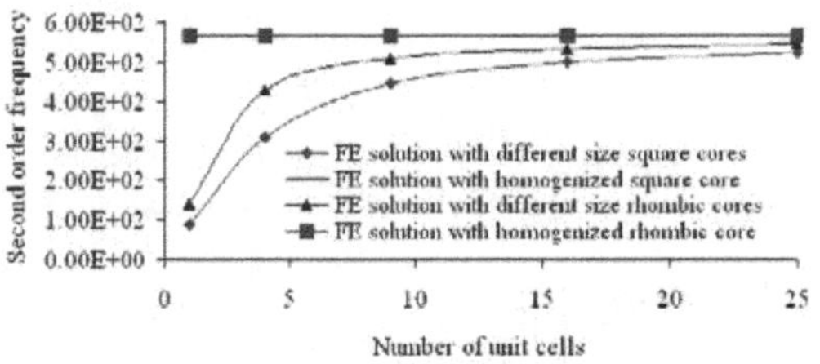

Fig.22. Frequency variation of the second order vibration with different size square and rhombic cores

Table 15. The second order vibration response with the different size square and rhombic cores

Number of unit cell	1×1	2×2	3×3	4×4	5×5
different sizes cores	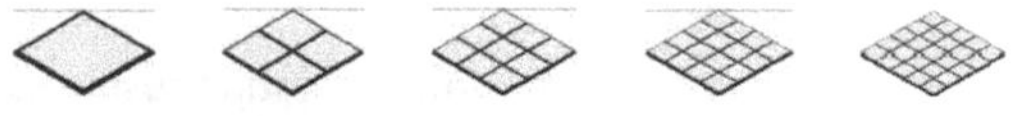				
Frequency	8.78E+1	3.10E+2	4.47E+2	4.98E+2	5.24E+2
Mode of sandwich panel	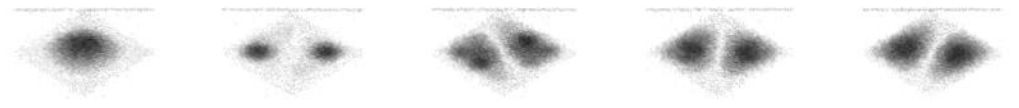				
different sizes cores	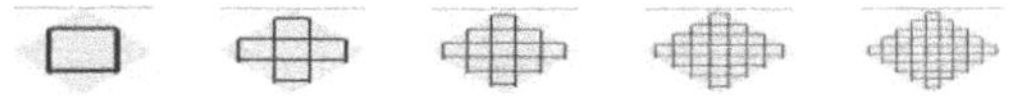				
Frequency	1.41E+2	4.28E+2	5.08E+2	5.35E+2	5.48E+2
Mode of sandwich panel					

Table 16. The third order vibration response with the different size square and rhombic cores

Number of unit cell	1×1	2×2	3×3	4×4	5×5
different sizes					

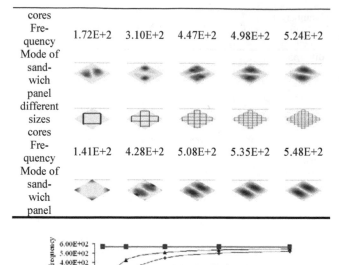

cores					
Frequency	1.72E+2	3.10E+2	4.47E+2	4.98E+2	5.24E+2
Mode of sandwich panel					
different sizes cores	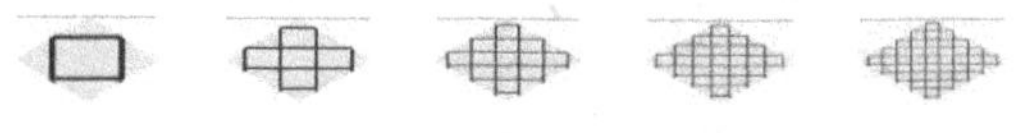				
Frequency	1.41E+2	4.28E+2	5.08E+2	5.35E+2	5.48E+2
Mode of sandwich panel	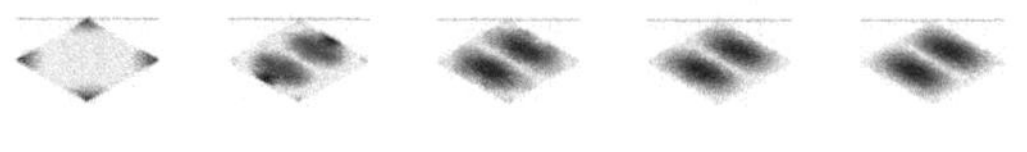				

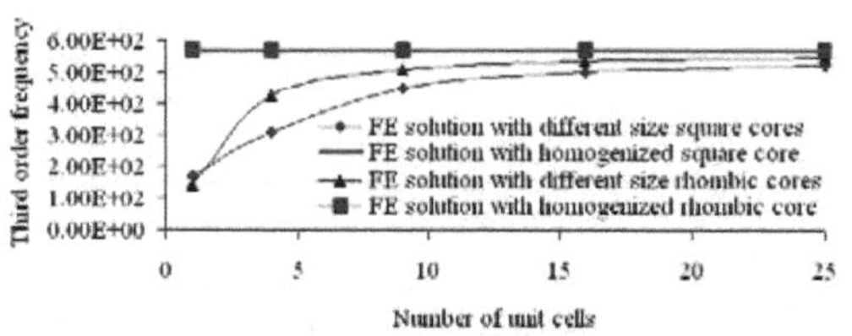

Fig.23. Frequency variation of the third order vibration with different size square and rhombic cores

4.4 Discussion

From Tables 6-10, Tables 12-16 and Figs.16-25, it is also demonstrated that the vibration frequencies and modes of sandwich panel approach the limit values with the homogenized cores with increasing the number of unit cells or decreasing the size of unit cells. Actually, these cases are reasonable. We can imagine that the material distributions are more and more homogeneous with the increasing number of unit cells under the same material amount and configurations of unit cells. Therefore the performance of sandwich panels for the free vibration is improved.

Table 17. The fourth order vibration response with the different size square and rhombic cores

Number of unit cell	1×1	2×2	3×3	4×4	5×5
different sizes cores	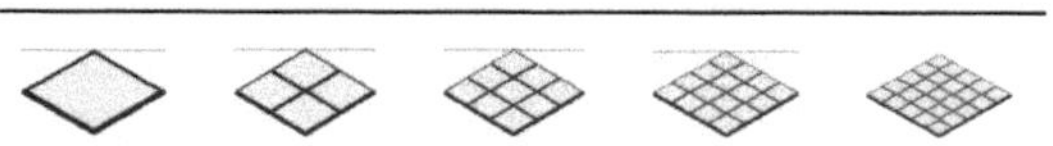				
Frequency	1.72E+2	3.31E+2	5.97E+2	6.98E+2	7.48E+2
Mode of sandwich panel	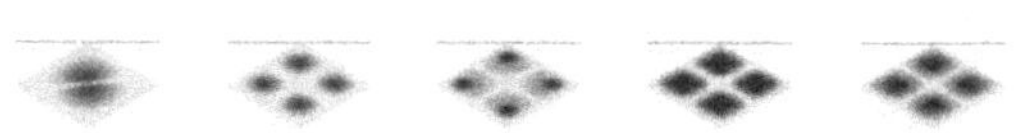				
different sizes cores	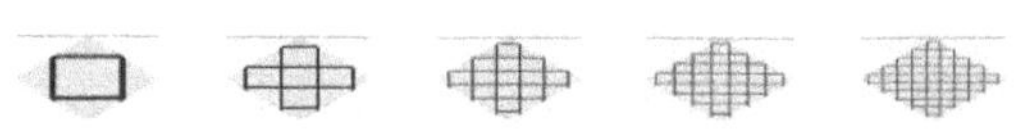				
Frequency	1.43E+2	5.41E+2	7.10E+2	7.68E+2	7.96E+2
Mode of sandwich panel	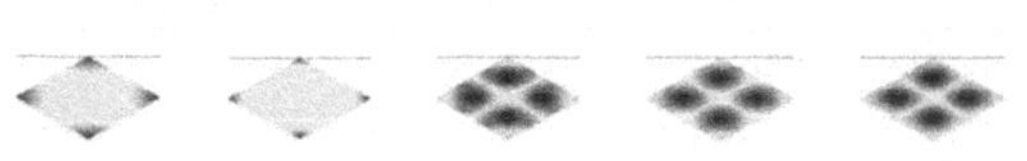				

Table 18. The fifth order vibration response with the different size square and rhombic cores

Number of unit cell	1×1	2×2	3×3	4×4	5×5
different sizes cores	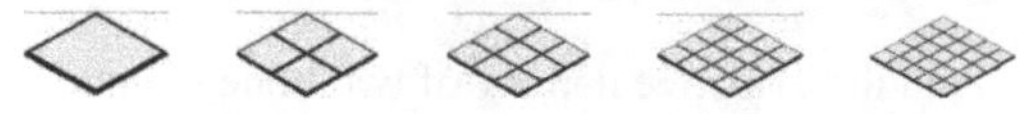				
Frequency	1.79E+2	3.38E+2	6.47E+2	7.82E+2	8.51E+2
Mode of sandwich panel	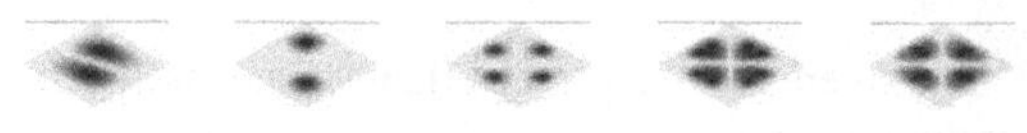				
different sizes cores	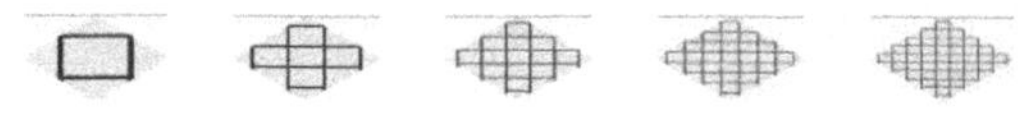				
Frequency	1.81E+2	5.41E+2	8.39E+2	9.0E+2	9.31E+2
Mode of sandwich panel					

In addition, the natural frequencies of sandwich panels are obtained with the laminated plate theory including the transverse shear deformation on the basis of the homogenized cores. The fundamental frequency occurs with $m=n=1$, which is for one half sine wave in each direction. Natural frequencies for the two sandwich panels are listed in Table 7 and Table 13 with the different m and n. Variation of m has greater influence on natural frequencies than n for sandwich panel with the hexagonal and rectangular cores because m is the number of x axial half-waves corresponding to the short side. Variation of m and n has the same influence on natural frequencies for sandwich panel with the square and rhombic cores. By observing the Fig.16 and Fig.21, the deviation between the analytical solution and the FE solution with homogenized square and rhombic cores is less than with homogenized hexagonal and rectangular cores. Similar to section 3.1, the ratio of the span dimensions to thickness ($\alpha = a/h$) is 17.73 for the hexagonal and rectangular cores which is less than for the square and rhombic cores ($\alpha = 22$). Therefore, the laminated plate theory for dynamic analysis is also more applicable to the thin plate.

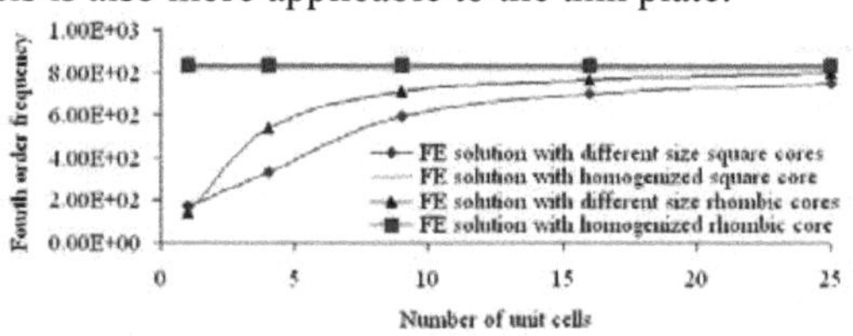

Fig.24. Frequency variation of the fourth order vibration with different size square and rhombic cores

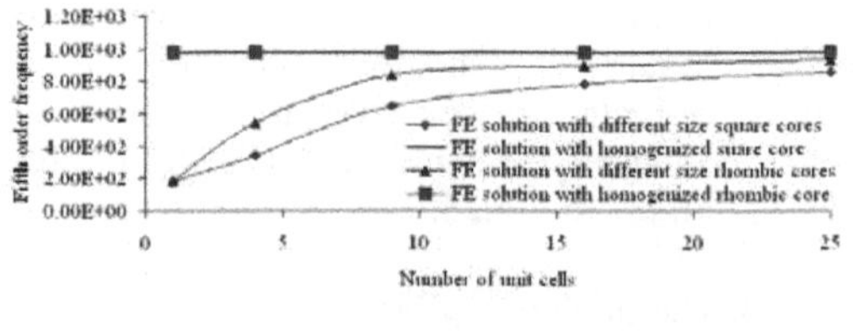

Fig.25. Frequency variation of the fifth order vibration with different size square and rhombic cores

And also we compare the dynamic response of sandwich panels with the different configuration of sandwich cores and with the same volume fraction. The FE analysis results show that the natural frequencies of sandwich panels with the hexagonal cores are bigger than the rectangular cores. And the natural frequencies of sandwich panels with the square cores are smaller than the rhombic cores. However their natural frequencies obtained by the analytical method are very close.

5 Conclusions and further works

In this paper, we analyzed the bending and dynamic responses of sandwich panels with the size variation of the different cores. Conclusions can be drawn as follows: (1) with decreasing the size of unit cells, the deformation and natural frequency of the sandwich panel with different size cores tends to the one with homogenized cores. So the homogenization method is valid in analyzing the sandwich panel when the number of core unit cells is many enough; (2) it is verified that the laminate plate theory is adapted to the static and dynamic analysis for sandwich panel with the homogenized sandwich core when the ratio α of span dimensions to thickness of sandwich panel satisfies the requirement of the lamination theory; (3) the size effect of cores is very obvious and important for the structural response of sandwich panels. Special attention must be paid when the core number is small; (4) the more suitable configuration of unit cells in sandwich cores can be chose under the given boundary condition and the analysis of structural responses.

The above examples also show that the Navier solution of sandwich panels with the square and rhombic cores and the analytical solution of dynamic responses are very close. The influence of configuration of sandwich cores on the structural response of sandwich panels cannot be reflected by using the classical laminate plate theory. Therefore, in further works, the high order laminate plate theory needs to be adopted in order to improve the analytical accuracy for sandwich panel with the homogenized cores. Besides, the influence of size effect on buckling and thermal responses of sandwich structures can be further studied. And the new configurations of sandwich cores that possess extraordinary properties are designed considering the integrated performances of sandwich panels by the multi-objective optimization.

References

1. L.J. Gibson, M.F. Ashby, *Cellular solids structure and properties* (Oxford, Pergamon Press, 1998).
2. N. Wicks, J.W. Hutchinson, *Performance of sandwich plates with truss cores.* Mechanics of Materials, **36**, 739-751 (2004).
3. A. Petras, M.P.F. Sutcliffe, *Failure mode maps for honeycomb sandwich panels.* Composite Structures. **44**, 237-252 (1999).
4. L. Valdevit, Z. Wei, C. Mercer, F.W. Zok, A.G. Evans, Structural performance of near-optimal sandwich panels with corrugated cores. *International Journal of Solids and Structures*, **43**, 4888-4905 (2006).
5. D. Lukkassen, A. Meidell, Advanced *Materials and Structures and their Fabrication Processes.* Third edition, (Narvik University College, HiN, 2003).
6. H. Zhu, B.V. Sankar, *Analysis of sandwich TPS panel with functionally graded foam core by Galerkin method.* Composite Structures, **77**, 280-287 (2007).
7. M. Styles, P. Compston, S. Kalyanasundaram, *The effect of core thickness on the flexural behaviour of aluminium-foam sandwich structures.* Composite Structures, **80**, 532-538 (2007).
8. N. Buannic, P. Cartraud, T. Quesnel, *Homogenization of corrugated core sandwich panels.* Composite Structures, **59**, 299-312 (2003).
9. F. Meraghni, F. Desrumaux, M.L. Benzeggagh, *Mechanical behavior of cellular core for structural sandwich panels.* Composites, Part A, **30**, 767-779 (1999).
10. X. F. Xu, P. Qiao, *Homogenized elastic properties of honeycomb sandwich with skin effect.* International Journal of Solids and Structures, **39**, 2153-2188 (2002).
11. J. Hohe, W. Becker, *An energetic homogenization procedure for the elastic properties of general cellular sandwich cores.* Composites, Part B, **32**, 185-197 (2001).
12. Z. Xue, J.W. Hutchinson, *Constitutive model for quasi-static deformation of metallic sandwich cores.* International Journal for Numerical Methods in Engineering, **61**, 2205–2238 (2004).
13. J. Romanoff, P. Varsta, *Bending response of web-core sandwich plates.* Composite Structures, **81**, 292-302 (2007).
14. C.E. Glenn, M.W. Hyer, *Bending behavior of low-cost sandwich plates*, Composites, Part A, **36**, 1449-1465 (2005).
15. J.K. Paik, A.K. Thayamballi, G.S. Kim, *The strength characteristics of aluminum honeycomb sandwich panels.* Thin-Walled Structures, **35**, 205–231 (1999).
16. V. Koissin, V. Skvortsov, S. Krahmalev, A. Shilpsha, *The elastic response of sandwich structures to local loading.* Composite Structures **63**, 375-385 (2004).
17. M. Meo, R. Vignjevic, G. Marengo, *The response of honeycomb sandwich panels under low-velocity impact loading.* International Journal of Mechanical Sciences, **47**, 1301-1325 (2005).
18. N. Pokharel, M. Mahendran, *Finite element analysis and design of sandwich panels subject to local buckling effects.* Thin-Walled Structures, **42**, 589-611 (2004).
19. Y. Frostig, O.T. Thomsen, *High-order free vibration of sandwich panels with a flexible core.* International Journal of Solids and Structures, **41**, 1697-1724 (2004).
20. W.S. Chang, E. Ventsel, T. Krauthammer, J. John, *Bending behavior of corrugated-core sandwich plates.* Composite Structures, **70**, 81-89 (2005).
21. C. Tekoglu, P.R. Onck, *Size effects in the mechanical behavior of cellular materials.* Journal of Materials Science, **40**, 5911-5917 (2005).
22. P.R. Onck, E.W. Andrews, L.J. Gibson, *Size effects in ductile cellular solids. Part I, modeling.* International Journal of Mechanical Sciences, **43**, 681-699 (2001).
23. G.M. Dai, W.H. Zhang, *Size effects of basic cell in static analysis of sandwich beams.* International Journal of Solids and Structures, **45**, 2512-2533 (2008).

24. B. Hassani, E. Hinton, *A review of homogenization and topology and topology optimization I-homogenization theory for media with periodic structure*. Computers & Structures, **69**, 707-717 (1998).
25. B. Hassani, E. Hinton, *A review of homogenization and topology and topology optimization II-analytical and numerical solution of homogenization equations.* Computers & Structures, **69**, 719-738 (1998).
26. J.R. Vinson, R.L. Sierakowski, *The behavior of structure composed of composite materials*. (Martinus Nijhoff Publishers, 1987).
27. J.N. Reddy, *Energy and variational methods in applied mechanics*. (Wiley-Interscience publication, 1984).

5

Minimum-cost planning of the multimodal transport of pipes with evolutionary computation

Begoña González[1], Gabriel Winter[1 a], José Maria Emperador[1], Blas Galván[1]

[1] Institute of Intelligent Systems and Numerical Applications in Engineering (SIANI), Laboratory of Evolutionary Computation and Applications (CEANI), University of Las Palmas de Gran Canaria, 35.017 Las Palmas de Gran Canaria, Spain

Abstract – Every day many kilometres of European highways are blocked by traffic jams. Congestion on roads and at airports adds the EU's fuel bill with a corresponding rise in pollution levels. In short, our present patterns of transport growth are unsustainable. One way of easing road congestion is to develop the efficient end-to-end movement of goods using two or more forms of transport in an integrated transport chain. We will focus on the multimodal transport problem that involves finding the most economical route in the distribution of cast iron ductile piping with or without mortar joint, both of different diameters and from different possible supply points to different points of destination over three transport networks, road, rail and sea, which may have routes in common. The orders are made for quantities in linear metres of pipes. The economic cost of the transport on the various routes is dependent on the number of lorries, freight wagons and platforms required, and as these quantities must be obviously integer numbers. In practical applications the search space is dimensionally very high, often there exist attractors into the search space due to the existence of multiple global optimum solutions, the cost function has discontinuities, many constraints, etc. The problem that has to be resolved is of great complexity, even using evolutionary algorithms. Our experience gained working several years in this optimization problem is described in this paper, to highlight that there is a need using evolutionary algorithms with certain learning ingredients and using strategies that progressively impose with more and more severity in the evolutionary optimization process the real scenario of the complex problem to get convergence to the global optimal solutions and simultaneously to obtain low computational cost total.

Key words: Minimum-cost planning, Multimodal transport problem, Evolutionary computation

1 Introduction

The transport problem that is considered here involves finding the most economical route in the distribution of cast iron ductile piping without mortar joint (CIDP) and cast iron ductile piping with mortar joint (CIDP-MJ), both of different diameters and from different possible supply points to different points of destination over three transport networks, road, rail and sea, which may have routes in common. The orders are made for quantities in linear metres ((lm) (with or without mortar joints) and are prepared in (tied) bundles of piping 6 metres long. Thus, the orders for each type and diameter of pipe should be in quantities (lm) that are multiples of 6.

The various networks considered are comprised of nodes (some belonging to different networks at the same time) which we have classified as factory-nodes (pipe supply points) and demand-nodes which cover both route-end-nodes (from which no product leaves for another destination point), and transhipment-nodes which can, in turn, satisfy a partial demand and serve as a link to another transhipment-node or to a route-end-node. A partial demand can be considered as a real order demand or as a fixed storage.

The transport cost, whether by road, rail or sea, of a certain amount or length (lm) of piping – of a certain type and specific diameter – is evaluated, for each route, by considering the number of lorries, freight wagons or platforms respectively required for this route and the unit cost per lorry, freight wagon or platform respectively associated with it, regardless of whether the lorries, freight wagons or platforms are full or not.

Since the economic cost of the transport on the various routes is dependent on the number of lorries, freight wagons and platforms required, and as these quantities are obviously integer numbers, the problem that has to be resolved is of great complexity, even using mathematical methods based on elements of artificial intelligence (genetic algorithms, evolutive strategies, etc.).

In addition, as a node can belong to more than one of the three transport networks considered, piping can leave and/or arrive from/to a same node via different means of transport, with which we have a very high number of situations or possible combinations to take into account when searching for the optimal route. This becomes extremely complex if we bear in mind that the ordered pipes can be of different diameter and type and that pipes of different diameters can be transported on the one same lorry, wagon or platform. In this situation, and if the possibility is also contemplated of a partial unloading of material at a transhipment node, thought has also to be given to the correct placement of the piping to facilitate its unloading so as not to have to unload and reload the piping that will continue to another demand-node.

[a] Corresponding author: gabw@step.es

Two factory-nodes have been considered. The cast iron ductile pipes without mortar joint are supplied from just one factory-node, while those with mortar joint can be supplied from both factory-nodes. Therefore, in this latter case, the selection of the most suitable factory-node to make the order from is contemplated amongst the optimal decisions to be obtained with the system.

The complexity of the multimodal transport system considered here lies in:

- Simultaneity of three different transport networks: we do not have just a road network, but also the possibilities of alternative routes by sea and/or rail.
- Specification of the various nodes and routes which comprise each of the networks considered.
- Each client can demand at the same time, in different physical places or demand-nodes, different amounts of piping of different types and of different diameters.
- The maximum full load of a lorry, freight wagon or platform depends on the type and diameter of the pipes to be transported. Thus, for each type and diameter of pipe the following will have to be taken into account:
  1. Number of pipes per bundle.
  2. Number of bundles per lorry, freight wagon and platform, respectively.
  3. Weight of each bundle.
  4. Volume of each bundle: length, height and width.

The filling of a means of transport (by availability of volume and weight) sometimes requires the use of non-standard sized bundles with less pipes than would correspond to it by type and diameter.

2 Intelligent system developed for the optimal planning of multimodal transport

A genetic algorithm (GA) has been used as an optimising tool, with selection and mutation, associated with an expert system (Galván and Winter [1]). Additionally, and in order to facilitate convergence to the global optimum, we have considered various stages in the optimisation which appreciably improve the performance of the optimiser. The fundamental items which describe the process carried out are as follows:

- Definition of the variables which comprise a possible solution (an individual or chromosome) of the GA considered. Thus, an individual will be made up of different variables which will be, for each cast iron ductile pipe of a certain class 'k' and a fixed diameter 'kk' the different lengths of pipe (lm) which are transported by road, rail or sea, from a departure node 'i' to an arrival node 'j' over a period of time 't'. These different lengths are represented by: x[i][j][k][t][kk] if the transport is by road, y[i][j][k][t][kk] if the transport is by rail, and z[i][j][k][t][kk] if the transport is by sea.
- Definition of the objective function that we wish to minimise and which in our case consists of two parts:
- The penalizing function which for a given demand-node is responsible for verifying that the quantity of a product that arrives at it is equal to the sum of the quantity of the product demanded by that node itself plus the product quantity which leaves it for other nodes.
- The cost function, which calculates the cost in function of the number of lorries, freight wagons and platforms used in the transport.
- Application of the developed intelligent system called Flexible Evolution Algorithm (FEA) (Winter et al. [2, 3, 4]). The FEA is subdivided into several functions, called 'engines'. These subroutines have been designed to group the diverse actions that are to be executed during the optimisation depending on their objectives. In this way, all the learning tasks will be clustered in a 'learning engine', and something similar will happen with all the selection schemes, sampling strategies or decision mechanisms. A general scheme of the Flexible Evolution Agent can be seen in Figure 1.

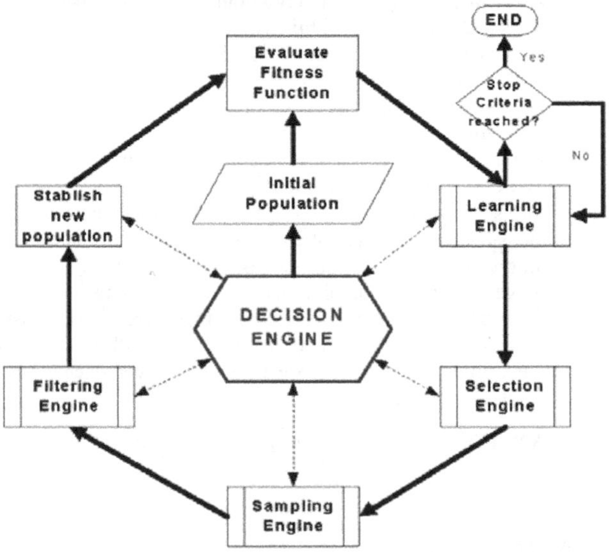

Fig. 1. Scheme of a Flexible Evolution Agent (FEA)

Starting with the initial population IP, and for all the iterations of the population obtained earlier, we evaluate the fitness function of each candidate solution and from here, and for each generation, the Decision Engine acts over all the different stages of the algorithm. So the decision engine will decide what kind of learning, selection and/or sampling strategy will be used in every generation until the stop criterion is reached, which is also determined by the Decision Engine. The Learning Engine stores everything that could be useful afterwards, such as information about the variables or statistics. The intention is to use this information to learn about the process and even to establish rules that could be fruitful and will be included in the decision engine afterwards.

The Selection Engine chooses which solutions are to be sampled and the sampling method that will be used, whereas the sampling engine carries out the mutation and crossover processes over the variables. Finally, the Filtering Engine removes the possible errors in the solutions before entering in the next iteration.

Main ingredients of the implementation of the FEA are: a Dynamic Structure of Operators (DSO), an Enlargement of the Genetic Code (EGC) of individuals and the use of a Central Control Mechanism (CCM). In order to obtain an efficient DSO two unique classes of operators have been defined: Selection and Sampling. Most existing crossover and mutation operators have been included in the Sampling class and the definition of two additional characteristics of all members of this class was also advisable: the Nature and the Range. The DSO enables the use of any of the operators at each step along every optimisation run depending on operator's previous contribution to the common task (to get the optimum). The genetic code of the individuals must be enlarged (EGC) in order to include useful information for the process control included in the CCM. After several implementations, the identification of the sampling method used to obtain each variable of the individuals has proved to be the most useful information, but only when a simple Probabilistic Control Mechanism (PCM) based on rules IF-THEN-ELSE is used as a CCM. The joint use of the DSO, the EGC and the CCM has permitted the elimination of the crossover and mutation probabilities. The PCM is responsible for reaching a trade-off between the exploration and the exploitation of the search space, which is equivalent to achieving a competitive and cooperative balance among the sampling operators.

Normally an evolutionary algorithm converge to a final population consists of the global optimum and solutions close to it. This causes difficulty when the function to optimize has multiple identical optimum solutions because in these problems there exist many attractors in which the algorithm can became directed to. To find different global optimum solutions we have incorporate in our Flexible Evolution Algorithm selection operators with sharing function proposed by Goldberg and Richardson [5].

In order to help the genetic algorithm in convergence to the optimum in our problem, two different fitness functions (FF) have been considered which differ basically in the weight given to the cost function (CF) and the penalizing function (PF): finally, the penalizing function weighs more. In addition, in the first time steps, a linear cost function has been considered.

The first objective function considered was: FF = CF + PF and the second one was FF = CF (1 + PF).

Table 1. Costs per lorry related to each route in the road network

Origin	Destination	Cost (€)
Germany	Bilbao	1779.63
Germany	Gijón	2083.23
Germany	León	2177.07
Germany	Vigo	2562.20
Germany	Porto	2592.33
Germany	Coimbra	2573.70
Germany	Lisbon	2969.76
Germany	Barcelona	1589.42
Germany	Lérida	1766.40
Germany	Madrid	2240.66
Germany	Salamanca	2219.85
Germany	Ciudad Real	2471.35
Germany	Valencia	1995.02
Germany	Murcia	2258.03
Germany	Málaga	2717.11
Germany	Seville	2854.30
Germany	Huelva	2860.05
Germany	Burgos	1950.15
Germany	Antwerp	750.00
Bilbao	Gijón	345.00
Bilbao	León	412.85
Bilbao	Lérida	533.60
Bilbao	Salamanca	454.25
Bilbao	Ciudad Real	672.75
Bilbao	Valencia	727.95
Bilbao	Murcia	915.40
Bilbao	Málaga	1079.85
Bilbao	Seville	1072.95
Bilbao	Huelva	1079.85
Bilbao	Tarragona	638.25
Bilbao	Burgos	181.70
Gijón	Bilbao	345.00
Gijón	León	141.45
Porto	Coimbra	218.50
Porto	Lisbon	460.00
Coimbra	Porto	218.50
Coimbra	Lisbon	241.50
Lisbon	Porto	460.00
Lisbon	Coimbra	241.50
Valencia	Murcia	277.15
Seville	Huelva	108.10
Austria	Bilbao	1779.63
Austria	Gijón	2083.23
Austria	León	2177.07
Austria	Vigo	2562.20
Austria	Porto	2592.33
Austria	Coimbra	2573.70
Austria	Lisbon	2969.76
Austria	Barcelona	1589.42
Austria	Lérida	1766.40
Austria	Madrid	2240.66
Austria	Salamanca	2219.85
Austria	Ciudad Real	2471.35
Austria	Valencia	1995.02
Austria	Murcia	2258.03
Austria	Málaga	2717.11
Austria	Seville	2854.30
Austria	Huelva	2860.05
Austria	Burgos	1950.15
Barcelona	León	901.60
Barcelona	Lérida	179.40
Barcelona	Salamanca	894.70
Barcelona	Ciudad Real	932.65
Barcelona	Valencia	401.35
Barcelona	Murcia	678.50
Barcelona	Málaga	1146.55
Barcelona	Seville	1202.90
Barcelona	Huelva	1079.85
Barcelona	Tarragona	112.70
Barcelona	Burgos	670.45
Madrid	León	382.95
Madrid	Lérida	179.40
Madrid	Salamanca	243.80
Madrid	Ciudad Real	218.50
Madrid	Valencia	404.80
Madrid	Murcia	461.15
Madrid	Málaga	625.60
Madrid	Seville	618.70
Madrid	Huelva	726.80
Madrid	Burgos	181.70

Tarragona	Madrid	614.10

3 Test application and results

A test application defined by the company COSTRUCTED S.A. (Winter et al. [6, 7], Gonzalez et al. [8]), together with the results obtained from the use of a first implementation of the Flexible Evolution Algorithm (FEA) (Winter et al. [2]) is presented.

A global network of 23 nodes of which two are factory-nodes is considered. There are 76 existing connections between these nodes for the road network (Table 1), 7 connections for the rail network (Table 2) and 12 for the sea network (Table 3). All train routes are also possible by road (http://ceani.ulpgc.es/transporte.php). The cast iron ductile pipes without mortar joint are only produced at one of the factory-nodes (Germany), while those with mortar joints are produced at both factory-nodes (Germany and Austria). The costs associated with each route of the various networks are shown in Tables 1-3.

Table 2. Costs per wagon related to each route in the rail network

Origin	Destination	Cost (€)
Germany	Antwerp	1002.80
Germany	Bilbao	1702.80
Germany	Barcelona	1520.20
Germany	Madrid	2142.80
Austria	Bilbao	1702.80
Austria	Barcelona	1520.20
Austria	Madrid	2142.80

Table 3. Costs per platform (lorry on routes Barcelona-Palma and Valencia-Palma) related to each route in the maritime network

Origin	Destination	Cost (€)
Antwerp	Bilbao	2260.00
Antwerp	Gijón	2260.00
Antwerp	Vigo	2260.00
Antwerp	Porto	2260.00
Antwerp	Lisbon	2260.00
Antwerp	Barcelona	2260.00
Antwerp	Valencia	2260.00
Antwerp	Palma	2260.00
Antwerp	Málaga	2260.00
Antwerp	Seville	2260.00
Barcelona	Palma	1430.00
Valencia	Palma	1430.00

In addition to the costs which appear in Table 3, other sea freight costs have to be added for the case of departure from Antwerp; the origin terminal handling charge, loading, bundling, destination terminal handling charge, goods handling charge, destination handling, etc. In the case of departure from Barcelona or Valencia to Palma, the destination terminal handling charge (165.00 Euros/lorry), goods handling charge (4.23 Euros/mt) and destination handling (100.00 Euros/lorry) have to be added.

Table 4 shows the pipe demand from the demand-nodes considered, and Tables 5 and 6 the breakdown of the optimal solution obtained: the penalizing function is zero (all restrictions are met), while the cost function is 1351.02 Euros for the Burgos demand, and 9802.52 Euros for the Valencia and Palma demand. Figure 2 shows the optimal route.

Table 4. Pipe demand from the demand-nodes considered

Demand node	Product	Diameter	Amount (lm)
Burgos	CIDP	100	3000
Valencia	CIDP-MJ	150	2004
Palma	CIDP-MJ	150	4002

Table 5. Optimal solution for the Burgos demand

Origin	Destination	Length (m)	Mode of Transport
Germany	Bilbao	3000	1 wagon
Bilbao	Burgos	3000	3 lorries

Table 6. Optimal solution for the Valencia and Palma demand. In Barcelona and Valencia the lorries board the ferry to Palma

Origin	Destination	Length (m)	Mode of Transport
Germany	Barcelona	6006	3 wagons
Barcelona	Valencia	2508	3 lorries
Barcelona	Palma	3498	4 lorries
Valencia	Palma	504	1 lorry

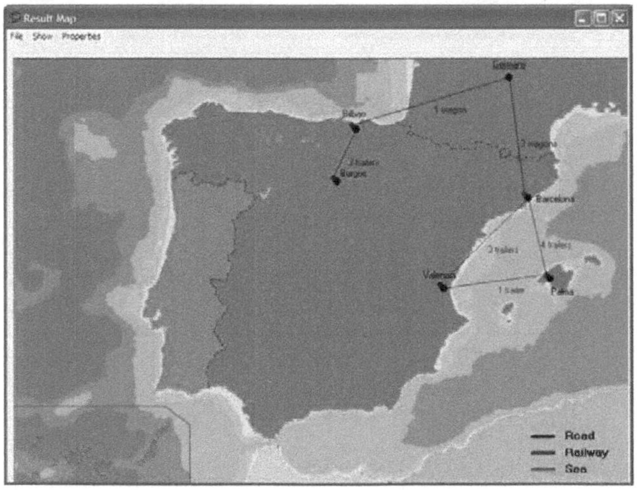

Fig. 2. Visualisation of the optimal route. In Barcelona and Valencia the lorries board a ferry to Palma.

This is a multimodal problem because the solution shown in Tables 7 and 8 is also an optimal solution with the same value of the cost function as the before optimal solution shown in Tables 5 and 6.

Table 7. Optimal solution for the Burgos demand

Origin	Destination	Length (m)	Mode of Transport
Germany	Bilbao	3000	1 wagon
Bilbao	Burgos	3000	3 lorries

Table 8. Optimal solution for the Valencia and Palma demand. In Barcelona and Valencia the lorries board the ferry to Palma

Origin	Destination	Length (m)	Mode of Transport
Germany	Barcelona	6006	3 wagons
Barcelona	Valencia	2508	3 lorries
Barcelona	Palma	3498	4 lorries
Valencia	Palma	504	1 lorry

3 Conclusions

We have applied our Flexible Evolution Algorithm (FEA), which has capacity to adapt the operators, the parameters and the algorithm to the circumstances faced at each step of every optimisation run. When the search space is dimensionally very high - as in the problem considered in this paper - there is a need for evolutive algorithms with certain learning ingredients, as well as strategies that progressively impose with more and more severity in the evolutive process the real scenario of the complex problem that has to be resolved.

References

1. B. Galván and G. Winter, *Evolución Flexible*, Report CEA-04-001 of CEANI-IUSIANI, University of Las Palmas de Gran Canaria, 2001.
2. G. Winter, B. Galván, S. Alonso and B. González, *Evolving from Genetic Algorithms to Flexible Evolution Agents, In* Late-Breaking Papers of the Genetic and Evolutionary Computation Conference, 466-473 (2002).
3. G. Winter, B. Galván, P.D. Cuesta and S. Alonso, *Flexible Evolution, In* Evolutionary Methods for Design, Optimization and Control with Applications to Industrial Problems, Barcelona: CIMNE, 89-94 (2002).
4. G. Winter, B. Galván, S. Alonso, B. González, D. Greiner, J.I. Jiménez, *Flexible Evolutionary Algorithms: cooperation and competition among real-coded evolutionary operators, In* Special Issue on solving real-world optimization problems using Real Coded Genetic Algorithms (RCGAs). Springer-Verlag Heidelberg, Soft Computing, **9**(4), 299-323 (2005).
5. D.E. Goldberg and J. Richardson, *Genetic algorithms with sharing for multimodal function optimization, In* Proceedings of the First International Conference on Genetic Algorithms and Their Applications, 41-49 (1987).
6. G. Winter, J.M. Emperador, B. González, D. Santos, B. Galván, F.O. López, *Diseño de un sistema de planificación óptima de transporte de productos mediante Algoritmos Genéticos*, Report CEA-12-002 of CEANI-IUSIANI, University of Las Palmas de Gran Canaria, 2002.
7. G. Winter, B. González, B. Galván, J.M. Emperador, *Sistema inteligente para la planificación óptima del transporte multimodal de mercancías, In* II Technological Innovations Forum for Transport: TRANSNOVA 2005, Las Palmas de Gran Canaria, 2005.
8. B. González, G. Winter, J.M. Emperador, B. Galván, *Sistema inteligente para la planificación con coste mínimo del transporte multimodal de tubos, In* Proceeding of the IV Congreso Español sobre Metaheurísticas, Algoritmos Evolutivos y Bioinspirados, 945-952 (2005).

6

Parameter Identification of Bladed Assemblies Using a Subspace Method

Bendali Salhi , Joseph Lardiès, and Marc Berthillier

Institute FEMTO-ST; UMR-CNRS 6174-Department LMARC, 25000, Besancon, France

Abstract – This paper is aimed at identifying a dynamical model for bladed assemblies such as turbines. Unknown excitation forces are applied to bladed disk assemblies leading to forced vibration responses. Non contact measurement of such vibrations using tip-timing has become an industrial standard procedure and current research focuses on analysis methods for interpretation of measured vibrations. Our purpose is to develop a subspace method for the identification of blade's natural frequencies, damping ratios and mode shapes using blade tip-timing data. The importance of the developed procedure results in the fact that in a narrow band frequency, less than 2 Hz, twenty two modes can be easily identified. A detailed description of this method and results are presented.

Key words: Modal parameters, Subspace method, Bladed disk assemblies, Aliasing, Signal reconstruction

1 Introduction

Bladed assemblies such as turbines are subject to several sources of excitation leading to forced vibration responses that appear near of blade's natural frequencies. Such structural vibration can affect the fatigue life, performance and integrity of bladed assemblies. Generally, blade vibrations during operation are difficult to measure and require many sensors in order to be detected fully. Two standard measuring methods are used to obtain blade vibrations: strain gages and frequency-modulated grid systems [1-3]. The first method requires the installation of strain gages on some of the blades. This is a very expensive process since it requires slip rings or high-quality telemetry and long installation times. For the second standard method, the frequency modulated grid systems, permanent magnets are fitted on the tips of some blades and a specially formed wire is installed in the compressor casing above the magnets. As a blade passes a wire, the magnet produces an alternating current in the wire. Blade vibrations are interpreted from the voltage modulation of this signal. No signal transmitter between the rotor and the stator is needed, but the wire requires a special casing and the number of blades monitored at a time is limited to three per rotor stage. An alternative method to the two standard measurement methods is the blade tip-timing (BTT) technique or non intrusive stress measurement which is based on optical, capacitive or magnetic probe technology. This method is briefly presented in section 2. To obtain the modal parameters of rotating bladed assemblies from BTT data a subspace method [4-5], which is an in-operation system identification method, is proposed. The ambient input is unknown and the subspace identification algorithm has to deal with output-only measurements. The basic description of the subspace identification method is to use a finite dimensional, discrete time, linear, time-invariant dynamic system to construct a sequence of real matrices known as Markov parameters. From these known parameters and using the singular value decomposition technique [6] we can identify the modal parameters of bladed assemblies. The subspace identification technique has recently attracted much attention owing to its advantages over traditional techniques such as the prediction error method. The prediction error method has problems of convergence and long running time as the number of parameters to identify becomes large. The subspace method does not entail such difficulties as the number of parameters increases, which often makes it more suitable for multi output system identification. This paper presents a contribution to the modal analysis of rotating machines using non contact measurements.

2 The blade tip-timing method

The basic concept of the blade tip-timing method has been developed in [1-3]. Several probes are installed in the engine casing above the rotor, and the blade transit times between the probes are measured. The basic principle of the method can be summarized as follows: two sensors are placed around the blades and they measure the passage time of each blade in front of the sensors. The angle between these two sensors is 180°. A third sensor is placed in the proximity of the engine shaft. It measures the once-per-revolution signal. When there are no blade vibrations, the blade transit times are a function of rotor speed, rotor radius and circumferential probe position. In the case of blade vibrations, the blade transit times deviate from those obtained in the undisturbed condition, with the blades passing the probes earlier or later than normal, depending on their instantaneous deflection. This technique provides notable advantages: it is non-contacting, it senses all blades and it reduces costs because it eliminates the need for rotor instrumentation and telemetry for signal transmission. However, one drawback is that the measurement sampling frequency is completely dependent of the rotor speed and the number of measurement probes.

Methods for analyzing blade tip timing data have been developed since 1970. However, given a limited number of probes, there are still no standard approaches that can identify synchronous response resonance frequencies with ade-

Corresponding Author joseph.lardies@univ-fcomte.fr

quate precisions. Let us recall that synchronous response occurs when a blade's vibration frequency is an integer multiple of the engine rotation speed and asynchronous response occurs when the blades frequency response is a non-integer multiple of the assembly rotation speed. Synchronous vibration can be caused by mechanical effects such as residual unbalance of the rotors and non-concentric casing, as well as aerodynamic effects. Asynchronous vibrations are typically caused by flutter, rotating stall, or by acoustic resonance. From experimental point of view, the problem is that it is impossible to know with enough accuracy which blade will produce the largest vibration amplitude. As rotating instrumentation is limited, a challenge for the monitoring of bladed assemblies such as turbines is the analysis of blade tip timing data.

3 The mathematical model

The blade tip timing data analysis method developed in this paper is applied to simulated time data obtained from a mathematical model of the forced response of a rotating bladed assembly. Figure 2 shows the basic layout of the mechanical model. For illustrative purposes only three blades represented by a mass-spring-damper system are shown in this figure and it is assumed that each blade in the assembly has one significant mode which is the first bending.

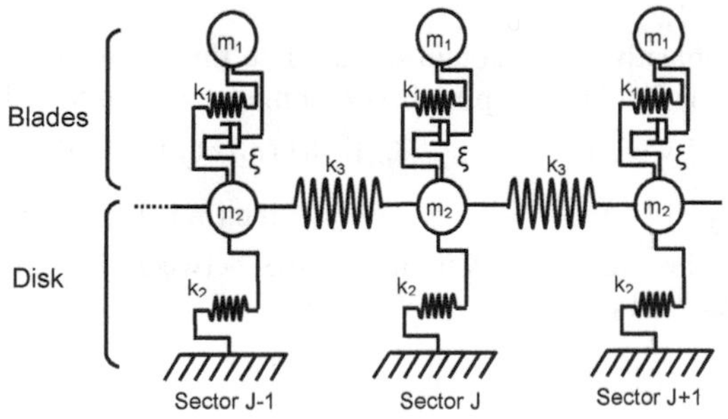

Fig. 1 Two degrees of freedom per sector model

This system has blade degrees of freedom (DOF) and disk (DOF) for each sector. Each disk is coupled to neighboring sectors by springs of stiffness k_c. A structural damping, whose damping ratio is ξ, is shown in the model. This model simulates the dynamic behavior of a blade assembly which has twenty two blades, and provides a temporal forced response of each blade. Random excitations are generated to obtain the forced responses of the system and only steady-state responses are considered for the identification of modal parameters. This model will provide the temporal forced response of each blade. The equations of motion for this model are:

$$M_0\ddot{q}(t)+C_0\dot{q}(t)+K_0 q(t)=F(t)_{aeroelastic}+F(t)_{aerodynamic} \quad (1)$$

where q(t) is the vector of displacements corresponding to the 2x22 degrees of freedom.

We pose $\eta(t)= F(t)_{aeroelastic}+ F(t)_{aerodynamic}$. The displacement in sector j is given by $q^j(t)=\begin{pmatrix} q_1^j(t) \\ q_2^j(t) \end{pmatrix}$, the subscript 1 represents the blade and the subscript 2 represents the disk. In fact, the displacement for all sectors is given by the global (44x1) vector : $q(t)=\begin{pmatrix} q^1(t) \\ . \\ . \\ q^{44}(t) \end{pmatrix}$; M_0 , C_0 and K_0 represent the structural mass, damping and stiffness matrices of dimension (n' x n') with n'=44. The mass matrix M_0 is given by

$$M_0=\begin{bmatrix} M_a & 0 & . & 0 \\ 0 & M_a & . & 0 \\ . & . & . & . \\ 0 & 0 & 0 & M_a \end{bmatrix} \quad (2)$$

with $M_a=\begin{bmatrix} m_1 & 0 \\ 0 & m_2 \end{bmatrix}$

The stiffness matrix K_0 is given by

$$K_0=\begin{bmatrix} K' & K'' & 0 & . & K'' \\ K'' & K' & K'' & . & 0 \\ 0 & K'' & K' & . & 0 \\ . & . & . & . & . \\ K'' & 0 & . & K'' & K' \end{bmatrix} \quad (3)$$

$$\text{with } K'=\begin{bmatrix} k_1 & -k_1 \\ -k_1 & k_1+k_2+2k_3 \end{bmatrix} ;\ K''=\begin{bmatrix} 0 & 0 \\ 0 & -k_3 \end{bmatrix} \quad (4)$$

The damping matrix is given by

$$C_0 = P^{-T}\,\mathrm{diag}(4\pi\xi_i\, f_i)\,P^{-1} \quad (5)$$

where f_i is the ith natural frequency, ξ_i is the ith damping ratio and P is the matrix containing the conservative mode shapes. An aeroelastic force $F(t)_{aeroelastic}$ has been introduced in the model, in the way of circulant matrices coefficients, considering only five different coefficients [7]. This aeroelastic force has been computed with a software developed by our research group. A white noise excitation simulates the aerodynamic forces $F(t)_{aerodynamic}$ and generates the time forced response. It is representative of turbulent excitation of the blades. The stiffness coefficients have been chosen in order that the blade modes are well separated from the disk modes: the blade modes family has frequencies around 60 Hz and the lowest frequency for a disk mode is close to 500 Hz. This tuned model is mistuned by the introduction of a different stiffness for each blade : $k_{1,i}=k_1(1+\delta_i)$, with i = 1, 22, where δ_i is the ith mistuning value which is given randomly.

Let m be the number of blades (m=22). To equation (1) is added the (mx1) observation equation [4]

$$y(t) = L\,q(t) + v(t) \quad (6)$$

where L is the (mxn') output influence matrix for the displacement, describing the relationship between the vector q(t) and the measurement vector y(t) and v(t) is an (mx1) additive noise disturbance, a vector of measurement errors simulated by a gaussian white noise. The modal characteristics (μ, Ψ) of the vibrating system are solutions of:

$$\det(M_o \mu^2 + C_o \mu + K_o) = 0 \; ; (M_o \mu^2 + C_o \mu + K_o)\, \Psi = 0 \tag{7}$$

where det( ) represents a determinant.
The system described by (1) and (6) is equivalent to the following continuous time state-space model [4]:

$$\dot{x}(t) = \tilde{A}\, x(t) + \tilde{B}\, \eta(t) \tag{8}$$

$$y(t) = C\, x(t) + v(t) \tag{9}$$

where x(t) is the state vector of dimension 2n' = n

$$x(t) = \begin{bmatrix} q(t) \\ \dot{q}(t) \end{bmatrix} \tag{10}$$

$\tilde{A}$ is the n by n state matrix, $\tilde{B}$ is the n by n' matrix containing the bloc matrix M_o^{-1} and C is the m by n output influence matrix including displacement only

$$\tilde{A} = \begin{bmatrix} 0 & I \\ -M_o^{-1}K_o & -M_o^{-1}C_o \end{bmatrix}; \quad \tilde{B} = \begin{bmatrix} 0 \\ M_o^{-1} \end{bmatrix}; \quad C = [L \;\; 0] \tag{11}$$

Equations (8) and (9) constitute a continuous time state space model of the dynamical system and the order of the system is the dimension of the state matrix. Given the initial condition $x(t_0)$ at some $t=t_0$ and solving for x(t) from equation (8) yields

$$x(t) = e^{\tilde{A}(t-t_0)} x(t_0) + \int_{t_0}^{t} e^{\tilde{A}(t-\tau)} \tilde{B}\eta(\tau)d\tau \tag{12}$$

This equation describes the variation with time of the state variable x(t) with respect to the initial condition $x(t_0)$ and the input $\eta(t)$. The evaluation of x(t) at equally spaced intervals of time t can be obtained by a discrete time representation of equation (12). Let the equally spaced times be given by 0, Δt, $2\Delta t$, ..., $(k+1)\Delta t$, ... where Δt is a constant sampling period. Consider $t = (k+1)\Delta t$ and $t_0 = k\Delta t$, equation (12) becomes

$$x\left[(k+1)\Delta t\right] = e^{\tilde{A}\Delta t} x(k\Delta t) + \int_{k\Delta t}^{(k+1)\Delta t} e^{\tilde{A}[(k+1)\Delta t-\tau]} \tilde{B}\eta(\tau)d\tau \tag{13}$$

Now, we define $A = e^{\tilde{A}\Delta t}$ the (nxn) discrete time state-space matrix, $x_{k+1} = x[(k+1)\Delta t]$ the discrete time state vector and $u_k = \int_{k\Delta t}^{(k+1)\Delta t} e^{\tilde{A}[(k+1)\Delta t-\tau]} \tilde{B}\eta(\tau)d\tau$ the global input vector. We obtain the following discrete time state-space model

$$x_{k+1} = A\, x_k + u_k \tag{14}$$

$$y_k = C\, x_k + v_k \tag{15}$$

y_k is the discrete time observation equation or output observation vector. The time responses of 22 blades are used in the identification process and the two discrete previous equations form the basis for the system identification procedure.

4 Identification of modal parameters

The matrix (nxn) of eigenvalues λ and the matrix (nxn) of eigenvectors Φ of the discrete time transition matrix A are related to the modal characteristics (7) by [9-10]

$$\lambda = e^{\mu\Delta t} \quad \text{and} \quad C\,\Phi = L\,\Psi \tag{16}$$

The global modal parameters: the natural frequencies f_i and damping ratios ξ_i of the vibrating system can be determined by

$$f_i = \frac{1}{2\pi\Delta t}\sqrt{\frac{[\ln(\lambda_i\lambda_i^*)]^2}{4} + [\cos^{-1}(\frac{\lambda_i+\lambda_i^*}{2\sqrt{\lambda_i\lambda_i^*}})]^2} \; ;$$

$$\zeta_i = \frac{1}{2\pi\Delta t}\sqrt{\frac{[\ln(\lambda_i\lambda_i^*)]^2}{4} + [\cos^{-1}(\frac{\lambda_i+\lambda_i^*}{2\sqrt{\lambda_i\lambda_i^*}})]^2} \tag{17}$$

for i = 1,2,. . .n'
Our objective is to obtain the discrete time transition matrix A (nxn) from the output observation vector y_k (mx1). Define $y_k^+ = [y^T_k, y^T_{k+1}, \ldots y^T_{k+f-1}]^T$ the (mfx1) future data vector and $y_{k-1}^- = [y^T_{k-1}, y^T_{k-2}, \ldots y^T_{k-p}]^T$ the (mpx1) past data vectors. The (mfxmp) covariance matrix between the future and the past is [4-5, 9-10]

$$H = E[y_k^+ y_{k-1}^{-T}] = \begin{bmatrix} R_1 & R_2 & . & R_p \\ R_2 & R_3 & . & R_{p+1} \\ . & . & . & . \\ R_f & R_{f+1} & . & R_{f+p-1} \end{bmatrix} \tag{18}$$

where E denotes the expectation operator, H is the block Hankel matrix (a block band counter diagonal matrix) formed with the (mxm) individual auto covariance matrices $R_i = E[y_{k+i}y^T_k] = CA^{i-1}G$, with $G=E[x_{k+1}y^T_k]$. The auto covariance matrices are estimated from T data points and computed by $\hat{R}_i = T^{-1}\sum_{k=1}^{T-1} y_{k+i}y_k^T$; i = 0,1, . . ., p+f and with these auto covariance matrices we form the block Hankel matrix. In order to identify the transition matrix A and the output influence matrix C two matrix factorizations of H are employed: the singular value decomposition of H which is given by $H=U\,S\,V^T$, with U^TU and V^TV identity matrices and S a diagonal matrix of singular values, and the factorization of H into its observability and controllability matrices [9-10]:

$$H=\begin{bmatrix} CA \\ CA^2 \\ \cdot \\ CA^{f-1} \end{bmatrix} [G\ \ AG\ldots A^{p-1}G] = O\,K \qquad (19)$$

The two factorizations of the block Hankel matrix are

$$H = (US^{1/2})(S^{1/2}V^T) = OK \qquad (20)$$

From this equation we obtain the observability matrix $O = US^{1/2}$. To identify the transition matrix A we consider the following property, deduced from the structure of the observability matrix O. Let $O^{\downarrow}$ be the m(f-1)xn matrix obtained from O by deleting the last block row of O and let $O^{\uparrow}$ be the m(f-1)xn matrix obtained from O by deleting the first block row of O. We have

$$O^{\downarrow}=\begin{bmatrix} C \\ CA \\ \cdot \\ CA^{f-2} \end{bmatrix} \quad \text{and} \quad O^{\uparrow}=\begin{bmatrix} CA \\ CA^2 \\ \cdot \\ CA^{f-1} \end{bmatrix} \qquad (21)$$

We obtain then

$$O^{\downarrow}\ A = O^{\uparrow} \qquad (22)$$

The least squares estimate of A is

$$A = (O^{\downarrow})^{+} O^{\uparrow} = \left[(US^{1/2})^{\downarrow}\right]^{+}\left[\ (US^{1/2})^{\uparrow}\right] \qquad (23)$$

The superscript $^{+}$ indicates a pseudo-inverse. The value of the matrix C is given by the first block row of the observability matrix O

$$C = O_{1R} = \{\text{first block row of } (US^{1/2})\} \qquad (24)$$

Once the transition matrix A has been identified its eigenvalues λ_i and the matrix of eigenvectors Φ are used to identify the modal characteristics of the system: eigenfrequencies f_i, damping ratios ζ_i and mode shapes.

5 Signal reconstruction

The subspace method requires signals without aliasing to identify modal parameters, whereas tip timing data gives signals with aliasing. To solve this problem and find a link between the subspace method and tip-timing data, we propose an interpolation technique based on the use of spline functions [8]. We apply the Hilbert transform to the real signal with aliasing obtained from BTT to obtain the analytical (complex) signal s_{AC}. Using the Ries theorem [8] the interpolated signal of bandwidth B and center frequency f_0 is :

$$s_{AR}(t) = \text{real}[\sum_{k=-\infty}^{+\infty} s_{AC}(\frac{k}{v_S})\text{sinc}(v_S t - k)\exp(i\,2\pi(f_0/v_S)(v_S t - k))] \qquad (25)$$

where k is the number of samples, sinc is the sinus cardinal function and v_S the sub-sampling rate which can be much smaller than twice the highest frequency ($f_0 + B/2$). Unfortunately, formula of this type are known to be impractical, since the sinc function decays very slowly, so that many terms of the series have to be evaluated for accurate reconstruction. An approach to avoid this problem in the complex envelope is to use reconstruction kernels K which are time-limited so that only a finite number of samples have to be considered. The general reconstruction formula is given by:

$$s_{AR}(t) = \text{real}[\sum_{k=-\infty}^{+\infty} s_{AC}(\frac{k}{v_S})K(v_S t - k)\exp(i\,2\pi(f_0/v_S)(v_S t - k))] \qquad (26)$$

where, K is piecewise continuous function. The optimum kernel for an arbitrary order m is given in time domain by [8]:

$$\text{Kopt}(t) = \sum_{l=0}^{[(m-1)/2]} (-1)^l\, b_{lm} B_m(t) \qquad (27)$$

where, B_m is the B-spline function of order m. It is a piecewise polynomial of degree (m-1) with finite support in [-m/2, m/2], defined recursively by:

$$B_m(t) = \frac{1}{(m-1)!}\sum_{k=0}^{[m/2-t]} (-1)^k \binom{m}{k}\left(\frac{m}{2} - |t| - k\right)^{(m-1)} \qquad (28)$$

and

$$B_m(t) = (B_{m-1} * B_1)(t) \qquad (29)$$

is the m-fold convolution of the rect-function, which is equal to B_1 with itself. The number b_{lm} is defined as:

$$\left(\frac{t/2}{\sin(t/2)}\right)^m = \sum_{l=0}^{\infty} b_{lm} t^{2l} \qquad (30)$$

6 Evaluation of the subspace algorithm

Figure 2 presents results obtained using the reconstruction function (26).

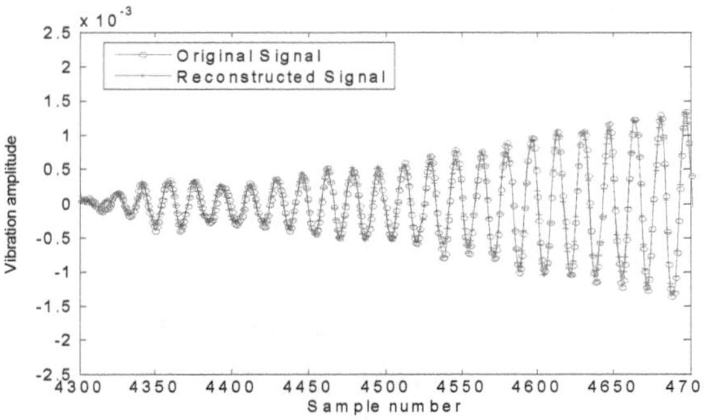

Fig.2 Comparison between the orignal and reconstructed signal

In this figure the reconstructed signal is compared to the original signal. The error given by the 2-norm of difference value between reconstructed and original signal is equal to $6\text{x}10^{-3}$. This reconstructed signal is used in the subspace algorithm for modal parameter identification. The stability diagram plotting the evolution of the identified eigen-values for various orders of the system is presented in figure 3.

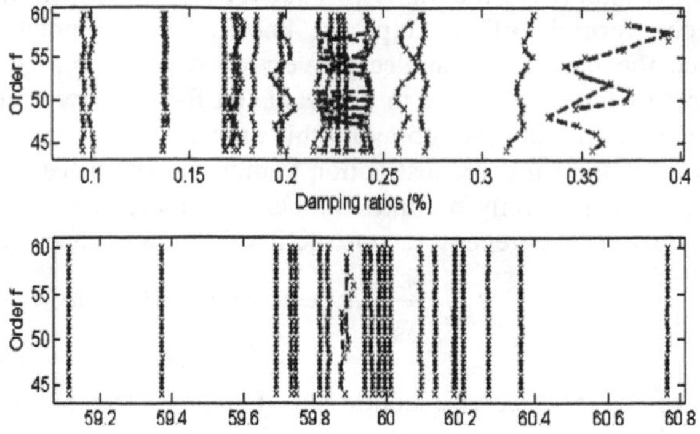

Fig.3 Stability diagrams on damping and eigenfrequencies

From these plots we can identify in the frequency band of the blades 22 eigenfrequencies and 22 damping ratios. We can see that all eigenfrequencies are stable. We plot in figures 4 and 5 the relative errors between exact and identified damping ratios and eigenfrequencies.

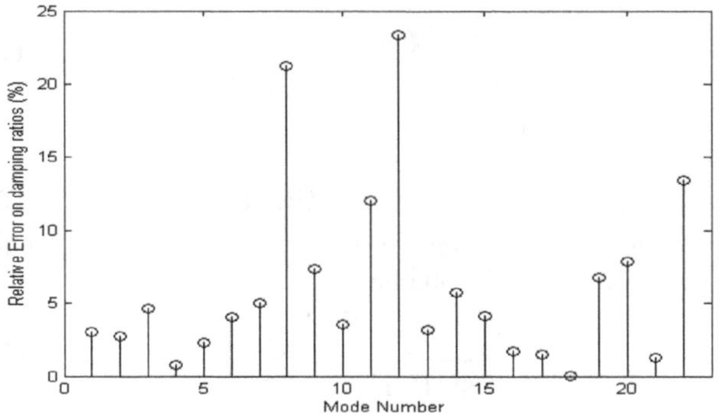

Fig.4 Relative errors on damping ratios

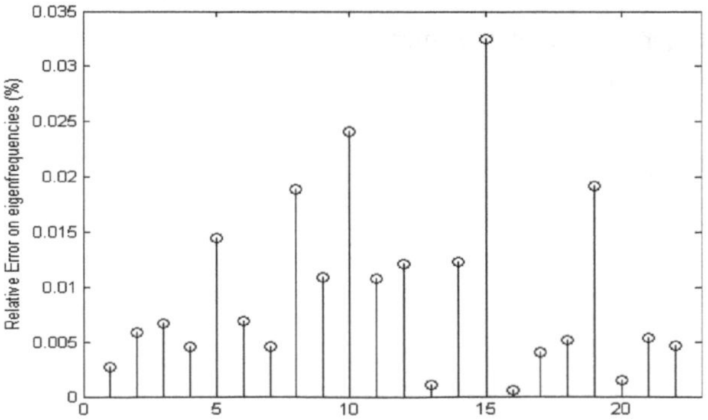

Fig.5 Relative errors on eigenfrequencies

Using the subspace method the eigenfrequencies can be identified with a reasonable error. However, the level of relative errors in damping ratios is high for certain blades. We are currently working to improve identification of damping ratios using a weighted subspace method. The exact mode shapes can be compared with the identified mode shapes using the modal assurance criterion (MAC) : let Φ_i be the ith exact mode shape and $\tilde{\Phi}_j$ the jth identified mode shape, the MAC matrix is defined as [11]:

$$(\mathrm{MAC})_{ij} = \frac{\left|\Phi_i^T \tilde{\Phi}_j\right|}{\sqrt{(\Phi_i^T \Phi_i)(\tilde{\Phi}_j^T \tilde{\Phi}_j)}} \tag{31}$$

The MAC indicates the degree of correlation between the mode shapes. For two vectors that are proportional the MAC equals 1 (perfect correlation) and values above 0,8 are very correlated. Values below 0,6 should be considered with much caution : the correlation is not well defined. Figure 6 shows the values of the MAC matrix for these 22 blades.

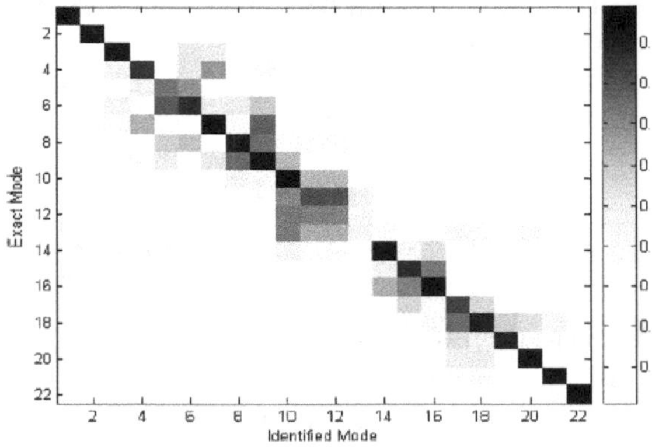

Fig.6 Comparison between mode shapes using the MAC

From this figure we can see that five modes: 5, 8, 11, 12 and 13 have not been found correctly by the identification process. The values of the MAC are lower than 0,6 for these five modes. For the remaining modes the correlation between exact and identified modes is acceptable or even excellent.

7 Conclusions

A new analysis method of blade tip timing data is proposed in this paper. This technique is based on the subspace method using the singular value decomposition of the block Hankel matrix. This method can identify very closely spaced eigenfrequencies and is a real improvement to the traditional FFT method. Despite the good results of the subspace method in eigenfrequency identification, it suffers from some disadvantages. One such disadvantage is that the subspace method, like others, is robust only if the signals are not aliased. To surpass this problem a reconstruction technique of the subsampled signal has been proposed. This reconstructed signal has been applied to the subspace algorithm. In the future we shall study the effect of signal to noise ratio in modal identification. The identification of aeroelastic coupling and aerodynamic excitation are also under investigation.

Acknowledgement

This work is supported by EDF R&D, France.

References

1. I. B. Carrington, J. Wright, J. E. Cooper, G. Dimitriadis, *A comparison of blade tip timing data analysis methods.* Jour. Aeros. Engin. **215**, 301-312 (2001).
2. C.P. Lawson, P.C. Ivey, *Turbo-machinery blade vibration amplitude measurement through tip timing with capacitance tip clearance probes*. Sensors and Actuators A, **118**, 14-24 (2005).
3. G. Dimitriadis, B. Carrington, J. WRIGHT, J.E. Cooper, *Blade tip timing measurement of synchronous vibrations of rotating bladed assemblies*, Mecha. Syst. and Sig. Process., **16,** 599-622 (2002).
4. J.N. Juang, *Applied System Identification*, (Prentice-Hall, Englewood Cliffs, NJ, 1994).
5. M.Aoki, *State Space Modeling of Time Series (2nd Edition)*, (Springer-Verlag, 1990).
6. G.H. Golub, C. Van Loan, *Matrix Computations (3rd Edition),* (Johns Hopkins University Press, 1996).
7. E.F. Crawley, *AGARD Manual on Aeroelasticity in Axial-Flow Turbomachines: Aeroelastic Formulation for Tuned and Mistuned Rotors* (1988).
8. S. Ries, *Digital time-delay beam forming with interpolated signals*, Sig. Process., **84**, 2403-2423 (2004).
9. J. Lardies, A *Stochastic realisation algorithm with application to modal parameter estimation*, Mecha. Syst. and Sig. Process.,, **15** , 275-285 (2001).
10. J. Lardies, *Estimation of parameters and model order in state space innovation forms*, Inv. Probl. in Enginee., **8**, 75-92 (2000).
11. L. Rigner, *Modal assurance criteria value for two orthogonal modal vectors*, 16th International Modal Analysis Conference, Santa Barbara CA, February 2-5 (1998).

7

Multiscale modelling and optimisation strategies for better understanding of biopolymer mechanical properties

Sofiane Guessasma[1,a]

[1] INRA, Reserach Unit Biopolymers Interactions and Assemblies (BIA), rue de la géraudière, 44316 Nantes, France

Abstract – Some biopolymers are considered as interesting natural materials for the replacement of oil-based products. Others are known as complex food systems for which texture properties determine the sensory perception. For both applications, the need to understand the mechanical behavior of biopolymers is essential. Control of texture, improvement of mechanical performance are some of the issues for which a growing research interest is noticed. The understanding of the mechanical properties cannot be considered without valuable information about the microstructure. For such materials, structural heterogeneities, which affect the behavior, appear to be dependent on several interacting scales. It is the aim of this work to shed more light on the possibility to use optimization techniques to either identify or optimize the mechanical properties of starch-based materials at different scales. We take the example of the starch cellular material, which proved to be necessitating a multiscale approach. The context of the present study is related to the investigation of elasticity behavior of cellular materials.

Key words: Biopolymers, Cellular materials, Composites, Elasticity, Microstructure, Optimization

1 Introduction

Cellular materials are known to allow interesting functional properties such as resistance to heat transfer, impact, noise propagation, etc. The structure of cellular materials plays a key role in the determination of their mechanical performance. One of the well known structural effect is the amount of void. Gibson and co-workers [1] have determined a correlation between the elastic parameters and the ratio of void in arbitrary cellular materials with periodic arrangement of cells. Such correlation writes as follows for the elastic modulus

$$E_Y = C\rho^n \qquad (1)$$

where E_Y is the modulus of elasticity, ρ is the relative density, i.e., density of the cellular materials over that of the dense material, C and n are constants to be determined.

Some other contributions fed the concerned literature with series of studies describing the role of other structural features such as cell size distribution, defects, etc [2-5].

Size effects have also been described leading to several limitations for the generalisation of the effective properties of cellular materials [6]. The main limitation is related to the contribution of free surfaces which affect significantly bulk properties if the cell size is comparable to the specimen size. Biopolymer cellular materials such as bread crumb [7] add another structural complexity (Fig. 1), which is related to the constitutive material. In fact, such material appears to be a composite with a randomly structured phases [8, 9]. Mechanical properties as well as microstructure of biopolymer cellular materials have been widely studied in the past decades [10-14].

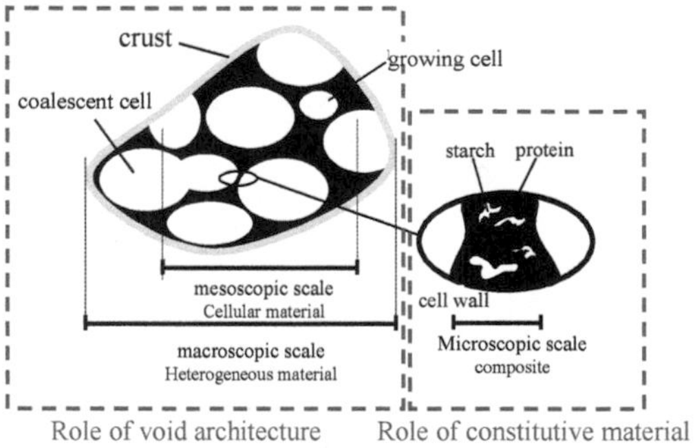

Fig. 1. Biopolymer cellular material within the multiscale approach (Example of the bread structure).

Finite element approach has been utilised to predict elastic parameters of cellular materials taking into account the explicit void architecture [15]. The technique is based on the conversion of voxels belonging to the solid phase to solid elements. This approach contrasts with other numerical approaches such as the effective medium theory [16, 17]. In the following is a description of the main advances realised on the assessment of biopolymer cellular material properties with respect to structural descriptors. Two main sections are considered. The first one is dedicated to the prediction of the mechanical properties of the struts, being considered as a composite material. The second section is dedicated to the optimisation of biopolymer cellular materials taking advantage of the architecture and the predicted strut behaviour.

[a] Corresponding author: sofiane.guessasma@nantes.inra.fr

2 Biopolymer-based composites

Fig.2 shows a typical microstructure of a starch-based composites revealed using SCLM (Confocal laser scanning microscopy) [18]. The dark gray levels represents starch whereas the light ones are relative to zein (protein). Because of phase compatibility, during the forming process, diffusion of both phases leads to a high level of percolation. In order to determine the effective properties we need to assess the following aspects:

- Mechanical behavior of intrinsic materials;
- Nature of the interface and its corresponding effect on the effective properties;
- Sensitivity of the mechanical behavior to the microstructure features.

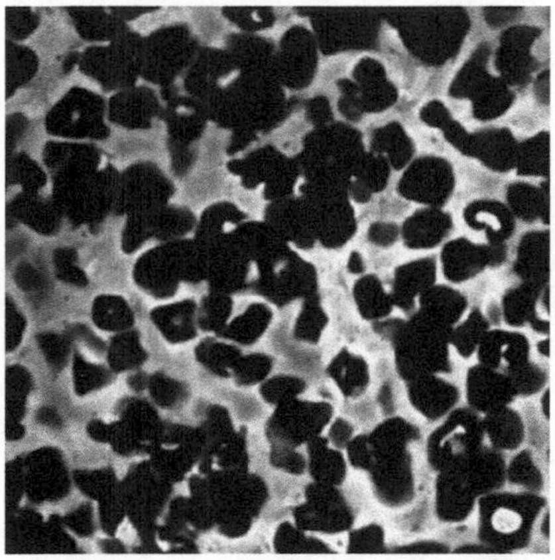

Fig. 2. Randomly structured microstructure of a typical biopolymer composite using SCLM. Image size about 140x140 μm².

In order to proceed with the first aspect, both macroscopic and microscopic investigations can be considered to determine the behavior of intrinsic materials. Macroscopic testing would , of course, require designing composites with similar feature to what is observed at the microscopic scale. Thermomoulding is a way of designing such materials, allowing the control of the phase ratio in the full range [19]. Extracting the mechanical parameters of the composite requires optimization technique to identify the optimal set of parameters fitting the observed response. For such purpose, three-point bending tests are performed on strips (38 x10 x 1 mm^3). Finite Element model is implemented to simulate sample bending under the same testing conditions (Fig. 3a). To each solid element is associated a material behavior that takes into account elasticity and plasticity stages. In our case, a bilinear model is considered because it describes the material behavior with a small number of mechanical parameters, namely Young's modulus, yield stress and tangent modulus [20]. If the simulation is performed in the first linear stage (Fig. 3b), one mechanical parameter is tuned in order to predict the optimal elastic modulus. The objective function can be written as follows

$$R = \frac{1}{N}\sum_{i=1}^{N}\left(F_{Exp}(\delta_i) - F_{Num}(\delta_i)\right) \quad (2)$$

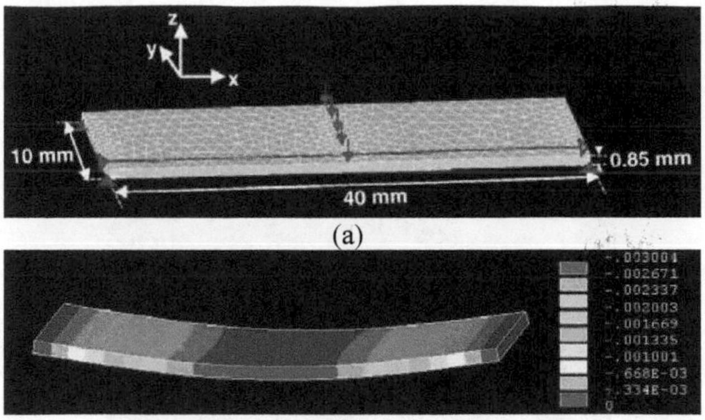

Fig. 3. (a) Loading conditions for the simulation of three-point bending test. (b)

Where F_{exp} and F_{num} are the experimental and numerical forces corresponding to a given deflection δ_i, respectively. N is the total number of deflection points for which the matching is searched.

The objective function is minimized by assuming a Newton-Raphson iterative scheme:

$$E_Y(t) = E_Y(t-1) - \alpha\frac{R(E_Y, t-1)}{R'(E_Y, t-1)} \quad (3)$$

where E_Y is the modulus of elasticity. R' is the first derivative of the objective function. t refers to the iteration level and α scales the rate of convergence.

The predicted results show that the modulus of elasticity is in the range 0.5 – 1.5 GPa for a composite containing 70% of starch [20].

Interface properties can be extracted from local measurements such as by nanoindentation [21]. Following the idea that the mechanical properties of biopolymers are sensitive to water content, viscoelasticity is investigated using a coupling between experimental and modeling techniques [22]. A grid of indents is performed near starch/zein interface to follow the change of mechanical properties across the interface. The experimental force – depth of penetration curves are compared to the equivalent numerical response taking into account a viscoelastic model. Such a model is described using three parameters, namely decay factor (β), initial (E_{YI}) and final moduli (E_{YF}). These parameters are related using the expression [22]

$$E_Y = E_{YF} + \left(E_{YI} - E_{YF}\right)e^{-\beta t} \quad (4)$$

The constitutive law is implemented in the Finite Element (FE) model using the meshing shown in Fig. 4.
Considering several combinations of the mechanical parameters (β, E_{YI}, E_{YF}), FE runs result in series of predicted force – depth of penetration curves. Identification of the experimental behavior is performed based on two criteria (Fmin, Fmax). These represent particular force values corresponding to the deepest penetration during loading and the final penetration during unloading, respectively.

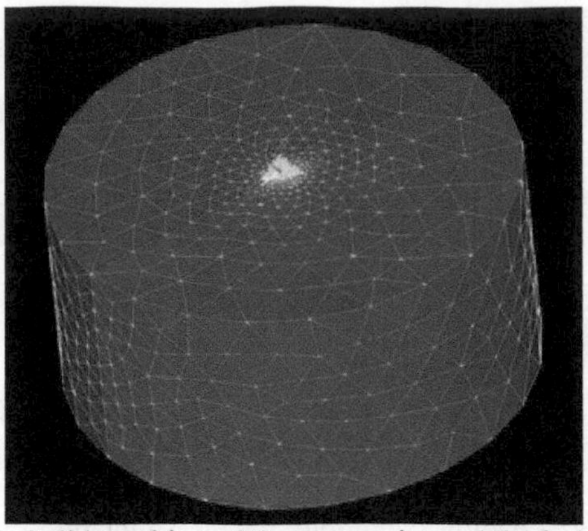

Fig. 4. Solid meshing of the composite and the indent to simulate nanoindentation at the interface of a starch/zein composite.

The application of an automatic fitting procedure gives the exact form of the objective functions relative to the force criteria.

$$R_{MIN} = \sqrt{\left(F_{MIN}^{\ EXP} - F_{MIN}^{\ NUM}\right)^2} \quad (5)$$

where R_{MIN} is the objective function corresponding to the criterion F_{MIN}. EXP and NUM subscripts refer to the numerical and experimental responses, respectively.

An equivalent expression is derived for R_{MAX}. The fitting procedure well shows that different expressions are predicted for starch and zein phases. These write

$$F^{ZEIN}{}_{i} = aE_{YI} + bE_{YF} + c\beta + d \quad (6)$$

$$F^{STARCH}{}_{i} = \exp\left(aE_{YI} + bE_{YF} + c\beta + d\right) \quad (7)$$

where i takes one of the following indices MIN or MAX.

Fitting parameters a, b, c and d are fully determined in each case with a correlation factor ranging from 0.85 to 1.00.

Equations (6) and (7) are used to determine, for each indent conditions, the optimal mechanical parameters. The predicted results show that both phases have similar mechanical properties. The relative difference between the intrinsic materials is 17%, 6% and 2%, for E_{YI}, E_{YF} and β, respectively.

Small difference between the intrinsic phase properties contrasts with the large deviation (up to 50%) of the numerical results with regard to those experimental conditions related to the interface indentation [22]. Such discrepancy is explained by the weak adhesion between constituents.
In order to determine the effective properties of the considered composite, FE simulation must take into account the weak adhesion effect. Such effect can be either approximated as an interphase [8] (third phase) which has intermediate properties with respect to intrinsic materials, or by considering imperfect interface action [23].
The former approximation allows the prediction of optimal interphase properties taking advantage of real microstructures and known intrinsic material properties. For such a purpose, SCLM images are converted into finite element meshes (Fig. 5). When an interface unit is detected, the surrounding region is attributed material properties different from the intrinsic materials. The interphase material is thus characterized by two main parameters (Young modulus Ei and thickness t).

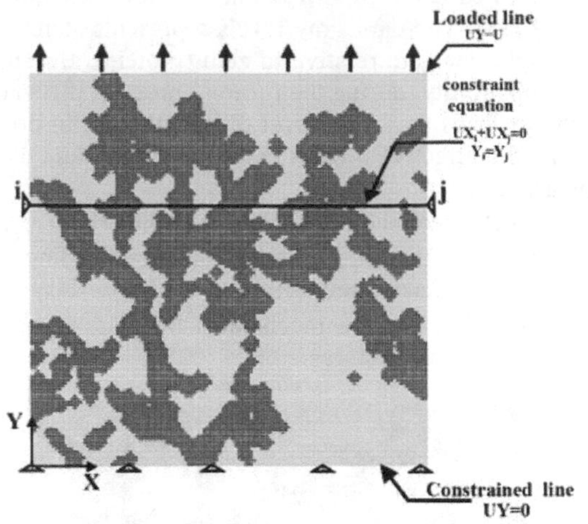

Fig. 5. Meshing and loading conditions for a composite microstructure under three-phase approximation.

The identification of the optimal interphase parameters requires experimental data that are available from three-point bending tests. The identification procedure is conducted by changing the interphase parameters (Ei, t) for each zein fraction considered in the experimental database. FE runs are performed to determine the effective modulus. Interpolation procedure is used to predict the optimal combination that allows the matching of the experimental and numerical moduli.

The predicted results show that the effective modulus is sensitive to the filler fraction and the ratio Ei/t [8]. The identification of the interphase parameters demonstrates that these are sensitive to the zein fraction. The interphase thickness varies between 0.31 an 1.24 µm, whereas the interphase modulus is found in the range 1.8 – 2.5 GPa.
It is worth mentioning that interphase approximation is mesh dependent. Interphase thickness less than the resolution of the image are not predictable. Moreover, interface action is not fully understood since the interphase region does not represent the true stress pattern near the interface. In order to overcome these difficulties, the implementation of the explicit interface behavior is suggested [23]. The model is based on the implementation of 1D interface elements characterized by tensile and shear effects. Indeed, to each element is associated a cohesive interface model characterized by the maximum traction, normal and shear separations. The simulation of tensile loading predicts different displacement patterns depending on the spatial distribution of phases. When the phase ratio is small, disconnected regions lead to local interface jumps [23]. When increasing further more the phase ratio, percolation of interfaces makes the interface effect stronger (Fig.6). At this stage, the predicted effective properties are the smallest ones at the percolation threshold. Any adjustment of the mechanical parameters associated to the cohesive model leads to lower performance when the interface content increases. Such effect is not confirmed by the experimental testing [8, 9]. More complex variations are instead observed. For instance, different water content equi-

libriums between the intrinsic phases change the interface properties. In order to determine the optimal interface parameters, neural computation and microstructure generation are exploited. Indeed, the search of optimal mechanical parameters cannot be decoupled from the microstructure information. Unfortunately, real microstructures such as that shown in Fig.2 are limited to allow independent following of all structural features. Microstructure generation is utilized to resolve such problem based on Monte Carlo technique [24]. The idea is to minimize interface energy and adjust generation parameters to control the interface content. Such algorithm requires several parameters to be tuned, which makes optimization difficult to perform without considering stochastic approaches. The idea behind neural network is to relate the generation parameters, interface and phase properties to the effective properties. By doing so, we are able to implicitly determine the shape of the objective function [24]. The predicted results show that tensile properties are more correlated to the maximum traction and the normal separation.

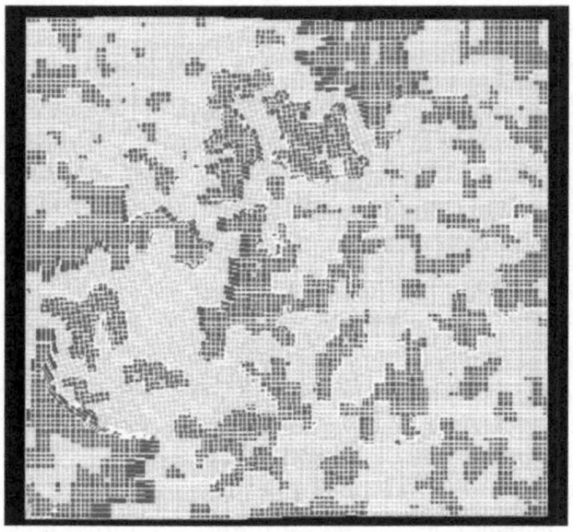

Fig. 6. Displacement pattern within a randomly structured composite showing interfacial displacement jumps.

3 Biopolymer-based cellular materials

As introduced above, cellular materials are dependent on the void ratio and on the mechanical properties of the intrinsic material. Since the effect of the former is elucidated, optimization techniques are used to assess the contribution of several structural features on the elasticity behavior of biopolymer cellular material. In this particular case, the forming process (ex. fermentation, extrusion) results in an open void structure. The void content occupies up to 90 % of the cellular material depending on the processing conditions. In order to represent the effect of void content, void size distribution and cell coalescence, microstructure generation is considered. Among the possible ways of void creation, Random Sequential Addition (RSA) [25] is a sequential process in which voids are positioned based on a spacing criterion δ (Fig. 7a). Such criterion writes

$$\delta \geq r_{ij} - \sum R_i \qquad (8)$$

where r_{ij} is the center-to-center distance between spherical voids, R_i is the radius of void i.

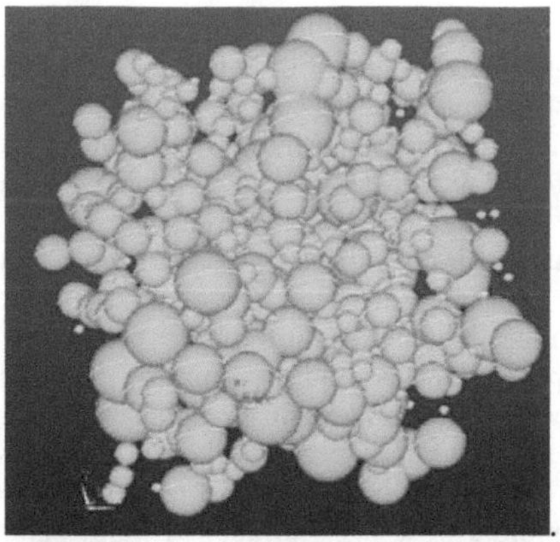

(a)

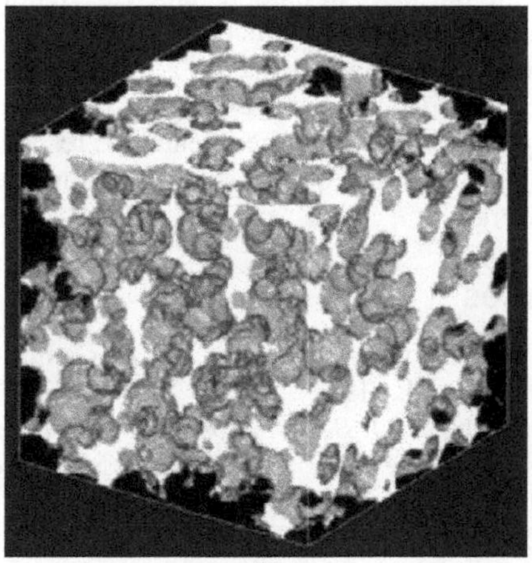

(b)

Fig. 7. (a) Generation of void structure using RSA (Random Sequential Addition). (b) Cellular material characterized by a void size distribution.

The void number is increased until the desired relative density is achieved. Note that any addition of voids would require that equation (8) being satisfied for all preceding voids. Size distribution is introduced by allowing Ri to be changed in equation 8 (Fig 7b). Gaussian size distribution can be considered with two control parameters: center and width of the void distribution [15].

3D images are converted into a FE model assuming that each voxel represents a solid element. Elastic properties of the intrinsic material are implemented. Uniaxial loading is simulated to allow the computation of the effective elastic parameters. The control of the effective properties, such as the elastic modulus requires the development of a hybrid strategy, which exploits a FE database representing the mechanical response for several combinations of input parameters. Neural computation is used to discover all causal correlations between the generation parameters, cellular structure and the mechanical parameters [26]. The generalization property of the optimized neural network predicts the iso-contours of the outputs as function of the input parameters in the hyperspace of the generation parameters.

4 Summary

The control of the mechanical behavior of biopolymer cellular materials requires a multiscale approach. Indeed, the effective properties are both affected by the cellular architecture and the properties of the solid material. The latter belongs to a particular category of composites characterized by random distribution of phases, weak contrast between phases and a prevailing role of interface. Optimization can be used in two different situations to help assessing the mechanical behavior of biopolymer-based materials.

It can be used, firstly, for the identification of mechanical parameters in a micromechanical model such as for the determination of the interface/interphase properties. For this purpose, optimization is used to minimize the difference between experimental and numerical responses.

Optimization is also used, secondarily, to realize a sensitivity analysis in which the control of the mechanical parameters requires handling of a large number of input parameters. In such a way, large FE database is necessary to address the correlations in the space of input parameters. Neural network is used to implicitly encode such correlations. The optimal neural network is obtained thanks to a training procedure in which the objective function represents the difference between the predicted and the experimental/FE responses. Such a function is dependent on the internal parameters of the neural network.

References

1. Gibson LJ, Ashby MF. *Cellular solids*. Cambridge: Pergamon Press Ltd., (1997).
2. Guo XE, Gibson LJ. *Behavior of intact and damaged honeycombs: a finite element study*. Int. J. Mech. Sci. **41**,85-105(1999).
3. Huang JS, Chang FM. *Effects of curved cell edges on the stiffness and strength of two-dimensional cellular solids*. Compos. Struct. **69**,183-191(2005).
4. Grenestedt JL. *Influence of wavy imperfections in cell walls on elastic stiffness of cellular solids*. J. Mech. Phys. Solids **46**,29-50(1998).
5. Silva MJ, Gibson LJ. *The effects of non-periodic microstructure and defects on the compressive strength of two-dimensional cellular solids*. Int. J. Mech. Sci. **39**,549-563(1997).
6. Onck PR, Andrews EW, Gibson LJ, Pw. *Size effects in ductile cellular solids. Part I: modeling*. Int. J. Mech. Sci. **43**,681-699(2001).
7. Lassoued N, Babin P, Valle GD, Devaux MF, Reguerre AL, Op. *Granulometry of bread crumb grain: Contributions of 2D and 3D image analysis at different scale*. Food Res. Int. **40**,1087-1097(2007).
8. Rjafiallah S, Guessasma S, Lourdin D. *Effective properties of biopolymer composites: A three-phase finite element model*. Composites Part a-Applied Science and Manufacturing **40**,130-136(2009).
9. Guessasma S, Hamdi A, Lourdin D. *Linear modelling of biopolymer systems and related mechanical properties*. Carbohydrate Polymers **76**,381-388(2009).
10. Scanlon MG, Zghal MC. *Bread properties and crumb structure*. Food Res. Int. **34**,841-864(2001).
11. Chanvrier H, Chaunier L, Colonna P, Valle Gd, Lourdin D. *Structural basis of the crispy properties of cereal products*. Using cereal science and technology for the benefit of consumers. Proceedings of the 12th International ICC Cereal and Bread Congress, Harrogate, UK, 23-26th May 2004,480-487(2005).
12. Keetels C, vanVliet T, Walstra P. *Relationship between the sponge structure of starch bread and its mechanical properties*. Journal of Cereal Science **24**,27-31(1996).
13. Hailemariam L, Okos M, Campanella O. *A mathematical model for the isothermal growth of bubbles in wheat dough*. J. Food Eng. **82**,466-477(2007).
14. Peleg M. *Review: Mechanical properties of dry cellular solid foods*. Food Science and Technology International **3**,227-240(1997).
15. Guessasma S, Babin P, Della Valle G, Dendievel R. *Relating cellular structure of open solid food foams to their Young's modulus : finite element calculation*. International Journal of Solids and Structures **45**,2881-2896(2008).
16. Garboczi EJ, Berryman JG. *Elastic moduli of a material containing composite inclusions: effective medium theory and finite element computations* Mech. Mater. **33**,455-470(2001).
17. Garboczi EJ, Day AR. *Algorithm for computing the effective elastic properties of heterogeneous materials - 3-dimensional results for composites with equal phase Poisson ratios* J. Mech. Phys. Solids **43**,1349-1362(1995).
18. Guessasma S, Hamdi A, Lourdin D. *Modelling of biopolymer systems and related mechanical properties*. Carbohydrate Polymers **76**,381-388(2009).
19. Chanvrier H, Colonna P, Della Valle G, Lourdin D. *Structure and mechanical behaviour of corn flour and starch-zein based materials in the glassy state*. Carbohydrate Polymers **59**,109-119(2005).
20. Guessasma S, Chaunier L, Lourdin D. *Finite element modelling of the mechanical behaviour of vitreous starch/protein composite*. J. Food Eng. **98**,150-158.
21. Ovaert TC, Kim BR, Wang JJ, An. *Multi-parameter models of the viscoelastic/plastic mechanical properties of coatings via combined nanoindentation and non-linear finite element modeling*. Progress in Organic Coatings **47**,312-323(2003).
22. Guessasma S, Sehaki M, Lourdin D, Bourmaud A. *Viscoelasticity properties of biopolymer composite materials determined using finite element calculation and nanoindentation*. Comput. Mater. Sci. **44**,371-377(2008).
23. Guessasma S, Benseddiq N. *Cohesive bonding interface model for the effective properties of randomly structured composites*. Comput. Mater. Sci. **47**,186-192(2009).
24. Guessasma S, Bassir H. *Identification of mechanical properties of biopolymer composites sensitive to interface effect using hybrid approach*. Mech. Mater. **42**,344-353(2010).
25. Sherwood JD. *Packing of spheroids in three-dimensional space by random sequential addition*. J. Phys. A-Math. Gen. **30**,L839-L843(1997).
26. Guessasma S, Bassir D. *Optimization of the mechanical properties of virtual porous solids using a hybrid approach*. Acta Mater. **58**,716-725(2010).

8

Comparison of Quantitative and Qualitative Information Provided by Different Structural Load Path Definitions

Kun Marhadi[1] , Satchi Venkataraman[2,a]

[1] Computational Science Research Center, San Diego State University, San Diego, United States
[2] Department of Aerospace Engineering and Engineering Mechanics, San Diego State University, San Diego, United States

Abstract – The structural mechanics community has developed several methods to identify and visualize load paths in structures. There is no single accepted approach or method to characterize, quantify, visualize and tailor load paths. This paper compares various methods proposed to characterize and visualize load paths. The comparison is performed for a two-dimensional (2-D) rectangular plate under plane stress conditions arising from different loading and boundary conditions. The effectiveness of each method is compared. The comparisons shows the methods provide different results and insights into the load transfer mechanisms. No single method appears to emerge as a clear choice for characterizing load paths. However, some methods provide more qualitative and quantitative information on the trajectory and efficiency of load transferred along load paths.

Key words: Structural load path definitions, Alternate load paths

1 Introduction

Structural design engineers need to be able to visualize how a load is transferred from its application point to the support or reaction points. Knowing how load "flows" in a structure is important at the design stage to make sure that a structure will perform its intended function properly. It is also important for optimum material utilization and for assessing the overall integrity of a structure. In case the structure is damaged, it is crucial to anticipate how the load flow will change in order to ensure that the structure can continue to perform its basic functions. Thus, it is important to identify alternate load paths in case the primary load path is damaged. In addition to identifying alternate load paths, engineers may want to be able to specifically tailor alternate load paths so that the structure can perform its basic functions under various unforeseen damage conditions.

Although it is clear why knowledge of load pathways is important, no commonly accepted approach has been developed to quantify, characterize, and visualize available load paths in a structure. Ideally, a method that visualizes load paths in a structure should be able to (1) visualize the overall paths of forces from the points of loading application to the reactions points, (2) indicate regions that need stiffness tailoring (more or less material utilization), and (3) indicate critical regions (regions with high stresses). The first criterion will help determine whether the structure carries loads as intended in the design. The second criterion provides information for optimum material utilization, and the last criterion helps anticipate regions with failure possibility. This work presents and compares different methods that have been developed for characterizing load paths. The methods are used to visualize load paths in a rectangular plate structure under various boundaries and loading conditions. Condition in which a hole exists in the structure (stiffness changes) is also considered. For each condition, the interpretation that can be obtained from visualization of each method is analyzed and checked whether it can meet criteria defined earlier.

2 Load Path Definitions

Over the years, the structural community has developed several methodologies that can be used to define load paths in a structure. Each method was derived differently, and therefore results in varied visualizations and interpretations of structural load paths. The different methods investigated in this work are explained in the following sections.

2.1 Using vectors aligned with directions of principal stresses

Principal stress vectors are readily available from post-processing program available in most commercial finite element analyses. As a result, the trajectory of principal direction vectors is interpreted as load paths. From theory of elasticity [1], in plane normal stress σ_n and shearing stress τ_{nt} acting at a point on an arbitrary plane of orientation angle θ with x axis stress equations are defined by Equations 1 and 2. The stresses are computed in terms of stresses: σ_x, σ_y, and $\tau_{xy} = \tau_{yx}$ along the coordinate axes as shown in Figure 1.

$$\sigma_n = \sigma_x \cos^2\theta + \sigma_y \sin^2\theta + \tau_{xy} \sin\theta\cos\theta \quad (1)$$

$$\tau_{nt} = -(\sigma_x - \sigma_y)\sin\theta\cos\theta + \tau_{xy}(\cos^2\theta - \sin^2\theta) \quad (2)$$

The principal stress directions (θ_p) obtained by setting equation 2 equal to zero provides the principal direction,

[a] Corresponding author: satchi@mail.sdsu.edu

expressed as

$$\tan 2\theta_p = \frac{2\tau_{xy}}{\sigma_x - \sigma_y}. \qquad (3)$$

The angles of major (σ_{p1}) and minor (σ_{p2}) principal stress directions are θ_{p1} and θ_{p2} respectively. The two angles θ_{p1} and θ_{p2} are 90° apart. The two principal stresses can be computed by replacing θ with θ_{p1} and θ_{p2} in Equation 1. The major principal stress σ_{p1} corresponds to the larger magnitude of the two stresses.

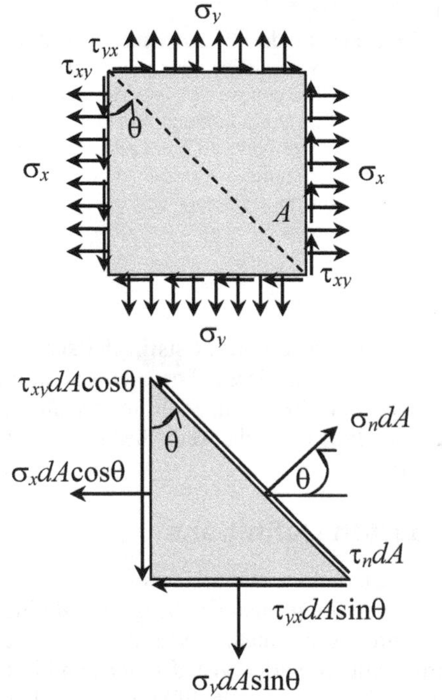

Fig 1. Geometry and notation for stress components acting on an arbitrary plane

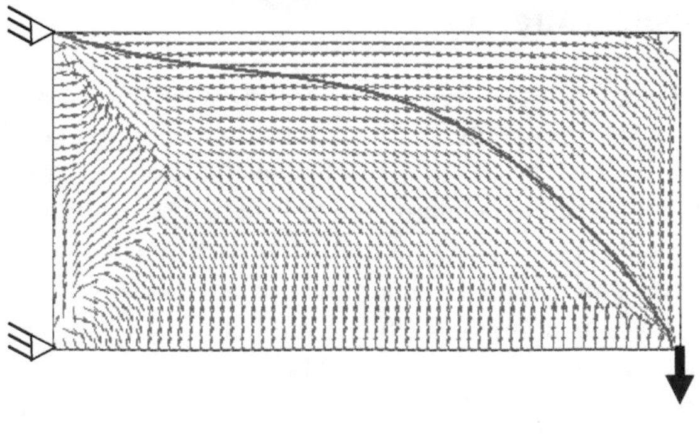

(a) Vector fields aligned with major principal stress σ_{p1}, load trajectory (red line) is traced from upper support

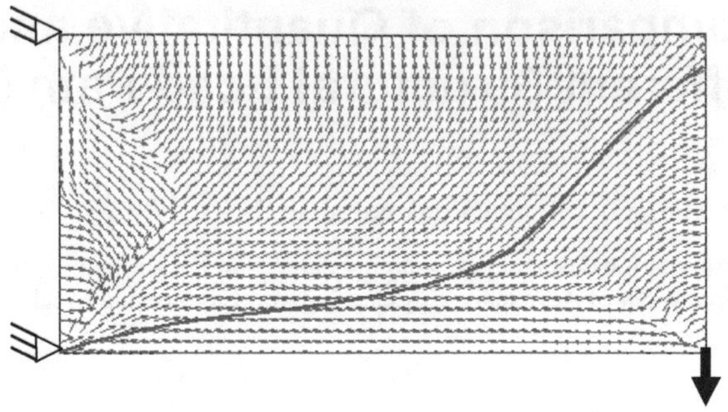

(b) Vector fields aligned with minor principal stress σ_{p2}, load trajectory is traced from lower support

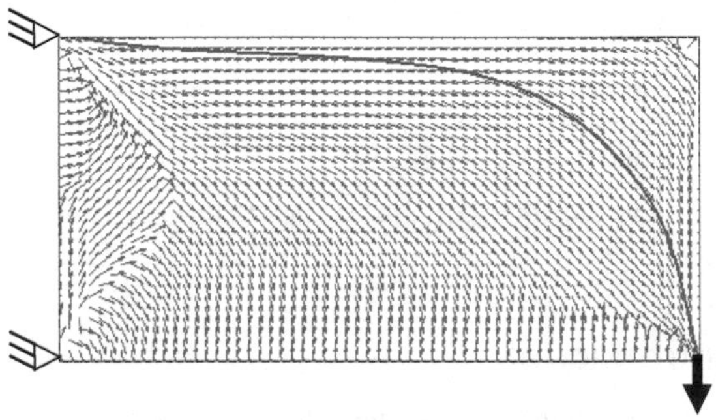

(c) Vector fields aligned with major principal stress σ_{p1} with load trajectory traced from the loading point

Fig. 2. A 2D homogeneous rectangular plate

Figure 2 shows an isotropic rectangular plate loaded vertically at its right bottom corner and constrained at the left corners. Stresses in the structure were computed using ABAQUS™ finite element analysis software. The rectangular plate is meshed with 30 by 60 4-noded quadrilateral plate finite elements with reduced integration. Figure 2 (a) and (b) show the principal stress (σ_{p1} and σ_{p2}) vectors (unit vectors) respectively at each element center in the structure. The red line indicates an attempt to trace trajectory of load following the principal direction from the reaction points to the point of loading application. This is a way to visualize paths of forces from the points of loading application to the reactions points. Tracing trajectory following the orientation of principal stresses from the point of loading application produces different results as opposed to following the trajectory from reaction points (see Figure 2 (c)). In the orientation of major principal stress, tracing trajectory from the upper support ends a location very close to the loading point. Similarly, tracing trajectory from the loading point ends at a location very close to the upper support. Ideally, trajectories that connect loading points and reaction points should be the same when they are traced from either the reaction or loading points.

In this example, the nature of loading on the structure is such that the loaded end (right side) of the plate is predominantly under shear load. However as we move towards the supports on the left, the structure develops bending and the load is resisted by a combination of shear and bending. By plotting orientation vectors of σ_{p1} and σ_{p2} separately, the flow of stresses in tensile (σ_{p1}) and in compression (σ_{p2}) can be visualized independently. σ_{p1} is maximum near the upper left support and diminish to zero at the lower side of the structure. Similarly, σ_{p2} is maximum near the lower left support and diminish to zero at the upper side of the structure. Since often times we are more interested in regions where the stresses (compression and tension) are high, it becomes more informative to plot the orientation vector of the maximum of the absolute value of either σ_{p1} or σ_{p2} (max(abs(σ_{p1}),abs(σ_{p2})) in each element at the same plot. This way, we can visualize the flow of high stresses (or load paths) as shown in Figure 3 (a). The upper half of the structure is predominantly under tensile stress, and the lower half is predominantly under compression stress. Tracing the trajectories from both supports by following the orientation vectors ends at the loaded point. Plotting the contour of maximum absolute value of principal stresses can indicate high stress regions as shown in Figure 3 (b). The contours are relatively similar with contours of von Misses stress of the structure as shown in Figure 3 (c). Here, high stress regions are near the supports and point of loading application.

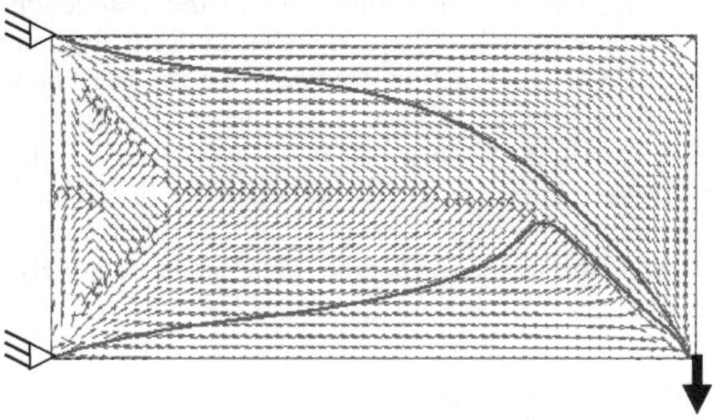

(a) Orientation vector of max(abs(σ_{p1}),abs(σ_{p2})) in each element

(b) Contours of magnitude of max(abs(σ_{p1}),abs(σ_{p2})) in each element

(c) Contours of von Misses stress.

Fig.3. Stresses on rectangular plate

The principal stresses and their directions indicate load distribution in the plate from the load introduction point to the support point. Kelly and Tosh [2] and Kelly et al. [3] explained that plotting orientations of the principal stresses does not indicate regions or contours where the load is constant as in a fluid flow streamline. Therefore tracing load trajectories based on these orientations will not result in trajectories where the loads being transferred are constant in the sense of streamlines in a fluid flow. To obtain trajectories that are similar to streamlines in a fluid flow, Kelly et al. [3] proposed a modified method for obtaining load trajectories from the stress field using fluid flow analogy. This is described in the next section.

2.2 Load path based on load flow

In the modified procedure of Kelly et al. [3], the load path is defined as the trajectory along which a constant force is being transferred. The concept is derived from fluid flow analogy. Although stress analysis does not obey the continuity law in the sense of fluid flow, continuity can be applied to the components of the force in an arbitrary set of orthogonal directions because of equilibrium requirements. This concept is illustrated with a hypothetical force "stream tube", shown in Figure 4.

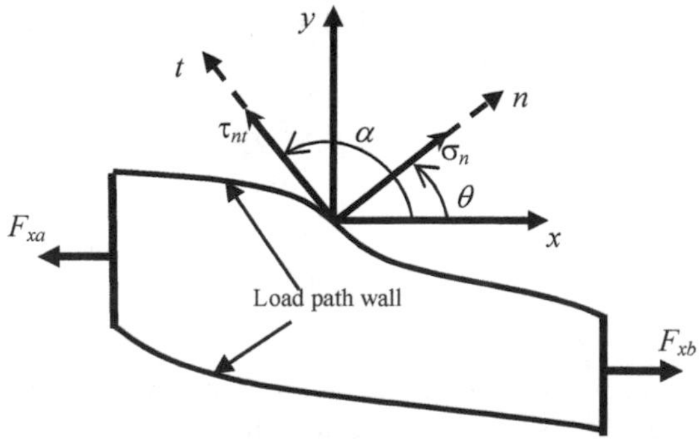

Fig. 4. Schematic of force "stream tube" that must satisfy equilibrium

Waldman et al. [4] summarized the theory originally derived by Kelly and Elsley [5] with some further clarification. They explained that for a particular force direction, such as the x-direction depicted in Figure 4, there is no flow of force across the boundary of the force tube. The load path is bounded by lines where there are no contributions to the force in the x-direction. Equilibrium over the tube that must be satisfied in the chosen direction (e.g. x-direction) can be expressed as

$$F_{xa} - F_{xb} = 0 . \quad (4)$$

There are two stress components acting on a plane that is tangent to the wall of the force tube, namely σ_n and τ_{nt}. σ_n is a local stress acting perpendicular to the plane, and τ_{nt} is acting along the plane (shear stress). The direction of σ_n is oriented by an angle θ with respect to x-axis in Figure 4. In this example, the load path is determined by resolving force equilibrium in the horizontal direction (x-axis). Similarly, the load path can be determined by resolving force equilibrium in the vertical direction (y-axis).

Equilibrium in any segment along the load path wall is achieved when the components of σ_n and τ_{nt} in the x-directions cancel out. This condition is satisfied by the following equation ($\theta = \theta_x$):

$$\sigma_n \cos\theta_x - \tau_{nt} \sin\theta_x = 0 . \quad (5)$$

When the force equilibrium is resolved in the y-direction, the equation is as follows ($\theta = \theta_y$):

$$\sigma_n \sin\theta_y + \tau_{nt} \cos\theta_y = 0 . \quad (6)$$

Substituting σ_n and τ_{nt} in Equations 5 and 6 with Equations 1 and 2 respectively, the orientation angles can be expressed as

$$\tan\theta_x = -\frac{\sigma_x}{\tau_{xy}} \quad (7)$$

$$\tan\theta_y = -\frac{\tau_{xy}}{\sigma_y} . \quad (8)$$

The local orientation of the load path along the wall of the force tube is expressed α, which is 90° apart from θ (see Figure 4). When the equilibrium is resolved into x and y directions, the angle can be expressed as

$$\alpha_x = \tan^{-1} \frac{\tau_{xy}}{\sigma_x} \quad (9)$$

$$\alpha_y = \tan^{-1} \frac{\sigma_y}{\tau_{xy}} . \quad (10)$$

Figures 5 (a) and (b) show load paths or orientations of the load flow calculated using the force "stream tube" concept, for the x and y-direction loads respectively. The arrows are unit vectors with orientation angles α_x and α_y. The red lines trace the trajectory of path obtained by following the load flow orientation vector from the support points where the load is reacted to the point of loading application. Here the trajectories, obtained using the load flow orientations connect the load to its support points for both forces with equilibrium along x and y directions. However, tracing the trajectories from the point of loading application produces different trajectories, such as shown in Figure 5 (c) for load flow with equilibrium in y-direction. For load flow with equilibrium in x-direction, no trajectories can be drawn when the starting point is the point of loading. In reality, the trajectory only connects the loading point and a point very closed to the upper reaction points. Similarly, when the trajectories are traced from the supports, they end at a point very closed to the loading point.

Analyzing load flow of x-direction forces reveals that the structure develops a bending moment due to the loading. The plots also indicate regions that have recirculation patterns (that resemble eddies in fluids) near the supports. These regions are typically low stress regions that do not contribute to loads in the specified load and support configuration. In the center line of the structure within the loop, the stresses are zero, and the vectors of load flow are perpendicular to the x-axis.

For load flow with equilibrium in the y-direction, the vectors show that loads are transferred from the point of application to the reaction points. Since the only non-zero component in the y-direction is shear, the vectors and trajectories indicate how shear is transferred. It is also evident from Figure 5 (b) that the regions with re-circulating patterns or eddies: one near the load application point and two near the reaction points, experience relatively low stress.

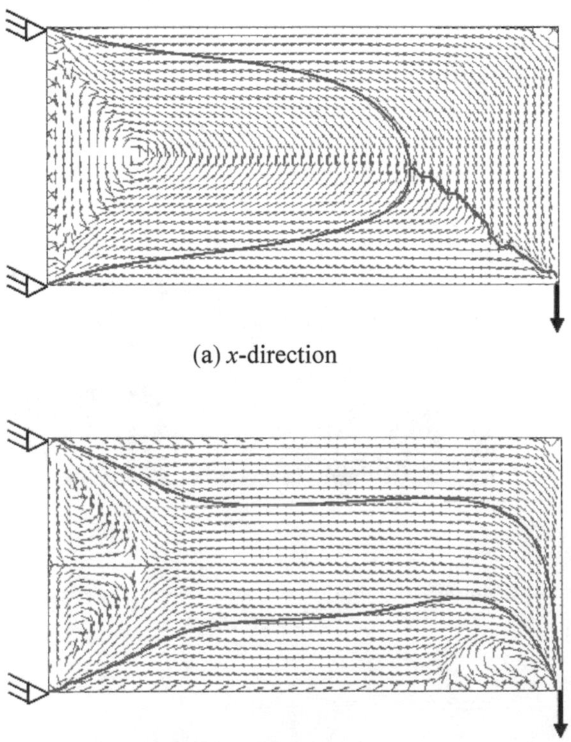

(a) x-direction

(b) *y-direction*

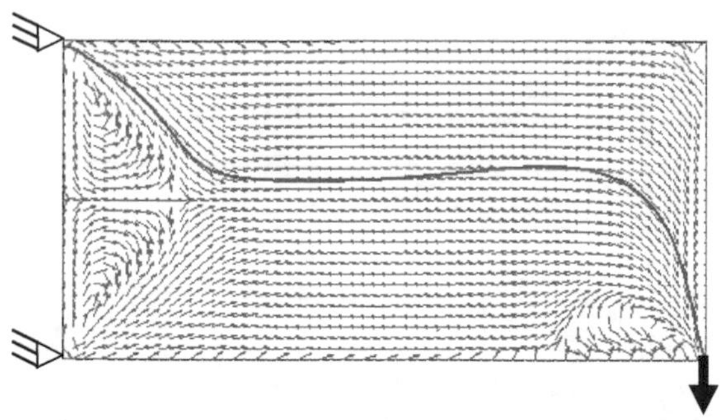

(c) Load flow orientation with force equilibrium in y-direction and trajectory traced from point of loading application

Fig. 5. Load flow orientation and load trajectories traced from reaction points with force equilibrium

2.3 Transferred and potential transferred force method

Harasaki and Arora [6] introduced the concept of transferred forces and potential transferred forces to investigate load paths in structures. Their idea is that a portion of the load is transferred through a region of the structure. The continuum representation of the structure shown in Figure 6 is used to explain this concept.

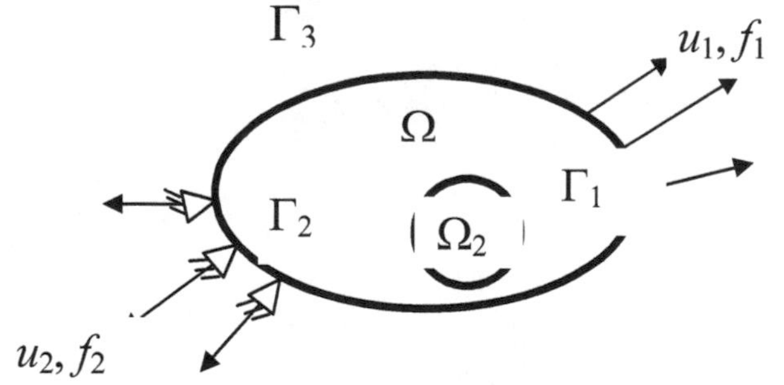

Fig. 6. Schematic representation of a continuum structure

Load f_1 applied on Γ_1 is transmitted to the supports on Γ_2 to generate reaction forces f_2. These forces can be obtained from solving the following equilibrium and boundary condition equations:

$$\begin{aligned} &\sigma_{ij,j} + b_i = 0 \text{ for } \Omega \text{ and } \Omega_2, \\ &\sigma_{ij} n_j = f_1 \text{ on } \Gamma_1, \\ &u_i = 0 \text{ on } \Gamma_2, \\ &\sigma_{ij} n_j = f_{2i} \text{ on } \Gamma_2, \\ &\sigma_{ij} n_j = 0 \text{ on } \Gamma_3. \end{aligned} \tag{11}$$

The force transmitted to Γ_2 has two components, one that goes through region Ω_2, and one that goes through the remaining region. The force components transferred through region Ω_2 are referred to as the transferred force. To calculate the transferred force through Ω_2, obtain the displacement u and the reaction force f_2 for the original problem by solving Equation (11). Next, set the stiffness of region Ω_2 to zero, apply the displacements calculated from the original solution on Γ_1 as enforced displacements, and obtain the new reaction load $\bar{f}_2$ (using the equations of equilibrium and boundary conditions shown in Equation (12)). Bar on the notations indicates a condition when stiffness of Ω_2 is set to zero.

$$\begin{aligned} &\bar{\sigma}_{ij,j} + b_i = 0 \text{ for } \Omega, \\ &\bar{\sigma}_{ij} = 0 \text{ for } \Omega_2, \\ &u_i = u_{1i} \text{ on } \Gamma_1, \\ &u_i = 0 \text{ on } \Gamma_2, \\ &\bar{\sigma}_{ij} n_j = \bar{f}_{2i} \text{ on } \Gamma_2, \\ &\bar{\sigma}_{ij} n_j = 0 \text{ on } \Gamma_3. \end{aligned} \tag{12}$$

The transferred force is then defined as the difference in the reaction loads.

$$\bar{F} = \bar{f}_{2i} - f_{2i} \quad \text{on } \Gamma_2. \tag{13}$$

The transferred force can be implemented in a finite element analysis, wherein the region Ω_2 can be either an element of the finite element mesh or a structural member in the finite element model of the structural assembly (e.g. truss and frame structures). Harasaki and Arora [6] also introduced the concept of potential transferred forces. Potential transferred forces are forces in a region Ω_2, in which the structure can transfer when this region is made to be rigid or to have very high value of stiffness approaching infinity. The potential transferred force gives an indication of how well stiffening the region will improve the stiffness of the structure.

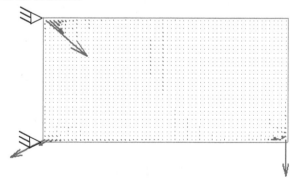

(a) Transferred force

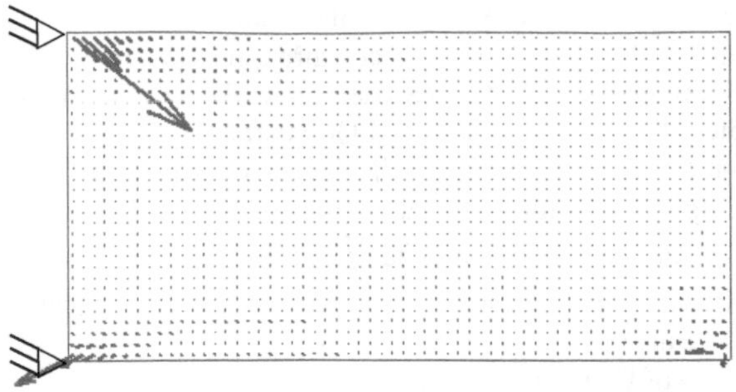

(b) Potential transferred force

Fig. 7. Transferred and potential transferred force to the reaction points

Figure 7 (a) shows an example of using transferred force method to visualize how each point on the plate contributes to the loads transfer to the support points in the homogeneous rectangular plate. Figure 7 (b) shows the potential of transferred force in the structure. The size of the arrows indicates magnitude of the transferred and potential transferred force. The transferred force and potential transferred forces plotted in Figure 7 (a) and (b) are obtained using a finite element mesh of 1800 (30 × 60) elements. When the structure is discretized finely, area of each element becomes smaller and thus contributes a smaller transferred force or presents a smaller potential transferred force through each element. To illustrate this point, the transferred and potential transferred forces are computed again for the structure with 50 elements (Figure 8). With coarser mesh, the contribution of each element in transferring force or its potential transfer force is larger as shown in the figure. This indicates the method is sensitive to the discretization length.

The plot of transferred force in Figure 7 (a) shows that stiffness reductions to elements near the supports and point of loading application leads to the largest changes in the load transfer (load paths). The regions with significant transferred forces are very similar with regions with high stresses (Figure 3). The plot of potential transferred force in Figure 7 (b) however shows that elements near the supports are most effective in changing the load transfer when their stiffness is increased. In subsequent papers [7] and [8], Harasaki and Arora demonstrated the attractiveness of this approach for tailoring direct stiffening or redesigning a structure such as in the case of topology optimization.

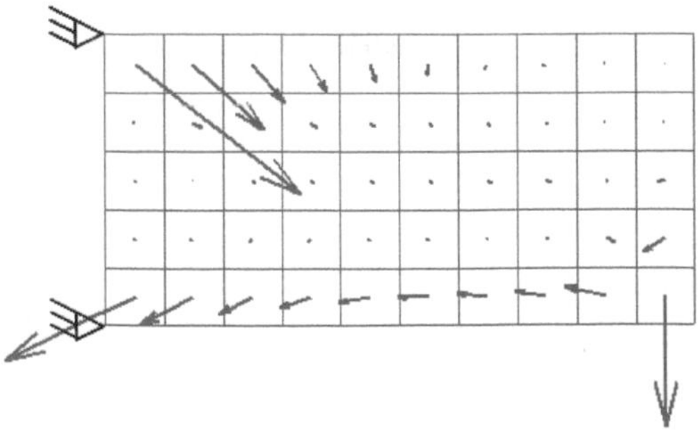

(a) Transferred force

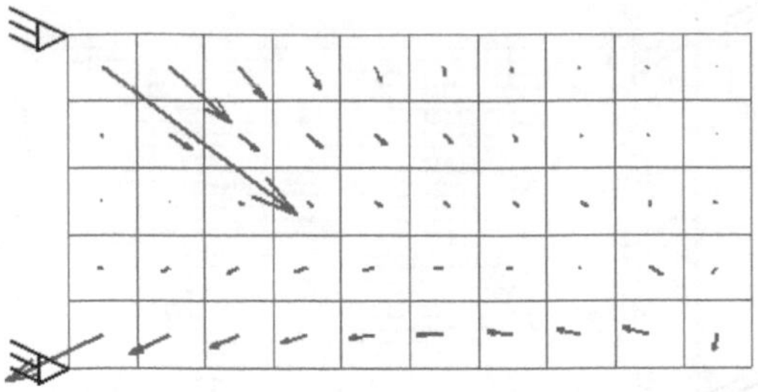

(b) Potential transferred force

Fig. 8. Transferred and potential transferred force to the reaction points with 50 elements

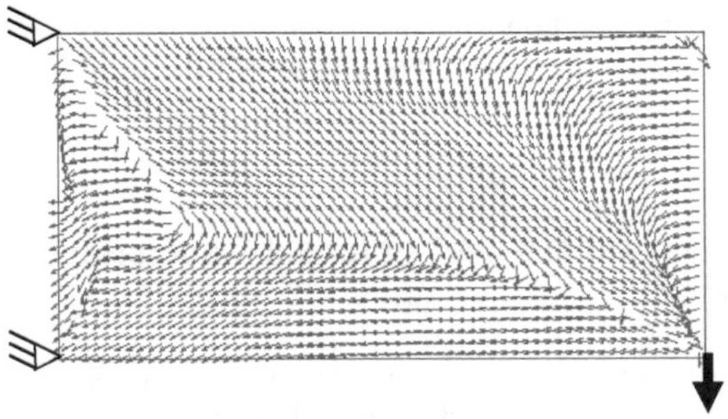

(a) Transferred force

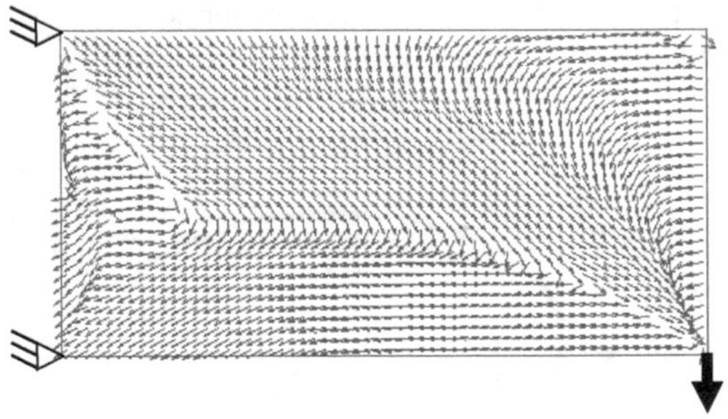

(b) Potential transferred force

Fig. 9. Orientations of the transferred and potential transferred force as unit vectors

Figure 9 shows the orientations of the transferred (a) and potential transferred force (b) as unit vectors without indicating the magnitudes. This way, the orientations of load being transferred (load paths) can be easily visualized. Both orientations are almost identical. Some differences in the orientations can be seen on thc upper right corner of the structure. These differences are mainly due to numerical error because the magnitude of both transferred and potential transferred force is actually very small, approaching zero. This kind of error or difference in orientation can be noted in other cases presented in this work. The loads are visualized to be transferred from the upper and right sides of the structure toward the application point. The flow then changes direction toward the lower support. The method only provides qualitative direction where the loads flow. No trajectories can be traced from the point of loading application to the reaction points. By plotting the magnitude of transferred or potential transferred force, the significance of some regions in load transfer can be identified. However, the visualization does not provide critical stress regions or regions with tension and compression.

2.4 Load path based on change in compliance of structure (U^* field)

Hoshino et al. [9] used a definition for load path based on the scalar field U^* that provides a measure of the participation of any point in the structure to load transfer. Figure 10 shows a schematic for the procedure to calculate U^* field. To obtain U^*, the displacements of the original structure under the applied loads are first calculated using Equation 11. The displacements calculated at the load points u_{1i} are then imposed as enforced displacement boundary conditions and the analysis is repeated. To obtain U^* at any point x_i in the structural domain Ω, displacement degrees of freedom at point x_i are held fixed (set to zero), and the problem is solved for displacements at other points in Ω (Equation 14).

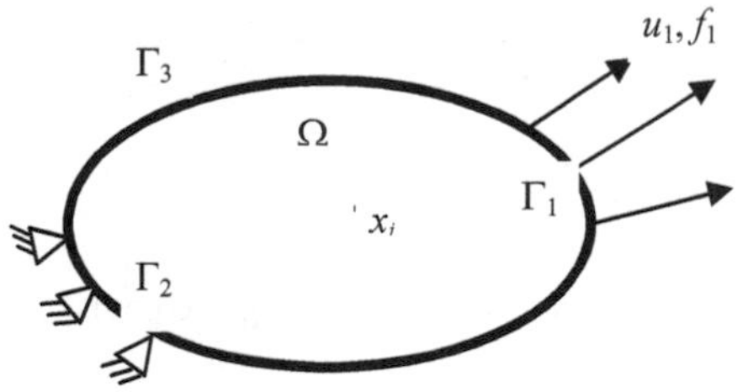

(a) Original structure with applied load f_1 and calculated displacement of u_1 on Γ_1

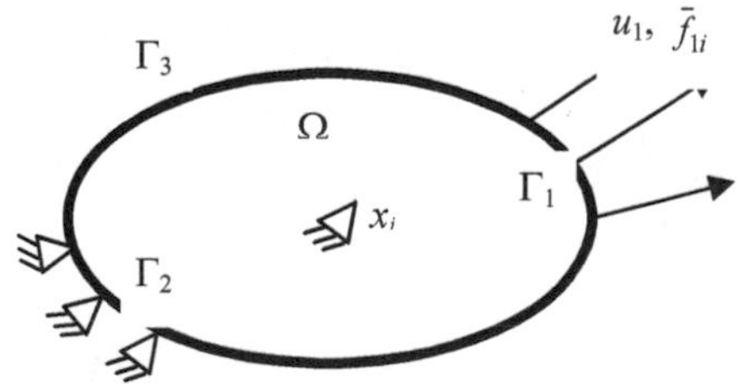

(b) Modified structure with imposed zero displacement at x_i and enforced displacement boundary condition of u_1 on Γ_1

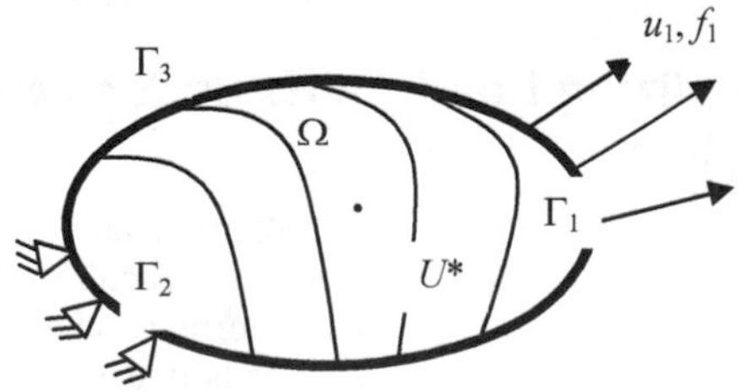

(c) Contour lines of U^* where $U^* = 0$ at support and $U^* = 1$ at load point

Fig. 10. Schematic of procedure for calculating U^*

$$\begin{aligned} &\bar{\sigma}_{ij,j} + b_i = 0 \text{ for } \Omega, \\ &u_i = u_{1i} \text{ on } \Gamma_1, \\ &u_i = 0 \text{ on } \Gamma_2, \\ &u_i = 0 \;\text{ at } x_i \in \Omega \\ &\bar{\sigma}_{ij} n_j = \bar{f}_{1i} \text{ on } \Gamma_1. \end{aligned} \tag{14}$$

In this approach, a scalar quantity of compliance change U^* is calculated to quantify the contribution of a point x_i to the load transfer path. Equation 15 shows U^* is calculated as:

$$U^* = 1 - \frac{U}{U'}, \tag{15}$$

where

$$\begin{aligned} &U = f_{1i} u_{1i}, \text{ and} \\ &U' = \bar{f}_{1i} u_{1i} \\ &f_{1i} = \sigma_{ij} n_j \text{ on } \Gamma_1 \cdot \\ &\bar{f}_{1i} = \bar{\sigma}_{ij} n_j \text{ on } \Gamma_1 \end{aligned} \tag{16}$$

The gradient of this scalar field is defined as the stiffness lines. The stiffness line that provides the steepest descent in U^* values from the load point to the support points is defined to be the load transfer path (load path) in the structure.

Hoshino et al. [9] explain that there are three conditions (termed uniformity, continuity, and consistency requirements) the U^* field must satisfy to achieve optimum stiffness distribution in a structure. The conditions are: (i) The U^* values along the load path must have a linear variation (uniformity); (ii) the curvature of the U^* field with respect to the coordinate along the load path must be zero (continuity); and (iii) the load paths traced from support to loads and loads to support must be coincident (consistency). The conditions are summarized in Figure 11, where s is the distance along a path from the point of application, and l is the whole length of a path.

The uniformity conditions indicate that the load transferred along the load path is constant. Large curvatures of U^* along the load path directions indicate large changes in loads transferred which implies large local shear transfer. This is the case that often arises in the presence of load path discontinuities that give rise to large stresses. Hoshino et al. [9] used the above criteria to directly tailor stiffness in automotive structures for reducing vibration. In their optimization, the area between the curve and the linear line in Figure 11 (a) is minimized along with constraints to impose the continuity and consistency requirements. They showed the optimized structure obtained corresponds to a maximum stiffness structure.

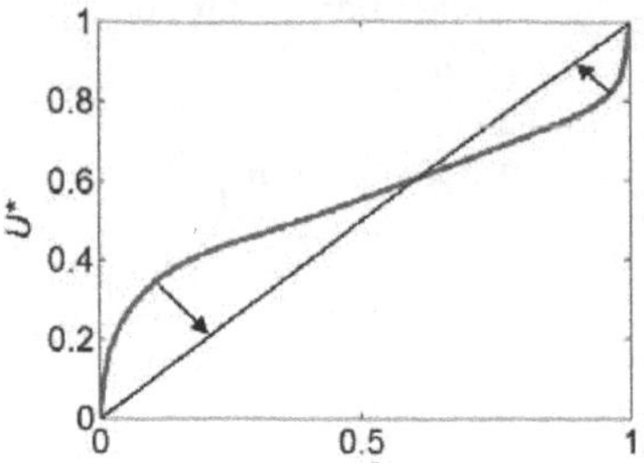

(a) Uniformity

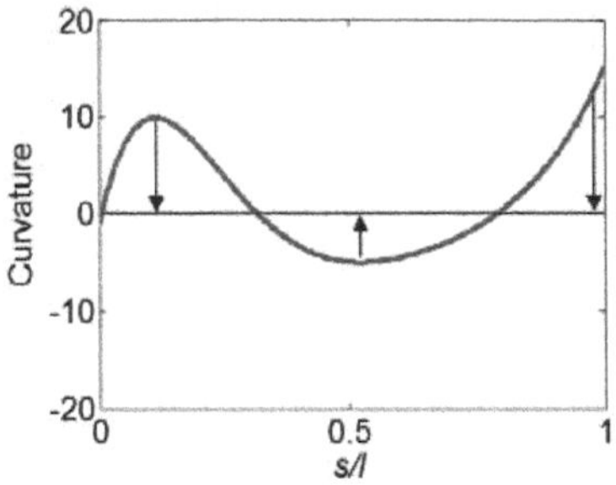

(b) Continuity

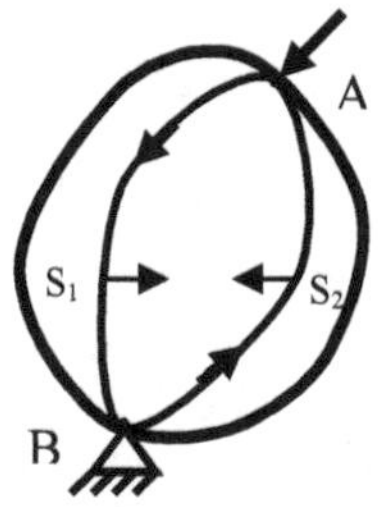

(c) Path consistency

Fig. 11. Conditions that need to be satisfied to achieve a desirable load path

Figure 12 (a) shows the contours of U^* field for the rectangular plate with loaded end. The path corresponding to the steepest gradient of the U^* from the support to the load is defined as the load path. The U^* values at the boundary points are zero and one at the application point. As shown in the figure, the trajectory connects the reaction points with the point of application. Figure 12 (b) and (c) show U^* variation along the paths and its curvature. Green indicates U^* variation and curvature from the upper path, and blue indicates information for lower path. The figures show that the structure does not meet uniformity and continuity requirements, indicating the stiffness distribution of the plate is not optimal. Large curvatures can be seen near the supports and loading point, which indicates location of high stresses. The indication is consistent with actual location of high stresses as shown in Figure 3.

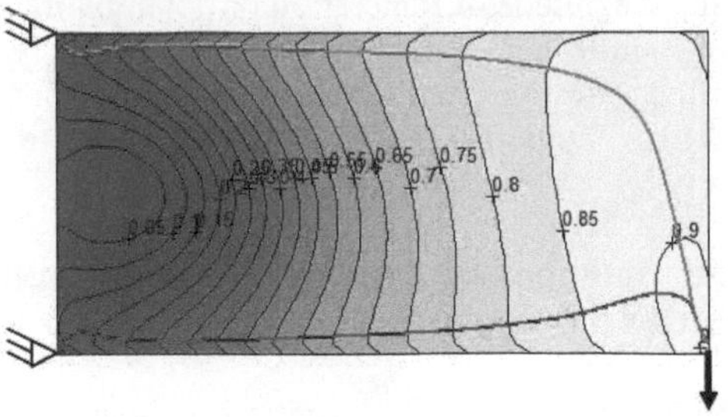

(a) Contour of U^* and steepest gradient of U^* as trajectory of load paths

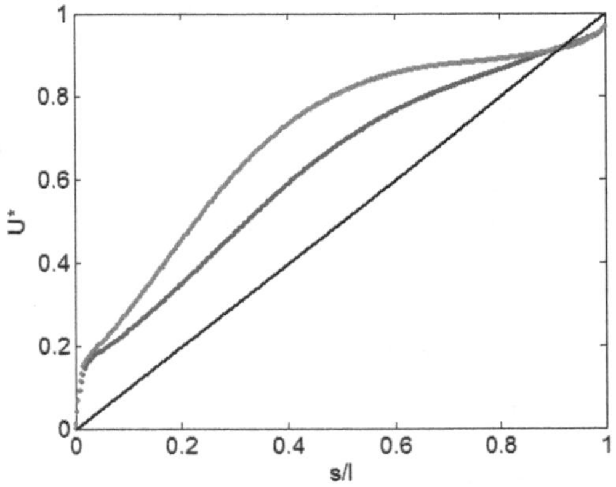

(b) U^* variation along the paths

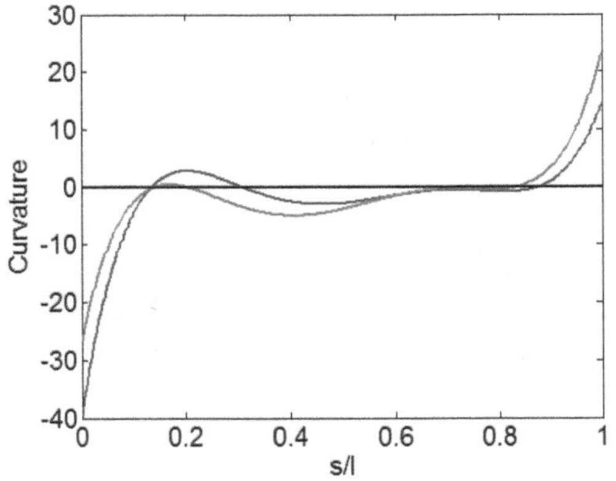

(c) Curvature of U^* along the paths

Fig. 12. Load paths based on U^*. Green indicates upper path and blue indicates lower path.

3 Visualizing Load Paths under Various Conditions

It is commonly understood that alternate and different load paths arise in a structure when the structure is modified. This modification can be in the form of changes in load distributions, changes in support or boundary conditions, or changes in the form of damage that changes (reduces) locally the stiffness of the structure. This section investigates the ability of the different load path definitions presented earlier in characterizing or visualizing the alternate load paths that arise in the plate structure.

3.1 Alternate load paths arising from changes in boundary condition

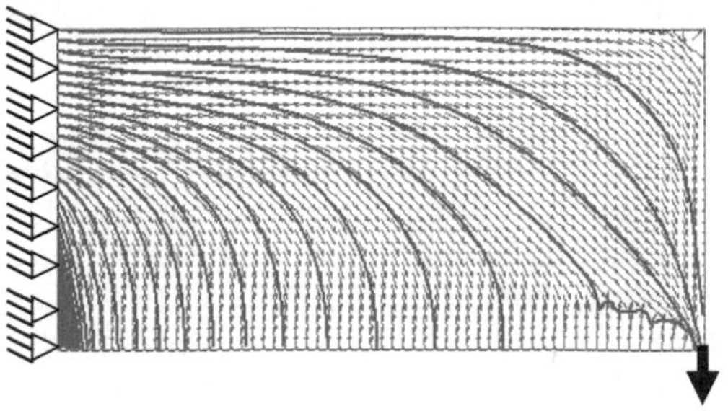

(a) Vector fields aligned with major principal stress σ_{p1}

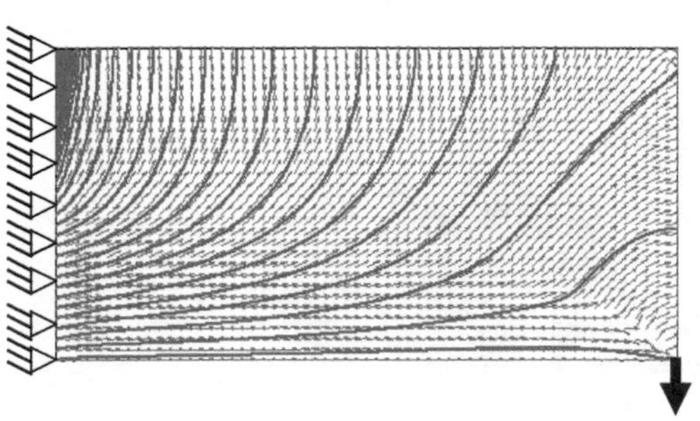

(b) Vector fields aligned with minor principal stress σ_{p2}.

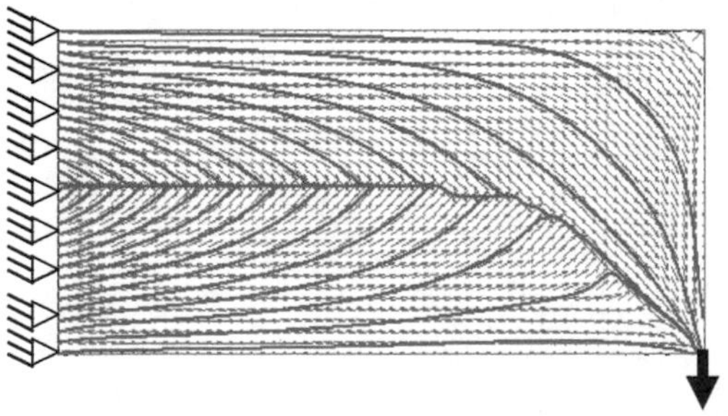

(c) Vector fields aligned with max(abs(σ_{p1}),abs(σ_{p2})) in each element

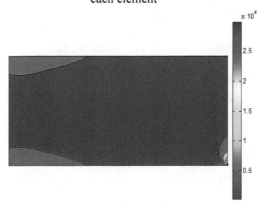

(d) Contours of magnitude of max(abs(σ_{p1}),abs(σ_{p2})) in each element

Fig. 13. Load paths based on principal stresses with left side of the structure fully constrained

The support boundary condition on the left side of the structure is constrained along the entire width. In the uniform plate, the load paths will distribute the applied load to the reaction points along the fixed edge. We now investigate how the different methods differentiate the change in load paths as a result of this change in boundary condition.

Figures 13 (a) and (b) show the vector fields oriented with σ_{p1} and σ_{p2} respectively at each element in the structure. Where there are two support points, tensile stress is highest at the top of the plate near the supports, and it diminishes to zero at the bottom side of the plate (Figure 13 (a)), except near the application point. High stress areas are spread closer to the upper half of the supports. Similarly, the structure experiences high compressive stress at the bottom side, and the stress goes to zero at the top of the structure (Figure 13 (b)). High compressive stress spreads near the lower half of the supports. In general, the stresses are more spread out when the left side of the structure is fully constrained. Figure 13 (c) shows the orientations of high stresses (tension and compression) by plotting max($|\sigma_{p1}|$,$|\sigma_{p2}|$). Figure 13 (d) shows the contours of max($|\sigma_{p1}|$,$|\sigma_{p2}|$), which indicates high stresses near the loading point. By combining the plots of orientations of both principal stresses, we can trace trajectories that connect point of loading application and reaction points. However, these trajectories do not indicate constant load transfer or load equilibrium along the trajectories.

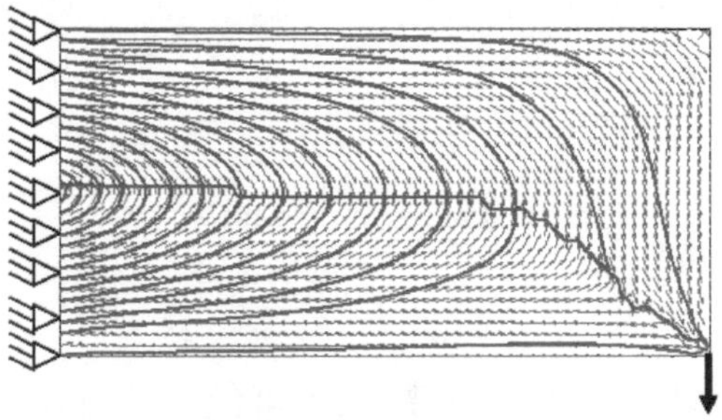

(a) Load flow with equilibrium in x-direction

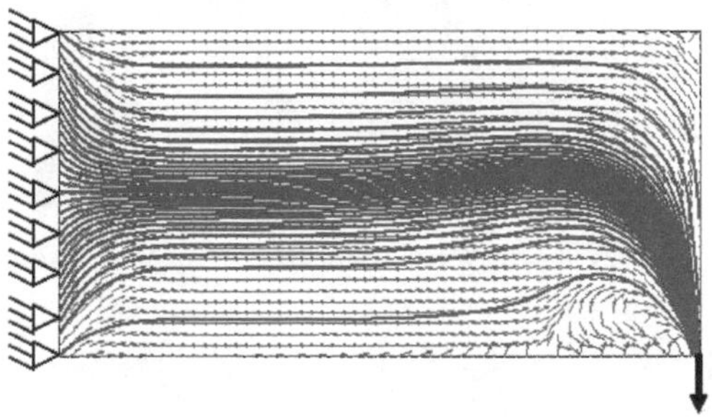

(b) Load flow with equilibrium in y-direction

Fig. 14. Orientation of load flow with left side of the structure fully constrained

Figure 14 shows load flow with load equilibrium in the x-direction (a) and the y-direction (b). Similar to the case of having two supports, load flow in the x-direction shows the structure reacts to bending moments. For load flow in the y-direction, shear is transferred from the application point to the reaction points. Unlike the case with only two support points, the region with a circulating pattern is only found near the application point. This shows that the shear is transferred more uniformly in the structure at the support. Qualitatively, the trajectories in Figure 14 (a) are very similar to the trajectories in Figure 13 (c). This indicates that dominant stress is σ_x, where non-zero principal stress directions are aligned with the x-direction.

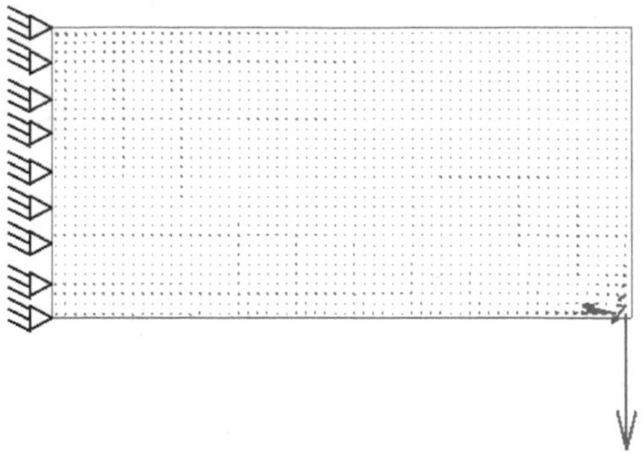

(a) Transferred force

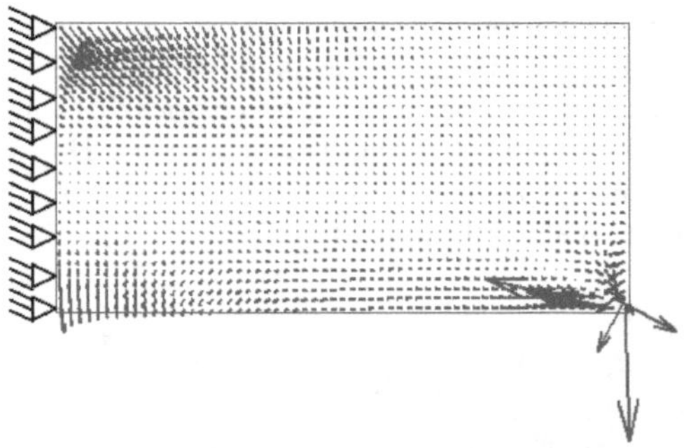

(b) Potential transferred force

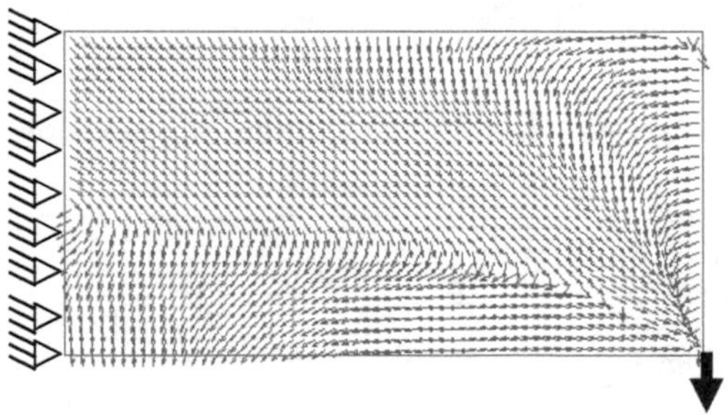

(c) Unit vectors showing orientations of transferred force

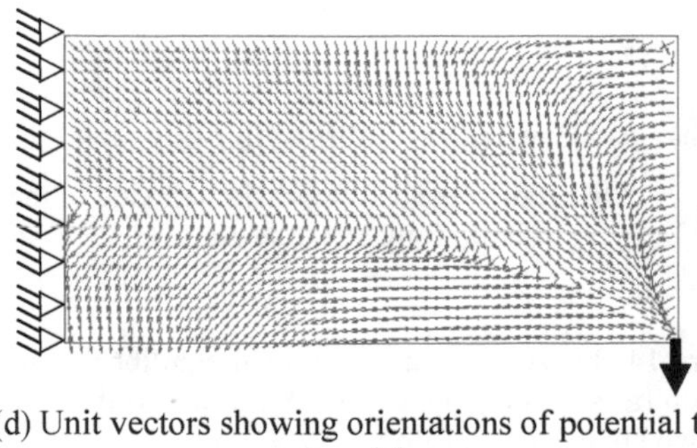

(d) Unit vectors showing orientations of potential transferred force

Fig. 15. Transferred and potential transferred force to the reaction points with left side fully constrained

Figure 15 shows transferred (a) and potential transferred (b) force when the isotropic rectangular plate is fully constrained on the left side. Plotting the transferred force shows that the only elements that contribute significantly in transferring force to the reaction points are the ones near the application point. The rest have small and almost equal contribution. This is because the force is transferred to more reaction points than in the case with only two reaction points. Plotting the potential transferred force shows many elements that can significantly change the load paths by increasing the stiffness of those elements. To visualize the flow of force being transferred, the orientations of the transferred and potential transferred force are plotted as unit vectors, shown in Figure 15 (c) and (d). Qualitatively, the orientations of transferred and potential transferred force are very similar.

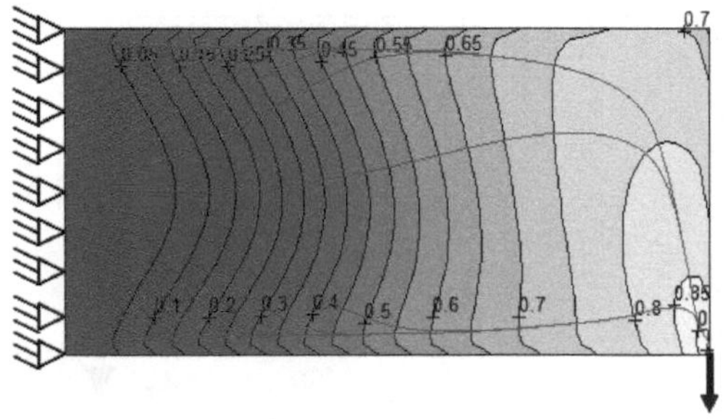

(a) U^* field and load path trajectories

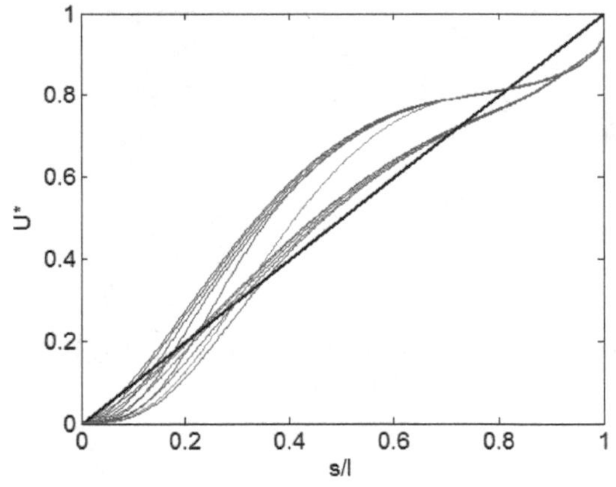

(b) U^* variation along the load paths

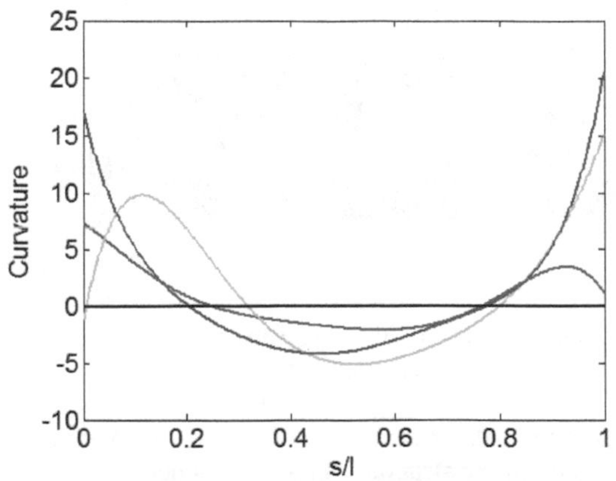

(c) Curvature of U^* along the paths

Fig. 16. Load paths based on U^* for rectangular structure with its left side fully constrained. Blue indicates lower path, green indicates paths from the center support, and red indicates upper path.

Figure 16 (a) shows the U^* field for the rectangular plate with its left side fully constrained. The load paths or steepest gradient of U^* field are also plotted from each support to the application point. Figure 16 (b) shows the variation of U^* along each path. The blue lines indicate load paths from the lower half of the supports, and the red lines indicate load paths from the upper half of the supports. The green line represents load path that comes from the center of the support. Load paths from the lower half have more linear variation of U^* than load paths from the upper half. Figure 16 (c) shows the curvatures of U^*. The curvatures plotted are from paths traced from a point closed the lower support (blue), a point near the upper support (red), and a point from the center support (green). The curvatures indicate there are high stresses near the lower and upper supports. A high stress region is also indicated in the path traced from the center support at 0.11 of s/l. In reality high stress region is only in the region near the loading application point as shown in Figure 13 (d). Thus a relation between high stress regions/stress concentrations and discontinuity in U^* curvature cannot be established in this case.

3.2 Alternate load paths arising from distributed loading

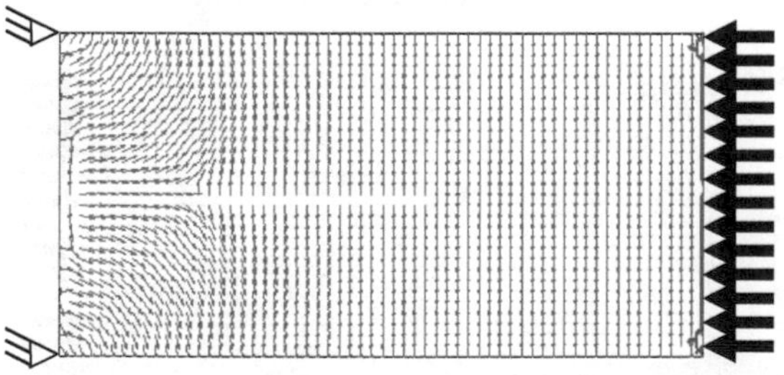

(a) Vector fields aligned with major principal stress σ_{p1}

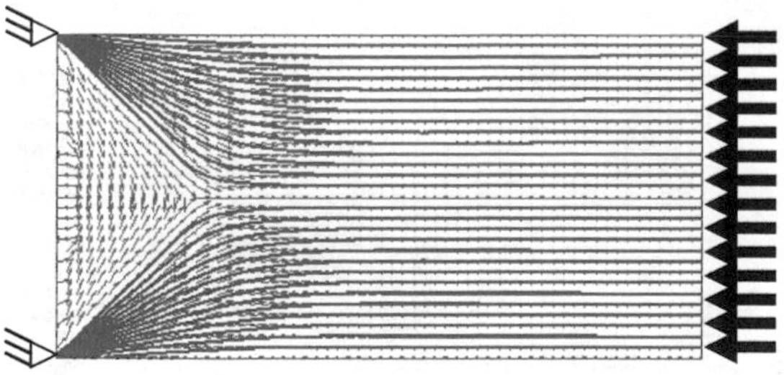

(b) Vector fields aligned with minor principal stress σ_{p2}

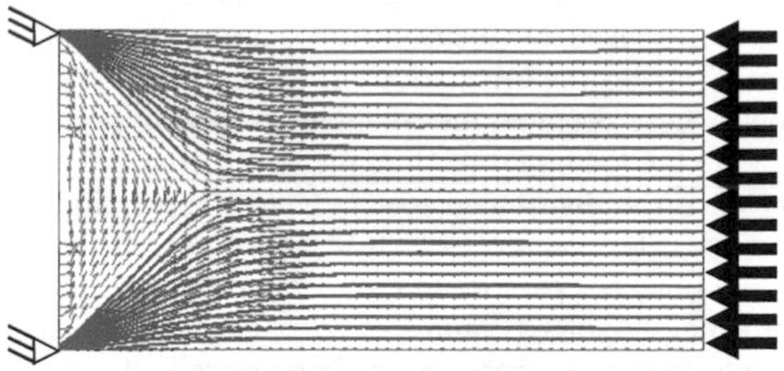

(c) Vector fields aligned with max(abs(σ_{p1}),abs(σ_{p2})) in each element

(d) Contours of magnitude of max(abs(σ_{p1}),abs(σ_{p2})) in each element

Fig. 17. Load paths based on principal stresses with distributed loading in the horizontal direction

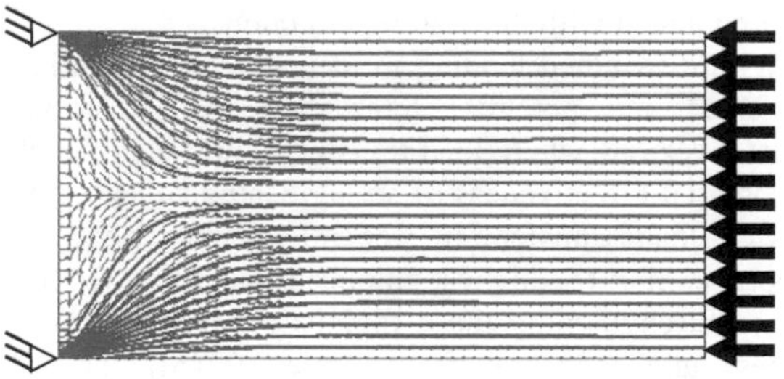

(a) Load flow with equilibrium in x-direction

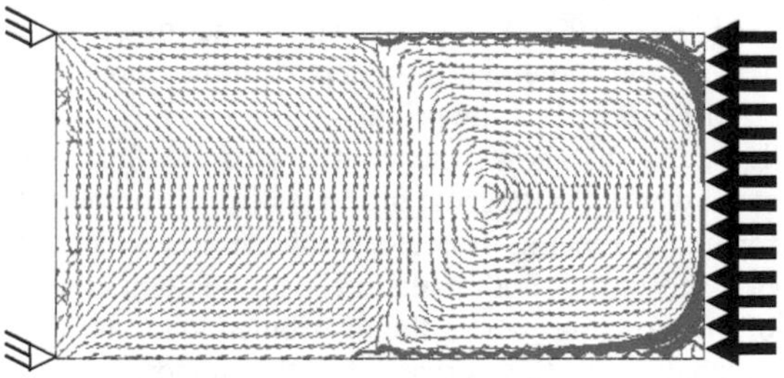

(b) Load flow with equilibrium in y-direction

Fig.18. Orientation of load flow with distributed loading in the x-direction

The load path definitions are also compared to visualize load paths caused by distributed loading in the structure. Figure 17 shows the orientations of principal stresses. In the regions where orientations of minor principal stresses are parallel to the loading direction, the major principal stress is zero. Since the distributed loads create compression in the plate, initially vectors of the minor principal stress (compression) are parallel to the loading direction then turn toward the supports (Figure 17 (b)). Trajectories can also trace the stress flow from the loading points to the supports. The highest compression occurs near the supports. Figure 17 (c) shows the orientation of max(abs(σ_{p1}),abs(σ_{p2})) in each element, which is almost identical to Figure 17 (b). This shows that the dominant stress in the structure is compressive stress. Figure 17 (d) shows the contours of max(abs(σ_{p1}),abs(σ_{p2})) in each element, which shows regions with high stresses are near the supports.

Figure 18 (a) shows that the load flow in the *x*-direction corresponds to the orientations of the minor principal stress. The same trajectories trace load flow from the loading points to the reaction points. Load flow in the *y*-direction plotted in Figure 18 (b), which complements load flow in the *x*-direction, shows circulating patterns in the right half of the plate. These patterns occur because of the equilibrium requirement explained by Kelly et al. [3]. Waldman et al. [4] explained that these circulatory patterns are self equilibrating because the *y*-components of the loads are zero. Orientations of minor principal stresses and orientations of load flow with equilibrium in *x*-direction are very similar (including their trajectories). Under distributed loads, the structure experiences compression along the *x*-direction. That is why orientations from minor principal stress (which indicate compression in the structure) are very similar to orientations from load flow in *x*-direction, which is again aligned with the loading direction.

With distributed loading in the *x*-direction, plotting the transferred and potential transferred force distributions indicates regions where load transfer is most significant and the potential effectiveness of strengthening some regions to improve load transfer. In general, regions next to the supports exhibit the highest amount of load transfer (Figure 19 (a)). Strengthening these regions consistently improves stiffness and load transfer (Figure 19 (b)). Thus both reducing and increasing stiffness of elements near the supports are effective in changing the load transfer (load paths). Figure 19 (c) and (d) show the orientations of transferred and potential transferred force more clearly. Both figures show that the orientations are almost identical.

Figure 20 (a) shows the contours of U^* field and the trajectory where the steepest gradients of the contours occur (load paths). Tracing trajectories from lower and upper supports shows that both paths meet at one point at the right side of the structure, where the distributed loads are applied. An explanation for this is that U^* at the supports is zero and U^* along the side where the loads are applied is one. Near the side where loads are applied there is only one location at each contour where the gradient of U^* is steepest. Thus, both paths meet at one location in the middle of the application side. Analyzing the U^* variation along both paths shows the variation to be identical in both paths (Figure 20 (b)). Figure 20 (c) shows the curvature of U^* along the paths, which is mostly zero with exception near the supports and loading points. Ideally, the curvature near the applied loads should be zero because there are no high stress regions near where the loads are applied. This is the drawback of using U^* method for distributed loading. A complimentary concept of U^* (a new index U^{**}) is introduced by Okano et al. [10] that can be used to investigate load paths in structures under distributed loading. The new index U^{**} is defined in terms of the complimentary strain energy instead of the work done by the load (compliance) in case of U^*.

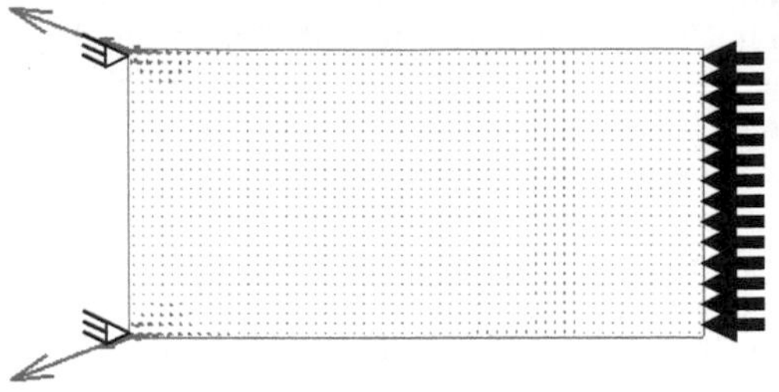

(a) Transferred force

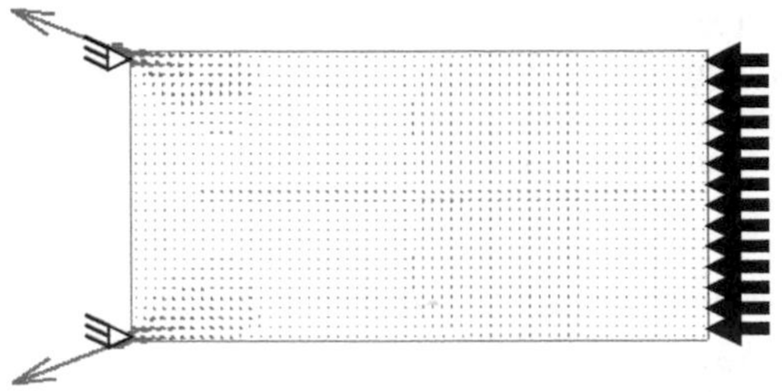

(b) Potential transferred force

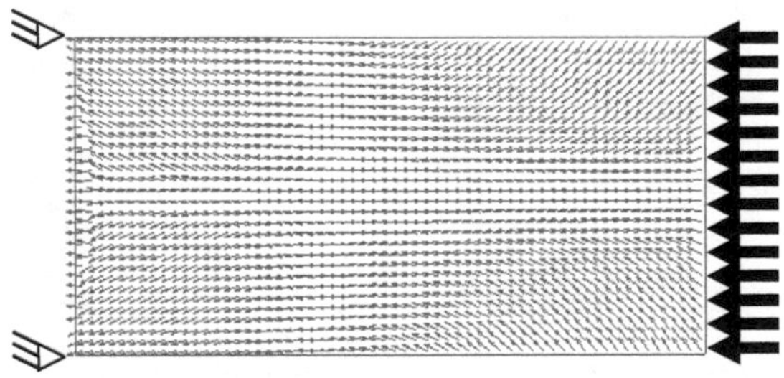

(c) Unit vectors showing orientations of transferred force

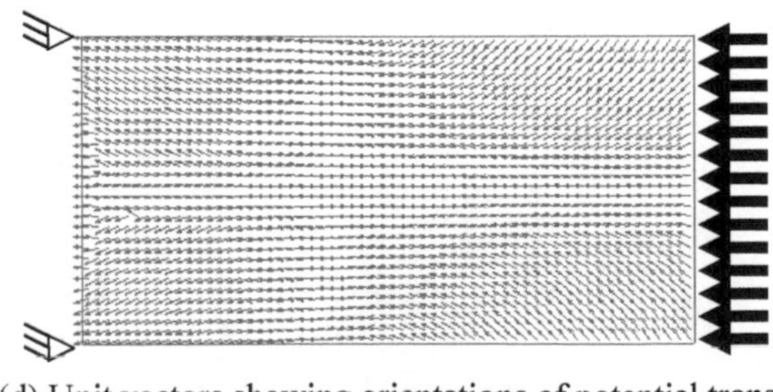

(d) Unit vectors showing orientations of potential transferred force

Fig. 19. Transferred and potential transferred force to the reaction points with distributed loading in the *x*-direction

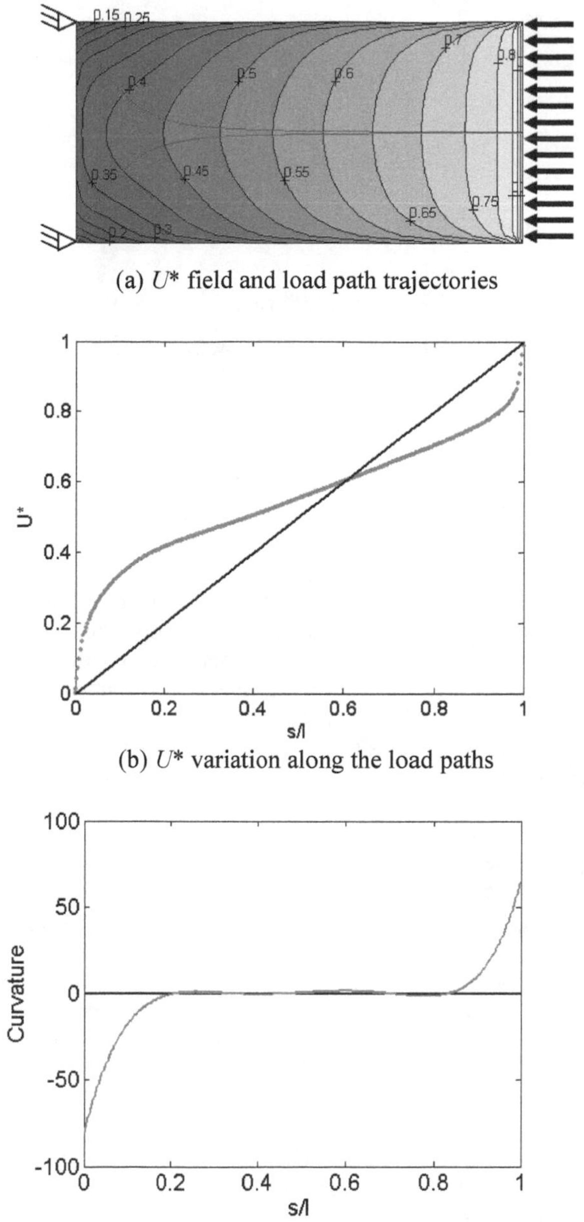

(a) U^* field and load path trajectories

(b) U^* variation along the load paths

(c) Curvature of U^* along the paths

Fig. 20. Load paths based on U^* for rectangular structure with distributed loading in the x-direction

3.3 Alternate load paths arising from introducing a hole

Engineers are particularly interested to see how load paths change in the events of damage to the structure. The idea is to check whether the alternative paths will enable the structure to perform its basic function. In this work, the damage introduced to the structure is a circular hole. Comparisons are made on the different ways the four load path definitions visualize alternative load paths.

Figure 21 shows the orientations of the principal stresses. Figure 21 (a) shows the orientation of the major principal stress vectors (tensile). As in the non-damage case, the plot of major principal stress orientations shows tension on the top side of the plate and the stress diminish to zero at the bottom side. Maximum tension occurs at the upper left support. Figure 21 (b) shows that the structure experiences compression at the bottom side (maximum compressive stress at the lower left support) and the compressive stress decreases to zero at the top side. The findings about orientation of σ_{p1} and σ_{p2} around the hole are similar to the results obtained by Waldman et al. in [4]. They noted that depending on the location along the free boundary of the hole, one of the two principal stresses will be zero. The non-zero principal stresses will be oriented tangent to the boundary of the hole. Due to the inherent numerical error in finite element method, the areas where orientations of the principal stresses are shown to be perpendicular to the hole are in fact areas with zero principal stresses. The trajectory from the upper support can be seen closely follows the boundary of the hole where the orientations of σ_{p1} are tangent to the hole boundary, and ends at the application point. On the other hand, trajectory from the lower support ends at the boundary of the hole where the orientations of the σ_{p2} are perpendicular to the hole boundary (where σ_{p2} is essentially zero). This is a major deficiency in using orientations of principal stresses because it is impossible for the load trajectory to end at the boundary of the hole or for the hole to transmit loads.

Plotting the orientation of max(abs(σ_{p1}),abs(σ_{p2})) in each element (Figure 21 (c)) shows how the stresses go around the hole. The orientations of σ_{p1} and σ_{p2} that are now plotted are the ones tangent to the surface of the hole. Tracing trajectory from the lower support ends at the loaded end, and tracing another one from the upper support ends at the right side of the plate. Figure 21 (d) shows the contour of magnitude of maximum principal stresses. High stresses are indicated to be near the supports and loading point.

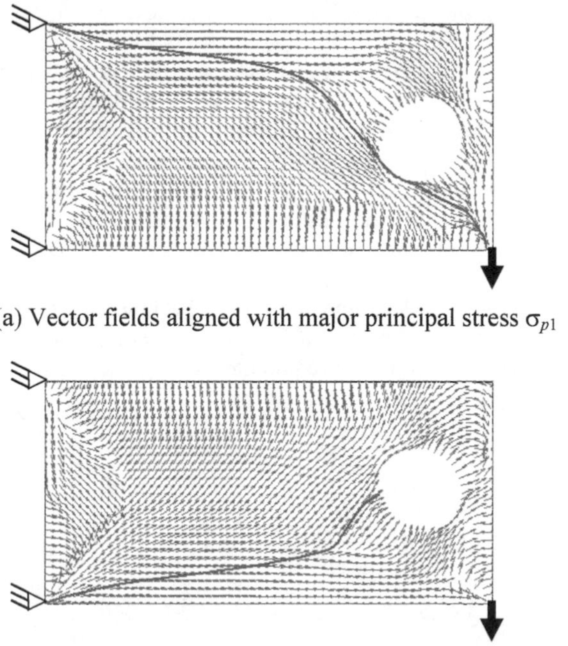

(a) Vector fields aligned with major principal stress σ_{p1}

(b) Vector fields aligned with minor principal stress σ_{p2}

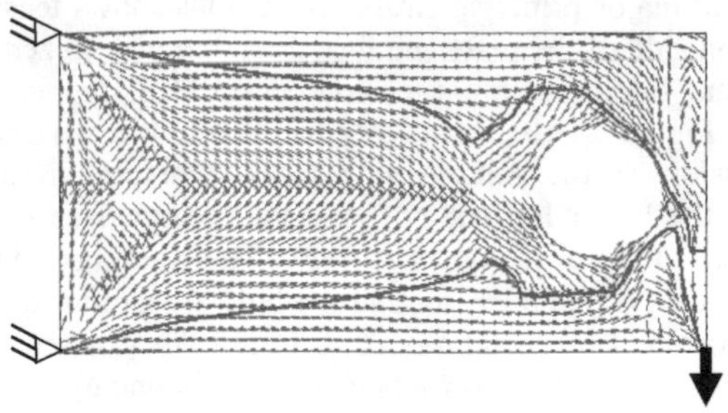

(c) Vector fields aligned with max(abs(σ_{p1}),abs(σ_{p2})) in each element

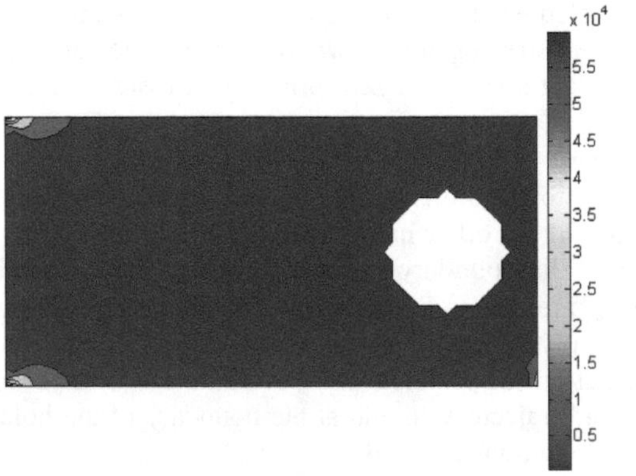

(d) Contours of magnitude of max(abs(σ_{p1}),abs(σ_{p2})) in each element

Fig. 21. Load paths based on principal stresses with a hole in the structure

Figure 22 (a) shows the distribution of load flow with load equilibrium in the *x*-direction. Similar to the case with no hole in the structure, the flow indicates bending in the structure. The hole changes the loops (red line trajectories) that used to connect between the two supports and to the application point. The load now flows around the hole, and end at the right side of the structure. There is also a region with circulatory patterns on the right side of the structure, which indicates region with low stress. Figure 22 (b) shows the distribution of load flow with load equilibrium in the *y*-direction. Similar to the case with no damage, shear is still transferred from the point load to the reaction points. The load has to travel around the hole. The hole creates more regions with circulatory patterns (near the hole) which have to satisfy the equilibrium requirements.

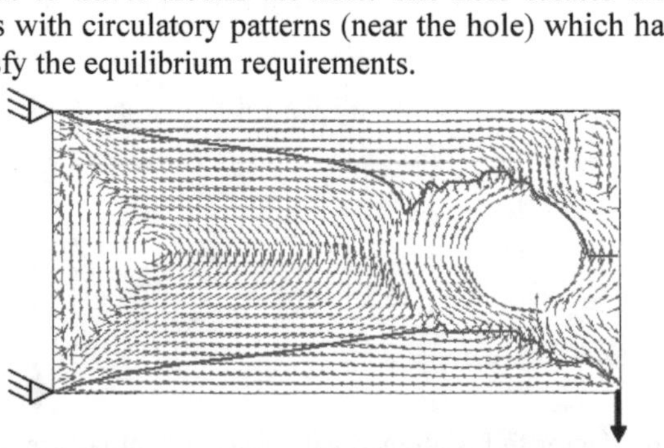

(a) Load flow with equilibrium in *x*-direction

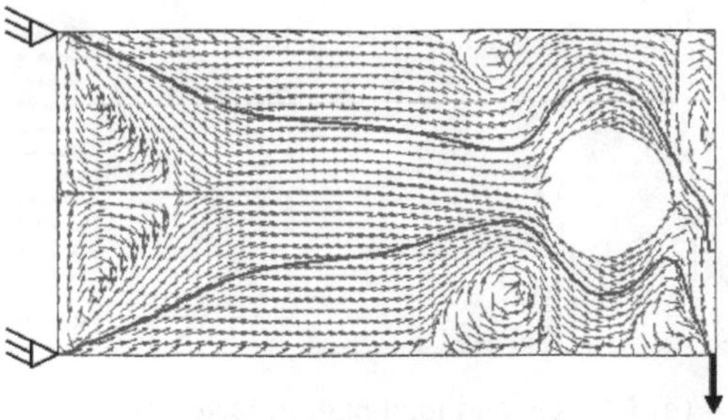

(b) Load flow with equilibrium in *y*-direction

Fig. 22. Orientation of load flow with a hole

The case with a hole for transferred and potential transferred force is shown in Figure 23. A quick inspection shows that differences in transferred and potential transferred force distribution between the case with a hole and no hole are subtle. An explanation for this is that the hole exists in the area where the elements contribute little to transferring force to the reaction points. Thus creating the hole does not make significant changes in the transferred and potential transferred force in other elements. This example gives the basis for removing materials in the structure during redesign process in later work by Harasaki and Arora [7 and 8]. By plotting the orientations of transferred and potential transferred force as unit vectors (Figure 23 (c) and (d)), we can visualize how the flow of transferred loads avoid the hole. Qualitatively, the orientations of transferred and potential transferred load are similar.

Using U^* field to identify load paths from the application point to the reaction points with a hole in the structure shows that the paths simply avoid the hole by taking a longer route (Figure 24 (a)). Changes in the paths are also evident in the plot of U^* variation along the paths (Figure 24 (b)). Non-linear variation of U^* along the paths indicates turns in the paths. The curvatures of U^* indicate high stresses near the supports and loading point by having large values of curvature. This observation is consistent with the actual location of high stress regions.

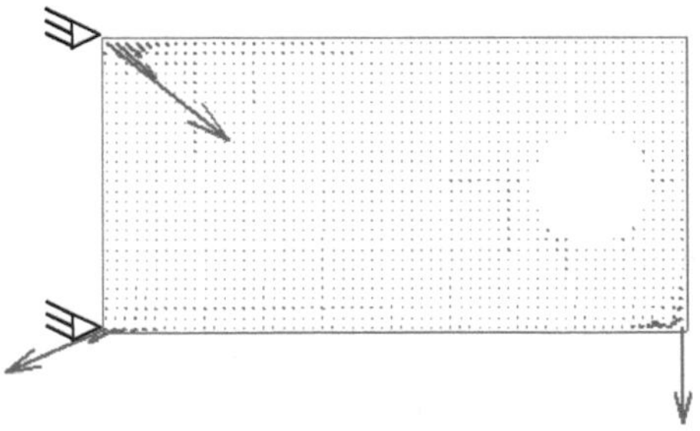

(a) Transferred force

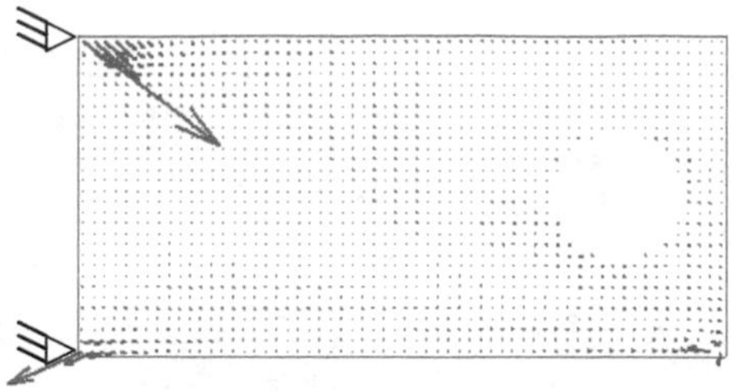

(b) Potential transferred force

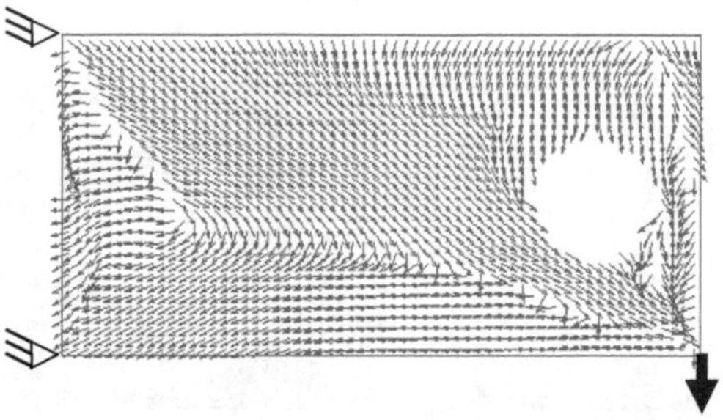

(c) Unit vectors showing orientations of transferred force

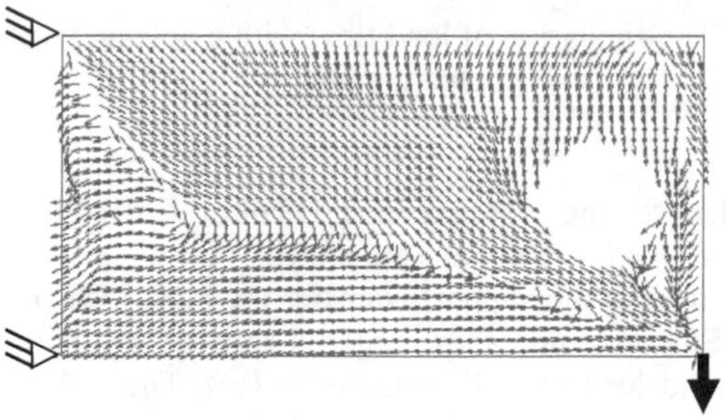

(d) Unit vectors showing orientations of potential transferred force

Fig. 23. Transferred and potential transferred force to the reaction points with a hole in the structure

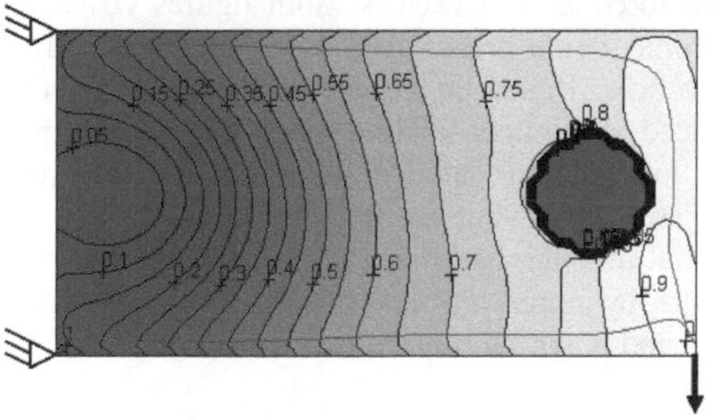

(a) U^* field and load path trajectories

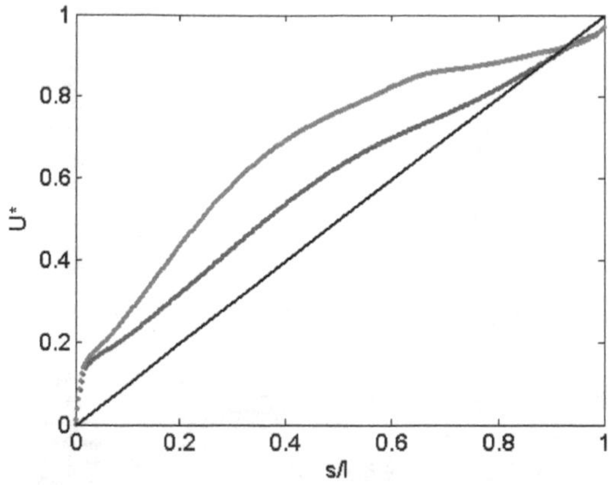

(b) U^* variation along the load paths

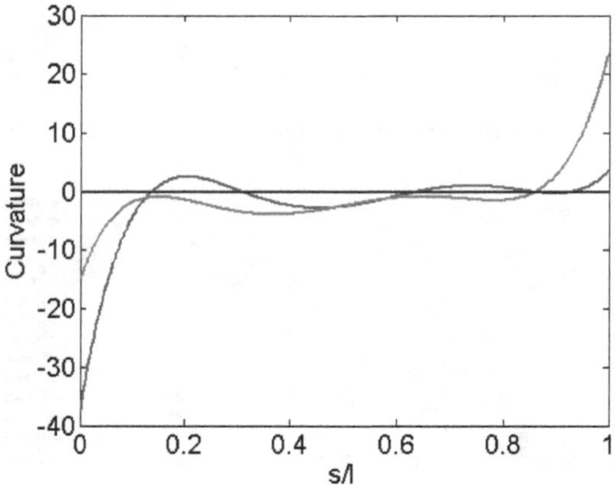

(c) Curvature of U^* along the paths

Fig. 24. Load paths based on U^* for rectangular structure with a hole in the structure

3.4 Alternate load paths arising from introducing a hole and having distributed loading

The load path definitions are compared to visualize alternate paths in the structure under distributed loading and when there is a hole. Figure 25 shows the orientation of the principal stresses under this condition. As in the case with distributed loading, the structure experiences compressive stress. On the upper and lower parts of the hole, σ_{p1} is mostly zero, and the orientations are also perpendicular to the hole boundary. In other parts of the structure, σ_{p1} is mostly zero, where the orientations are perpendicular to the direction of applied loads (Figure 25 (a)). Vectors of the minor principal stress (compressive) can be seen parallel to the loading direction initially. They pass the hole, and turn toward the supports. This is evident by tracing the trajectories from the application side to the supports in Figure 25 (b). Plotting orientations of $\max(\text{abs}(\sigma_{p1}),\text{abs}(\sigma_{p2}))$ in Figure 25 (c) shows that the trajectories are identical to the ones in Figure 25 (b). Clearly, the dominant stress in the structure is compressive stress. Also, the orientations of σ_{p1} and σ_{p2} can now be seen all tangent to the surface of the hole. Figure 25 (d) shows that high stresses are only near the supports.

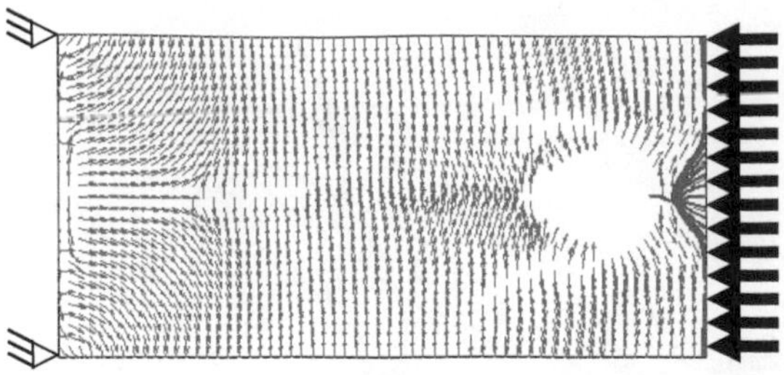

(a) Vector fields aligned with major principal stress σ_{p1}

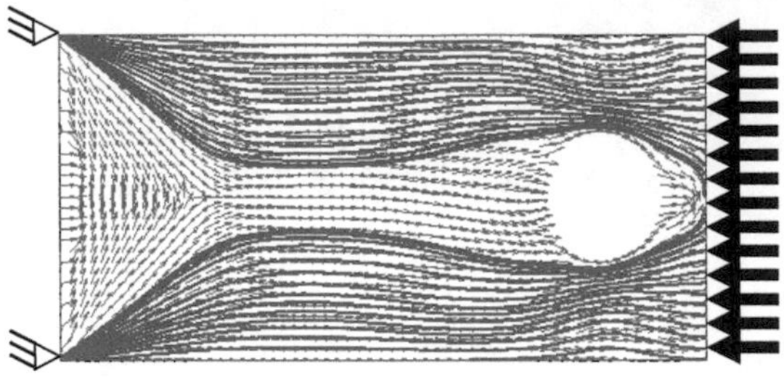

(b) Vector fields aligned with minor principal stress σ_{p2}

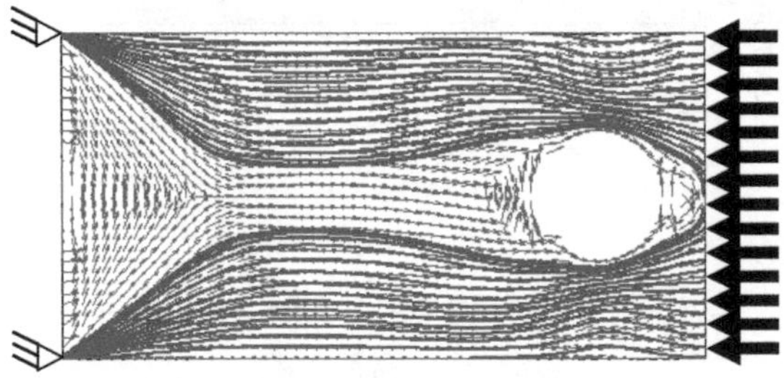

(c) Vector fields aligned with max(abs(σ_{p1}),abs(σ_{p2})) in each element

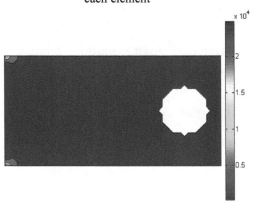

(d) Contours of magnitude of max(abs(σ_{p1}),abs(σ_{p2})) in each element

Fig. 25. Load paths based on principal stresses with a hole and distributed loading in the structure

Again, the load flow with equilibrium in *x*-direction is the counterpart of minor principal stress (Figure 26 (a)). The patterns are more complex for load flow with equilibrium in *y*-direction (Figure 26 (b)). There are many regions with circulatory patterns in the *y*-direction load flow, especially near the hole. The circulatory patterns are self equilibrating because the *y*-components of the loads are zero.

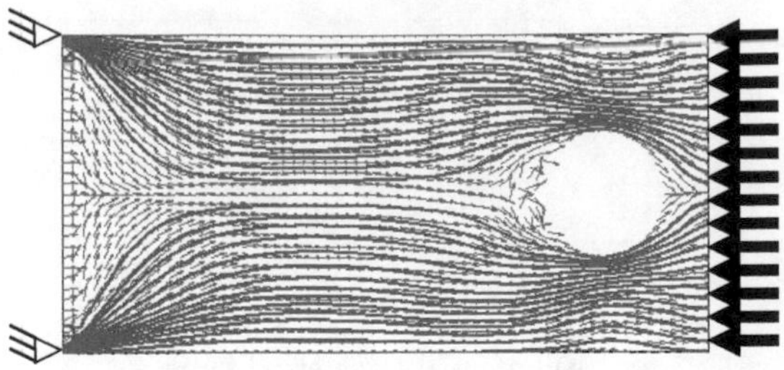

(a) Load flow with equilibrium in *x*-direction

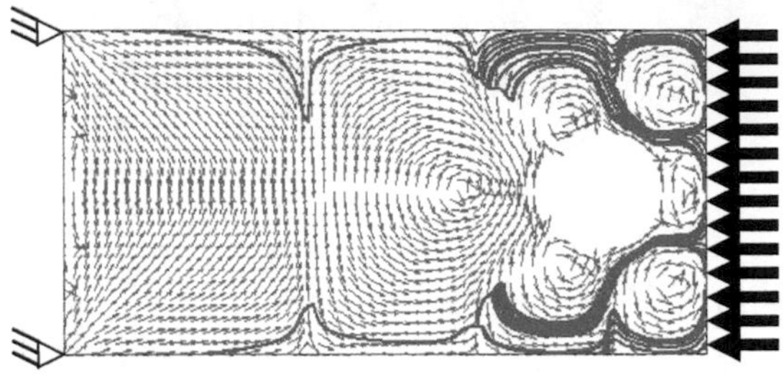

(b) Load flow with equilibrium in *y*-direction

Fig. 26. Orientation of load flow with a hole and distributed loading

Similar to the case with no hole, distributions of transferred and potential transferred force show that elements next to the supports transfer the most load (Figure 27 (a)). Strengthening these regions consistently improves stiffness and load transfer (Figure 27 (b)). The differences between the case with hole and no hole are subtle. This is because the hole is in the region where the contributions of elements in transferring loads are minimal. Thus removing elements to create the hole does not significantly change overall load transferred by the other elements. Figure 27 (c) and (d) present orientations of transferred and potential transferred force as unit vectors. Both figures visualize the flow of force being transferred across the structure and around the hole. Based on the orientations, no trajectories can be traced to connect loading point and reaction points. Also, the information obtained does not indicate regions with high stresses. Using the magnitude of the transferred and potential transferred force enables stiffness tailoring of the structure by removing material from regions with low transferred and potential transferred force.

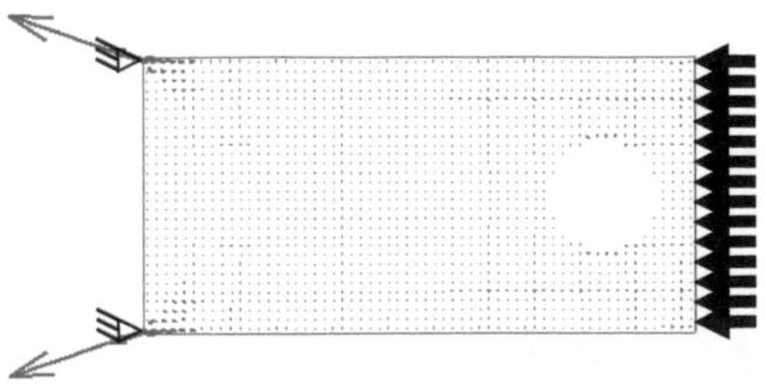

(a) Transferred force

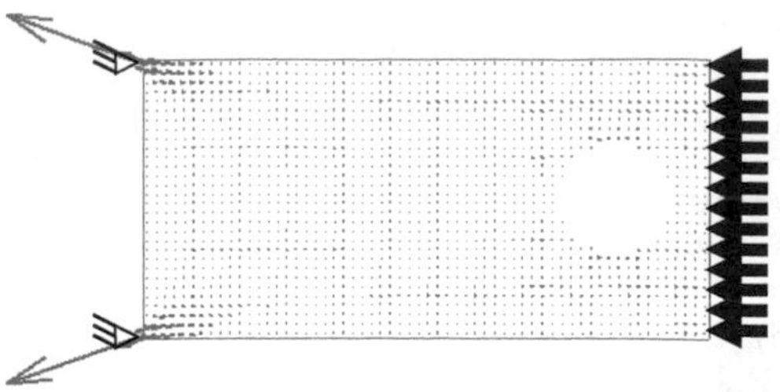

(b) Potential transferred force

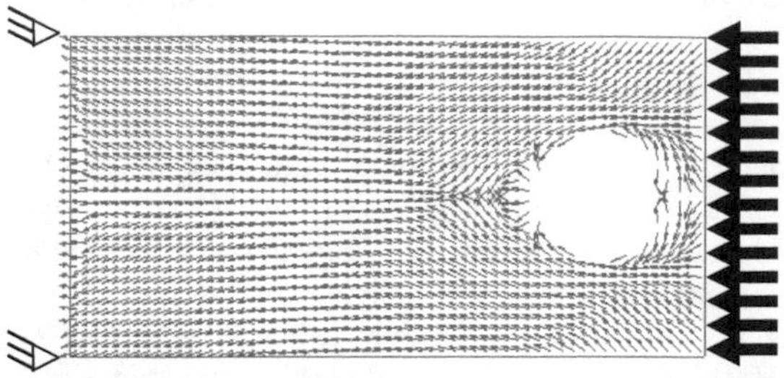

(c) Unit vectors showing orientations of transferred force

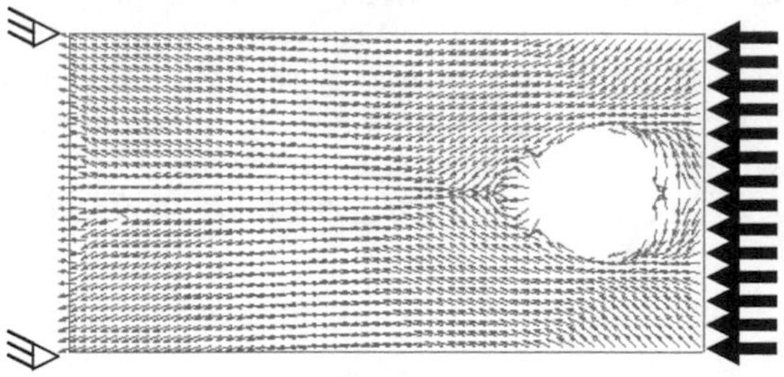

(d) Unit vectors showing orientations of potential transferred force

Fig. 27. Transferred and potential transferred force to the reaction points with a hole and distributed loading in the structure

Figure 28 (a) shows the contours of U^* field for the plate structure with a hole and distributed load. The load paths trace trajectories from the supports, around the hole, and to the application side. Since the structure is symmetric, the U^* variation along both lower and upper paths are identical as shown in Figure 28 (b). The two paths also end at two locations at the loading application side, where U^* value is one along the side. The slope of U^* variation changes at the location where the hole exists (Figure 28 (b)), which also indicates the paths turn to go around the hole. Another drawback of using U^* method to analyze load paths in a structure under distributed loading is shown here. High stresses are only observed near the supports. However, large non-zero values of curvature near the supports and loading points indicate otherwise.

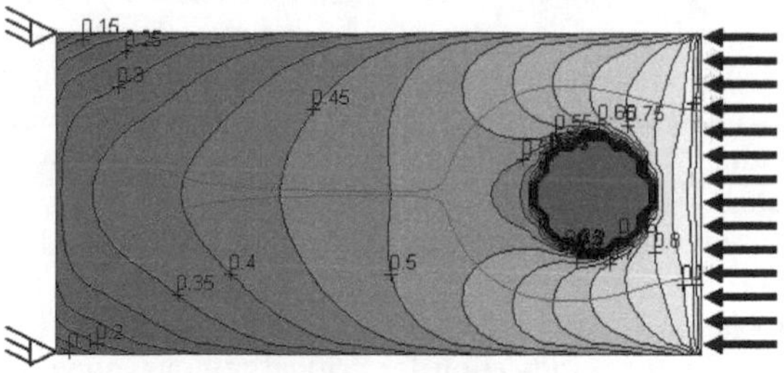

(a) U^* field and load path trajectories

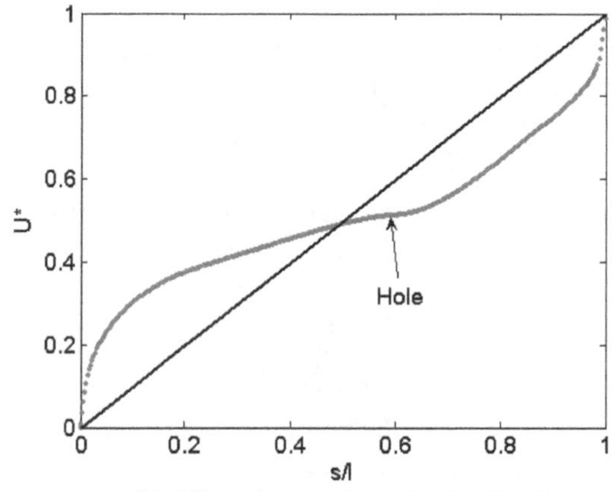

(b) U^* variation along the load paths

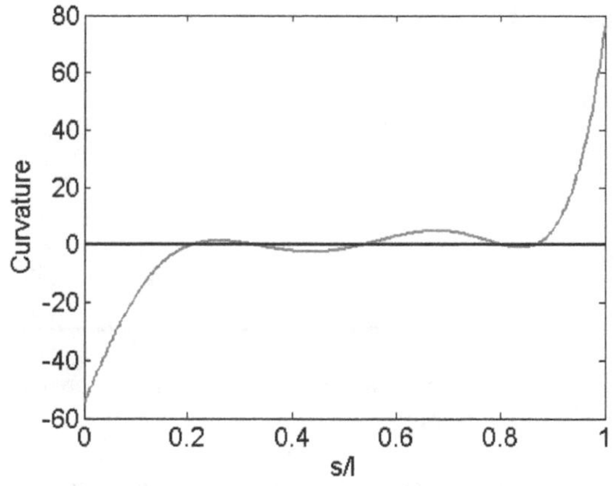

(c) Curvature of U^* along the paths

Fig. 28. Load paths based on U^* for rectangular structure with a hole and distributed loading in the structure

4 Summary and Conclusions

In summary the different definitions and methods that have been developed to characterize and visualized load paths in a structure were compared. The methods compared are: (1) using directions of major and minor principal stresses, (2) load flow defined by orthogonal axes in which load equilibrium must be satisfied, (3) transferred and potential transferred force method, and (4) load path based on change in compliance (U^* field). The different methods are compared for characterizing load paths in a rectangular plate structure under various conditions, namely: (a) two points and fully constrained boundary conditions, (b) distributed loading in x-direction, (c) a hole in the structure, and (d) a hole in the structure with distributed loading. All definitions compared can provide identification and visualization of load flow in the structure.

Based on the pre-defined criteria that a load path characterization method should have, namely: (a) visualization of load trajectories, (b) indication for stiffness tailoring, and (c) indication for critical regions, none of the methods compared has clear advantages over the others. Table 1 provides a summary of the methods as they are checked for criteria initially defined.

Table 1. Summary of comparison of various load path definitions against the pre-defined criteria

	Orientation of principal stresses	Load flow based on load equilibrium in a set of orthogonal axes	Transferred and potential transferred force method	Load paths based on U^*
Visualization of load trajectories		x		x
Indication for stiffness tailoring			x	
Indication for critical regions	x			

In several cases and aspects, some methods provide similar results. The examples are:

1. Trajectories from minor principal stress and load flow with equilibrium in x-direction under distributed loads.
2. Trajectories from combined principal stresses and load flow with equilibrium in x-direction under fixed supports.
3. Regions of high stresses and regions with significant transferred forces.

Further study is needed to have a common approach to characterize and visualize load paths that will meet the pre-defined criteria.

References

1. A.P. Boresi, K.P. Chong, *Elasticity in engineering mechanics 2nd edition* (John Wiley & Sons, New York, 2000)
2. D.W. Kelly, M.W. Tosh, *Interpreting load paths and stress trajectories in elasticity*, Engineering Computations, **17**(2), 117-135 (2000).
3. D.W. Kelly, P. Hsu, M.W. Tosh, *Load paths and load flow in finite element analysis*, Engineering Computations, **18**(1/2), 304-313 (2001).
4. W. Waldman, M. Heller, R. Kaye, F. Rose, *Advances in two-dimensional structural loadflow visualization*, Engineering Computations, **19**(2), 305-326 (2002).
5. D.W. Kelly, M. Elsley, *A procedure for determining load paths in elastic continua*, Engineering Computations, **12**(5), 415-424 (1995).
6. J.S. Harasaki, J.S. Arora, *New concepts of transferred and potential transferred forces in structures*, Computer Methods in Applied Mechanics and Engineering, **191**(3-5), 385-406 (2001).
7. J.S. Harasaki, J.S. Arora, *A new class of evolutionary methods based on the concept of transferred force for structural design*, Structural and Multidisciplinary Optimization, **22**(1), 35-36 (2001).
8. J.S. Harasaki, J.S. Arora, *Topology design based on transferred and potential transferred forces*, Structural and Multidisciplinary Optimization, **23**(5), 372-381 (2002).
9. H. Hoshino, T. Sakurai, K. Takahashi, *Vibration reduction in the cabin of heavy-duty trucks using the theory of load transfer paths*, JSAE Review, **24** 165-171 (2003).
10. Y. Okano, T. Matsunaga, S. Maruyama, M. Hanazato, K. Takahashi, *Load path analysis of vehicle body structures under eigenmode deformation of bending vibration*, SAE International, (2009). Available via https://shop.sae.org/technical/papers/2009-01-0770.

9

An efficient optimization method to obtain the set of most promising minima in multimodal problems

Álvaro Noriega[1,a], Ricardo Vijande[1], Jose Luis Cortizo[1], Eduardo Rodríguez[1], Jose Manuel Sierra[1]

[1] Department of Mechanical Engineering, University of Oviedo. Campus de Viesques, 33204 Gijón, Asturias, Spain

Abstract – This paper propounds a new evolution strategy, the Discrete Directions Mutation Evolution Strategy (DDM-ES), with the aim of obtaining the set of most promising minima in multimodal functions and making this process as efficient as possible. First, DDM-ES is compared with a Genetic Algorithm (GA) on two scaleable test functions with 5, 10, 15 and 20 dimensions, showing better behaviour than GA when the objective function is unimodal but not being as global as the GA in highly multimodal ones. Later, the multimodal search nature of DDM-ES is shown applying this ES on two functions with multiple minima. Finally, an application of DDM-ES to the problem of the initial position of a mechanism is shown.

Key words: Evolution strategy; Multimodal function; Mechanisms, Initial position problem

1 Introduction

The unconstrained optimization problem of a single function (called objective function) can be formulated as a minimization problem as follows:

$$\min f(\mathbf{x}) \qquad (1)$$

$$\text{with } \mathbf{x} \in \Re^n \text{ and } \mathbf{x} \in \Omega$$

Ω being the search space in a hyperbox shape. In Ω, every variable can take any value between $\mathbf{l}_i$ and $\mathbf{u}_i$ with i=1,…,n where n is the number of variables.

In the search space there can be a single minimum (unimodal function) or several minima (multimodal function). In this latter case, there can be one or several global minima and one or several local minima.

There exist several classifications of the optimization methods [5,17]. Chronologically, the first optimization methods looked to obtain a minimum of the objective function in the most efficient possible way. For do so, certain suppositions about the continuity and derivability of the objective function in the neighbourhood of a minimum are made, producing the mathematical programming methods. These methods [5] need an initial point and they usually obtain the closest minimum to that initial point in a, more or less, efficient way. For this reason, these methods have local behaviour.

Later, and in view of the possibility of more than one minimum existing, the necessity of a minimum search with more global nature arises. This, linked with the fact that in many types of problems the conditions of continuity and derivability cited before cannot be assured and that the derivatives are very expensive to calculate, motivates that the stochastic optimization methods were developed.

These methods consider the objective function as a black box and they try to find its global minimum. Some examples of this type of method are the simulated annealing (SA) [12], the random search (RS) [9,11] and the evolutive algorithms (EA) [3,13] where the genetic algorithms (GA) [7,10] and the evolutions strategies (ES) [2,18] are the best-known. Some of them have global behaviour (RS and GA) and others, instead, have a more local behaviour (SA and ES).

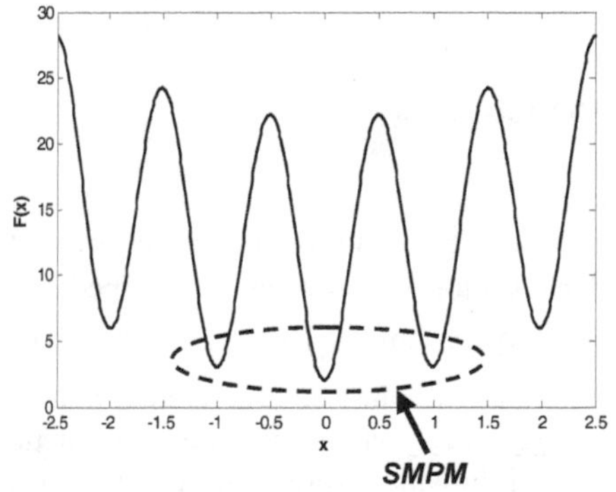

Fig. 1. Example of SMPM

However, many of these methods continue centering the global minimum search, considering it as unique, when, in many problems, the user is interested in knowing if one or several minima of similar values exist. These minima can be called Set of Most Promising Minima (SMPM) and it is composed of all the global minima (in case more than one exists) and the local minima whose values are closer to the global one as well, as is shown in the example of Fig. 1. The size of SMPM depends on the user, who can select the final solution among the solutions contained in this set taking into account additional criteria in a similar way to the Pareto Optimal Front (POF) in multiobjective optimization [1].

The goal of this paper is to propound an optimization method to obtain the SMPM or an approximation of it. This method must:

[a] Corresponding author: noriegaalvaro@uniovi.es

a) Differentiate between the different minima allowing the knowledge of the user about the topology of the objective function to be increased and offering more possibilities to select the final solution.

b) Make the process as efficient as possible.

The paper is organized as follows: In Section 2, the new optimization method, called Discrete Directions Mutation Evolution Strategy (DDM-ES), is described. In Section 3, the results of two benchmark tests between the DDM-ES and a GA are shown. They show that DDM-ES has the desired features a) and b). In Section 4, a real application with multiple global solutions is shown and DDM-ES is used to solve it in a satisfactory way. In Section 5, a set of conclusions are extracted about the new method proposed.

2 Description of the DDM-ES

The Discrete Directions Mutation Evolution Strategy [15,16] is an evolution strategy of type $(\mu+\lambda)-ES$ which is characterized by its mutation operator.

This mechanism of mutation consists of adding to the vector that represents the parent $\mathbf{x}_{parent}$, a vector $\nu \cdot \mathbf{d}$ that represents the mutation. The unitary vector $\mathbf{d}$ represents the direction of mutation in the n-dimensional space and ν is the mutation step:

$$\mathbf{x}_{offspring} = \mathbf{x}_{parent} + \nu \cdot \mathbf{d} \qquad (2)$$

Moreover, the DDM-ES has the following additional specific features.

2.1 Specific features

Workspace

The population $\mathbf{P}$ is made by a set of individuals represented by vectors $\mathbf{x}'$, which are defined in a workspace where every variable $\mathbf{x}'_i$ belongs to the interval [0,1]. When an individual $\mathbf{x}'$ must be evaluated, it must be scaled first to the search space where the objective function is defined using the following expression applied to each component:

$$\mathbf{x}_i = \mathbf{l}_i + (\mathbf{u}_i - \mathbf{l}_i) \cdot \mathbf{x}'_i \qquad (3)$$

where $\mathbf{x}$ is the vector that represents the individual $\mathbf{x}'$ in the search space, $\mathbf{l}$ is the vector that contains the lower bound of the variables and $\mathbf{u}$ is the vector with the upper bound of the variables.

The vector $\mathbf{d}$ which represents the direction of mutation is defined in the workspace.

Discrete directions of mutation

This is the most important feature of this method and the one that gives it its name (DDM-ES).

The classical method to generate unitary n-dimensional vectors with uniform distribution in the space consists of randomly generating points inside a hypercube according to a uniform distribution of probability. The vector that joins the centre of the hypercube with the generated point defines the direction of the unitary vector. Only the points generated inside the hypersphere inscribed in the hypercube are valid and, then, every direction has the same probability of being selected. The drawback is that the hypercube's volume (and, therefore, the probability of generating individuals in its volume) is concentrated in the vertexes when the number of dimensions increases as can be seen in Table 1 where the quotient between the volumes of the hypercube and the hypersphere inscribed on it is shown when the number of dimensions increases. Thus, the probability of generating individuals in the hypersphere tends to 0 when the number of dimensions increases. Although there exist some methods to generate random samples in and on a hyperpshere [8,14], there is not an efficient method to generate n-dimensional unitary vectors with randomly and uniformly distributed directions.

Table 1. Variation of volume quotient

Number of dimensions	$V_{hypersphere}/V_{hypercube}$
1	1
2	0,7854
3	0,5236
4	0,3084
5	0,1645
6	0,0807

For this reason, it is proposed to discretize the infinite possible directions to a finite set that allows easy and efficient generation and that, furthermore, these directions are distributed in quite a homogeneous way over the hypersphere's volume.

To carry out this discretization the following method is proposed. First of all, a unit hypercube is generated with the individual to mutate situated in its centre. Secondly, a face of the hypercube is randomly selected and on this face is generated a grid of equally-spaced nodes. Then, one node of this grid is randomly selected. Finally, the vector that joins the hypercube's centre with the selected point indicates the mutation direction. A graphic representation of this method can be seen in Fig. 2.

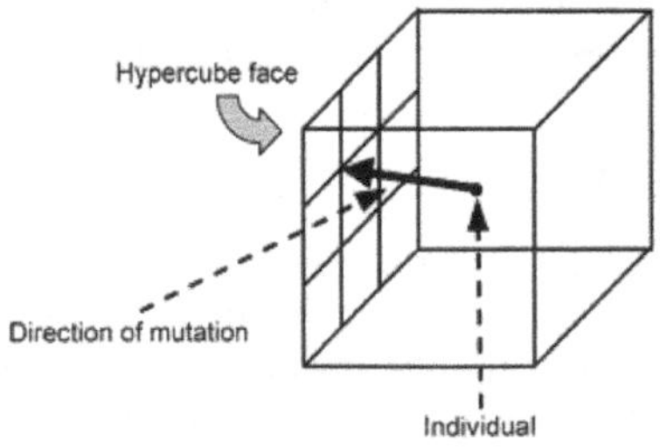

Fig. 2. Discrete direction generation

The number of nodes in the grid generated in the hypercube's face is controlled by means of a parameter of the method called n_{dv} which allows the discretization (number of possible directions for mutation) to be controlled. The bigger this parameter is, the smaller the homogeneity of the distribution of the directions is.

Mutation step

As is indicated at the beginning of this section, the mutation step v is unique and it is randomly generated according to a normal distribution with mean 0 and standard deviation σ (called mutation strength) for every offspring. Both of them, v and σ, are always referred to the workspace.

Dynamic control of mutation strength

The mutation strength decreases with the generations according to an expression fixed by the user of the algorithm. This idea is similar to the one used in simulated annealing to modify the temperature. The expression selected for the DDM-ES is the following:

$$\sigma_j = \left(1 - \frac{R}{100}\right) \cdot \sigma_{j-1} \qquad (4)$$

where j is the number of the current generation and R is the percentage decrease of the mutation strength from a generation σ_j with regard to the previous generation σ_{j-1}. This expression allows the automatic advancing of several generations or advancing from one generation to the next one manually.

Valid and non valid individuals

Inside a population of offsprings generated by mutation from their parents, the ones that belong to the workspace are called valid individuals, and the ones that are outside the workspace, non-valid individuals. The appearance of non-valid individuals is possible due to the fact that the mutation step v is generated according to a normal distribution which is defined between $-\infty$ and $+\infty$, and as a result, the offspring can be outside the workspace.

Independent individuals

There also exists another type of individual, called independent individuals, which are generated in the workspace according to a uniform distribution of probability.

The independent individuals have a mission to provide global convergence to the DDM-ES since they make a pure random search. Their effect is similar to the mutation in a GA.

In DDM-ES, the population of offsprings (individuals generated by mutation and independent individuals) has a constant size μ, but the amount of individuals of every type is variable depending on the search progress. The number of independent individuals of every generation increases (parameter Δ_{ii}) if the search is stagnated and is reduced to a minimum (parameter n_{ii}) when the search obtains an improvement with regard to the previous generation.

The initial population is generated with μ independent individuals.

2.2 Pseudocode

The detailed pseudocode of the DDM-ES is shown below:

Input: μ (Population size)
g (Number of generations)
σ_1 (Initial mutation strength)
R (% decrease of σ in every generation)
n_{ii} (Initial independent individuals)
Δ_{ii} (Increase of independent individuals)
n_{dv} (Divisions per variable)
$\mathbf{l}, \mathbf{u}$ (Vectors with lower and upper bounds)

Output: m (Optimal individual)
fm (Optimal individual evaluation)

Step 1: Initialization: Set the number of variables n. Generate initial population $\mathbf{P}_0$. Initialize the number of independent individuals $n_{indep} = n_{ii}$.

Step 2: Evaluation and saving: Evaluate $\mathbf{P}_0$ to obtain $\mathbf{F}_0 = f(\mathbf{P}_0)$. Initialize m and fm with the best individual found in $\mathbf{F}_0$.

Step 3: Main loop: For $j = 1$ to $j = g$

a) Calculate σ_j

b) Generate offspring population $\mathbf{P}_{offspring}$

Repeat $\mu - n_{indep}$ times:
Random selection of a parent
Random generation of a mutation direction
Generate an offspring by mutation of the parent
If offspring is non valid:
Replace offspring with an independent individual

c) Evaluate $\mathbf{P}_{offspring}$ to obtain $\mathbf{F}_{offspring}$

d) Sorting $\{\mathbf{F}_{j-1}, \mathbf{F}_{offspring}\}$ and $\{\mathbf{P}_{j-1}, \mathbf{P}_{offspring}\}$

e) Selection of the $\mu - n_{indep}$ best offsprings of reordered $\{\mathbf{P}_{j-1}, \mathbf{P}_{offspring}\}$ to obtain $\mathbf{P}_{best}$ and $\mathbf{F}_{best}$

g) Generate and evaluate indep. individuals to obtain $\mathbf{P}_{indep}$ and $\mathbf{F}_{indep}$

h) Build the new population: $\mathbf{P}_j = \{\mathbf{P}_{best}, \mathbf{P}_{indep}\}$ and $\mathbf{F}_j = \{\mathbf{F}_{best}, \mathbf{F}_{indep}\}$

i) Obtain the best individual m_{new} and its evaluation fm_{new}

j) Update n_{indep}

if $fm = fm_{new}$ and $n_{indep} < \mu - 1$
$n_{indep} = n_{indep} + \Delta_{ii}$
if $\mu - 1 < n_{indep}$
$n_{indep} = \mu - 1$
else if $fm_{new} < fm$
$n_{indep} = n_{ii}$

2.3 Parameter setting

The population size μ is chosen taking into account the possible multimodality of the objective function. The bigger the number of minima expected in the objective function is, the bigger the population size must be. It is also possible to relate the population size to the number of dimensions of the search space n. Based on the test made by the authors, the empirical expression $\mu = 50 \cdot n$ is proposed.

The number of generations g and the value of the percentage decrease R between generations affect to the variation of the mutation strength σ. Based on several tests made, the recommended values are $R = 5$ and $g = 50$ which make the DDM-ES converge to the minima very quickly unless the function is very complex.

For the mutation strength of the first generation σ_1, the following expression is proposed:

$$\sigma_1 = \frac{\sqrt{n}}{2} \cdot \left(\frac{1}{\mu}\right)^{\frac{1}{n}} \quad (5)$$

This expression arises from considering the hypervolume of the workspace (whose value is 1) equitably shared among the μ individuals of the population and supposing that the hypervolume corresponding to each individual adopts the shape of a hypercube. Then, the initial mutation strength is the distance between the centre of the hypercube and one vertex of it. A graphical example of this idea can be seen in Fig. 3.

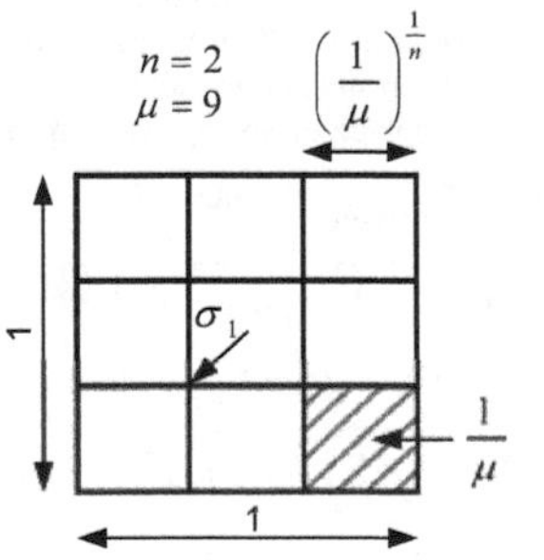

Fig. 3 Graphical example of the meaning of σ_1

The number of initial independent individuals n_{ii} must be set as a small value and thus not decrease the exploitation ability of the algorithm. A recommended value is 0. The increase in the number of independent individuals when the evolution is stagnated Δ_{ii} will be a small value compared with μ, for instance, 5%. When you do not want to hinder the convergence to the minima found, the value of Δ_{ii} is set to 0.

The number of divisions of the grid per variable n_{dv} used in the test made is 3 and no obvious improvement is observed when this value increases.

3 Benchmarking

In this section, the outcomes of two benchmark tests between the DDM-ES and a GA are shown. The platform used was Matlab® where the code of DDM-ES is programmed. Moreover, the Genetic Algorithm and Direct Search Toolbox that implements a highly adjustable GA was used.

3.1 Test 1

In this test, it is intended to compare the performance, as optimization algorithms, of the DDM-ES and the GA when they have the same computational cost.

Objective functions and conditions

For this test, two standard and scaleable test functions are selected. Their features are shown in Table 4.

The main difference between both functions is the total number of minima. While the hyper-sphere function is unimodal, the Rastrigin's function is highly multimodal and its number of minima increases with the number of variable (11^n minima), increasing its complexity a great deal.

5, 10, 15 and 20 variables are used with every test function. The population size and the number of generations are the same with every combination of test function and number of variables. The test will be repeated 30 times. In each repetition, the initial population is randomly generated outside the algorithm and it will be common to both of them.

Both algorithms evolve from the same initial population for the same number of generations and the mean evolution of the minima found in every generation is extracted. This evolution will be shown by means of a semilogarithmic graph to compare the accuracy and the value of the minima reached with each algorithm. As the two test functions selected have a global minimum of value 0, the value of this function coincides with the absolute error and it can also be used to verify if an algorithm converges to the global minimum or to a local minimum.

The runtime is also extracted with every test function with both algorithms and in every repetition to calculate the mean of the runtime for the 30 repetitions.

The number of generations g for both algorithms will be 100 and the population size μ and the initial mutation strength σ_1 will be the ones indicated in 2.3.

The specific parameters used with the DDM-ES are shown in Table 2 and the specific parameters for the GA are shown in Table 3.

Table 2. Parameters for DDM-ES

Parameter	Value
μ	$50 \cdot n$
g	100
σ_1	(see Section 2.3)
R	5
n_{ii}	0
Δ_{ii}	n
n_{dv}	3

The ga_out function allows the best value obtained on each generation to be externally saved. The computer used for this test has a processor Intel® Pentium® IV, 3.0 GHz and 1 GB of RAM.

Outcomes and discussion

The outcomes of the benchmarking on the function hyper-sphere are shown in Fig. 4. On it, it can be seen that the DDM-ES reaches the minimum with higher precision than the GA in all cases. Observing the evolution of accuracy with the generations, the DDM-ES improves the accuracy according to a law that can be set to a logarithmic equation while the GA obtains a faster initial improvement of the accuracy. However, later, this improvement slows down and the DDM-ES always finishes by overcoming the GA in accuracy.

Table 4. Test functions

Name	Expression	Global minimum		Features
		Location	Value	
Hyper-sphere	$f(\mathbf{x})=\sum_{i=1}^{n}\mathbf{x}_i^2$ $-5.12 \le \mathbf{x}_i \le 5.12$	$\mathbf{x}_i = 0$	0	Unimodal
Rastrigin	$f(\mathbf{x})=10\cdot n+\sum_{i=1}^{n}\left(\mathbf{x}_i^2-10\cdot\cos\left(2\cdot\pi\cdot\mathbf{x}_i\right)\right)$ $-5.12 \le \mathbf{x}_i \le 5.12$	$\mathbf{x}_i = 0$	0	Multimodal
MGM	$f(\mathbf{x})=\sum_{i=1}^{n}\left(\mathbf{x}_i^2-2\right)^2$ $-2.5 \le \mathbf{x}_i \le 2.5$	$\mathbf{x}_i = \pm 2$	0	Multimodal

Table 3. Parameters for GA

Population		Reproduction	
Population type	Double	Elite count	2
Population size	$50\cdot n$	Crossover fraction	0,8
Initial population	-	**Migration:**	None
Bounds	-	**Algorithm settings:**	By default
Fitness Scaling		**Hybrid function: None**	
Scaling function	Proportional	**Stopping criteria**	
Selection		Generations	100
Selection function	Roulette	Time limit	Inf
Mutation		Fitness limit	-Inf
Mutation function	Gaussian	Stall generations	100
Scale	1	Stall time limit	3600
Shrink	1	Function tolerance	1e-6
Crossover		**Output function: ga_out**	
Crossover function	Single point	**Vectorized: Off**	

The outcomes of the benchmarking on the Rastrigin's function are shown in Fig. 5. In the case of 5 variables, the GA is able to find the global minimum while the DDM-ES obtains a nearby local minimum. In the other cases, both algorithms obtain a local minimum, with the minimum obtained by the GA always being better.

In Table 5 the mean runtimes are shown and you can notice that the DDM-ES is faster than the GA in all cases. As the number of function evaluations is the same for both algorithms, you can conclude that the DDM-ES has an internal computational cost smaller than the GA. The improvement in runtime of the DDM-ES over the GA increases when the number of variables increases and it approximately varies between 25% with 5 variables and 57% with 20 variables.

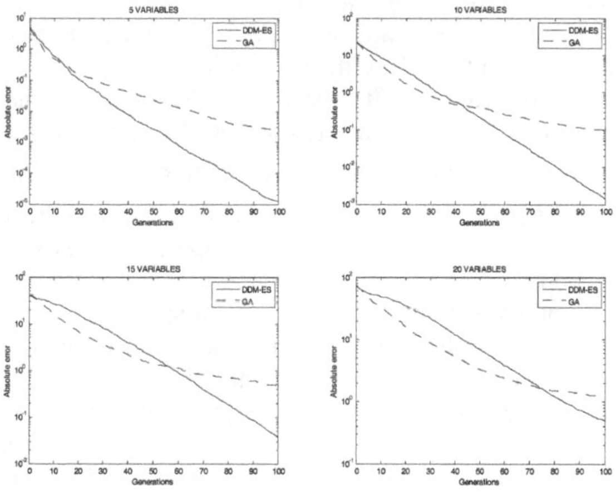

Fig. 4 Outcomes of Hyper-sphere function

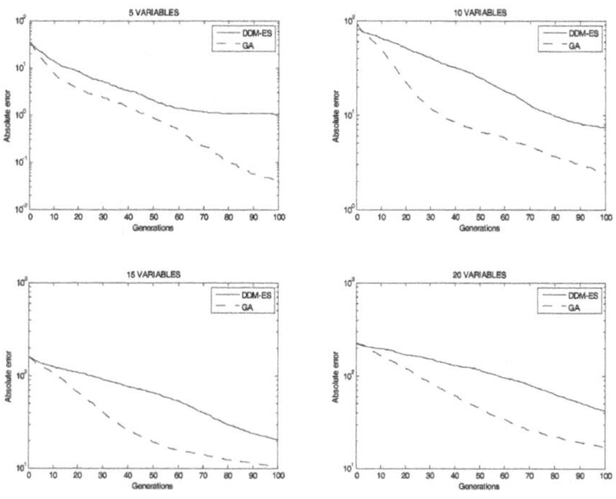

Fig. 5 Outcomes of Rastrigin's function

Table 5. Mean runtime (s)

Function	Algorithm	Number of variables			
		5	10	15	20
Hyper-sphere	DDM-ES	3.4895	8.5762	16.6997	26.6708
	GA	4.6739	13.4234	31.6905	61.9313
Rastrigin	DDM-ES	3.5729	8.6705	16.5921	26.9703
	GA	5.0889	15.8101	32.1995	54.7577

3.2 Test 2

In this test, it is intended to compare the computational cost needed to obtain the SMPM with enough definition and accuracy.

Objective function and conditions

In this case, two test functions have been selected: the Rastrigin's function with 2 variables and the function MGM (Multiple Global Minima) with four variables. This last function (proposed by the authors of this paper) is scaleable, multimodal and it has the special feature that its 2^n minima are all global. Its features are shown in Table 4.

One run will be made with every optimization method (DDM-ES and GA) from the same initial population of size 200 and evolving for 50 generations. The other parameters used will be the ones indicated in Test 1 except for the parameter Δ_{ii} which is set to 0 so as not to hinder the convergence to the minima already found and to improve the definition which you can observe the graphical representation of this process.

To compare both algorithms, the populations of some generations will be shown. In the case of Rastrigin's function, the individuals will be directly shown in the search space. In the case of function MGM, the individuals will be shown in the workspace using a representation by means of parallel coordinates similar to the one used in the decision space of multiobjective optimization [4].

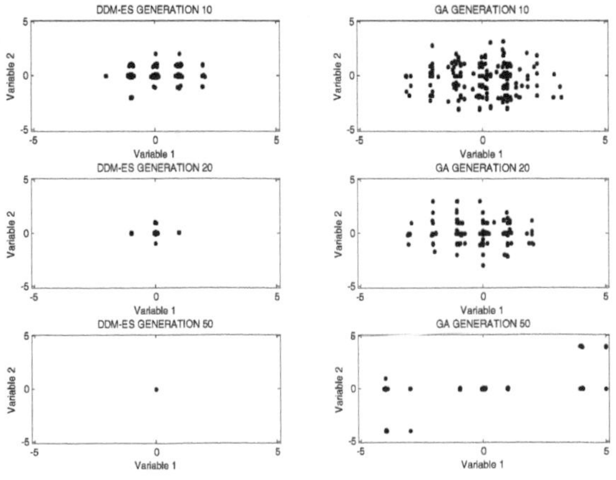

Fig. 6 Populations with Rastrigin's function with 2 variables

Outcomes and discussion

The outcomes of the Rastrigin's function are shown in Fig. 6. In the three generations shown, the population of the DDM-ES is more crowded than the population of the GA, defining with more clarity the location of the minima. In the case of the DDM-ES, it is noticed that the population is concentrated on the global minimum and on the minima located in its neighbourhood, that is to say, the SMPM. The set of minima that makes up the SMPM in every generation decreases monotonously with the generations since the global minimum is alone. In the case of the GA, there exists a decrease in the number of minima defined by the population but they do not concentrate around the global minimum.

Moreover, it is noticed that the DDM-ES converges to the minima in a more efficient way than the GA. For instance, the DDM-ES in generation 20 shows a set of 5 minima with a high degree of definition while the GA in the generation 50 still has 12 minima with a similar definition but with more spreading.

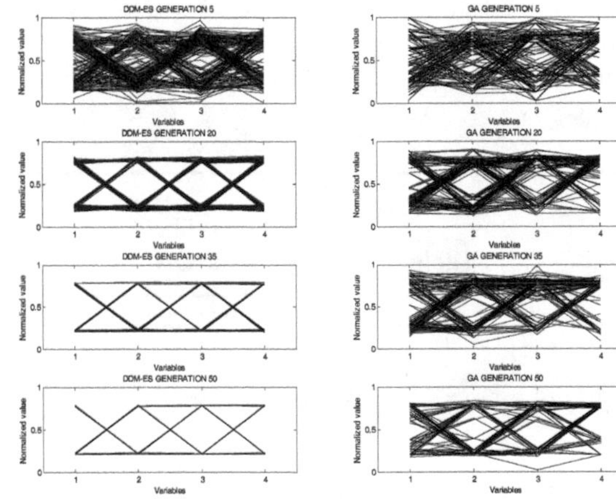

Fig. 7 Populations with function MGM with 4 variables

The outcomes of the test on the function MGM are shown in Fig. 7. In this figure, you can see that the DDM-ES converges to the 16 global minima (depending on the generation) with more definition and efficiency since in the generation 20, the DDM-ES has clearly obtained the location of all the minima of the function while the GA does not obtain the same definition of the minima even in the generation 50 with a computational cost 2.5 times greater. Furthermore, with the passing of generations, the DDM-ES refines the minima found since the strip around every minimum become tighter and it means that the individuals are more grouped around the minimum and, therefore, they represent more precise solutions. This refining process is slower with the GA.

Looking at these outcomes, it is possible to state that the DDM-ES makes a more efficient use of the computational effort made than the GA, supplying a more refined SMPM as well.

4 Application to the problem of initial position of a mechanism

4.1 Problem description

The problem is about determining all the initial positions that the mechanism of six bars of Watt (shown in Fig. 8) can have when the value of its degree of freedom α is set. Every possible initial position has caused a different kinematic simulation of the mechanism.

The lengths of the bars are known and the locations of the joint with the frame too. All these parameters are shown in Table 6.

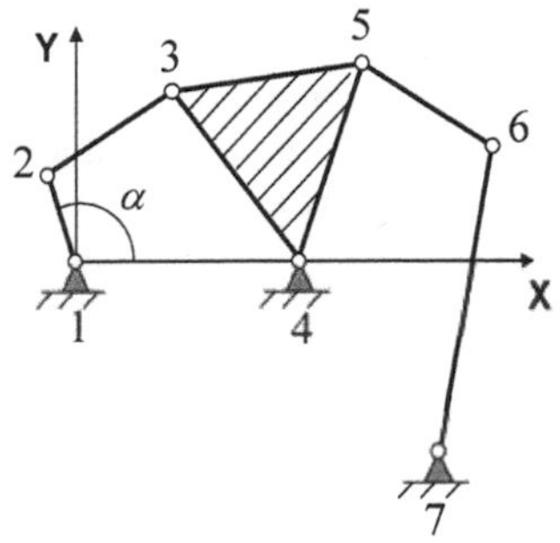

Fig. 8 Mechanism of six bars of Watt

Table 6. Dimensional parameters

$x_1 = 0$	$L_{12} = 2$
$y_1 = 0$	$L_{23} = 5$
$x_4 = 5$	$L_{34} = 5$
$y_4 = 0$	$L_{35} = 5$
$x_7 = 9$	$L_{45} = 6$
$y_7 = -5$	$L_{56} = 4$
$\alpha = 120°$	$L_{67} = 8$

This mechanism can be modelized by means of natural coordinates [6] generating the following constraint equations:

$$(x_1 - x_2)^2 + (y_1 - y_2)^2 - L_{12}^2 = 0 \quad (6)$$

$$(x_2 - x_3)^2 + (y_2 - y_3)^2 - L_{23}^2 = 0 \quad (7)$$

$$(x_3 - x_4)^2 + (y_3 - y_4)^2 - L_{34}^2 = 0 \quad (8)$$

$$(x_3 - x_5)^2 + (y_3 - y_5)^2 - L_{35}^2 = 0 \quad (9)$$

$$(x_4 - x_5)^2 + (y_4 - y_5)^2 - L_{45}^2 = 0 \quad (10)$$

$$(x_5 - x_6)^2 + (y_5 - y_6)^2 - L_{56}^2 = 0 \quad (11)$$

$$(x_6 - x_7)^2 + (y_6 - y_7)^2 - L_{67}^2 = 0 \quad (12)$$

$$(x_2 - x_1) - L_{12} \cdot \cos\alpha = 0 \quad (13)$$

$$(y_2 - y_1) - L_{12} \cdot \sin\alpha = 0 \quad (14)$$

The 9 constraint equations can be represented in a more compact way as:

$$\mathbf{\Phi}(\mathbf{q}) = \mathbf{0} \quad (15)$$

$\mathbf{\Phi}(\mathbf{q})$ being a column vector of 9 components where the left sides of the constraint equations are stored and $\mathbf{q}$ is the vector where the cartesian coordinates of the mobile nodes of the mechanism are stored:

$$\mathbf{q} = \begin{bmatrix} x_2 & y_2 & x_3 & y_3 & x_5 & y_5 & x_6 & y_6 \end{bmatrix} \quad (16)$$

The non-linear system of equations shown can usually be solved using Newton's method, which needs an initial approximation and it obtains one solution.

However, this system of equations can have more than one solution. To determine all the existing solutions, the problem of finding the roots can be converted in an error minimization problem where the error measures the simultaneous fulfilment of the constraint equations.

The error made by a vector of coordinates $\mathbf{q}$ is defined as:

$$error(\mathbf{q}) = \sum_{i=1}^{9} \mathbf{\Phi}_i^2(\mathbf{q})$$

(17)

Those solutions $\mathbf{q}$ that make the error 0 will be the solutions of the non-linear system of equations posed.

4.2 Parameters used with DDM-ES

The lower and upper bounds of the variables are defined, depending on the type of coordinate, in the following way:

$$x \in [-5, 15]$$
$$y \in [-10, 10] \quad (18)$$

The parameters used with the DDM-ES are shown in Table 7.

Table 7. Parameters of DDM-ES

Parameter	Value
μ	1000
g	50
σ_1	0.5964
R	5
n_{ii}	0
Δ_{ii}	0
n_{dv}	3

4.3 Filtering and refinement of solutions

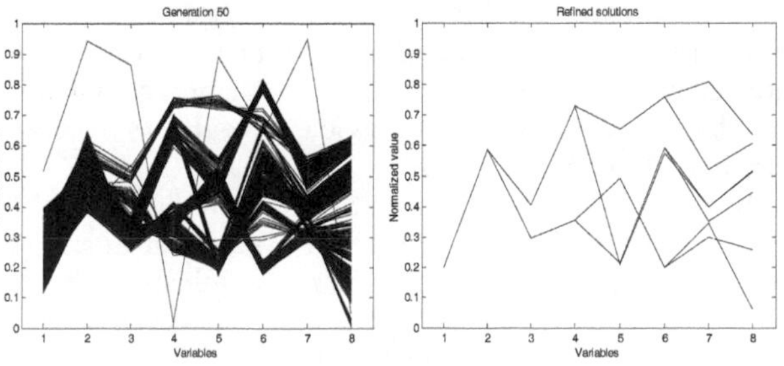

a) b)

Fig. 9 Population in generation 50 and filtered and refined solutions

After running the DDM-ES with the parameters indicated before, the final population shown in Fig. 9.a is obtained.

The individuals of this population must be filtered to eliminate redundant individuals. During the filtering process, the individuals closer to one, which acts as a reference, and which have greater error than the reference individual are eliminated.

The individuals which have passed the filter are used as initial approximations for a deterministic optimization method of second order. The method used in this application is a quasi-Newton method that uses the BFGS technique to update the Hessian matrix [5]. The individuals of the population that have passed the processes of filtering and refining can be seen in Fig. 9.b.

The refining process of the filtered individuals has a very low cost because the initial approximations are close to the final solution (they are the solutions obtained by the DDM-ES) and because this method is very efficient.

4.4 Discussion

The filtered and refined population offers, with high precision, 7 of the 8 possible solutions for the problem of initial solution of the mechanism. As an example, two of these solutions, which correspond to two possible configurations of the mechanism, which furthermore, are far away from each other, can be seen in Fig. 10.

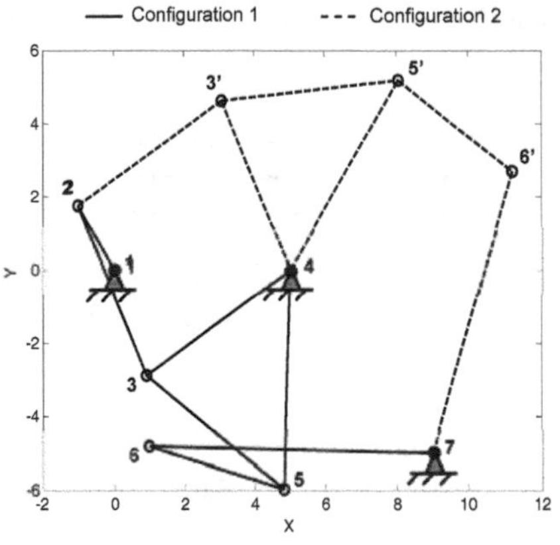

Fig. 10 Two possible configurations for the mechanism

5 Conclusions

The evolution strategy called DDM-ES and proposed in this paper constitutes an optimization method which shows greater precision than a GA with the same computational cost but it does not show a behaviour as global as the GA on highly multimodal functions.

However, the DDM-ES allows an approximation of the set of most promising minima (SMPM) to be obtained. This set monotonously reduces its size, eliminating the less promising minima during the successive generations because its visual monitoring by the user is very intuitive. Moreover, these minima are defined with greater precision than with the GA. Finally, the obtaining of SMPM is more efficient than with the GA.

This feature contributes to obtaining a better knowledge by the user about the interesting part of the objective function's topology when it has several minima, allowing the user to make his choice among several optima according to criteria not specified in the problem definition as sensitivity of the minima or fulfilment of constraints not specified before.

The DDM-ES has been applied to the problem of obtaining the initial position of a mechanism, which can be solved before making its kinematic or dynamic simulation. This problem is multimodal and it has several global minima.

For the practical solving of this problem, the DDM-ES has been modified by adding a stage of filtering to eliminate the redundant individuals of the population and later a stage of refining the filtered individuals. In this case, the DDM-ES allows almost all the solutions of the problem to be obtained with high precision.

References

1. J. Andersson, *A survey of multiobjective optimization in engineering design*, Technical Report LiTH-IKP-R-1097, Sweden (2000)
2. T. Bäck, F. Hoffmeister, H.P. Schwefel, A Survey of Evolution Strategies, In *Proceedings of the Fourth International Conference on Genetic Algorithms* (Los Altos, California, USA, 1991)
3. T. Bäck, *Evolutionary algorithms in theory and practice*, (Oxford University Press, 1996)
4. C.M. Fonseca, *Multiobjective Genetic Algorithms with Applications to Control Engineering Problems*, PhD Thesis, University of Sheffield (1995)
5. R.L. Fox, *Optimization Methods for Engineering Design*, (Addison-Wesley, Reading, Massachusetts, 1971)
6. J. García de Jalón, E. Bayo, *Kinematic and dynamic simulation of multibody systems. The real-time challenge*, (Springer-Verlag, New Cork, 1994)
7. D.E. Goldberg, *Genetic Algorithms in Search, Optimization and Machine Learning*, (Addinson-Wesley, Reading, Massachusetts, 1989)
8. G. Guralnik, C. Zemach, T. Warnock, *An algorithm for uniform random sampling of points in and on a hypersphere*, Inf. Process. Lett. 21(1), 17-21 (1985)
9. C. Hamzaçebi, F. Kutay, *A heuristic approach for finding the global minimum: Adaptive random search technique*, Appl. Math. Comput. 173(2), 1323-1333 (2006)
10. J.H. Holland, *Adaptation on Natural and Artificial Systems*, (MIT Press, Cambridge, Massachusetts, 1975)
11. J. Jezowski, R. Bochenek, G. Ziomek, *Random search optimization approach for highly multi-modal nonlinear problems*, Adv. Eng. Softw. 36, 504–517 (2005)
12. S. Kirkpatrick, C.D. Gelatt, M.P. Vecchi, *Optimization by Simulated Annealing*, Science 220, 671-680 (1983)
13. Z. Michalewicz, *Genetic Algorithms + Data Structures = Evolution Programs*, (Springer-Verlag, 1992)
14. J. Nie, B.R. Ellingwood, *Directional methods for structural reliability analysis*, Struct. Saf. 22, 233-249 (2000)
15. A. Noriega, E. Rodríguez, J.L. Cortizo, R. Vijande, J.M. Sierra, A new evolution strategy for the unconstrained optimization problem. In *Proceedings of Second International Conference on Multidisciplinary Design Optimization and Applications*, (Gijón, Spain, 2008)
16. A. Noriega, *Síntesis dimensional óptima de mecanismos mediante estrategias evolutivas*, PhD. Thesis, University

of Oviedo (2008)
17. S.S. Rao, *Engineering Optimization, Theory and Practice*, (John Wiley & Sons, New York, 1996)
18. H.P. Schwefel, *Evolution and Optimum Seeking*, (John Wiley & Sons, New York, 1995)

10

Woven thermoplastic composite forming simulation with solid-shell element method

Q.Q. Chen [1], A. Saouab [1,a], P. Boisse [2], C.H. Park [1], J. Bréard [1]

[1] Laboratoire Ondes et Milieux Complexes, FRE 3102, CNRS, Université du Havre, France
[2] Laboratoire de Mécanique des Contacts et des Structures, UMR 5259, CNRS, INSA Lyon, France

Abstract – Textile composites become more and more popular in aeronautic industries, due to their high performances. In this work, based on the model shown in the paper [9], a solid-shell element is used to simulate the woven composite forming. Comparing with other shell elements, a distinctive advantage of solid-shell elements is that the complication on handing finite rotations does not exist. Accounting the specific mechanical behaviors of woven composite material, the tensile, in-plane shear, bending and compressive energies are taken into account depending on the fiber direction, and then the total strain energy is computed to be the sum of those energies. The necessary material data for the simulation come from standard tensile, compressive and bias test experiments. Some forming simulations are performed with this method, and we can observe the wrinkles that exhibit the influence of bending stiffness. The results show the efficiency of the approach.

Key words: Solid-shell element, Woven thermoplastic composite, forming simulation

1 Introduction

Woven composites are now gaining the popularity in manufacturing automotive and aerospace parts due to their high mechanical performances. This calls for a development of adequate design and analysis methods and reliable simulation tools considering the large deformations of textile reinforcements in composite forming process. Indeed, during the forming stage, the possible deformation modes of the composite are those of the reinforcement. The woven reinforcement behaviors are very special. The tensile stiffness plays a major role in the fiber direction, and the others stiffnesses, such as the in-plane shear, bending and compressive stiffnesses are very small compared to it. Even so, they are important in some simulation. For example, the in-plane shear stiffness causes the wrinkles and the bending stiffness can change the form of wrinkle. The compressive stiffness can't be ignored in the consolidation and injection case.

For modeling the performing of woven reinforcements, two different approaches exist: the geometrical approach and the finite element approach. The models based on the geometrical approach are called fishnet algorithms [1-2]. An alternative to these geometrical methods is the use of finite element approaches. Some of them are obtained by homogenizing the mechanical behavior of the underlying meso-structure and considering the fabric as an anisotropic continuum [3-4]. Conversely, some discrete models are also developed for fabric in which each yarn is modeled and is assumed to be a straight or a curved beam or truss [5]. And other authors have proposed the semi-discrete element methods [6-8]. All those models have been proved to be efficient and fast in the suitable cases. However, we note that the bending and compressive stiffness are rarely considered in those models.

In the present work, solid-shell element model has been proposed for the simulation of fabric shaping process, which is based on a meso-macro approach. This type of element has only the translational but no rotational nodal degree of freedoms. Fabric forming is a typical geometric nonlinear problem, in which the strains in the yarn directions are small (less than 2% for the glass fabric), while the displacement and the rotation are large. Thus, the strain energy is considered in the field of large strain kinematics. The tensile, bending and shear energies can be expressed as simple functions of the nodal displacements, with the explicit method. Subsequently, we can obtain the internal force in function of the nodal displacements.

2 Solid-shell element

In this section, the formulation of the solid-shell element is discussed.

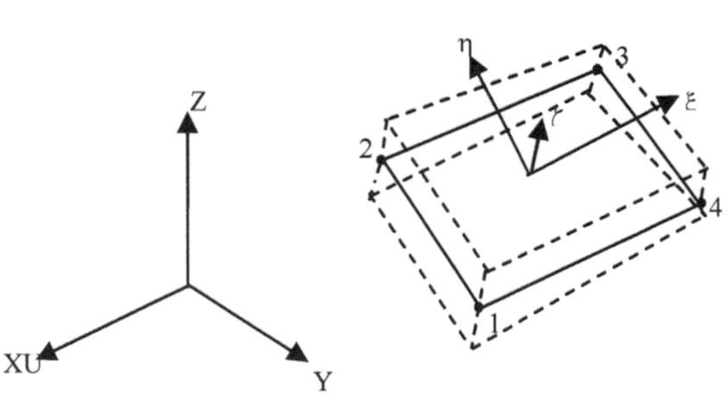

Fig 1 Solid-shell element

With reference to the solid-element in figure 1, the undeformed position vector X and the displacement vector U can be written as:

[a] Corresponding author: abdelghani.saouab@univ-lehavre.fr

$$X(\varepsilon,\eta,\zeta)=X_o(\varepsilon,\eta)+\zeta X_n(\varepsilon,\eta)=\sum_{i=1}^{4}N_i(\varepsilon,\eta)X_{oi}+\zeta\sum_{i=1}^{4}N_i(\varepsilon,\eta)X_{ni} \quad (1)$$

$$U(\varepsilon,\eta,\zeta)=U_o(\varepsilon,\eta)+\zeta U_n(\varepsilon,\eta)=\sum_{i=1}^{4}N_i(\varepsilon,\eta)(U_{oi}+\zeta U_{ni})=[N \quad \zeta N]u \quad (2)$$

where $X_o=X|_{\zeta=0}$, $U_o=U|_{\zeta=0}$, $X_n=X|_{\zeta=+h/2}-X|_{\zeta=-h/2}$, $U_n=U|_{\zeta=+h/2}-U|_{\zeta=-h/2}$. The interpolation function is:

$$\{N\}=\begin{Bmatrix}N_1(\varepsilon,\eta)\\N_2(\varepsilon,\eta)\\N_3(\varepsilon,\eta)\\N_4(\varepsilon,\eta)\end{Bmatrix}=\frac{1}{4}\left(\begin{Bmatrix}1\\1\\1\\1\end{Bmatrix}+\varepsilon\begin{Bmatrix}-1\\1\\1\\-1\end{Bmatrix}+\eta\begin{Bmatrix}-1\\-1\\1\\1\end{Bmatrix}+\varepsilon\eta\begin{Bmatrix}1\\-1\\1\\-1\end{Bmatrix}\right) \quad (3)$$

$$\mathrm{N}=[IN_1 \quad IN_2 \quad IN_3 \quad IN_4]$$

It can be seen that the undeformed and deformed nodal directors are X_{ni} and $X_{ni}+U_{ni}$ respectively. $\zeta=0$ represents the mid-surface and X_{ni} is of unit length. The natural Green strain is:

$$\varepsilon_{ij}=\varepsilon_{ij}(U)=(\overline{X}_{,i}^T\cdot\overline{U}_{,j}+\overline{X}_{,j}^T\cdot\overline{U}_{,i})/2+(\overline{U}_{,i}^T\cdot\overline{U}_{,j}+\overline{U}_{,j}^T\cdot\overline{U}_{,i})/4 \quad (4)$$

Then the in-plane strain can be written as:

$$\varepsilon_{ij}=\varepsilon_{ij}^{(0)}+\xi\varepsilon_{ij}^{(1)}+\xi^2\varepsilon_{ij}^{(2)} \quad (5)$$

where $i,j=\zeta,\eta$. In the in-plane natural strains, the zeroth and first-order ζ-terms are commonly known as the membrane and bending strains, respectively. The second-order z-terms are dropped. Thus, equation (5) can be simplified as:

$$\varepsilon_{ij}=\varepsilon_{ij}^m+\varepsilon_{ij}^b \quad (6)$$

With equation (3), we can express the bending strains and the membrane strains respectively:

$$\begin{aligned}\varepsilon^b{}_{ij}&=\varsigma(\overline{X}_{n,i}^T\cdot\overline{U}_{o,j}+\overline{X}_{o,i}^T\cdot\overline{U}_{n,j}+\overline{X}_{n,j}^T\cdot\overline{U}_{o,i}+\overline{X}_{o,j}^T\cdot\overline{U}_{n,i})/2\\&+\varsigma(\overline{U}_{o,i}^T\cdot\overline{U}_{n,j}+\overline{U}_{o,j}^T\cdot\overline{U}_{o,i}+\overline{U}_{n,i}^T\cdot\overline{U}_{o,j}+\overline{U}_{n,j}^T\cdot\overline{U}_{o,i})/4\end{aligned} \quad (7)$$

$$\begin{aligned}\varepsilon^m{}_{ij}&=(\overline{X}_{o,i}^T\cdot\overline{U}_{o,j}+\overline{X}_{o,j}^T\cdot\overline{U}_{o,i})/2\\&+(\overline{U}_{o,i}^T\cdot\overline{U}_{o,j}+\overline{U}_{o,j}^T\cdot\overline{U}_{o,i})/4\end{aligned} \quad (8)$$

We can also define the compressive normal strain as:

$$\varepsilon_{\varsigma\varsigma}=N_1\varepsilon_{\varsigma\varsigma}\big|_{\varepsilon=-1,\eta=-1}+N_2\varepsilon_{\varsigma\varsigma}\big|_{\varepsilon=1,\eta=-1}+N_3\varepsilon_{\varsigma\varsigma}\big|_{\varepsilon=1,\eta=1}+N_4\varepsilon_{\varsigma\varsigma}\big|_{\varepsilon=-1,\eta=1} \quad (9)$$

3 Dynamic equation

Usually, the forming process can be considered as the quasi-static case, and the majority of codes for the material forming simulations are based on the explicit dynamic approach:

$$[M]\{\ddot{U}\}+[C]\{\dot{U}\}+\{F_{int}\}=\{F_{ext}\} \quad (10)$$

The textile geometry is particular. It consists of the yarns that intertwined with each other, and the yarns are made of the fiber filaments with very small diameter (5 to 7 μm for carbon, 10-20 μm for aramid, 5-25 μm for glass). The particular geometry results in the particular mechanical behaviors. During the forming process, we can consider that the yarn has the tensile stiffness only in the fiber direction. In some types of analysis, however, it is also noted that it is necessary to take into account the other stiffnesses, because they play a significant role (for example, it is shown that the main stiffening effect due to shear makes the wrinkles when the shear limit angle is surpassed, and the bending stiffness can change the wrinkle form). Hence, in order to obtain the total internal virtual work, we consider the internal virtual works of the warp and the weft caused by tensile loads, bending moment, compressive force as well as by shear.

$$\begin{aligned}-W_{\text{int}}&=\sum\left(\varepsilon^m{}_{warp}(\overline{u})\sigma^m{}_{warp}+\varepsilon^m{}_{weft}(\overline{u})\sigma^m{}_{weft}+\gamma(\overline{u})C_y\right.\\&\left.+\varepsilon^m{}_{warp}(\overline{u})\sigma^m{}_{warp}+\varepsilon^b{}_{weft}(\overline{u})\sigma^b{}_{weft}+\varepsilon_{\varsigma\varsigma}(\overline{u})\sigma_{\varsigma\varsigma}\right)\end{aligned} \quad (11)$$

3.1 Internal work of tension

To calculate the internal work caused by tension, we should calculate the strain of yarn. We take a unit yarn to analyze, the strain of this unit yarn can be described as:

$$\varepsilon=\frac{(ds-dS)}{dS}=\frac{dX^TEdX}{2dS^2} \quad (12)$$

Here ε is the Green strain tensor, dX is the initial direction of yarn, and dS is the initial length of unit yarn, and ds is the length of unit yarn after the deformation.

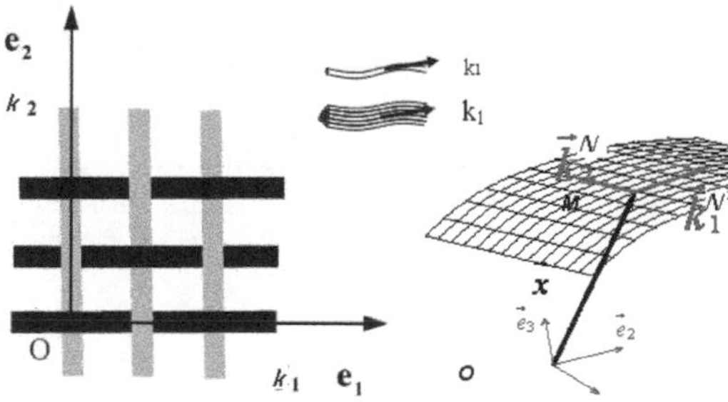

Fig 2: Schematic of the coordinate system

We define a global coordinate frame $\{e_1,e_2,e_3\}$ (see figure 2), in which the initial yarn directions can be represented as:

$$\overline{k}_i=r_{i1}\overline{e}_1+r_{i2}\overline{e}_2 \quad (13)$$

Then, the strain of yarn can be obtained by a following relation.

$$\varepsilon^T{}_{ii}=\varepsilon^m{}_{11}r_{i1}^2+\varepsilon^m{}_{22}r_{i2}^2+2\varepsilon^m{}_{12}r_{i1}r_{i2} \quad (14)$$

A number of experiments have proved that the yarns can be assumed to be elastic. The stress caused by tensile loads is expressed as:

$$\sigma_{ii} = E\varepsilon_{ii} \qquad (15)$$

where E is the Young's modulus of yarn. Hence, the internal work caused by tensile load can be obtained as:

$$-W^{m}_{\text{int}} = \sum(\varepsilon^{m}_{warp}(\bar{u})\sigma^{m}_{warp} + \varepsilon^{m}_{weft}(\bar{u})\sigma^{m}_{weft})$$
$$= \sum(\varepsilon^{m}_{warp}E_{warp}\varepsilon^{m}_{warp} + \varepsilon^{m}_{weft}E_{weft}\varepsilon^{m}_{weft}) \qquad (16)$$

3.2 Internal work of shear

The experimental observations of the shear tests of the woven reinforcements have shown that the fabric deformation is the result of a relative rotation between the warp and the weft yarns but not of a fiber shearing. The relative rotations of the warp and the weft yarns lead to a torque applied at the yarn intersections. The value of this shear torque for a shear angle is experimentally obtained by the bias-test.

The increment of shear strain $\Delta\gamma_i$ is assumed to be the sum of the increment of weft and warp rotations.

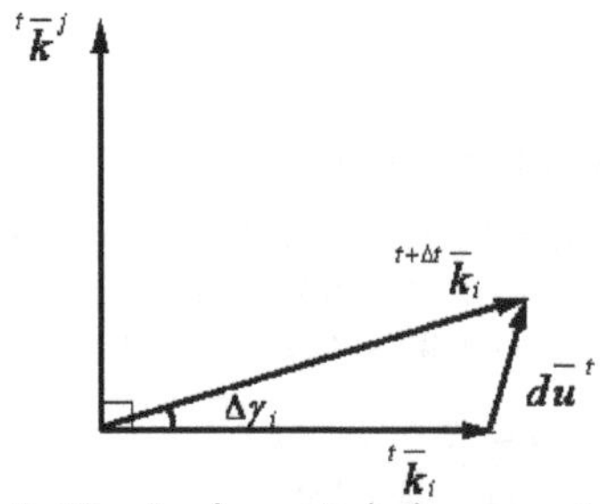

Fig 3: Yarn's shear strain increment

To calculate the yarn shear strain increment, we suppose that $\Delta\gamma_i$ is small (see figure 3). Then we can consider:

$$\Delta\gamma = \sin(\Delta\gamma) \qquad (17)$$

With the geometry shown in figure 3, we can derive:

$$\sin(\Delta\gamma) = \frac{{}^{t+\Delta t}\bar{k}_i \cdot {}^{t}\bar{k}^{j}}{\left\|{}^{t+\Delta t}\bar{k}_i\right\|\left\|{}^{t}\bar{k}^{j}\right\|} = \frac{\bar{du} \cdot {}^{t}\bar{k}^{j}}{\left\|{}^{t+\Delta t}\bar{k}_i\right\|\left\|{}^{t}\bar{k}^{j}\right\|} \cong \frac{\bar{du} \cdot {}^{t}\bar{k}^{j}}{\left\|{}^{\Delta t}\bar{k}_i\right\|\left\|{}^{t}\bar{k}^{j}\right\|} \qquad (18)$$

where $i \neq j$. Then, we obtain:

$$\Delta\gamma_i = \sin(\Delta\gamma_i) = \left(\frac{\partial\Delta\bar{u}}{\partial X_1}\cdot\bar{k}^{j}\right)r_{i1} + \left(\frac{\partial\Delta\bar{u}}{\partial X_2}\cdot\bar{k}^{j}\right)r_{i2} \qquad (19)$$

Since $\Delta\gamma_i$ is the shear strain increment of one yarn for the fabric, the shear strain is :

$$\Delta\gamma = \Delta\gamma_1 + \Delta\gamma_2 \qquad (20)$$

The internal work caused by shear can be defined as:

$$-W_{\text{int}} = \sum(\gamma(\bar{u})C_y) \qquad (21)$$

where C_y is the shear torque which is the function of γ_i and is obtained by a bias-test.

3.3 Internal work of bending

To obtain the internal work of bending, we should find out the bending strains of fabric. In equation (8), we can obtain the bending strains. With the similar relation as equation (14), we can obtain:

$$\varepsilon^{b}_{ii} = \varepsilon^{b}_{11}r_{i1}^2 + \varepsilon^{b}_{22}r_{i2}^2 + 2\varepsilon^{b}_{12}r_{i1}r_{i2} \qquad (22)$$

Then, with the bending stiffness, we can easily obtain the internal work of bending

$$-W^{b}_{\text{int}} = \sum(\varepsilon^{b}_{warp}C^{b}_{warp}\varepsilon^{b}_{warp} + \varepsilon^{m}_{weft}C^{b}_{weft}\varepsilon^{b}_{weft}) \qquad (23)$$

3.4 Internal work of compression

We have already presented the compressive normal strain in equation (9). If we obtain the compressive stress, we obtain the internal work of compression. The experiment shows that the relation between compressive strain and compressive stress is nonlinear. Thus, in this paper, the compressive stress is express as a function of the compressive strain, in form of polynomial as:

$$\sigma^{c} = 111.17\varepsilon_c^3 - 26.862\varepsilon_c^2 + 2.683\varepsilon_c + 0.0078 \qquad (24)$$

Then we obtain the internal work of compression:

$$-W^{C}_{\text{int}} = \sum(\varepsilon^{C}\sigma^{C}) \qquad (25)$$

4 Model validations

Some validations are presented in this section. Those tests come from the special behaviors of fabric, and usually are used to verify the validity of the model for fabric simulation.

4.1 Picture frame test

The picture frame test is conducted to consider a pure shear case. It offers a direct method to measure the response of woven yarns in a deformation mode. In this case, a hinged frame with four equal bars is assembled in a tensile testing machine. A tensile force is applied across diagonally opposing corners of the picture frame rig causing the picture frame to move from an initially square configuration into a rhomboid, like figure 4. As in-plane shear causes the shear stress only, the stresses in the yarn directions must be zero in the case of simple shear of woven fabric. The result of picture frame test is shown in figure 5.

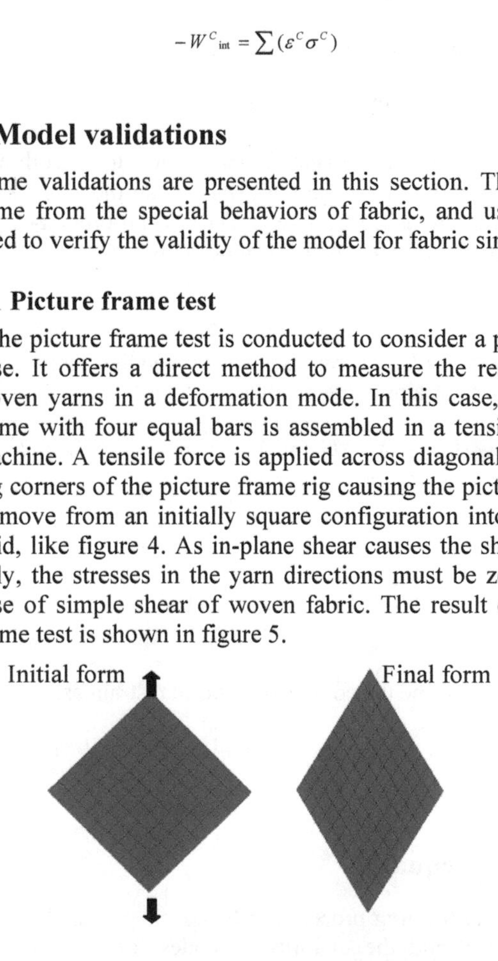

Fig 4: Simulation of picture frame

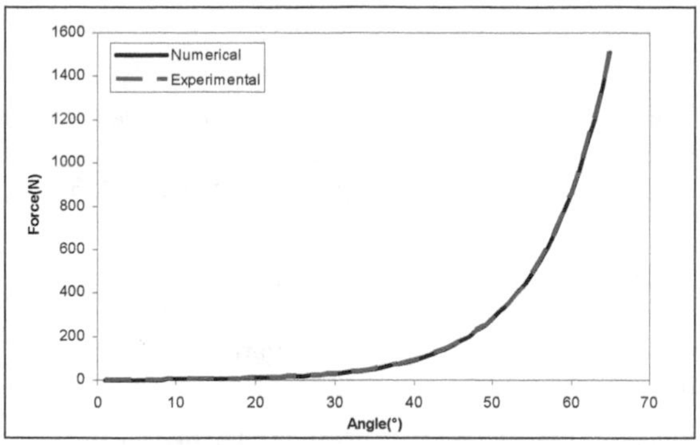

Fig 5: Diagonal force vs shear angle

4.2 Bias test

Bias extension test is performed with a fabric sample of a length normally twice greater than the size of width where the fibres are oriented at 45° to the loading direction (see figure 6). During this test, the central area is sheared whereas four others areas are half-sheared and the clamping areas are not sheared. This test allows to consider the second order stiffness contributions and to determine the continuous material parameters. We can see the result of bias test in figure 7.

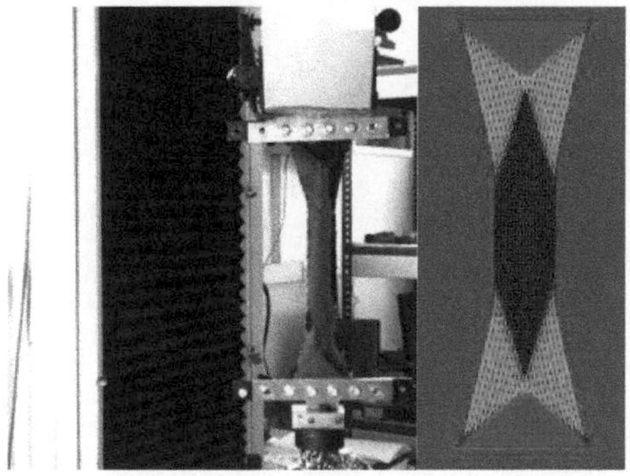

Fig6: Experimental and simulation results of bias test

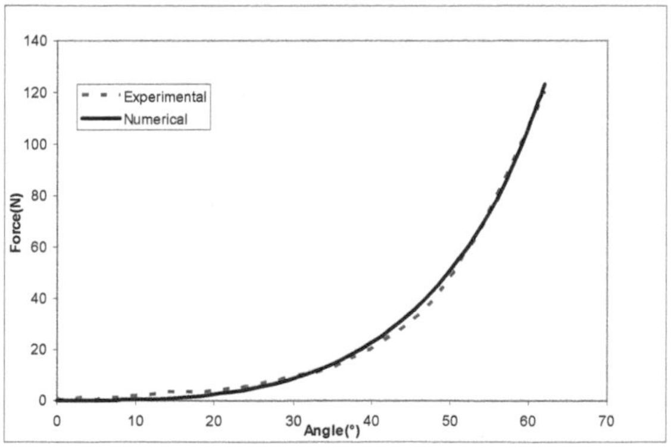

Fig 7: Tensile force vs shear angle

4.3 Compression test

An experimental device developed at the University of Le Havre (figure 8) is used for the compression test. Twenty layers woven fabrics which have the same fiber direction are tested by this machine. We use the displacement control and outputs are the compressive normal strain and the normal compressive stress (figure 9).

Fig 8: Experimental setup for compression test

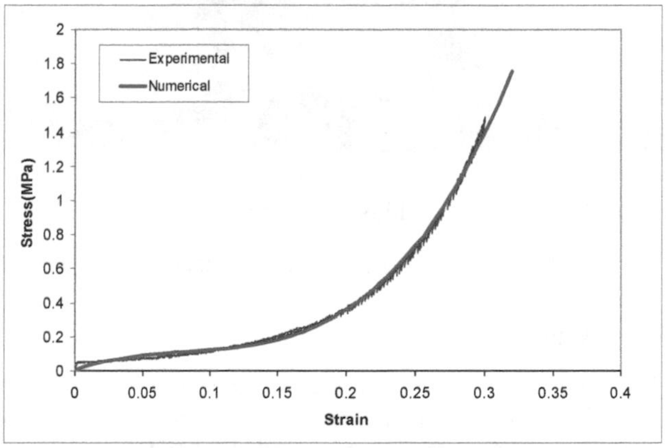

Fig 9: Normal stress vs normal strain

5 Simulation results

5.1 Hemisphere forming simulation

Hemisphere forming is a classical forming simulation test. From this test, we can observe that the final form is different if the fibre direction is different. Figure 10 and figure 11 show the simulation results of this test, in which the fibre direction is -45/45. The result show us the change of angle between weft and wrap (figure 10), and the normal strain (figure 11).

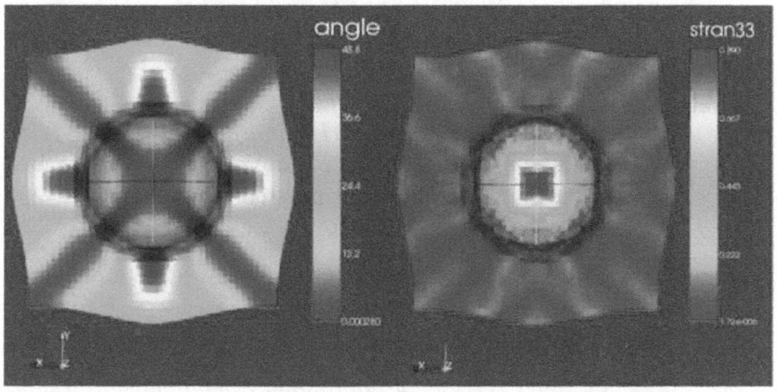

Fig 10: Change of angle Fig 11: Normal strain

5.1 Square box deep drawing simulation

Square box deep drawing simulations have been conducted real woven sheet forming of this geometry is difficult, because it leads to large variations of angle between warp and weft in the radius. Three types of simulation have been done with the consideration of the tension only and of both the tension and the shear, finally of the bending as well. Figure 12 presents three deformed shapes of the woven fabric at the end of the forming. There is no wrinkling in the tensile only solution because there is no source of instability in this case. On the other hand, some wrinkles are developed in the consideration of both the tension and the shear. The wrinkles are caused by the fabric shear locking that leads to out-of-plane deformation. We can observe that the form of wrinkle changes if the bending stiffness is also considered.

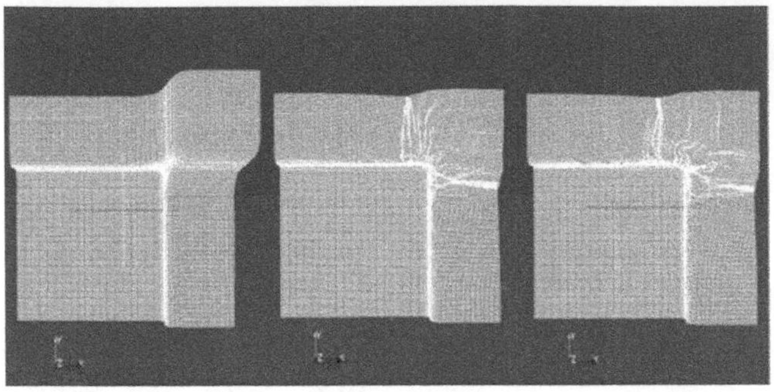

Without shear without bending — With shear without bending — With shear with bending

Fig 12: Simulation results of square box deep drawing test

6 Conclusions

We proposed a model for the woven composite forming simulation. We presented a model to describe the woven's tensile behavior, shear behavior and the bending behavior. Compared with the tensile stiffness, shear stiffness and bending stiffness are actually very small for most textile fabrics. When some wrinkles appear, however, the model with the shear stiffness yields better results than those based on tensile properties only. And the result of the model with bending stiffness show that bending stiffness changes the wrinkle form. Based on the current model, the future work is to develop a model for the woven composite forming simulation to consider also the behavior of resin.

Acknowledgement

The authors would like to acknowledge the financial support to this work by the AIRCELLE/SAFRAN.

References

[1] O. K. Bergsm, J. Huisman, *Deep drawing of fabric reinforced thermoplastics*. In 2nd conference on computer aided design in composite material technology, P. 323-333, 1988.

[2] V. Der, F. Ween, *Algorithms for draping fabrics on doubly curved surfaces*. Int J Numer Method Eng, P. 1414-1426, 1991.

[3] X. Q. Peng, J. Cao, *A continuum mechanics-based non-orthogonal constitutive model for woven composite fabrics*, Composites Part A, Vol. 36, P. 859–874, 2005.

[4] W. R .Yu, F. Pourboghrat, *Non-orthogonal constitutive equation for woven fabric reinforced thermoplastic composites*. Composites Part A, P. 1095-1105, 2002.

[5] B. V. West, R. B. Pipes, M. Keefe, *A simulation of the draping of bidirectional fabrics over arbitrary surfaces*. J Text Inst, P. 448-460, 1990.

[6] P. Boisse, M. Borr, K. Buet, A. Cherouat, *Finite element simulations of textile composite forming including the biaxial fabric behavior*. Composites Part B, P. 453-464, 1997.

[7] N. Hamila, P. Boisse, *Simulations of textile composite reinforcement draping using a new semi-discrete three node finite element*. Composites Part B, P. 999-1010, 2008.

[8] B. Zouari, J. L. Daniel, P. Boisse, *A woven reinforcement forming simulation method influence of the shear stiffness*. Computers and Structures, P. 351-363, 2006.

[9] Q. Q. Chen, P. Boisse, N. Hamila, A. Saouab, J. Bréard, C. H. Park, *A finite element method for the forming simulation of the reinforcements of thermoplastic composite*. In ESAFORM 2009.

11

A Uniform Optimum Material Based Model for Concurrent Optimization of Thermoelastic Structures and Materials

Jun Yan[1a], Geng-dong Cheng [1], Ling Liu [1]

[1] State Key Lab of Structural Analysis for Industrial Equipment and Department of Engineering Mechanics, Dalian University of Technology, Dalian, 116024, P.R.China

Abstract –This paper presents an optimization technique for structures composed of uniform cellular materials in macro scale. The optimization aims at to obtain optimal configurations of macro scale structures and microstructures of material under certain mechanical and thermal loads with specific base material volume. A concurrent topology optimization method is proposed for structures and materials to minimize compliance of thermoelastic structures. In this method macro and micro densities are introduced as the design variables for structure and material microstructure independently. Penalization approaches are adopted at both scales to ensure clear topologies, i.e. SIMP (Solid Isotropic Material Penalization) in micro-scale and PAMP (Porous Anisotropic Material Penalization) in macro-scale. Optimizations in two scales are integrated into one system with homogenization theory and the distribution of base material between two scales can be decided automatically by the optimization model. Microstructure of materials is assumed to be uniform at macro scale to reduce manufacturing cost. The proposed method and computational model are validated by the numerical experiments. The effects of temperature differential, volume of base material, numerical parameters on the optimum results are also discussed. At last, for cases in which both mechanical and thermal loads apply, the configuration of porous material can help to reduce the system compliance.

Key words: Topology optimization, thermoelasticity, concurrent optimization, porous anisotropic material, homogenization

1 Introduction

With shortage of global resources and the intense of enterprises' competition, structural optimization design is drawing more and more attention from academicians and engineers. Different from dimensional or shape optimization, structural topology optimization can achieve more efficient conception/configuration design at the stage of initial design, and it is a hot topic in recent two decades. The pioneer work of structural topology optimization for continuum can be traced back to 1981, when Cheng and Olhoff[1] introduced the concept of microstructure to structural optimization in their studies of optimum thickness design of a solid elastic plate with minimum compliance. After that, Homogenization method[2] and SIMP(Solid Isotropic Material with Penalization) method[3] were developed and became two main branches of topology optimization.

Structures could be frequently applied with mechanical and thermal loads simultaneously in automobile, electronic, nuclear, aerospace and aircraft industries. It is worth of mentioning that some new materials that sustain extreme temperature are often bear mechanical loads also in practical structures. Thus studies of optimization design of this kind of thermoelastic structures are becoming a very attractive area. But there are no enough papers to deal with the topology optimization for structures and materials with combined mechanical and thermal loads, especially for the concurrent optimization for the two scales simultaneously to consider the coupled effects of macro-structure and micro-structure. [4; 5].

This paper presents an optimization technique for thermoelastic structures composed of uniform cellular materials in macro scale. The optimization aims at to obtain optimal configurations of macro scale structures and microstructures of material under certain mechanical and thermal loads with specific base material volume. A concurrent topology optimization method is proposed for structures and materials to minimize compliance of structures. In this method macro and micro densities are introduced as the design variables for structure and material microstructure independently. Penalization approaches are adopted at both scales to ensure clear topologies, i.e. SIMP (Solid Isotropic Material Penalization) in micro-scale and PAMP (Porous Anisotropic Material Penalization) in macro-scale. Optimizations in two scales are integrated into one system with homogenization theory and the distribution of base material between two scales can be decided automatically by the optimization model. Microstructure of materials is assumed to be uniform at macro scale to reduce manufacturing cost. The proposed method and computational model are validated by the numerical experiments. The effects of temperature differential, volume of base material, numerical parameters on the optimum results are also discussed. At last, for cases in which both mechanical and thermal loads apply, the configuration of porous material can help to reduce the system compliance.

2 Concurrent optimization of structures and materials

Microstructure with some simple specific configurations is introduced into topology optimizations in homogenization

[a] Corresponding author: yanjun@dlut.edu.cn

method and is assumed with infinite periods normally. Then structural topology optimization can be solved by size optimization in micro scale. The "Black-White" design of macro structures can be realized according to the relative density of unit cells of materials. Cells with large cavities (representing "white") are treated as void, while those with small cavities (representing "black") denote solid part and form the structure. Though unit cells are introduced into homogenization method, the optimization at micro scale is limited to be within the scope of size optimization.

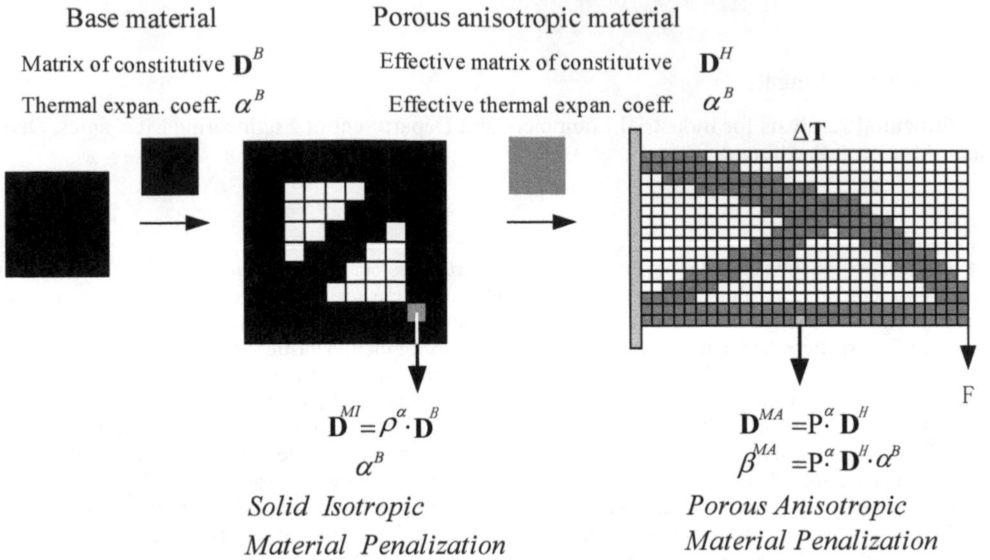

Fig. 1. Penalization-based concurrent optimization with two classes of density as design variables

An alternative approach to implement structural topology optimization is the so-called SIMP method. Densities of elements are set as design variables to interpolate the transition between solid material and void. Relationship between the design variable and the material properties is established based on power laws, which are mental assumptions. Though having been proposed to match with the intermediate densities in the sense of effective elastic properties[6], microstructures are introduced merely for validating the material interpolation model but not integrated into the optimization.

Application of the above two approaches often leads to structural design containing gray area, which is neither solid nor void, and checkerboard pattern. To achieve clear "black-white" topology, various techniques [3] have been developed, such as enforcing an upper bound on the perimeter of structures [7], introducing a filtering function[8] and imposing constraints on the slope of the parameters defining the geometry[9].

Rodrigues et al.[10] proposed a hieratical design method for structure and material to achieve minimum system compliance with a homogenization method . This method is characterized by the varying microstructural configurations from point to point in macro-scale, which results in a "varying gray" look of the structural design. Such results could bring about some manufacturing difficulty. It must be pointed out that the design variables for macro and micro scales in this method are dependent, that is to say, the ratio of integration of micro-density (micro design variables) over micro unit cell to the volume of micro unit cell is set to be equal to the macro-density(macro design variables).

The ultra-light material includes metal cellular materials with perfect periodic micro-structural arrangement, such as metal honeycomb materials, metal linear cellular alloys and truss-like materials. With rapid developments in manufacturing techniques, ultra-light material are increasingly widely used in applications such as ultra-light weight structures, heat exchangers, energy absorption systems, vibration control and acoustical scattering[11; 12; 13]. But a new problem rises in field of topology optimization with the increasing use of ultra-light materials in which macro relative density is no longer 1 but an intermediate value between 0 and 1. That is how to design an optimal structure and corresponding material microstructure with homogeneous cellular material in macro scale. And we note that many research works[14; 15; 16; 17] for ultra-light materials aim only at developing materials with prescribed or extreme properties, i.e., optimizing material microstructure in terms of certain equivalent properties(pure tension, bending or torsion) which is not guaranteed to be the most efficient when constructing the structure, since both structural configuration and boundary condition may vary dramatically in practical use.

The present work attempts to achieve a "single gray-white" design as shown in Fig 1. In macro scale, the "gray domain" is occupied by macro homogeneous porous material; the "white domain" has no material distribution. In micro scale, for porous material in "gray domain", the "black domain" in microstructure is occupied by base material such as aluminum or its alloy; and the "white domain" has no material. Especially the porous materials are usually anisotropic and its microstructures are free from any assumptions about its configurations (e.g. cellular materials with square and rectangular holes, ranked laminates). To obtain such a design, we will establish the mathematics formulae for concurrent optimization in next section.

3 Formulation of optimization

Both problems at macro-structure and micro-structure scales as shown in Fig 1 can be dealt with as classical layout designs, for which topology optimization is a powerful tool. First as shown in Figure 1, macro domain Ω is meshed into N elements and micro domain Y is meshed into n elements. Each element is then assigned a unique density value varying between 0 and 1, e.g. P_i for the *ith* (i=1,2,...N) element in macro-scale and ρ_j (i=1,2,...n) for the *jth* element in micro-scale. Since elements in macro-scale is composed of porous material, its physical density equals to $\rho^{PAM} \times P_i(X)$, where $\rho^{PAM} = \int_Y \rho dy / V^{MI}$, relative density of the porous anisotropic material, is included here. In single-scaled topology optimization, the relative density ρ^{PAM} should equal to 1. Y represents micro design domain and V^{MI} is the area of micro design domain. The macro design domain Ω is subjected to external forces **F** and uniform temperature differential ΔT, then the formulation of optimization for the minimum compliance can be expressed as

$$Min: C = \int_\Omega \mathbf{F}\cdot\mathbf{U}d\Omega + \int_\Omega \boldsymbol{\beta}^{MA}\cdot\boldsymbol{\varepsilon}\cdot\Delta T d\Omega \quad (1)$$

$$s.t.: \mathbf{K}\left(P^\alpha E^H(\rho)\right)\cdot\mathbf{U} = \mathbf{F}^{Me} + \mathbf{F}^{TEM}\left(P^\alpha \beta^H(\rho)\right) \quad (2)$$

$$s.t.: \ \varsigma = \frac{\rho^{PAM}\cdot\int_\Omega Pd\Omega}{V^{MA}} \le \bar{\varsigma} \quad (3)$$

$$s.t.: \gamma = \sum_{k=1}^{m} l_k\cdot(\rho_{k1}-\rho_{k2})^2 \le \bar{\gamma} \quad (4)$$

$$s.t.: 0<\delta\le P\le 1,\ 0<\delta\le\rho\le 1 \quad (5)$$

where C denotes structural compliance and U, ε represent structural deformation vector and stain tensor, $\boldsymbol{\beta}^{MA}$ represents the effective thermal stress tensor of porous material in macro scale.

Constraint I represents the balance equation for macro-structure system which shows how the two independent design variables (P,ρ) influence the stiffness matrix **K** and thermo-load vector $\mathbf{F}^{TEM}$. More detailed explanations about this constraint can be found at section 4.

Constraint II sets a limit on the total available base material by defining relative density ς and its upper bound $\bar{\varsigma}$. V^{MA} is the area of macro design domain Ω.

To limit the complexity of designs and suppress the checkerboard pattern, Constraint III, a so called "perimeter-like" constraint[18] is introduced in this research where m is the number of share edge in finite element mesh, l_k is the length of share edge, ρ_{k1}, ρ_{k2} are the micro densities of neighbor elements who share the *kth* edge, and $\bar{\gamma}$ is specific upper bounds of perimeter.

Constraint IV sets bounds for density variables at two scales to avoid numerical singularity of optimization, where δ is a small predetermined value that is set as $\delta = 0.001$ here.

4 Structure and sensitivity analysis for thermoelastic structures

4.1 Structural analysis for thermoelastic structures

The compliance of thermoelastic structures show in Eq. [1] can be obtained by Finite element analysis. The formula are shown as follows,

$$\mathbf{K}\cdot\mathbf{U} = \mathbf{F}^{Me} + \mathbf{F}^{TEM} \quad (6)$$

$$\mathbf{K} = \int_\Omega \mathbf{B}^T\mathbf{D}^{MA}\mathbf{B}d\Omega \quad (7)$$

$$\mathbf{F}^{TEM} = \int_\Omega \mathbf{B}\cdot\boldsymbol{\beta}^{MA}\cdot\Delta T d\Omega \quad (8)$$

Here, **K** is stiffness matrix of structures and **B** is the strain-displacement matrix. **U** and ΔT are the vectors composed of the nodal values of **U** and ΔT. $\mathbf{F}^{Me}$ and $\mathbf{F}^{TEM}$ represent the vectors of mechanical loads and thermal loads respectively. $\mathbf{D}^{MA}$ and $\boldsymbol{\beta}^{MA}$ are the elastic constitutive matrix and the thermal stress matrix of macro material points to be determined by the following equations.

$$\mathbf{D}^{MA} = \mathrm{P}^\alpha\cdot\mathbf{D}^H \quad (9)$$

$$\boldsymbol{\beta}^{\mathbf{MA}} = \mathrm{P}^\alpha\cdot\mathbf{D}^{\mathbf{H}}\cdot\boldsymbol{\alpha}^{\mathbf{H}} \quad (10)$$

P is the design variable defined as the macro density, α denotes the exponent of penalization and α = 3 here. $\boldsymbol{\alpha}^H$ represents effective thermal expansion coefficients matrix. According to reference [19], no matter what configuration of micro unit cell has, we always have $\boldsymbol{\alpha}^H = \boldsymbol{\alpha}^B$ for porous anisotropic material composed of one pure base material, $\boldsymbol{\alpha}^B$ being thermal expansion coefficients matrix of base material. $\mathbf{D}^H$ is the equivalent macro elastic constitutive matrix with corresponding macro relative density being 1. The computation of $\mathbf{D}^H$ could follow the classical homogenization procedures[2] :

$$\mathbf{D}^H = \frac{1}{|Y|}\int_Y \mathbf{D}^{MI}\cdot(\mathbf{I}-\mathbf{b}\cdot\boldsymbol{\varphi})dY \quad (11)$$

$$\mathbf{D}^{MI} = \rho^\alpha\cdot\mathbf{D}^B \quad (12)$$

Assuming $\mathbf{D}^{MI}$ represents constitutive matrix of the material points with relative density ρ at micro-scale, $\mathbf{D}^B$ represents the constitutive matrix of isotropic base material, where **I**(3×3) is a unit matrix in two-dimensional case and $|Y|$ is the area of a unit cell, **b** is the strain/displacement matrix. Generalized deformations of microstructure $\boldsymbol{\varphi}$ could be obtained from the two equations below,

$$\mathbf{k}\cdot\boldsymbol{\varphi} = \int_Y \mathbf{b}^T\cdot\mathbf{D}^{MI}dY \quad (13)$$

$$\mathbf{k} = \int_Y \mathbf{b}^T\cdot\mathbf{D}^{MI}\cdot\mathbf{b}dY \quad (14)$$

where deformation $\boldsymbol{\varphi}$ is a matrix which is composed of three deformation fields in two dimensional case, and Eq.

(13) is a multiple loads FEM analysis with three different loads (stiffness matrix is unchanged) for two dimensional case.

By virtue of Eqs. (6-14), we have completed the structural analysis at two scales and got the structural deformation **U**. Then one can further obtain current objective function C based on the current design variables. The basic idea of the process above was summarized in Fig 1.

4.2 Sensitivity analysis of concurrent optimization for thermoelastic structures and materials

Sensitivity analysis is important to enhance the efficiency of the sensitivity based algorithm. Based on the equations above, it is readily to obtain the following two derivatives of objective function with respect to design variables.

$$\begin{aligned}\frac{\partial C}{\partial P_i} &= -\mathbf{U}^T \frac{\partial \mathbf{K}}{\partial P_i}\mathbf{U} + 2\cdot\mathbf{U}^T \sum_{r=1}^{N}\int_{\Omega^e} \mathbf{B}^T \frac{\partial \boldsymbol{\beta}^{MA}}{\partial P_i}\Delta\mathbf{T}d\Omega^e \\ &= -\mathbf{u}_i^T\left[\left(\alpha\cdot P_i^{\alpha-1}\right)\int_{\Omega^e}\mathbf{B}^T D_i^H \mathbf{B}d\Omega^e\right]\mathbf{u}_i \\ &+2\cdot u_i^T\cdot\alpha\cdot P_i^{\alpha-1}\int_{\Omega^e}\mathbf{B}^T\boldsymbol{\beta}_i^H\Delta\mathbf{T}d\Omega^e \\ &= -\frac{\alpha}{P_i}\mathbf{u}_i^T\left[\int_{\Omega^e}\mathbf{B}^T D_i^{MA}\mathbf{B}d\Omega^e\right]\mathbf{u}_i \\ &+2\cdot\frac{\alpha}{P_i}u_i^T\int_{\Omega^e}\mathbf{B}^T\boldsymbol{\beta}_i^{MA}\Delta\mathbf{T}d\Omega^e\end{aligned} \tag{15}$$

$$\begin{aligned}\frac{\partial C}{\partial \rho_j} &= -\mathbf{U}^T \frac{\partial \mathbf{K}}{\partial \rho_j}\mathbf{U} + 2\cdot\mathbf{U}^T \sum_{r=1}^{N}\int_{\Omega^e} \mathbf{B}^T \frac{\partial \boldsymbol{\beta}^{MA}}{\partial \rho_j}\Delta\mathbf{T}d\Omega^e \\ &= -\sum_{r=1}^{N}\mathbf{u}_r^T\left(\int_{\Omega^r}\mathbf{B}^T P_r^{\alpha}\frac{\partial \mathbf{D}_r^H}{\partial \rho_j}\mathbf{B}d\Omega^r\right)\mathbf{u}_r \\ &+2\cdot\sum_{r=1}^{N}\mathbf{u}_r^T\left(\int_{\Omega^r}\mathbf{B}^T P_r^{\alpha}\frac{\partial \mathbf{D}_r^H}{\partial \rho_j}\boldsymbol{\alpha}^B\Delta\mathbf{T}d\Omega^r\right)\end{aligned} \tag{16}$$

where the derivative of $\mathbf{D}^H$ with respect to ρ_j can be computed following references [20] as

$$\frac{\partial \mathbf{D}^H}{\partial \rho_j} = \int_Y (\mathbf{I}-\mathbf{b}\cdot\boldsymbol{\varphi})^T\cdot\frac{\partial \mathbf{D}^{MI}}{\partial \rho_j}\cdot(\mathbf{I}-\mathbf{b}\cdot\boldsymbol{\varphi})dY \tag{17}$$

Combined with equation(12), the equation above leads to

$$\frac{\partial \mathbf{D}^H}{\partial \rho_j} = \frac{\alpha}{\rho_j}\frac{1}{|Y|}\int_Y\left(\mathbf{I}-\boldsymbol{\varepsilon}_y^T(\boldsymbol{\varphi})\right)\mathbf{D}^{MI}\left(\mathbf{I}-\boldsymbol{\varepsilon}_y(\boldsymbol{\varphi})\right)dY \tag{18}$$

The derivatives of Constraint Ⅰ with respect to design variables can be written as,

For the perimeter control only is applied on the micro-scale, then

$$\frac{\partial \varsigma}{\partial P_i} = \frac{\rho^{PAM}A_i^{MA}}{V^{MA}\bar{\varsigma}}\ ;\quad \frac{\partial \varsigma}{\partial \rho_j} = \frac{a_j^{MI}\cdot\int_\Omega P d\Omega}{V^{MA}\cdot V^{MI}\cdot\bar{\varsigma}} \tag{19}$$

The derivatives of Constraint Ⅱ with respect to design variables can be written as,

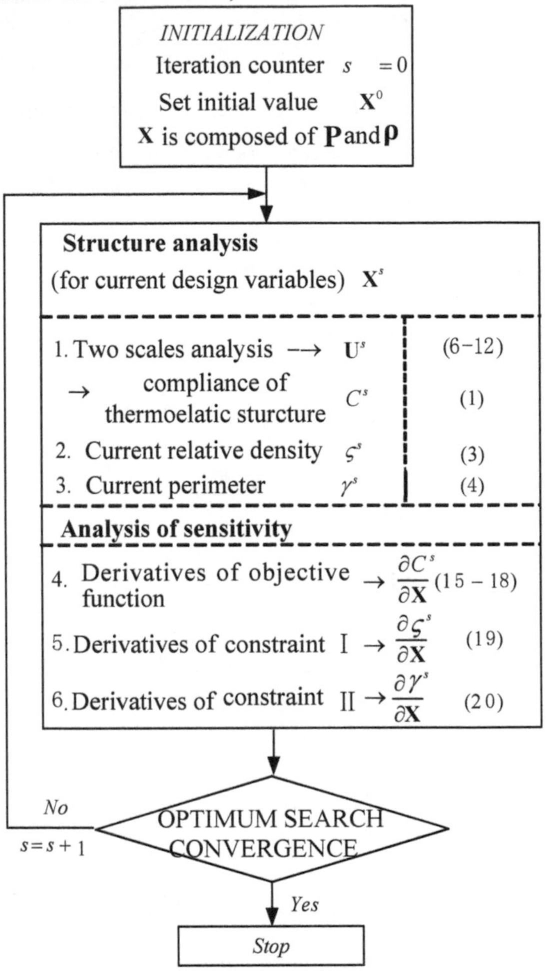

Fig. 2. Flow chart of concurrent optimization for thermoelastic structure and material

$$\frac{\partial \gamma}{\partial P_i} = 0\ ;\quad \frac{\partial \gamma}{\partial \rho_j} = \frac{2\cdot\sum_{j=1}^{m} l_j\left(\rho_{j1}-\rho_{j2}\right)}{\bar{\gamma}} \tag{20}$$

A^{MA}, a^{MI}, V^{MA} and V^{MI} represents the area of elements and design domain at macro- and micro- scales. Now, we have completed the structural analysis and sensitivity analysis. A flow chart of key steps and corresponding equations is given in Fig 2.

Table 1. The influence of temperature differential on the concurrent design results

T	Structural topology	Microstructural topology	
		Unit Cell	3×3 arrays
0° C	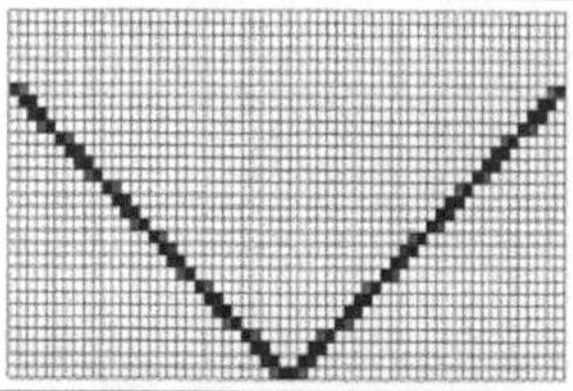		
4° C	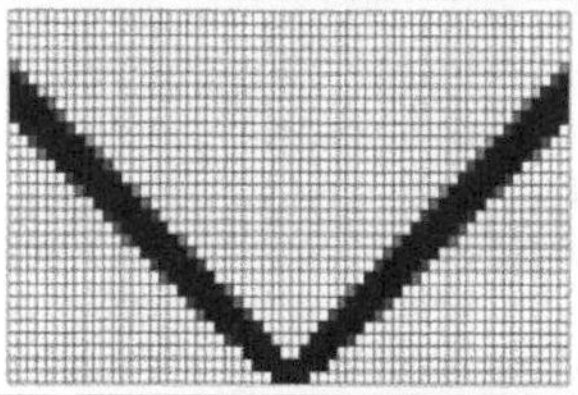	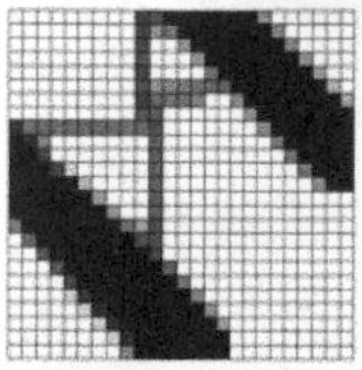	
20° C	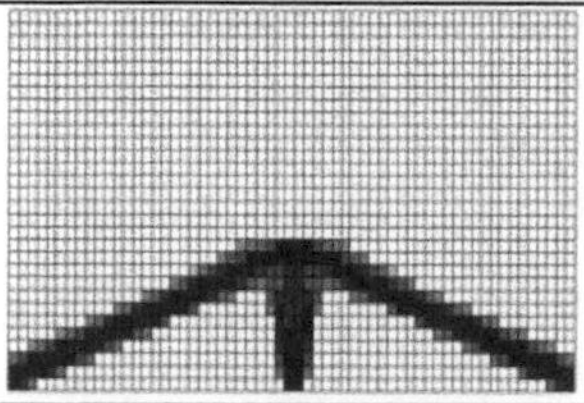	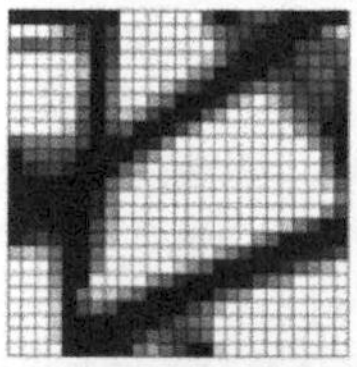	
40° C	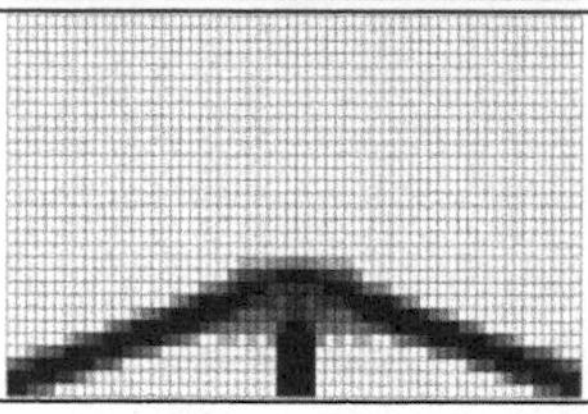	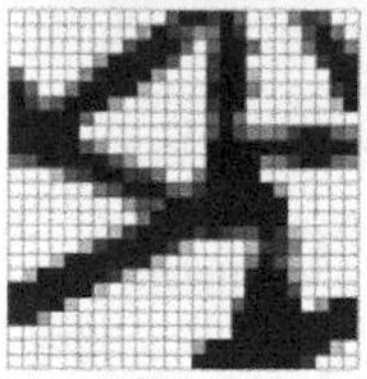	

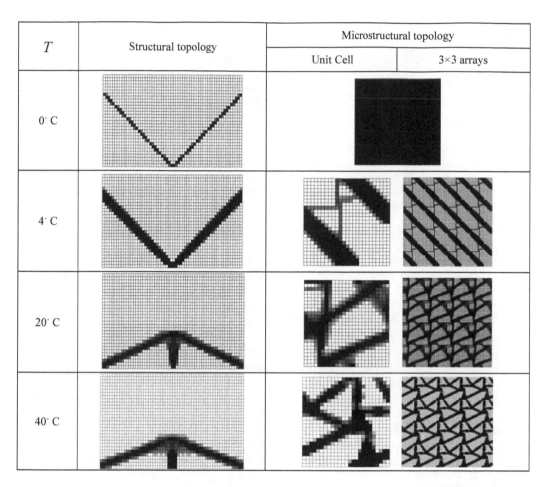

Table 2 Influence of base material volume on the concurrent optimization design

V	P^{SIM}	ρ^{PAM}	Compliance	Structural topology	Microstructural topology	
					Unit Cell	3×3 arrays
5%	0.1326	0.3772	47770	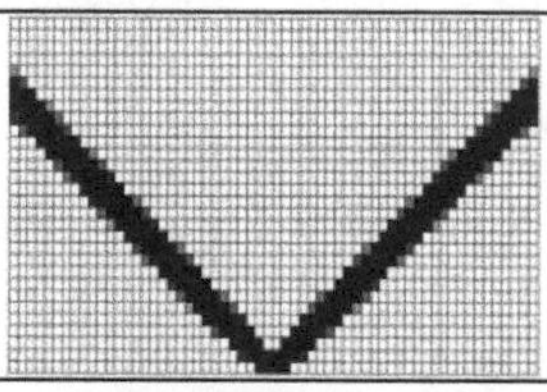	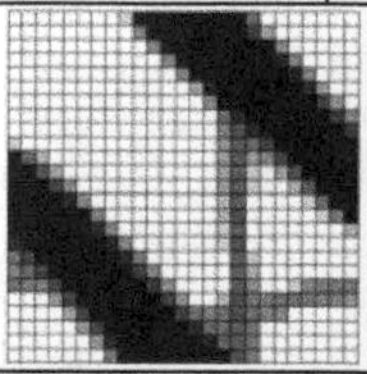	
20%	0.2191	0.9126	17664	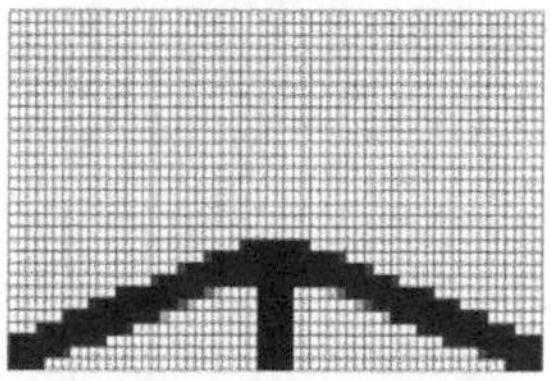	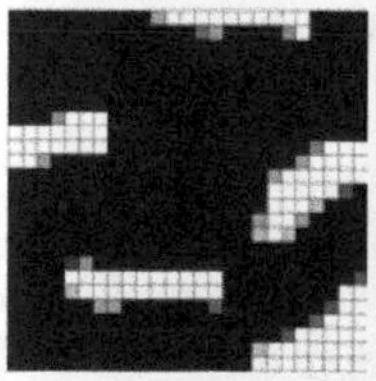	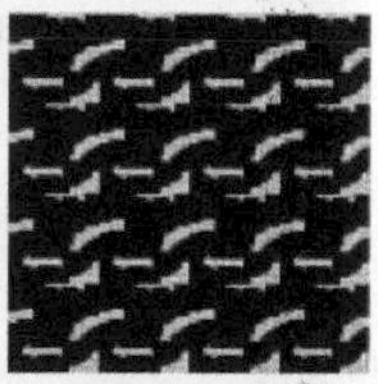
30%	0.3409	0.8742	14597	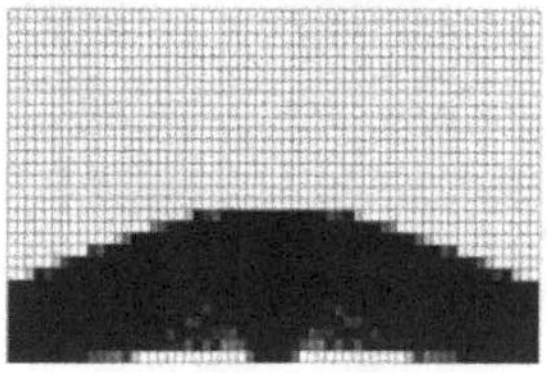		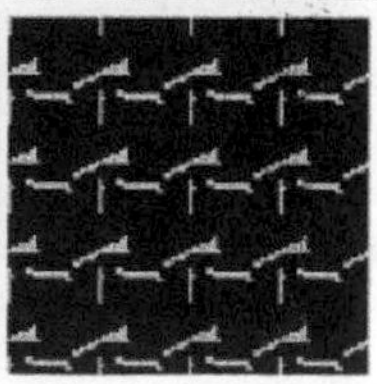

5 Numerical Examples

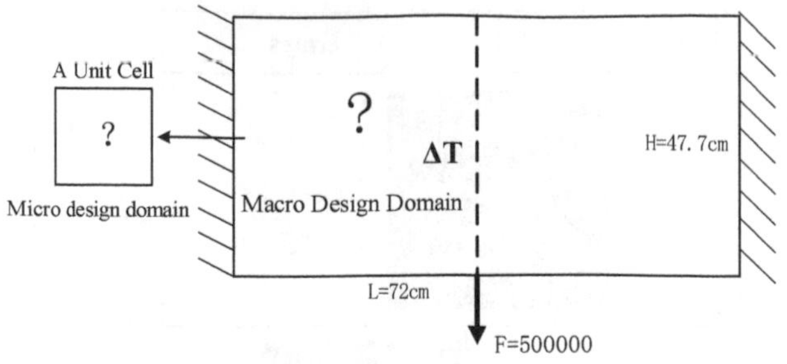

Fig. 3. Numerical example

The initial design domain is shown in Fig 3. The dimensions are 72cm×47.7cm×1cm, the applied load has a value of F=500000N, the right and left sides of the structure are clamped and the whole design domain has a temperature differential of **ΔT**. Base material is assumed to have Young's modulus E^B = 100GPa, Poisson's ratio $\nu^B = 0.3$ and thermal expansion coefficient of $\alpha^B=\{1.0\times10^{-5}, 1.0\times10^{-5}, 0\}^T$. Due to the symmetry of the problem, only the left half part is considered as macro design domain (the configuration of micro-structure in right part can be obtained as mirror of counterpart of left part). The mesh is 60×30 for macro design domain and 25×25 for the microstructure (8-Node Planar Element). OPTIMUM SEARCH is implemented by the optimization package DOT using the SQP (Sequential Quadratic Programming) algorithm [21].

The influence of temperature differential on the concurrent design results are discussed in Table 1. Here upper bound of perimeter constraint is set to be $\bar{\gamma}$, and the volume constraint is equal to 5% of the total volume.

The first row of the Table 1 shows the case of no effects due to thermal loads, i.e. **ΔT=0**, case in which the concurrent optimization for thermoelastic structures degenerates to optimization for elastic structure with mechanical loads alone. In this case, it is interesting to note that the "two-bar like" configuration appears for the macro-structure and there is no cellular structure in the result configuration of microstructures, equivalently the optimum microstructure is isotropic solid material ($\rho_{Opt}^{PAM} = 1$). Is the use of porous material not good for improving stiffness of the structures with mechanical loads only? More numerical examples indicate it is true except for the structures in a uniaxial stress case as far as the authors know. The reason for this, we believe, is the assumption of uniform configuration of micro-structure. States of stress in the structures are usually complex and the directions of principle stress at different material points could be arbitrary and the best design for material configuration is to distribute the base material along the directions of principle stress at certain material point. Thus to meet the different requirements of material distribution at different points in structures with uniform micro-structure configuration, the isotropic solid material might be the best choice. On the other hand, the microstructual configuration of porous material actually imposes a kind of constraint on the distribution of base material in whole structure system with an assumed uniform micro-structure configuration. Compared with the constrained distribution when porous material is used, the base material can be distributed more freely when the isotropic solid material is used to obtain better system performance. More explanations could be done from the point view of sensitivity analysis, which might be done in the near future study.

When $\Delta\mathbf{T} \neq 0$, the thermal loads, together with the mechanical loads, have effects on the optimization results, and in this case we found the cellular material could help to reduce the compliance of system from the observations of the results in the 2nd to 5th rows of Table 1. As we can see in rows 2-5, when the temperature differential is small, the mechanical loads governing, the configuration of macro-structure shows a "two-bar" configuration. With increasing of temperature differential, it tends to transform to "three-bar" configuration that reflects greater effect of thermal loads. For "three-bar" configuration, central force could be balanced partly by the sum force from the two oblique bars due to temperature improvement. Then the displacements, also the system compliance, could be reduced by this configuration. When the mechanical loads dominate, the base material is distributed along the direction of axis of "macro-bar" at micro-scale; when no load dominate, a complex configuration appears which reflects combined effects of mechanical and thermal loads.

Table 2 shows optimization results with varying volume fraction of base material $\bar{\varsigma}$, where the upper bound of perimeter constraint is set to be a proper value $\bar{\gamma} = 2$ based on experience obtained from numerical simulation, and the temperature differential is set to be $\Delta\mathbf{T} = 2^{\circ}C$. $P^{SIM} = \frac{\int_{\Omega} P_i d\Omega}{V^{MA}}$ and ρ^{PAM} represent the distribution volume fractions of base material at macro and micro scales.

As shown in the table above, relative density of micro unit cell ρ^{PAM} and macro scale P^{SIM} both increase as volume fraction of base material increase from 5% to 20%, but the increasing rate of relative density of micro unit cell far exceeds its counterpart. At the same time, the configuration of macro-structure transforms from the "two-bar" to the "three-bar" and there is a corresponding reduction in system compliance. But when the volume fraction of base material increase further from 20% to 30%, the relative density of micro unit cell does not approach ρ^{PAM} =1 as expected, but begins to reduce. The volume fraction of macro-structure tends to increase substantially and the system compliance can reduce further when the configuration of macro-structure tends to be a horizontal bar.

And Figs. 4 and 5 give the trends of actually used material volume fraction and macro/micro volume fraction with increasing of specified material volume fraction. In figure 4, we can see a linear increase of actually used material volume fraction with that of specifying when the specified volume fraction is less than 35%. After that, an obvious plateau in the figure can be observed, which is corresponding to the optimum material volume fraction mentioned above. The macro/micro volume fractions and configuration remain stable after the optimum volume fraction. And the volume constraint, constraint II, is no longer an active one after the optimum volume fraction also.

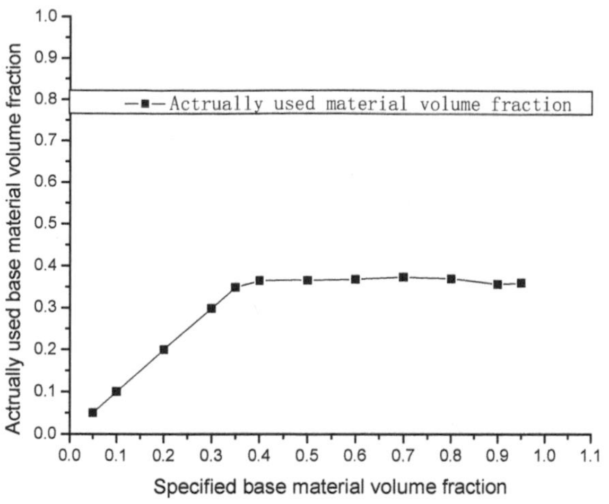

Fig. 4. Trend of actually used material volume with increasing of specified material volume fraction

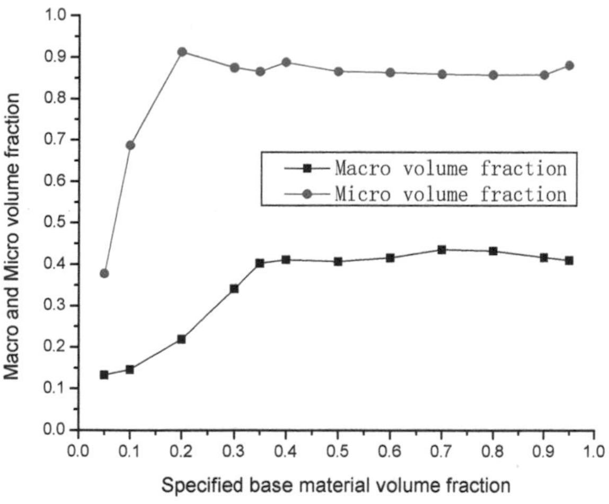

Fig. 5. Trend of macro/micro volume fraction with increasing of specified material volume fraction

6 Conclusion remarks

A new strategy of concurrent optimization design of macro-structure and micro-structure for the thermoelastic structures under combined mechanical and thermal loads is proposed. By this method, the optimum material microstructure configuration according to different macro structure configurations, loads and constraints could be obtained for thermoelastic structures. Macro and micro densities are chosen as the design variables for structure and material microstructure independently and integrated into one system with the help of homogenization theory and the penalization approaches (SIMP at micro-scale and PAMP at macro-scale) to ensure clear topologies. The distribution of base material between the structure and material can be decided automatically by the optimization model. At the same time, microstructure is assumed to be uniform in macro-scale to reduce manufacturing cost. Numerical results in this paper proved the viability of the method and model. With this strategy it is found that for the cases in which only mechanical loads apply, micro-structure of isotropic solid material is best for achieving the minimum structural compliance; while for the cases in which both mechanical and thermal loads apply, the configuration of porous material is more effective to reduce the system compliance. So it will be an interesting and challenging work to extend this concurrent optimization method to multifunctional applications, e.g. integrate heat transfer, vibration isolation and mechanical requirements into one system.

Acknowledgements

The financial support for this research was provided by National Basic Research Program of China through Grant No. 2006CB601205 and the Major Program (10332010) and the Innovative Research Team Program (10421002) of NSFC and the start funds for research of DUT. These supports are gratefully appreciated.

References

1. G.D. Cheng. *On Non-Smoothness in Optimal Design of Solid Elastic Plates.* International Journal of Solids and Structures, **17**, 795-810 (1981).
2. B. Hassani, E. Hinton. *A review of homogenization and topology optimization III - topology optimization using optimality criteria.* Computers and Structures, **69,** 739-756 (1998).
3. M.P. Bendsoe, O. Sigmund. *Topology Optimization: Theory Methods and Applocations.* (Berlin: Springer-Verlag, 2003).
4. H. Rodrigues, P. Fernandes. *A material based model for topology optimization of thermoelastic structures.* International Jornal for numerical methods in engineering, **38,** 1951-1965 (1995).
5. B. Wang. *Design of cellular structures for optimum efficiency of heat dissipation.* Structural and Multidisciplinary Optimization, **30,** 447-458 (2005).
6. M.P. Bendsoe, O. Sigmund. *Material interpolation schemes in topology optimization.* Archive Of Applied Mechanics, **69,** 635-654 (1999).
7. R.B. Haber, C.S. Jog, M.P. Bendsoe. *A new approach to variable-topology shape design using a constraint on perimeter.* Structural Optimization, **11**, 1-12 (1996).
8. O. Sigmund. *Design of material structures using topology optimization*, PhD thesis, (Department of Solid Mechanics, Technical University of Denmark, 1994).
9. O. Sigmund, J. Petersson. *Numerical instabilities in topology optimization: A survey on procedures dealing with checkerboards, mesh-dependencies and local minima.* Structural Optimization, **16**, 68-75 (1996).
10. H. Rodrigues, J.M. Guedes, M.P. Bendsoe. *Hierarchical optimization of material and structure.* Structural And Multidisciplinary Optimization, **24**, 1-10, (2002).
11. L. J. Gibson, M. F. Ashby. *Cellular Solids: Structure and Properties.* (Cambridge: Cambridge University Press, 1997.)
12. e. a. A.M. Hayes. *Mechanics of linear cellular alloys.* Mechanics of Materials, **36**, 691-713, (2004).
13. N. Wicks, J.W. Hutchinson. *Optimal truss plates.* International Journal of Solids and Structures, **38,** 5165-5183,

(2001).
14. S. Hyun, S. Torquato. *Optimal and manufacturable two-dimensional, Kagome-like cellular solids.* Journal Of Materials Research, **17,** 137-144, (2002).
15. S. Gu, T.J. Lu, A.G. Evans. *On the design of two-dimensional cellular metals for combined heat dissipation and structural load capacity*. International Journal of Heat and Mass Transfer, **44**, 2163-2175, (2001).
16. O. Sigmund. *Tailoring materials with prescribed elastic properties.* Mechanics of Materials, **20**, 351-368, (1995).
17. J. Yan, L. Ling, G. Cheng, *Comparison of and Scale effects on prediction of equivalent elastic property and the shape optimization of truss material with periodic microstructure.* Internatioanl Journal of Mechanical Science, **48,** 400-413, (2006).
18. W.H. Zhang, P. Duysinx. *Dual approach using a variant perimeter constraint and efficient sub-iteration scheme for topology optimization.* Computers & Structures, **81,** 2173-2181, (2003).
19. S. Liu, G. Cheng. *Homogenization-based method for prediciing thermal expansion coefficients of composite materials*. Journal of Dalian University of Technology, **35**, 451-457, (1995).
20. S. Liu, G. Cheng, Y. Gu. *Mapping method for sensitivity analysis of composite material property*. Structural And Multidisciplinary Optimization, **24**, 212-217, (2002).
21. G. N. Vanderplaats. *Design optimization tools user's manual*, (Vanderplaats Research & Development Inc., Colorado, 1999).

12

Numerical Optimization applied to structure sizing at AIRBUS: A multi-step process

S. Grihon[1a], L. Krog[2], D. Bassir[3]

[1] AIRBUS, Toulouse, France,
[2] AIRBUS, Filton, United Kingdom
[3] TUDelft, Delft, The Netherlands.

Abstract – Structure optimization at airframe level is mainly focused on sizing design variables detailing the thin-walled properties of aircraft structures. Typical design variables are cross sectional dimensions for 1D and 2D elements with an additional complexity brought by composite materials with their directional and multi-layer aspects. Even if the scope of these design variables is clear and well understood, the vision of the structure behaviour is multi-criteria and encompasses various fidelity levels. Its design requires several stages from the future project to the detailed definition of structural parts using various analysis tools from different disciplines. These several stages require adequate structural optimization processes to offer the best response with the right level of details to answer questions being sought at each maturity level of the design. A review of methods & tools developed and applied at AIRBUS to deliver automated sizing for aircraft structures along their development will be presented. Ways forward and major stakes for the future will be discussed.

Key words: structure optimization, aeronautical design, mathematical programming, composite materials, multi-level optimization

1. Introduction

In this paper a multi-step sizing process for aeronautical structures will be discussed. The described sizing process does not come from a single attempt at the problem, rather the process should be seen as a result of a multi-year effort in structural optimization [1-6]. For this reason it is important to first describe the history of structural optimization at AIRBUS, and show the development of ideas, which has lead to today's vision.

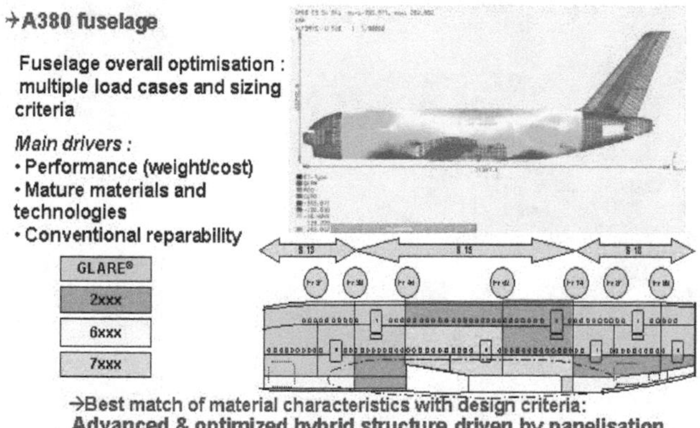
→A380 fuselage
Fuselage overall optimisation : multiple load cases and sizing criteria
Main drivers :
• Performance (weight/cost)
• Mature materials and technologies
• Conventional reparability
GLARE®
2xxx
6xxx
7xxx
→Best match of material characteristics with design criteria:
Advanced & optimized hybrid structure driven by panelisation (worksharing) ⇒ local optimisation of stiffened panels

Fig. 1. Optimization of A380 Fuselage with ISSY

In a second part of the paper we describe sizing processes suited to support aircraft development from early concept design thought to detailed design. Three sizing stages have been identified and associated with sizing processes, which has been named: rapid sizing, preliminary sizing and detailed sizing. Sizing stages are described in reverse order of aircraft development starting from detailed sizing and going up to rapid sizing, integrating progressively the sizing process from the part level to the full aircraft level [7-10]. The two extremes of the sizing optimization process, which are considered today bottlenecks and therefore also the subject of intensive internal research, will then be discussed. This discussion considers how to address optimization at the finest level designing composite materials at ply level and considers how to address optimization at the highest level optimizing the full aircraft. Finally the consistency of the overall process and the continuity between the subsequent sizing stages will be commented. The conclusion will give the ways forward envisaged in the running projects

2. A history of structural optimization at AIRBUS

2.1 From A340 to A380

Structural optimization at AIRBUS was first implemented through sizing processes guided by engineer experience. Efficient tools, like ISSY (Fig. 1) for sizing of fuselages and later SOMBRA (Fig. 2) for sizing of wings, were developed implementing iterative re-sizing loops incorporating recalculation of internal loads. Today, tools are still used to provide an initial sizing for aircraft structures.

With the progress of computational means, sizing processes based on numerical optimization using gradient-based mathematical programming theory appeared. At the time where AIRBUS partners still had their own finite element software, in-house developments were made to add an optimization capability. An example of such early developments is ASELF from AIRBUS-France, which was developed to compute sensitivities of structural finite

(a) Corresponding author : stephane.grihon@airbus.com

element responses and connected to gradient-based optimizers. Another example is the code STARS, which was developed in the 80s by ERA (today Qinetiq) in collaboration with AIRBUS-Germany. With the arrival of NASTRAN [11] as a common Finite Element (FE) package at AIRBUS, the optimization module of NASTRAN, SOL200, became widely used to address simple sizing optimization problems aiming to control direct NASTRAN responses. An example of a direct use of NASTRAN SOL200 is the work performed at the beginning of the A380 development to reduce running loads at the fuselage-wing intersection (Fig. 3).

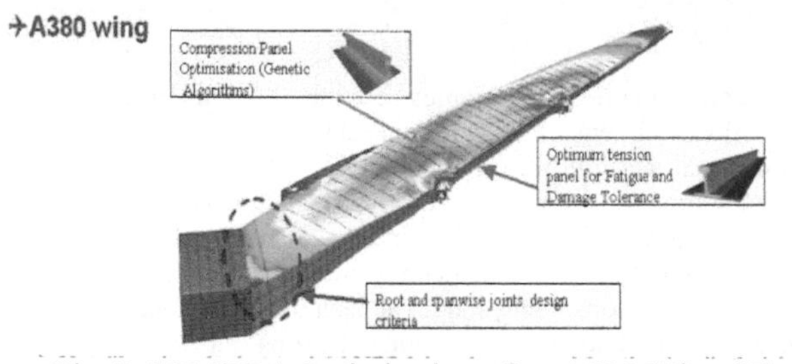

Fig. 2. SOMBRA Optimization of an A380 Wing (The SOMBRA sizing optimization is performed to determine optimum skin/stringer cross sections for a range of loading. Optimised local designs are stored into design curves that in the second level are used to update finite element properties in an iterative and global re-sizing process).

The use of SOL200 is here limited to stress allowable and running loads constraints (direct NASTRAN responses). NASTRAN was also used to compute sensitivities of global responses and chain these in complex multidisciplinary optimization processes. An example is the flutter and stress optimization chain developed in the 90s by AIRBUS-France. This was a stiffness driven sizing process and a first Multidisciplinary Design Optimization experience at AIRBUS.

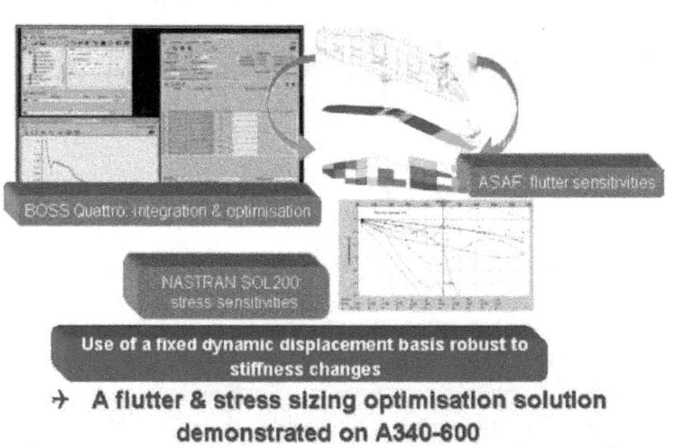

Fig. 3. Integrated flutter and stress optimization applied to A340-600 engine pylons

Another and more advanced example on a direct use of NASTRAN SOL200 is the SOL tool developed for sizing of composite wings (Fig. 3). The SOL tool embeds not only strain requirements but also engineer equations for buckling into a NASTRAN SOL200 input deck to provide a fast preliminary sizing and laminate optimization capability for a composite wing box.

$$N_x^{crit} = \frac{2 \cdot \pi^2}{b^2} \left(\sqrt{D11 \cdot D22} + D12 + 2 \cdot D33 \right)$$

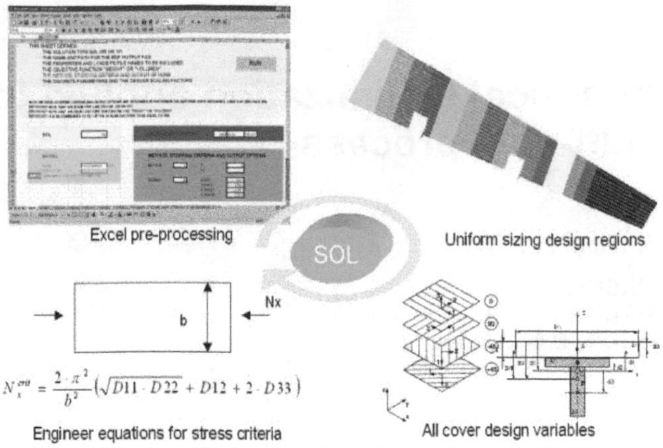

Fig. 4. Fast preliminary sizing of wing boxes with SOL (SOL200 customization)

At the same time a parallel trend was to investigate sizing optimization based on more complex stress tools. These tools are the stress tools used for hand sizing at AIRBUS. They are generally still based on analytical (semi-empirical) approaches, but they chain a long list of equations with potential branching conditions (if then else) and/or integrate iterations and solvers (eigenvalue calculations for example). Such skill tools cannot be easily integrated in SOL200 as done for engineer equations in SOL.

However, due to the restricted number of variables and the small computation times, it was easy by using finite differences to integrate these skill tools inside open optimization frameworks and build automated sizing tools. A good example of application for this kind of tool is the weight saving campaigns made for A380, where many stiffened panels have been optimized thanks to fast integration of stress tools inside an open framework for optimization such BOSS Quattro [12-15] software (Fig. 5).

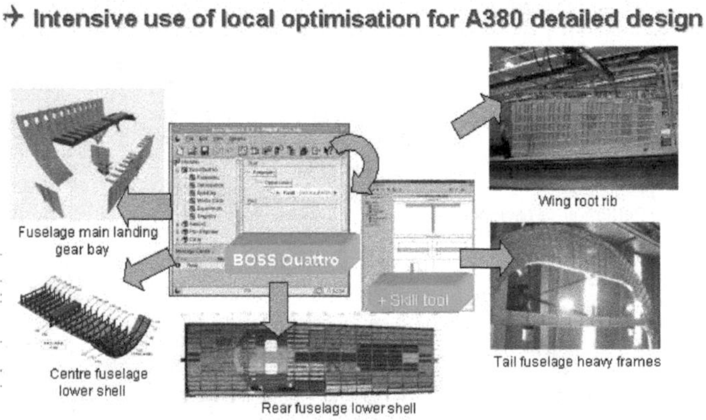

Fig. 5. A380 Weight Savings

2.2 For A350 XWB

It is important at this stage to make understand the sizing process of a structure at AIRBUS to position the various approaches.

Typically tools like SOMBRA, ISSY would automate this sizing process, but without considering more sophisticated stiffness effects, like control of internal load paths. In a way it is just an automation of a set of local optimizations with internal loads updates. Also processes, automating a set of

local optimizations, would have difficulties dealing with global continuity aspects for composite designs.

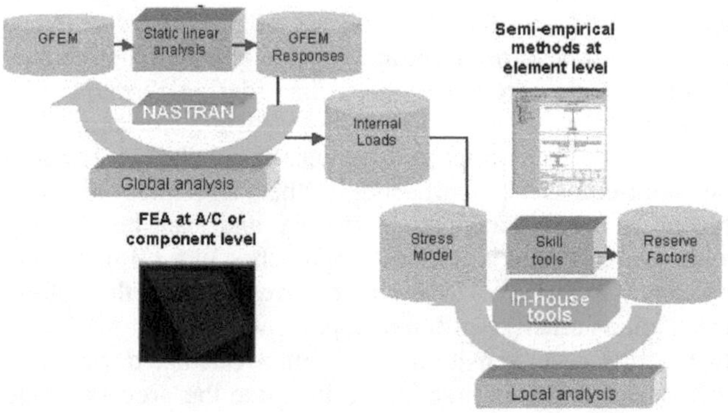

Fig. 6. Hand stress process at AIRBUS

So regarding the sizing approaches based on optimization or mathematical programming it is interesting to make a difference between optimization tools before and after A350. Before A350 there were essentially two kinds of optimization: global optimizations and local optimization. A good example of global optimization is the SOL process. Here the added value is in the consideration of internal load sensitivities with the potential to drive an optimum load path. It is also possible to add constraints on elements not considered in the optimization process with some elements not necessarily driven by stress considerations. This kind of approach is interesting for conceptual design but as the exact stress tools are not used but simplified engineering equations it is not applicable to further stages and especially to the preliminary sizing where a consolidated sizing is required. Another approach is local optimization. Local optimization means essentially that the Global Finite Element Model is not inside the optimization process. A good example is the use of local optimization for A380 weight saving campaigns. This kind of optimization is often made based on fixed internal loads applied to the part to be sized. For this reason it is limited to detailed design (Fig.7). Finally and more recently, a synthesis was made to integrate the first family of tools based on FE analysis and the second level based on stress tools. A tool was developed to mix FE based optimization with skill tool based.

2.3 Summary

Across this history, it is quite clear that there exist 3 families of tools:

- tools based on simple stress criteria and focused on GFEM behavior and stiffness criteria (aeroelastics, loads). These tools are to be used in early design stages in cooperation with Flight Physics to have a good initial sizing of the airframe. An exact stress analysis is not necessary here.
- tools based on advanced stress criteria and using GFEM to address the redistribution of internal loads or still considering some stiffness constraints. These tools have to be used in the transition from architecture to detailed design to consolidate the sizing before finer studies. This is the kind of tool to be used for preliminary sizing to have a good vision of the overall component sizing.
- tools based on skill tools again and focused on the use of skill tools as stand alone. This is the kind of tool to be used for detailed sizing to address part by part sizing. In certain cases we can also have fully FE based optimization.

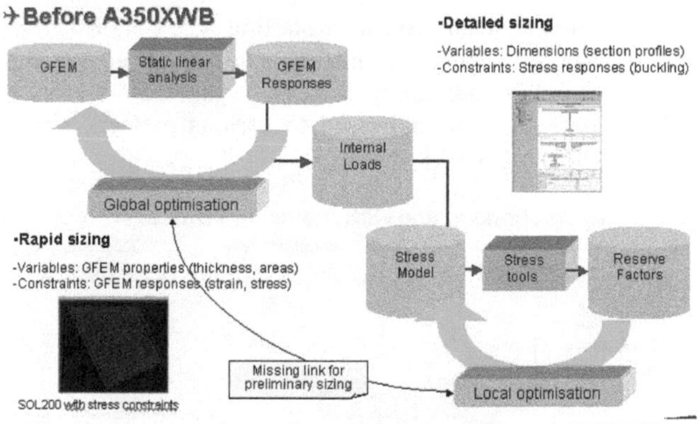

Fig. 7. Sizing optimization approaches before A350XWB

3. A multi-step design process requires various sizing solutions

It is standard in the aeronautical community to see the aircraft design split along three subsequent stages:

- conceptual design
- preliminary design
- detailed design

Conceptual design is an upstream task to optimize the aircraft configuration in terms of high level parameters like external geometry (3-side view), structural lay-out (frame and rib pitch), big choices in terms of materials (composite or metallic). Preliminary design is addressing more refined trade-offs selecting stringer pitch, choosing ply angles and addressing best compromises in terms of weights and costs. Detailed design comes after a good overall definition of airframe external structure (covers) and will deal with the detailed design of all structural parts down to system brackets for example. A way at AIRBUS to distinguish these three different stages is to define milestones linked to the development of an aircraft.

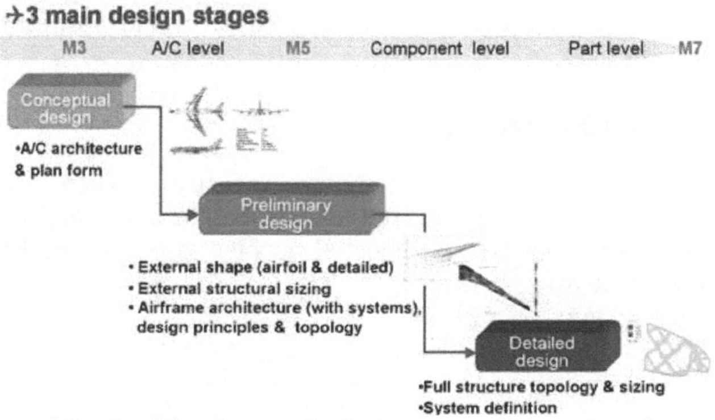

Fig. 8.a. The three main design stages for an aircraft

The main milestones for optimization are:

- M3: the aircraft concept is selected and the optimization of the configuration is starting at aircraft level

- M5: The detailed aircraft configuration is validated and the detailed definition is starting
- M7: The definition is completed at component level and the manufacturing is starting
- M5 is an important milestone because from M5, the structure definition will be organized into work packages and addressed to various partners across the world (work sharing).

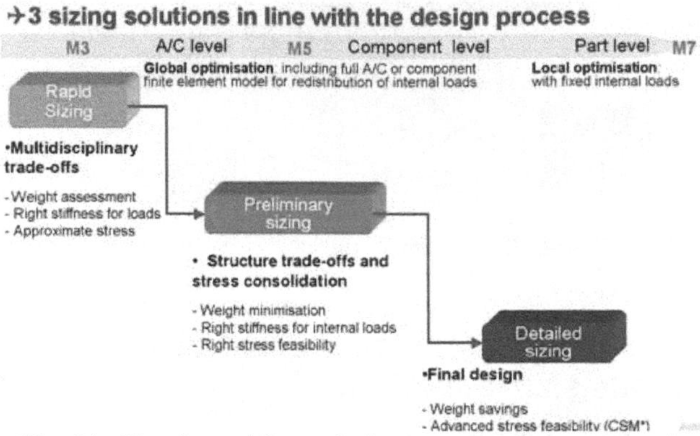

Fig. 8.b. The three sizing solutions proposed to support the three main design stages

For each stage and depending on the level of trade-offs and on the maturity of data, it is necessary to use a particular sizing process and particular sizing methods & tools (Fig. 8 a & b). For multidisciplinary trade-offs, when the focus is on weight assessment, we can accept an approximate stress estimate and use simplified equations. The number of open design variables can also be reduced through assumptions for secondary ones. For structure trade-offs and stress consolidation required before sharing the structure design work, it is necessary to consider agreed stress criteria and proper weight minimisation to give the right stiffness for external and internal loads. The final design focuses on latest weight savings and can used Computational Structure Mechanics for final design checks and updates. We will further describe each design stage detailing the way it was implemented today at AIRBUS. This description will be made from the detailed sizing addressing the most refined level of details up to the full aircraft level and upstream design stages.

4.Detailed sizing

Detailed sizing is the lower level of sizing. There are different approaches to address this detailed sizing. The problem to be solved is almost always the same and can be formulated as:

$$\begin{aligned} & Min \quad w(x) \\ & x \in \Re^n \\ & s.t. \begin{cases} RF_j(x, N_k) \geq 1 & \mathrm{j=1,n_c;k=1,n_{lc}} \\ d_l(x) \geq 0 & \mathrm{l=1,n_d} \end{cases} \end{aligned} \tag{1}$$

The loading is kept constant, there are only local design constraints and reserve factor constraints for stress feasibility (RF>1)

Note that internal loads are here to be considered as external loads because we are at part level. So this optimization, especially if the analysis is finite element based can include an internal load re-distribution (for the part). These different approaches depend on the way the part to be optimised is analysed and justified by stress people. Typically if we consider primary structures and especially external structures (covers) there are very particular design criteria like reparability and damage tolerance (especially for composite structures), which suppose to use analytical skill tools based on semi-empirical approaches. Other structures are less linked to such certification criteria and can be directly addressed via pure numerical approaches like refined finite element analysis. These major trends for the stress calculations orient to different approaches.

In the first case, sensitivities are often calculated via finite differences and it is practical to integrate the process inside an open optimization framework to perform the optimization. This is the approach used in the A380 weight saving campaign and pursued today on the A350XWB. This kind of approach is particularly in line with the works of stress people in the detailed design phase, because they often need to adapt the stress process and stress calculations and have to be very reactive in terms of sizing delivery. The possibility with BOSS Quattro for example to quickly assemble a calculation process, integrate and encapsulate inside an optimization process based on finite difference sensitivities is particularly suited to this care of reactivity. In the second case, the optimization process is more numerically based and requires advanced sensitivity analysis based on semi-analytical approaches. This is particularly the case when addressing buckling or post-buckling. For this kind of optimization various software can be used linked to the kind of optimization performed. For pure sizing optimization, the use of NASTRAN SOL200 is frequent based on detailed model dedicated to buckling analysis.

When topology or shape variables are considered [16-17] it is often more efficient to use ALTAIR Hyperworks suite for its pre-processing capabilities (Fig. 9), but the process is about the same: FE-based optimization.

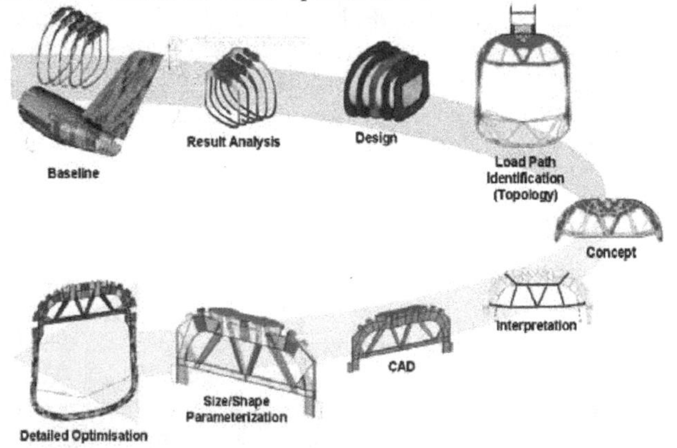

Fig. 9. Example of FE-based detail optimization when chained with topology optimization. A350XWB rear fuselage frames.

Today there is probably a lack of integration between both approaches and it would be welcome to have a joint optimization using numerical FE simulation with semi-analytical stress tools. Another lack is with respect to a wide application of optimization at all skill tool levels for all structural elements. A wide stress analysis framework has been recently developed by AIRBUS, this framework called ISAMI (Fig. 10) is capable to address stress analysis of an entire aircraft structure. This is the proper place where local optimization should be embedded for repetitive parts, which does not exclude finite element approaches.

5. Preliminary sizing

For the special M5 milestone a good preliminary sizing must be ready at full component level. For this reason we need to have a good control of internal loads while using the appropriate skill tools for stress criteria. Hence the full global optimization problem must be addressed:

$$\begin{aligned} &Min \sum_{i=1}^{n_s} W_i\,(y_i) \\ &x \in \Re^N \\ &s.t. \begin{cases} y_i = f_i\,(x_i) \in \Re^{n_i} \\ RF_j\,(x_i, N_k^i(y)) \geq 1 \quad j=1,n_c; k=1,n_{lc} \\ d_l\,(x) \geq 0 \quad l=1,n_d \\ g_m(y) \geq 0 \quad m=1,n_g \end{cases} \end{aligned} \tag{2}$$

Internal loads are updated and optimized for weight minimization. Global constraints (stiffness or design) can be considered. A full structure can be optimized.

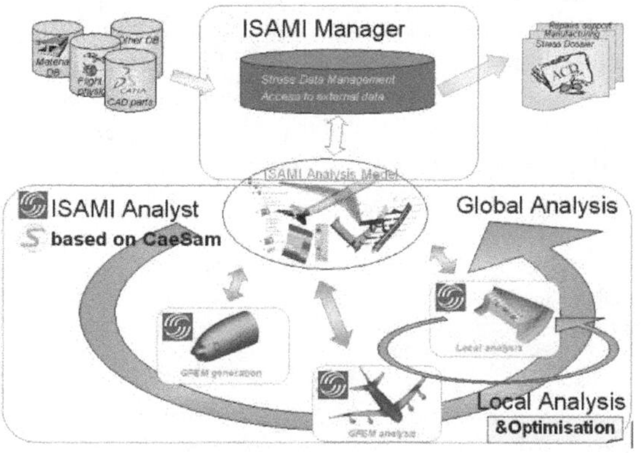

Fig. 10. ISAMI and optimization

This is the reason why AIRBUS has launched with A350 a new generation of optimization tools in order to do so. This kind of tool is integrating GFEM and skill tool analysis and makes a global/local optimization [18-22] link (Fig. 11). It was first developed for a composite wing then extended to all aircraft boxes, hence its name: COMBOX for COMposite BOXes. This tool has recently been extended to COMposite FUSElage with COMFUSE. The optimization process for COMBOX and COMFUSE is identical and is based on chain-ruling of sensitivities between global responses (internal loads) and local responses (reserve factors).

The pre-processing of an optimization process for covers was also automated. From groups of finite elements provided by the user, structural elements are built, then calculation points are assembled as groups of structural elements. Groups of structural elements are also built to define optimization regions with uniform sizing and reduce the optimization problem. To each structural element and calculation point can be attached every necessary stress information to manage the optimization and the stress analysis (materials, stringer profiles, sizing properties, calculation hypothesis).

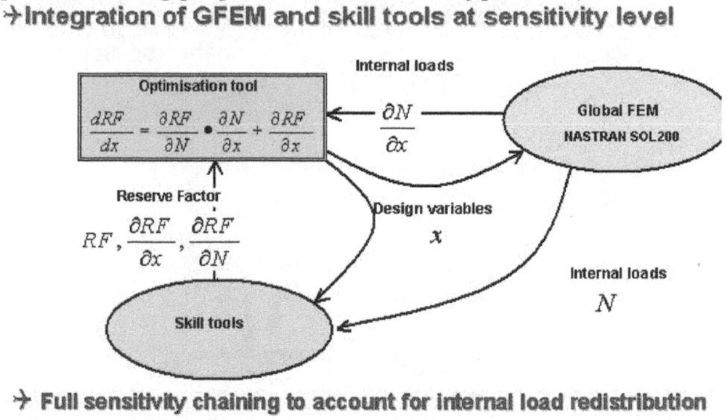

Fig. 11. Chain ruling of sensitivities inside COMBOX for a global-local optimization link

The pre and post-processing and the management of the stress model is addressed with a specific tool called CAESAM developed by the SAMTECH company, while the management of the full optimization process embedding NASTRAN SOL200 sensitivities and skill tools, is performed with BOSS Quattro. The optimization algorithm used is taken in the BOSS Quattro library (GCM: Globally Convergent Method). All the standard variables for composite materials are considered (Fig. 12). The total thickness and percentages for 0°/-45°/45°/90° orientations can be taken as design variables. The order of magnitude of thickness is large enough to consider a material homogenization and address the stacking sequence in a next step more manufacturing-oriented. All composite design criteria are addressed:

- buckling/post-buckling
- reparability
- damage tolerance

Buckling/post-buckling are classical criteria. They are calculated via a Rayleigh-Ritz approach, which is a precursor of the finite element method. There is an eigenvalue solver behind to estimate the global buckling of the cover elementary pattern (super-stringer). For this reason buckling analysis is the most computationally heavy part of the stress process. Reparability and damage tolerance are less usual. Reparability anticipates the possibility of small shocks on covers, which can be repaired via metallic bolted plates: reparability criteria are in fact special cases of bearing/by-pass criteria for assemblies. Damage tolerance criterion considers the residual strength of composite covers after an impact specified by certification authorities and occurrence probabilities linked to the location in the aircraft and to the loading.

At this point the computational times needed for Reserve Factor sensitivity analysis is to be stressed. Indeed if we consider that this sensitivity analysis is performed via finite differences and that it is to be done for each calculation point and for each load case, the computational times can be very heavy (Fig. 13). The extension of COMBOX, called COMFUSE to fuselage is today under validation. The intent to run it on full fuselage is strong but the computational time and resources needed is today a brake. The skill tool used inside is more computational heavy than for boxes because it has to address the curvature of fuselage panels. Moreover the complexity of a fuselage structure is higher: there are more bays than on a wing. For this reason the application to a full fuselage will probably require hundreds of processors (Fig. 14). A decomposition approach will probably be necessary before addressing such an integrated optimization.

Design variables
Skin angle thicknesses / stringer section parameters

%0, %45   %0, %45

Different Stringer Geometries

Design criteria

All composite design criteria are considered:
- stability: Rayleigh Ritz approach & Karman theory for post-buckling

- damage tolerance

- reparability: bearing, by-pass

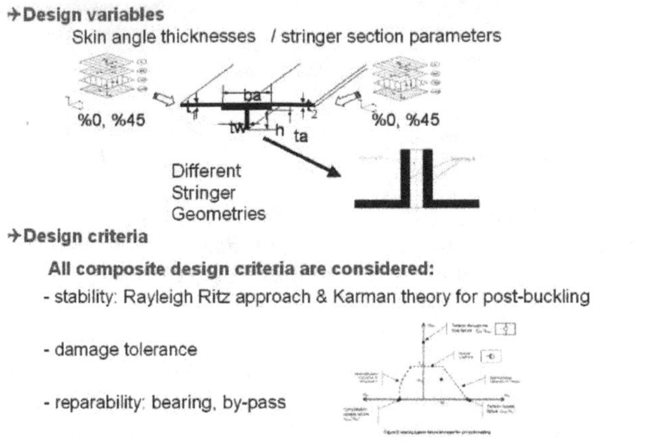

Fig. 12. Composite design & stress process inside COMBOX

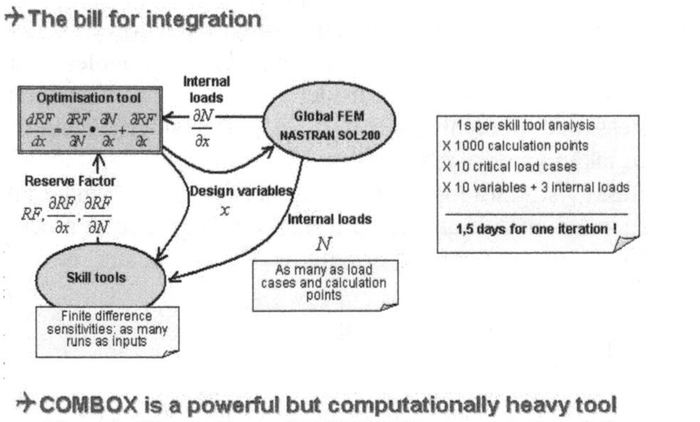

The bill for integration

$$\frac{\partial RF}{\partial x} = \frac{\partial RF}{\partial N} \cdot \frac{\partial N}{\partial x} + \frac{\partial RF}{\partial x}$$

Optimisation tool

Internal loads $\frac{\partial N}{\partial x}$

Global FEM NASTRAN SOL200

1 s per skill tool analysis
X 1000 calculation points
X 10 critical load cases
X 10 variables + 3 internal loads

1,5 days for one iteration !

Reserve Factor $RF, \frac{\partial RF}{\partial x}, \frac{\partial RF}{\partial N}$

Design variables x

Internal loads N

Skill tools

As many as load cases and calculation points

Finite difference sensitivities: as many runs as inputs

COMBOX is a powerful but computationally heavy tool
Fig. 13. Illustration of COMBOX computational times

→ Stress process comparable with boxes:
  - stability
  - damage tolerance
  - reparability

→ Fuselage specificities like hat stringer profile and large damage capability taken into account

→ First demonstration on centre fuselage

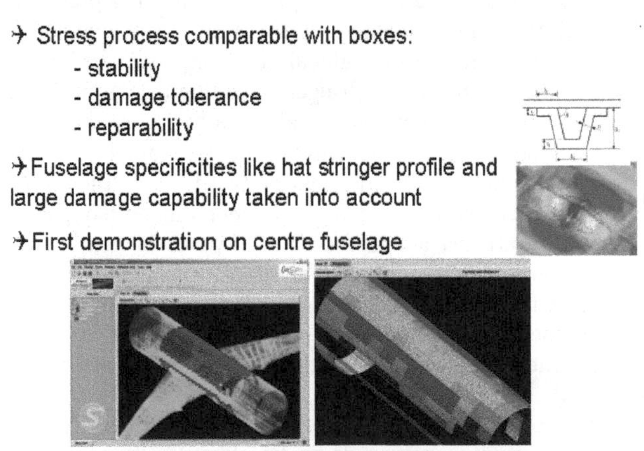

Fig. 14. Illustration of COMFUSE tool

Clearly this optimization stage appear as necessary to address the preliminary sizing at component level and be sure that the stiffness of the component and the stress are adequate for the next sizing stage where the sizing of covers will be refined or where the sizing will be extended to internal components. But this tool is clearly not what we can use today to address

full aircraft sizing in multidisciplinary trade-offs. COMBOX as developed for the A350 is not the convenient tool for a rapid sizing. Meanwhile the COMBOX process itself based on a global-local optimization is to be kept in order to master both stiffness and stress in early design stages and ensure a continuity with the preliminary sizing stage.

6. Rapid sizing

Rapid sizing was developed at AIRBUS with such a spirit: keeping but lightening the COMBOX optimization process. In a way the topic was to reduce the COMBOX optimization process in terms of design variables and in terms of stress analysis. In another way it was to be extended to be able to address the full airframe structure with potential novel concepts.

To reduce both the design variables and stress analysis a principle of "design curves" was put in place. This principle is approximated (Fig. 15) and will be discussed further but quite efficient for this level of sizing. It consists in prior intensive local optimizations in order to derivate the minimum sizing required for a given structural pattern (here a super-stringer). Here is the principle

The minimum skin thickness and stringer area as a function of internal loads as given by the approximation is then integrated as a lower bound in the global optimization process. In this way we have built a fast sizing criteria addressing only finite element properties and not detailed stringer profiles as in the previous schemes. So the process is reduced by itself. However this approach is sometimes a rough approximation, as shown in Fig. 16. This is particularly true when thickness is driven by another criterion. For this it is possible to build design curves function of thickness. Another approach to reduce a stress criteria is to use a profile library.

→ **Construction of approximate stress criteria**
  ➤ **A design curve service**

Restriction of design space

Filling space Design of Experiment

Local Optimisation

Assumptions
Typical loading (bounds)

Approximation with a surrogate model (polynomial, neural nets)

DESIGN CURVES

Stringer Area$_{min}$(N,pitch)
Skin Thickness$_{min}$(N,pitch)

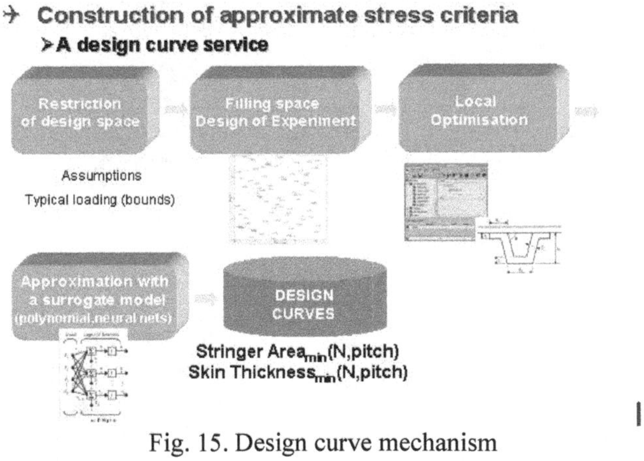

Fig. 15. Design curve mechanism

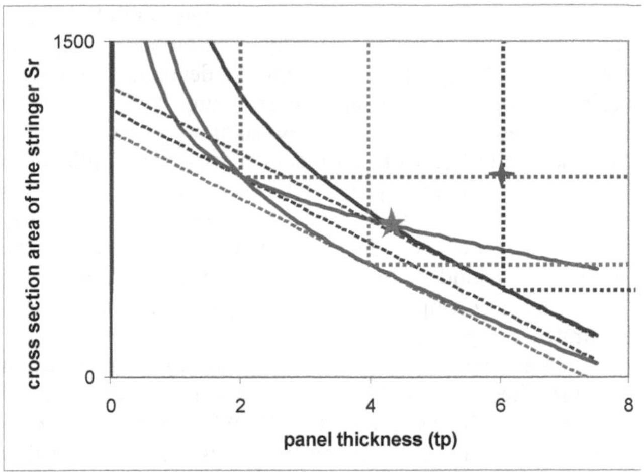

Fig. 16. Approximation of feasibility domain yielded by design curve

This rapid sizing solution was also improved in terms of scope. With COMBOX and COMFUSE today we can only address covers. The ambition with RHAPSODY (Fig. 17-18) is to address the full structure: both internal and external structure. For this reason, new Structural Elements have been added to extend the optimization process to the full structure. The full list of Structural Elements based on today structural design principles was addressed. Another important point is the flexibility in terms of stress criteria. For this we have introduced a new concept of generic skill tool, which is able to address any of the structural elements mentioned before.

First example applications have been run to demonstrate the capability to address:

- different components like wing and fuselage separately
- different components simultaneously
- external and internal structure

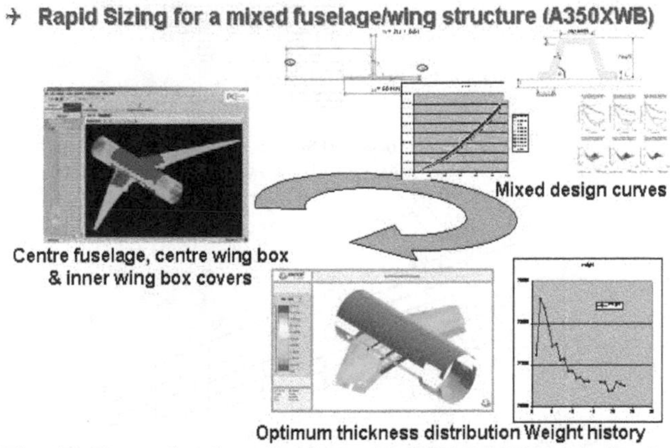

Fig. 17. Example of application with RHAPSODY (A simultaneous optimization of wing and fuselage structures was performed successfully with different design curves)

For commonality between different sizing levels inside the same interface we have kept the COMBOX framework for integration.

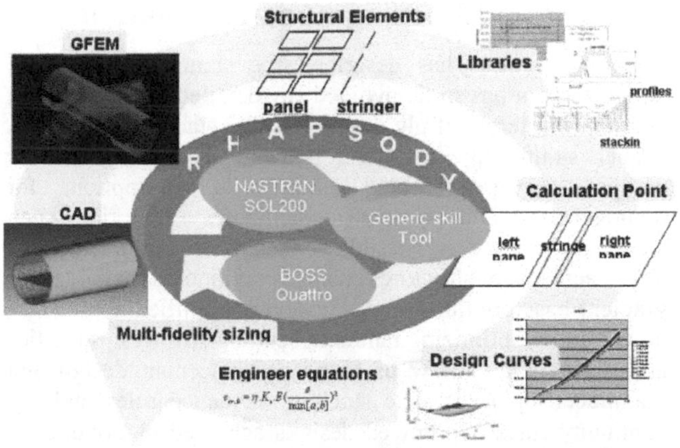

Fig. 18: RHAPSODY at a glance (With the same principles as COMBOX a lightened version was implemented focussed on Global Finite Element Model sizing)

The intent in a very next future at AIRBUS is to couple the rapid sizing capability with parameterised CAD digital mock-ups. In a further step topology optimization applied to architecture could be the source for the first CAD mock-up to have a support to architectural innovation in the numerical design process.

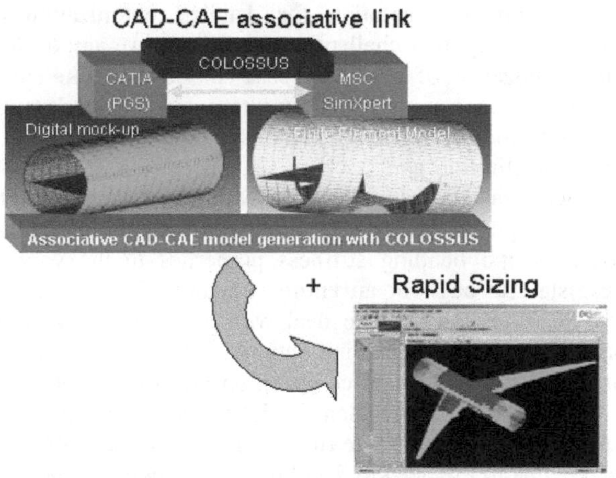

Fig. 19. A fully parameterized sizing tool

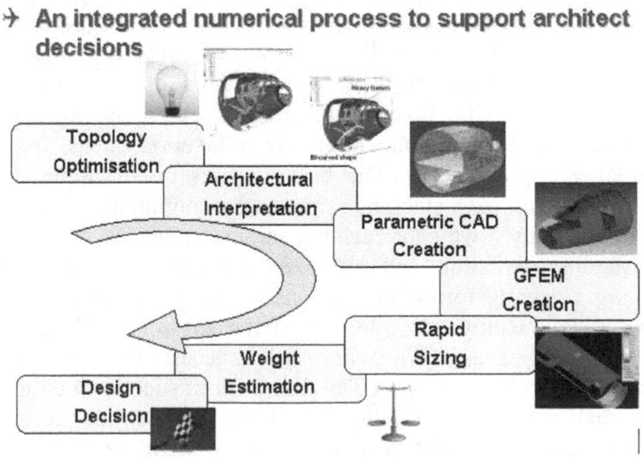

Fig. 20. From architecture creation to sizing and weight estimate

7. How to address composite materials

Previous sections has described the sizing of composite structures, but has so far avoided any detailed optimization of laminates in terms of ply definitions and stacking sequences. Rather simple thickness and percentage formulations for composites were adopted along with assumptions for homogeneous and symmetric laminates. Adopting such simplistic ideas it is possible to deal with optimization of large aerospace structures using continuous methods for gradient-based optimization. However simplified approaches do not allow optimizing laminate bending stiffness properties and also do not allow us to properly account design and manufacturing rules, like stacking sequence rules and ply continuity rules. Optimized designs achieved by continuous and homogeneous approaches are therefore often considered as structural designs only and is the starting point for further design efforts to ultimately detail laminates for manufacturing. During the further detailing of the composite solution additional weight is added when rationalizing the structural optimization solution and adding details such as for example allowed ramp rates and ply continuity / ply termination rules. Clearly it would be a beneficial both in terms of both weight saving and time saving if such requirements could be dealt with by the structural optimization process.

But developing a solution for detailed optimization of composites is quite a challenge. Not only do we aim to deal with optimization of large aerospace components, like entire wing or fuselage panels, but simultaneously methods must allow a detailed definition of composite laminates in terms of both ply-definition and stacking sequences (Fig. 21-22). To complicate matters ultimately we would like to be able to utilize composite design freedom and tailor both directional properties and bending stiffness properties to the varying stress state throughout an entire structure. The problem is large scale, as we need to deal with optimization of large composite structure including optimization of cross sectional dimensions and laminate composition and ply orientations. At the same time the problem is global due to ply continuity requirements and ramp rate rules. And finally the problem is discrete due to the need to detail discrete stacking sequences. In an attempt to develop a complete process this is currently an active area of research with multiple ideas being pursued. The following presents two such ideas, but without revealing full details as these are still active areas of research.

In a first approach to deal with detailed optimization of composites it is being attempted to develop a fully continuous formulation, by using relaxation ideas from topology optimization. The basic idea is quite simple. In order to optimize a stacking sequence by continuous methods of optimization we split each ply into sub-plies, each having different orientation, and optimize the thickness of sub-plies using a penalty formulation to ensure that in the end of the optimization only a single one of the sub-plies will exist. Such approaches have with some success been already investigated in Refs (7-8). The drawback of such formulation is that they introduce a very large number of design variables. To achieve a manageable problem size for full scale aerospace applications, ideas from Refs (8-9) are being combined with the use of stacking sequence tables and to introduce additional design freedom we introduce local ply orientations as design variables. Combining multiple ideas it is possible to develop a fully continuous composite optimization formulation applicable to detailed preliminary design of large-scale composite structures keeping design variable counts reasonably to a few 1000's.

To make such ideas work for practical aerospace applications the overall calculation process needs to be developed with extensive use of intermediate variables for sensitivity analysis in order to reduce calculation requirements. The basic ideas behind this continuous optimization formulation for composite sizing and stacking sequence optimization is illustrated in Fig. 21.

In a second approach to deal with the detailed optimization of composites a two-step approach is being developed. In the first step COMBOX and/or COMFUSE are being used to develop an optimized design in terms of cross section dimensions and laminate ply percentages. In the second step pre-sizing results generated by COMBOX and/or COMFUSE are first interpreted into global ply definitions using level set ideas and a stacking sequence optimization is then being performed by simply shuffling a fixed and limited set of global ply definitions. As a key for this approach to work the COMBOX/COMFUSE pre-sizing is being performed imposing smoothness constraints, thickness ramp rate constraint and laminate percentage evolution constraints in order to ensure that ply-definitions in the second level of optimization process are continuous and well connected. Fig. 22 below illustrates how a global optimization solution via level curves are interpreted into ply definitions for a global stacking sequence optimization. This two level approach to composite optimization is still subject to further developments allowing for optimization of ply-count rounding.

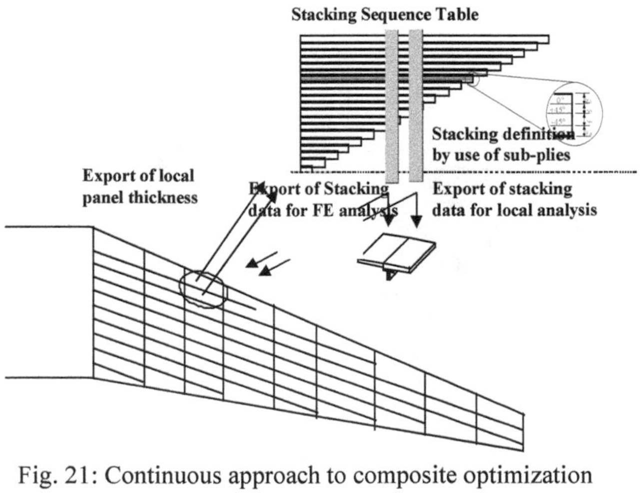

Fig. 21: Continuous approach to composite optimization

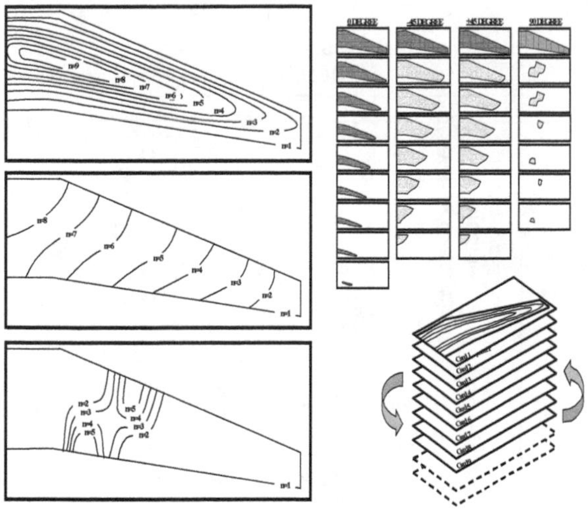

Fig. 22: Left) Thickness distributions for a 0, +/-45 and 90 degree plies with level curves showing where 1, 2, 3, 4 .. plies are required. Top right) Level curves are interpreted into global ply definitions. Bottom Right) A global stacking sequence optimization is performed shuffling global ply definition cards. This step is performed using a perturbation GA.

8.How to reach a full airframe sizing

8.1 Decomposition/coordination approaches (MAAXIMUS) [23]

Whatever the algorithm used, the resolution of a continuous optimization problem via a gradient-based approach is equivalent to the resolution of the Karush-Kuhn Tucker equations which is a $O((N+M)^3)$ operation, with N the number of variables and M the number of constraints.

In this point of view the unique way for very large size problems to face this, is to divide N and M, that is to say, to decompose the structure optimization problem in the optimization of smaller parts.

This is practically, what is done by stress people, when they size the structure structural element per structural element, except that they have no way to guarantee optimum load path or manufacturing constraints between structural elements. This is the reason why a more rigorous scheme is needed to guarantee the equivalence between the resolution of all local optimization problems and the resolution of the global one. For this we need an appropriate coordination scheme to ensure that the optimization stays correct even if decomposed.

To do so many approaches have been investigated in the literature, particularly in the area of Multidisciplinary Design Optimization. Multidisciplinary Design Optimization often uses such decomposition schemes based on disciplines (Fig. 23). One reason is that the disciplines usually have their own optimization processes, so the preferred approach is more to have a coordination of these single discipline optimizations than to solve the all-in-one problem. It is also more in adequacy with the organizational schemes of a company.

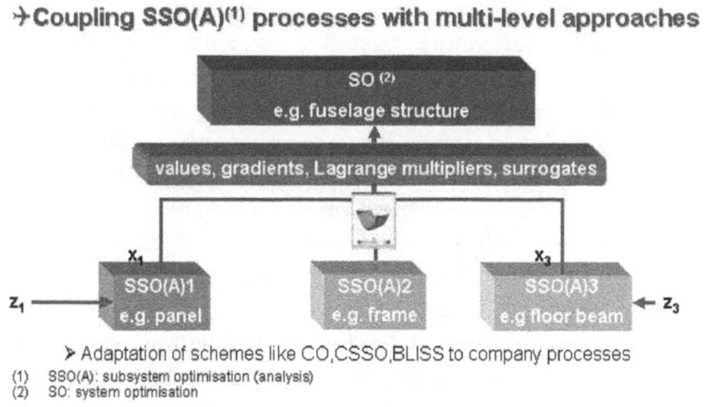

Fig. 23. Multi-level optimization applied to optimization of systems of systems for a large structure

Some preliminary successful tests were made in a previous PhD Thesis showing the possibility to put in place such schemes. A scheme called min-masse was put in place and has shown good results considering also heavily hyper-static configurations. Efforts are now made to consolidate this approach and extend to composite materials. One important point for such decomposition approaches is the robustness (Fig. 24). When using an all-in-one approach the difficulty is that the full structural responses and sensitivities are necessary to move to the next iteration. In a decomposition-coordination approach as the optimization is decomposed, it is easier to face an error in one of the sub-system optimizations.

Another approach is to keep the all-in-one scheme but to use as much as possible the topology of the problem (sparsity of the Jacobian matrices) in order to be able to parallelize. Approximate resolution of the Karush Kuhn-Tucker equations can also be used to limit the number of operations.

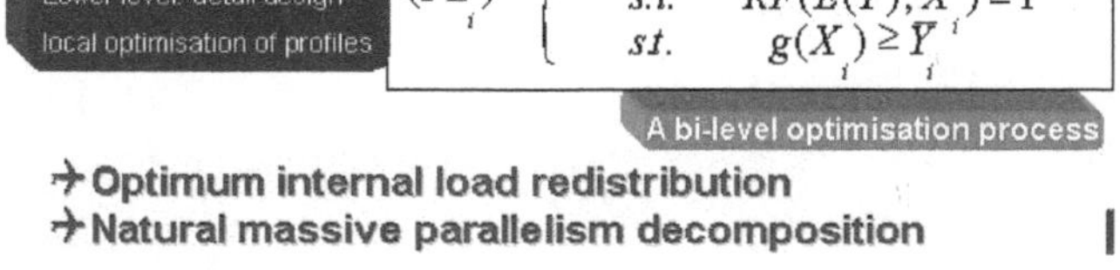

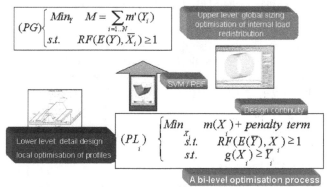

Fig. 24. A candidate solution for a multi-level decomposition scheme

8.2 Very large size optimization approaches with parallelism (MDOW)

A current research task within a larger program on Multi Disciplinary Optimization for Wings (MDOW) considers development of an optimization system for multi objective optimization of advanced composite structures. This task links the ambition to both perform very large-scale optimization and more detailed optimization of the composite structure. As part of this task a modular research framework is being developed allowing us to also experiment to with distributed computing at different levels of the optimization process and for example allow us to experiment with simple ideas for optimization decomposition.

The basic idea behind this development is to develop a number of highly efficient analysis and sensitivity analysis engines. Specific analysis modules are currently being developed for weight calculations, structural/aero-elastic analysis and for evaluation of manufacturing constraints. Each module will where required be developed to support distribute computing, in order to enable efficient management of overall runtime of the system. Fig. 25 illustrates the system set up in its most basic form, with each module drawing on a common database detailing for example the global design description and its link to an underlying FE model.

Each analysis module in Fig. 25 will perform a specific analysis and sensitivity analysis according to instructions provided in the structural optimization data base and export analysis results and sensitivity analysis results. Analysis and sensitivity analysis results are assembled to a global optimization problem description that is then passed to a gradient-based optimizer.

The modular architecture of this system, which is being created as a research framework opens up to multiple uses, with analysis/sensitivity analysis modules being used as building blocks to build/solve an overall larger optimization task. For example one could relatively easily rearrange the analysis modules such as to create an analysis process for optimization of multiple models via separate optimization streams. Also already now it would be perfectly feasible to call the structural analysis module twice in the same optimization cycle. This capability allows us to distribute computing from a very high level by managing analysis / sensitivity analysis for different load cases via individual computing streams. Also this capability allows us to call the structural analysis module with different FE models as input variables, allowing us directly to analyses and calculate sensitivities for an aircraft in different configurations.

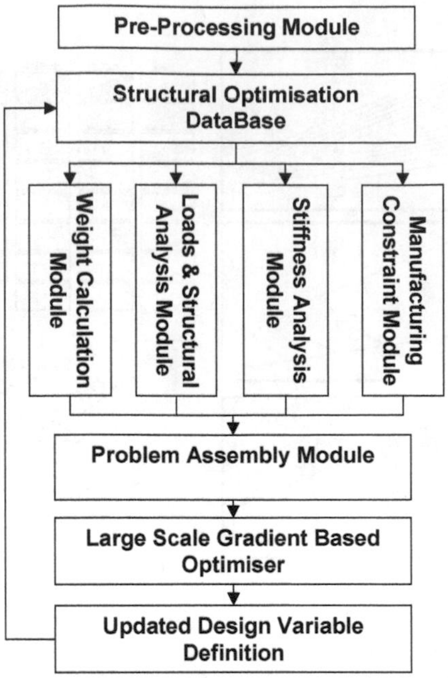

Fig. 25: Top level modular architecture and distributed computing model for optimization developments in MDOW.

A main objective of developments in MDOW is however to develop an optimization system for advanced composite optimization, allowing us to research optimization formulations such as in Section 7 before exporting ideas into industrial tools like COMBOX/COMFUSE.

9. How to ensure a smooth transition between sizing stages

A multi-stage sizing process for structures was presented but a few words were said in terms of continuity between the various stages. How to ensure continuity between rapid sizing and preliminary sizing, preliminary sizing and detailed sizing and last but not least detailed sizing and manufacturing. An effort was made to close the gap between rapid sizing and preliminary sizing defining specific methods for construction of rapid sizing criteria based on agreed skill tools. Two methods have been proposed for that: either a design curve construction based on approximation of reserve factors or a direct approximation of reserve factors based on the use of libraries which can be previously built. In both cases even if the agreed skill tools are used to build the simplified stress criteria there are some simplifications made for the feasible domain that are not really quantified. In the case of design curves we are not sure that the solution is really feasible at the end. In the case of profile library and reserve factor optimization, we are sure to have a feasible solution but it is not optimum because variable are linked. So an experience is to be gained in both cases to quantify the gap with preliminary sizing. This can only be done via practice. Considering the gap between the preliminary sizing and the detailed sizing, there is again an effort in terms of stress tools. It depends in fact the kind of stress tools that are used at detailed sizing level. More and more refined finite element analysis is not only used to check the structure behavior (virtual testing) but also to size this structure. In this

point of view, it is important to understand the gap there can be between an analytical stress tool and a refined finite element modeling approach. This is to be formalized in our design and stress processes. An important point to be addressed at detailed sizing level is also the gap there can be in terms of internal load redistribution and optimum load path. Indeed detailed sizing is often made with fixed internal loads and the internal loads are thereafter updated. But this can lead to surprises showing that the separate optimums do not lead to an overall optimum. For this the schemes proposed to enable very large size optimization via decomposition-coordination have to be considered to help to control the work-shared detailed sizing. Decomposition/coordination approach must converge to a softer scheme to control a work-shared design at AIRBUS. A final point to be considered and is very important especially for composite materials is to guarantee a continuity between detailed sizing and the next phase which is manufacturing.
For that smoothness constraints have to be integrated in the optimization problems and not only at the detailed sizing levels but at any level from the rapid sizing level. Indeed manufacturing constraints can have a very large impact on structure weight. A typical example of manufacturing constraints with a large impact is the ramp-rate constraints for CFRP panels. These ramp-rate constraints limit the composite ply drop-offs over the distance: these ply drop-offs cannot be too quick or you will create a bad through thickness behaviour of your panel (interlaminate stresses). This is why some bounds are to be respected for these interlaminate constraints. An example where this kind of constraints can be very important for weight is the example of a lower wing cover: there are large thicknesses around man holes and these large thicknesses can have an impact on the full cover thickness distribution due to the ramp-rates. To summarize there are three kinds of continuity to be ensured in the multi-stage sizing processes: continuity of stress feasibility: ensure that a design for one step is feasible or not too far from feasibility for the next steps continuity of manufacturing feasibility: ensuring manufacturing constraints are satisfied at each level. Continuity of weight optimality: guaranteeing that we do not go too far from the previously obtained optimum.

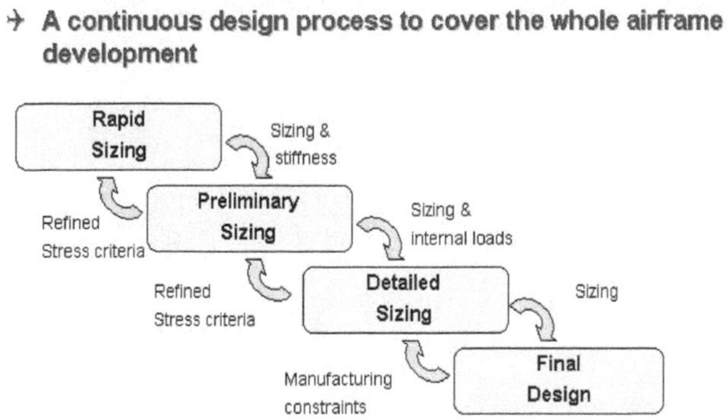

Fig. 26: Cascade of sizing stages and potential feed-backs

10. Conclusion and ways forward

A good set of tools for sizing has been established at AIRBUS but all challenges have not yet been addressed. A systematic process for optimization at structural element level is not yet in place and is really the starting point for a 100% integration of optimization in the design and stress process: this is the necessary building block that can be assembled to a full aircraft optimization process. This must include refined FE based analysis.

Niche applications for specific parts with 3D models will always be necessary, but there should be a way to connect stress tools. The Rapid Sizing optimization is to be pushed at full A/C level and used to prototype a full A/C preliminary sizing optimization that should go to a coordination of a work-shared detailed sizing process. Regarding composite optimization, an integration of optimization at ply level is still needed and should be put in place in the frame of MAAXIMUS project. For unconventional composite laminates, the topic is still quite open how to integrate in our processes.

References

1. L.A. Schmit, R.H. Mallet, *Structural synthesis and design parameter hierarchy*, Proceedings of the 3rd ASCE Conference on Electronic Computation, 269-300 (1963).
2. A. Remouchamps, Y. Radovcic, *BOSS Quattro: an open system for parametric design*, Structural & Multidisciplinary Optimization, **23**, 140-152 (2002).
3. B. Colson, M. Bruyneel, S. Grihon, C. Raick, A. Remouchamps, *Optimization methods for advanced design of aircraft panels: a comparison*, Optimization and Engineering.
4. L. Krog, *A distributed computing process for optimum pre-sizing of composite aircraft box structures*, Samtech 2007 User's Conference (2007).
5. AIRBUS France, *MTS004. Manuel de calcul statique pour matériaux métalliques* (2000).
6. A. Carpentier, S. Grihon, L. Michel, J.J. Barrau, *Buckling optimization of composite panels via lay up tables*, 3rd European Conference on Computational Mechanics Solids, Structures and Coupled Problems in Engineering, Lisbon (2006).
7. A. Carpentier, L. Michel, S. Grihon, J.J. Barrau, *Optimization Methodology of Composite Panels*. 4th European Conference on Computational Mechanics Solids, Structures and Coupled Problems in Engineering, Biarritz (2007).
8. A. Merval, M. Samuelidès, S. Grihon, *Multi-level Optimization with local mass minimization*, 2nd European Conference for Aerospace Sciences - EUCASS (2007).
9. A. Merval, M. Samuelidès, S. Grihon, *Lagrange kuhn-tucker coordination for multilevel sizing of aeronautical structures*, 49th conference on AIAA /ASME /ASCE /AHS /ASC Structures, Structural Dynamics & Material Conference (2008).
10. A. Remouchamps, S. Grihon, C. Raick, B. Colson, M. Bruyneel, *Numerical optimization. a design space odyssey.* International Workshop, 2007: Advancements in Design Optimization of Materials, Structures and mechanical Systems, Xi'an China (2007).
11. MSC.Software, *NASTRAN Linear Static Analysis User's Guide* (2000).
12. SAMTECH, *BOSS Quattro user's handbook – Release*

6.0-02 (2008).

13. C. Fleury, *Dual methods for convex separable problems in optimization of large structural systems*, Kluwer Academic Publishers, The Netherlands, 509-530 (1993)
14. M. Bruyneel, P. Duysinx, C. Fleury, *A family of MMA approximations for structural optimization*, Structural & Multidisciplinary Optimization, **24**, 263-276 (2002).
15. A. Merval, M. Samuelides, S. Grihon, *Application of Response Surface methodology to stiffened panel optimization*, 47th conference on AIAA/ASME/ASCE/AHS/ASC Structures, Structural Dynamics & Material Conference (2006)
16. J.H. Zhu, W.H. Zhang, D. Bassir, *Validity improvement of evolutionary topology optimization: procedure with element replaceable method*, Int. J. Simul & Multidisc Des Opt. **3**, 347-355 (2009)
17. M. Bruyneel, *A general and effective approach for the optimal design of fibres reinforced composite structures*, Composites Science & Technology, **66**, 1303-1314 (2006).
18. S. Guessasma, D. Bassir, *Comparing heuristic and deterministic approaches to optimise mechanical parameters of biopolymer composite materials*, Mechanics of Advanced Materials and Structures. **16**, 293-299 (2009).
19. S. Guessasma, D. Bassir, *Optimization of mechanical properties of virtual porous solids using a hybrid approach*, Acta Materiala, **58**, 716-725 (2010).
20. D. Bassir, S. Guessasma, Boubakar M.L, *Hybrid computational strategy based on ANN and GAPS: Application for identification of a non linear composite material*, Journal of Composite Structures, **88**, 262-270 (2009).
21. R.J. Balling, J. Sobieszczanski-Sobieski, *An Algorithm for solving the System-level Problem in Multi-Level Optimization*, NASA Contractor Report 195015 (1994).
22. L.A.Jr. Schmit, R.K. Ramanathan, *Multilevel Approach to Minimum Weight Design including Buckling Constraints*, AIAA Journal **16** (1978).
23. "MAAXIMUS" Integrated Project, 7th Framework, 2008-2013.

13

Control of the finite element discretization error during the convergence of structural shape optimization algorithms

Gabriel Bugeda[1,3,a], Juan José Ródenas[2], José Albelda[2], Eugenio Oñate[3]

[1] Escola Universitària d'Enginyeria Tècnica Industrial de Barcelona (EUETIB), Universitat Politècnica de Catalunya (UPC), C/ Comte d'Urgell, 187, 08036, Barcelona, Spain

[2] Centro de Investigación de Tecnología de Vehículos (CITV), Universidad Politécnica de Valencia (UPV), Camino de Vera s/n, 46022, Valencia, Spain

3 International Center for Numerical Methods in Engineering (CIMNE), Universitat Politècnica de Catalunya (UPC), C/ Gran Capitán s/n, Campus Nord UPC, Módulo C1, 08034, Barcelona, Spain

Abstract – This work analyzes the influence of the discretization error contained in the Finite Element (FE) analyses of each design configuration proposed by structural shape optimization algorithms over the behaviour of the algorithm. If the FE analyses are not accurate enough, the final solution will neither be optimal nor satisfy the constraints. The need for the use of adaptive FE analysis techniques in shape optimum design will be shown. The paper also proposes the use of the algorithm described in [1] in order to reduce the computational cost associated to the adaptive FE analysis of each geometrical configuration when evolutive optimization algorithms are used.

Key words: Structural shape optimization, Adaptive remeshing, Sensitivity analysis, Evolutionary algorithms

1 Introduction

From a mathematical point of view, the treatment of an optimization problem can be viewed as the minimization of a function $f(\mathbf{x})$ depending on a set of variables $\mathbf{x}$ and subjected to some constraints. The general form of such a problem is:

$$\begin{array}{lll} \text{minimize}: & f(\mathbf{x}); \mathbf{x} = \{x_i\} & ; i = 1, \dots, n \\ \text{with}: & \mathbf{g}(\mathbf{x}) = \{g_j(\mathbf{x})\} & ; j = 1, \dots, m \\ \text{verifying}: & g_j(\mathbf{x}) \le 0 & ; j = 1, \dots, m \\ & a_i \le x_i \le b_i & ; i = 1, \dots, n \end{array} \qquad (1)$$

where f is the objective function (OF), x_i are the design variables and g_j are inequality constraints which, for structural problems, are normally expressed in terms of stresses and/or displacements. The values a_i and b_i define lateral constraints. Each individual is characterized by a set of values of $\mathbf{x}$ that correspond to a specific structural design. The definition of each design in terms of the values of $\mathbf{x}$ is called the parameterization of the optimization problem. The resolution of the optimum design problem consists of finding the values of $\mathbf{x}$ defining the best design.

The algorithms used to solve optimization problems are generally iterative. Whichever the algorithm used, it would be necessary to evaluate the values f and $\mathbf{g}$ for each of the different designs during the iterative optimization process. In this work we have considered structural shape optimization. The values for f and $\mathbf{g}$ in this kind of problems are usually obtained by the use of the finite element method (FEM). Hence, one should create a specific mesh for each of the different designs to be considered and then use the FEM to obtain the structural response of each design and, if necessary, the corresponding sensitivities with respect to the design variables. Two main aspects relative to the evaluation of f and $\mathbf{g}$ by means of the FEM, which have a great importance over the global behavior of the optimization process, must be taken into account: the computational effort required for the numerical evaluation of each individual (geometrical configuration) and the accuracy of the FEM results.

The importance of the computational effort required for the evaluation of each geometrical configuration is evident. In optimization problems, like those under consideration, most of the computational cost is devoted to the analysis of individuals in order to obtain the values of the OF and the degree of satisfaction of the constraints.

On the other hand, and related to the accuracy of the results, we have to be aware that this numerical analysis techniques only provide approximate values for the data required by the optimization algorithm (OF and constraints). If these values are not accurate enough, an excessive amount of noise can be introduced in the optimization process. This could decrease the rate of convergence of the optimization process to the optimal solution, produce the convergence of the process to a non-optimal solution or, simply, avoid convergence. In the context of the FEM, the so called *h*-adaptive techniques, the *p*-adaptive techniques and the *hp*-adaptive techniques can be used to obtain solutions with the prescribed accuracy level. However, the use of these techniques implies a big computational cost that reduces the computational efficiency of the optimization process.

This paper shows that the correct behavior of the optimization process is only obtained if a minimum quality of the results of the analysis of each design, used to drive the optimization process, is ensured. To do this we will show the effect of the prescribed maximum error in energy norm over the final results obtained by means of a gradient-based deterministic algorithm and those obtained with an evolutionary algorithm.

[a] Corresponding author: bugeda@cimne.upc.edu

As previously commented, adaptive FEM techniques can be used to obtain solutions with a prescribed accuracy level. However, in the traditional adaptive techniques this implies the successive analysis of numerical models with increasing accuracy, automatically adapted to the characteristics of the solution of the problem. The computational cost related to the use of these traditional adaptive analysis techniques can be critical when evolutionary algorithms are used. To solve this problem, in this paper we propose the use of the *h*-adaptive analysis technique for the individuals of each generation described in [1], that avoids the full *h*-adaptive remeshing loop for the vast majority of them. We also propose to increase the required level of accuracy in the FE analyses during the evolution of the optimization process in order to decrease the computational cost at the early stages of the process while ensuring the quality of the final results of the optimization.

2 Case study and motivation. Pipe cross section

Here we present the results of the solution of an optimization problem, with a known analytical solution, using different levels of the controlled discretization error, as a motivation for the developments presented in this paper. Both, evolutionary and deterministic optimization algorithms have been considered. The part to be optimized corresponds to the cross-section of a pipe subjected to an internal pressure. Two perpendicular planes of symmetry have been considered; therefore, only one quarter of the section has been modeled, as shown in Figure 1. The shape is defined by a total of 8 points, 5 of these points describe a circular internal shape and 3 describe the external boundary of the pipe. The optimization problem consists of finding the shape for the external boundary keeping the internal one fixed and minimizing the total area. The 4 design variables V_i, $i = 1...4$, shown in Figure 1 correspond with the coordinates of the points that define the external boundary.

The maximum von-Mises stresses along the boundary of the model have been restricted to $2{,}0\text{x}10^6$.

The area of the analytical solution for this optimization problem (1/4 of cross section) is $A_{\text{opt}} = 69{,}725903$. This corresponds to an external radius $R_o = 10{,}666666$.

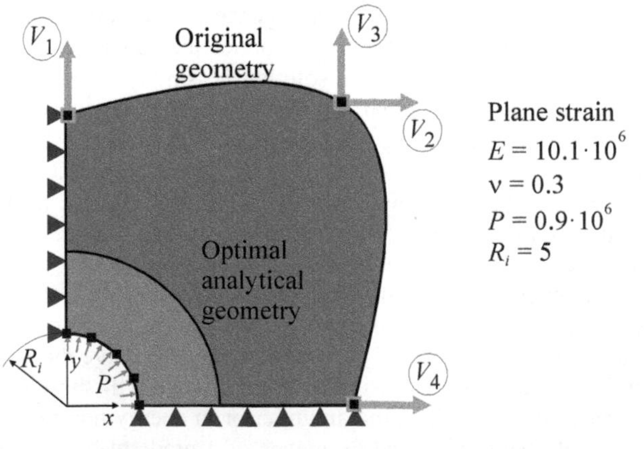

Fig. 1. Pipe cross section. Analysis data, original model, optimal analytical solution and design variables

2.1 Evolutive algorithm

For these numerical analyses we have used the *Differential Evolution* (DE) algorithm. DE is an evolutionary algorithm that has shown a robust performance yielding good results, even when applied to very different types of problems. DE was developed by Storn and Price in 1995 (see [2]). Its key idea is the differential operator, which serves the same purpose as the crossover parameter in a standard genetic algorithm, namely to exchange information between parents when creating offspring. We have used the DE1 classical version of the Differential Evolution proposed by Storn and Price.

The initial values of the design variables and their allowed data range and constraints for the Pipe cross section problem are shown in Table I.

Table 1. Pipe cross section. Values of design variables

Design variable	Initial value	Range	Constraints
V_1	20	[5.2 – 50.0]	
V_2	19	[4.0 – 50.0]	
V_3	19	[4.0 – 50.0]	$V_3 < V_1 - 0.5$
V_4	20	[5.2 – 50.0]	$V_4 < V_2 + 0.5$

Observe that we have used constraint equations between the values of the design variables in order to minimize the production of geometrically unfeasible individuals.

2.2 Gradient-based algorithm

The deterministic optimization algorithm considered in this work defines the new values of the design variables for a new design using the results of the numerical analyses associated to the behavior of the existing design, and their sensitivity analysis. The methodology used in this paper corresponds to the algorithm developed by Navarrina [3]. Once the *k*-th design has been analyzed, the values for the design variables for the next design are defined as:

$$\mathbf{x}_{k+1} = \mathbf{x}_k + \theta_k \mathbf{s}_k \tag{2}$$

where $\mathbf{x}_k$ is the vector containing the values of the design variables for the *k*-th geometry, $\mathbf{x}_{k+1}$ is the vector corresponding to the next geometry, $\mathbf{s}_k$ is a unit vector defining the direction of change in the space of the design variables and θ_k is a scaling factor in this direction.

The algorithm computes the direction of change $\mathbf{s}_k$ by using a SIMPLEX method with information coming from an exact first order sensitivity analysis of the OF and the constraints. Next, the scaling factor θ_k is computed by performing a line search minimization using second order directional sensitivity analysis.

2.3 H-Adaptive Finite Element Analysis

We have used an *h*-adaptive finite element analysis code to obtain the values of the objective function and the degree of satisfaction of the constraints for each of the different geometrical configurations proposed by the optimization algorithms. The use of the *h*-adaptive strategy ensures the quality of the analysis providing FE solutions with a relative estimated discretization error in energy norm γ lower than that specified by the analyst. The program uses the Zienkiewicz-Zhu error estimator in energy norm [4] to guide the h-adaptive analysis. Hence, the following expression is used to evaluate the error estimation in energy norm for each element, η_e:

$$\eta_e^2 = \int_{\Omega_e} \left(\boldsymbol{\sigma}^* - \boldsymbol{\sigma}_h\right)^T \mathbf{D}^{-1} \left(\boldsymbol{\sigma}^* - \boldsymbol{\sigma}_h\right) d\Omega \qquad (3)$$

where $\boldsymbol{\sigma}_h$ is the stress field directly obtained from the FE analysis, $\boldsymbol{\sigma}^*$ is a recovered stress field, $\mathbf{D}$ relates strains with stresses as $\boldsymbol{\sigma} = \mathbf{D}\boldsymbol{\varepsilon}$ and Ω_e is the domain of element e.

In the numerical examples, triangular elements have been used due to their big flexibility when generating adapted unstructured meshes. Quadratic (6 noded) instead of linear (3 noded) triangular elements have been used in order to improve accuracy. We have used the global least squares smoothing technique [4] to obtain the recovered stress field $\boldsymbol{\sigma}^*$ required by the Zienkiewicz-Zhu error estimator. Other recovery techniques like the Superconvergent Patch Recovery technique (SPR) by Zienkiewicz and Zhu[5] or any other improvement of this recovery technique could also be used [6-8].

Cubic B-splines [9] have been used to define each of the geometrical configurations in terms of the coordinates of some definition points (parameterization).

In order to see the effect of the amount of discretization error over the behavior of the optimization algorithms (both evolutionary and deterministic) 6 different situations corresponding to different prescribed error levels have been studied. The maximum error values prescribed for the first 5 analyses were 1%, 2.5%, 5%, 10% and 20%. In the 6th case a γ<100% tolerance has been specified, which in practical terms implies that the accuracy of the solution is not controlled and the number of elements is only depending on geometrical criteria (see examples in Figure 2).

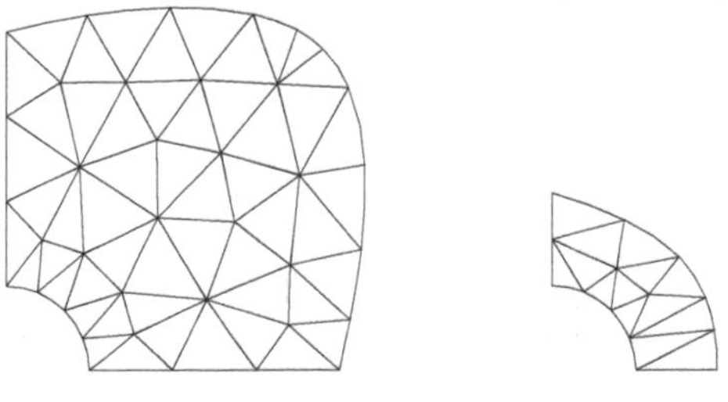

Fig. 2. Examples of initial meshes

2.4 Solution using the evolutionary algorithm. Influence of the discretization error

Figure 3 shows the effect of the prescribed maximum estimated relative error in energy norm γ over the evolution of the area of the pipe cross section. It can be observed that, at least for this problem, the global aspect of the results for all the situations is quite similar.

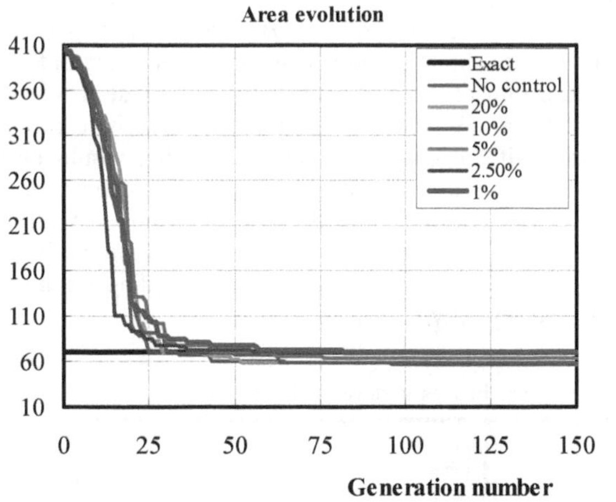

Fig. 3. Influence of γ over the evolution of the objective function

However, as shown in Figure 4, the effect of γ over the evolution of the optimization process is especially significant if we compare the final results obtained with each different degree of the discretization error. Figure 4 shows, in relative terms, the evolution of the difference between the area provided by the best individual obtained up to each generation and the area of the optimal analytical solution. The graph shows that the final solution associated to each analysis is significantly different to the analytical solution for the cases with higher values of the prescribed error γ, but approaches to the exact solution for the lower values of γ.

Figure 5 represents the effect of γ over the final solution provided by the optimization algorithm. It can be clearly observed that for high values of γ the algorithm converges to shapes that are quite different to the optimal analytical solution. However, the final solution provided by the optimization process approaches to the analytical solution for decreasing values of γ. Observe that the difference between the exact solution and that obtained for γ = 1% is only 0.46%. In any case, one should take into account that the optimal analytical external boundary (circular shape) cannot be exactly obtained because the B-splines used to define de boundary are unable to exactly reproduce an exact circular shape.

The finite element method usually underestimates the maximum stress value. The level of this underestimation of stresses increases with the size of the elements used in the analysis. In order to quantify the quality of the solutions obtained with the different degrees of discretization error, we have performed a full h-adaptive analysis requiring a final estimated error in energy norm γ < 0.3% over each of the geometries displayed in Figure 5. This has produced much more accurate approximations of the stress distributions and, therefore, a much more accurate evaluation of the degree of satisfaction of the stress constraints. Figure 6 displays the difference between the maximum von Mises stresses finally obtained for each design and the maximum allowed value for this magnitude. It is clearly shown that the obtained optimal solutions underestimate the maximum value of the von Mises stress. Hence, the accurate evaluation of these designs reveals that they would severely exceed this magnitude. The same figure also shows the difference between the final area obtained for each value of γ and the area of the analytical solution. It can be clearly observed that both graphs are closely related. Basically, due to the underestimation of the maximum von Mises stress the optimization algorithm reduces the area until this value reaches the specified limit. Hence, the optimization algorithm provides solutions with a lower area than those that would be obtained with an accurate evaluation of the maximum von Mises stress. Observe that the solution obtained with $\gamma \leq 1\%$ is almost identical to the analytical solution, with a difference in areas of only +0.46% and exceeding the allowable stresses by only 0.68%.

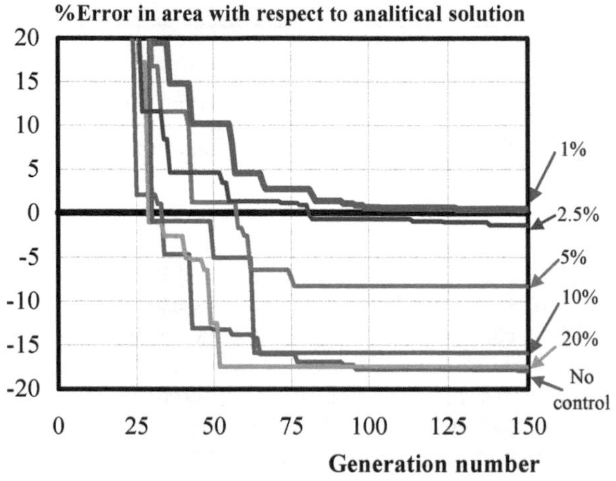

Fig. 4. Influence of γ over the evolution of the error in the objective function with respect to the analytical solution

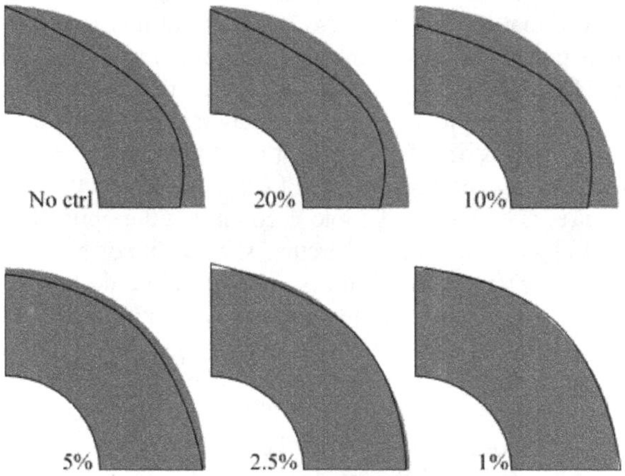

Fig. 5. Influence of γ over the optimal solution found (black contour) and comparison with optimal analytical solution (shaded area)

2.5 Solution using the gradient-based deterministic algorithm. Influence of the discretization error

Figure 7 shows a comparison between the convergence curves obtained with the different levels of prescribed discretization error for the case of the gradient-based deterministic algorithm. First, it can be seen that in all cases the convergence is much faster than with the evolutionary algorithm. Nevertheless, it can also been seen that after an initial quick drop of the OF, its evolution is different depending on the amount of the allowed discretization error.

During the first 10 iterations the convergence is not depending on the level of discretization error. This is because in these initial iterations the obtained designs are far away from the optimal one and the corresponding stress values are still far away from the restricted ones. Therefore, the constraints are not yet active and thus the process is still independent of the degree of accuracy in the evaluation of the constraints.

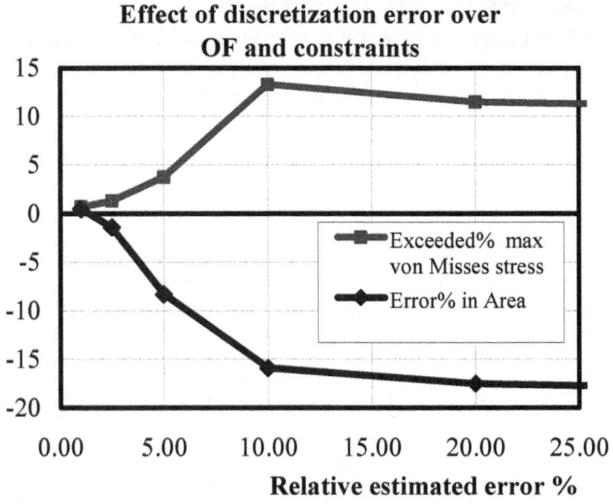

Fig. 6. Influence of γ over the accuracy of the objective function and the degree of satisfaction of stress constraint equations

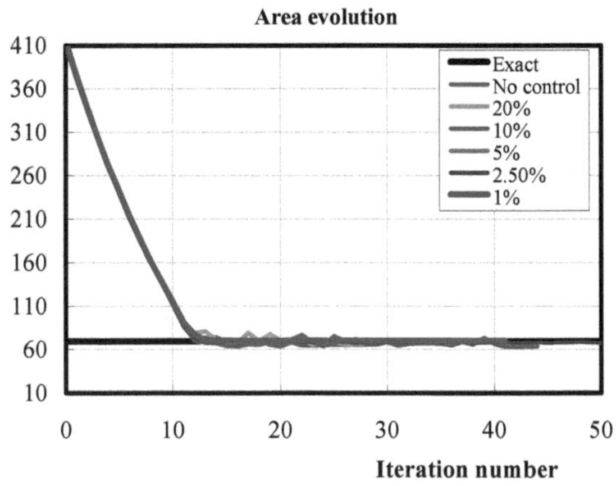

Fig. 7. Deterministic algorithm. Influence of γ over the evolution of the objective function

Fig. 8 shows the detailed evolution of the OF after the initial iterations. In this case, the evolution of the relative differences between the cross sectional area obtained at each iteration and the optimal analytical one is represented. It can be seen how a quick convergence to a practically exact value is obtained when γ is fixed to 1%. On the other hand, when higher values of γ are employed, the evolution of the OF shows big oscillations and the process stops with final designs that, in fact, are not feasible because a more accurate analysis also shows too high values of the von Mises stress. The main reason of all this behavior is the lack of reliability of the obtained values for the von Mises stress that drive all the optimization process. These values change every time the mesh is modified, introducing a lot of "noise" in the convergence of the process and in the lack of reliability of the final design. This noise would not appear if a single mesh, conveniently adapted to each geometry, had been used. In this case, this noise wouldn't be present and wouldn't produce oscillations, but the final optimum design wouldn't be reliable because the degree of reliability of the computed von Mises stress would be very low.

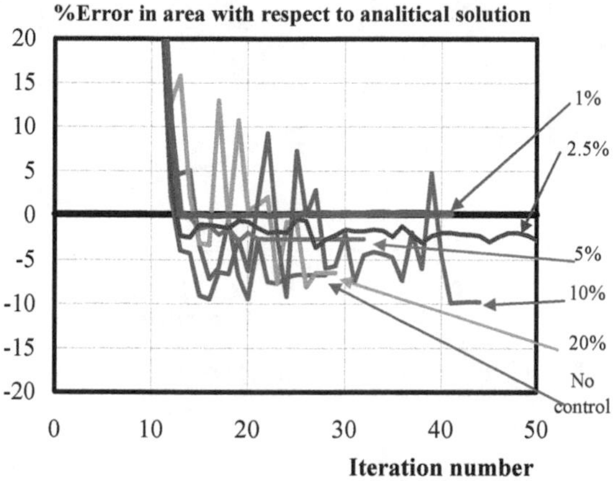

Fig. 8. Deterministic algorithm. Influence of γ over the evolution of the difference between the obtained objective function and the analytical solution

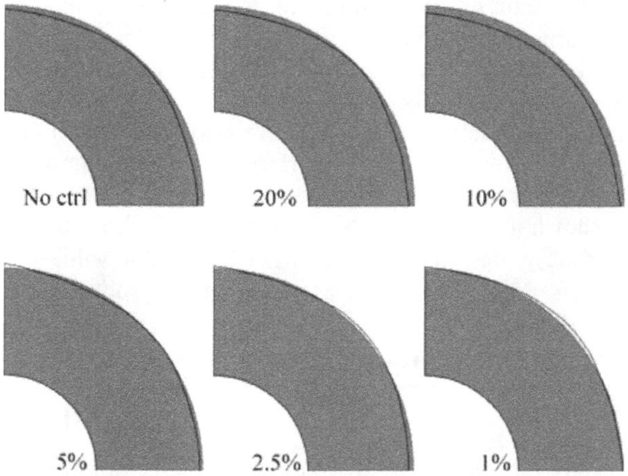

Fig. 9. Deterministic algorithm. Influence of γ over the optimal solution found (black contour) and comparison with optimal analytical solution (shaded area).

As in the case of the evolutionary algorithm, and in order to quantify the quality of the solutions obtained with the different degrees of discretization error, a full *h*-adaptive analysis requiring a final estimated error in energy norm $\gamma < 0.3\%$ was performed over each of the geometries displayed in Fig. 9. These analyses produced much more accurate approximations of the stress distributions and, thus, much more accurate evaluation of the degree of satisfaction of the stress constraints. Fig.10 displays the difference between the maximum von Mises stresses finally obtained for each design and the maximum allowed value for this magnitude. The results are similar to those previously shown for the evolutionary algorithm: the optimal solutions provided by the optimization process underestimate the maximum value of the von Mises stress that would be obtained with more accurate FE models. Solutions with a lower area than those that would be obtained with an accurate evaluation of the maximum von Mises stress are, thus, obtained. However, the results obtained in this case are more accurate than those obtained with the evolutionary algorithm. The solution obtained with $\gamma \leq 1\%$ is again quite close to the analytical solution, with a difference in areas of only +0.061% and exceeding the allowable stresses by only 0.33%.

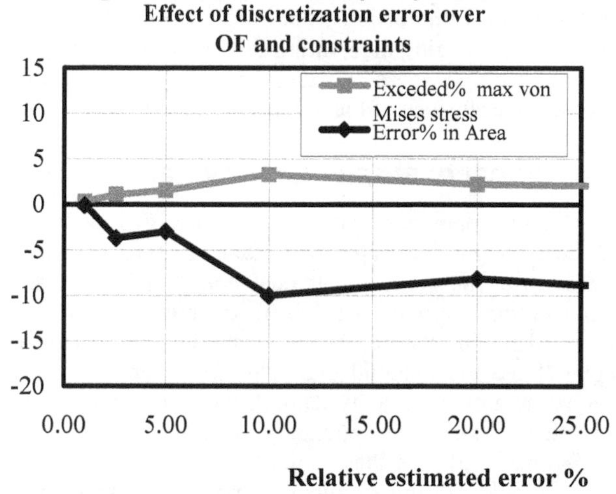

Fig. 10. Deterministic algorithm. Influence of γ over the accuracy of the objective function and the degree of satisfaction of stress constraint equations.

3 Error-control strategies for evolutionary algorithms

The numerical results previously exposed have clearly shown the importance of the accuracy of the FE analysis on the final results of both types of optimization algorithms. Mesh refinement in FE analyses is directly associated to error control techniques. In fact, to minimize the total amount of calculations one should preferably use some kind of adaptive analysis technique such us the automatic *h*-adaptive mesh refinement technique previously mentioned as they tend to produce the solution with the prescribed accuracy at the lowest computational cost. The use of such techniques is especially critical when evolutionary algorithms are used due to the large amount of different geometrical configurations to be analyzed. In this case, and in order to reduce the computational cost associated to the creation of an adapted mesh for each of the individuals to be analyzed, we propose the use of the *h*-adaptive strategy for the analysis of generations of individuals described in [1]. This technique has been used in the numerical example presented in the following section. The origin of this technique, and its application to deterministic optimization algorithms, can be seen in references [10-12]. The work in [1] presents a strategy that allows generating an adapted mesh for each individual of a generation without the necessity of performing a full adaptive remeshing procedure for each of them. It makes use of sensitivity analysis of all magnitudes related with adaptive remeshing (location of nodes, error estimation, etc.) in a reference geometry with respect to the design variables. This sensitivity analysis is then used to project the results from the reference geometry to all other geometrical configurations. This information allows generating an appropriate *h*-adapted mesh for each geometry, thus avoiding the full *h*-adaptive loop over each individual.

However, the results previously presented have also shown that the accuracy of the analyses, prescribed by γ, does not significantly modify the early stages of the optimization process. This suggests the use of a very simple error control technique to reduce the total amount of calculations involved in the optimization process. The error control technique consists of using high values of γ at the early stages of the optimization process and to successively decrease this value with the advance of the optimization process.

4 Numerical example: Gravity dam

The gravity dam represented in Figure 9 was analyzed. Both dead weight and water hydrostatic pressure were considered in the analysis. The model does not include any sharp reentrant corners. The shape optimization problem consists of finding the best shape for the internal boundary, keeping fixed the external one. This minimizes the cross sectional area of the gravity dam. A total of 7 points were used to define the internal boundary. As indicated in Fig. 10, the coordinates of 5 of these points were considered as the design variables for this problem. The maximum von-Mises stresses along the boundary of the model have been restricted to $2{,}75 \cdot 10^6$ Pa.

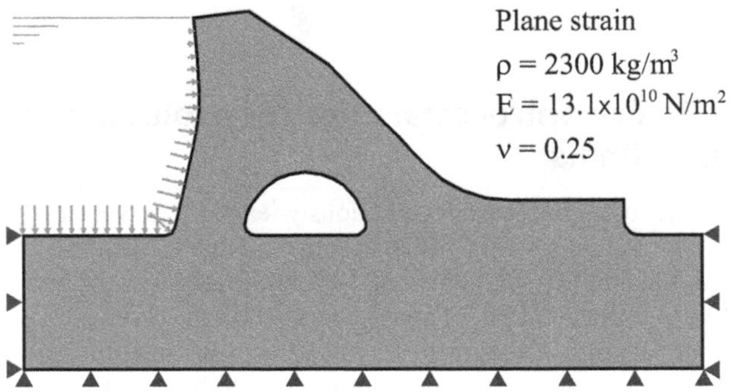

Fig. 9. Gravity dam. Analysis model

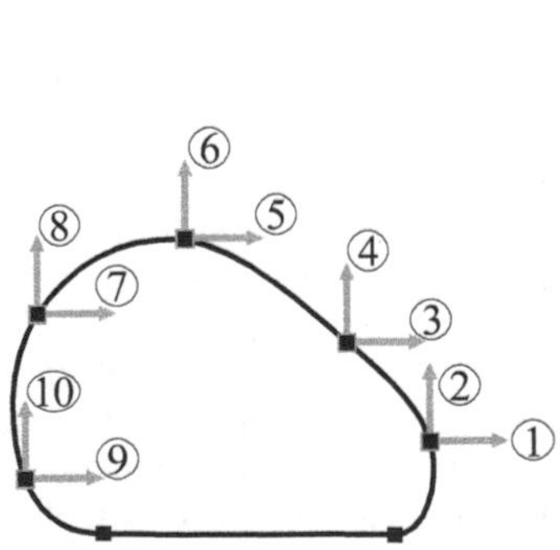

Fig. 10. Gravity dam. Design variables

30 individuals per generation were used in the analysis. The analysis ran for a total of 100 generations. A maximum estimated relative error in energy norm γ = 2.5% was required for the analysis of the final solution. We specified a geometrical variation of the estimated error in energy norm from γ = 20% in the first generation to γ = 2.5% in the last one (see Fig. 11) to reduce the computational cost associated to the early stages of the optimization process.

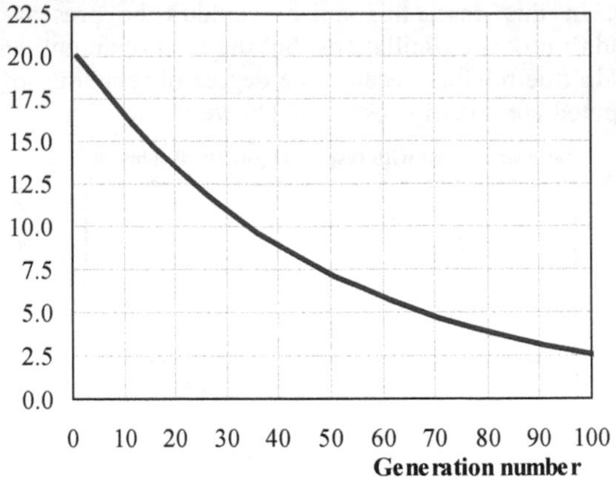

Fig. 11. Evolution of the prescribed value of γ.

In this test case, the use of the error projection technique previously described [1] provided the appropriate mesh for the FE analysis of 95% of the individuals considered in the optimization process, further reducing the computational cost of the optimization.

Fig. 12 shows the evolution of the objective function (area) during the optimization process. Fig. 13 clearly shows the difference between the original and the optimized designs. After the analysis of 100 generations, a previous test, where the maximum estimated relative error in energy norm was prescribed as γ = 3% for the whole optimization process, provided an area whose difference with respect to the final result shown in Fig. 12 is only 0.7%. As expected, the use of the previously described strategy where a variable value γ is prescribed, does not put the accuracy of the optimization process at risk.

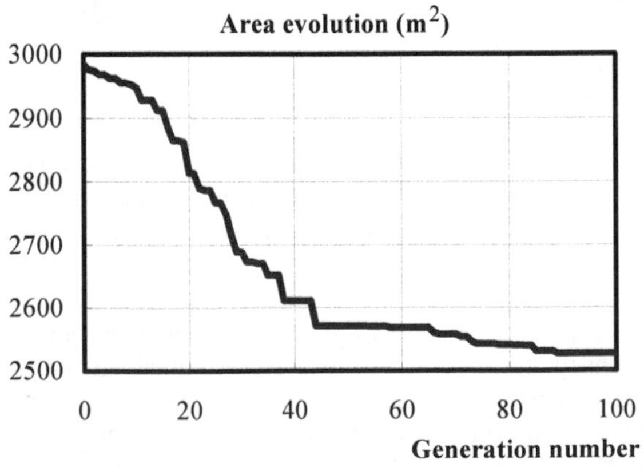

Fig. 12. Gravity dam. Area evolution

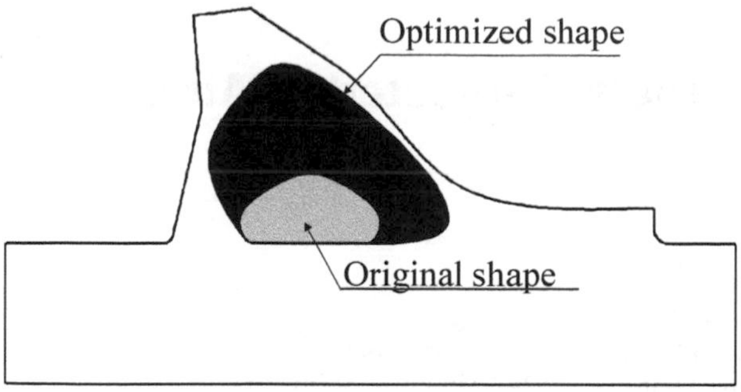

Fig. 13. Gravity dam. Optimized geometry *versus* original geometry

5 Conclusions

This paper has shown that a minimum quality of the results used to drive structural shape optimization processes must be ensured; otherwise the process will not converge to the optimal solution, providing solutions that could notably violate the satisfaction of the constraint equations. Therefore, the optimization processes that make use of the finite element method to evaluate the objective function and the degree of satisfaction of constraints require for the use of FE model refinement analysis techniques to ensure the quality of the results.

Due to the high number of individuals to be analyzed, the computational cost associated to the use of adaptive analysis techniques can be critical when evolutionary algorithms are considered. For this kind of optimization algorithms we propose the use of the technique for the *h*-adaptive analysis of generations of individuals presented in [1]. This technique uses the projection of the estimated discretization error in energy norm to obtain the meshes required for the analysis of the individuals considered in each generation. The results presented show the efficiency of this technique which in the vast majority of cases avoids the full adaptive remeshing process.

Preliminary results have shown that the maximum discretization error level imposed over the FE analyses at the beginning of the optimization has no significant effect over the final results of the optimization process. Hence, we have proposed the use of a technique where the maximum discretization error level decreases with the progress of the optimization process. This technique considerably reduces the computational cost associated to the analysis of the first generations of individuals without affecting the accuracy of the results corresponding to the last steps of the optimization process.

Acknowledgement

The authors have been sponsored by the Spanish Ministerio de Ciencia e Innovación through the projects DPI2008-05250 (first author) and DPI2007-66773-C02-01 (second and third authors). The second and third authors have also been sponsored by the Generalitat Valenciana and the Universidad Politécnica de Valencia.

References

1. G. Bugeda, J. J. Ródenas, E. Oñate, *An integration of a low cost adaptive remeshing strategy in the solution of structural shape optimization problems using evolutionary methods*, Computers & Structures, **86**, 1563-1578 (2008).
2. R. Storn, K. Price. *Differential evolution - A simple and efficient adaptive scheme for global optimization over continuous space*. International Computer Science Institute, Berkeley, CA, USA (1995). Available: ftp://ftp.icsi.berkeley.edu/pub/techreports/1995/tr-95-012.pdf
3. F. Navarrina, *Una metodología general para optimización structural en diseño assitido por ordenador*, Phd Thesis, Universitat Politècnica de Catalunya, in spanish (1987).
4. O. C. Zienkiewicz, J. Z. Zhu, *A simple error estimator and adaptive procedure for practical engineering analysis*, International Journal for Numerical Methods in Engineering, **24**, 337-357 (1987).
5. O. C. Zienkiewicz, J. Z. Zhu, *The superconvergent patch recovery and A posteriori error estimates. Part 1: The recovery technique*, International Journal for Numerical Methods in Engineering, **33**, 1331-1364 (1992).
6. N. E. Wiberg, F. Abdulwahab, S. Ziukas, *Enhanced superconvergent patch recovery incorporating equilibrium and boundary conditions*, International Journal for Numerical Methods in Engineering, **37**, 3417-3440 (1994).
7. J. J. Ródenas, M. Tur, F. J. Fuenmayor, A. Vercher, *Improvement of the superconvergent patch recovery technique by the use of constraint equations: the SPR-C technique*, International Journal for Numerical Methods in Engineering, **70**, 705-727 (2007).
8. P. Díez, J. J. Ródenas, O. C. Zienkiewicz, *Equilibrated patch recovery error estimates: simple and accurate upper bounds of the error*, International Journal for Numerical Methods in Engineering, **69**, 2075-2098 (2007).
9. I. D. Faux, M. J. Pratt, *Computational Geometry for Design and Manufacture*. [5th. reprint.] ed.Chichester: Ellis Horwood (1987).
10. G. Bugeda, Oliver, *A general methodology for structural shape optimization problems using automatic adaptive remeshing*, International Journal for Numerical Methods in Engineering, **36**, 3161-3185 (1993).
11. G. Bugeda, E. Oñate, *A methodology for adaptive mesh refinement in optimum shape design problems*, Computing Systems in Engineering, **5**, 91-102 (1994).
12. F. J. Fuenmayor, J. L. Oliver, J. J. Ródenas, *Extension of the Zienkiewicz–Zhu error estimator to shape sensitivity analysis*, International Journal for Numerical Methods in Engineering, **40**, 1413-1433 (1997).

MPI-enabled Shape Optimization of Panels Subjected to Air Blast Loading

V. Argod[1], A.D. Belegundu[1], A. Aziz[2], V. Agrawala[2], R. Jain[3] and S. D. Rajan[3,a]

[1] Mechanical & Nuclear Engineering, Pennsylvania State University, University Park, PA 16802, USA
[2] Research Computing & Cyberinfrastructure, Pennsylvania State University, University Park, PA 16802, USA
[3] Civil, Environmental and Sustainable Engineering, Arizona State University, Tempe, AZ 85287, USA

Abstract –The problem of finding the optimal shape of an aluminum plate to mitigate air blast loading is considered. The goal is to minimize the dynamic displacement of the plate relative to the test fixture, while monitoring plastic strain values, mass, and envelope constraints. This is a computationally challenging problem owing to (a) difficulty with finding optimal shapes with higher dimensional shape variations, (b) non-differentiable, non-convex and computationally expensive objective and constraint functions, and (c) difficulties in controlling mesh distortion that occur during explicit finite element analysis. An approach based on coupling LS-DYNA finite element software and a differential evolution (DE) optimizer is presented. Since DE involves a population of designs which are then crossed-over and mutated to yield an improved generation, it is possible to use coarse parallelization wherein a computing cluster is used to evaluate fitness of the entire population simultaneously. However, owing to highly dissimilar computing time per analysis, a result of mesh distortion and minimum time step in explicit finite element analysis, implementation of the parallelization scheme is challenging. Sinusoidal basis shapes are used to obtain an optimized 'double-bulge' shape.

Key words: structural optimization, shape optimization, blast loads, MPI, load balancing, differential evolution, parallel computing

Nomenclature

$\mathbf{x}$	=	design variables vector
$\mathbf{x}^L$	=	lower limit on design variables
$\mathbf{x}^U$	=	upper limit on design variables
FEA	=	Finite Element Analysis
$\mathbf{G}$	=	vector of x-, y-, z- coordinates of nodes in FE model
$\mathbf{q}^i$	=	i^{th} velocity field (or trial shape change) vector
w	=	z- or plate normal displacement
k	=	number of design variables
ε_{max}	=	maximum plastic strain at failure
ε	=	equivalent plastic strain
M	=	total mass of the structure
M_{max}	=	upper limit for the mass of the structure
T	=	thickness of the structure (plate) at any (x, y) location in the plate
t_{min}	=	Minimum thickness allowed
$\mathbf{z}$	=	vector of z-coordinate of the nodes
$\mathbf{z}^U$	=	upper limit on z-coordinate
$\mathbf{z}^L$	=	lower limit on z-coordinate
$(\det J_j)$	=	smallest value of the Jacobian of the jth hexahedral element at all the eight nodes
n_{pop}	=	Population size
n_{gen}	=	Number of generations
n_{eval}	=	Number of function evaluations
n_p	=	Number of processors

1 Introduction

Shape optimization of panels subjected to dynamic loading has unique challenges one of which is the considerable compute time required for carrying out the finite element analysis, an integral part of function evaluation [1, 2]. The analysis of metallic and composite panels subjected to both ballistic and blast load has been carried out by many researchers. Dharaneepathy and Sudhesh [3] investigate stiffener patterns on a square plate subject to blast loads modeled using Friedlander's exponential function. They demonstrate that stiffeners provide significant advantage in comparison to an unstiffened panel of same weight. They also show disadvantages of a waffle design. Hou [4] considers the effect of stiffener size on blast response. Yen, Skaags and Cheeseman [5] show that significant reduction in the maximum stress amplitude propagating within the protected components can be achieved by suitable selection of honeycomb material with proper crush strength. Icardi and Ferrero [6] study optimum fiber orientations in a laminated composite to absorb energy while maintaining stiffness. Main and Gazonas [7] have studied the effect of blast loading on sandwich plates and on cellular material sandwiched between plates. In contrast to these works, this paper uses formal shape optimization procedures in arriving at optimal shapes of solid aluminum plates. LS-DYNA is used to perform explicit finite element analysis of the structure subject to air blast loading.

While numerical optimization methodologies are fairly mature, their use on engineering design problems for dynamic loading with damage evolution, involving explicit

[a] Corresponding author: s.rajan@asu.edu

finite element analyses, is fairly limited. We use one of the more promising global optimization techniques, viz. Differential Evolution (DE). It is a stochastic direct search method utilizing the concepts developed from the broad class of evolutionary algorithms and can handle non-differentiable objective functions. DE has shown faster convergence compared to other contemporary evolutionary methods (EAs) [8, 9]. DE is similar to GA (genetic algorithms) in that a population of designs are evaluated, mutated and crossed-over a fixed number of generations while storing the best design obtained during the process. Differences between DE and GA exist in the manner of cross-over and mutation and in representing variables. Like most of the EAs, DE can also be easily parallelized since each member of the population can be evaluated individually.

In fact, use of a simpler differentiable optimizer was first attempted but without success, as the non-differentiability of the functions was identified in the process. For this particular problem, DE performs better than an in-house GA code. Response surface optimization, used successfully on crashworthiness optimization with LS-DYNA is another possible route, but has not been chosen here. That is, the route chosen here is to directly couple accurate finite element analysis with optimization. Comparison of these two approaches may be worth studying in future as noted towards the end of the paper.

There are two popular schemes for parallelization of DE (or GA for that matter) [10]. The first scheme employs the Master-Worker model. This is a simple method where the master process controls the program by assigning tasks to worker processes. A 'coarse-grained' parallelization is possible under this scenario. Typically, any function evaluation is done by workers while the master process generates new population using the worker-generated information. The second model [11], which we refer to as 'fine-grained' parallelization, divides the population into subpopulations and associates every entire subpopulation (also called islands) to a process. Each subpopulation converges to its own solution and the relevant information is then exchanged between processes – periodically, best individual from each process is moved to other process (migration). Both these schemes have been implemented and used successfully in solving various types of problems [12, 13]. In this paper, we have implemented a DE optimizer with coarse-grained parallelization.

In most parallelization schemes, the time taken by each function evaluation varies in a narrow range. However, in this work, there is a huge variation in computation time among members in the population, primarily owing to some meshes being distorted for which finite element analysis cannot be carried out and secondarily owing to differences in element thicknesses affecting the time steps used during explicit finite element analysis. Thus, within the framework of coarse-grained parallelization, two different schemes have been studied with respect to obtaining respectable speedup ratios.

The paper is divided into five sections. Section 2 deals with details of the design optimization problem. We look at the design problem statement, the finite element model required for efficient function evaluation, the shape optimization methodology and the generation of velocity field (shape changes). In Section 3, we discuss parallelization strategies needed to decrease the wall clock time required to obtain the solution. Results are presented in Section 4, where the shape of the plate is optimized with three design variables and with a larger space of nine variables. Finally, findings, limitations and future work are discussed in Section 5.

2 Problem Definition

In this paper we use a generic but specific example to illustrate our design optimization methodology for both sequential and parallel implementations. The schematics of the specific example are shown in Fig. 1. The standoff distance of the charge is taken to be 0.4064 m. It should be noted that the plate is a part of a 'grip' assembly (Fig. 2) used to model the experimental condition as explained subsequently. The design optimization problem is as follows.

Given a set of basis shapes that controls the shape and thickness of the plate, a mass limit for the structure, plastic strain limits representing fracture strength, a minimum thickness for the panel, and a geometric envelope within which the structure must lie, determine the best possible combination of these basis shapes that minimizes the deflection (at the first peak in time).

Find $\mathbf{G}(\mathbf{x})$

minimize $\|w(\mathbf{x})\|_r$ (1)

subject to $\varepsilon_j \le \varepsilon_{\max}$ for each element j

$M \le M_{\max}$

$t \ge t_{\min}$

$\mathbf{x}^L \le \mathbf{x} \le \mathbf{x}^U$

$\det J_j(\mathbf{x}) \ge 0$ for each element j

$\mathbf{z}^L \le \mathbf{z} \le \mathbf{z}^U$ (geometric envelope)

where the notation is explained at the beginning of the paper.

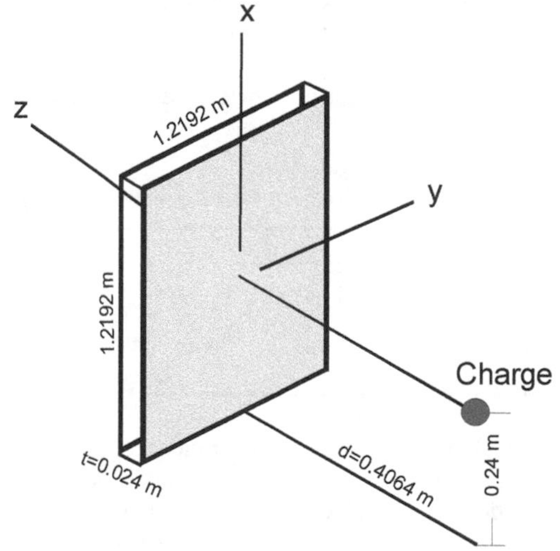

Fig. 1. Baseline structural model details

The defined problem has the following characteristics.

(a) Euclidean norm of the relative z-displacement of nodes in the plate is taken as the objective function (i.e. r = 2 in Eqn. (1)). x- and y- displacements are not significant and are

not considered. The term ‘relative’ is explained subsequently. The displacement is a function of time and value at first peak is monitored.
(b) Plastic strain, also a function of time, stabilizes after a certain time. This stabilized value is used in the constraint.
(c) M refers to the combined mass of the assembly (Fig. 2).
(d) Plate thickness is computed from nodal coordinates of the hexahedral elements used in the FE model.

2.1 FE Modeling Considerations

Our baseline design is a square plate with a grip system or assembly that holds the plate as shown in Fig. 2.

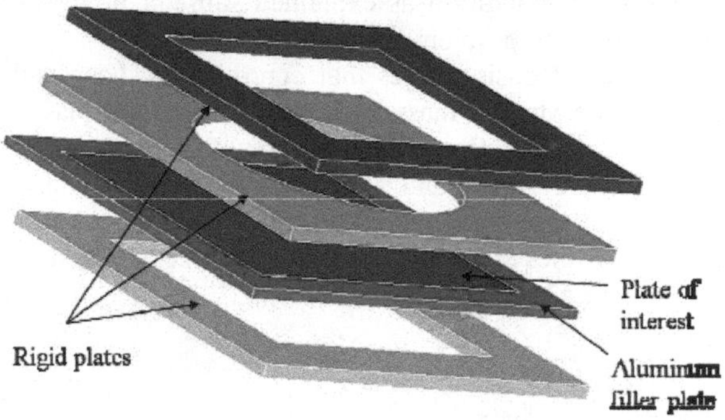

Fig. 2. Exploded view of the structural model

The grip assembly (plate of interest, filler plate and 3 rigid plates) is used in the experimental evaluation of similar panels and is included in the FE model. Appropriate boundary conditions with contact surfaces are used in the assembly. Blast load exerted is calculated using the CONWEP function in LS-DYNA computer program. Given the charge mass and the type of blast, the CONWEP function calculates the pressure values and then applies them to the appropriate surfaces. Since the pressure values are recomputed during every function evaluation, changes in the loading due to shape change are automatically calculated during the design optimization process. Details of the blast parameters can be found in Table 1.

Table 1. Blast Load Input Data

Property	Value
Equivalent mass of TNT	1 kg
Blast Location	(0, 0, -0.4064) m
Type of Burst	Air Blast (spherical charge)

The plate of interest and the surrounding filler plate are made of Aluminum 5083. In the FE model, elasto-plastic material model is used to describe the behavior (Table 2). All the parts are meshed using eight-noded solid elements. Our initial mesh convergence studies showed the FE analysis time for one complete analysis to vary between 90 s for the 4862-element model to 900 s for the 51902-element model on an Intel P4-3.6 GHz machine with 3 GB RAM. Noting that the peak response values (time required for plastic strain to stabilize at a constant value) can shift during the design optimization process due to shape changes in the FE model, the simulation time was taken conservatively to be 11 ms. The plate assembly is unrestrained; hence, the whole assembly is free to move during the blast loading. To eliminate the rigid body component in the objective function in Eqn. (1), $w(\mathbf{x})$ is taken to be the ‘relative’ displacement obtained by subtracting the nodal displacement at a point in the plate from the displacement of a reference node in the grip.

Table 2. Plate Material Properties

Property	Value
Mass Density	2700 kg/m^3
Young’s Modulus	68.9 GPa
Poisson’s Ratio	0.33
Yield Stress	225 GPa
Tangent Modulus	633 GPa
Hardening Parameter	1.0
Failure Strain	0.39

2.2 Shape Optimization Methodology

Shape changes are allowed to take place in a square portion of the model at the center of plate. This ensures that changes in plate shape do not result in changes in the grip system (see the circular hole cover plate directly above the plate of interest in Fig. 2). However, a thickness change in the plate has to be matched by an equal thickness change in the filler plate for the assembly to function. The key equation to implement shape optimization is [14, 15, 16]

$$\mathbf{G}(x) = \mathbf{G}_{original} + \sum_{i=1}^{k} x_i\, \mathbf{q}^i \tag{2}$$

where G is vector of nodal or grid coordinates representing x-, y-, z- coordinates of all nodes in the model. Each xi is the amplitude of a permissible shape change vector, $\mathbf{q}^i$. Vectors $\mathbf{q}^i$ are generated before the start of the iterative optimization loop. $\mathbf{G}_{original}$ contains the grid coordinates of the original flat plate. The optimizer chooses $\mathbf{x}^{\text{opt}}$ so that the corresponding shape $\mathbf{G}(\mathbf{x}^{\text{opt}})$ is optimum. As $\mathbf{x}$ is iteratively changed by the optimizer and the grid point coordinates $\mathbf{G}$ are updated, the LS-DYNA input file is recreated with the updated nodal coordinates. The overall algorithm and flow of information can be written as follows.

(1) Read the FE model.
(2) Read the design model including all the $\mathbf{q}^i$ vectors (velocity field matrix).
(3) Transfer control to the optimizer,
(4) Start new generation.
(5) Optimizer calls for function evaluations for an entire population of designs.
(6) Construct the updated nodal coordinates using Eqn. (2) and recreate the FE input file.
(7) Carry out the FE analysis.
(8) Read FE results and compute the objective function and constraint values.
(9) Check stopping criteria. If not met, optimizer generates a new generation using crossover and mutation. Go to Step (5).

A pictorial diagram of the algorithm is presented in Fig. 3.

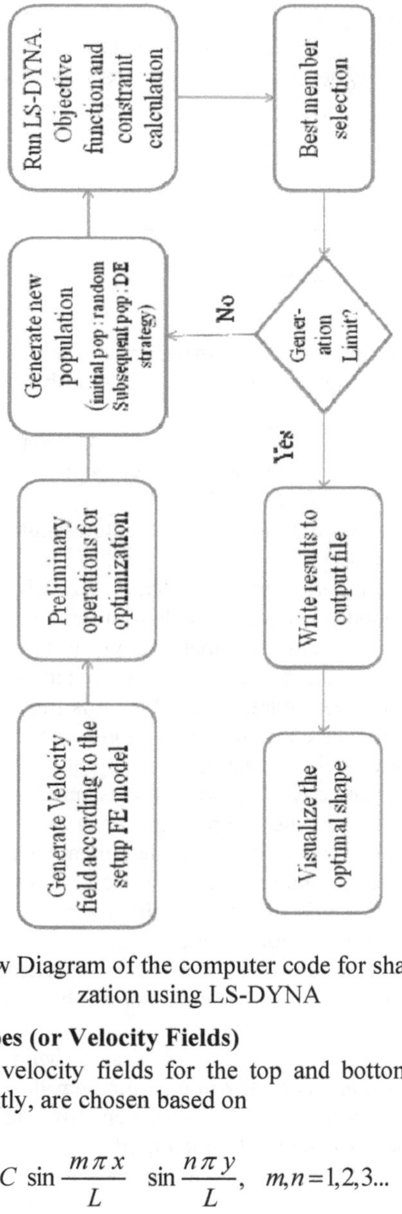

Fig. 3. Flow Diagram of the computer code for shape optimization using LS-DYNA

Basis Shapes (or Velocity Fields)

Sinusoidal velocity fields for the top and bottom surfaces, independently, are chosen based on

$$f(m,n) = C \sin\frac{m\pi x}{L} \sin\frac{n\pi y}{L}, \quad m,n = 1,2,3... \tag{3}$$

where C is a suitable normalization factor. In this paper, optimization results are presented for the three different cases.

3-DV (Three Design Variables) Case: $m = n = 1$. This gives a total of three (3) *symmetric* basis shapes corresponding to $q^1 \equiv f(1,1)$ for the top surface, $q^2 \equiv f(1,1)$ for the bottom surface, and q^3 = thickness change. Specifically, q^1 represents a bulge in the shape of the top surface while bottom surface is fixed (other thru-thickness nodes are moved to preserve equal spacing), q^2 represents a bulge on the bottom surface while top surface is fixed, and q^3 = a thickness change only. The design variable vector is $x = [x_1, x_2, x_3]^T$ and the optimizer tries to determine an optimum combination of these three basis shapes. Basis shape corresponding to q^1 is illustrated in Fig. 4(a). Note that the bulge can be positive or negative depending on the sign of x_i.

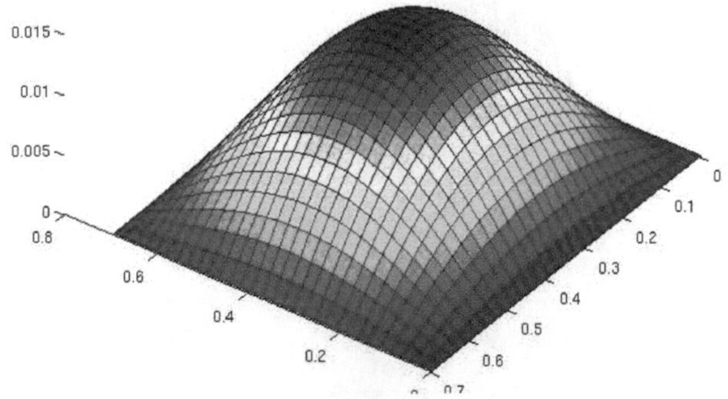

(a)

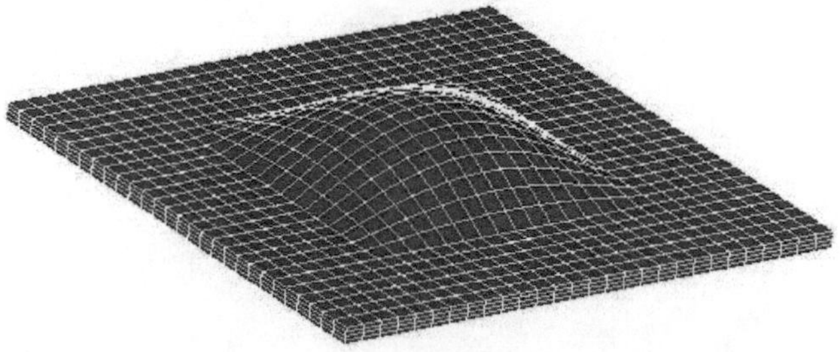

(b)

Fig. 4. (a) 3-DV basis shape corresponding to top surface bulge (exaggerated for visualization), (b) Full plate showing the domain for shape optimization of the plate

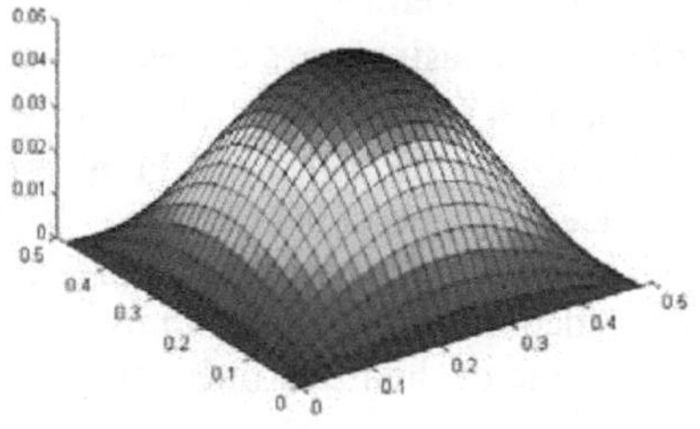

(a)

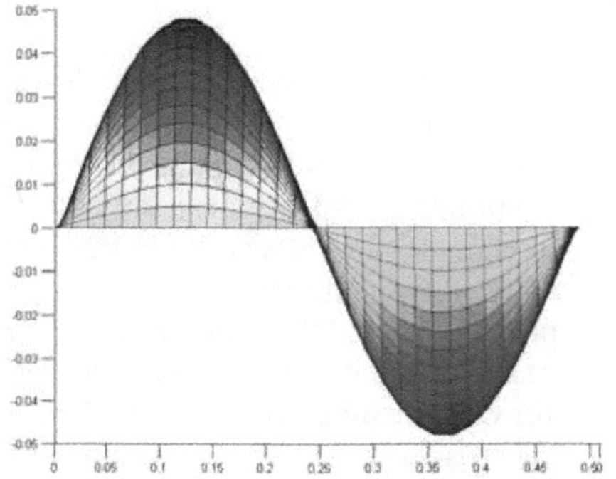

(b)

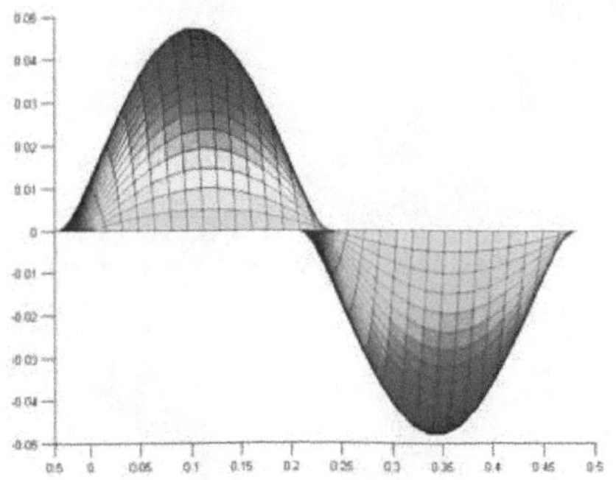

(c)

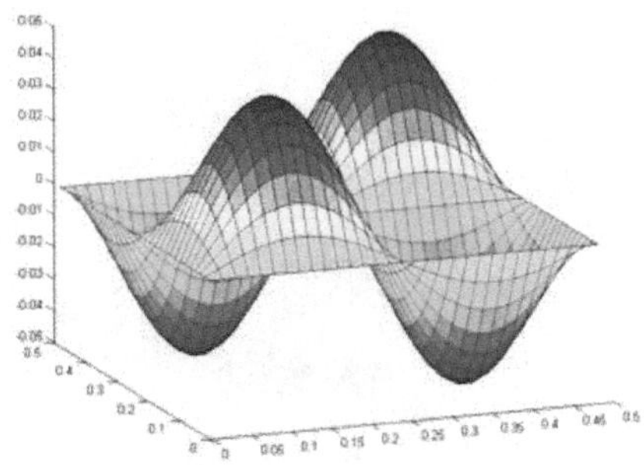

(d)

Fig. 5. Some of the basis shapes for the 9-DV problem (Note that Fig.(b) is the front view of q^2 whereas Fig.(c) is the side view of q^3)

9-DV (Nine Design Variables) Case: $m = n = 2$. This gives a total of nine (9) basis shapes corresponding to $\mathbf{q}^1 \equiv f$ (1,1), $\mathbf{q}^2 \equiv f$ (1,2), $\mathbf{q}^3 \equiv f$ (2,1), $\mathbf{q}^4 \equiv f$ (2,2) for the top surface, $\mathbf{q}^5 \equiv f$ (1,1), $\mathbf{q}^6 \equiv f$ (1,2), $\mathbf{q}^7 \equiv f$ (2,1), $\mathbf{q}^8 \equiv f$ (2,2) for the bottom surface, $\mathbf{q}^9$ = thickness change. It should be noted that unlike the 3-DV Case above, presence of unsymmetric basis shapes may lead to an unsymmetric final optimum shape. Some of the more interesting basis shapes are shown in Fig. 5.

3 Differential Evolution with Coarse Parallelization

Computational experiments showed that downhill or descent search directions did not always lead to a reduction in the objective function even for small steps when using a gradient-based optimizer. The problem was seen to be clearly non-differentiable. The stochastic Differential Evolution (DE) optimizer was chosen for this work. From a computational point of view, DE is similar to GA. An initial population of designs is generated, function evaluations are carried out for each member in the population followed by mutation and crossover operations, leading to a new generation. Salient aspects of DE are as follows.

(i) Function evaluation (here, a finite element analysis with LS-DYNA) of a population of designs can be done independently, on separate processors. Thus, a computing cluster is very attractive to reduce time (as with GA), as clearly, the most time-consuming step is the function or fitness evaluation (FEA).

(ii) The total number of analyses equals product of population size and number of generations. Thus, the total computing time for a job can be ascertained ahead of time in terms of n_p, n_{pop}, and n_{gen} (as with GA).

(iii) Real-valued design variables are stored as such, whereas in GA, a conversion to binary or other representation is involved.

(iv) The mutation and crossover operations are different than GA. Specifically, the following is one strategy used for mutation and crossover:

$$\mathbf{v} = \mathbf{x}_i + \lambda\left(\mathbf{x}_{best} - \mathbf{x}_i\right) + F\left(\mathbf{x}_{r2} - \mathbf{x}_{r3}\right) \tag{4a}$$

$$\mathbf{x}_i^{new} = \left(1 - p\right)\mathbf{x}_i + p\mathbf{v} \tag{4b}$$

where $\mathbf{x}_i$ = member in the population, $r2$ and $r3$ are random numbers pointing to random members in the population, λ and F are user-defined parameters, p = probability factor, say 0.5.

In view of (i) above, a multi-processor computing cluster is used. However, different implementations have/need to be researched owing to different computing times for each member in the population, the latter occurring due to two main reasons:

(A) *Due to finite element distortion*. Specifically, each design in the population corresponds to a generally different shape or grid of nodal coordinates as per Eqn. (2). The Jacobian for each finite element is computed at the eight nodes for each hexahedral element. If it is negative at any node, then the element is distorted (non-convex) and finite element analysis (FEA) cannot and is not carried out. A suitably large objective function value is simply returned to the optimizer. Thus, the computing time is essentially zero. It is not possible to avoid this, as new member designs are obtained using a random procedure (Eqn. 4). On the other hand, if the mesh is undistorted, then typically the FEA takes, say, 5 minutes for the mesh size used in this paper. Hence, a large variation in times for each function evaluation exists depending on whether the mesh is distorted or not.

(B) *Each function evaluation involves solving differential equations in time*. The maximum time step depends on the thickness and more generally on element size and shape. The time per analysis can vary by factors of 4:1.

Two parallelization schemes have been implemented, herein called the SATR and LB. Each scheme was successively motivated by the performance of the previous scheme. Details are as given below.

Send-all-then-receive (SATR) Scheme [10]: In this approach, master process divides all the members of the population equally among all the processors. It first sends values of all the design variables associated with each member of the population to appropriate workers. Every worker, once it receives the information, carries out the function evaluation. After finishing all the function evaluation assigned, each worker sends the function values to master. Even though this is a simple scheme, due to variation in the computation time for each function evaluation, there can be unnecessary wait time for the processes that have finished their function evaluations successfully (see (3) above) or cannot evaluate due to problems with the FE model distortion. This can be illustrated with the following sample data. Let n_{pop} = 8, n_p = 4, and FEA time for each member in the population as given in

Table 3 below. The '0 min' FE time indicates distorted meshes for which no FE analysis is carried out.

Table 3. Sample Data to Illustrate Parallel Schemes

Member	1	2	3	4	5	6	7	8
FE time (min)	2	0	6	3	0	3	2	0

From Table 3 we see that a single processor will take 16 min for all 8 evaluations. With 4 processors, with P1 acting both as a master and a worker, the distribution of computations is as indicated in Fig. 6. The 8 function evaluations are distributed in two stages to the 4 processors. Thus, total time for all 8 evaluations equals 6+3 = 9 min. Thus, actual speedup is 16/9 = 1.78, much less than ideal of 4.0 which would occur if each FEA takes equal time.

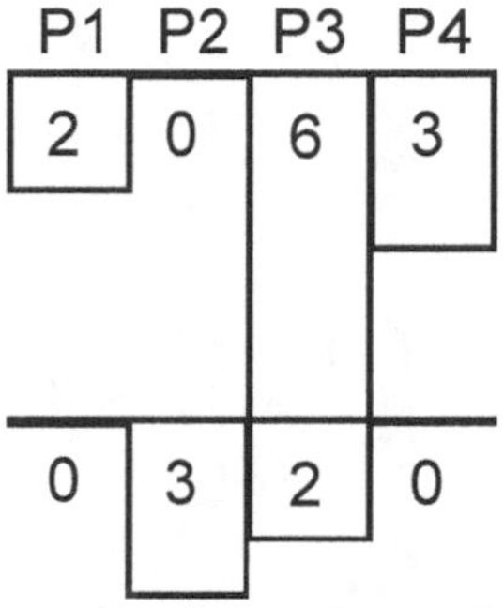

Fig. 6. SATR scheme (numbers refer to minutes, P*i* refers to processor *i*)

Load-balanced (LB) Scheme [10]: A modified scheme is used where send and receive takes place one after another depending on how the availability of the worker process. The master process sends only one individual (of the population) to each worker initially. Once the worker process completes the function evaluation and communicates the function values to the master process, the next individual in the population is sent to the worker for evaluation. In other words, the master process continues to send and receive until all members of population have been evaluated. The overall algorithm is explained next.

Steps in Master Process

(1) Broadcast details of entire population (design variable values) to all the worker processes.

(2) Set number of members already evaluated, $n_{sent} = 0$.

(3) Loop through $i = 1, \ldots, \min(n_{pop}, n_p)$.

(4) Increment n_{sent}.

(5) Ask process i to evaluate member n_{sent}.

(6) End loop

(7) Loop through all the members of the population, $j = 1, 2, \ldots, n_{pop}$

(8) Receive function values from process i.

(9) If $n_{sent} < n_{pop}$, increment n_{sent} and ask process i to evaluate member n_{sent}. Else inform process i that there is no more function evaluation to conduct (**no-more-work** message).

(10) End loop.

Steps in Worker Process (only for process $i < n_{pop}$)

(1) Receive the broadcast message and store all the design variables.

(2) Loop till no-more-work message is received from the master process.

(3) Receive the population index, compute and send function values to master process.

(4) End loop.

It should be noted that only the master process executes DE and takes a very small compute time compared to the time taken for a typical function evaluation. On the sample data in Table 3, with P1 acting as the master and P2-P4 doing the FEA, Fig. 7 shows the distribution of computations. We see that maximum time is 6 min. Thus, even with one processor not sharing in FEA, the speedup is 16/6 = 2.67 > 1.78 by SATR Scheme.

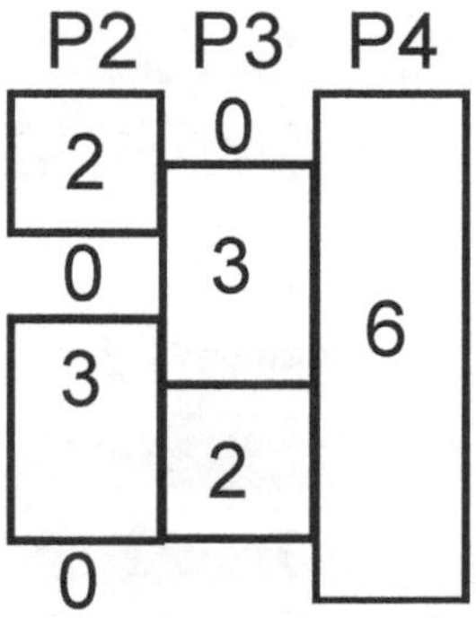

Fig. 7. LB scheme (numbers refer to minutes, P*i* refers to processor *i*)

These parallel algorithms were implemented and executed on the LION-XC cluster located at Pennsylvania State University's Research Computing and Cyberinfrastructure. The compute nodes are dual 3.0-GHz Intel Xeon 3160 (Woodcrest) Dual-Core Processors each with 16 GB of ECC RAM and with Myrinet interconnect. The program was written in FORTRAN and message passing was achieved via MPICH2 calls.

4 Numerical Results

In this section, we look at finding the optimal shapes using 3 and 9 design variables using the parallel shape optimization methodology discussed in the previous sections.

4.1 Distribution of Computing Times for Each Member of the Population

We first study the distribution of computing times for FE analysis of each member of the design population. As noted in Section 3, the unequal FEA times creates challenges to obtain good speedup. Results for the 3-DV (three design variable) problem are used here. Figure 8 shows how the iteration time for every processor varies with optimization iterations with np = 4. The length of each bar represents the time taken for each iteration. Computations for the next generation can commence only after all the processors finish function evaluations for the current generation. This slows down the progress as some processors wait for other processors to finish their computations. The iteration time for any processor is the sum of time taken by all the function evaluations allocated to that processor. Potentially, each worker can get a different number of function evaluations as the master processor tries to balance the computational load. Next, Fig. 9 shows the distribution of the FE (LS-DYNA function evaluation) times. Bin represents the function evaluation time while frequency gives the number of evaluations in a given bin. Majority of the function evaluations required about 150 s. However, a significant number of members in the generation turn out to be invalid/distorted designs requiring almost zero compute time. Finally, in Fig. 10, the normalized computation time of each iteration is plotted against the iteration number. Departure from equal-time analyses, indicated by a horizontal line, is again evident.

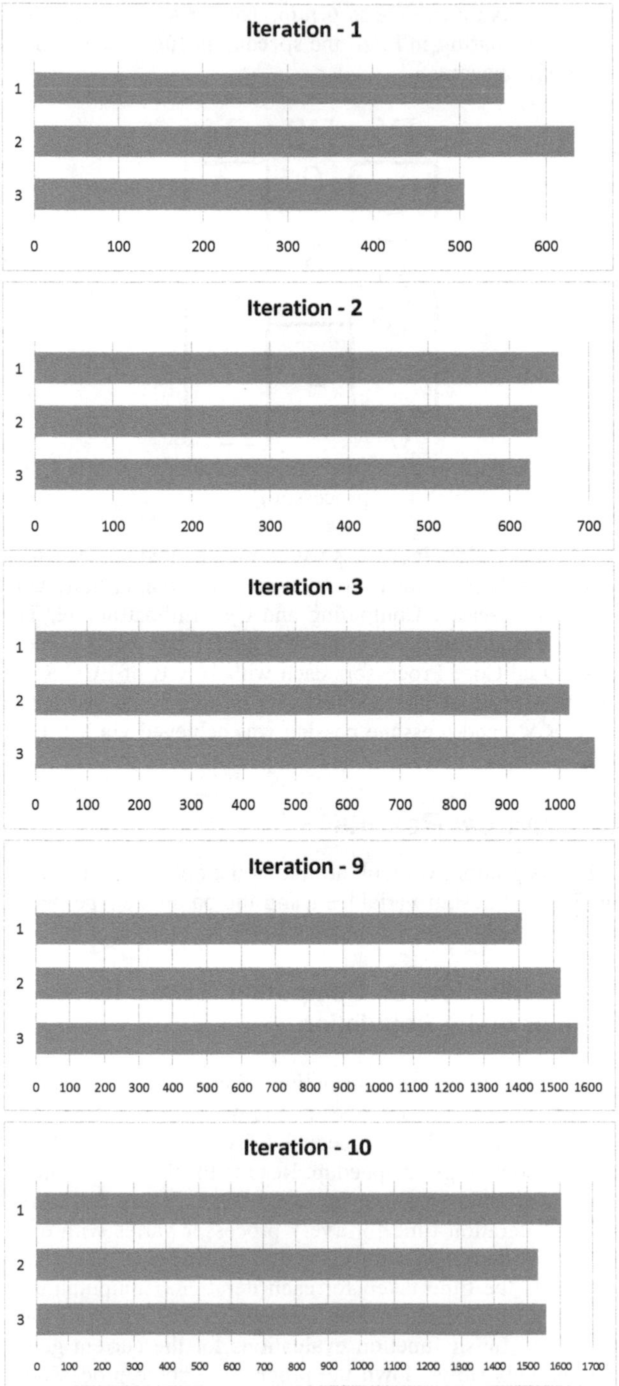

Fig. 8. Bar chart to show iteration time (in seconds for) every processor (for $n_p = 4$) for 3-DV case

4.2 Obtained Speedups

The SATR and LB schemes were used to solve the design optimization problem described in Section 2. Speedups obtained by the two schemes discussed in Section 3 are shown for the 3-DV and 9-DV cases, respectively, in Figs. 11, 12 and corresponding Tables 4, 5. Speedup is defined in the usual way as $S = T(n_{ref}) / T(n_p)$, where n_{ref} = number of processors used in the. In the 3-DV case in Table 4 (Fig. 11), $n_{ref} = 1$, while in the 9-DV case in Table 5 (Fig. 12), $n_{ref} = 4$ (the 9-DV problem cannot be solved with less processors in reasonable time). Note that the speedup with SATR, when n_p is very low, is better than LB since the latter uses one of the processors as a master which does not share in FEA. As is to be expected, LB overtakes SATR with increasing n_p. Compared to ideal speedup, both fall short, owing to the continuing presence of assorted computing times per FEA as explained in Section 3.

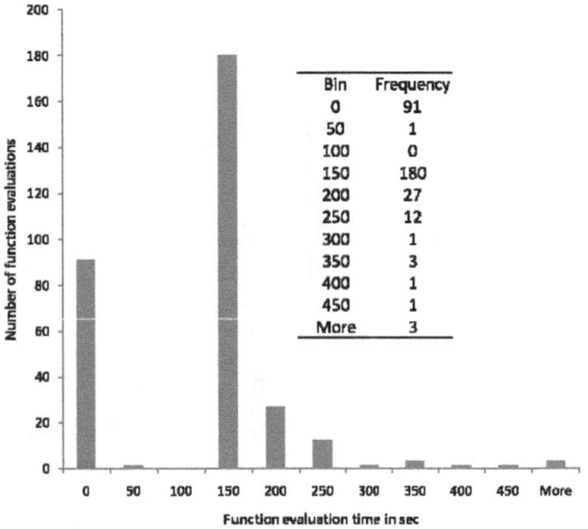

Fig. 9. Histogram of function evaluation times for 3-DV for LB Scheme

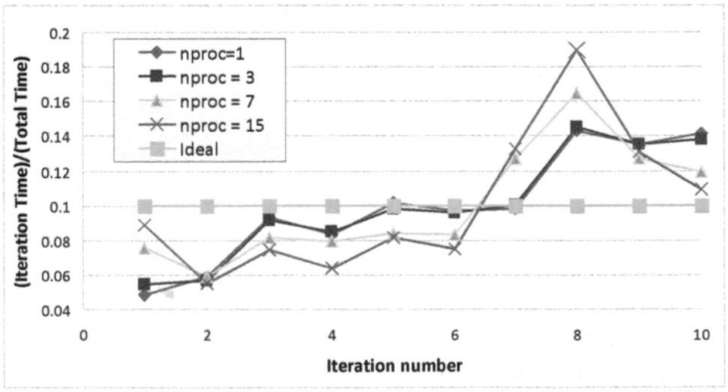

Fig. 10. Plot showing the variation of computation time of every iteration for different number of processors (SATR Scheme)

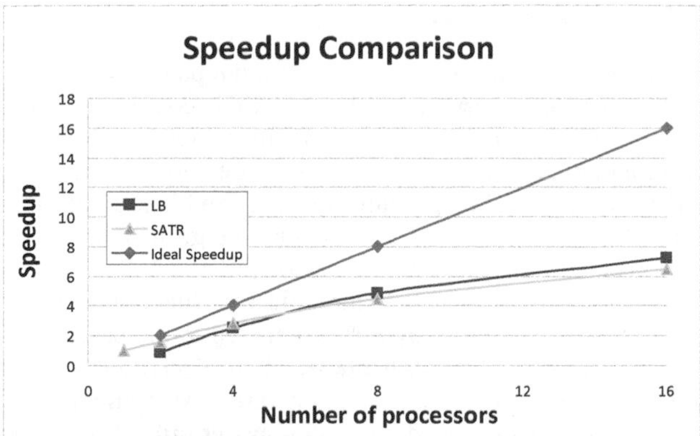

Fig. 11. Speedup comparisons of SATR and LB schemes for 3-DV case

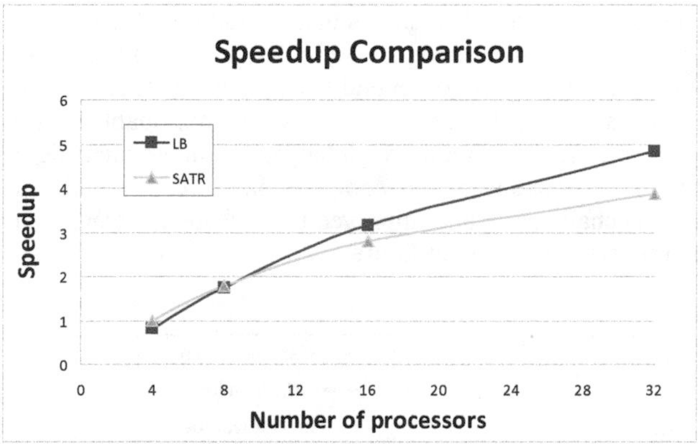

Fig. 12. Speedup comparison of SATR and LB schemes for 9-DV case

4.3 Structural Optimization Aspects

Regarding the structural aspects, the performance metrics associated with the baseline (i.e. flat plate) and optimized designs, for both 3-DV and 9-DV cases, are shown in Table 6.

Baseline and optimized plates within the grip assembly are shown in Fig. 13(a) and (b). The optimized shape turns out to be a double bulge. Overall thickness is reduced from 0.0381m to 0.0241m with bulges on both sides. There is a greater bulge towards the charge (Fig. 13(c)). Plastic strain is maximum at center for the baseline design while it is around the borders of domain for the optimized panel (Fig. 14), indicating greater utilization of material. Maximum relative displacement of optimized designs versus baseline design is shown in Fig. 15(a), where we see an 80% reduction through optimization. The displacement reaches its peak at t = 1.1 ms. The total impulse responses of optimized designs are compared to those of baseline design in Fig. 15(b). Finally, Fig. 16 shows the double bulge shape for the 9-DV problem. This is slightly unsymmetric, owing to the choice of basis shapes used (Section 2).

Limitation: An attempt was made to solve the same problem using 19 design variables (with $m = n = 3$ in Eqn. (3). However, the DE optimizer did not produce optimum solutions. Thus, more interesting shapes need to be explored through improved optimizers and velocity field generators.

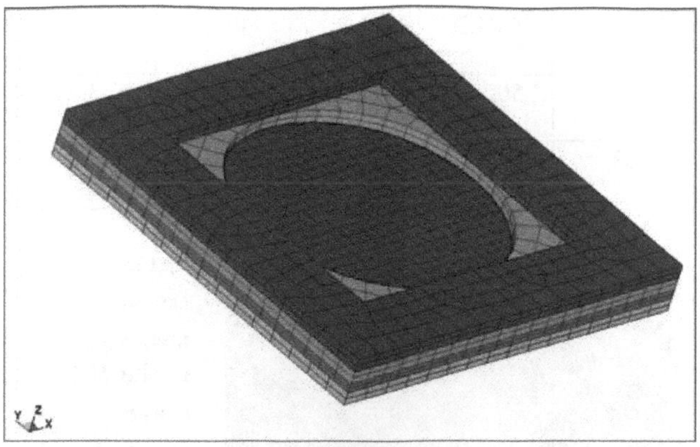

(a)

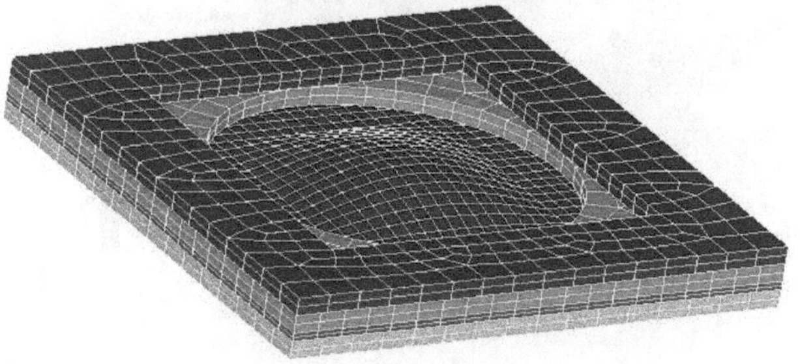

(b)

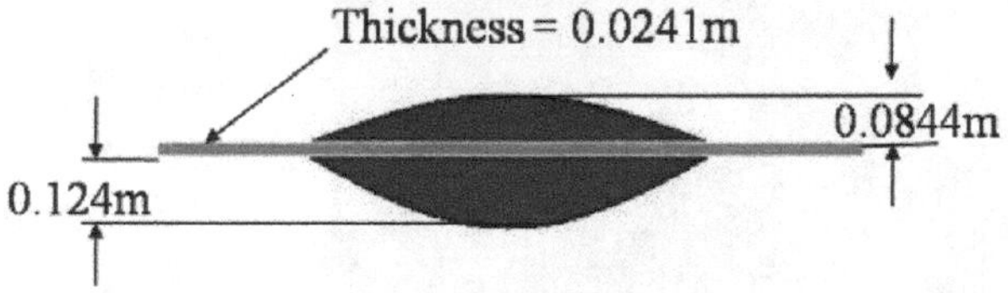

(c)

Fig. 13. (a) Baseline design (uniform thickness) (b) Optimized plate-double bulge (for large envelope case) (c) Optimized plate dimensions

Table 4. Parallel computation for 3 DV, n_{pop} = 32, n_{gen} = 10

n_p	SATR		LB	
	Time (min)	Speedup	Time (min)	Speedup
1	487.6	1.0		
2	306.5	1.6	544.1	0.9
4	171.3	2.8	192.3	2.5
8	109.1	4.5	101.2	4.8
16	75.4	6.5	67.4	7.2

Table 5. Parallel computation for 3 DV, n_{pop} = 100, n_{gen} = 30

n_p	SATR		LB	
	Time (min)	Speedup	Time (min)	Speedup
4	1402.5	1.0	1701.0	0.8

8	784.2	1.8	806.0	1.7
16	502.24	2.8	445.0	3.2
32	362.4	3.9	290.0	4.8

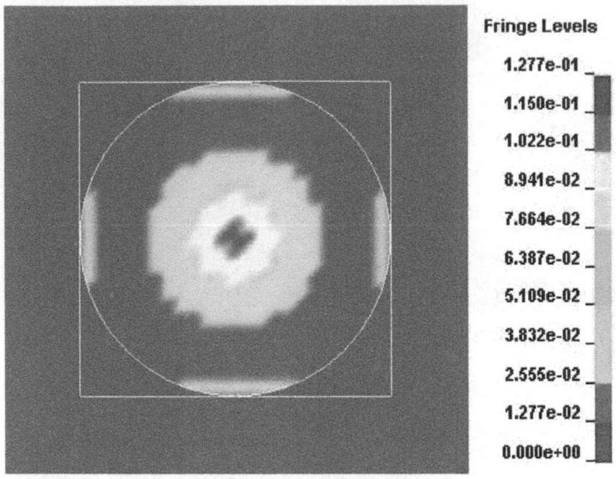

(a)

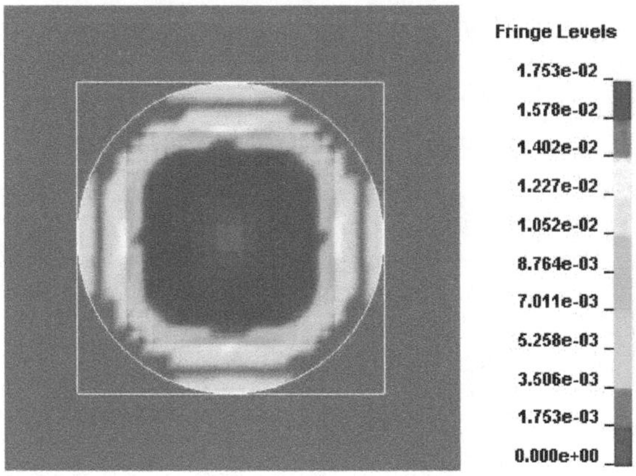

(b)

Fig. 14. Plastic strain plot for (a) baseline design (b) optimized design

Table 6. Results for Baseline and Optimized Designs

Properties	Baseline Design	3-DV	9-DV
Objective Function (mm)	20.51	4.49	4.28
Max Relative Displacement (mm)	58.43	7.68	7.79
Max plastic strain	0.1277	0.02	0.02
Total Mass (kg)	1872.2	1894.5	1895.3
Saturated impulse, (kg-m/s)	6254.3	5401.4	5313.6

5 Concluding Remarks

Shape optimization of a solid aluminum panel for air blast load mitigation is carried out. LS-DYNA is coupled to a stochastic DE optimizer using a modular FORTRAN code. Three and nine sinusoidal basis shapes are chosen to find the optimum shapes. The optimum shape, a combination of these basis shapes, turns out to be a double-bulge in both cases, with unequal bulges on both sides of the plate. The panel's RMS displacement which is the objective function, relative to the fixture, decreased by 80% compared to the baseline or flat plate design. Maximum plastic strain decreased as well and was well within the constraint limit. At optimum, the plastic strain was smeared, indicating better utilization of the material. Parallelization of the DE optimizer makes the design optimization approach viable. Two schemes are used to implement the coarse parallelization: A study of the two schemes SATR and LB, shows that the latter methodology is better able to handle unequal compute times per FE analysis. When attempting to go beyond 9 basis shapes (i.e. 9 design variables), the optimizer fails to provide a reasonable design. Thus, the task of finding a global optimum in such highly nonlinear, nonconvex and computationally expensive functions is challenging and improved basis shape generators and optimizers are needed in future.

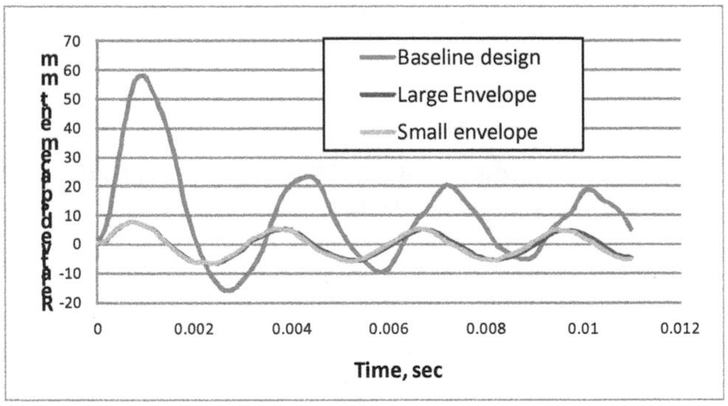

(a)

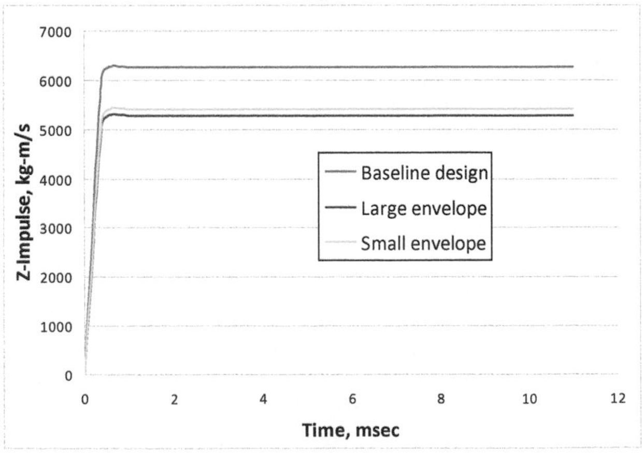

(b)

Fig. 15. Comparison of (a) relative displacement (b) impulse response

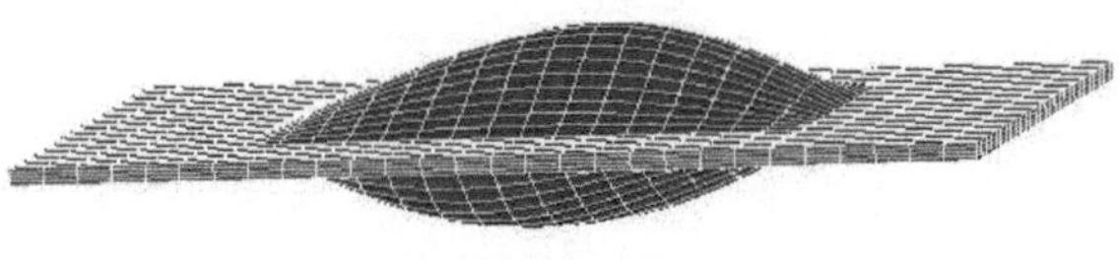

Fig. 16. Optimized shape 9-DV

Acknowledgement

This paper is based on the research work supported by the U.S. Army Research Office (Proposal Number 50490-EG. Technical Monitor: Dr. Bruce LaMattina). We thank Dr. B.A. Cheeseman and Dr. C. Yen of the Army Research Lab for valuable discussions and suggestions. Partial financial and computational support from the High Performance Computing Group at Penn State under Mr. Vijay Agarwala is gratefully acknowledged.

References

1. A. D. Belegundu, V. Argod, S. D. Rajan, K. Krishnan, *Shape optimization of panels subjected to blast loading modeled with LS-DYNA*, *In* 49th AIAA/ASME/ASCE/-AHS/ASC Structures, Structural Dynamics, and Materials. AIAA 2008-2285 (2008).
2. A. D. Belegundu, V. Argod, S. D. Rajan, R. Jain, *Shape optimization of solid isotropic plates to mitigate the effects of air blast loading*, submitted to Intl J of Impact Engineering (2008).
3. M.V. Dharaneepathy, K. G. Sudhesh, *Optimal Stiffening of square plates subjected to air-blast loading*, Computers & Structures, **36**(5), 891-899 (1999).
4. Hai-Liang Hou, *Study on failure mode of stiffened plate and optimized design of structure subjected to blast load*, Explosion and Shock Waves [in Chinese], **27**, 26-33(2007).
5. C.F. Yen, R. Skaggs, B.A. Cheeseman, *Modeling of shock mitigation sandwich structures for blast protection*, The 3rd First International Conference on Structural Stability and Dynamics, Kissimmee, Florida, June 19-22 (2005).
6. U. Icardi, L. Ferrero, *Impact and blast pulse: Improving energy absorption of fibre-reinforced composites through optimized tailoring*, Proc of ESDA 2006: 8th Biennial ASME Conference on Engineering Systems Design and Analysis, Torino, Italy, July 4-7 (2006).
7. J.A. Main, G.A. Gazonas, *Uniaxial crushing of sandwich plates under air blast: Influence of mass distribution*, International Journal of Solids and Structures. **45**, 2297–2321 (2008).
8. R. Storn, *System design by constraint adaptation and differential evolution*, IEEE Transactions on Evolutionary Computation, 22-34 (1999).
9. D.K. Tasoulis, N.G. Pavlidis, V.P. Plagianakos, M.N. Vrahatis, *Parallel Differential Evolution*, Congress on Evolutionary Computation (CEC 2004), Portland, Oregon (2004).
10. S.D. Rajan, D.T. Nguyen, *Design Optimization of discrete structural systems using MPI-enabled genetic algorithm*, Structural Multidisciplinary Optimization, **27**, 1-9 (2004).
11. W. Kwedlo, *Parallelizing Evolutionary Algorithms for Clustering Data*, Springer-Verlag Berlin Heidelberg. PPAM 2005, LNCS 3911, 430-438 (2006).
12. L. Singh, S. Kumar, *Parallel Evolutionary Asymmetric Subsethood Product Fuzzy –Neural Inference System with Applications*, IEEE International Conference on Fuzzy Systems (2006).
13. C.C. Liang, M.F. Yang, P.W. Wu, *Optimum design of metallic corrugated core sandwich panels subjected to blast loads*, Ocean Engineering, **28**, 825–861 (2001).
14. A.D. Belegundu, S.D. Rajan, *A Shape Optimization Approach Based on Natural Design Variables and Shape Functions*, J. Computer Methods in Applied Mechanics and Engineering, **66**, 87-106 (1998).
15. A.D. Belegundu, T.R. Chandrupatla, *Optimization Concepts and Applications in Engineering*, Prentice-Hall, New Jersey (1999).
16. S.D. Rajan, S-W. Chin, L.Gani, *Towards a Practical Design Optimization Tool*, Microcomputers in Civil Engineering, **11**, 259-274 (1996).

15

Fault Tolerant Control: Application of GIMC structure to a PLL Identifier Module

Thabet Assem [1,2,a], Hamdaoui Rim[1,2], Abdelkrim M.N[1,2]

[1] Unit Modeling, Analyzes and Control of Systems (MACS), Street Omar Iben Elkhattab Zrig-6029-Gabés (Tunisia)
[2] National School of Engineers of Gabés, Omar Iben Elkhattab Zrig-6029-Gabés (Tunisia)

Abstract – In this paper, we present a study dealing with stabilizing and robust controllers synthesis, precisely the Fault Tolerant Control (FTC). The case where these controllers are calculated by GIMC (Generalized Internal Model Control) structure will be developed and applied to a Phase-locked Loop (PLL) Identifier Module. In each case, we will focus on the control and the system output evolutions in the defects event. We will show the control quality and the advantages offered by GIMC structure in the transitory mode and the permanent one.

Key words: Fault Tolerant Control, stability, residue, GIMC structure, Phase Locked Loop (PLL).

1 Introduction

In order to ensure the systems reliability and human safety, the problem of systems control with presence of defects was largely studied by several researchers. The major part of research was devoted to study the Fault Detection and Diagnosis (FDD) problem and so the determination of the system's operating condition (Normal or defected), Iserman [1].

Under the assumption of a block of diagnosis providing information related to the detection and the localization of the defect, it is possible either to compensate the defect effect (accommodation) or to reconfigurate the control laws in order to bring the system in the possible nearest state to its normal one(called commonly reconfiguration or reorganization). These procedures to be implemented at the time of the defect occurrence were developed by several strategies defined under the expression of the Fault Tolerant Control Systems FTCS), Iserman [1] and Eterno [2].

This paper will be organized as follows. Section 2 studies the Fault Tolerant Control problem. Section 3 presents the GIMC structure. Section 4 gives a basic theory of Phase-Locked Loop Identifier Module. Finally, in section 5 a numerical example is illustrated showing the results.

2 Fault Tolerant Control (FTC)

The purpose of the FTC is to put up itself automatically with the effect of the defects while being able to maintain the stability and at best the nominal performances of the system. The consequence is to avoid the immediate system's arrest and to allow its function in a degradation mode. The FTC is generally classified into two distinct approaches: a passive approach (Passive Fault Tolerant Control, PFTC) and an active approach (Active Fault Tolerant Control, AFTC).

2.1 Passive methods

PFTC methods use the techniques of the robust control to ensure that the closed loop system remains insensitive to certain defects with constant regulators and without using online defects information on the system, Eterno [2]. This approach doesn't require a diagram of fault detection nor a control law reconfiguration but its tolerance capacity remains limited to some defects.

2.1 Active methods

The first active methods of accommodation were developed and applied in the aeronautics field of beginning in year 80. Contrary to the passive methods, the active methods react to the appearance of one or several defects by the reconfiguration of the control system. Their main aim is as to compensate the fault effect of the defects on the system so that the stability and the performances are maintained while exploiting the robustness of the control which must be improved with each detection of a defect.

These methods, Thabet [3], are based on one of the following principles: the linear quadratic control, the pseudo reverse method, the adaptive control, the predictive control, techniques by multi-models, Fuzzy logic/Neuronal networks. In this work, we will present GIMC structure as an AFTC method.

3 Generalized Internal Model Control structure

The parameterization of Youla offers an adequate architecture for the design of an AFTC law, Youla [4]. This parameterization allows description the whole of all the correctors stabilizing a system and satisfying a given performance level. The idea is to use $H\infty$ standard synthesis to elaborate a nominal corrector and the parameterization of Youla to parameterize it, in order to make it robust and to respect a class of predetermined defects. The latter are then considered as model uncertainties (multiplicative defects) or exogenic disturbances (additive defects).

[a] Corresponding author: assem.thabet@yahoo.fr

To formalize this idea, we consider $G_0(s) \in \Re H_\infty$, the matrix of transfer obtained starting from the state representation (A, B, C, D) of the nominal system:

$$G_0 = C(sI - A)^{-1}B + D$$

Supposing that K_0 is a corrector stabilizing G_0, and then it exists left and right factorizations coprimes, $U, V, \tilde{U}, \tilde{V}, \tilde{M}, \tilde{N}, M$ and N such as:

$$K_0(s) = U(s)V(s)^{-1} = \tilde{V}(s)^{-1}\tilde{U}(s)$$
$$G_0(s) = \tilde{M}(s)^{-1}\tilde{N}(s) = N(s)M(s)^{-1} \qquad (1)$$

Any regulator K stabilizing G_0 can then be deduced from $\tilde{U}, \tilde{V}, \tilde{M}, \tilde{N}$ and a transfer matrix Q called Youla parameter. The structure of K is illustrated on the following figure (Fig.1). We note K_0 is the regulator corresponding to the particular choice $Q = 0$ and called central corrector.

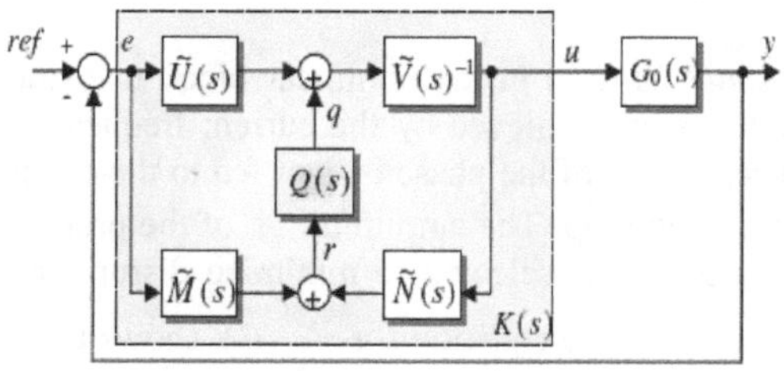

Fig. 1. Youla Parameterization

The idea consists in rewriting the structure of Fig.1 the way illustrated by Fig.2 and to synthesize the Youla parameter Q such as the control law is tolerant to the defects, Cieslak [5]. This particular structure is called GIMC structure (Generalized Internal Model Control structure). We can notice on Figure 1 that if we choose $Q = 0$, we find the central corrector. Considering the vector of residues as being defined in the following general form, Zhou [6]:

$$r(s) = \tilde{N}(s)u(s) - \tilde{M}(s)y(s) \qquad (2)$$

where: $\tilde{M}$ and $\tilde{N}$ define a decomposition coprime on the left model of the system under G_0 normal functioning.

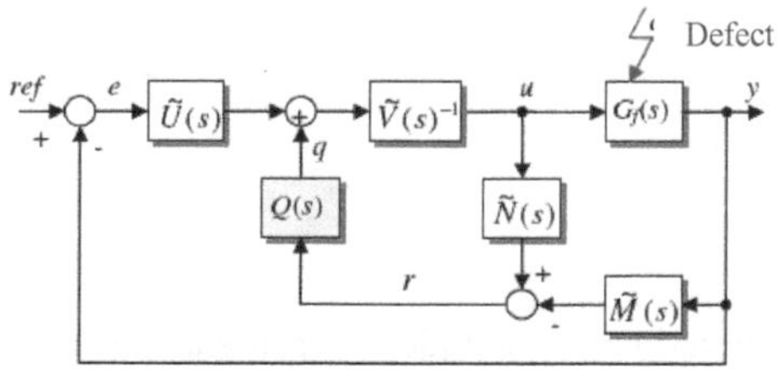

Fig.2. GIMC Structure

r can be used as a defect indicating signal. The control law illustrated on Fig.2 is then written as a function of the residue vector r:

$$u(t) = \tilde{V}(s)^{-1}(\tilde{U}(s)e(t) + r(t)) \qquad (3)$$

This illustrates well the philosophy of AFTC since the control depends now on the residue vector. So that Q can be synthesize either starting from the objectives of diagnosis or starting from the objectives of control, or by managing a compromise between the performances specifications in control and diagnosis. In this paper, the idea of using the Youla parameterization of which was taken again by Delgado [7] and [8] to accommodate the failures actuators and sensors is interesting.

$$G_f(s) = G_0(s) + W_1(s)\Delta_f(s)W_2(s), \Delta_f \in H_\infty \qquad (4)$$

where G_0 indicate the nominal system given by the state representation (A, B, C, D), G_f present failing system. Δ_f is an unstructured uncertainty block modeling the defects such as $\|\Delta_f\|_\infty \le 1$. W_1 and W_2 are selected ponderation in an adequate way. Thus $G_f(s) = (I + \Delta_f(s))G_0(s)$ with $W_1(s) = G_0(s)$ and $W_2(s) = I$ representing the sensors defects, and $G_f(s) = G_0(s)(I + \Delta_f(s))$ with $W_1(s) = I$ and $W_2(s) = G_0(s)$ representing the actuators defects. The objective is to synthesize the Youla parameter Q minimizing the influence of the defects effect on the system with the H_∞ direction. In a formal way, this problem is written as:

$$Q = \arg\min \|T_{zw}\|_\infty \qquad (5)$$

where T_{zw} is the transfer function in closed loop of $w \rightarrow z$ (see Fig.3)

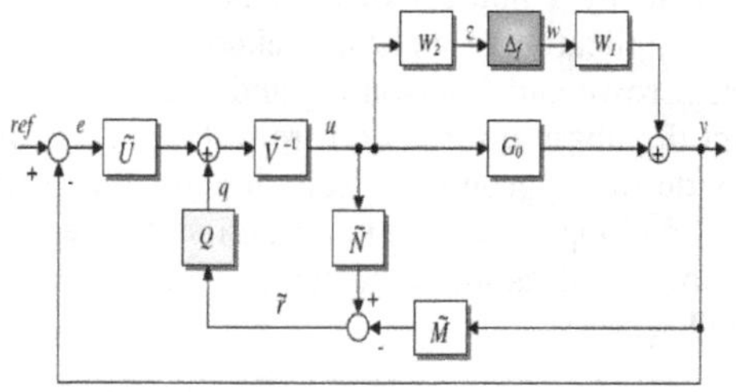

Fig.3. GIMC structure with multiplicative defects.

The solution to this problem is then given by the following theorem:

Theorem 1 (Delgado [7])

Supposing that $W_1(s), W_2(s) \in \Re H_\infty, G_0(s) \in \Re H_\infty$ and $K_0(s) = \tilde{V}(s)^{-1}\tilde{U}(s)$ is a corrector stabilizing G_0 while ensuring a certain closed loop performance. Then, the relation:

$$Q(s) = -\tilde{U}(s)\tilde{M}(s)^{-1} \qquad (6)$$

is the optimal solution to the optimization problem (5) where $\tilde{M}$ and $\tilde{N}$ are the left decomposition coprime of G_0. Indeed, for this choice of Q, the criterion (5) is null.

However, it is not always desirable to have the compensation signal q active all the time. In fact, authors show that the solution (6) doesn't guarantee neither the robustness against model errors, nor the robustness against exogenic disturbances. To resolve this problem, the authors propose to adopt a FTC structure where the compensation signal q is added to the nominal control signal since the fault detection and location. The activation of FTC strategy is carried out using commutation logic (see Fig.4). Whereas FTC corrector is in open loop for a no failing situation. It is important to mention that with the Figure 4 configuration, the closed loop system is not linear any more due to the introduction of commutation logic into the loop. This logic gives a hybrid character to the closed loop system and returns its analysis of complex stability. No real solution to this problem is presented by the research. The latter simply propose to operate commutation only once and to maintain it until the operation cycle in progress is finished.

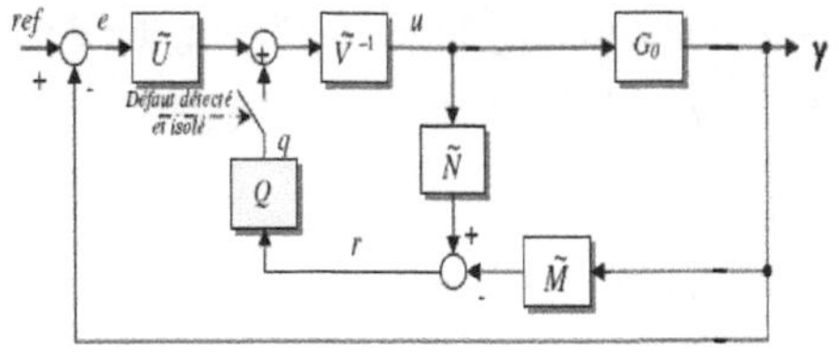

Fig.4. GIMC structure with commutation logic.

4 Phase-Locked Loop Identifier Module-Basic Theory:

Phase-locked loops have been used in a number of applications ranged from speed control loops to the detection of FM signals for radio receivers. The analysis of phase-locked loop systems used in the above applications has been covered in detail by a number of authors, Crowe and Johnson [9]. In the application of a phase-locked loop to system identification, Crowe and Johnson [9] and [10], the loop is used to extract the phase information from the process under test and provide the appropriate excitation for the system. The phase-locked loop system which was first devised was based on a number of ideas implemented as an analogue circuit as shown in Fig.5.

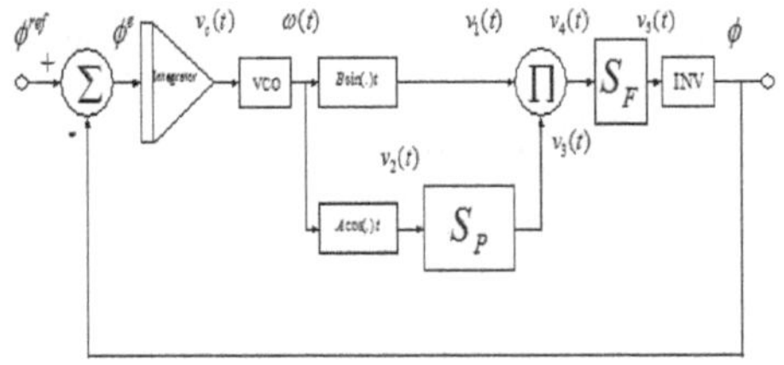

Fig.5. Phase-locked loop identifier module - Analogue prototype

The identifier module of Fig.5 was conceived as a feedback circuit around a voltage-controlled oscillator (VCO). The reference input to the loop was the desired process phase angle, so to drive the loop towards the critical frequency, the phase reference is $\phi^{ref} = -\pi$. Thus at the comparator, the phase error signal input to the integrator is given by $\phi^{e}(t) = \phi^{ref}(t) - \phi(t)$. The integrator in the loop is designed to ensure that the constant phase reference signal is attained in steady state conditions. The integrator equation is straightforwardly $v_c(t) = \int_0^t \varphi^{e}(\tau)d\tau$. A voltage-controlled oscillator produces the sinusoidal excitation signals of appropriate frequency. This frequency is proportional to the integral of phase reference error, $\omega(t) = K_{VCO}v_c(t)$, where the gain of the voltage controlled oscillator is denoted, K_{VCO}. The voltage-controlled oscillator generates two sinusoidal signals, $v_1(t) = B\sin\omega t$ and $v_2(t) = A\cos\omega t$. The signal $v_2(t)$ is used to excite the process and after transients have decayed, yields the steady state output signal,

$$v_3^{SS}(t) = S_p(v_2(t)) = A\left|G_p(j\omega)\right|\cos(\omega t + \varphi(\omega)) \quad (7)$$

Across the multiplier, the steady state output is,

$$\begin{aligned} v_4^{SS}(t) &= v_1(t)v_3^{SS}(t) \\ &= \frac{AB}{2}\left|G_p(j\omega)\right|\left[\sin(2\omega t + \varphi(\omega)) - \sin\varphi(\omega)\right] \end{aligned} \quad (8)$$

This signal is used in the nonlinear block to extract and identify the phase achieved by the current frequency value. This current value of the phase is then fed to the comparator to complete the loop. The amplitude A of the process excitation signal is user selected to minimize disruption to the process outputs. The equation for $v_4^{SS}(t)$ shows that a convenient choice for amplitude B is to use $B = 2/A$. In this way, the dependence of the signal $v_4^{SS}(t)$ on signal amplitudes A and B through the multiplier $AB/2$ is removed. The concepts in this analogue prototype were used to construct a phase-locked loop identifier module that retained the feature of continuous-time process excitation and used digital processing in the data extraction components of the outer loop.

All the sinusoidal signals in the module below (Fig.6) are transformed and adapted in square signals (SSC) and the comparator of phase used is a pump charges(PPC), Acco [11], and this module be used in the application.

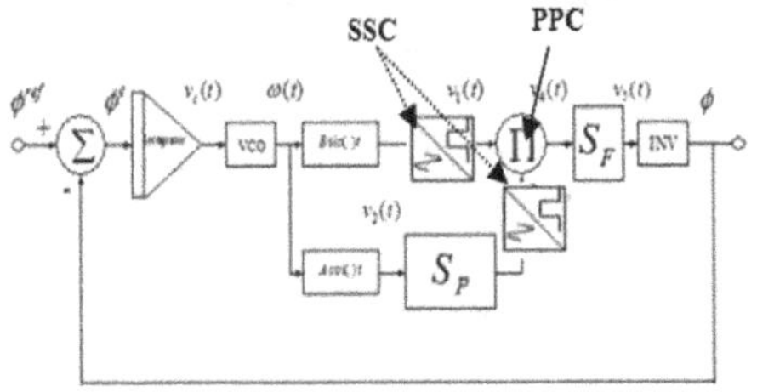

Fig.6. Phase-locked loop identifier module using adapted signals

5 Application

Considering the system with following transfer function

$$H(s) = \frac{1}{0.0032 * s + 1}$$

(Frequency for -45°=50Hz). Parameters of the loop are: the VCO gain is $K_{VCO} = 0.25\text{Hz/V}$, the filter used is 1 st order (low-pass) such as its cut-off frequency is $2\pi rad/\sec$; the current Ic of pump Charge is 1A. For a reference phase equal to -45°, we will present the evolution of the various sizes of the loop in the case without defects:

According to Fig.7 we note dephasing between the signal exciting the system to be identified and that of output (dephasing of -45°) in permanent mode.

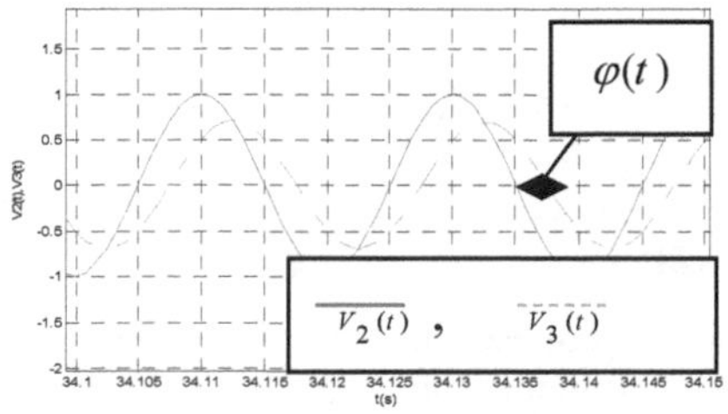

Fig.7. Evolution of $V_2(t)$ and $V_3(t)$ in permanent mode

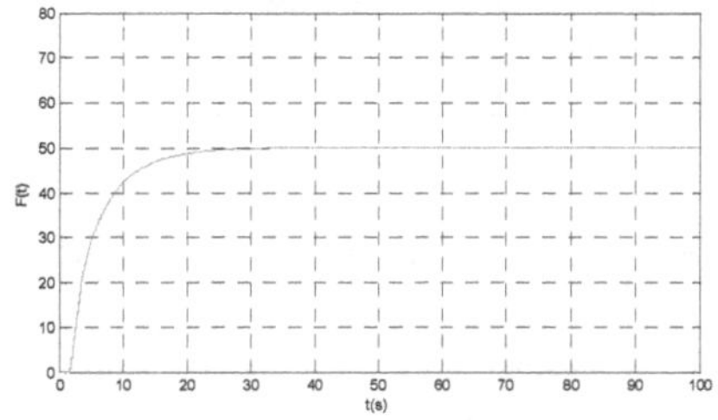

Fig.8. Frequency evolution *F(t)*

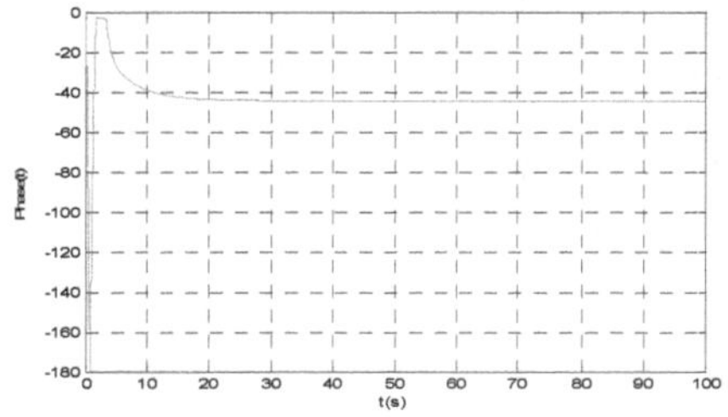

Fig.9.a. Phase evolution $\varphi(t)$

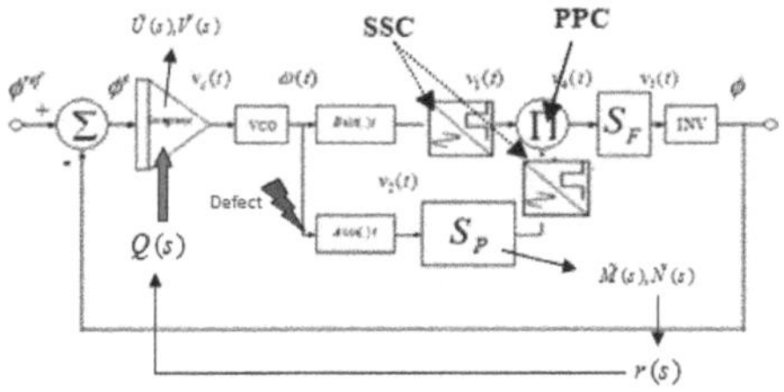

Fig.9.b. Application of GIMC structure on the module

Fig.8 and Fig.9.a show well the control quality of the frequency and the phase for the same reference phase.

We inject then a defect on the actuator of the loop (on the system input variation from + 3: very strong excitation on the static gain of the actuator which is almost equal to 3 times its face value) between the moments 20s → 25s (transitory mode) and we observe the variation of the loop controlled variables with and without application of the GIMC structure.

1 - For the decomposition [5] we choose $L = 1, (A - LC)$ and $F = 1, (A - BF)$ for the transfer function and the regulator nominal also, such as: $\tilde{M}(s) = \dfrac{s+312.5}{s+313.5}$ and $\tilde{N}(s) = \dfrac{625}{2s+627}$, $K_0(s) = \dfrac{1}{s}$ the regulator nominal of the loop, from where: $\tilde{U}(s) = \dfrac{1}{s+1}$ and $\tilde{V}^{-1}(s) = \dfrac{s+1}{s}$ thus: $Q(s) = -\dfrac{s+313.5}{s+312.5}$, for the commutation logic we have chosen a binary test on value 0 of the residue ($r \neq 0$).

2 - The application diagram of GIMC structure on the module is showed as in Fig. 9(b).

In a first place we observe the residue *r(t)* variation indicating the occurrence of a defect:

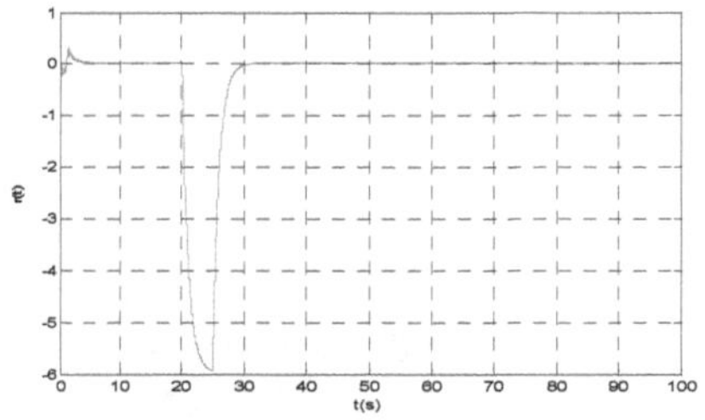

Fig.10. Residue variation *r(t)*

In a second place, we notice according to these figures above, during the presence of the defect (application of the defect in transitory mode), that for the case where we applied GIMC structure and according to Fig.11: the frequency evolution is better than that at faulty case since it is not of strong value of frequency (maximum at fault $F_{GIMC}(t)$= *51,4Hz* however, for the preceding case is almost $F_d(t)$= *68Hz*); The control loop variation (Fig.12): $Vc_{GIMC}(t)$ is about 20% of that in nominal case while $Vc_d(t)$ is about 47%, thus the elimination of the actuator's over-excitation risk.

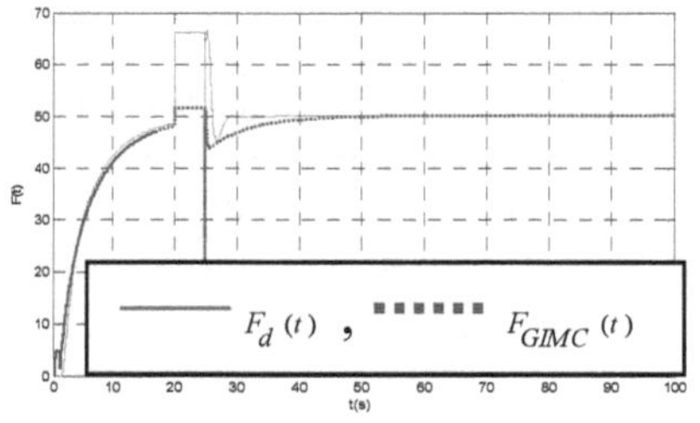

Fig.11. Frequency variation : $F_d(t)$ and $F_{GIMC}(t)$

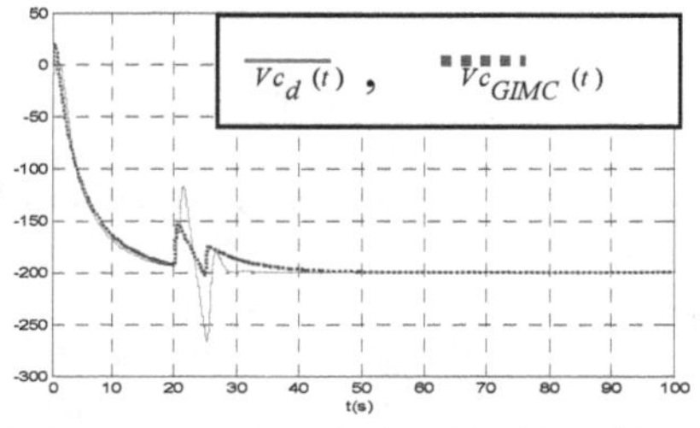

Fig.12. Loop control variation $Vc_d(t)$ and $Vc_{GIMC}(t)$

According to Figure 13, the module output variation (the phase) is better while applying GIMC structure. It offers a stabilization time better:

$Td_{stabilization}$=*29s* and $TGIMC_{stabilization}$=*26s*.

Now, we inject the same defect but at the moments 50s →60s (permanent mode) and we observe the system Outputs/Inputs variations.

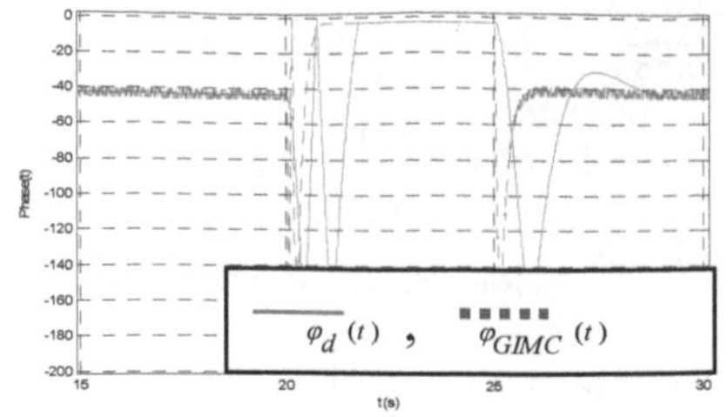

Fig.13. Phase variation: $\varphi_d(t)$ and $\varphi_{GIMC}(t)$

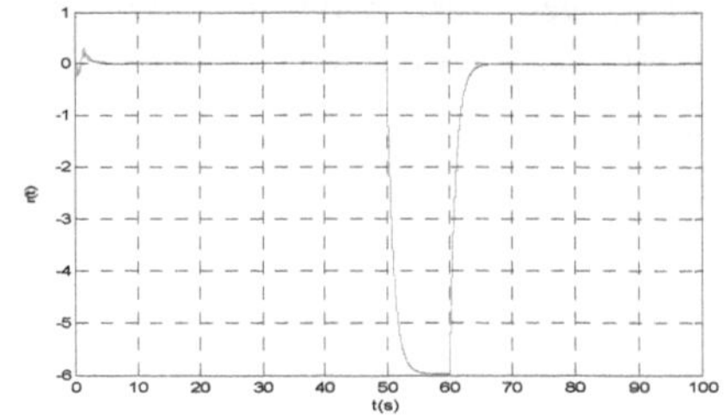

Fig.14. Residue variation *r(t)*

We notice according to Figures 15-17, during the presence of the defect (application of the defect in permanent mode), that for the case where we applied GIMC structure, we see almost same qualities and performances offered in the application of the method to the transitory mode with Just small value variations (Fig.15 and 16).

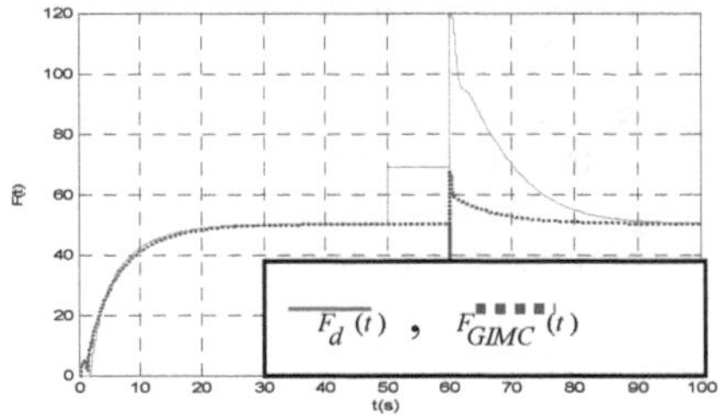

Fig.15. Frequency variation $F_d(t)$ and $F_{GIMC}(t)$

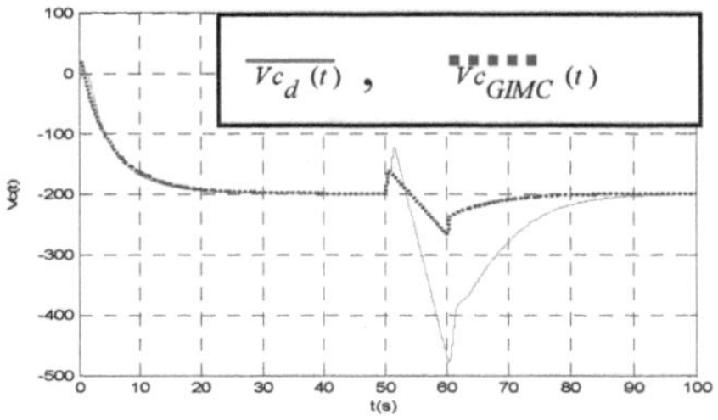

Fig.16. Loop control variation $Vc_d(t)$ and $Vc_{GIMC}(t)$

The only exception is the frequency variation and according to Fig.17 we see that:

$Td_{stabilization} > TGIMC_{stabilization}$.

Thus the solution offered by GIMC structure makes it possible to avoid strong deviation of frequency and maintains it near the rated frequency even in faulty case (an increase of 2.8%) as well as a small variation of the Loop control eliminating the risk from unhooking of the loop and a better phase control, from where a solution allowing to maintain as well as possible the nominal performances of the system in the occurrence of a defect even if this defect is injected into the transitory mode.

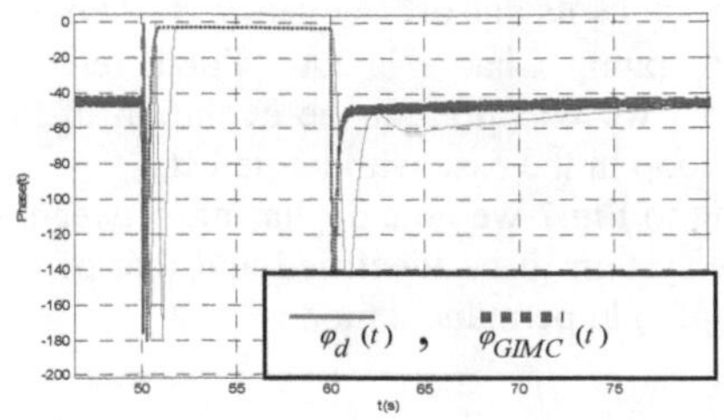

Fig.17. Phase variation: $\varphi_d(t)$ and $\varphi_{GIMC}(t)$

6 Conclusion

In this work, we proposed an application a method of AFTC called: GIMC structure on Phase-locked Loop Identifier Module. This application has presented very important results, showing, clearly, the quality of control and performances which are closer to that of nominal case and an acceptable control value at the defects occurrence. The results obtained seem to be encouraging and consequently, this application can be used in the case of the PLL regulators auto-parameter setting, Crowe and Johnson [10].

References

1. R. Isermann, *Process fault detection based on modeling and estimation methods -a survey*. Automatica, **20**(4), 387–404 (1984).
2. J.S. Eterno, D.P. Looze, J.L. Weiss, A.S. Willsky, *Design issues for fault tolerant restructurable aircraft control*. In: Proc. of the 24th IEEE Conference onDecision and Control, Fort Lauderdale (1985).
3. A. Thabet et.al, *Commande tolérante aux défauts: méthode pseudo-inverse (PIM) et méthode Linéaire Quadratique (LQR)*. La cinquième Conférence Internationale d'Electrotechnique et d'Automatique (JTEA),2008, Tunisie, 354-359 (2008).
4. D.C. Youla, J.J. Jabr, H.A. Bongiorno *Modern Wiener-Hopf design of optimal controllers – Part II: The multivariable case*. IEEE Transactions on Automatic Control, **21**(3), 319-338 (1976).
5. M.J. Cieslak, *Analyse et synthèse d'une architecture coopérative pour la commande tolérante aux défauts : Application à un système aéronautique*. Phd thesis. École doctorale des sciences physiques et de l'ingénieur. L'Université Bordeaux I (2007).
6. K. Zhou, Z. Ren, *A New Controller Architecture for High Performance, Robust and Fault Tolerant Control*," IEEE Transactions on Automatic Control, **46**, 1613-1618 (2001).
7. D.U. Campos-Delagado, K. Zhou, *Reconfigurable fault tolerant control using GIMC structure*, IEEE Transactions on Automatic .Control, **48**, 832-838 (2003).
8. D.U. Campos-Delagado, S. Martinez, K. Zhou, *Integrated Fault tolerant scheme with disturbance feed forward*. In Proceeding of the 2004 American Control Conference, Boston, 1799-1804 (2004)
9. J. Crowe, M.A. Johnson, *Towards autonomous PI control satisfying classical robustness specifications,* IEEE Proc-Control Theory Appl., **149**, 26-31 (2002)

10. J. Crowe, M.A. Johnson, *Automated PI controller tuning using a phase locked loop identifier module*. Industrial Electronics Society, IECON 2000.
11. P. Acco. *Etude de la boucle à verrouillage de phase par impulsions de charge. Prise en compte des aspects hybrides*. Phd thesis. Institut National des Sciences Appliquées de Toulouse, France (2003).

Recent progress in the optimal design of composite structures: industrial solution procedures on case studies

Michael Bruyneel[1,a], Benoît Colson[1], Philippe Jetteur[1], Caroline Raick[1], Alain Remouchamps[1], Stéphane Grihon[2]

[1] SAMTECH s.a., Liège Science Park, 8 Rue des chasseurs-ardennais, 4031, Angleur, Belgium
[2] Airbus France, 316 Route de Bayonne, 31060, Toulouse, France

Abstract – In this paper, recent developments carried out in the SAMCEF finite element code and in the BOSS quattro optimization toolbox are presented. Those developments aim at simulating high non linear effects in laminated composite structures (post-buckling, collapse, delamination) and at optimising the composites with respect to those structural responses. The use of Sequential Convex Programming and of Surrogate-Based Optimization methods is discussed on industrial optimization problems.

Key words: optimization methods, composite structures, industrial application, delamination

1 Introduction

In order to decrease the lead time, virtual testing and numerical optimization techniques are increasingly used in the different fields of engineering. This is especially the case for composite structures, where two main issues have recently been identified. Firstly, reliable methods are required to analyse post-buckling [1], collapse and delamination, which is a specific failure mode of laminated structures [2]. Secondly, designing real composite structures such as aircraft wings implies handling a large number of design variables and restrictions, resulting in a large scale optimization problem that is difficult to both define and solve [3]. Moreover, local optimization of aircraft components should involve advanced non linear analyses simulating delamination, post-buckling and collapse.

This paper presents an overview and a synthesis of the solution procedures recently developed in the SAMCEF finite element code [4] and in the BOSS Quattro multidisciplinary optimization platform [5] for solving such problems at an industrial level. The advanced buckling and collapse analysis capabilities are first presented, together with a discussion on the related sensitivity analyses, and an approach to evaluate delamination risks [6]. Then two optimization techniques used in this paper are recalled: a specific Sequential Convex Programming algorithm [7] and a Surrogate-Based Optimization method [8]. Finally, three applications are presented. The first one tackles the optimization of laminates with respect to damage tolerance considerations, based on a detailed (high fidelity) analysis of delamination. The second one aims at designing composite structures to withstand buckling and collapse [9,10]. The last application presents the results obtained for the optimal pre-design of a wing box of the Airbus A350, in which local criteria are used in an optimization problem including around 1000 design variables and about 100000 design restrictions [8,11].

2 Advanced structural analyses

This section, briefly describes the analyses involved in the optimization problems. The SAMCEF Finite Element code [4] is used to compute the structural responses.

2.1 Stability analysis

Structural stability analysis

Stability analysis consists in solving an eigen-value problem of the form (1), where **K** is the structural stiffness matrix, **L** the geometric stiffness matrix (also termed the initial stress stiffness matrix), $\mathbf{\Phi}_j$ the jth buckling mode and λ_j the associated buckling load. The components of vector $\mathbf{\Phi}_j$ are the structure's degrees of freedom, usually the displacements (translations and rotations). The buckling load must be interpreted as the factor by which the external loads must be multiplied for the structure to become unstable.

$$\mathbf{K}\mathbf{\Phi}_j - \lambda_j \mathbf{L}\mathbf{\Phi}_j = 0\,,\ j = 1,2,... \tag{1}$$

Typically, Reserve Factors are used in the optimization problem. For example $RF_j = \lambda_j / 1.2$, where 1.2 is a safety factor.

Sensitivity analysis of the buckling loads

The analytical first order derivative of the buckling load λ_j is derived in [12] and its implementation in an industrial software is discussed in [9]. It is given by:

$$\frac{\partial \lambda_j}{\partial x_i} = \mathbf{\Phi}_j^T \left(\frac{\partial \mathbf{K}}{\partial x_i} - \lambda_j \frac{\partial \mathbf{L}}{\partial x_i} \right) \mathbf{\Phi}_j\,,\ j = 1,2,... \tag{2}$$

As shown in this paper and in [9], in order to avoid excessive oscillations during the optimization process, a large number of load factors (and associated modes) must be taken into account, to ensure that the structure is sensitive to local

[a] Corresponding author: michael.bruyneel@samcef.com

modes everywhere. The sensitivity of RF_j is easily obtained from (2).

2.2 Post-buckling and collapse analyses

Structural non linear analysis and continuation method

Although the stability analysis provides an estimation of the bifurcation points, it is based on a linear approach, and is therefore only an approximation. Moreover, once buckling has occurred, some thin walled structures can sometimes still sustain an increasing loading up to the final collapse [1]. This is illustrated in Figure 1 in the case of a stiffened composite panel.

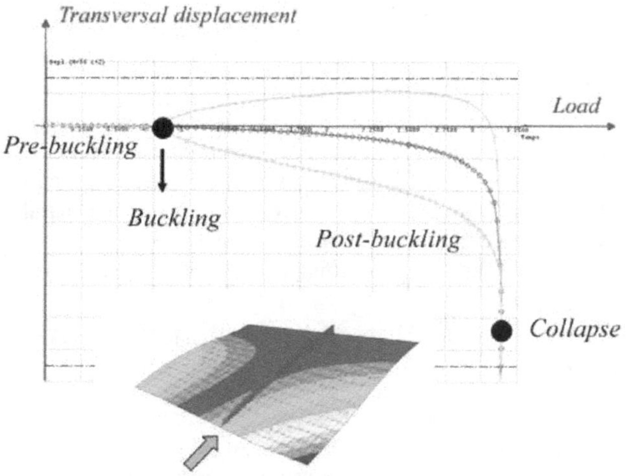

Fig. 1. Illustration of the post-buckling analysis of a stiffened composite panel

To simulate the large displacements appearing in a structure beyond its bifurcation point, a geometric non linear analysis is required, in which, contrary to (1), the stiffness matrix changes all over the loading. A non linear system of equilibrium equations (3) is therefore solved, for an imposed load factor λ or displacements q. When a limit point (e.g. collapse) must be identified, the classical Newton-Raphson method can present problems, and a continuation method (also called arc length or Riks method) must be used. In this method, **q** and λ are unknown and linked to an additional parameter, called the arc length [13], with equation (4). This parameter is controlled over the iterations. The complete set of equations can now be now written as:

$$\mathbf{F}(\mathbf{q},\lambda)=0 \qquad (3)$$

$$c(\mathbf{q},\lambda)=0 \qquad (4)$$

The Reserve Factor associated with the collapse load is given by the load increment λ, i.e. $RF = \lambda_{collapse}$. At the solution, RF must be larger than or equal to 1, implying that collapse will not occur at a loading lower than the nominal one.

Sensitivity analysis of the collapse load

The goal here is to compute the value $d\lambda/dx_i$, where x_i is the ith design variable and λ is the load factor. Starting from the equilibrium equations and knowing that the forces depend on the displacement **q**, the load increment λ and the set of design variables **x**, it follows that

$$\frac{\partial \mathbf{F}}{\partial \mathbf{q}}d\mathbf{q}+\frac{\partial \mathbf{F}}{\partial \mathbf{x}}d\mathbf{x}+\frac{\partial \mathbf{F}}{\partial \lambda}d\lambda=0 \qquad (5)$$

The unknown vector is also constrained to be orthogonal to the load-displacement curve rather than being a simple measure based on the vertical gap Δλ. This allows a better accuracy of the sensitivity measure. It turns out that $d\lambda/d\mathbf{x}$ can be computed from the tangent stiffness matrix; the variation of the internal forces with respect to the design variables is computed by finite differences. Details are given in [10,14].

2.3 Advanced damage tolerance analysis

When the fracture mechanics approach is applied to the delamination of laminated composites [2,6], the finite element method is used to model the cracked structure and to compute the energy release rates G_I, G_{II} and G_{III}, related to each of the three modes (I, II and III) of inter-laminar fracture (crack lips opening, sliding shear and tearing, respectively). Once these values are computed at each node defining the crack front, they are inserted in a criterion such as (5) and compared to G_{IC}, G_{IIC} and G_{IIIC}, which characterize the inter-laminar fracture toughness in the three individual modes.

$$\frac{G_I}{G_{IC}}+\frac{G_{II}}{G_{IIC}}+\frac{G_{III}}{G_{IIIC}}<1 \qquad (5)$$

When the value in (5) reaches unity, it is assumed that the crack will propagate in the structure. In this paper a specific Virtual Crack Extension method is used to compute G_I, G_{II} and G_{III}. This computation is carried out in a linear analysis. The method is decomposed into two steps. In the first, the variation of the total potential energy π at equilibrium is evaluated:

$$G_T=-\frac{d\pi}{dA}=G_I+G_{II}+G_{III} \qquad (6)$$

Considering the expression of π in linear elasticity, and taking the derivative with respect to the crack length (surface) A, it turns out that:

$$\pi=\frac{1}{2}\mathbf{q}^T\mathbf{K}\mathbf{q}-\mathbf{g}^T\mathbf{q}$$

$$=> \frac{d\pi}{dA}=\frac{1}{2}\mathbf{q}^T\frac{d\mathbf{K}}{dA}\mathbf{q}-\mathbf{q}^T\frac{d\mathbf{g}}{dA}$$

where **q** are the nodal displacements and **g** is the vector of applied nodal forces. In a semi-analytical approach, $d\mathbf{K}/dA$ can be replaced by $\Delta\mathbf{K}/\Delta A$. The total energy release rate G_T in (6) is finally obtained from (7), where the index *init* corresponds to the initial (actual) crack length, and *pert* denotes a perturbed configuration of the crack associated with a virtual (very small) advance in its local plane. Equations (6) and (7) clearly show how the sensitivity analysis for structural optimization and the calculation of the energy release rate in a fracture mechanics problem are related.

$$G_T=-\frac{d\pi}{dA}\cong-\frac{(\pi_{pert}-\pi_{init})}{\Delta A} \qquad (7)$$

In the second step, the total energy release rate given by (7) is distributed over the three modes G_I, G_{II} and G_{III}, considering the relative displacements of the lips and the reactions to the crack opening, sliding and tearing at the crack front. The VCE method is used in SAMCEF to identify the most critical cracks in a structure, and to estimate the propagation load, i.e. the amplitude of the load leading to at least one crack propagation, according to criteria such as (5). This method is illustrated in Figure 2, for mode I.

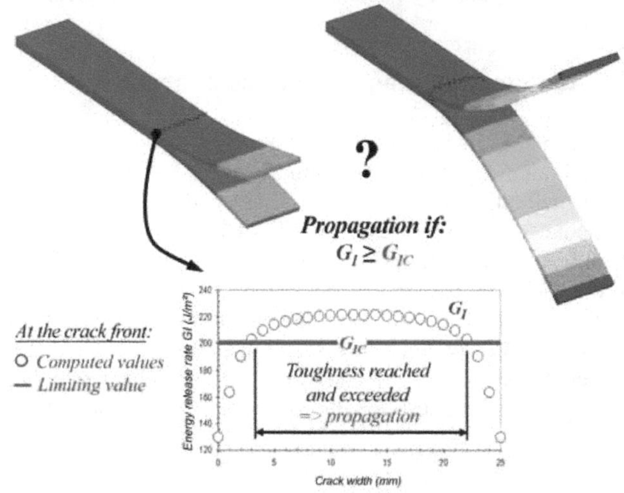

Fig. 2. Principle of the VCE method illustrated on a Double Cantilever Beam (DCB)

A semi-analytical sensitivity analysis of the energy release rate with respect to ply thickness and fibres orientation has not yet been developed in SAMCEF, but is somehow related to the structural stiffness. Moreover, as explained in Section 4, some uncertainties still exist concerning the formulation of the optimization problem.

2.4 Pre-design criteria for composite aircraft structures

Structural analysis

A wing is divided into a set of super-stiffeners, made of a portion of the skin and a T-stiffener (Figure 3). The Reserve Factors are computed at the local level, i.e. in each super-stiffener. According to [3,11,15], several criteria can appear in the formulation of the pre-design of a composite aircraft wing. In this case, Reserve Factors reflect buckling, damage tolerance, reparability and some design rules at the super-stiffener level. The values of these *RFs* vary with respect to design variables, which are the panel thickness, the proportions of fibres oriented at 0°, ±45° and 90°, and dimensions of the stiffeners (web and flange height, web thickness, etc). The *RFs* are also functions of internal forces, N, computed from a global finite element model of the wing as depicted in Figure 3. The *RFs* values at the local level (in the super-stiffeners) are calculated using analytical formulas.

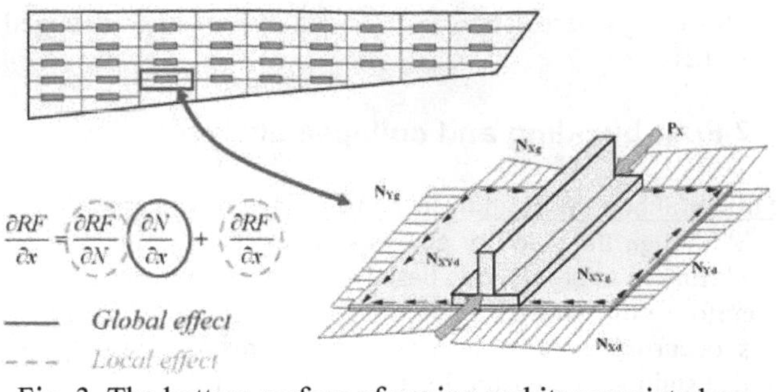

Fig. 3. The bottom surface of a wing and its associated super-stiffeners where local computations are carried out

Sensitivity analysis

The interaction between the local and the global effects is taken into account by the sensitivity analysis, as illustrated in Figure 3, through the modification of the internal forces N with respect to a change in each design variable *x*. While the computation of global sensitivities are based on semi-analytical derivatives, finite differences and massive parallelism are used for computing the derivatives of the local values, on the set of super-stiffeners. For details, see [8,11].

3 Basic description of the optimization methods

Several optimization methods are used in this paper, depending on the application. The selection of an efficient optimization method depends on the problem to be solved. When derivatives are available and when the problem includes a large number of design variables and design functions, it is recommended to use a gradient-based method, such as a Sequential Convex Programming method (SCP). On the other hand, when derivatives are not available, either because the problem is non differentiable, or simply because they have not be implemented, the use of a Genetic Algorithm (GA) is certainly a good choice, assuming that the computational time for a structural analysis is very low and that the problem includes few design variables. When non linear structural analyses are conducted, a Surrogate Based Optimization method (SBO) is preferred to a Genetic Algorithm. In this case the number of design variables must however remain relatively small. To conclude therefore, it is important to note that a gradient based optimization method will not generally provide the global optimum of the problem, while a Genetic Algorithm will, for a large population. Moreover, when working with discrete design variables, GA is a natural and easy choice. In the following applications, continuous design variables are considered, and SCP and SBO methods are used.

3.1 The general optimization problem

The optimization problem to be solved takes the following form:

$$\begin{aligned} &\min FOB(\mathbf{x}) \\ &RF_j(\mathbf{x}) \geq 1 \quad j = 1,\ldots,m \\ &\underline{x_i} \leq x_i \leq \overline{x_i} \quad i = 1,\ldots,n \end{aligned} \tag{8}$$

where **x** is the set of design variables, FOB is the objective function (weight or total energy release rate in the following applications), and RF_j is the jth Reserve Factor. Two methods are used in what follows. For a detailed presentation of optimization methods, the reader should refer to [7,8].

3.2 Sequential Convex Programming - SCP

In this gradient-based approach, the solution of the initial optimization problem (8) is replaced by the solution of successive explicit approximations, as illustrated in Figure 4 for an unconstrained optimisation problem. A generalization of the MMA approximation, developed in [7] and available in the BOSS Quattro optimization toolbox, is used. This method automatically generates monotonous or non monotonous approximations of the structural response with respect to the design variables, in order to have an accurate model of the initial optimization problem. An approximation of problem (8) is generated based on the functions value and their first order derivatives (obtained from structural and sensitivity analyses, respectively). Once the solution of an approximated problem is obtained, it is checked to see whether convergence has been reached. If this is not the case, a new approximation is built, and the process is continued until convergence to a desired accuracy is achieved. The advantage of this method is that it requires a small number of iterations to reach the solution (say between 10 and 25) irrespective of the number of design variables. However, derivatives must be available, and generally only local optima can be identified. For constrained optimisation problem, a dual approach is used (see [7]).

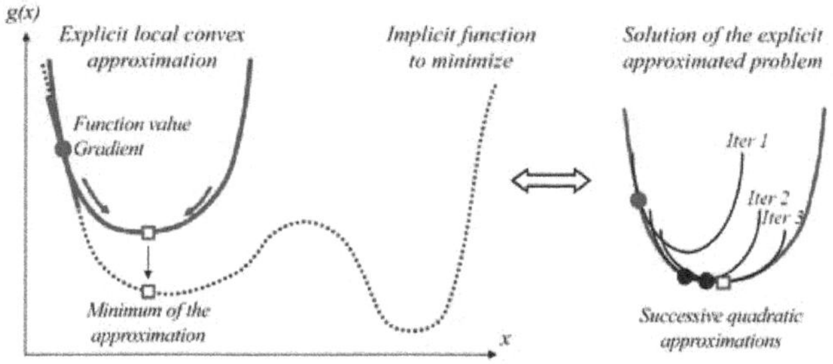

Fig. 4. Illustration of the Sequential Convex Programming approach

3.3 Surrogate Based optimization - SBO

In this method [8], only the function values are used to build a global approximation of the design domain, as illustrated in Figure 5. A response surface is generated based on a Neural Network (NN) or a Radial Basis Function (RBF). The optimum of this global approximation is obtained with a genetic algorithm. The new point is then used to build a new response surface, and the process is repeated until convergence. The advantage of this approach lies in the fact that it can be used when the derivatives are not available. On the other hand, it results in a prohibitively long computational time when a large number of design variables is used. However, parallelism allows a reduction – to some extent – of the time needed to find a solution. For constrained optimisation problems, a penalty is used.

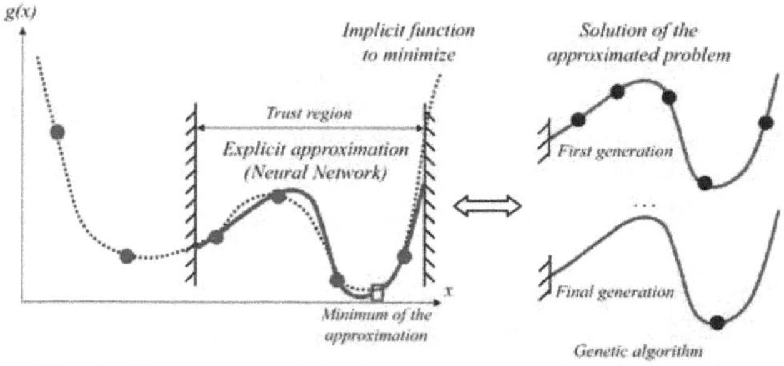

Fig. 5. Illustration of the Surrogate Based Optimization approach

4 case study 1: design with respect to delamination

Designing a composite structure with respect to damage tolerance is becoming a challenge. Although simplified formulations may be used at a global level for a pre-design (e.g. a complete wing [11]), more sophisticated high fidelity approaches should be selected when local detailed structural components are studied. An ENF (End Notched Flexure) specimen is considered here (Figure 6). The function to be minimized is the total energy release rate G_T (6) over the crack front, in order to design a laminate less sensitive to delamination. Since the value of G_T varies along the crack front, minimum, mean and maximum values are therefore minimized, in order to obtain a laminate less prone to crack propagation. Only one design variable is selected: it is the angle of the following lay-up: [±θ /0/- θ /0/ θ /0$_4$/ θ /0/- θ /0/- θ / θ /*d*/- θ / θ /0/ θ /0/- θ /0$_4$/- θ /0/ θ /0/± θ]. The initial value of θ is 30°.

The inter-laminar toughnesses G_{IC}, G_{IIC} and G_{IIIC} used in the criterion (5) depend on the fibre orientations across the interface [16]. Moreover, a large dispersion in the inter-laminar toughness values exists. In the simplified approach adopted here, a constant value of G_C is considered. For the sake of accuracy this variation of G_C should be included in the formulation of the optimization problem, and robust optimization methods should be used [17]. The current approach is therefore not rigorous and aims rather at comparing optimization methods. The results must therefore be interpreted with care.

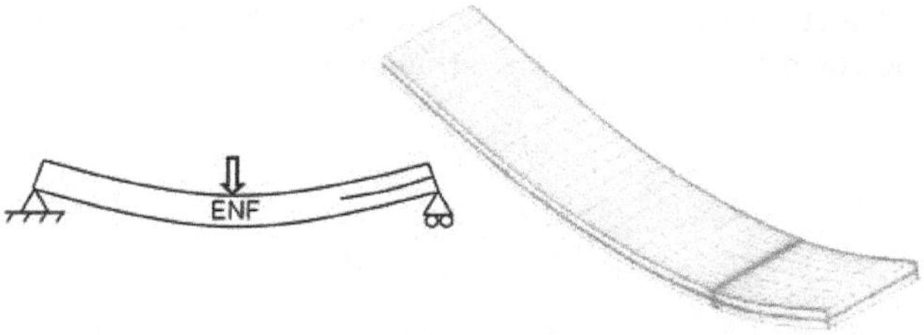

Fig. 6. The ENF test case, and its finite element model

First the SCP method presented in [7] is used, and the sensitivities are up-to-now computed by finite differences. The results of the iterative optimization process are presented in Figure 7a. The optimal value of θ (0-deg) is obtained after 8 iterations, and 15 structural analyses.

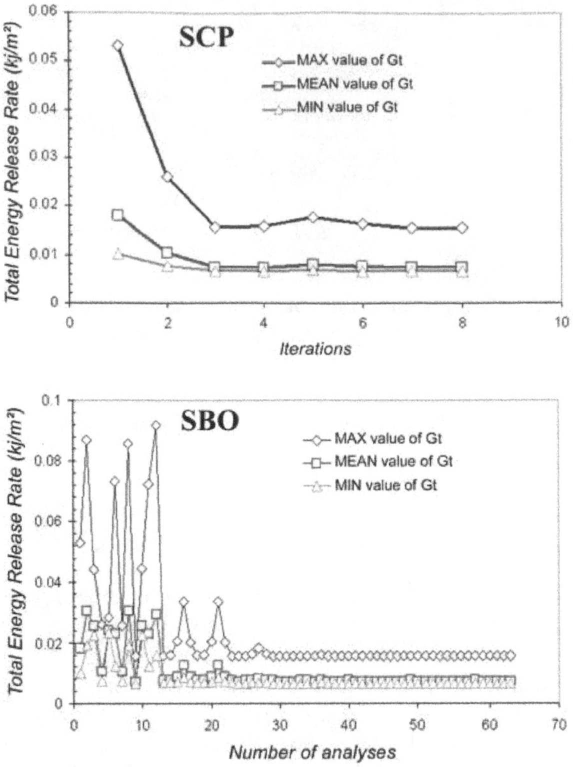

Fig. 7. The ENF test case, on its finite element model

Surrogate Based Optimization methods [8] – where Neural Networks or other response surfaces are used to generate a global approximation of the design problem – may be efficient for treating the damage tolerance problem, as was the case in [1] for post-buckling optimization of composite structures. In this case, their main advantage is that analyses are run on parallel processors, which is not possible with a sequential gradient-based approach such as SCP. Applying such a method to the problem depicted in Figure 6 provides the solution after 63 structural analyses, which is competitive with the SCP method since 4 processors were used for the parallel solution (Figure 7b). The formulation of this kind of problems should be further investigated.

5 case study 2: design of a stiffened panel

A hat-stiffened curved composite panel subjected to shear and compression is considered (Figure 8).

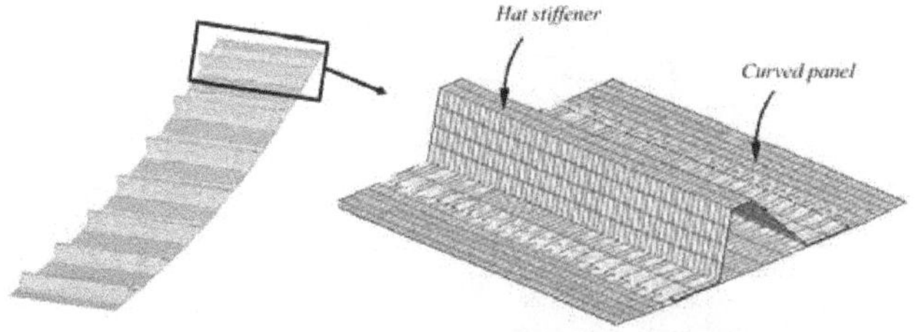

Fig. 8. Curved composite panel and its super-stiffeners

In each super-stiffener (Figure 8b), three design variables are related to the thickness of the plies oriented at 0°, ±45° and 90° to the skin, and three other design variables are defined for the corresponding values in the stiffener. Since seven panels are used to form the structure, 42 design variables are defined in the problem.

5.1 Optimization with respect to buckling

The goal is to find the values of the ply thickness that minimize the weight while satisfying RF ≥ 1, according to (1). It can be seen in Figure 9 that when only the first 12 load factors are considered in the design problem, large oscillations appear. Given the local character of the associated buckling modes, some structural parts may become insensitive to buckling, and the modes start to move all over the structure during the iterative optimization process, leading to oscillations. In contrast, when a large number of buckling loads are taken into account, the whole structure remains sensitive to buckling and, insofar as a reliable optimization method is used, the solution can be obtained in a small number of iterations (Figure 9). More details can be found in [9].

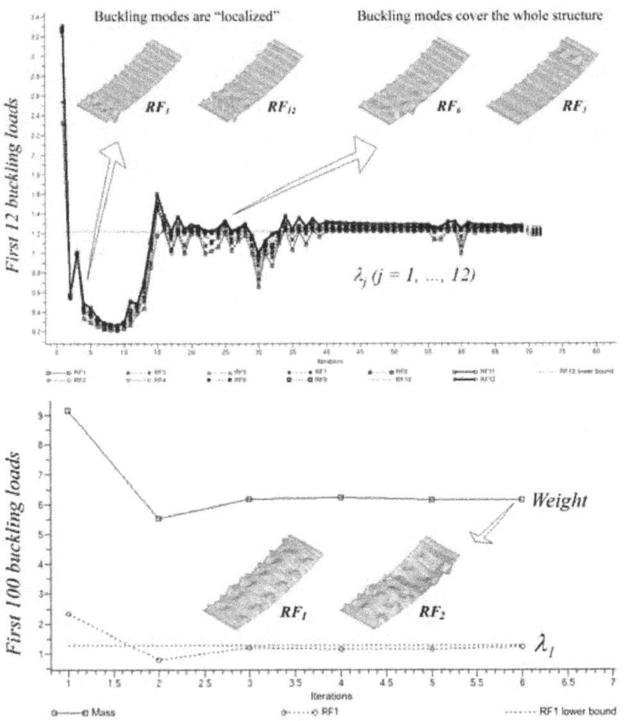

Fig. 9. Convergence history for 12 and 100 buckling modes

5.2 Optimization with respect to buckling and collapse

This problem can be solved when post-buckling behaviour is considered as well. In this case, post-buckling is allowed to develop in the structure, and the buckling loads are prescribed to be larger than 0.76. The collapse must appear for $\lambda_{collapse} \geq 1$. The results are presented in Figure 10, where 100 buckling modes are taken into account. The solution is obtained after 17 iterations. As in the previous section, convergence problems (oscillations) are observed when a small number of buckling modes is used.

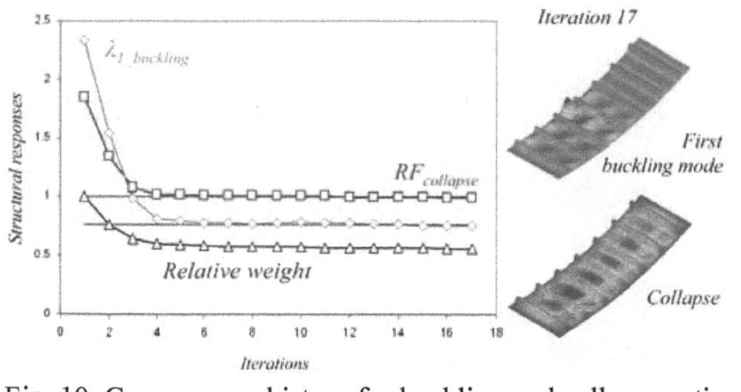

Fig. 10. Convergence history for buckling and collapse optimization

6 case study 3: large scale optimization of a composite aircraft component

Only a part of the composite box structure of a wing is considered in this optimization problem. Based on Section 2.4, the mass is to be minimized, while 71552 restrictions on buckling, damage tolerance and reparability are defined on the several super-stiffeners composing the wing box. The problem includes 630 design variables (panel thickness, and size of the stiffeners). As illustrated in Figure 11, the solution is found after 10 iterations. More details on a full wing optimization are available in [9,11].

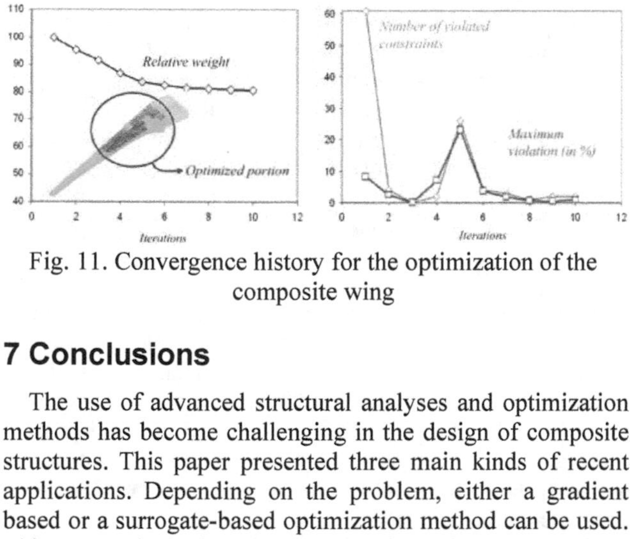

Fig. 11. Convergence history for the optimization of the composite wing

7 Conclusions

The use of advanced structural analyses and optimization methods has become challenging in the design of composite structures. This paper presented three main kinds of recent applications. Depending on the problem, either a gradient based or a surrogate-based optimization method can be used. This comparison should be further investigated, especially when local non linear analyses, such as delamination, post-buckling and collapse, are considered. Indeed, in such cases, few design variables are used, and both methods could become competitive.

Acknowledgement

The support of the European Commission (VIVACE Project) and of the Walloon Region of Belgium (OPTISTACK Project) is gratefully acknowledged.

References

1. L. Lanzi, V. Giavotto, *Post-buckling optimization of composite stiffened panels: computations and experiments*, Compos. Struct. **73**, 208-230 (2006).
2. R. Krueger, Computational fracture mechanics for composites – State of the art and challenges, In *NAFEMS Seminar – Prediction and Modelling of Failure Using FEA* (2006).
3. F. Huttner, M. Grosspietsch, S*olving very large scale structural optimization problems*, AIAA J **45**(11), 2729-2736 (2007).
4 SAMCEF. Système d'Analyse des Milieux Continus par Eléments Finis. www.samcef.com
5. Y. Radovcic, A. Remouchamps, *BOSS quattro: an open system for parametric design*, Struct. Multidiscipl. Optim. **23**, 140-152 (2002).
6. M. Bruyneel, J.P. Delsemme, F. Germain, Ph. Jetteur, A study of complex delaminations in laminated composite structures with SAMCEF, In *Fourth International Conference on Advanced Computational Methods in Engineering* (2008).
7. M. Bruyneel *A general and effective approach for the optimal design of fibers reinforced composite structures*, Compos. Sci. Technol. **66**, 1303-1314 (2006).
8. A. Remouchamps, S. Grihon, B. Colson, C. Raick, M. Bruyneel, Numerical optimization: a design space odyssey, In *1st International Conference on Advancements in Design Optimization of Materials, Structures and Mechanical Systems* (2007).
9. M. Bruyneel, B. Colson, A. Remouchamps. *Discussion on some convergence problems in buckling optimization*, Struct. Multidiscipl. Optim. **35**, 181-186 (2008).
10. B. Colson, M. Bruyneel, Ph. Jetteur, P. Morelle, A. Remouchamps, Composite panel optimization with non linear finite element analysis and semi-analytical sensitivities, In *NAFEMS Seminar – Simulating Composite Materials and Structures* (2007).
11. L. Krog., M. Bruyneel, A. Remouchamps, C. Fleury, COMBOX: a distributed computing process for optimum pre-sizing of composite aircraft box structures, In *10th SAMTECH Users Conference* (2007).
12. H. Adelman, R.T. Haftka, A *discourse on sensitivity analysis for discretely-modelled structures*, NASA Technical Memorandum 104065.
13. E. Riks, C. Rankin, F. Brogan, *On the solution of mode jumping phenomena in thin walled shell structures*, Comp. Meth. Appl. Mech. Engng. **136**, 59-92 (1996).
14. M. Bruyneel, B. Coslon, J.P. Delsemme., Ph. Jetteur, A. Remouchamps, S. Grihon, *Exploiting semi-analytical sensitivities from linear and non-linear finite element analyses for composite panel optimization*, to appear in Int. J. Struct. Stability & Dynamics (2009).
15. D. Weiss, *Optimization in aircraft pre-design with sizing criteria*, Diploma Thesis N° IMES-ST 06-019, Swiss Federal Institute of Technology Zurich (2006).
16. O. Allix, D. Lévêque, L. Perret, *Identification and forecast of delamination in composite laminates by an interlaminar interface model*, Compos. Sci. Technol., **58**, 671-678 (1998).
17. H.G. Beyer, B. Sendhoff, *Robust Optimization – A Comprehensive Survey*, Comput0 Meth. Appl. Mech. Engng. **196**, 3190-3218 (2007).

17

Numerical prediction of the effective coefficient of thermal expansion of 3D braided C/SiC composite

Yingjie Xu[1, a], Weihong Zhang[1]

[1] Key Laboratory of Contemporary Design & Integrated Manufacturing Technology, Northwestern Polytechnical University, 710072, Xi'an, Shaanxi, China

Abstract –This paper is focused on the microstructure modeling and evaluation of effective coefficient of thermal expansion (CTE) of 3D braided carbon fiber-reinforced silicon carbide composites (C/SiC). Regarding the multi-scale characteristics of the composite, the microstructure modeling is carried out sequentially from the fiber scale to tow scale. Effective elastic properties are obtained based on the sequential homogenization from the fiber scale to the tow scale. A stain energy model is developed for the prediction of the effective CTE of composite materials. This model is based on the relationship established between the strain energy of the microstructure and that of the homogenized equivalent model under specific thermo-elastic boundary conditions. Expressions of closed-form are derived for the effective CTE in terms of the strain energy and effective elastic tensor. Numerical results obtained by the proposed model show a good agreement with the results measured experimentally.

Key words: 3D braided C/SiC composite, Coefficient of thermal expansion, Microstructure modeling, Strain energy, Numerical prediction

1 Introduction

Under extreme high-temperature environment, the basic concern is to use materials which can maintain their superior character during exposure to hostile temperature environment ranging between 800℃ and 1100℃ [1]. C/SiC composites have been purposefully engineered according to these service requirements. 3D braided C/SiC composites are widely used in high temperature air-breathing, space, and nuclear applications [1]. Introduction of SiC matrix into composites has boosted the possibility of having materials that could provide dimensional stability along with sustained thermo-physical properties in an environment prone to rapid corrosion and severe thermal shock.

Complicated spatial architecture and material heterogeneity of 3D braided C/SiC composites constitute the challenges to understand their physical properties. Revelation of the intrinsic relations between the effective physical properties and the complex materials microstructure is thus the key for practical applications of 3D braided C/SiC composites. The common numerical approach for characterizing the composite materials is to create a representative volume cell (RVC) that captures the major features of the underlying microstructure. A variety of RVC models and strategies were proposed to determine mechanical properties of 3D braided composite [2-12], but the work for characterization of 3D C/SiC composites has been limited compared to polymer and metal matrix composites. [1]

This study aims at the microstructure modeling and numerical prediction of effective CTE of 3-D braided C/SiC composite. Regarding the multi-scale characteristics of the composite, the microstructure modeling is carried out sequentially from the fiber-scale to tow-scale. Effective thermal-elastic properties are obtained based on the sequential homogenization. A stain energy model is developed for the prediction of the effective CTE. Numerical results obtained by the proposed model and are then compared with the results measured experimentally.

2 Strain energy model for evaluation of CTE of composite

In the present work, the relationship between the strain energy of unit cell and homogenized equivalent model is studied for 3D orthotropic materials. To make things clear, consider a unit cell model with heterogeneous microstructure depicted in Fig. 1a. It consists of two material phases (the dark color represent the fiber while the light color represent the matrix) and can be regarded as a homogenized equivalent model depicted in Fig. 1b.

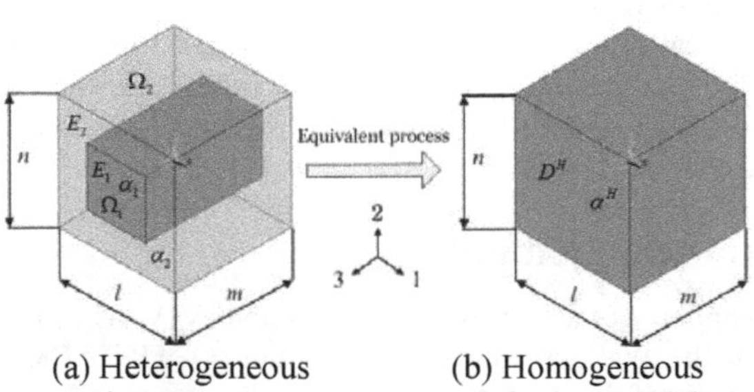

(a) Heterogeneous microstructure (b) Homogeneous equivalent model

Fig. 1. Illustration of RVC

In thermo-elastic regime, the macroscopic behaviors of the RVC can be characterized by the effective stress tensor $\bar{\boldsymbol{\sigma}}$ and strain tensor $\bar{\boldsymbol{\varepsilon}}$ over the homogeneous equivalent model:

[a] Corresponding author: xyj1014@gmail.com

$$\overline{\boldsymbol{\sigma}} = \boldsymbol{D}^H\left(\overline{\boldsymbol{\varepsilon}} - \boldsymbol{\alpha}^H \Delta T\right) \quad (1)$$

where ΔT is the temperature increase. $\boldsymbol{D}^H$ and $\boldsymbol{\alpha}^H$ represent the effective stiffness matrix and thermal expansion coefficient matrix, respectively. Further more, $\boldsymbol{D}^H$ and $\boldsymbol{\alpha}^H$ can be written as:

$$\boldsymbol{D}^H = \begin{bmatrix} D_{1111}^H & D_{1122}^H & D_{1133}^H & 0 & 0 & 0 \\ D_{1122}^H & D_{2222}^H & D_{2233}^H & 0 & 0 & 0 \\ D_{1133}^H & D_{2233}^H & D_{3333}^H & 0 & 0 & 0 \\ 0 & 0 & 0 & D_{1212}^H & 0 & 0 \\ 0 & 0 & 0 & 0 & D_{2323}^H & 0 \\ 0 & 0 & 0 & 0 & 0 & D_{3131}^H \end{bmatrix} \quad (2)$$

$$\boldsymbol{\alpha}^H = \begin{bmatrix} \alpha_{11}^H & \alpha_{22}^H & \alpha_{33}^H \end{bmatrix}^T \quad (3)$$

note that here $\boldsymbol{D}^H$ consists of known coefficients, which have been obtained by using the strain energy of microstructure but only considering elastic boundary conditions. Details about the implementation procedure were discussed in our previous work [14].

Thus, the relationship between effective stress and strain caused by the temperature increase of ΔT can be then given as:

$$\begin{aligned} \overline{\sigma}_{11} &= D_{1111}^H(\overline{\varepsilon}_{11} - \alpha_{11}^H \Delta T) + D_{1122}^H(\overline{\varepsilon}_{22} - \alpha_{22}^H \Delta T) \\ &\quad + D_{1133}^H(\overline{\varepsilon}_{33} - \alpha_{33}^H \Delta T) \\ \overline{\sigma}_{22} &= D_{1122}^H(\overline{\varepsilon}_{11} - \alpha_{11}^H \Delta T) + D_{2222}^H(\overline{\varepsilon}_{22} - \alpha_{22}^H \Delta T) \\ &\quad + D_{2233}^H(\overline{\varepsilon}_{33} - \alpha_{33}^H \Delta T) \\ \overline{\sigma}_{33} &= D_{1133}^H(\overline{\varepsilon}_{11} - \alpha_{11}^H \Delta T) + D_{2233}^H(\overline{\varepsilon}_{22} - \alpha_{22}^H \Delta T) \\ &\quad + D_{3333}^H(\overline{\varepsilon}_{33} - \alpha_{33}^H \Delta T) \end{aligned} \quad (4)$$

The strain energy related to the RVC is equal to:

$$C = \int_{\Omega} \boldsymbol{\sigma}^T \boldsymbol{\varepsilon} d\Omega \quad (5)$$

note that $\boldsymbol{\sigma}$ and $\boldsymbol{\varepsilon}$ are the stress and strain tensor over the RVC, respectively.

Now, consider the following three kinds of boundary condition depicted in Figs. 2, 3 and 4, respectively.

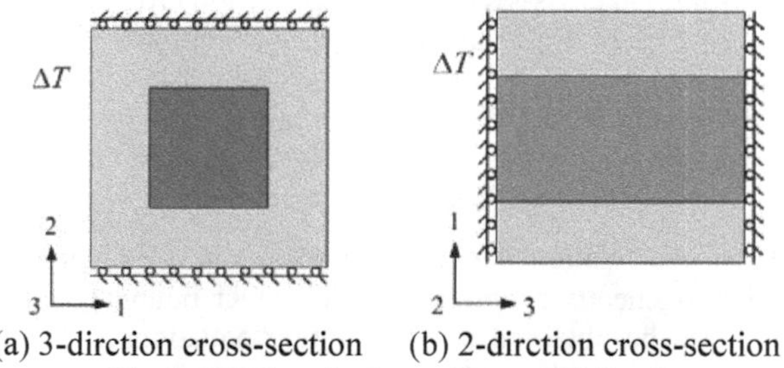

(a) 3-dirction cross-section (b) 2-dirction cross-section

Fig. 2. RVC under boundary condition 1

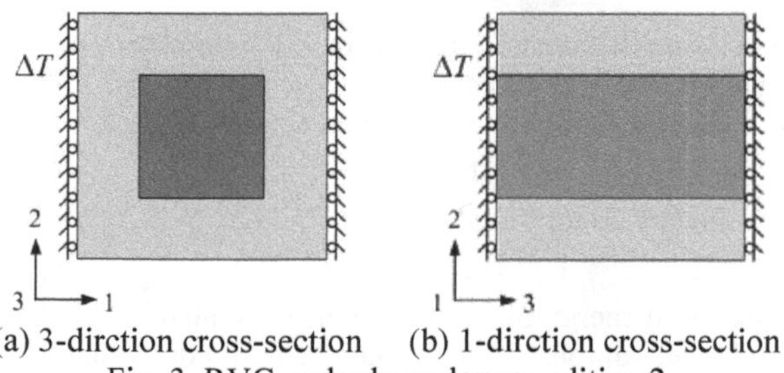

(a) 3-dirction cross-section (b) 1-dirction cross-section

Fig. 3. RVC under boundary condition 2

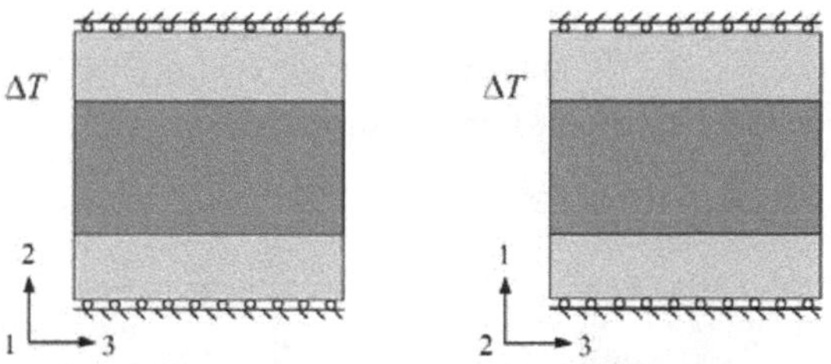

(a) 1-dirction cross-section (b) 2-dirction cross-section

Fig. 4. RVC under boundary condition 3

The RVC under boundary condition 1 is restricted to move in the 2, 3 directions but free in the 1 direction, which leads to the deformation caused by the temperature increase is free in the 1 direction while restricted in the 2, 3 direction. The following effective stress and strain conditions can be obtained, note that the superscript (1) represents the first boundary condition:

$$\overline{\sigma}_{11}^{(1)} = 0,\ \overline{\varepsilon}_{22}^{(1)} = 0,\ \overline{\varepsilon}_{33}^{(1)} = 0 \quad (6)$$

Inverting equation (6) into equation (4), one obtains the following expressions:

$$\begin{aligned} \overline{\varepsilon}_{11}^{(1)} &= \alpha_{11}^H \Delta T + \frac{D_{1122}^H}{D_{1111}^H}\alpha_{22}^H \Delta T + \frac{D_{1133}^H}{D_{1111}^H}\alpha_{33}^H \Delta T \\ \overline{\sigma}_{22}^{(1)} &= \left(\frac{D_{1122}^H D_{1122}^H}{D_{1111}^H} - D_{2222}^H\right)\alpha_{22}^H \Delta T + \left(\frac{D_{1122}^H D_{1133}^H}{D_{1111}^H} - D_{2233}^H\right)\alpha_{33}^H \Delta T \\ \overline{\sigma}_{33}^{(1)} &= \left(\frac{D_{1133}^H D_{1122}^H}{D_{1111}^H} - D_{2233}^H\right)\alpha_{22}^H \Delta T + \left(\frac{D_{1133}^H D_{1133}^H}{D_{1111}^H} - D_{3333}^H\right)\alpha_{33}^H \Delta T \end{aligned} \quad (7)$$

The same demonstrations can be made for the other two boundary conditions, and the following expressions can be obtained:

$$\begin{aligned} \overline{\varepsilon}_{22}^{(1)} &= \alpha_{22}^H \Delta T + \frac{D_{1122}^H}{D_{2222}^H}\alpha_{11}^H \Delta T + \frac{D_{2233}^H}{D_{2222}^H}\alpha_{33}^H \Delta T \\ \overline{\sigma}_{11}^{(1)} &= \left(\frac{D_{1122}^H D_{1122}^H}{D_{2222}^H} - D_{1111}^H\right)\alpha_{11}^H \Delta T + \left(\frac{D_{1122}^H D_{2233}^H}{D_{2222}^H} - D_{1133}^H\right)\alpha_{33}^H \Delta T \\ \overline{\sigma}_{33}^{(1)} &= \left(\frac{D_{2233}^H D_{1122}^H}{D_{2222}^H} - D_{1133}^H\right)\alpha_{11}^H \Delta T + \left(\frac{D_{2233}^H D_{2233}^H}{D_{2222}^H} - D_{3333}^H\right)\alpha_{33}^H \Delta T \end{aligned} \quad (8)$$

$$\begin{aligned} \overline{\varepsilon}_{33}^{(1)} &= \alpha_{33}^H \Delta T + \frac{D_{1133}^H}{D_{3333}^H}\alpha_{11}^H \Delta T + \frac{D_{2233}^H}{D_{3333}^H}\alpha_{22}^H \Delta T \\ \overline{\sigma}_{11}^{(1)} &= \left(\frac{D_{1133}^H D_{1133}^H}{D_{3333}^H} - D_{1111}^H\right)\alpha_{11}^H \Delta T + \left(\frac{D_{1133}^H D_{2233}^H}{D_{3333}^H} - D_{1122}^H\right)\alpha_{22}^H \Delta T \\ \overline{\sigma}_{22}^{(1)} &= \left(\frac{D_{2233}^H D_{1133}^H}{D_{3333}^H} - D_{1122}^H\right)\alpha_{11}^H \Delta T + \left(\frac{D_{2233}^H D_{2233}^H}{D_{3333}^H} - D_{2222}^H\right)\alpha_{22}^H \Delta T \end{aligned} \quad (9)$$

Considering the RVC under boundary condition 1, the relationship between the strain energy of RVC and homogeneous equivalent model is illustrated below. Here, boundary condition 4 is imposed on the RVC, as shown in Fig. 5. The displacement u_1 and interface force f are equivalent to the displacement and interface force caused by the thermal deformation under boundary condition 1, which are expressed as:

$$u_1 = \left(\alpha_{11}^H \Delta T + \frac{D_{1122}^H}{D_{1111}^H}\alpha_{22}^H \Delta T + \frac{D_{1133}^H}{D_{1111}^H}\alpha_{33}^H \Delta T\right) l \quad (10)$$

$$f = \int_S \left[\boldsymbol{D}(E_1)\boldsymbol{\alpha}(\alpha_1) - \boldsymbol{D}(E_2)\boldsymbol{\alpha}(\alpha_2)\right] \Delta T ds \quad (11)$$

Obviously, the RVC under boundary condition 4 has the same deformation field as that under boundary condition 1 and thus the strain energies of RVC under both two boundary conditions are equivalent:

$$C_R^{(1)} = C_R^{(4)} \tag{12}$$

where $C_R^{(1)}$ and $C_R^{(4)}$ indicate the strain energy of RVC under boundary condition 1 and 4, respectively.

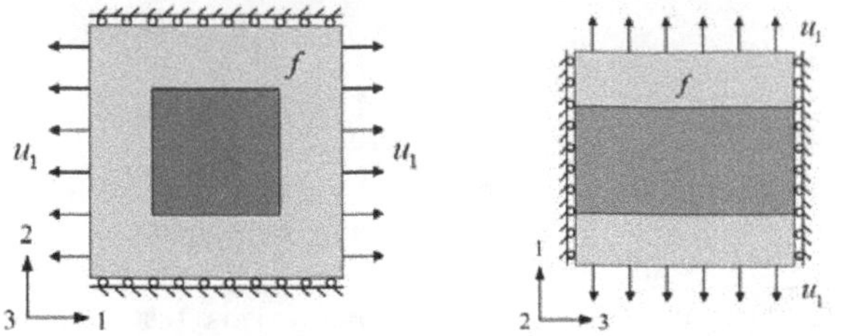

(a) 3-dirction cross-section (b) 2-dirction cross-section
Fig. 5. RVC under boundary condition 4

Similar demonstration can be made for the homogeneous equivalent model. The equivalent model under boundary condition 1 (depicted in Fig. 6) has the same deformation field as that under boundary condition 5 (depicted in Fig. 7), and the strain energy of equivalent model under these two boundary conditions are equivalent:

$$C_H^{(1)} = C_H^{(5)} \tag{13}$$

where $C_H^{(1)}$ and $C_H^{(5)}$ refer to the strain energy of homogeneous equivalent model under boundary condition 1 and 5, respectively.

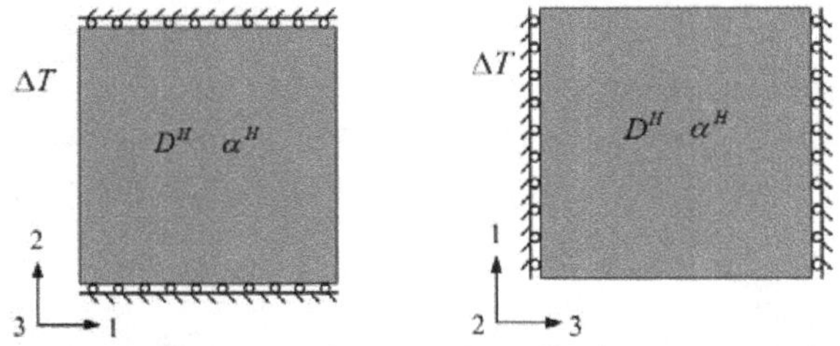

(a) 3-dirction cross-section (b) 2-dirction cross-section
Fig. 6. Homogeneous equivalent model under boundary condition 1

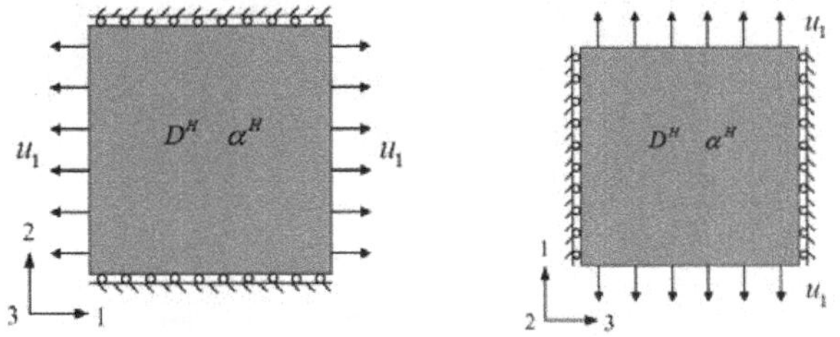

(a) 3-dirction cross-section (b) 2-dirction cross-section
Fig. 7. Homogeneous equivalent model under boundary condition 5

It can be demonstrated that the strain energy related to the RVC is equal to that of the homogeneous equivalent model under uniformly distributed loading boundary conditions. Hence, the strain energy of RVC under boundary condition 5 (depicted in Fig. 8), $C_R^{(5)}$, can be expressed as:

$$C_R^{(5)} = C_H^{(5)} \tag{14}$$

Comparing equation (14) with equation (13) results in:

$$C_R^{(5)} = C_H^{(1)} \tag{15}$$

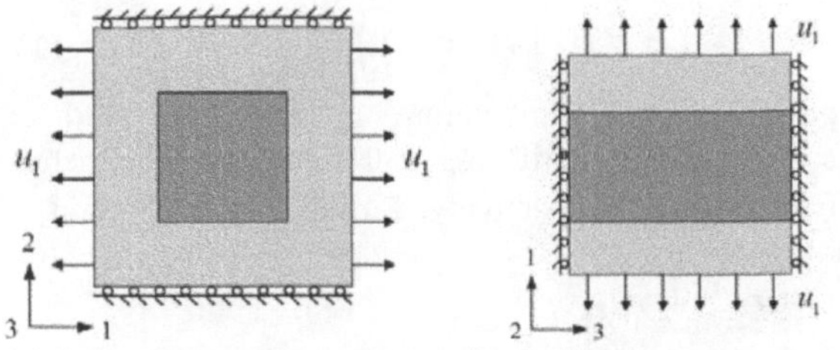

(a) 3-dirction cross-section (b) 2-dirction cross-section
Fig. 8. RVC under boundary condition 5

Boundary conditions 6 and 7, as illustrated in Figs 9 and 10, are then imposed on the RVC respectively. The interface force f denoted in Fig 10 is equivalent to that caused by the thermal deformation under boundary condition 6. Hence, the strain energies of RVC under both two boundary conditions are equivalent:

$$C_R^{(6)} = C_R^{(7)} \tag{16}$$

where $C_R^{(6)}$ and $C_R^{(7)}$ refer to the strain energy of RVC under boundary condition 6 and 7, respectively.

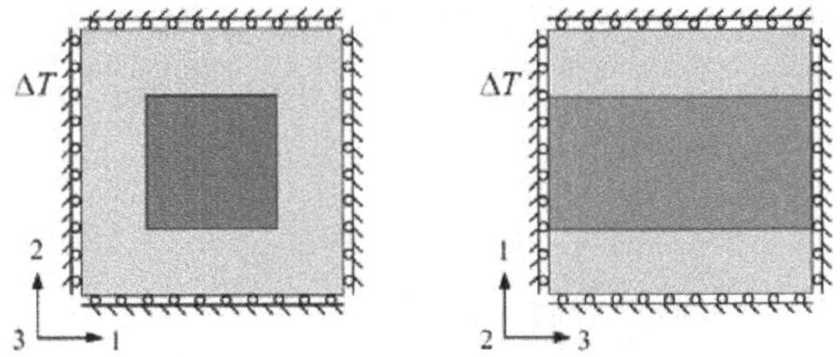

(a) 3-dirction cross-section (b) 2-dirction cross-section
Fig. 9. RVC under boundary condition 6

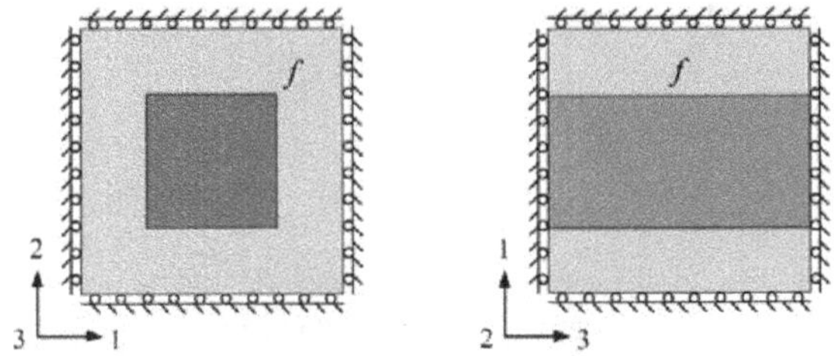

(a) 3-dirction cross-section (b) 2-dirction cross-section
Fig. 10. RVC under boundary condition 7

Considering the RVC under boundary conditions 4, 5 and 7, one can explicitly derive the following expression:

$$C_R^{(5)} + C_R^{(7)} = C_R^{(4)} \tag{17}$$

Then, the relation between the strain energy of unit cell and homogeneous equivalent model under boundary condition 1 can be obtained by substituting equations (12), (15) and (16) into equation (17):

$$C_R^{(1)} = C_R^{(6)} + C_H^{(1)} \tag{18}$$

The same demonstrations can be made to obtain the relationship between the strain energy of unit cell and homogeneous equivalent model under boundary condition 2:

$$C_R^{(2)} = C_R^{(6)} + C_H^{(2)} \tag{19}$$

and boundary condition 3:

$$C_R^{(3)} = C_R^{(6)} + C_H^{(3)} \tag{20}$$

The strain energy of homogeneous equivalent model under boundary conditions 1, 2 and 3 can be easily determined as:

$$C_H^{(1)} = D_{1111}^H \left(\alpha_{11}^H \Delta T + \frac{D_{1122}^H}{D_{1111}^H} \alpha_{22}^H \Delta T + \frac{D_{1133}^H}{D_{1111}^H} \alpha_{33}^H \Delta T \right)^2 V \tag{21}$$

$$C_H^{(2)} = D_{2222}^H \left(\alpha_{22}^H \Delta T + \frac{D_{1122}^H}{D_{2222}^H} \alpha_{11}^H \Delta T + \frac{D_{2233}^H}{D_{2222}^H} \alpha_{33}^H \Delta T \right)^2 V \tag{22}$$

$$C_H^{(3)} = D_{3333}^H \left(\alpha_{33}^H \Delta T + \frac{D_{1133}^H}{D_{3333}^H} \alpha_{11}^H \Delta T + \frac{D_{2233}^H}{D_{3333}^H} \alpha_{22}^H \Delta T \right)^2 V \tag{23}$$

note that V is the volume of unit cell. By replacing $C_H^{(1)}$, $C_H^{(2)}$ and $C_H^{(3)}$ into equation (18), (19) and (20), respectively, one obtains the following expressions:

$$C_R^{(1)} - C_R^{(6)} = D_{1111}^H \left(\alpha_{11}^H \Delta T + \frac{D_{1122}^H}{D_{1111}^H} \alpha_{22}^H \Delta T + \frac{D_{1133}^H}{D_{1111}^H} \alpha_{33}^H \Delta T \right)^2 V \tag{24}$$

$$C_R^{(2)} - C_R^{(6)} = D_{2222}^H \left(\alpha_{22}^H \Delta T + \frac{D_{1122}^H}{D_{2222}^H} \alpha_{11}^H \Delta T + \frac{D_{2233}^H}{D_{2222}^H} \alpha_{33}^H \Delta T \right)^2 V \tag{25}$$

$$C_R^{(3)} - C_R^{(6)} = D_{3333}^H \left(\alpha_{33}^H \Delta T + \frac{D_{1133}^H}{D_{3333}^H} \alpha_{11}^H \Delta T + \frac{D_{2233}^H}{D_{3333}^H} \alpha_{22}^H \Delta T \right)^2 V \tag{26}$$

Solving equations (24)-(26) finally yields the effective CTEs of RVC:

$$\alpha_{11}^H = \frac{\left(\frac{D_{1122}^H}{D_{1111}^H} \frac{D_{2233}^H}{D_{2222}^H} - \frac{D_{1133}^H}{D_{1111}^H} \right) \left(\frac{D_{2233}^H}{D_{3333}^H} Q - R \right) - \left(\frac{D_{2233}^H}{D_{3333}^H} \frac{D_{2233}^H}{D_{2222}^H} - 1 \right) \left(\frac{D_{1122}^H}{D_{1111}^H} Q - P \right)}{\left(\frac{D_{1122}^H}{D_{1111}^H} \frac{D_{2233}^H}{D_{2222}^H} - \frac{D_{1133}^H}{D_{1111}^H} \right) \left(\frac{D_{2233}^H}{D_{3333}^H} \frac{D_{1122}^H}{D_{2222}^H} - \frac{D_{1133}^H}{D_{3333}^H} \right) - \left(\frac{D_{2233}^H}{D_{3333}^H} \frac{D_{2233}^H}{D_{2222}^H} - 1 \right) \left(\frac{D_{1122}^H}{D_{1111}^H} \frac{D_{1122}^H}{D_{2222}^H} - 1 \right)} \tag{27}$$

$$\alpha_{22}^H = \frac{\left(\frac{D_{1122}^H}{D_{2222}^H} \frac{D_{1133}^H}{D_{1111}^H} - \frac{D_{2233}^H}{D_{2222}^H} \right) \left(\frac{D_{1133}^H}{D_{3333}^H} P - R \right) - \left(\frac{D_{1133}^H}{D_{3333}^H} \frac{D_{1133}^H}{D_{1111}^H} - 1 \right) \left(\frac{D_{1122}^H}{D_{2222}^H} P - Q \right)}{\left(\frac{D_{1122}^H}{D_{2222}^H} \frac{D_{1133}^H}{D_{1111}^H} - \frac{D_{2233}^H}{D_{2222}^H} \right) \left(\frac{D_{1133}^H}{D_{3333}^H} \frac{D_{1122}^H}{D_{1111}^H} - \frac{D_{2233}^H}{D_{3333}^H} \right) - \left(\frac{D_{1133}^H}{D_{3333}^H} \frac{D_{1133}^H}{D_{1111}^H} - 1 \right) \left(\frac{D_{1122}^H}{D_{2222}^H} \frac{D_{1122}^H}{D_{1111}^H} - 1 \right)} \tag{28}$$

$$\alpha_{33}^H = \frac{\left(\frac{D_{1133}^H}{D_{3333}^H} \frac{D_{1122}^H}{D_{1111}^H} - \frac{D_{2233}^H}{D_{3333}^H} \right) \left(\frac{D_{1122}^H}{D_{2222}^H} P - Q \right) - \left(\frac{D_{1122}^H}{D_{2222}^H} \frac{D_{1122}^H}{D_{1111}^H} - 1 \right) \left(\frac{D_{1133}^H}{D_{3333}^H} P - R \right)}{\left(\frac{D_{1133}^H}{D_{3333}^H} \frac{D_{1122}^H}{D_{1111}^H} - \frac{D_{2233}^H}{D_{3333}^H} \right) \left(\frac{D_{1122}^H}{D_{2222}^H} \frac{D_{1133}^H}{D_{1111}^H} - \frac{D_{2233}^H}{D_{2222}^H} \right) - \left(\frac{D_{1122}^H}{D_{2222}^H} \frac{D_{1122}^H}{D_{1111}^H} - 1 \right) \left(\frac{D_{1133}^H}{D_{3333}^H} \frac{D_{1133}^H}{D_{1111}^H} - 1 \right)} \tag{29}$$

where $P = \sqrt{\frac{C_R^{(1)} - C_R^{(6)}}{D_{1111}^H (\Delta T)^2 V}}$, $Q = \sqrt{\frac{C_R^{(2)} - C_R^{(6)}}{D_{2222}^H (\Delta T)^2 V}}$ and $R = \sqrt{\frac{C_R^{(3)} - C_R^{(6)}}{D_{3333}^H (\Delta T)^2 V}}$. Regarding the above equations, an important point to be noted is that the explicit closed-form expressions can be established between the effective CTEs and the elastic tensors by virtue of the strain energy model. In practice, the considered RVC will be discretized into a finite element model on which the above four boundary conditions 1, 2, 3 and 6 will be imposed to evaluate the corresponding strain energies, respectively.

3 Multi-scale modeling of RVC

The 3D 4-step braided C/SiC composite is considered in the present study. The RVC model of the 3D 4-step braided C/SiC composite involves two scales: fiber scale and tow scale. The first scale concerns the modeling of RVC for tows and the second scale concerns the modeling of RVC for 3D 4-step braided composites. Considering the multi-scale characteristics, the multi-scale analysis procedure are carried out for the analysis: (a). On the fiber scale, finite element model is built to obtain the effective thermo-elastic properties of the fiber-scale RVC, and the results are used for the tows that are treated as a homogeneous transversely isotropic material. (b). Finite element model of the tow-scale RVC is created to evaluate effective thermo-elastic properties of the composite. Here, RVC models of both scales are established using ANSYS finite element software.

3.1 Fiber-scale model

The fiber-scale concerns the tows which are considered as unidirectional fiber reinforced composites. Fig. 11 shows the finite element model of the RVC with a 60% fiber volume fraction of C/SiC unidirectional composite. Similar finite element models can be created for other volume fractions.

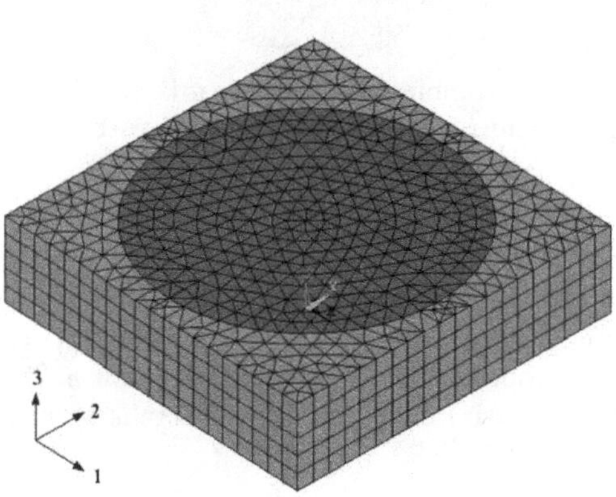

Fig. 11. Finite element model of the fiber-scale RVC

3.2 Tow-scale model

Over the last decades, extensive investigations have been mainly carried out [2-12] about the modeling of 3D braided composites. 4-step method is widely used as the basic forming technique of 3D braiding composites. In the 4-step braiding process, the braider tows are intertwined through their relative displacements. The braiding pattern is termed 1×1 because of the identical distance traveled by all the rows or columns in each step. Four steps of motion constitute one machine cycle which will braid the tows. As these steps of motion are repeated, the tows move throughout the cross-section and are interlaced to form the braided structure. More details about the 4-step braiding process can be found in Ref. [6].

The RVC structure used in this paper is followed from which described in Ref. [12]: the cross-section of tow is hexagonal; the braided structure is uniform and all the tows are straight within the braided preform; all tows in the braided preform have identical constituent material, size and flexibility. Fig. 12 shows the finite element model of the RVC of a 22° braiding angle 3D 4-step braided C/SiC composite.

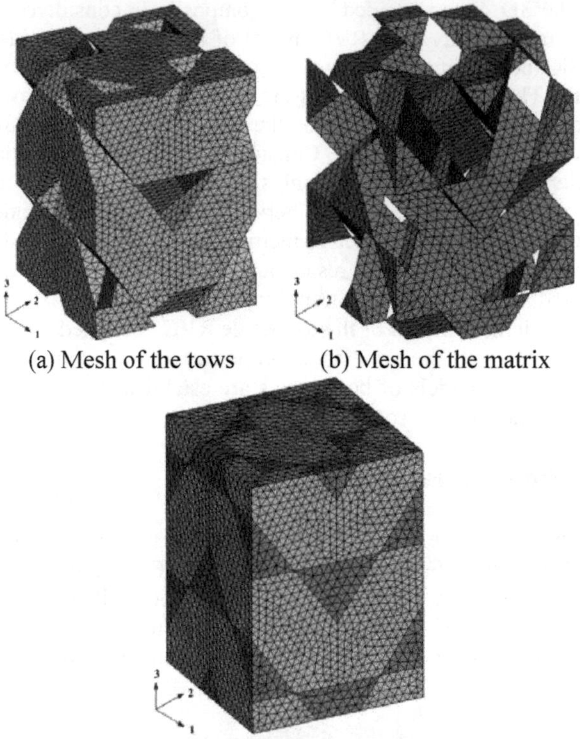

(a) Mesh of the tows (b) Mesh of the matrix

(c) Combined tows and matrix mesh

Fig. 12. Finite element model of the tow-scale RVC

4 Numerical examples

The CTE for 3D braided C/SiC composite under different temperatures are investigated experimentally [13]. The thermo-elastic properties of its constituents (Carbon fiber, Silicon carbide matrix) under various temperatures are summarized in Table 1.

Table 1. Properties of the constituents

		200□	500□	700□	800□
E_{11} (GPa)	C fiber	22	22	22	22
	SiC matrix	350	350	350	350
E_{33} (GPa)	C fiber	220	220	220	220
	SiC matrix	350	350	350	350
G_{23} (GPa)	C fiber	4.8	4.8	4.8	4.8
	SiC matrix	145.8	145.8	145.8	145.8
ν_{12}	C fiber	0.4	0.4	0.4	0.4
	SiC matrix	0.2	0.2	0.2	0.2
ν_{23}	C fiber	0.12	0.12	0.12	0.12
	SiC matrix	0.2	0.2	0.2	0.2
α_{11} $(10^{-6}/°C)$	C fiber	8.85	8.85	8.85	8.85
	SiC matrix	1.9	3.7	4.6	4.9
α_{33} $(10^{-6}/°C)$	C fiber	0.0	1.5	1.5	1.5
	SiC matrix	1.9	3.7	4.6	4.9

The orthotropic thermo-elastic tow properties are firstly generated using strain energy model, followed by computation of the effective thermo-elastic properties for 3D braided C/SiC composite.

In Table2, the CTEs obtained by the strain energy model are compared with experimental results given in Ref. [13]. It can be seen that the predicted results coincide well with the experiments.

Table 2. Comparison of computed CTEs with experimental and numerical results

		200□	500□	700□	800□
α_{11} $(10^{-6}/°C)$	Strain energy model	3.31	4.63	5.18	5.38
	Experiment	3.76	5.31	6.08	6.53
α_{33} $(10^{-6}/°C)$	Strain energy model	1.79	3.26	3.64	3.77
	Experiment	1.67	3.02	3.98	4.70

5 Conclusions

In this paper, the predicting of effective CTEs for 3D braided C/SiC composite is presented. Finite element modeling of the 3D braided C/SiC composite is carried out. The strain energy model is presented as an efficient homogenization approach and effective CTE are obtained based on the sequential homogenization from the fiber scale to the tow scale. The significance of strain energy model lies in its simplicity in numerical implementation. In addition, by applying the strain energy model, the closed-form expressions between the effective CTEs and the elastic tensors can be established explicitly. The comparison with the experimental results shows the validity and the rationality of the present model.

References

1. R. Naslain. *Design, preparation and properties of non-oxide CMCs for application in engines and nuclear reactors: an overview.* Compos. Sci. Technol. **64**, 155-170 (2004).
2. Y.Q. Wang, A.S.D. Wang. *On the topological yarn structure of 3-D rectangular and tubular braided performs.* Compos. Sci. Technol. **51**, 575-586 (1994).
3. Y.Q. Wang, A.S.D. Wang. *Microstructure/property relationships in three dimensional braided fiber composites.* Compos. Sci. Technol. **53**, 213-222 (1995).
4. R. Pandey, H.T. Hahn. *Designing with 4-step braided fabric composites.* Compos. Sci. Technol. **56**, 623-634 (1996).
5. H.Y. Sun, X. Qiao. *Prediction of the mechanical properties of three-dimensionally braided composites.* Compos. Sci. Technol. **57**, 623-629 (1997).
6. L. Chen, X.M. Tao, C.L. Choy. *On the microstructure of three dimensional braided preforms.* Compos. Sci. Technol. **59**, 391-404 (1999).
7. L. Chen, X.M. Tao, C.L. Choy. *Mechanical analysis of 3-D braided composites by the finite multiphase element method.* Compos. Sci. Technol. **59**, 2383-2391 (1999).
8. Z.X. Tang, R. Postle. *Mechanics of three-dimensional braided structures for composite materials-part□: fabric structure and fibre volume fraction.* Compos. Struct. **49**, 451-459 (2000).
9. Z.X. Tang, R. Postle. *Mechanics of three-dimensional braided structures for composite materials-part II: pre-*

diction of the elastic moduli. Compos. Struct. **51**, 451-457 (2001).

10. X.K. Sun, C.J. Sun. *Mechanical properties of three-dimensional braided composites*. Compos. Struct. **65**, 485-492 (2004).
11. K. Xu, X.W. Xu. *Finite element analysis of mechanical properties of 3D five-directional braided composites*. Mater. Sci. Eng. A **487**: 499-509 (2008).
12. G.D. Fang, J. Liang. B.L. Wang. *Progressive damage and nonlinear analysis of 3D four-directional braided composites under unidirectional tension*. Compos. Struct. **89**, 126-133 (2009).
13. Q. Zhang, L.F. Cheng, L.T. Zhang, et al. *Thermal expansion behavior of carbon fiber reinforced chemical-vapor-infiltrated silicon carbide composites from room temperature to 1400 °C*. Mater. Lett. **60**, 3245-3247 (2006).
14. Y.J. Xu, W.H. Zhang, H.B. Wang. *Prediction of effective elastic modulus of plain weave multiphase and multilayer silicon carbide ceramic matrix composite*. Mater. Sci. Technol. **24**, 435-442 (2008).

Optimal Modeling Study of Flooding Phenomenon in Urban Area (Dam break case)

M. Rezoug[1,A], R.El Meouche[1], R. Hamzaoui[1], J.F Khreim[1], Z.Q Feng[2], D. Bassir[1]

[1] FIT / ESTP/ Constructibility Research Institute. 28, avenue du Président Wilson - 94234 Cachan cedex, France.
[2] EVRY Laboratory *LME-Evry*. Evry University, 40 rue du Pelvoux, 91020 Evry, France.

Abstract – In this paper a numerical study of urban flooding caused by dam break has been undertaken. **Problem statement:** This study illustrated the influence of the different versions of K-epsilon turbulence model on the water flow behavior, predicted by Computational Fluid Dynamic (CFD) and validated through experiment. **Approach:** The water velocity, free surface profile and also secondary circulation flow along with the pressure through the city are simulated and proved. **Results:** Results are obtained with numerical simulation using standard k-epsilon, are relatively good agreement with the experimental results. **Conclusion/Recommendations:** In the present study, the velocity and the water depth are investigated to check the real capabilities of a 3D numerical code ANSYS-CFX and especially to define the optimal parameters (Mesh, boundary conditions, turbulence model,) able to simulate the flow behavior through the complex urban area, with the best accuracy.

Keywords: Urban flooding; Turbulence models; Free surface flow; VOF; Computational Fluid Dynamic (CFD); ANSYS-CFX.

1 Introduction

Various computational fluid dynamics methods have already been used in order to simulate flood progress in cities [1-4]. In recent years there have been advances in modelling the interaction between sewer models and models describing the flow on the surface. Two dimensional models originally developed for use in estuaries and oceanic modeling has been modified to interact with the drainage system, i.e. MIKE 2 [5], TUFLOW [6] and RMA-2 [7]. Other models have been developed specifically to describe overland flooding, such as DELFT-FLS [8] and GIS based pathway models [9]. This will allow for more complex systems to be better described and modeled. The results are encouraging but there is still a lack of knowledge in the accuracy of the risk assessment.

In view of the flow, singularities, sewage systems, the presence of storage volumes (water entry through doors of buildings, cellars, gardens, lawns, parking garages, etc.) are the origin of losses of hydraulic head due to the turbulence created. These losses are difficult to quantify, as they are tributary of the flow properties and the fluid, they also depend on the precise shape of an obstacle, its orientation and its surface roughness, etc. Note the flow near an obstacle has a fully three-dimensional structure with a strong component of vertical velocity, this implies that near the obstacles, the use of a 2D codes based on SaintVenant equations is not strictly correct [10, 11].

The aim of this work is to check the real capabilities of a 3D numerical code ANSYS-CFX to simulate an urban flood. To find good results, three mesh types (hexahedral, tetrahedral with refinement and tetrahedral with inflation) have taken and applied to three turbulence models for each mesh type (Standard k-ε, RNG and Realizable k-ε model). To validate numerical results, an experimental test case of flood in a simplified city, have been taken as a base of comparison [12], it consists to study the flow around a buildings where the reflections of the wave on the walls and recirculation behind the obstacles are two parameters which have a major importance. The comparisons between the experimental and numerical records should permit to check the difficulties remaining when simulating an urban flood numerically.

2 Presentation of the test case

The experimental device is located at the Catholic University of Louvain (Belgium) [12]. This is a great channel with a length of 36 meters and a width of 3.6 meters with a horizontal bottom (Figure 1). A narrowing of a section and a door are arranged in the channel to simulate a dam break.

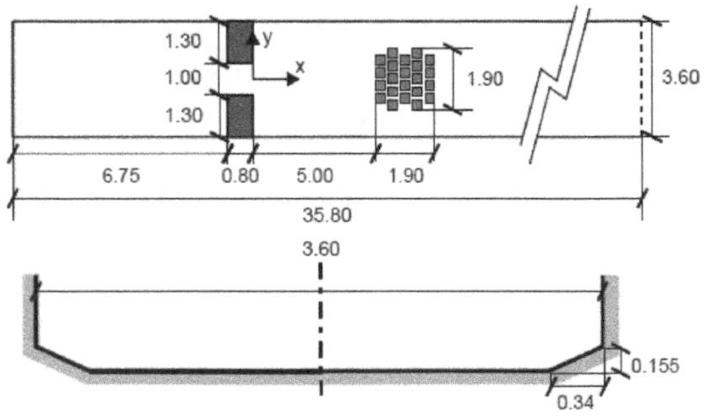

Fig. 1. Experimental device, dimensions of the channel (meters) and simplified arrangement of the city (J. Lhomme et al., 2006)

In this study, a Permanent flow (95 L / s) is simulated by keeping the door opened and pumping water from one end to the other of the channel. A simplified city is arranged in the channel with a staggered arrangement of buildings. The coefficient of Strickler channel is equal to100 m1/3/s.

[a] Corresponding author: rezoug@profs.estp.fr

Two methods of measurement have been used. The RTDs (Resistance Temperature Detectors) allow the recording of changes in depth, and digital imaging technique was used to track the movement of tracers (polystyrene beads) on the surface of the water, and allow obtaining the field of velocity at the surface [13].

3 Three-dimensional multiphase model

The three-dimensional multiphase approach is based on the numerical resolution of the incompressible Navier-Stokes equations. To maintain the multiphase nature of the flow, there are currently two approaches widely used: the Euler-Lagrange approach and the Euler-Euler approach. In the latter approach, the different phases are taken into account by considering that the volume of a phase cannot be occupied by other phases. Then the concept of phase volume fractions as continuous functions of space and time is introduced.
In this paper, the so-called Volume of Fluid (VOF) method is used [14, 15]. The VOF method is a surface tracking technique applied to a fixed Eulerian mesh, in which a specie transport equation is used to determine the relative volume fraction of the two phases, or phase fraction, in each computational cell. Practically, a single set of Reynolds- averaged Navier-Stokes equations is solved and shared by the fluids and for the additional phase, its volume fraction γ is tracked throughout the domain.
Therefore, the full sets of governing equations for the fluid flow are [16]:

$$\frac{\partial}{\partial x_i}(\rho_m u_i) = 0 \tag{1}$$

$$\frac{\partial \rho_m u_i}{\partial t} + \frac{\partial}{\partial x_i}(\rho_m u_i u_j) = -\frac{\partial p}{\partial x_j} + \frac{\partial}{\partial x_i}\left(\mu_m\left[\frac{\partial u_i}{\partial x_j} + \frac{\partial u_j}{\partial x_i}\right]\right) + \frac{\partial}{\partial x_i}(-\rho_m \overline{u_i' u_j'}) + \rho_m g_j \tag{2}$$

$$\frac{\partial \alpha}{\partial t} + \vec{u}.\nabla \alpha = 0 \tag{3}$$

For the incompressible phase volume fraction, α the following three conditions are possible:

– $0 < \alpha < 1$: when the infinitesimal volume contains the interface between the q-th fluid and one or more other fluids;
- $\alpha = 0$: volume occupied by air;
- $\alpha = 1$ volume occupied by water.

The nature of the VOF method means that an interface between the species is not explicitly computed, but rather emerges as a property of the phase fraction field. Since the phase fraction can have any value between 0 and 1, the interface is never sharply defined, but occupies a volume around the region where a sharp interface should exist.

3.1 Turbulence modeling

Modeling turbulent flow in a multi-phase model is highly challenging because of the complexity associated with strong turbulence anisotropy, streamline curvature, and rotation.

In present calculations fully homogeneous buoyant models are used with air and water as continuous fluids because of a requirement for more accurate representation of the turbulent transport of momentum in order to achieve an improved prediction of the flow field around obstacles. This goal may be realized through the use of three mathematical models of turbulence namely the model (Standard k-ε, RNG k-ε and Realizable k-ε model).

- The main differences between the three models are:
- The turbulent Prandtl number governing the turbulent diffusion.
- The production and destruction terms in the equation for epsilon.

The methods to calculate the turbulent viscosity.

3.1.1 Standard k-ε model

This standard model has been proposed b is based on the concept Bousinesq (1977). The two equations of this model are [17, 18]:

For turbulent kinetic energy K

$$\frac{\partial}{\partial t}(\rho k) + \frac{\partial}{\partial x_i}(\rho k u_i) = \frac{\partial}{\partial x_j}\left[\left(\mu + \frac{\mu_t}{\sigma_k}\right)\frac{\partial k}{\partial x_j}\right] + G_k + G_b - \rho\varepsilon - Y_M + S_K \tag{4}$$

For dissipation ε

$$\frac{\partial}{\partial t}(\rho \varepsilon) + \frac{\partial}{\partial x_i}(\rho \varepsilon u_i) = \frac{\partial}{\partial x_j}\left[\left(\mu + \frac{\mu_t}{\sigma_\varepsilon}\right)\frac{\partial \varepsilon}{\partial x_j}\right] + C_{1\varepsilon}\frac{\varepsilon}{k}(G_k + C_{3\varepsilon}G_b) - C_{2\varepsilon}\rho\frac{\varepsilon^2}{k} + S_\varepsilon \tag{5}$$

G_k is the production of turbulent kinetic energy

$$G_k = -\rho \overline{u_i' u_j'} \frac{\partial u_j}{\partial x_i} \tag{6}$$

Effect of buoyancy

$$G_b = \beta g_i \frac{\mu_t}{\mathrm{Pr}_t}\frac{\partial T}{\partial x_i} \tag{7}$$

Where Pr_t is the turbulent Prandtl number for energy and g_i is the component of the gravitational vector in the ith direction. For the standard and realizable - models, the default value of Pr_t is 0.85.

Y_M represents the expansion of the turbulent fluctuations. S and S_k are terms of sources.

$$Y_M = 2\rho\varepsilon M_t^2 \tag{8}$$

Turbulent viscosity is modeled as:

$$\mu_t = \rho C_\mu \frac{k^2}{\varepsilon} \tag{9}$$

$C_{\varepsilon 1}$, $C_{\varepsilon 2}$ and C_μ are constants that were determined experimentally and are given in table 1.
σ_ε and σ_k represents respectively the Prandtl number for turbulent kinetic energy and dissipation rate, these are also given in Table 1.

Table 1. Constant values of k –ε model

C_μ	$C_{\varepsilon 1}$	$C_{\varepsilon 2}$	σ_k	σ_ε
0.09	1.44	1.92	1	1.3

3.1.2 RNG k –ε Model

The RNG model, developed by the renormalization group (Yakhot & Smith) [19, 20] is an estimate in the calculation of the constant $C\varepsilon_1$, replaced in the equation of dissipation $C''_{\varepsilon 1}$. This expression adds a term function of strain rate η in the equation of dissipation, making it less diffusive.

$$\eta = \frac{k}{\varepsilon}\sqrt{\frac{p}{\eta_t}} \tag{10}$$

With

$$c''_{\varepsilon 1} = c_{\varepsilon 1} - \frac{\eta\left(1-\frac{\eta}{\eta_0}\right)}{1+\beta\eta^3} \tag{11}$$

The RNG model constants are given in Table2.

Table 2. Constant values of RNG k –ε model

C_μ	$C_{\varepsilon 1}$	$C_{\varepsilon 2}$	σ_ε	η_0	β
0.085	1.42	1.62	0.7179	4.38	0.015

The main difference between standard version and RNG k-ε is in the equation of the rate of turbulent dissipation of energy. In flows with high levels of constraint, the RNG model provides a low turbulent viscosity (that is to say a high dissipation rate ε and production of turbulence k low) than the standard model.

Although the RNG k-ε model was found to work better than the standard model for flows with large curvature of the streamlines, it has not yet been validated extensively by researchers opposed to the k-ε model. The standard version k - ε and RNG k-ε is valid for turbulent flows away from the walls.

3.1.3 Realizable k-epsilon model:

The realizable k-epsilon model is recently developed by Shih (1995); he uses another form of turbulent viscosity and dissipation equations [21, 22]:

$$\frac{\partial}{\partial t}(\rho k) + \frac{\partial}{\partial x_i}(\rho k u_i) = \frac{\partial}{\partial x_j}\left[\left(\mu + \frac{\mu_t}{\sigma_k}\right)\frac{\partial k}{\partial x_j}\right] + G_k + G_b - \rho\varepsilon - Y_M + S_K \tag{12}$$

$$\frac{\partial}{\partial t}(\rho\varepsilon) + \frac{\partial}{\partial x_i}(\rho\varepsilon u_i) = \frac{\partial}{\partial x_j}\left[\left(\mu + \frac{\mu_t}{\sigma_\varepsilon}\right)\frac{\partial \varepsilon}{\partial x_j}\right] + \rho C_1 S\varepsilon - \rho C_2\frac{\varepsilon^2}{k+\sqrt{\nu\varepsilon}} + C_{1\varepsilon}\frac{\varepsilon}{k}C_{3\varepsilon}G_b + S_\varepsilon \tag{13}$$

The turbulent viscosity is determined by the equation below, which is identical with the standard model, but in this model Cμ is variable.

$$\mu_t = \rho C_\mu \frac{k^2}{\varepsilon} \tag{14}$$

Where

$$C_\mu = \frac{1}{A_0 + A_s\frac{kU^*}{\varepsilon}} \tag{15}$$

$$U^* = \sqrt{S_{ij}S_{ij} + \widetilde{\Omega}_{ij}\widetilde{\Omega}_{ij}} \tag{16}$$

$$\widetilde{\Omega}_{ij} = \overline{\Omega_{ij}} - \varepsilon_{ijk}\omega_k - 2\varepsilon_{ijk}\omega_k \tag{17}$$

$\overline{\Omega_{ij}}$: The average rotation velocity

ω_k : Angular velocity

$A_0=4.04 \quad A_s = \sqrt{6}\cos\phi$

With:

$$\phi = \frac{1}{3}\cos^{-1}\left(\sqrt{6}\frac{S_{ij}S_{jk}S_{ki}}{\tilde{S}^3}\right) \tag{18}$$

$$\tilde{S} = \sqrt{S_{ij}S_{ij}} \tag{19}$$

$$S_{ij} = \frac{1}{2}\left(\frac{\partial u_j}{\partial x_i} + \frac{\partial u_i}{\partial x_j}\right) \tag{20}$$

The constants of this model are given in Table 3.

Table 3. Constant values of K-ε realizable model

$C_{\varepsilon 1}$	C_2	σ_k	σ_ε
1.44	1.9	0.7179	4.38

3.2 Calculation Domain: Boundary conditions

An Inlet boundary condition is used as flow is directed into the domain at location 'Inflow' shown in (Figure 2). Inlet velocity is taken as 0.26 m/s. Turbulence intensity I=u / U is 5% at inlet boundary condition in which, 'U' is the vector of velocity $U_{x,y}$ and 'u' being fluctuating velocity component in turbulent flow. At pressure outlets, the elevation of the water must usually be known as part of the problem definition. The mechanism used to enforce this elevation is to set a pressure profile consistent with the known elevation. Top and bottom boundary are free slip condition. In this case, the velocity component parallel to wall has a finite value (which is computed), but the velocity normal to the wall, and wall shear stress, are both set to 0: $U_{N,\,Wall}=0$ and $\tau_w=0$. For 2-D both sides are taken as symmetry plane boundary condition which 'mirror' the flow on either side. The normal velocity component at the symmetry plane boundary and the scalar variable gradients normal to the boundary are set to zero.

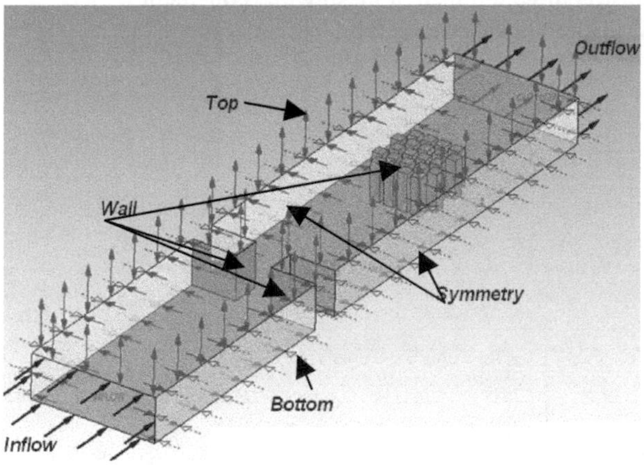

Fig. 2. Calculation domain showing 3D boundary conditions

3.3 Mesh Generation

To accurately predict the flow over the complex terrain, a great deal will depend on the good mesh generation, by keeping always in mind the importance of the memory and computing time. To capture the flow effects near the boundary wall of the ground, and to predict accurately the Water height, size and density of mesh are two parameters which have a major importance. According to the literature, three methods of mesh presented below (Figure 3 to 5), are among the recommended methods for calculating the fluid flow, each one has its advantages and disadvantages.

The first method consists to mesh the domain with unstructured tetrahedral mesh, using inflation option, from bottom to the estimated height of water (figure 3). Inflation refers to the generation of prism layers next to the wall to increase the resolution of gradients normal to the wall. This is accomplished with the boundary layer function in ANSYS-CFX mesh. In the second method, unstructured tetrahedral mesh has been exploited also, except near the boundary wall (obstacles walls, bottom) mesh refinement method has been employed instead of inflation method (Figure 4). In the third method, a structured hexahedral volume mesh in throughout domain is applied, fewer cells are needed for a hexahedral mesh, and the convergence is better (Figure 5).

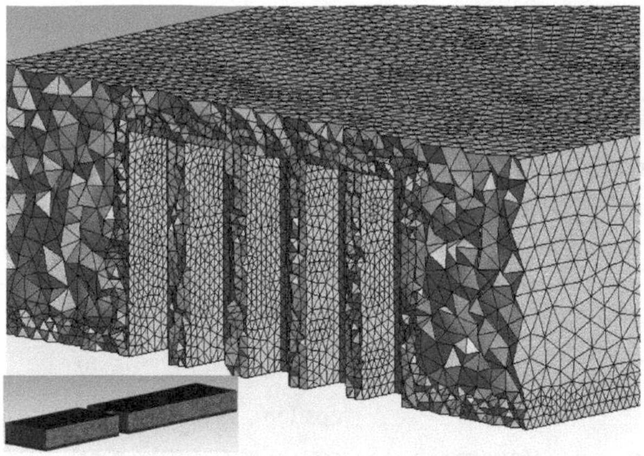

Fig. 3. Unstructured tetrahedral mesh with inflation

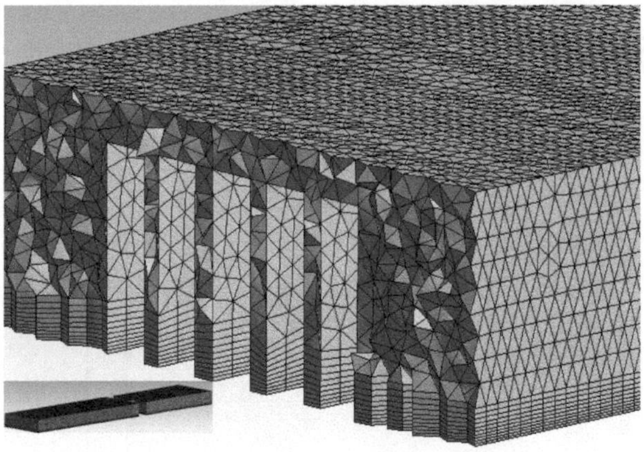

Fig. 4. Unstructured tetrahedral mesh with refinement

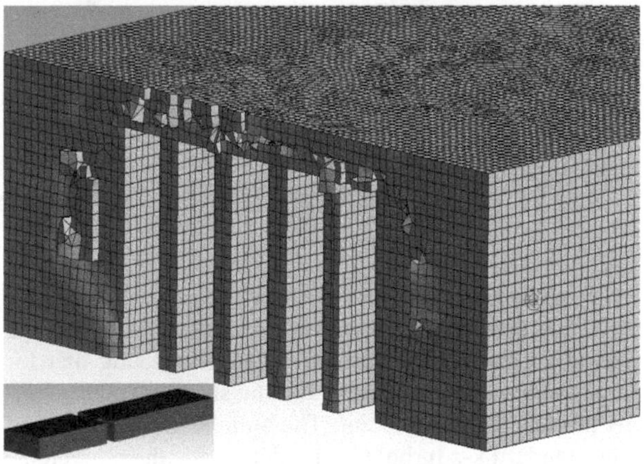

Fig. 5. Structured hexahedral mesh

In order to find the most suitable one of this study case, 9 simulation tests are performed as shown in the table 4.

Table 4. Plan of simulation

Types of mesh	Elements number	Turbulences model	Computing time(hour)
1	677653	k-epsilon	6.56
2	1388735	k-epsilon	9.1
3	655347	k-epsilon	7.45
1	677653	RNG K-epsilon	6.49
2	1388735	RNG K-epsilon	8.55
3	655347	RNG K-epsilon	7.45
1	677653	RSM	7.15
2	1388735	RSM	9.3
3	655347	RSM	7.22

With:

1: Unstructured tetrahedral mesh with inflation
2: Unstructured tetrahedral mesh with refinement
3: Structured hexahedral mesh

4 Results and discussion

4.1 Effect of mesh

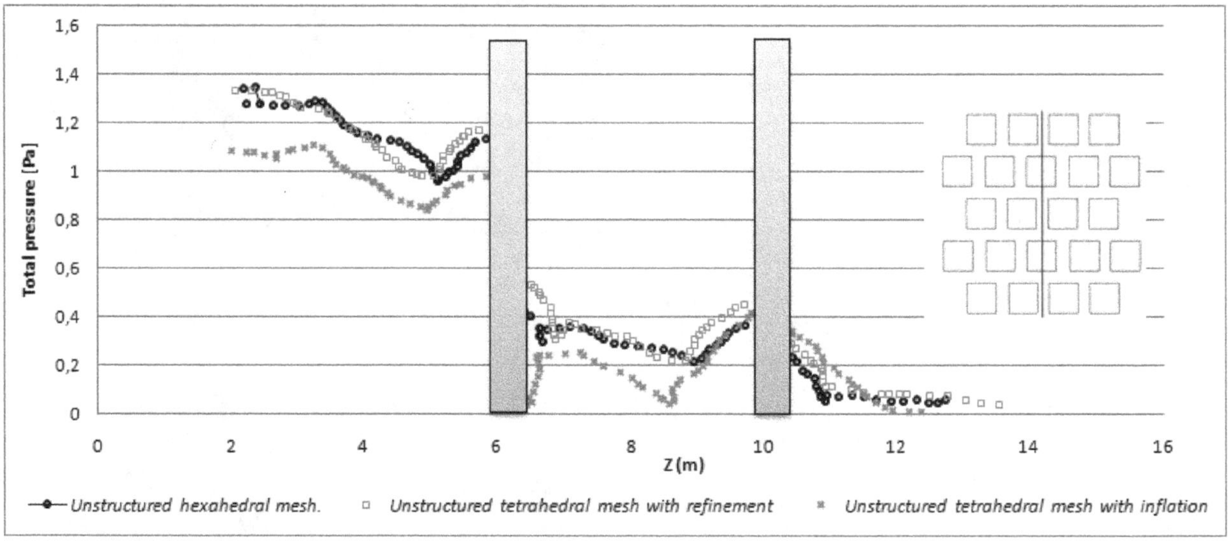

Fig. 6. Total pressure profiles according to type of mesh along Z axes.

A preliminary mesh convergence study is carried out in order to verify that the solution is meshing independent. Using the three meshing methods described above, it is found that for the same computing parameters and the same boundary conditions the results are deferent. The simulation is performed with the standard k-ε turbulence model for the three methods. Figure 6, shows the profiles of Total pressure along the Z axis. It is observed that the tetrahedral mesh with refinement and the hexahedral mesh methods give very similar profiles of pressure which differ numerically by less than 2%. The profile for the method of the tetrahedral volume mesh with inflation however, is clearly different, and numerically the results differ by up to 23%.

Figure 7 shows clearly the difference between the three results, depending on the meshing. Concerning the solutions (a, b), it is observed that pressure fields are so better between and around obstacles than in solution (c) , because of small size of elements mesh in this area.
It means that the tetrahedral mesh with refinement and the hexahedral mesh methods can provide more information about the behavior of the flow through the buildings network despite the complexity of the area. The maximum pressure values noticed in this area for different solutions (a, b, c) are: 420 Pa, 390 Pa, and 90 Pa respectively.

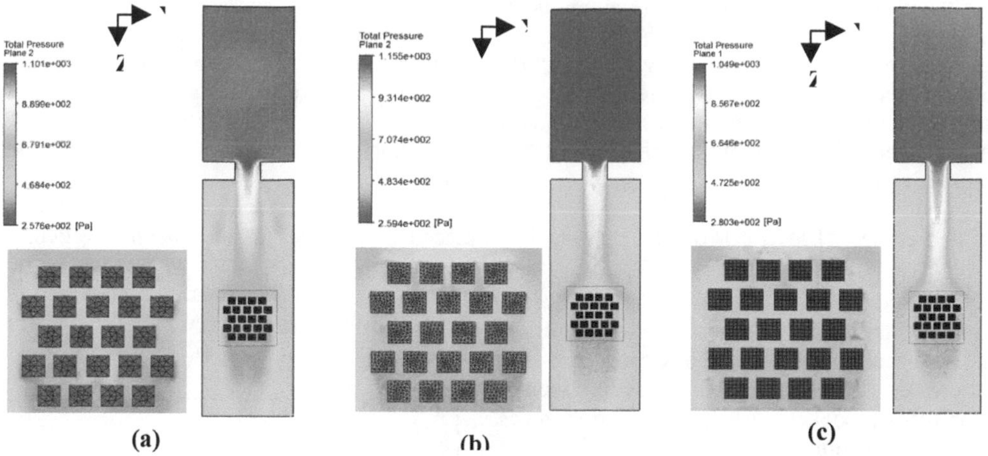

Fig. 7. Pressure field calculated for the three kinds of mesh in the ZX plan. (a)Unstructured tetrahedral volume mesh with inflation; (b) Unstructured tetrahedral volume mesh with refinement; (c) Structured hexahedral volume mesh

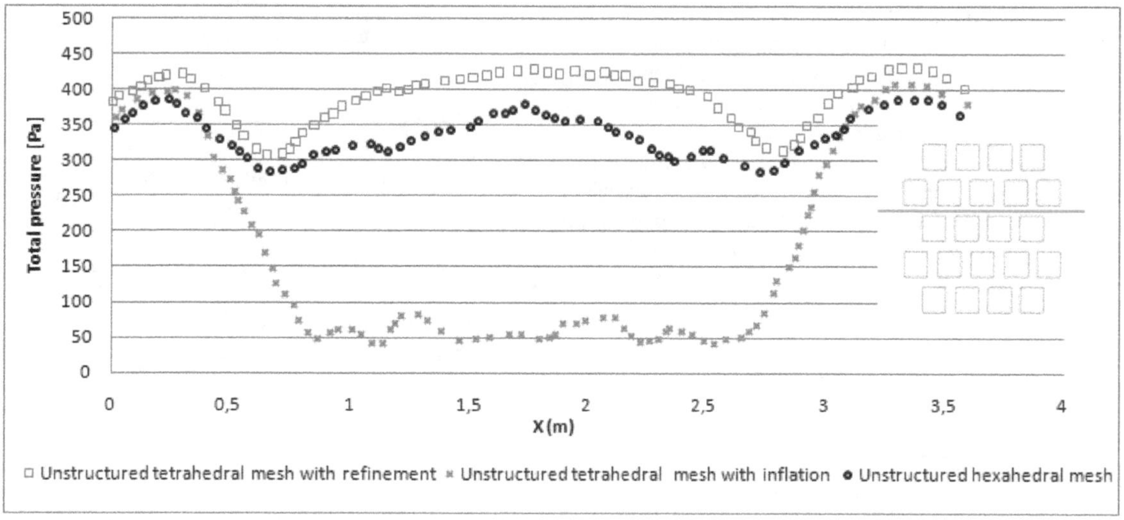

Fig. 8. Total pressure profiles according to type of mesh along X axes

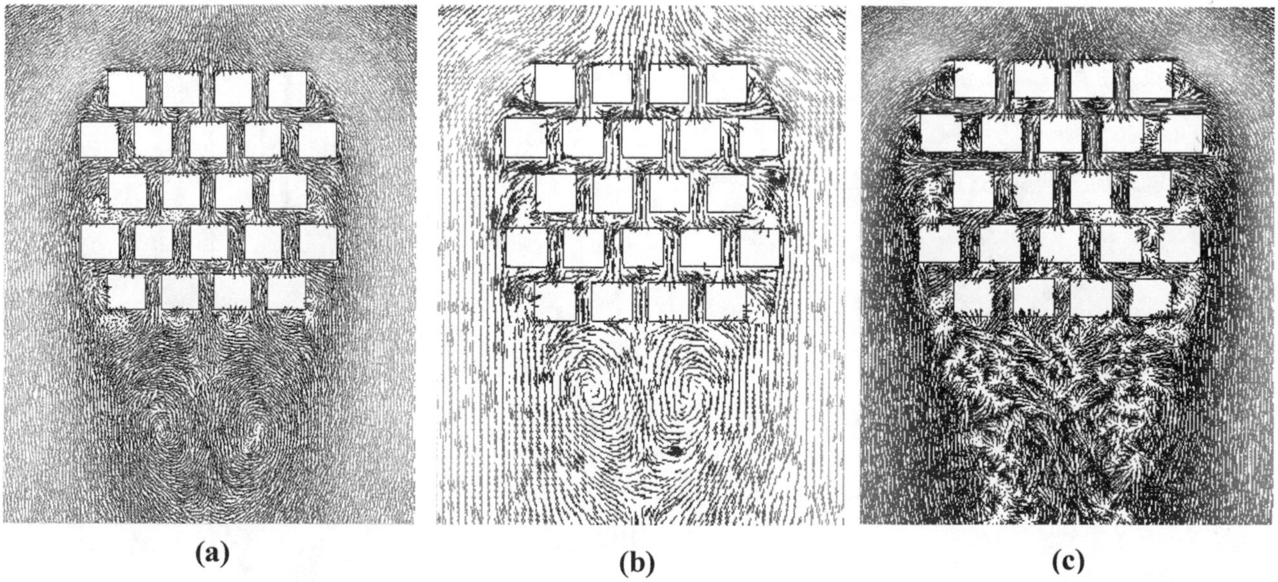

Fig. 9. Comparison between the velocity vectors simulated. (a) Standard k-ε; (b) RNG; (c) realizable k-ε

Figure 8 shows the profile of the total pressure along the X axis on the line just before the last group of buildings. It is remarked that the differences between the two simulations results for methods tetrahedral mesh with refinement and hexahedral mesh are minor. However, the hexahedral mesh method is employed for the simulation performed in this work is for reducing computational requirements.

4.2 Comparison of Turbulence Models

After the rapid opening of the gate, the strong dam-break wave reflects against the building, almost submerging it and the flow separates forming a series of shock waves crossing each other and creates a complicated flow structure, including several captured air pockets. Also, recirculation zones can be identified near the building.

4.2.1 Comparison of experimental and numerical velocity fields

The effect of the turbulence model was investigated using three isotropic models, the standard k-ε, Realizable k-ε and the RNG model. The experimental velocity vector plot using digital imaging technique [12] is compared with those of the three turbulence models in Figures 9.

In a general aspect, the two models RNG and standard k-ε, give flow patterns very alike (Figures 9 (a), (b)). They show almost similar field of vector velocity with the experimental one. This similitude is not observed with the realizable k-ε model, where it appears that the field of velocity vector behind the buildings is very disturbed and the velocity is close to zero.

Some small differences are noticed however between the two models; RNG and standard k-ε in the Distance of the onset of the vortex behind the group of buildings. Moreover the figure 10 shown the streamlines given by the three models, where there appears to be a slight deformation of the secondary circulation loop predicted by the RNG model behind the buildings , that is not observed with the standard k-ε model.

In the experiment performed, the Doppler velocimeter is placed in 9 points in the channel (Figure 11) and several measurements were made vertically. More the measuring point is near the urban area, the more the influence is strong and the differences between measure and simulation will be larger.

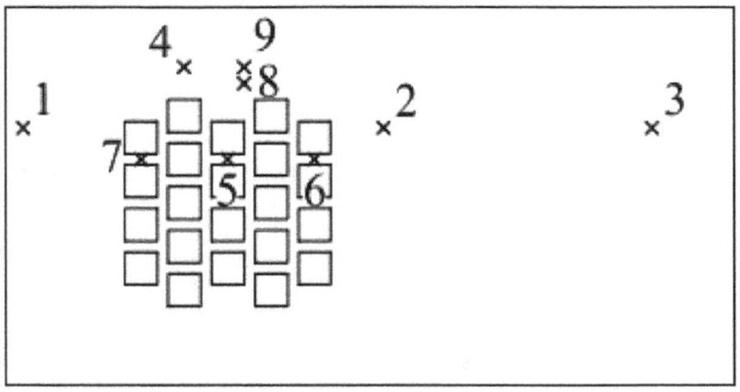

Fig.11. Positions of measurement points with Doplller velocimeter

Table 5 shows the measured and simulated values of the velocity vector in points 1, 2, 3, 4, 9 and 8 positioned in the channel as shown in Figure 11. At point 1, 4 and 9, the angle of the experimental velocity vector is almost constant and

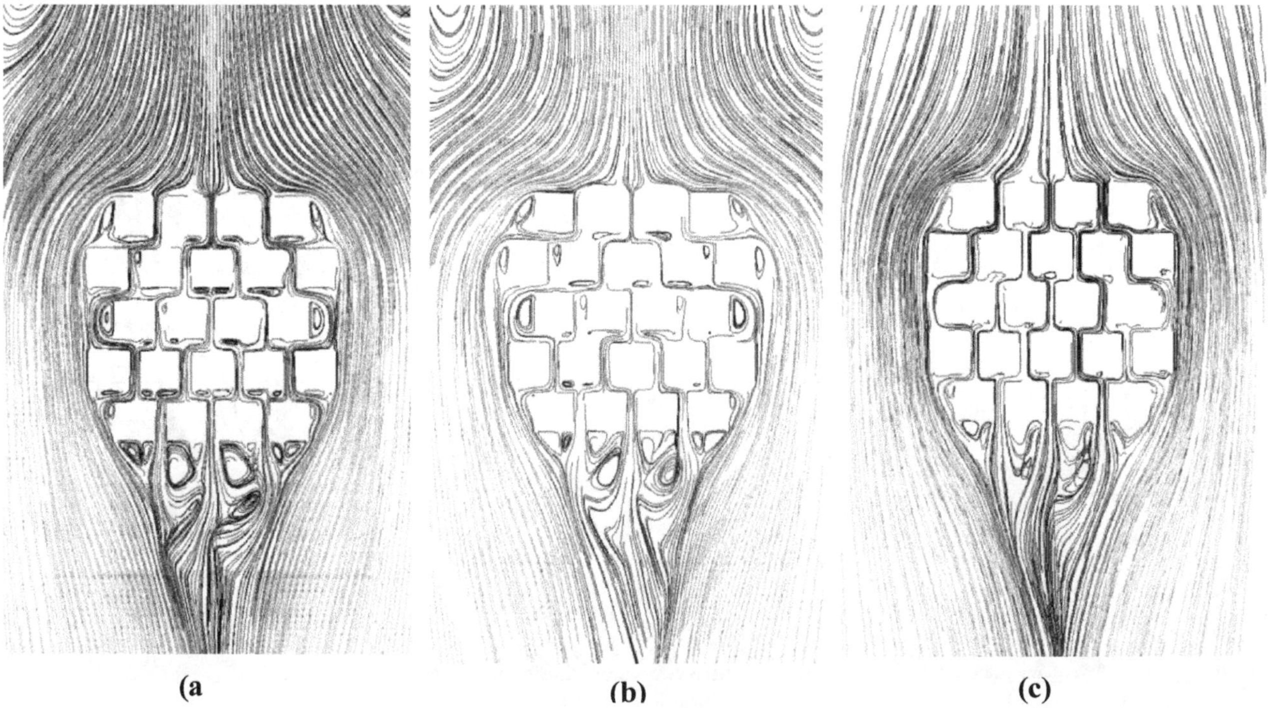

Fig. 10. Streamlines with different simulated turbulence models. (a) Standard k-ε; (b) RNG; (c) realizable k-ε

very close to the angle of the velocity vector simulated with the all turbulences model. V_x and V_y velocity components simulated with realizable k-ε are slightly Higher than V_x experimental, while the V_x and V_y velocity components simulated with standard k-ε and RNG model are well estimated. The measuring point 2 is located in the recirculation zone located in the "wake" of the city. It is noticed that in Figure 10 (a) and (b) obtained by the RNG model and standard k-ε, two complete rotations of the velocity vector, whereas it is observed no complete rotation of the velocity vector simulated with the realizable k-ε model, but rather an oscillation generally between -90° and 90 °. The average of the V_x measured velocity component at point 2, is very close to zero (which is normal since the velocity vector is rotating), as the Vx simulated component.

The measuring point 3 is located 3m behind the urban area. Vy and Vx velocity components simulated are well estimated for every Turbulences model. The measuring point 8 is located on the same cross section as points 9, but it is a little closer to the urban area. The influence of the lateral recirculation (which occurs between the 2nd and 3rd row of buildings) is stronger. The values of the components of velocity simulated with standard k-ε and RNG turbulences model are very similar to the measured velocity vector. The Vx component simulated with realizable model is highly overestimated, while the Vy one is well estimated. The measuring points 5, 6 and 7 are located inside the urban area. With the simulation the flow enters the streets where are the three points, continuously at a velocity of 0.15 m / s, whereas from the experimental measurements of velocity components measured are almost nil. It can be explained by the fact that the width of the streets may be too low for the probe has a sufficient sample volume [12]. This shows that the simulated velocities with standard k-ε and RNG turbulences model are closer to the measured velocities (with some variation) than the realizable k-ε model.

4.2.2 Comparison of experimental and numerical profiles along the free surface

Table 5. The measured and simulated values of the velocity vector

Points	V_x and V_y Velocity	Experimental Values	Simulated values (standard k-ε)	Simulated values(RNG)	Simulated values (Realizable k-ε)
Point 1	V_x (m/s)	0,279	0,265	0,245	0,262
	V_y (m/s)	-0,086	-0,081	-0,072	-0,104
Point 4	V_x (m/s)	0,483	0,451	0,361	0,412
	V_y (m/s)	-0,074	-0,07	-0,066	-0,087
Point 9	V_x (m/s)	0,326	0,318	0,308	0,317
	V_y (m/s)	-0,005	-0,005	-0,004	-0,011
Point 2	V_x (m/s)	0,005	0,003	0,002	0,01
	V_y (m/s)	-0,037	-0,033	-0,020	-0,06
Point 3	V_x (m/s)	0,060	0,062	0,041	0,05
	V_y (m/s)	0,029	0,027	0,027	0,04
Point 8	V_x (m/s)	0,113	0,107	0,102	0,098
	V_y (m/s)	-0,013	-0,01	-0,012	-0,008

After the dam break, the water flows to the obstacles. Once it reaches this, a part of the wave is reflected and forms a negative bore travelling back in the upstream direction. The comparison between experimental and numerical results of the three turbulence models, in terms of free surface at different position along the longitudinal axis X is given in Figure 12.

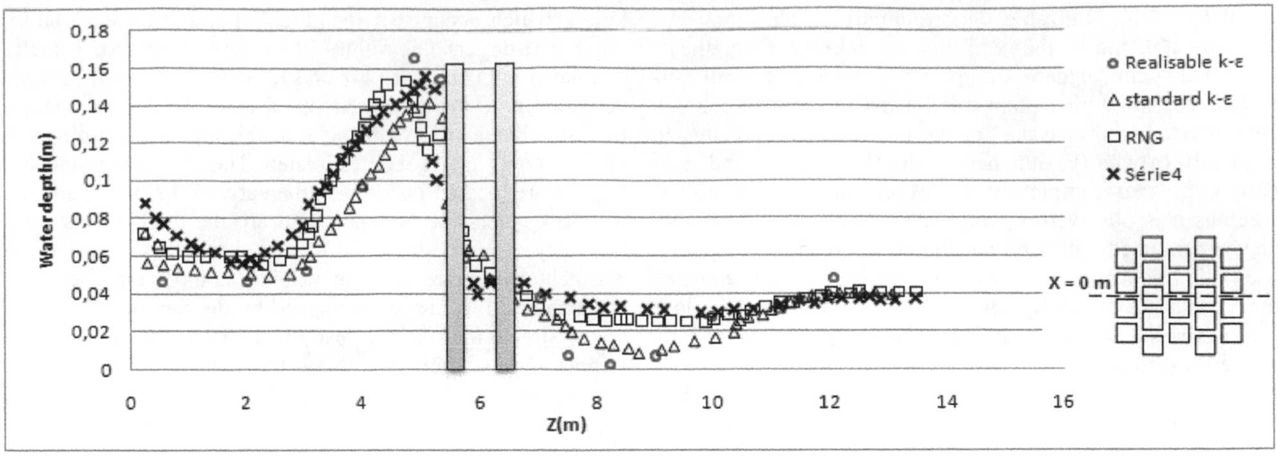

(a)

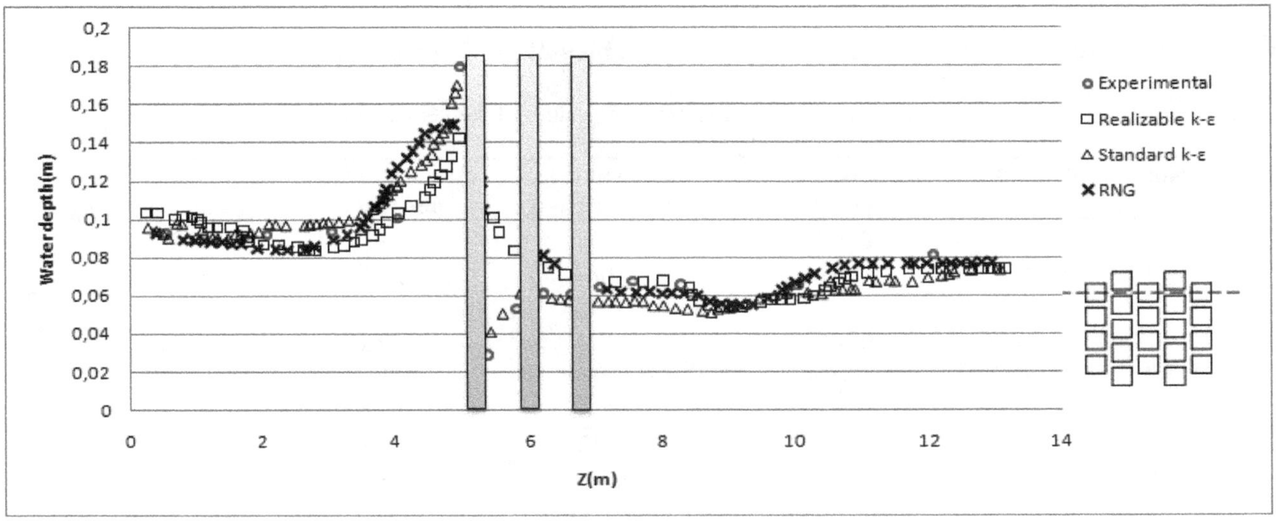

(b)

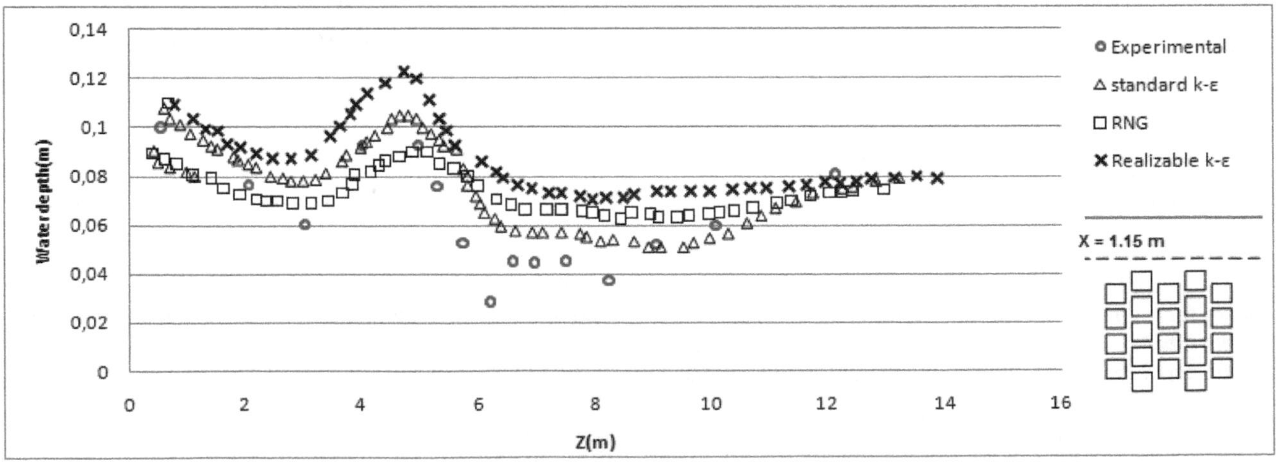

(c)

Fig. 12. Profiles along the free surface for the three turbulence models along the axis X. (a) For X = 0 m, (b) For X = 0.6m and (c) For X = 1.15m

The simulated free surface profiles are very close to that given by the measures experimental for any position of the X axis (Figure 13(a) X = 0m, 13(b)X = 0.6m, and13(c) X = 1.15m) but the standard k-ε seems to give the best profile. The free surface elevation upstream of the urban areas is well reproduced and it is less important along the axis z = 1.15 since it is located outside the urban area.

5 Conclusion

This study consist to show the influence of the different versions of K-epsilon turbulence model on the water flow behavior applied to three mesh types (hexahedral, tetrahedral with refinement and tetrahedral with inflation) predicted by Computational Fluid Dynamic (CFD) and validated through experiment. The summarizing pertinent results are:

Structured hexahedral mesh throughout the domain and k-epsilon model as a turbulence model can accurately represent the physical phenomena expected to occur in the real case of dam break such as turbulence zones near obstacles, and the free surface elevation upstream of the obstacle. The simulation results are in good agreement with the one obtained by experimental measure.

The set of results originating from these simulations shows that the dam break problem is characterized by three-dimensional aspects that have a great impact on water surface elevation and submersed wave travelling downstream.

The comparison between simulated and experimental results clearly shows that the three-dimensional model represents quite well the unsteady flow behavior.

References

1. J – M. Hervouet, R. Samie, B. Moreau. *Modelling urban areas in dam-break flood wave numerical simulations*. Proceedings of RESCDAM workshop. Seinäjoki, Finland: Finnish Environment Institute (2000).
2. Khan, R. Cadavid, S. S. Y. Wang. *Simulation of channel confluence and bifurcation using the CCHE2D model*. Water and Maritime Engineering. **142**, 97-102, (2000).
3. V. S. Neary, et F. Sotiropoulos. *Numerical investigation of laminar flows through 90-degree diversions of rectangular cross-section*. Computers and Fluids. **25**, 95-118, (1996).
4. L. S. Nania. PhD thesis: *Metodologia numérico-experimental para el analisis del riesgo asociado a la escorrentia pluvial en una redde calles*. Departamento de Ingéniera Hidraulica, Maritima y Ambiental Barcelona, Universitat politècnica de Catalunya (1999).
5. DHI Water and Environment, Reference Manual Mike Flood (2008). http://www.dhigroup.com, visited Marts 2008.
6. W. J. Sume. *Modelling of Bends and Hydraulic Structures in a Two-Dimensional Scheme*. Conference on Hydraulics in Civil Engineering, Hobart,. The Institution of Engineers, 28-30 (Australia, November 2001).
7. P. King, B.P. Donnel. Users Guide to RMA2 WES Version 4.5. US Army, Engineer research and Development Center. Waterways Experiment Station and Hydraulics Laboratory. USA (2006)
8. Deltares (2008), Reference Manual DELFT-FLS, http://www.wldelft.nl, visited Marts 2008.
9. S. Boonya-aroonnet, Č. Maksimović, D. Prodanović, S. Djordjević. *Urban pluvial flooding: development of GIS based pathway model for surface flooding and interface with surcharged sewer model,* Desbordes M. and B. Chocat (eds): Sustainable Techniques and Strategies in Urban Water Management. Proc. 6th Int. Conf. Novatech 2007, **1**, 481-488, France, (Lyon June 2007)
10. K. El Kadi Abderrezzak, A. Paquier and E. Mignot. *Modelling flash flood propagation in urban areas using a two-dimensional numerical model*, Natural Hazards, **50**, 433 - 460 (2009).
11. E. Mignot, A. Paquier and S. Haider, *Modeling floods in a dense urban area using 2D shallow water equations*, J. Hydrol., **327**(1-2), 186-199, (2006).
12. J. Lhomme, C. Bouvier, E.Mignot and A. Paquier. *One-dimensional GIS-based model compared to two-dimensional model in urban floods simulations*. Water Science and Technology, **54**(67), 83-91 (2006).
13. H. Capart, D. L. Young, Y. Zech. *Voronoï imaging methods for the measurement of granular flows*. Experiments in Fluids, **32**, 121-135, (2002).
14. D. B. Kothe, R. C. Mjolsness and M. D. Torrey. *RIPPLE: a computer program for incompressible flows with free surfaces*, Los Alamos National Laboratory, Report LA 12007 MS (1991).
15. P. Lin and P. L. -F. Liu. *Turbulence transport, vorticity dynamics, and solute mixing under plunging breaking waves in surfzone,* J. Geophys. Res., **103**, 15677-15694, (1998).
16. W. Rodi. *Turbulence Models and Their Application in Hydraulics*, International Association of Hydraulic Engineering (IAHR) Monograph, Delft, The Netherlands, (1980).
17. E. Launder and D. B. Spalding. *The numerical computation of turbulent flows*. Computer Methods in Applied Mechanics and Engineering. **3**, 269-289, (1974).
18. Y. Yang, M. Gu, S. Chen and X. Jin. *New inflow boundary conditions for modelling the neutral equilibrium atmospheric boundary layer in computational wind engineering*. Journal of Wind Engineering and Industrial Aerodynamics, **97**, 88-95 (2009).
19. V. Yakhot, S. A. Orszag. *Renormalization group analysis of turbulence*. Journal of Scientific Computing **1**, 3–51, (1986).
20. V. Yakhot, L. M. Smith, *The renormalization group, the ε-expansion and derivation of turbulence models*, J. Sci. Comput, **7**, 35-61, (1992).
21. T. –H. Shih, W. W. Liou, A. Shabbir and J. Zhu. A *New k-ε Eddy-Viscosity Model for High Reynolds Number Turbulent Flows - Model Development and Validation*, Computers & Fluids, **24**(3), 227-238 (1995).
22. C. Wilcox. Turbulence Modeling for CFD, 2nd Edition, DCW Industries, Inc (1988).

19

Finite Element Simulation and Experimental Investigation of Hot Embossing of Thin Polymer Film

Mohamed Sahli[1,a], Thierry Barrière[1], Jean-Claude Gelin[1]

[1] Femto-st Institute, Applied Mechanics dept., CNRS UMR 6174, ENSMM, 25030 Besancon, France

Abstract – The modelling of the hot embossing process requires accurate determination of the polymer flows. The present work is focussed on experiments and numerical simulations of the hot embossing processes consisting in the replication of polymers plates on engraved shapes in the metallic plates that are used for the tests. In the proposed analysis consisting of the micro-indentation of the polymer plate, axisymmetrical and 2D FE models are used to analyse the cavity filling capabilities vs. strain rates, strains and temperature contours. The numerical simulation results show that profile deformation is largely influenced by the forming pressure and temperature, velocity of movement of upper plate and fluidity of the polymer during the embossing step. These results showed also the flow behaviour of COC inside the mould during hot embossing process. This may assist future improvement of manufacturing quality and production throughput. Hot embossing experiments were also conducted and the results obtained were compared with the simulated ones. The predicted workpiece geometry shows good agreement with experimental result. It is found that the finite element simulation results are in reasonable agreement with the experimental observation.

Key words: Hot embossing, Flow behavior, Simulation, Polymers

1 Introduction

Hot embossing is becoming a key technology to manufacture high precision and high quality plastic microstructures, using a range of thermoplastic polymers including PMMA, polycarbonate and cellulose acetate [1-4], Fig. 1. It provides several advantages such as low-cost for moulds, high replication accuracy for micro-features and simple operation [5,6]. This process include three steps, the first one consists in heating and applying pressure step, the second is remaining temperature and pressure step and the third one consists in demoulding step. The important parameters that govern the success of hot embossing process include temperature (usually heating the polymer substrate to above its glass transition temperature T_g, is required), pressure and embossing time. The protocol associated with this technology, as shows in Fig. 2; need to guarantee both the dimensional accuracy, even for complex shapes and replication of topographical surface states [7]. Numerous of studies have been conducted in recent years to investigate the hot embossing process for micro or nanostructures. The pressure profiles on the surface of the polymer during hot embossing process have been investigated. The results indicate that a higher embossing pressure results in more uniform shrinkage in the elastically deformed state during cooling [8].

Chang and Yang [9] reported an innovative method for hot embossing by applying gas pressure directly to press the mould and the substrate. This can improve replication accuracy because more uniform embossing pressure was applied across the entire substrate. Becker and Heim also concluded some suggestions in processing conditions for the hot embossing of polymer parts with micro-sized features [10].

Li et al. [12] carried out a series of experiments to investigate the processing of micro-components by hot embossing. The results indicate that the replication accuracy strongly depends on the processing conditions, in particular on the processing temperature and pressure.

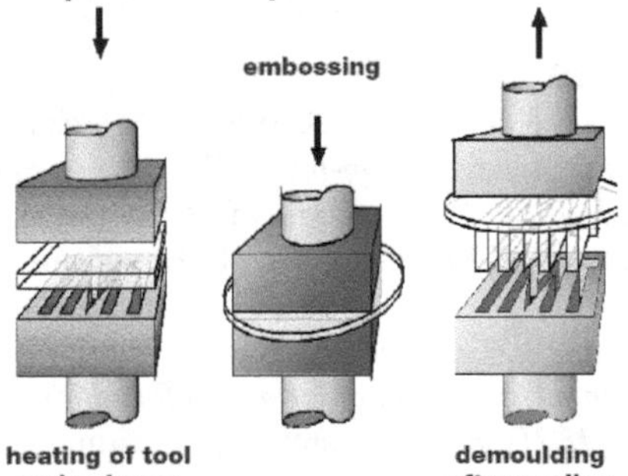

Fig. 1. Principle scheme of the hot embossing process [7]

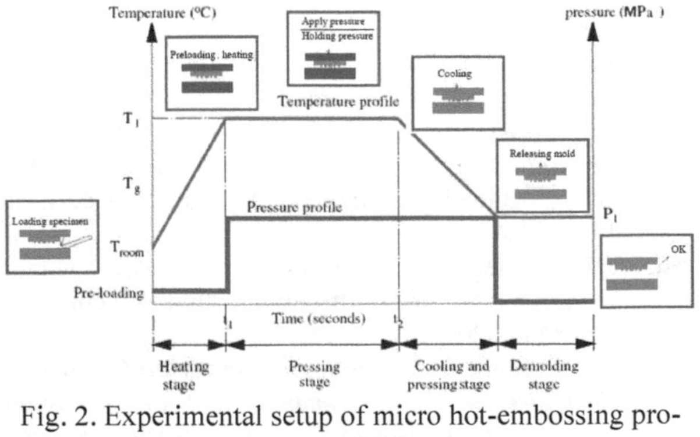

Fig. 2. Experimental setup of micro hot-embossing process [11]

[a] Corresponding author: Mohamed.sahli@ens2m.fr

However, to date, only a limited number of contributions are focussed in numerical analysis concerning the forming by the hot embossing process in the mould cavity. Recently, Wang et al. [13] studied the hot embossing of forming micro-gear with Zr-Cu-Ni-Al bulk metallic glass was analyzed by the finite element simulation with Deform 3D software and they report also experimental investigations. It was found that the finite element simulation results were in reasonable agreement with the experimental observations.

Chang et al. [14] studied the micro-imprinting replications using the finite element simulation method. In this study, they consider the viscous flow behaviour of the metallic and the amorphous polymer PMMA at temperatures slightly above their glass transition temperature. The result reveals that pressure level of 400kPa and forming time equal 4min are good combinations to replicate micro-lens array. The results were in reasonable agreement with the experimental observation.

In this study, the finite element method has been used to perform modelling of hot embossing process using the LsDyna® software in order to describe the behaviour of polymers plate during the forming process. A mechanical characterization of a COC polymer material by tensile tests was conducted at temperatures close to the glass transition temperature (T_g) to assess to the behaviour of the polymer as a function of strain, strain rate and temperature. Then the results were considered to identify the material model that is used for the numerical simulations based on the finite elements method using the LsDyna® software.

2 Finite elements model

2.1 Constitutive relations

In 1983, Johnson and Cook [15,16] proposed a constitutive model for materials which captures the strain rate and temperature dependency of the material, expression in the following form:

$$\sigma_y = \left[A + B\left(\varepsilon^{p}_{eff_y}\right)^n\right]\left[1 + C\ln\dot{\varepsilon}\right]\left[1 - \left(T_H\right)^m\right] \tag{1}$$

where σ is the the true stress, A is the yield stress at room temperature and reference strain rate, B is the strain hardening coefficient, n is the strain hardening exponent, ε is the plastic strain, $\dot{\varepsilon}$ is the plastic strain rate and T_H is the homologous temperature and expressed as:

$$T_H = T - T_{room} / T_{melt} - T_{room} \tag{2}$$

with T standing for the current absolute temperature, T_{melt} the melting temperature and T_{room} is the ambient temperature ($T \geq T_{room}$). The minimum temperature of the matrix is taken as the reference temperature. Here it is limited to the interval $0 \leq T_H \leq 1$.

In Eq. (1) the terms within the first set of parentheses imposes a power-law relationship on the true stress versus effective plastic strain. The second term in parentheses introduces a logarithmic dependence on strain-rate. The final term gives the stress an exponential decay as temperature increases.

2.2 Finite elements method

With the data obtained through tensile test experiments, the simulation of hot embossing on COC polymers has been carried out with LsDyna. Fig. 3a illustrates the geometry, dimensions and boundary conditions of hot embossing, in which a circular shaped die is used. The initial FE mesh of the polymer part and the die mould are shown in Fig. 3b. Under the assumption of plain-strain forming conditions, FE results of the material flow and displacement contours on the polymer plate have been obtained. Moreover due to symmetry, only the right part of the system was considered. Other assumptions are proposed to describe boundary conditions. First of all, one considers that the polymer material exhibits a viscoplastic behaviour and the die mould remains rigid and not deformable. The mesh of the polymer plate and die mould were respectively composed of 4016, 300 and 1898 elements. It is assumed that the friction with the contact surfaces between polymer plate and die mould meet Coulomb friction law and remains unchanged during hot embossing process (f=0.1). The speed of upper die varies from 10 to 40mm/s (in steps of 10) and is kept constant during the simulation. A uniform mesh with an adaptive remeshing and hourglass control are employed to reduce the distortion of the elements and control the zero energy modes.

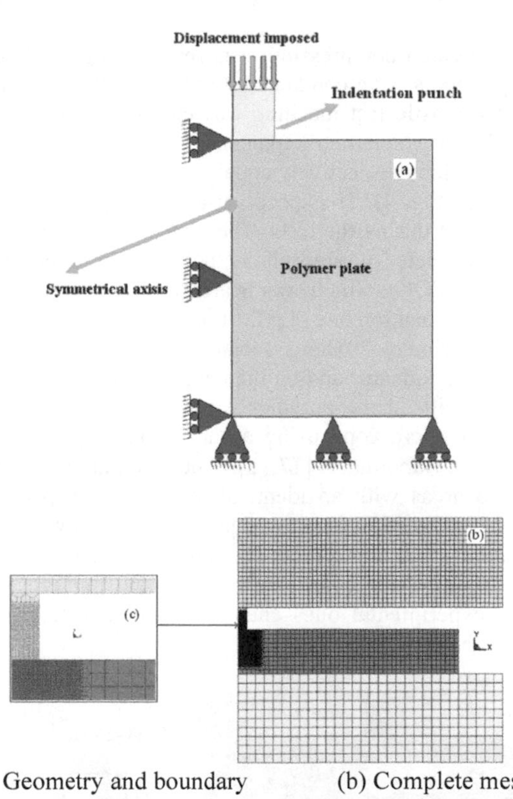

(a) Geometry and boundary conditions (b) Complete mesh (c) Zoom close to contact

Fig. 3. Finite element model used for the numerical simulations of hot embossing

3 Experimental method

3.1 Materials

In this analysis, COC in plate shape provided by Ticona® Company was used as substrate. It is a glassy polymer at room temperature, with a melt flow index between 14 and

48g/10min as determined under a constant load of 2.16kg. The glass transition temperature of COC provided by supplier is about 130-140°C. Each substrate with a thickness of 1mm was cut to 20mm×20mm square pieces. The details of the mechanical and thermal properties of the considered materials are listed in Table 1.

Table 1. Main characteristics of the COC polymers

Polymers grades	COC 5013	COC 6013
Density	1.02	1.02
Young modulus (MPa)	3220	2900
Glass transition temperature (°C)	140	135
Poisson's ratio	0.40	0.40
Coefficient of linear thermal expansion ($x10^{-4}K^{-1}$)	0.60	0.60
Thermal conductivity (W/mK)	0.15	0.15

3.2 Method

Instrumented compression tests reproducing the hot embossing process were conducted. For this analysis, the upper plate of a tensile test machine was equipped with a mould that includes a symmetric punch of cylindrical shape and with dimensions respectively equal to Ø=200µm et h=800µm (depicted in Fig. 4). The speed varied from 10 to 40mm/s is kept constant during the tests. The material part used in this study is a plate of amorphous polymer of cyclo-olefin-copolymer (COC), which was heated to a temperature close to the glass transition one (T_g+20°C).

The experimental data associated to the geometry produced by the indentor and on the negative shape corresponding to a cavity in the polymer was conducted by scanning mechanical microscopy using an apparatus that was developed in our laboratory [17,18]. The comparative profiles related to areas with an identical location were performed using N=5000 sampled points, equidistant with a value equal of p=2µm, that represents a sampled total length of L=Np=10mm. The correlation between the numerical data and the experimental ones enables to adopt a deformation model to the hot embossing process.

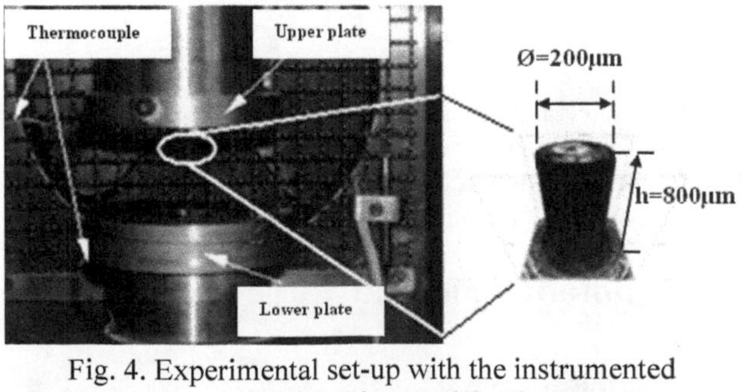

Fig. 4. Experimental set-up with the instrumented compression machine used for the tests

3.3 Identification of material model parameters

An experimental investigation on COC test tensile specimens subjected to tensile tests has been carried out. The cyclo-olefin copolymer has been first polymer injected in the cold room die mould in order to obtain the tensile test specimen with a hydraulic injection moulding equipment. The filling of the mould cavity was optimized at injection temperature and pressure equal to 260°C and between 10MPa respectively. Than, the tensile tests were performed on an Instron 6025 testing electrical equipment operating with axial speed control (1mm/min). The equipment is instrumented with an isothermal enclosure providing test temperatures from 20 to 300°C with ± 2% temperature regulation accuracy. Four temperatures have been tested: 100, 120, 140 and 160°C. Two tensile strain rates for each temperature were used, ie. 10^{-3} and $10^{-1}s^{-1}$. The strain is measured using an extensometer positioned at the centre of the useful part of the tensile tests for temperatures below 130°C. For temperature above 130°C for which the specimen becomes too extendable, the deformation was obtained as a function of the cross beam displacement. These experimental results were used to identification of constitutive material model parameters. A schematic view of the experimental setup is shown in Fig. 5.

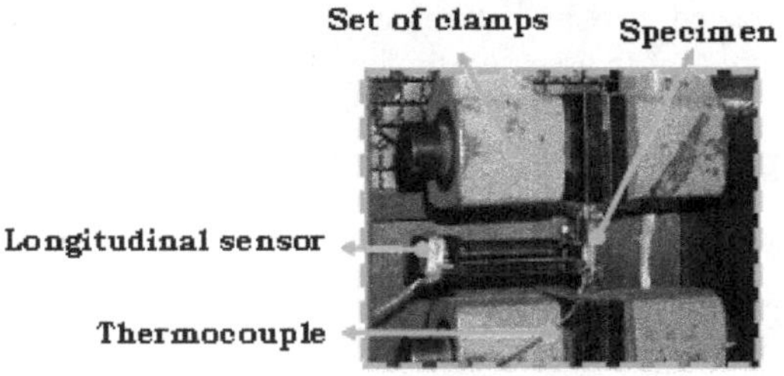

(a) Testing setup

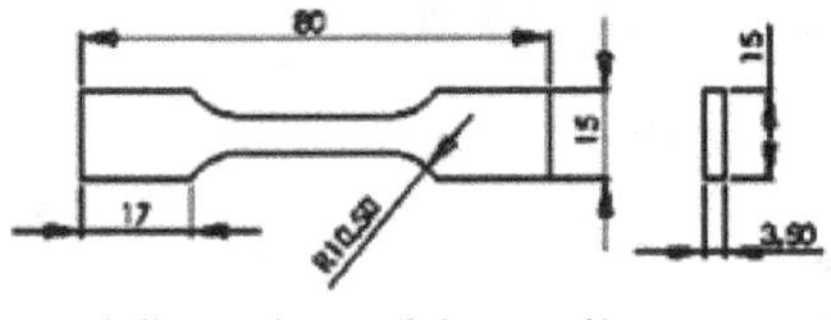

(b) Size and dimensions of the tensile tests specimens

Fig. 5. Experimental set-up for the tensile tests

Table 2. Material parameters corresponding to follow stress over of the COC

	COC 5013	COC 6013
$\dot{\varepsilon}$	10^{-3}	10^{-3}
n	0.27	0.25
m	0.70	0.70
A	0.45	0.20
B	1.10	0.80
C	0.27	0.35

The mechanical data recorded during the tensile test make it possible to derive the stress/strain relationship. In the case of thermo-elastic polymers, the selected behaviour law takes into account the accumulated plastic deformation, the temperature and the deformation rate. The material parameters corresponding to the model are listed in Table 2. As an example, the stress versus strain curve of the specimens at 160°C is shown in Fig. 6. Fig. 6 reveals a proper agreement between the experimental results and numerical solutions for the principal stresses.

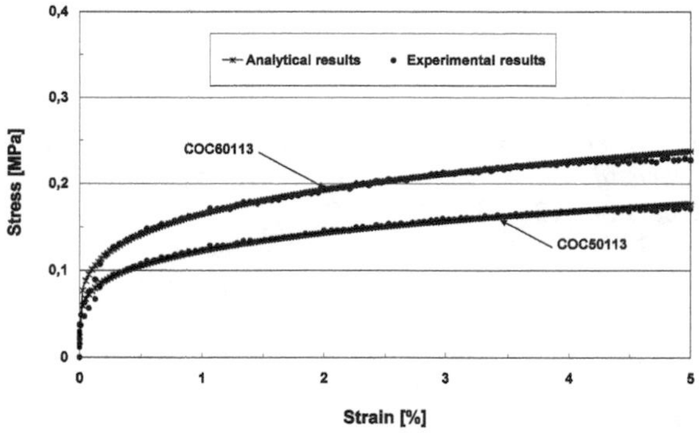

Fig. 6. Comparison of the flow stress curves obtained through tensile test specimens

4 Results and discussions

Fig. 7 shows the displacement contour in the polymer substrate during hot embossed. One can remark that during forming, the profile replication is associated with a correct filling. We remark again that the profile replication is consistent with expectations.

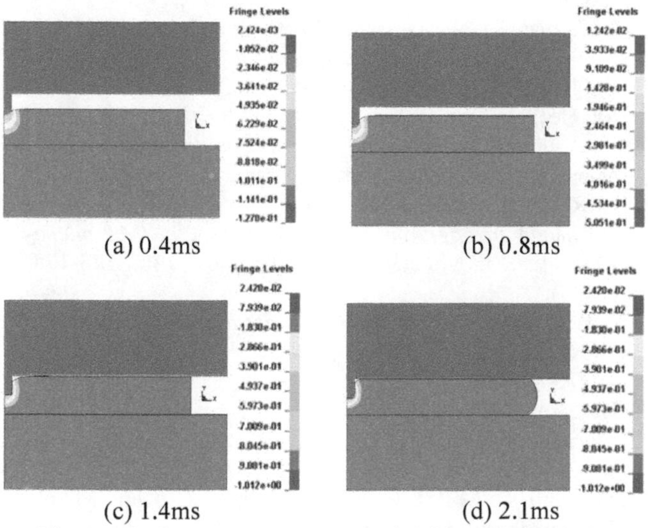

(a) 0.4ms (b) 0.8ms

(c) 1.4ms (d) 2.1ms

Fig. 7. Displacement contours obtained by FE simulation during hot embossing process at different instants

The graphs related in Fig. 8 reveal very similar trends for the deformed surface as a function of the imposed displacement. Moreover the appearance of visco-plastic polymer cushion increases continuously with the imposed displacement, which is linked to the sensitivity to strain rate in polymers. The area requested by the indenter is indeed greater when penetration increases.

Different simulations were carried out in order to optimize the forming parameter for hot embossing of polymer plate. Fig. 9 relates the variation of the value of the filling rate vs. the flow of viscoplastic polymers. One found that higher the melt flow is increased; the rate filling increases, leading thereby to replicas of the geometry shapes corresponds to the original. This Fig. shows off well the progressive filling of cavities that takes place in proper conditions. The filling of sharp edges of the cavities is more or less important almost equivalent linked to problems of material flow during the hot embossing process. One can notice that the trend is consistent with those ones reported in the literature.

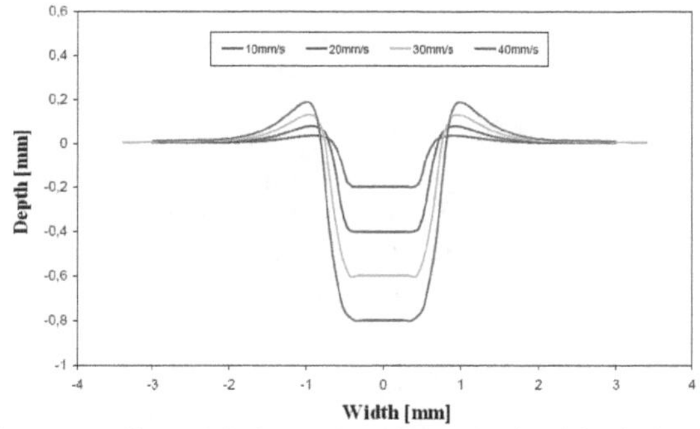

Fig. 8. Profiles of deformed surface obtained by indentation with the flat base cylindrical punch

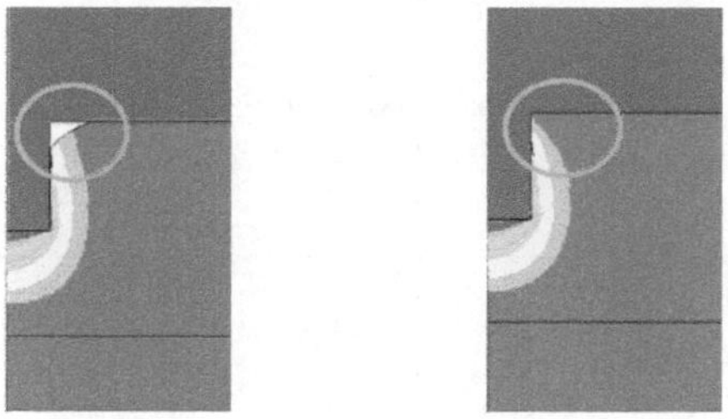

(a) COC 6013 (b) COC 5013

Fig. 9. The filling of the mould cavity for different values of the imposed displacements

5 Experimental validations

The approach was reinforced by experimental studying the features of hollow imprints made by rigid indentation in the COC polymers plates. Fig. 10 reveals the fact that, the lower the young's modulus of the polymer, the deeper the imprint within is moreover, the temperature more increases with increasing depth.

The profiles of COC replications are related in Fig. 11. The curves related indicate that the responses obtained using this numerical model is rather similar to the experimental responses. The main difference take place in the part that is closes to the surface. These results help to understand and analysis the various observations resulting from the shaping of thermoplastic polymers using hot embossing.

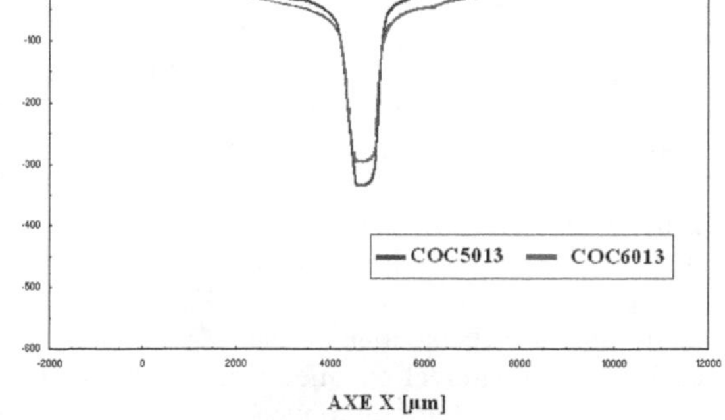

(a) Different polymers

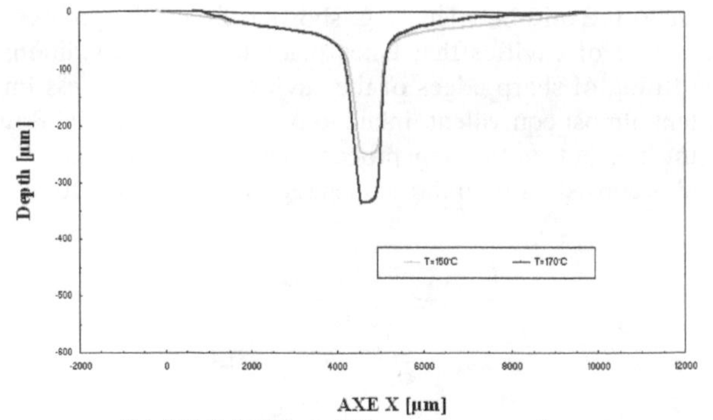

(b) COC 5013 at different temperatures

Fig. 10. Profile of deformed surface under a constant pressure

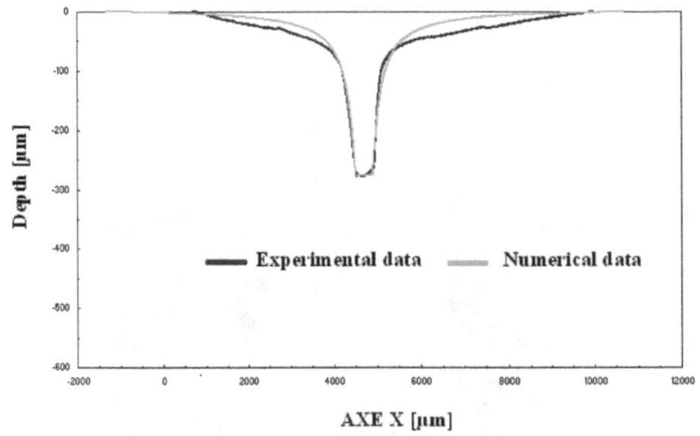

(a)

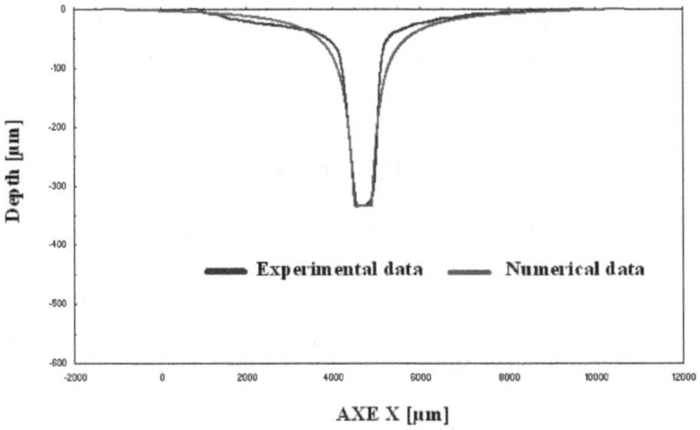

(b)

Fig. 11. Comparison between experimental results and modelling of the deformation of the surface under a constant pressure

5 Conclusions

This study focused on the numerical and experimental analysis concerning forming of polymers using hot embossing for the manufacturing of micro-components. In the proposed study, a simulation approach was developed based on a viscous model to analyze the polymer flow behaviour during the hot embossing process. Moreover, to have the proper conditions for replication, one has to know the polymer behaviour during the hot embossing process.

In the first part, the tensile tests are performed to identify the adequate material behaviour. The study consists in reproducing the uni-axial behaviour of the COC at 160°C. One can confirm that the model parameters are well identified as the stress/strain profiles are reproduced correctly. In the second part, numerical simulations of hot embossing process were carried out integrating the physical and mechanical behaviour of the polymer as well as the conditions under which the forming process is conducted. Experimental validations of the numerical simulations are proposed. The results show that the calculated values vary in the same manner as the experimental data, and the agreement between the numerical model and the experimental results is good.

References

1. H. Becker, U. Heim. *Hot embossing as amethod for the fabrication of polymer high aspect ratio structures*. Sens. Actuators, 130-135, (2000).
2. M. Sahli, C. Millot, C. Roques-Carmes, C. Khan Malek, T. Barriere, J-C. Gelin. *Quality assessment of polymer replication by hot embossing and micro-injection moulding processes using scanning mechanical microscopy*. Journal of Materials Processing Technology, 5851-5861, (2009).
3. K. F. Leil, W. J. Li. *Effects of contact-stress on hot-embossed PMMA microchannel wall profile*. Microsyst. Technol. **11**, 113-119, (2005).
4. M. Sahli, C. Millot, C. Roques-Carmes, C. Khan Malek, T. Barrière, J-C. Gelin. *Optimization of hot embossing demoulding for improvement of quality replication of circular grooved shapes in cycloolefin polymer*. Steel Res. Int., 513-520, (2008).
5. Y. J. Huang, L. L. James. *Hot embossing in microfabrication.* Parte I. Experimental. Polym. Eng. Sci. **42**, 539-550, (2002).
6. Y. J. Juang, L. L. James. *Hot embossing in microfabrication II. Rheological characterization and process analysis*. Polym. Eng. Sci. **42**, 539-550, (2002).
7. M. Heckele, W. Bacher, K. D. Müller. *Hot embossing: the moulding technique for plastic microstructures*. Microsyst. Technol., 122-124, (1998).
8. C. R. Lin, R. H. Chen, C. Hung. *Preventing non-uniform shrinkage in open-die hot embossing of PMMA microstructures*. J. Mater. Process. Technol. **140**, 173-178, (2003).
9. J. H. Chang, S. Y. Yang. *Gas pressurized hot embossing for transcription of micro-features*. Microsyst. Technol. **10**, 76-80, (2003).
10. H. Becker, U. Heim. *Hot embossing as a method for the fabrication of polymer high aspect ratio structures*. Sensors and Actuators A **83**, 130-135, (2000).
11. M. Sahli, C. Millot, C. Roques-Carmes, C. Khan Malek. *Experimental analysis and numerical modelling of the forming process of polypropylene replicas of micro-cavities using hot embossing*. Microsyst Technol, 827-83, (2009).
12. J. M. Li, C. Liu, J. Peng. *Effect of hot embossing process parameters on polymer flow and microchannel accuracy produced without vacuum*. Journal of materials processing technology **207**, 163-171, (2008).
13. D. Wang, T. Shi, J. Pan, G. Liao, Z. Tang, L. Liu. *Finite element simulation and experimental investigation of forming micro-gear with Zr-Cu-Ni-Al bulk metallic glass*. Journal of Materials Processing Technology, **210**, 684-688, (2010).
14. Y. C. Chang, T. T. Wu, M. F. Chen, C. J. Lee, J. C. Huang, C. T. Pan. *Finite element simulation of micro-imprinting in Mg–Cu–Y amorphous alloy.* Materials Sci-

ence and Engineering A **499**, 153-156, (2009).

15. Y. C. Chang, T. T. Wu, M. F. Chen, C. J. Lee, J. C. Huang, C. T. Pan. *Finite element simulation of micro-imprinting in Mg–Cu–Y amorphous alloy.* Materials Science and Engineering A **499**, 153-156, (2009).
16. G. R. Johnson, W. H. Cook. *A constitutive model and data for metals subjected to large strains, high strain-rates and high temperatures.* Proc. 7th Int. Symposium on Ballistics, 541-547, (1983).
17. G. R. Johnson, W. H. Cook. *Fracture characteristics of three metals subjected to various strains, strain rates, temperatures and pressures.* Engineering Fracture Mechanics **21**, 31-48, (1985).
18. C. Roques-Carmes, N. Bodin, G. Monteil, J. F. Quiniou. *Description of rough surfaces using conformal equivalent structure concept Part 1. Stereological approach.* Wear **248**, 82-91, (2001).
19. D. Wehbi, G. Monteil, C. Roques-Carmes. *Notion de rugosité de surface et méthodes de mesure.* Le vide, les couches minces **224**, 107, (1985).

Investigation on Buckling of Orthotropic Circular and Annular Plates of Continuously Variable Thickness by Optimized Ritz Method

Fatemeh Farhatnia [1,a], Arash Golshah[2]

[1] Islamic Azad University-Branch of Khomeinishahr,Mechanical Engineering Faculty, Boulvard Manzarie, Khomeinishahr, Isfahan, Iran
[2] Iran Aircraft Manufacturing (HESA), Moallem Highway, Isfahan, Iran

Abstract – This paper investigates symmetrical buckling of orthotropic circular and annular plates of continuous variable thickness. Uniform compression loading is applied at the plate outer boundary. Thickness varies linearly along radial direction. Inner edge is free, while outer edge has different boundary conditions: clamped, simply and elastically restraint against rotation. The optimized Ritz method is applied for buckling analysis. In this method, a polynomial function that is based on static deformation of orthotropic circular plates in bending is used. Also, by employing an exponential parameter in deformation function, eigenvalue is minimized in respect to this parameter. The obtained results show that in plate with identical thickness, increasing of outer radius decreases the buckling load factor

Keywords: Buckling, Orthotropic circular and annular plates, Optimized Ritz, Variable thickness.

1 Introduction

Orthotropic circular and annular plates are always used by mechanical, civil, aerospace and structural engineers and designers. Some applications of these systems are pressure vessel valve, reinforced circular plates by radial and circumference supporter, composite plates, cylinder head cover, bulkhead plates in submarines, separated plates in aircraft, optical lenses, and acoustic transducers in rockets. For first time Woinosky[1], studied the problem of elastic stability of orthotropic circular plates. He introduced numeric results by using Bessel function for buckling of plates. Menk *et al.*[2], studied on variation of thickness on buckling of orthotropic rectangular plate. Laura *et al.* [3], found critical load of buckling for isotropic annular plate with constant thickness by optimized Ritz method. Imposed boundary condition of plate for inner edge either outer edge was under different supports. Cianco [4] studied on buckling of circular and annular isotropic plate with variable thickness that used as a part of submarine. This plate was considered with free support on inner edge and clamped support and resistant of rotation for outer edge. The thickness of plate is exponential function of its radius. He analyzed the plate by optimized Ritz method. Bremec *et al.* [5] also introduced one optimized rate of variation of thickness for buckling of isotropic plates which both in inner edge and outer edge was under constant radial load and thickness was varied in radial direction. Buckling function was in linear fashion and solved by numeric method under simply and clamped supported. Coutierrez *et al.* [6] considered buckling and vibration of the isotropic plate with variable thickness on elastic support using Ritz method, and obtained acceptable results. Liang *et al.* [7] found natural frequencies of one orthotropic circular and annular plate with variable thickness using Ritz method and compared with the result of finite element method that were good in agreement between them.

In this paper, buckling of orthotropic circular and annular plates with linear variation of thickness under constant compressive radial loading is studied. The boundary condition of annular plates are F-C plates (free inner, and clamped outer edge) or clamped circular solid ones, F-S plates (free inner, simply outer edge) or simply supported solid circular ones, and annular plates with free inner support and resistant elastic against rotation outer edge. Circular plates contain plates with clamped, simply and elastic resistant against rotation boundary condition. Solving buckling differential equation of orthotropic circular or annular plate with variable thickness is impossible by analytical method and it should be solved using numerical or energy method. For this reason optimized - Ritz method is used. The results of this method is more precisely than Ritz method. For optimization of Ritz method, one exponential parameter in approximate function is considered eigenvalues (buckling load factor) that is obtained, are minimized according to this exponential parameter. Furthermore, the comparison between results of this method and the results of finite element procedure is done. The effects of thickness variation, boundary conditions, young module ratio in radius and circumference axis, variation of ratio of inner radius to outer one on buckling load factor are considered.

2 Theory

2.1 Basic formulation of the problem

The formulation of the problem is derived under the following assumptions:

1. The plate is in the state of plane stress.
2. The stress-strain relationship follows of orthotropic material.

[a] Corresponding author: farhatnia@iaukhsh.ac.ir

3. The plate is thin, therefore the Kirchhoff assumptions incorporated.
4. The thickness is varied in the direction of radius of the plate.

Consider a circular annular plate with variable thickness h(r), a, b inner and outer radius, respectively as shown in Figure (1). For buckling analysis, the in-plane displacement u and v may be neglected and only out-of-plane deformation w is considered.

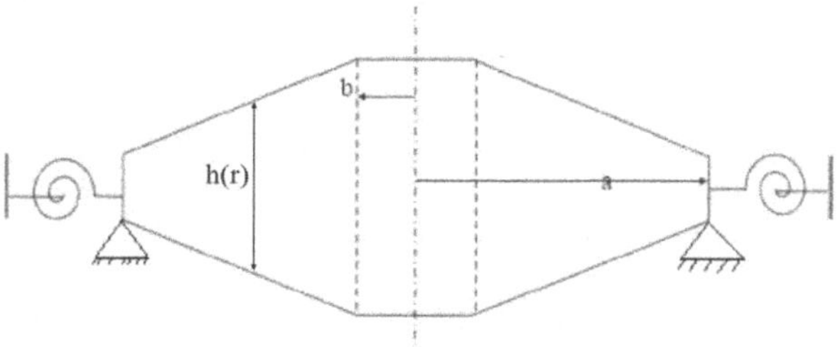

Fig. 1. Schematic view of annular plate with variable thickness

The governing energy functional can be given by:

$$J=U+V \tag{1}$$

Where U is the stored strain energy per unit volume that in the polar coordinate system for plane stress is given as follows [8]:

$$U=\frac{1}{2}\iiint_V(\sigma_r\varepsilon_r+\sigma_\theta\varepsilon_\theta+\tau_{r\theta}\gamma_{r\theta})rdrd\theta dz \tag{2}$$

The work done by in-plane radial force is given as:

$$V=\frac{1}{2}\iint_A\left[N_r\left(\frac{\partial w}{\partial r}\right)^2+N_\theta\left(\frac{\partial w}{\partial \theta}\right)^2\right]rdrd\theta \tag{3}$$

In present study, the axial radial symmetry is assumed, so plate is independent of azimuthal variable:

$$V=\pi\int_b^a N_r\left(\frac{\partial w}{\partial r}\right)^2 rdr \tag{4}$$

For orthotropic annular plate, V is derived as follows [9]:

$$V=\pi\int_b^a\frac{-N_0}{h_a}\frac{a^{\beta+1}}{a^{2\beta}-b^{2\beta}}\left[r^{\beta-1}-\frac{b^{2\beta}}{r^{\beta+1}}\right]\left(\frac{\partial w}{\partial r}\right)^2 rdr \tag{5}$$

Also, using the stress-strain relation for orthotropic material, substituting into equation (1), one may obtain:

$$U=\frac{1}{2}\iiint_V\frac{z^2}{1-\upsilon_r\upsilon_\theta}\left[E_r\left(\frac{d^2w}{dr^2}\right)^2+2E_r\upsilon_\theta\left(\frac{d^2w}{dr^2}\right)\left(\frac{dw}{dr}\right)+E_\theta\left(\frac{dw}{rdr}\right)^2\right]rdrd\theta dz \tag{6}$$

where,

$$D_r(r)=\frac{E_rh^3(r)}{12(1-\upsilon_r\upsilon_\theta)}\quad,\quad\frac{E_\theta}{E_r}=\frac{D_\theta(r)}{D_r(r)}=\beta^2 \tag{7}$$

In above equation, $D_r(r), D_\theta(r)$ denote circumferential and radial bending stiffness of the plate, respectively.

In this study, annular and solid circular plates with continuously varying thickness are considered. The variation of thickness along the radius direction can be expressed as follows:

$$h(r)=h_o\left(1+\gamma\left(\frac{r}{a}\right)^n\right) \tag{9}$$

where *ho* and *a* represent the thickness in the centre (inner radius for annular plate) and the outer radius of plate, respectively.

In order to consider the influence of non uniform thickness on buckling load factor, two values are assigned for the parameter n, n=0, 1 for uniform and linearly varying thickness, respectively. γ is non-dimensional geometric parameter that may be positive (centrally thinner circular plate) or negative (centrally thicker circular plate) and is defined as follows:

For circular solid plates:

$$\gamma=\frac{h_a}{h_o}-1 \tag{10}$$

For circular annular plates:

$$\gamma=\frac{h_b-h_o}{h_o(r_b)^n} \tag{11}$$

In above equation, r_b is the ratio of inner radius to the outer one $(=\frac{b}{a})$.

In the sake of convenience, the variables in equations (7) and (15) are transformed to dimensionless one, so the total potential energy functional is as follows:

$$\frac{a^2}{\pi D_0}J(w)=\int_{r_b}^1\left\{g(R)\left[\left(\frac{d^2w}{dR^2}\right)^2+2\upsilon_\theta\left(\frac{d^2w}{dR^2}\right)\left(\frac{dw}{RdR}\right)+\beta^2\left(\frac{dw}{RdR}\right)^2\right]-\frac{\lambda}{1-r_b^{2\beta}}\left[R^{\beta-1}-\frac{r_b^{2\beta}}{R^{\beta+1}}\right]\left(\frac{dw}{dR}\right)^2\right\}RdR \tag{12}$$

that,

$$g(R)=(1+\gamma R)^3,\quad D_0=\frac{E_rh_o^3}{12(1-\upsilon_r\upsilon_\theta)},\quad R=\frac{r}{a} \tag{13}$$

λ is the buckling load factor that is related to buckling load as follows:

$$\lambda=\frac{N_0a^2}{D_0} \tag{14}$$

2.2 Optimized Ritz method

Regarding to this fact that Ritz method is an upper bound method, so determined eigenvalue is more than real one, therefore if one can optimized it somehow, the results will be closer to real one. In general, if the function which introducing the unknown quantity, is a linear combination of shape modes φ_n, as follows:

$$f(x)=\sum_{n=1}^N c_n\varphi_n(x) \tag{15}$$

where c_n is the unknown constants. Regarding to the idea of optimization, by performing the optimized Ritz method, it is quite convenient to approximate the displacement amplitude W(R) by means of a summation [4]:

$$f(x)=\sum_{n=1}^N c_n\varphi_n(x,k) \tag{16}$$

Note that *k* in above equation is the exponential optimization parameter. Regarding to the equation (15), out-plane displacement is given as follows:

$$w(R)=\sum_{i=1}^N c_iw_i(R,k) \tag{17}$$

By minimizing potential energy functional in Ritz method:

$$\frac{\partial J}{\partial c_i}=0 \qquad i=1,\dots,N \tag{18}$$

Total number of N linear homogenous algebraic equations are generated that the unknowns are constants c_n. It forms the eigenvalue problem that the eigenvlaues are the values of buckling load parameter. The non-trivially condition leads to a transcendental equation in whose lowest root is the desired buckling load factor [4].

Since $\frac{\partial\lambda}{\partial k}=0$, by requiring one is able to optimize the fundamental eigenvalue.

2.3 Buckling of annular circular plate

Regarding to the equation (15), $w_i(R)$ is defined as follows [9]:

$$w_i(R,k)=\left(a_iR^k+b_iR^{1+\beta}+1\right)R^{i-1} \tag{19}$$

Unknown constants a_i and b_i are determined by applying boundary conditions.

2.3.1 Clamped outer edge (F-C) plate

For a clamped outer edge; in r=a or R=1, the governing boundary conditions are:

$$\begin{cases} w_i(1)=0 \\ \frac{dw_i}{dR}(1)=0 \end{cases} \tag{20}$$

By substitution eq. (19) into eq. (20), the a_i and b_i values are determined as follows:

$$a_i=\frac{-1-\beta}{1+\beta-k} \qquad b_i=\frac{k}{1+\beta-k} \tag{21}$$

2.3.2 Simply supported outer edge(S-F) plate

For a simply supported outer edge, the out-plane displacement w, must be satisfied the following conditions:

$$\begin{cases} w(1)=0 \\ \frac{d^2w}{dR^2}(1)+\upsilon_\theta\frac{dw}{dR}(1)=0 \end{cases} \tag{22}$$

Regarding to the boundary condition in outer edge, the a_i and b_i values are determined:

$$a_i=\frac{(1+\beta)(-2+2i+\beta+\upsilon_\theta)}{(-1-\beta+k)(-2+2i+k+\beta+\upsilon_\theta)}$$
$$b_i=-\frac{k(-3+2i+k+\upsilon_\theta)}{(-1-\beta+k)(-2+2i+k+\beta+\upsilon_\theta)} \tag{23}$$

2.3.3 Elastically restrained rotation

For the case of elastically restrained rotation:

$$\begin{cases} w_i(1)=0 \\ \varphi\frac{dw_i}{dR}(1)=-g(R)\left[\frac{d^2w_i}{dR^2}(1)+\upsilon_\theta\frac{dw_i}{dR}(1)\right] \end{cases} \tag{24}$$

the a_i and b_i values are determined as follows:

$$a_i=-\frac{Q_i-L_i}{S_i-L_i}, \quad b_i=-\frac{S_i-Q_i}{S_i-L_i} \tag{25}$$

In above equation, S_i, Q_i, L_i are defined as follows:

$$\begin{aligned} S_i&=(k+i-1)[1+g(R)\varphi(-2+i+k+\upsilon_\theta)] \\ L_i&=(i+\beta)[1+g(R)\varphi(-1+i+\beta+\upsilon_\theta)] \\ Q_i&=(i-1)[1+g(R)\varphi(-2+i+\upsilon_\theta)] \end{aligned} \tag{26}$$

$\varphi=\frac{ak_\varphi}{D_0}$ represents the dimensionless flexibility coefficient. Using the equation (18), total number of N linear homogenous algebraic equations is generated. The non-trivially condition leads to set zero the determinant of coefficients matrix, as follows:

$$|A-\lambda B|=0 \tag{27}$$

Where A_{ij} and B_{ij} are determined as follows:

$$A_{ij}=\int_{r_b}^{1}g(r)\left[\left(\frac{d^2w_i}{dR^2}\right)\left(\frac{d^2w_j}{dR^2}\right)+2\upsilon_\theta\left(\frac{d^2w_i}{dR^2}\right)\left(\frac{dw_j}{RdR}\right)+\beta^2\left(\frac{dw_i}{RdR}\right)\left(\frac{dw_j}{RdR}\right)\right]RdR+\varphi\left(\frac{dw_i}{dR}\right)\left(\frac{dw_j}{dR}\right) \tag{28}$$

$$B_{ij}=\frac{\lambda}{1-r_b^{2\beta}}\left[R^{\beta-1}-\frac{r_b^{2\beta}}{R^{\beta+1}}\right]\int_{r_b}^{1}\left(\frac{dw_i}{dR}\right)\left(\frac{dw_j}{dR}\right)RdR \tag{29}$$

In the above equation, for the case of simply supported and clamped in outer edge, φ=0 , φ=∞ respectively.

2.4 Buckling of circular solid plate

Regarding to equation (17), for circular solid plate $w_i(R)$ is defined as follows [9]:

$$w_i(R,k)=\left(a_iR^k+b_iR^{1+\beta}+1\right)R^{2(i-1)} \tag{30}$$

In order to obtain a_i and b_i as constants, the following boundary conditions must be satisfied:

2.4.1 Clamped outer edge, (C-F) plate

$$b_i = \frac{k}{1+\beta-k}, \quad a_i = \frac{-1-\beta}{1+\beta-k} \tag{31}$$

2.4.2 Simply supported outer edge, (S-F) plate

$$a_i = \frac{(1+\beta)(-4+4i+\beta+\upsilon_\theta)}{(-1-\beta+k)(-4+4i+k+\beta+\upsilon_\theta)}$$
$$b_i = -\frac{k(-5+4i+k+\upsilon_\theta)}{(-1-\beta+k)(-4+4i+k+\beta+\upsilon_\theta)} \tag{32}$$

2.4.3 Elastically restrained rotation

$$a_i = -\frac{Q_i-L_i}{S_i-L_i} \qquad b_i = -\frac{S_i-Q_i}{S_i-L_i} \tag{33}$$

where,

$$S_i = (k+2i-2)\left[1+g(R)K_\phi(-3+2i+k+\upsilon_\theta)\right]$$
$$L_i = (2i+\beta-1)\left[1+g(R)K_\phi(-2+2i+\beta+\upsilon_\theta)\right] \tag{33}$$
$$Q_i = 2(i-1)\left[1+g(R)K_\phi(-3+2i+\upsilon_\theta)\right]$$

A $_{ij}$ and B$_{ij}$ are determined as follows:

$$A_{ij} = \int_0^1 g(R)\left[\left(\frac{d^2w_i}{dR^2}\right)\left(\frac{d^2w_j}{dR^2}\right) + 2\upsilon_\theta\left(\frac{d^2w_i}{dR^2}\right)\left(\frac{dw_j}{RdR}\right)\right. \tag{34}$$
$$\left. + \beta^2\left(\frac{dw_i}{RdR}\right)\left(\frac{dw_j}{RdR}\right)\right] + \varphi\left(\frac{dw_i(1)}{RdR}\right)\left(\frac{dw_j(1)}{RdR}\right)$$

$$B_{ij} = \lambda R^{\beta-1}\int_0^1\left(\frac{dw_i}{dR}\right)\left(\frac{dw_j}{dR}\right)RdR \tag{35}$$

Like before, in the above equation, for the case of simply supported φ=0 and clamped in outer edge, φ=∞.

3. Numerical results

This section presents a number of numerical examples that shows the good performance of the proposed method, which was implemented in *Mathematica 5.1* computer program. The results of the developed optimized Ritz method are compared with some other results obtained from FE method. All calculation has been performed for E_r =10000 Mpa, υ_θ =.3, a=1 m, h_o=.08 m. It was revealed that convergent buckling load factor is obtained with 4-term series. Table (1) shows this convergence for centrally thicker annular orthotropic plate. In presenting results, the dimensionless buckling load factor is used. Value of this factor is obtained for plates of uniform and linearly continuously thickness.

Table (1): Convergence study for annular orthotropic plate

γ	r_b	m				
		1	2	3	4	5
-0.3	0.1	8.06227	7.82111	7.80585	7.65965	7.65696
	0.3	7.64248	7.26206	7.24417	7.15621	7.15612
	0.5	10.7017	10.6339	10.6283	10.6069	10.6066

Annular plate

Table (2) depicts the influence of parameters γ, β^2, r_b on the buckling load factor. It is observed with increasing the amount of β, buckling load factor is increased too. One observes that orthotropic plate ($\beta^2 > 1$) has more stiffness against buckling occasion in comparison to isotropic one. Furthermore increasing parameter γ toward positive values makes the buckling load factor to increase. Regarding to table (1), some values of r_b (r_b>.1) decreases the buckling load factor λ, meanwhile some other values makes it decrease. As shown in table (3), as it was expected, clamped boundary condition represents the highest value of factor while the simply supported one, shows the lowest. The influence of parameters γ, β^2, r_b is the same as clamped case.

Table 2. Buckling load factor variation with simply supported outer edge

β^2	γ	r_b				
		0.1	0.2	0.3	0.4	0.5
1	-0.3	7.65965	7.08443	7.15621	8.17407	10.6069
	-0.1	11.6538	11.1526	11.9511	14.4785	19.7288
	0	14.0102	13.6272	14.9707	18.5588	25.7602
	0.1	16.605	16.4169	18.4444	23.3258	32.8914
	0.3	23.5623	23.0035	26.8698	35.1226	50.8109
2	-0.3	12.2977	11.7989	11.3131	11.6165	13.4416
	-0.1	19.4974	18.8195	18.6013	20.0802	24.5068
	0	23.8244	23.0811	23.1413	25.5038	31.7732
	0.1	28.6657	27.8789	28.3333	31.807	40.3339
	0.3	39.9593	39.1814	40.8333	47.3052	61.7521
5	-0.3	23.331	23.2335	22.7974	22.1416	22.4007
	-0.1	39.3318	39.151	38.4959	38.0138	39.9237
	0	49.2861	49.0655	48.3052	48.0918	51.309
	0.1	60.6435	60.3648	59.3648	59.7502	64.6481
	0.3	87.8954	87.4584	86.6497	88.2489	97.7947
10	-0.3	39.4051	39.2595	39.2595	38.7452	37.9053
	-0.1	69.3379	69.0895	69.0894	68.2961	67.7093
	0	88.3379	88.4204	88.1414	87.2232	87.0211
	0.1	110.615	110.568	110.221	109.203	109.61
	0.3	164.852	164.774	164.275	163.176	165.608

Table 3. Buckling load factor variation with clamped outer edge

β^2	γ	r_b				
		0.1	0.2	0.3	0.4	0.5
1	-0.3	2.38864	2.08242	1.74291	1.45192	1.22152
	-0.1	3.40413	2.99726	2.59067	2.25996	2.00307
	0	3.99418	3.53995	3.10666	2.76324	2.50023
	0.1	4.64426	4.14536	3.69047	3.33985	3.007638
	0.3	6.13934	5.56135	5.8046	4.7343	4.48982
2	-0.3	3.865	3.70686	3.37779	2.95803	2.54578
	-0.1	5.91459	5.67527	5.2282	4.70576	4.21785
	0	7.14892	6.86634	6.36338	5.79828	5.28355
	0.1	8.53568	8.20873	7.65316	7.05245	6.51991
	0.3	11.8043	11.3873	10.7398	10.0932	9.5504
5	-0.3	7.44953	7.42653	7.29997	6.95221	6.35169
	-0.1	12.4039	12.3628	12.1571	11.6415	10.8251
	0	15.5186	15.467	15.2169	14.6124	13.6953
	0.1	19.1024	19.0392	18.7421	18.0519	17.0371
	0.3	27.8088	27.7192	27.3225	26.4616	25.2822
10	-0.3	12.7613	12.7592	12.7332	12.5904	12.1299
	-0.1	22.434	22.4299	22.3826	22.1401	21.4237
	0	28.6802	28.6739	28.6134	28.3129	27.4558
	0.1	35.9679	35.9621	35.889	35.5252	34.5213
	0.3	54.0108	54.0021	53.8957	53.3922	52.0821

Tables (4-6) depict the influence of rotational constant φ on buckling load factor for different value of β^2. It is revealed that when $\varphi \rightarrow 0$, the boundary condition is closer to simply supported case and the loading factor shows the lower than when $\varphi \rightarrow \infty$ the outer edge is clamped and stiff against rotation.

Table 4. Buckling load factor variation with edge elastically restrained $(\beta = 1)$

γ	φ	r_b				
		0.1	0.2	0.3	0.4	0.5
-0.3	0	2.39267	2.08653	1.74474	1.45248	1.22165
	10	7.02073	6.47188	6.4328	7.14899	8.92773
	∞	7.78485	7.17253	7.20876	8.21381	10.6283
-0.1	0	3.4185	3.00976	2.59598	2.26171	2.00357
	10	10.1649	9.62109	9.92857	11.3968	14.4472
	∞	11.7928	11.2945	12.0246	14.5139	19.7524
0	0	4.0144	3.55674	3.11384	2.76572	2.50097
	10	11.7538	11.2724	11.8074	13.6684	17.3273
	∞	14.1309	13.7553	15.0361	18.5922	25.7854
0.1	0	4.66952	4.16614	3.6995	3.34309	3.07739
	10	13.3724	12.9663	13.7373	15.9742	20.1736
	∞	16.7082	16.5284	18.5018	23.357	32.9186
0.3	0	6.17125	5.5881	5.0932	4.73918	4.49148
	10	16.6434	16.4146	17.6377	20.5221	25.5586
	∞	22.6	23.0801	26.9097	35.1488	50.8404

Table 5. load factor variation with edge elastically restrained $(\beta = \sqrt{2})$

γ	φ	r_b				
		0.1	0.2	0.3	0.4	0.5
-0.3	0	3.86494	3.70778	3.37948	2.95904	2.54614
	10	11.1494	10.7466	10.2355	10.2921	11.4907
	∞	12.3941	11.9712	11.429	11.7022	13.4887
-0.1	0	5.92078	5.68816	5.23808	4.71045	4.21952
	10	16.3925	15.9406	15.5214	16.0831	18.3679
	∞	19.6007	19.0235	18.7609	20.168	24.5558
0	0	7.16249	6.88791	6.37831	5.80537	5.28613
	10	19.173	18.6768	18.3597	19.2084	22.0132
	∞	23.9331	23.2797	23.2917	25.5881	31.8244
0.1	0	8.55772	8.23958	7.67409	7.06221	6.52353
	10	22.0216	21.1903	21.2775	22.4076	25.679
	∞	28.762	28.062	28.4736	31.8876	40.388
0.3	0	11.8246	11.4362	10.7724	10.1088	9.56313
	10	27.8305	27.2711	27.2789	28.8982	32.897
	∞	40.0193	39.3203	40.9454	47.3759	61.8092

Table 6. load factor variation with edge elastically restrained $(\beta = \sqrt{5})$

γ	φ	r_b				
		0.1	0.2	0.3	0.4	0.5
-0.3	0	7.44981	7.42763	7.30188	6.95214	6.35201
	10	20.398	20.3231	19.9702	19.3557	19.2569
	∞	23.5367	23.4633	23.0736	23.396	22.5735
-0.1	0	12.4127	12.3628	12.1602	11.6479	10.83
	10	31.3392	31.2815	30.8997	30.2359	30.5775
	∞	39.4941	39.3991	38.8456	38.3133	40.103
0	0	15.5204	15.469	15.2275	14.6276	13.70421
	10	37.136	37.0678	36.654	36.058	36.6338
	∞	49.4286	49.3058	48.672	48.401	51.4971
0.1	0	19.1036	19.0485	18.764	18.0745	17.0509
	10	43.1385	43.0614	42.6181	42.0768	42.8725
	∞	60.7884	60.6234	59.9327	60.0692	64.8462
0.3	0	27.8251	27.7559	27.3754	26.5071	25.3083
	10	55.7733	55.6721	55.182	54.7283	55.8625
	∞	88.0433	87.7881	87.0796	88.5781	98.01

3.2 circular solid plate

Figures (2) and (3) illustrate the variation of bucking load factor respect to boundary condition case, orthotropic and geometry β^2 and γ.

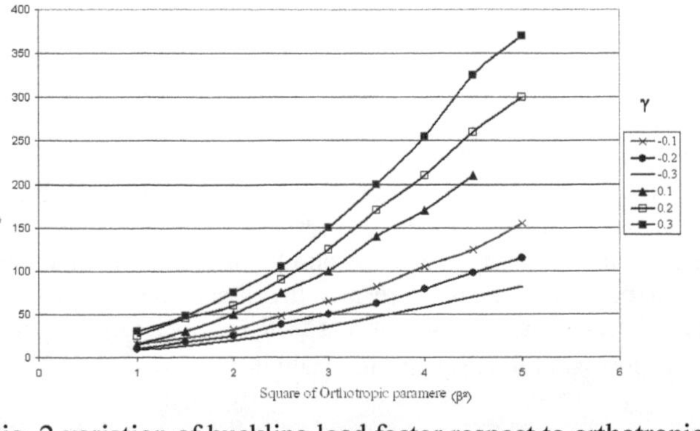

Fig. 2 variation of buckling load factor respect to orthotropic parameter and non-dimensional geometric parameter with clamped outer edge

As shown, plate with $\gamma < 0$ (centrally thicker solid plate, $\frac{ha}{h0} < 1$) has lower buckling load factor than plate with $\gamma > 0$ (centrally thinner circular plate, $\frac{ha}{h0} > 1$). Buckling factor pattern for all boundary conditions are similar.

Figure (4) illustrates the influence of rotational constant φ on buckling load factor for different value of β^2. For different boundary conditions, the obtained result is the same as the annular plate In fact, for simply supported outer edg, the evaluated buckling load factor is lower than clamped and elastically restrained against rotation in outer edge.

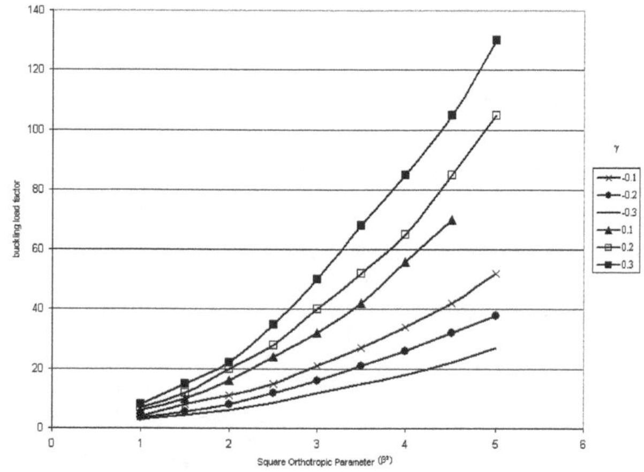

Fig. 3. Variation of buckling load factor respect to orthotropic parameter and non-dimensional geometric parameter with simply supported outer edge

As shown in Table (6), the results obtained from present method, compare very well with obtained from finite element procedure. This confirms the accuracy of Optimized Ritz method in buckling analyzing of circular plates.

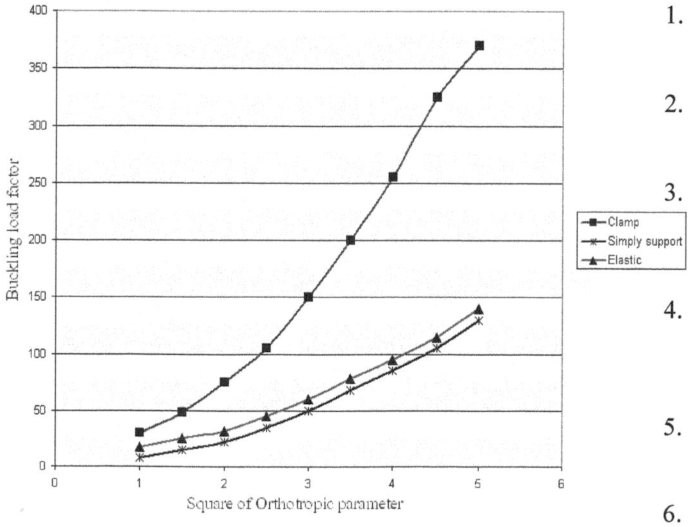

Fig. 4. Variation of buckling load factor respect to orthotropic parameter for different boundary conditions

Table 7. Comparison of results for buckling load factor in Optimized Ritz method (I) and FEM (II)

β^2		γ						
		-0.3	-0.2	-0.1	0	0.1	0.2	0.3
1	I	8.05	10.03	12.24	14.68	17.36	20.28	23.43
	II	7.8	9.825	12.11	14.68	17.53	20.69	24.15
1.4	I	9.87	12.43	15.32	18.54	22.1	26.04	30.26
	II	9.72	12.31	15.24	18.54	22.21	26.28	30.75
1.8	I	11.56	14.69	18.25	22.24	26.67	31.57	36.94
	II	11.55	14.67	18.23	22.23	26.7	31.66	37.11

4 Conclusion

The buckling analysis of orthotropic circular annular and solid plates under uniform radial compression loading with uniform and linearly varying thickness was presented. The inner edge is free while the outer edge is under different types of classical boundary conditions and also with edges elastically restrained against rotation. This is implemented by optimized Ritz method. In this method, an optimization exponential parameter is utilized that buckling load factor was minimized respect to it. Following are some of the concluding remarks:

- Increasing orthotropic parameter and radius ratio (inner to outer radius), increases the resistance of plate against buckling phenomena.
- Plate with clamped boundary condition exhibits the higher value of the buckling parameter, while the simply supported case shows lowest. Also plate with edges elastically restrained against rotation has value of between two boundary condition cases.
- Centrally thinner circular plate has higher buckling parameter than centrally thicker one.

5 References

1. S.Woinowski-Krieger, *Buckling stability of circular plates with circular cylindrical Aeolotropy*, Ingenieur-Archiv, **26**, 129-13, (1958).
2. T. Meink, S. Huybrechts, J. Ganley, *The effect of varying thickness on the buckling of orthotropic plate*, J. Composite Materials, **33**, 1048-1061, (1999).
3. P.A.A, Laura, R.H. Gutierrez, H.C. Sanzi, G. Elvira, *Buckling of circular, solid and annular plates with an intermediate circular support*, J. Ocean Engineering, **27**, 749-755, (2000).
4. P.M. Ciancio, J.A. Reyes, *Buckling of circular annular plates of continuously variable thickness used as internal bulkheads in submersibles*, J. Ocean engineering, **30**, 1323-1333, (2003).
5. B. Bremec , F. Kosel ,*Thickness optimization of circular annular plates at buckling*, Thin-Walled Structures, **32,** 74-81, (2006).
6. R.H. Gutierrez, E. Romanlli, P.A.A Laura, *Vibration and elastic stability of thin circular plates with variable profile,* J. sound and vibration, **195,** 391-399, (1996).
7. B. Liang , Sh. Zhang , D. Chen, Natural *frequencies of circular annular plates with variable thickness by a*

new method, J. pressure vessels and piping, **84,** 293-297, (2007).

8. S.P. Timoshenko, J. M. Gere, *Theory of elastic stability*, (McGraw-Hill, New York, 1961).
9. U.S. Gupta, R. Lal, C.P Verm, *Buckling and vibrations of polar orthotropic annular plates of variable thickness,* J. sound and vibration, **104**, 357-369, (1985).

21

Automatic Generation of Computer Models through the Integration of Production Systems Design Software Tools

Pavel Vik[1], Dias Luís, Pereira Guilherme and José Oliveira

University of Minho, Centro ALGORITMI, Campus de Gualtar, Braga, 4710 - 057, Portugal

Abstract – The design of production and logistic systems is a process of managing both technical and organizational variants in order to identify the best solution for a given system. This is a very well-known industrial engineering issue, where the objectives for designing such a system have been changing over the last decades. Former approaches were concerned about material handling costs only but more recent works include re-layout and product mix costs, together with a great concern on processes – high service levels, optimal scheduling policies, setup times and costs, etc. Nowadays, the rapid technological progress and the associated competitive problems lead to a great need of fast and successful solutions to deal with continuous change (re-design) of the currently used industrial systems. Flexibility, modularity, efficiency and robustness are generally highly desired system properties. For general design of industrial systems, three basic types of software tools are used: Computer Aided Design, Simulation and Information Systems. These tools help on improving the utilization of system resources like equipment, manpower, materials, space, energy, information, etc. Nevertheless these three types of software tools have been used with low levels of integration. This absence of an adequate data connection and integration of outputs cause time delays in the design process, duplication of work and could also be a source of errors. In this work, Production Systems Design software tools integration possibilities are discussed and a unified system architecture solution, implemented on AutoCAD (layout design), Witness (Simulation) and MS-Access (Information Systems) is presented. The aim is to focus on the need of data coherence between different software tools, exploring ways of dealing with data diversity and assuring valid and efficient solutions. MS-Access supports the specification of the system and data exchange between Witness and AutoCAD. Based on the database specification, our application automatically generates simulation programs and also different spatial patterns of project layouts. These tasks are implemented in Visual Basic code. Iteratively the results from the simulations are used to improve AutoCAD layouts and AutoCAD layouts are used in new simulations. The use of our application, in the examples showed in this paper, proved to get quick, valid and efficient solutions.

Key words: production system design, computer simulation, CAD system, database system, automatic generated simulation models, automatic generated layouts.

1 Introduction

This paper describes an internal logistic system in the automotive industry – namely a manufacturer of plastic parts for cars. Its production and logistic system is strictly based on customer requirements and it is very hard to establish optimal solution and a static optimal system configuration. For this purposes, it is common to use computer simulation which can be used in many ways.

Constructing a simulation model is time consuming. Adapting a previous simulation model could also be time consuming. However simulation proved to be an important tool to deal with production and logistic systems design. In this project we propose a way of automatically generating simulation models. We also propose a way of automatically generating layout designs. Furthermore we propose to integrate both approaches and iteratively get better solutions for our production and logistic system. Both tools would interact with a suggested database that would be able to correctly describe the whole system under study. Advantages and disadvantages are then discussed. The problem under analysis in this paper has been previously approached by the conventional way – models manually constructed (Jareš 9); The approach proposed in this paper – models created automatically, is part of our current research work (Vik 19, 20, 21).

Assembly lines in the automotive industry produce hundreds of cars per day. It is critical to supply the correct component to the correct line at the appropriate time. Nowadays mass customization leads to the possibility of choosing a car according to specific customer requirements. This impels companies to provide a very large set of product variants. It is then possible to reach over 50 000 real variants for a particular type of car – virtually more than 8 billion different possible combinations.

To tackle the problem of large quantities of product variants, and due essentially to capital and storage limitations, production strategies have emerged - JIT (Just in Time) or even JIS (Just in Sequence). These strategies imply that components are just supplied to production line when they are needed (Hutchins 8), so reducing storages and buffers. These production approaches make it possible to anticipate to suppliers an exact production schedule, exact production sequences, etc.

Nevertheless models developed in this work do include the possibility of changing production sequences (as a conse-

[1] Corresponding author: vikpavel@seznam.cz

quence of changing assembling sequences) in the internal logistic system, combining production and storage areas. Logistics of production systems became one of the most important issues in the automotive industry. Companies in this area don't differ too much in technology and equipment used. Essentially quality of products and services, especially logistic services would make the difference. Critical aspects for a successful company would then include:

- flexibility to customers' requirements
- rapid adaptation to customers' requirements
- permanent flexibility to actual market needs
- permanent need of quality increasing
- short time reactions to any type of changes

The time pressure in the design of production systems and frequent changes mentioned above leads to our suggested approach of currently used software tools integration in the area of production systems design. These tools would refer to project data analysis, design and consequent validation, namely:

- Databases
- CAD systems
- Discrete simulation

These tools are usually used with low levels of integration, leading to redundant work and absence of data coherence. Our approach supports the integration of a CAD system with a simulation tool through a common database together with some developed functions for data exchange.

This integration approach has the following aims:

- Designing a unique database for a set of different projects, with all detailed production system behaviour specified
- Constructing automatic functions (for data analysis, for generating simulation models, for generating layout alternatives)
- Avoiding redundant project work
- Reducing sources of human errors (in design, in modelling, in coding, etc.). This reduction is due to integrated system coherence and use of automatic model generators.
- Easy feedback processing
- Producing specific documents for an easy balance of different alternatives
- Standardizing design phase

Traditional use of simulation can then be divided into the following steps (phases):

1. Definition of project tasks
    - Definition of exact project targets
    - Decision of using computer simulation as the solving tool
    - Setting of system's boundaries and level of detail
    - Team building and its responsibility
2. Processing and obtaining data
    - Technical data (facilities data, product data, information about material flows, production areas, breakdowns etc.)
    - Organizational data (production scheduling)
    - Business data (costs, orders)
3. Creation of the simulation model
    - Conceptual model (schematic)
    - Interlacing model
    - Computer model
4. Simulation run and experiments
    - Setting of parameters (e.g. length of simulation run)
    - Model validation and verification
5. Interpretation of results and implementation
    - Data evaluation
    - Interpretation of results and presentation (graphs, tables, animation)

This method is based on "Systematic layout planning" developed by Muther 15, Zelenka [23], Francis et al. 6
Our project shows some possibilities of saving time through the automatic generation of solutions, especially in these phases:

- Creation of the simulation model
- Layout design (CAD drawing)
- Presentation of results (statistical graphs, display of material flows in layout (Havlík et al. 7)

2 Project Description

This project describes a part of the internal logistic system, in the production of plastic car parts (bumpers). The simple schema of production is shown in Fig. 1.

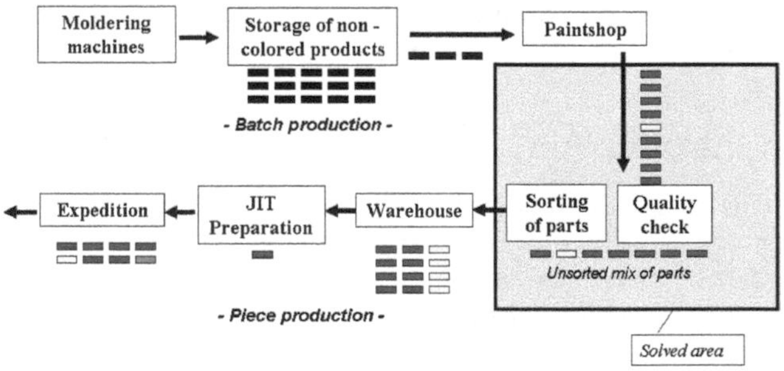

Fig. 1. Schema of production processes

Injection molding machines produce non-coloured bumpers and these are consequently painted in paint shop. Bumpers are divided according to the frequency of their production into large-lot (around 80% of production) and small-lot production (20% - mainly some unusual colours). This is the reason why there are two paint shop lines for each type of production. After painting, bumpers are transported by conveyors into quality checking places. Five different classifications apply - perfect (around 65% of the production), locally repairable by brushing (15%), able to local repainting (15%), need of complete repainting (5%) and scrap product (5%). Perfect and repairable products are hitched back to conveyor. At the end of the conveyor the products are put into transport boxes according to shape and colour. Transport boxes (crates) are different based on shape of bumpers and they have also different capacities. Crates are stored in the warehouse. From

the warehouse, the parts are delivered do assembly workshop according to JIT system demands.
Production consists of over two hundred variants of bumpers depending on shapes (front or back, car type) and colours. In this area, it is fundamental to use a good logistic system, mainly because of the following reasons:

- Large range of product types (two hundred specific variants);
- High daily production (thousands of products);
- Strict JIT customer demands (time between ordering and supplying is around four hours), each final product after assembly has unique properties (type and colour of main bumper parts, combined with assembled components as holder of identification mark, lights, parking sensors etc.);
- Batch Production in the paint shop is stocked in an intermediate super market to supply the assembly task that behaves following a JIT production philosophy depending on customer orders;

Specific area studied
This paper focuses on a specific area of the factory - modelled and studied through simulation. It is the area between the paint shop and the warehouse. Painted parts leave paint shop in sorted batch sequences, respective quality is checked, and the good ones are transported on a conveyor next to the warehouse. Then they are hung down and stored into transport crates in the warehouse. Parts arrive randomly and it is then necessary to have a temporary storage for crates not full.

Tasks
The main objective for this work is to find out the best way for a systematic adaptation to new customer requirements, introducing the adequate changes in production and suppliers. This paper then discusses possible changes on the current logistic system (transportation system, storage system and material flow).
The following parameters were identified, to which special attention should be driven:

- Number of operators to hang down bumpers from the conveyor
- Number of transport boxes and size of storage space
- Number of fork-lifts
- Size of temporary storage area (capacity) where transport boxes (partially filled) are stored
- Brush workplaces

Solving
The main tool for performing with these tasks is Discrete Computer Simulation, useful to:

- Deal with the stochastic system behaviour (product quality, processing times, batch sequences)
- Gain easy testing and evaluating alternatives
- Reach the ability to deal with large and complex systems

The following chapters would then describe two different approaches for solving the same type of task and would compare them, showing advantages and disadvantages – in fact, the main focus of this paper.

3 Manually created models – conventional way

For solving the given tasks, the following software tools were used:

- MS Excel 2003 as a data storage tool
- Witness 2008 as a simulation tool (Dias et al. 5, Markt et al. 11)
- AutoCAD 2004 as a layout design tool

It was developed according to the following phases:

1) Definition of project tasks
2) Processing and obtaining input data
3) Creation of simulation model
4) Simulation run and experiments
5) Interpretation of results and implementation

3.1 Definition of project tasks and input data (phase 1 and 2)

Project tasks specification is identical for both approaches as well as input data:

- Technological processes and operations specification
- Part routes in the studied area
- Production scenarios (output sequences of bumpers from paint shop, defining colour and shape of each bumper, transport box capacity, etc.)
- Stochastic behaviour for bumpers according to quality level and checking performing times. These data were obtained from company databases (monitoring each workplace and its outputs)
- Size of temporary storage (buffer) for transport boxes
- Statistic data for fork-lifts – measuring of transport times

3.2 Creation of simulation model (phase 3)

A conceptual model was then created, with description of inputs, outputs and logic control (Fig. 2).

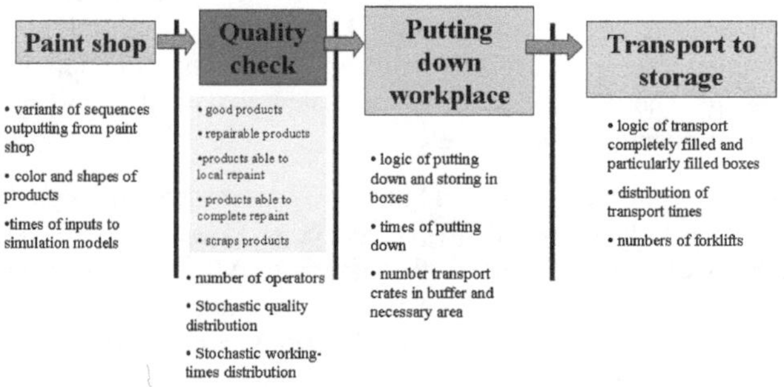

Fig. 2. Conceptual model

According to this conceptual model a simulation model was developed. Fig. 3 shows a part of this model created in Witness 2008 simulation tool.

3.3 Simulation run and experiments (phase 4)

Several experiments were performed and feedback from system's reactions was monitored. Different scenarios of paint shop production scheduling were tested according to different tact times of paint shop and different outputting sequences. The experiments performed also tested different values for some parameters e.g. incrementing/decrementing time out for moving partially filled boxes, changing number of operators, forklifts etc.

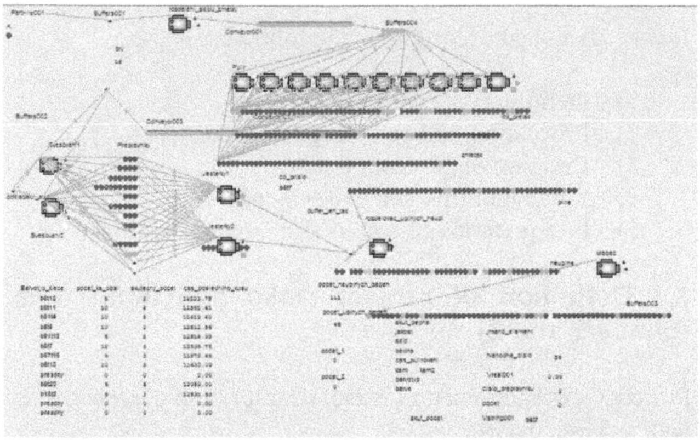

Fig. 3. Screenshot of simulation model and example of simulation results

3.4 Interpretation of results and implementation

Simulation model was created to evaluate all important parameters of the real system. Simulation results have shown that current production system would be adequate by simply changing some parameters and that changes in process logic control, capacities or space would not be necessary. These results (e.g. utilization of operators, forklifts or storage area) for each sequence were compared and it was found that the structure of any sequence does not influence the functionality of the system. Fig. 3 shows some results.

4 Automatic models generation – new approach

The essential part of this approach consists of the integration of software tools, commonly used in systems design (Moorthy [12], Mecklenburg [11], Aleisa et al. [1]) – Database system; CAD system; and Computer Simulation. Fig. 4 shows the purpose of each tool and also the interconnection possibilities.

Similar approach is used in "holistic" systems called "digital factories" (Bureš et al. [3], Chen et al [4], Neil [16])The kernel of our approach is the database (MS Access 2003) which is the storage for all project data and also includes functions for its analysis and functions for generation of computer simulation programs in Witness Simulation tool 2008.

Simulation model and experiments make it possible numerically evaluate and compare different scenarios which give important results such as utilization of system resources, material flows, buffers occupation etc. The results are automatically updated in specific tables of the database. That data is then used in the automatic generation of production system layout in CAD tool (AutoCAD 2004). In such a layout it is possible to identify the position of facilities (using alternative icons symbols or accurate facility drawing); material flows (with different arrows accordingly to actual flows from simulation results); entities; and specific place for storages and buffers, etc. (Benjaafar [2], Kulturel [10], Sly [17], Moorthy [13]).

Following chapters describe details of each tool and integration functions.

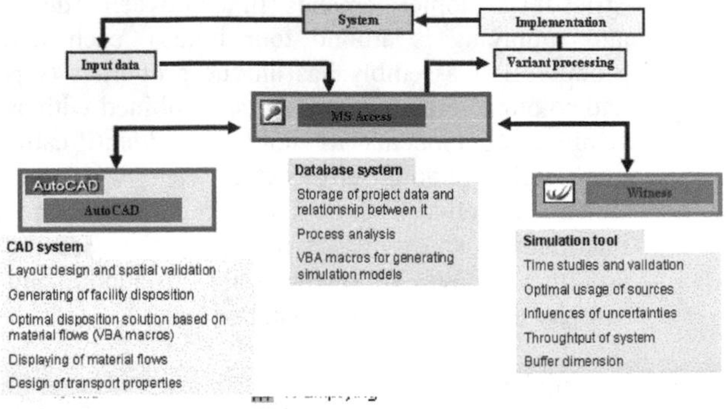

Fig. 4. Most common functionalities of each integrated software tool

4.1 Database system

The system database (MS Access) serves as the source and repository for project data (with input and output data from simulation and CAD), and it builds a basic interconnection element. The database includes VBA macros for automatic generation of simulation elements (machines, buffers, etc.) and their properties with minimum user intervention.

So, this database connects all necessary project data by appropriate relationship between them.

The required data for the simulation model is (Taylor [18]):

- Definition of operations (input and output parts/entities, batches sizes, assembly information, process times, etc.);
- Production sequences of parts/entities (i.e. their routing through production facilities);
- Type of crates and transported quantity;
- Productive and non-productive facilities (machines and handling equipment) and their properties (setup times, transport speeds, etc.);
- Scheduling of production;
- Workers and their properties.

Fig. 5 displays a set of selected tables (nearly half of the database), representations and relationships from the relational database. For example, inputs for operations, material flow between stations and table of priorities for each operation and process are described in the database.

In the top right corner of this screenshot there are three tables "ListOfInventory", related to "Library_Blocks_process" by the table "Tbl_CAD_Inventory". This association assigns different AutoCAD drawings to each element in the inventory, which are representations for system resources or production facilities. Connected to "ListOfInventory" we can find the table "Tbl_working_possible" that relates the resources with "ListOfOperation", associating feasible operations for each resource/facility. Table "ListOfOperation" includes a list of operations and some properties of the operations like production times, setup times, possible production facility locations, etc. Each operation has input (table "Inputs") and output (table "Outputs") definition, describing incoming and outgoing parts, quantities (batch sizes), type of container (crate) used, etc. There are also tables to define parts/entities ("ListOfParts") and transport crates ("ListOfCrates"), also with relationship with CAD data tables ("Library_blocks_part", "Library_blocks_crate") that includes references and properties of CAD drawing blocks. There is similar structure for definition of space, and also some other specific tables describing material flows, production scheduling, human resources, tables including results from simulation (statistics) and from CAD layout (coordinates for objects).

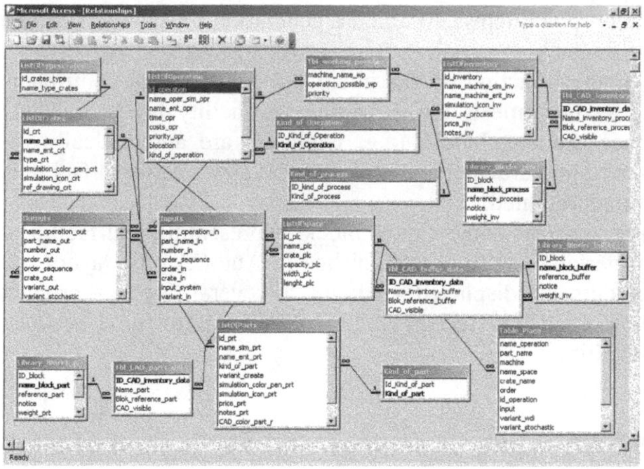

Fig. 5. Snapshot from MS Access relational database

The database, moreover, contains VBA macros for automatic loading of CAD objects into AutoCAD - also with minimum operator intervention - and elements of fundamental analysis (mainly PQ analysis helps to identify the most important product family and also optimal layout type – flow line, flow shop, job shop, etc.).

Material flow analysis from-to table and simple heuristic optimization methods based on material flow values identify optimal location of system resources. Cluster analysis helps finding similar sequences of technological processes (and designing production cells or production lines).

4.2 Simulation System

The generated simulation model consists of the previously mentioned elements and other elements such as lists (operations, facilities, parts, etc.), modules for project database establishment and modules involving SQL queries for data loading. These modules automatically feed simulation elements with appropriate data, configuring and updating them. The system can also configure the simulation runs according to database information (performing model's initialization in the beginning of each simulation run). As a consequence, users only need to change data in the database directly or through user-friendly forms in order to manage the simulation model.

After the generation and configuration of the model, subsequent simulation runs and experimentations are performed, and the obtained data are recorded back to the database. Output data are mainly results of stochastic behaviour in material flows, average and maximum occupation of buffers (this information is used in design of the CAD layout), resources utilization (machines, operators and handling equipment), bottlenecks, system throughputs, etc.

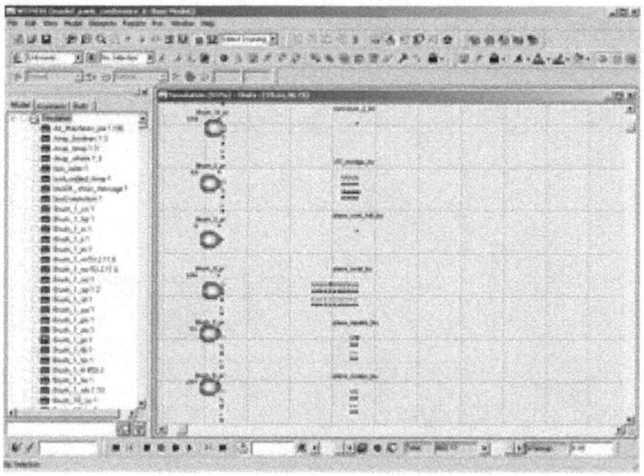

Fig. 6. Illustration of Witness simulation model

Fig. 6 contains a screenshot of a generated simulation model - actual occupation of buffers (queues), utilization of facilities (pie graphs) and a list of additional information (list of facilities, parts, and operations) (Mujber [14] and Vilarinho[22])

4.3 CAD System

The CAD system (Autodesk AutoCAD v. 2004) is mainly used for identifying best locations for all facilities and displaying them in the selected layout. For this purpose, VBA macros enable the identification of the optimal positions, currently according to a simple constructive heuristic method - a triangular algorithm based on ranking of material flow data.

The detailed layout is influenced by several factors and limitations (e.g. current production facilities or building constraints).

Fig. 6 shows an automatically generated layout (left side of figure) of a system with material flows of specific entities (ideal and real). Each machine/operation is represented by a small rectangle followed by the output buffer (blue rectangles). Flows are represented by line segments with different widths accordingly to the actual entities movements evaluated numerically in the simulated model (in witness). In fact, actual material flow is a major criterion for selection of the best solution. In the

Fig. 6 (right side), there is a layout limited by constraints (current production facilities, architectonics limitation as walls, pillars and others).

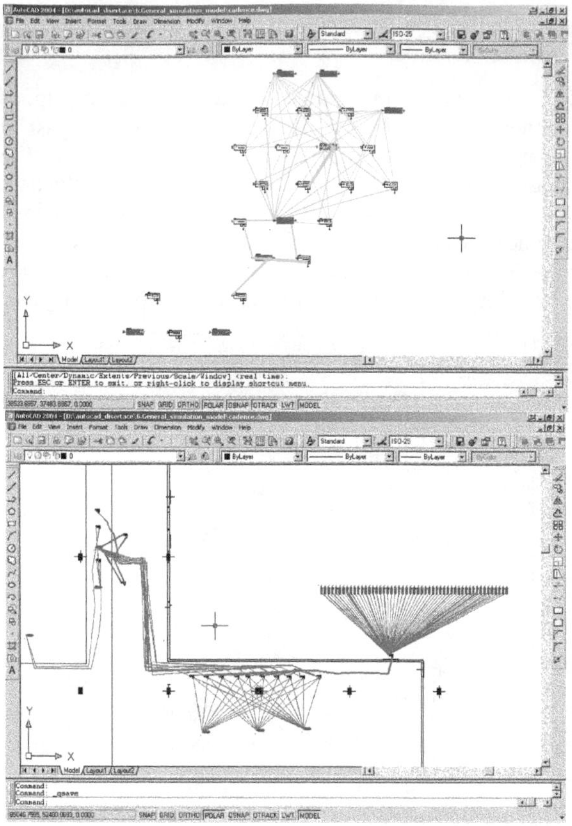

Fig. 6. Snapshots of layout from AutoCAD for a model with material flows (ideal and real)

Information related to material flows can have different units (e.g. weight transported in a time period or frequency of transport movement). Flows can be displayed according to various parameters – related to specific parts, to pallet transportation or to any transport facility.

5 Comparing both approaches

We described two approaches for solving the same set of tasks – a model constructed manually by the user and a model automatically generated by a solution tool integration. In this Chapter we compare them in different ways:

- Results
- Speed and time requirements
- Changing of settings and application of feedbacks
- Explanation of results, clearness, graphics
- Documentation

5.1 Results

These values are related to the same facilities in the manually created model and the automatically generated one. As far as facilities utilizations statistics are concerned (
Fig. 7), results are very similar, with differences around 5% (which could be acceptable due to stochastic system behaviour).

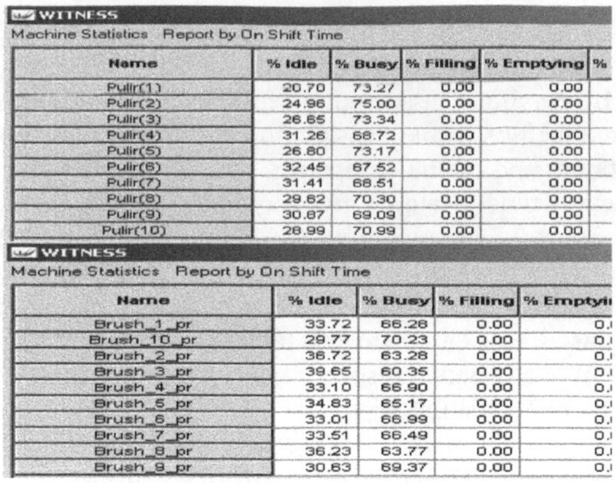

WITNESS

Machine Statistics Report by On Shift Time

Name	% Idle	% Busy	% Filling	% Emptying	%
Pulir(1)	20.70	73.27	0.00	0.00	
Pulir(2)	24.96	75.00	0.00	0.00	
Pulir(3)	26.65	73.34	0.00	0.00	
Pulir(4)	31.26	68.72	0.00	0.00	
Pulir(5)	26.80	73.17	0.00	0.00	
Pulir(6)	32.45	67.52	0.00	0.00	
Pulir(7)	31.41	68.51	0.00	0.00	
Pulir(8)	29.62	70.30	0.00	0.00	
Pulir(9)	30.87	69.09	0.00	0.00	
Pulir(10)	28.99	70.99	0.00	0.00	

WITNESS

Machine Statistics Report by On Shift Time

Name	% Idle	% Busy	% Filling	% Emptyi
Brush_1_pr	33.72	66.28	0.00	0.
Brush_10_pr	29.77	70.23	0.00	0.
Brush_2_pr	36.72	63.28	0.00	0.
Brush_3_pr	39.65	60.35	0.00	0.
Brush_4_pr	33.10	66.90	0.00	0.
Brush_5_pr	34.83	65.17	0.00	0.
Brush_6_pr	33.01	66.99	0.00	0.
Brush_7_pr	33.51	66.49	0.00	0.
Brush_8_pr	36.23	63.77	0.00	0.
Brush_9_pr	30.63	69.37	0.00	0.

Fig. 7. Comparing of results

5.2 Time requirements for creating simulation model

Manual creation of the model took around 2 days of a simulation practitioner. Automatic generation took only a couple of minutes.

Another function of this integrated solution that contributes to saving time is the generation of facility layout in CAD once drawing blocks (e.g. facilities) are automatically inserted into drawing and also material flows between facilities are represented.

Fig. 6 shows some simple blocks representing real facilities. Material flows are distinguished in AutoCAD by layers and colours and displayed according to several factors – product type, used crate (box, pallets etc.) or a sum of flows between facilities.

5.3 Changing of settings and application of feedbacks

As shown on example of production times, the Fig. 8 shows two ways of changing a specific cycle time. In the manually created model, user must find an element and change cycle time property in Witness (Fig. 8, left side)

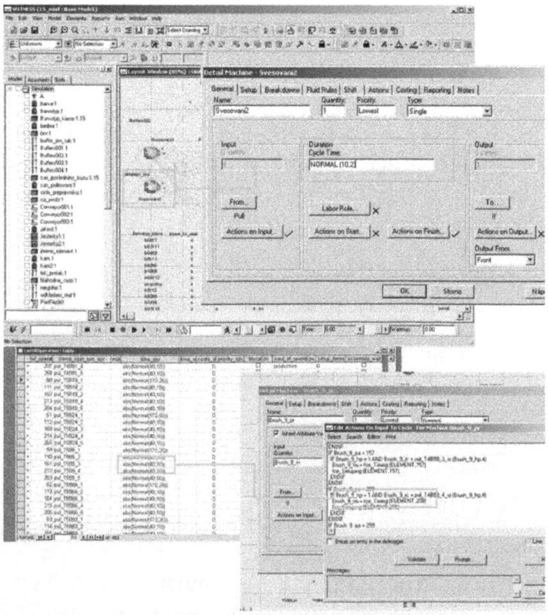

Fig. 8. Changing of settings

In the integrated approach with simulation model automatic generation, information is changed in project database; all model data are in one common database and it is easy to changing it (Fig. 8, right side). If the data are changed, simulation model is automatically updated in the initialization phase of next simulation run. Or if it is necessary (as by adding a new object), a new model would be generated.

5.4 Explanation of results, clearness, graphic

Generated simulation model is not built for animation view; it is mainly for "background" simulation and it is not as clear as in the case of manually created models. On the other hand, generated models contain some other functions for making results more clear. These functions are used automatically, without user intervention. For example:

- Maximum occupation for each product in the buffers (Fig. 9 – left side)
- Occupation - time graphs for estimating storage size (Fig. 9 – right side)
- Table with process results – waiting times, setup times and also a list of processed operation (their name, number and time) for each facility (Fig.10)

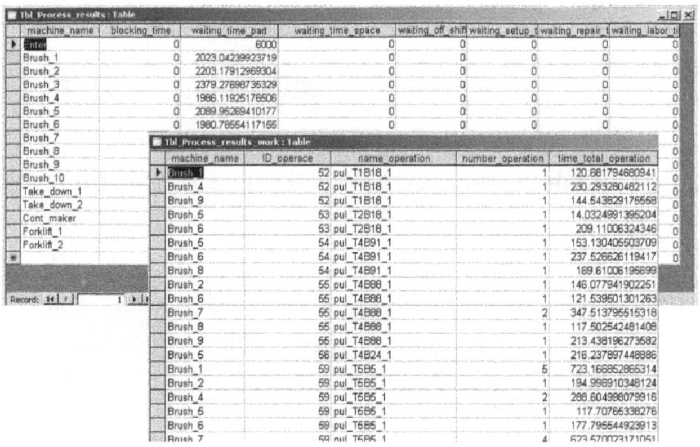

Fig.10. Detailed processes statistics

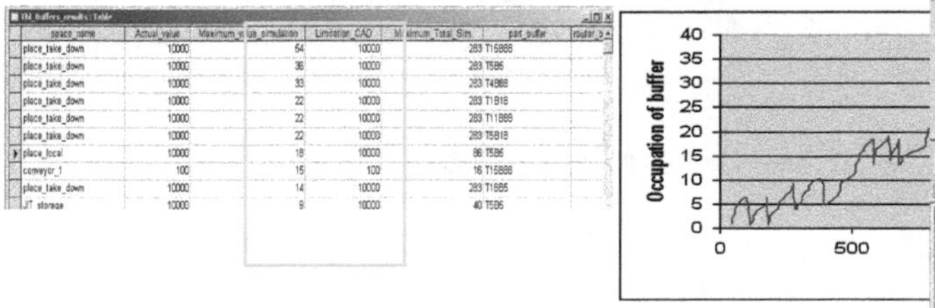

Fig. 9. Maximum occupation for each part and storage occupation plot (right side)

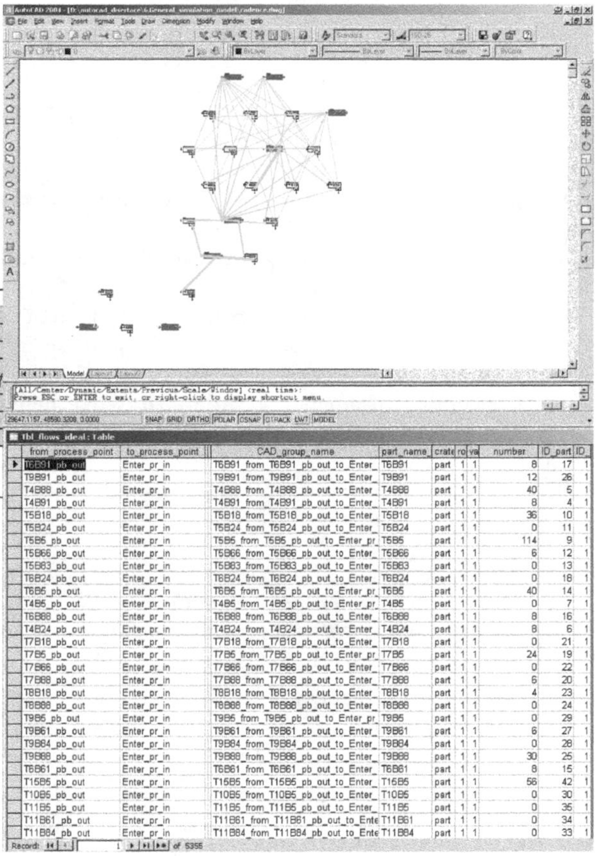

Fig. 11. Displaying of material flows

5.5 Material flows

Another function for making project data more clear is the display of material flows. Information about part flows in simulation model is recorded into database (in Fig.12), and then flows are displayed as lines with starting point (origin of the flow) and final points (destination of the flow). Weights of the flows symbolize a throughput between these two production facilities. Different colors of lines identify different part types (or type of crate used) and it is possible to filter them by switching on/off their AutoCAD layers. Material flow information helps for better facilities positioning – it helps to realize which facilities must be closer to each other.

6 Conclusion

At the end, both approaches would best be adequate for certain project phases where the following fundamental advantages would apply:

The phases of designing production systems can be divided into the following four phases, according to "Systematic layout design" developed by Richard Muther 15:

1. Location – determination of space and another important resources
2. Overall layout – arrangement of areas and transport aisles

3. Detail layout – determination of specific machinery and equipment
4. Installation – detailed specification of the system

For the first two phases (overall system design) of a production system design project, the automatic generation of models would be appropriate. Mainly because of the following reasons:

- To avoid fundamental errors in early project phases
- The fast creation of models and immediate results to be used in the comparison of different alternatives, enable choosing good solutions rapidly
- Included feedbacks support configuration changes very quickly
- The connection to a common database for simulation tool and CAD system allows to work on all system resources together and also to work on the overall system optimization

In detail layout project phase it seems to be better to use models manually created. Mainly for these reasons:

- Detailed logic control (like in complex material flows)
- Specific 3D space limits (instead of the 2D limitations of the automated approach)
- Refined 3D animation (for better visualization of the designed system). Could be useful for some specific issue like check 3D collision of moving entities.
- Concerning of another specific factors like human ergonomics, vibration, noise, pollution etc.

References

1. Aleisa E., Lin L., *For effective facilities planning: layout optimization then simulation, or vice versa?* In: *Proceedings of the Winter Simulation Conference*, 1381-1385, (2005)
2. Benjaafar, S., Heragu, S. S., Irani S., *Next generation Factory layouts: Research challenges and recent progress*, Interface (2002)
3. Bureš M., Ulrych Z.,Leeder E. *Digitální fabrika – softwarové produkty pro oblast digitální fabriky*, Mopp – Modelování a optimalizace podnikový procesů, Plzeň 8.-9. 2. ISBN 978–80–7043–535-9 (2007)
4. Chen D., Kjellberg T., Euler A. *Software Tools for the Digital Factory – An Evaluation and Discussion*, Proceedings of the 6th CIRP-Sponsored International Conference on Digital Enterprise Technology, Springer Berlin, ISSN1615-3871 (2009)
5. Dias, L.,Pereira, G. and Rodrigues, G., *A Shortlist of the Most Popular Discrete Simulation Tools*, Simulation News Europe, **17**(1), 33-36, ISSN 0929-2268 (April 2007)
6. Francis R.L., McGinnis L.F., White J.A., *Facility Layout and Location: An Analytical Approach*, 2nd edition, Prentice-Hall, Englewood Clifs, NJ, USA. (1992)
7. Havlík, R.; Manlig, F., *Vom 2D Layout bis zur virtuellen Realität*, Priemyselne inženierstvo. Sborník příspěvků mezinárodní konference, Dolný Smokovec 07.-08.10.04., 2004, Košice: TU v Košiciach,
8. Hutchins D., *Just in Time*, Gower Publishing Company, ISBN 978-0566077982 (1999)
9. Jareš, D. *Počítačová simulace transportního systému v podniku X*, Liberec. Bachelor work (2007)
10. Kulturel S., *Approaches to uncertainties in facility layout problems: Perspectives at the beginning of the 21th Century*, Springer Science and Business Media, Springer Netherlands, ISSN 0956-5515 (2007)
11. Markt L.,Mayer M., *Witness simulation software a flexible suite of simulation tools*, Proceedings of the 1997 Winter Simulation Conference, 711-717 (1997)
12. Mecklenburg K., *Seamless integration of layout and simulation*, Proceedings of 2001 Winter Simulation Conference, 1487- 1491.
13. Moorthy S., *Integrating the CAD model with dynamic simulation: simulation data exchange*, Proceedings of the 1999 Winter Simulation Conference, 276-281 (1999)
14. Mujber T.S., Szecsi T., Hashmi M., *A new hybrid dynamic modelling approach for process planning*, Journal of Materials Processing Technology **167**, (2005)
15. Muther R. *Systematické projektování (SLP)*, SNTL, Praha (1973)
16. Neil S., *The Digital factory*, Managing Automation (USA), **22**(10), (2007)
17. Sly David P., *A systematic approach to factory layout and design with Factoryplan, Factoryopt and Factoryflow*, Proceedings of the Winter Simulation Conference, 584-587, (1996)
18. Taylor G. *Introduction to logistics engineering*, New York, Taylor & Francis Group (2008)
19. Vik P., *Integration of CAD systems and computer simulation and its usage in designing of manufacturing systems,* 3. mezinárodní konference Výrobní systémy dnes a zítra, 27– 28.11.2008
20. Vik P., Dias L., Pereira G., *Software Tools Integration for the Design of Manufacturing Systems*, Industrial Simulation Conference 2009, June 1-3, 2009, Loughborough,UK, ISBN 978-90-77381-4-89
21. Vik P., Dias L., Pereira G., *Integration possibilities of software tools used in design of manufacturing systems*, ACC Journal. XV, (2009) ISSN 1803-9782
22. Vilarinho P., Guimaraes R., *A Facility Layout Design Support System*, Investigacao Operacional **23**, 145–161, (2003)
23. Zelenka A., Král M., *Projektování výrobních systémů*, Praha: ČVUT, 1995,ISBN80–01-013302-2

22

Automatic Optimization of Air Conduct Design Using Experimental Data and Numerical Results

Luis Toussaint [1,2a], Nadhir Lebaal[2], Daniel Schlegel[2], Samuel Gomes[2]

[(1)]Mark IV Systèmes Moteurs, ZA Les grands près N°6, 68370 Orbey, France
[(2)]M3M Laboratory, Université de Technologie de Belfort-Montbéliard, 90010 Belfort Cedex, France

Abstract - The development of a new product is a process that goes through several phases, each of them requiring the capitalization of data, information, knowledge and experiences gathered from previous projects. This knowledge is kept by a limited number "Experts", and is not necessarily captured in a practical, reusable way, which translates into a loss of time and a delay for the projects. Our approach involves exporting the client's specifications from a PLM platform and constructing a generic product, an automotive air conduct, from them. This generic product is then fed through an optimization cycle to determine the best position and geometrical shape for all its elements. This multi-criteria optimization requires several constraints and objective functions in order to improve the part quality and process reliability needed expected by the Original Equipment Manufacturer (OEM). The need to have a design process less dependent on personal "expert" knowledge was the driving idea behind this work. The automatic optimization of the design of an air conduct still remains a challenge and the purpose of this work is to contribute to the development of an automatic design tools capable of doing this.

Keywords - Design for Manufacturing, Optimization, Knowledge Based Engineering, Simulation.

1 Introduction

Designing a product, from the definition of the client's needs right up to its fabrication is a process that requires time, attention and the capitalization of data, information, knowledge [1] and experiences gathered from previous projects [2, 3]. This knowledge is kept by a limited number of people, usually called "Experts" and is not necessarily capitalized in a practical, reusable way, which can be translated into a loss of time and a delay for the projects.
Traditionally, an air conduct for a car engine is designed following the Original Equipment Manufacturers (OEM) functional specifications, which establish the length of the line, its footprint or size to comply to and the engine's functional clearance. The engine's functional clearance is assured through the use of bellows within the form of the conduct. Due to the evolving nature of car engines, all these parameters are never standard and an expert has to validate them at every step of the design phase. These validations raise the cost and time involved in the design of an air conduct and need several iterations before reaching an optimal solution.

Our approach involves exporting the client's specifications from a PLM platform and constructing a generic conduct from them. This generic conduct is then fed through an optimization cycle to determine the best position and geometrical shape for all its elements, the height, fillets and angles of each element being given, we optimize the number of convolutions which will determine the clearance angles and the reach of the air conduct in use. These optimization cycles give out an optimal set of parameters which will enable the designer to build an air conduct which respects the OEM's functional requirements without requiring an expert's intervention at every step.

2 Expert knowledge in product development

Knowledge Based Engineering (KBE) applications are a way of involving product knowledge, be it process or product related, during the design phases of said product [4]. In contrast with traditional CAD tools, KBE applications allow the design intentions, answering the "why" and the "how" of a product to come forth, along with the description of the "what" [5]. These applications are also very promising, not only for academic purposes, but in the industrial milieu as well [6-8]. However, the development of KBE applications demands a full investment for industries using them. They have to stay simple or modular enough to facilitate their maintenance and evolution.
Hew *et al.* [5] establish the beneficial link of KBE applications with CAD modeling on three levels, the creation of 3D models, their analysis via expert tools and the modification and reutilization of these models. All KBE approaches share three common steps for their construction:

- The identification of elements linked to a mathematical equation of the problem to solve. Once the technological and mechanism configurations are chosen, it is possible to describe the mechanism by a certain number of parameters;
- The construction of the interface and the 3D models from the parameters established in the preceding step, as well as the knowledge retained by the company;

[a] Corresponding author: luis.toussaint-manuel@utbm.fr

- The interaction of the designers for the development of new products, always with the possibility of updating the knowledge retained on the models and the interface.

Examples of the use of KBE applications exist on the literature, for the development of new complex products with the aid of axiomatic design and Case Based Reasoning (CBR) [9], for the development of product catalogs with captured knowledge and MOKA or CommonKADS [10], coupled with CAD modeling software like CATIA V5 [11]. They are also often coupled with optimization algorithms to improve the product design choices made [12].
The coupling with an optimization algorithm can effectively raise the utility of a KBE application. Since the interest of a KBE application is to involve product/process knowledge in the product's design, the use of optimization can improve the flexibility of results obtained during the design phase. All optimization problems can be divided into five categories [12]. Each one of these favors a different interpretation of the optimization problem, which can be solve according to:

- Its design variables [13, 14];
- The existence of constraints within the optimization problem [15, 16];
- Their objective function (qualitative, quantitative, analytical, etc.) [17, 18];
- The domain of the problem (single, multiple or interdependent) [19];
- The environment of the optimization (completeness of knowledge, designer implication, unknown variables, etc.) [20].

For every interpretation of an optimization problem, there is an algorithmic method of resolution that can better solve it. They can be either multi-objective, multi-modal, constrained, increasing designer confidence or dealing with real life design requirements [12]. We will work with certain gradient type (Sequential Quadratic Programming – SQP and Broyden, Fletcher, Goldfarb, Shanno – BFGS) and nondeterministic or stochastic methods (Simplex) algorithms [18] in this research paper, in order to improve the results offered by our approach. This KBE application is coupled with the FaBK methodology described in [21] in order to help designers develop better products, with more respect of design and process rules, in less time and with less effort.

3 Product optimization and its algorithms

This research paper is conducted within the R&D department of an automobile supplier, for the design of an air conduct that communicates between the radiator and the air compressor feeding air to the engine. When a car's Original Equipment Manufacturer (OEM) makes a call for offers from a supplier, they deliver a document that lists all the specifics the product will have to fulfill in order to be accepted. They range from material requirements to validation tests, including every detail of form and function for the concept they expect. In addition to the items in this list, a rough geometrical envelope or form is also needed to complete the product. For the type of product this paper describes at least the general path (1), the location and orientation of its sub-elements (2) and the type of connection to the vehicle required are needed (Fig1).

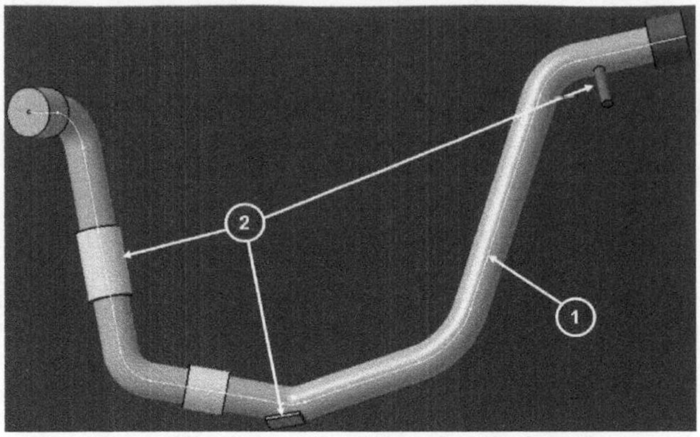

Fig. 1. Client's requirements - first draft model

One of these sub-elements, the bellows, assures the flexibility of the product when the engine moves forwards and backwards through its regular function. Since the radiator is a fixed point on the chassis, and the engine oscillates between a Full Back Position (FBP) on acceleration and a Full Front Position (FFP) upon braking, the bellows maintain the integrity of the conduct and allow it to deform and reach these positions. The path from the FBP to the FFP is otherwise known as the clearance. The proper geometry and exact position of these bellows is important, as it can reduce undue constraints during the production and the service of the conduct.

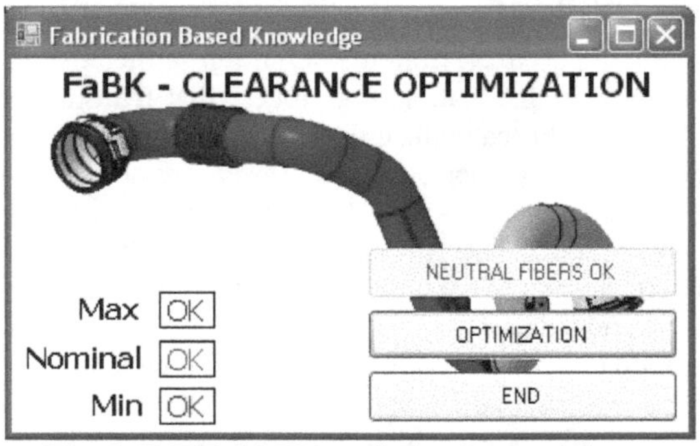

Fig. 2. FaBK CATIA optimization module

In our research we have created a KBE application that effectively aids the designer by guiding him through the development of a conduct by joining the client's specifications and the product/process knowledge rules to his design work. This application, better described in [22], was coupled with optimization algorithms and a native VBA application in CATIA V5 to best place the bellows in a conduct based on product/process knowledge (as seen in figure 2).

4 Approach towards product design optimization

A basic optimization approach is the development through trial and error. However, often enough the number of involved variables and their interactions prevent any optimization through trial and error, as the number of evaluations needed may become very high. When formulating the optimization of an air duct, various criteria must be satisfied, so several constraints and objective functions should be defined in order to improve the part quality and process reliability.

In the current work, an optimization problem was formulated to find an optimal bellows position and optimal design of the bellows geometry which allows the minimization of the development cost and respecting the clearance imposed by the OEM. In order to describe the clearance (objective function), an algorithm was developed in MATLAB, this algorithm permits the simulation of the clearance using a spherical link at each bellows.

According to the initial shape of the conduct we define neutral fiber. Once the neutral fiber is generated, a spherical link is then imposed at each bellows position. This spherical link is controlled by six optimization variables. They correspond to the bellows functional angles (two angles by bellows) obtained by the bellows geometry (number of convolutions) located at different heights of the air conduct and two bellows positions. The optimization variables are constrained using lower and upper bounds, corresponding respectively to the lower and upper parameters obtained by an experimental data using a design of experiment.

The choice of the optimization algorithm is closely related to the type of objective function. In our application, we attempt to minimize a nonlinear real-valued function, subject to bound constraints. In addition, strong geometric nonlinearities could induce the non linearity of the objective function, but we haven't a significant numerical instability [23], therefore the objective function is differentiable. As a consequence, the gradient-based algorithm is adapted to this type of problem [24]. In this work, several optimization algorithms are used and compared regarding the CPU time, optimal solution and number of functions evaluation.

5 Robust optimization based on product knowledge

In this section, we propose to couple some optimization algorithms to numerical simulations of the clearance of the air conduct in order to optimize the bellows geometry (angles). Through empirical experimentation we have determined a direct link between the angle of bend required and a set of geometrical parameters that give form to the bellows. The goal will be to equal the clearance imposed by the OEM through calculations and then retrieve the geometrical parameters that assure this clearance.

For this an optimization problem (P) was formulated to find an optimal angle for the bellows which guarantees the clearance between the FFP and FBP positions of the engine imposed by the OEM.

The optimization problem is formulated as follows:

$$(P): \begin{cases} Min\ J_1(X)\ and\ J_2(X) \\ Such\ that \\ X^u \le X \le X^v \end{cases} \qquad (1)$$

5.1 Parameterization and Constraints

In order to describe the clearance (objective function), we consider four optimization variables. They correspond to the bellows functional angles obtained by the bellows geometry (number of convolutions) located at different heights of the conduit, as illustrated by Fig. 3. The optimization variables are constrained using lower and upper bounds, corresponding respectively to the minimal and the maximal angles obtained by an experimental data, $x^u = 0°$ and $x^v = 20°$ are respectively the min and max value of the design variables.

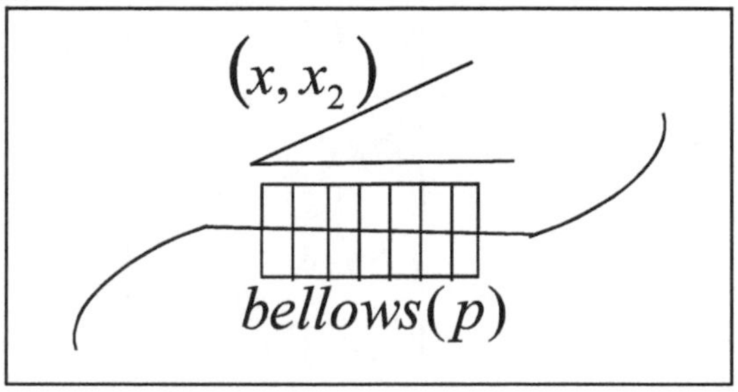

Fig. 3. Bellows angles x and x_2

5.2 Objective function

In this application, we attempt to provide a similar clearance to the one imposed by the OEM. This objective must be mathematically formulated by an appropriate cost function. Because the clearance is defined by two positions (the frontal and full back positions), and because the OEM imposes the respect of the coordinate points of the FBP and FFP positions we define two objective functions. The simplest way to proceed is to define these objective functions by the standard deviation of the computed and imposed coordinates the frontal and back positions.

For this optimization problem we optimize the bellows geometry (number of convolutions) to minimize the objective function J. The optimization problem is formulated as follows:

$$J_1(X) = \left| \sqrt{\left(x_{imp}^{FBP} - x_{cal}\right)^2 + \left(y_{imp}^{FBP} - y_{cal}\right)^2 + \left(z_{imp}^{FBP} - z_{cal}\right)^2} \right| \qquad (2)$$

$$J_2(X) = \left| \sqrt{\left(x_{imp}^{FFP} - x_{cal}\right)^2 + \left(y_{imp}^{FFP} - y_{cal}\right)^2 + \left(z_{imp}^{FFP} - z_{cal}\right)^2} \right| \qquad (3)$$

where $J(\mathbf{x})$ is the objective function, x, y, z are the coordinate of the frontal or full back positions, and X represent the design variables vector (bellows functional angles). Each formula represents the optimization of either the FFP or the FBP.

All numerical results reported in this paper were obtained on a 2.6 GHz-2 Gb Pentium 4.

Automotive air duct – Case Study

According to the optimization algorithm used, three optimization cases are formulated:

- Case 1: BFGS algorithm
- Case 2: Simplex
- Case 3: SQP

A representative convergence history during an optimization process on the both objective functions (J_1 and J_2) is represented in table 1.

Table 1: BFGS iterations converging towards 0

BFGS					
Iteration	J1	J2	Iteration	J1	J2
1	193.991	44.0619	19	0.0132765	0.125377
2	70.6264	40.2027	20	0.00809803	0.0657592
3	31.3168	35.481	21	0.00438403	0.0378795
4	20.9375	34.9968	22	0.00243004	0.0231421
5	17.287	34.7887	23	0.00148619	0.0137858
6	16.5466	34.5106	24	0.000921544	0.00825104
7	12.6317	33.2837	25	0.000555993	0.00445277
8	7.28338	30.0027	26	0.000311855	0.00263807
9	2.98848	21.8941	27	0.000181649	0.00161385
10	1.73986	15.9233	28	0.000178322	0.000947654
11	1.01979	7.42503	29	7.1908e-005	0.000548009
12	0.545869	4.87194	30	6.15485e-005	0.000305545
13	0.292263	2.81168	31	4.88144e-005	0.000187385
14	0.186999	1.90315	32		0.000161301
15	0.118748	1.00296	33		0.000160178
16	0.0669474	0.556147	34		0.000110312
17	0.0356434	0.329875	35		7.89125e-005
18	0.0208356	0.195604	36		6.26737e-005

After ten iterations, the objective function approaches the zero value. And at the iteration thirty the objective function falls below the cut-off threshold of 10−8 and the simulation stops with a reduction of 99.99 % of the objective function's initial value (193mm).

For the second optimization (to minimize the distance between calculated and imposed coordinates of the FBP), we note that the second objective function decreases gradually and converges starting from the fifteenth iteration. The optimal value of this objective function is obtained at the thirty-sixth iteration (Fig. 4.). The result of the initial and optimal design is reported in figure 5. The optimization algorithm and objective function chosen for this problem prove their capacity to obtain an optimal solution with a very fast convergence. This same procedure was carried out with the Simplex and SQP algorithms to compare between them and chose the one most likely to work with our design problem.

A summary of the optimization results obtained for the two optimization (*J1* and *J2*), is reported in table 2.

Table 2: Optimization results summary

	BFGS		Simplex		SQP	
	J1	J2	J1	J2	J1	J2
α_1 (x1)	-12,24°	9.47°	-4,26°	-0,89°	-13,45°	16,68°
α_2 (x2)	-10.71°	8.27°	- 12,34°	14,63°	-9,51°	-2,47°
θ_1 (x1)	13,28°	-8.26°	3,20°	5,45°	15,03°	-19,39°
θ_2 (x2)	15,13°	-11.49°	17,15°	- 19,02°	13,60°	1,63°
Objective function	4.881e-005	6.267e-005	7,2967	0,0018	1,711e-005	3.477e-005
Iterations	30	36	121	117	43	46
Maximum clearance						
L_{cl}	44,06mm					
$L_{cl} + C_s * L_{cl}$	52,872mm					

Fig. 4 displays the decrease of the objective-function value in terms of the number of optimization iterations. We observe that the objective function is reduced by 90% of its initial value after the second iteration, and by more than 99.99% at the end of the optimization process. Consequently, the maximum clearance is 99.99 % equal to the one imposed by the OEM (multiplied by a security factor), equal to 52.87mm. The algorithm converges after 10 iterations. Fig. 5 illustrates respectively the air conduct with the maximum (red) and minimum (blue) clearances as well as the neutral fiber (black) obtained by the optimization.

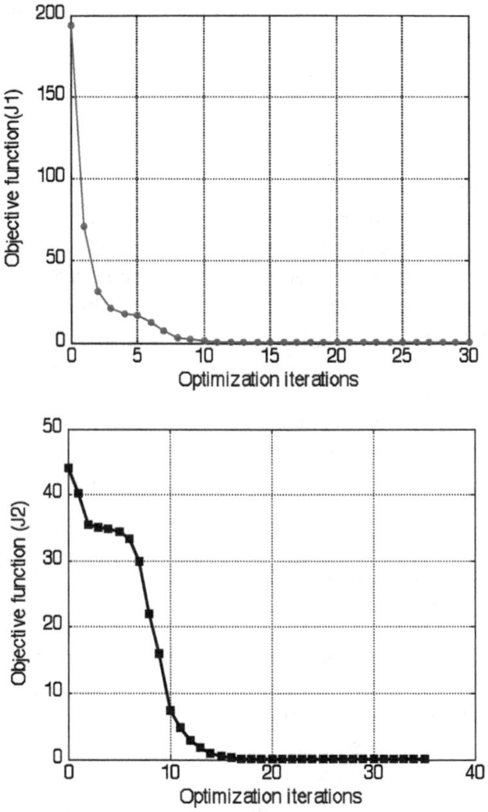

Fig. 4. BFGS Iterations

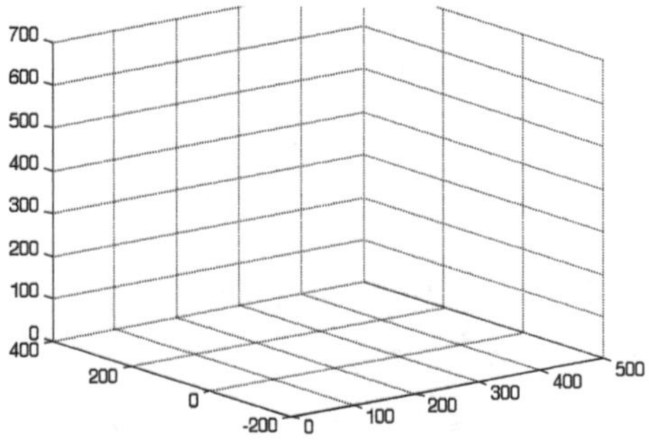

Fig. 5. BFGS module on the MATLAB application

Figures 6 and 7 show the same procedure with the Simplex algorithm applied, while figures 8 and 9 show the application of the SQP algorithm with its corresponding iterations.

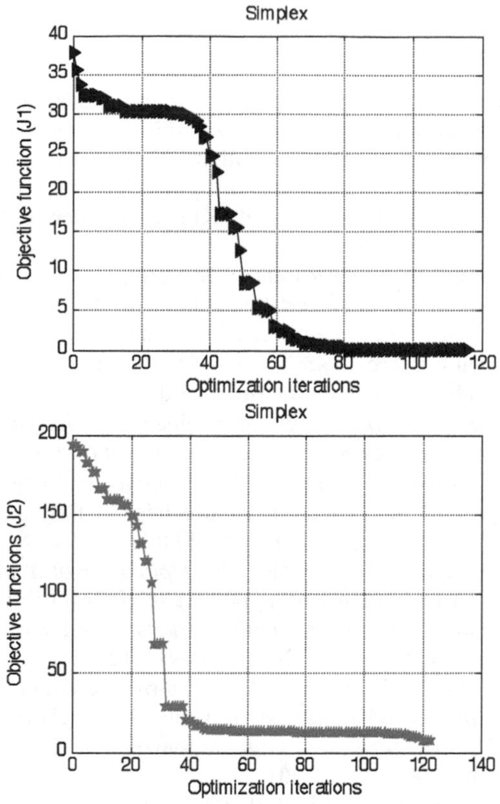

Fig. 6. Simplex iterations

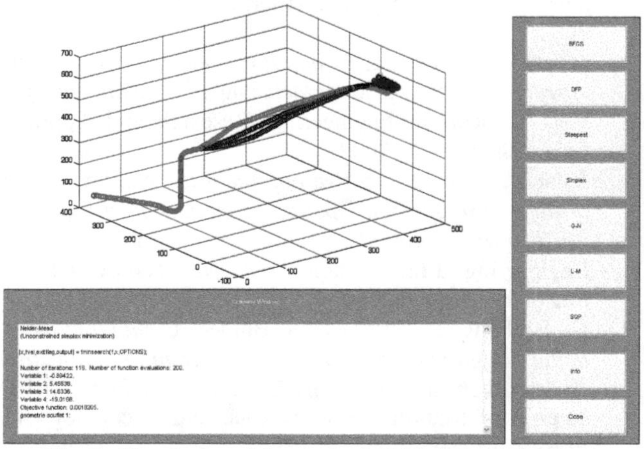
Fig. 7. Simplex module on the MATLAB application

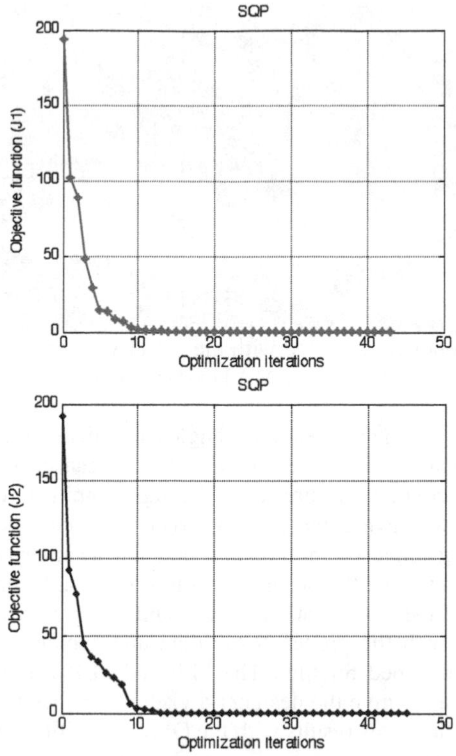

Figure 8: SQP Iterations

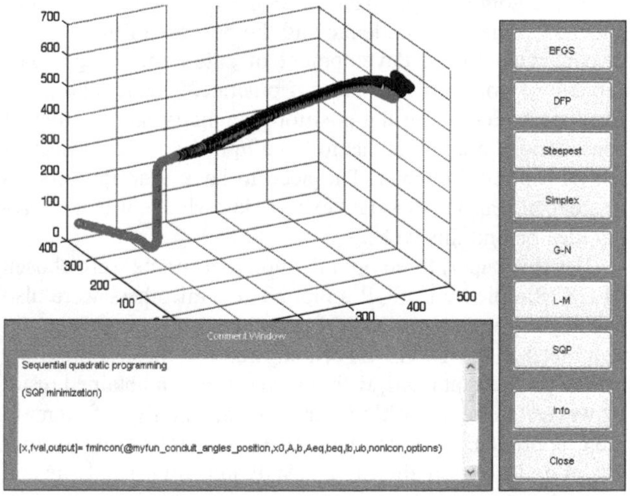

Fig. 9. SQP module on the MATLAB application

From these optimizations we can see that the algorithm best suited to our example is the BFGS, with the lowest number of iterations and therefore the quickest answer to the problem at hand. We can also see that the Simplex algorithm stagnated on a local objective and did not reach a 99.99% reduction of the objective function, as the other two did. But for the future applications, if the objective function is not differentiable the simplex algorithm will be adequate for this type of problem.

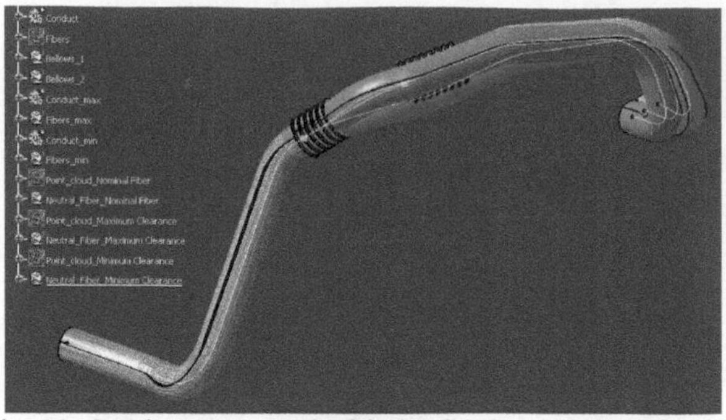

Fig. 10. Conduct generated with the CATIA V5 optimization module and MATLAB results

Once the optimized clearance angles are determined, the KBE application developed for CATIA V5 can generate an optimized conduct (figure 10). Through empirical experimentation we have determined a direct correlation between the bending angle of the conduct and the geometry of the bellows to use. All the designer has to do is run the application, select the optimization results and a conduct will be generated, with the proper positioning and geometry of the bellows developed for him. The FFP and FBP will also be generated, as to give the designer a visual reference to correlate and validate his results with the OEMs specifications.

6 Conclusions and perspectives

The automatic optimization of the design of an air conduct still remains a challenge and the purpose of this work is to contribute to the development of automatic design tools capable of doing this. In current practice, product and process experts determine the position, geometry and number of convolutions a conduct has to have in order to better answer the OEMs requirements. The need to have a design process less dependent on personal "expert" knowledge was the driving idea behind this work.

For this paper, three optimization algorithms were chosen, BFGS, Simplex and SQP although several others were also developed for the approach. From then we were able to determine that the BFGS algorithm was the most appropriate for the problem at hand, with a fewer iteration obtained result. However, these algorithms are fundamentally different in their approach, two gradient based constraint and unconstraint optimization algorithms (SQP and BFGS) and one non deterministic algorithm to resolve a non differentiable objective functions Simplex. Even though the current problem is unconstraint problem, and the objective function is differentiable, the inclusion of the Simplex algorithm and SQP algorithm was done to prepare future work where the complexity of the problem will require it. As we can see in figures 7, 9 and 11, the path combinations for the conduct to reach the FFP and FBP are close to infinite, so the option to work with several solution possibilities guarantees the designer certain flexibility when developing a product.

Actually, the KBE application and the optimization module are still distinct applications within their own operating software (CATIA and MATLAB). Even though the designer is no longer dependent on the interaction of an expert, he still has to work with two software modules in order to achieve the best results. Our future work is to congeal both modules into a single application, as well as integrating other design concerns into it. This, in order to tackle the axiom that, in engineering, 80% of efforts go towards routine design and only 20% to true engineering work [25]. In helping the designers to do faster their routine work and with more robust results, the free time can be dedicated to development of better products through innovation

References

1. S. Gomes, J.C. Sagot, *A concurrent engineering experience based on a cooperative and objective oriented design methodology*, 3rd International Conference on Integrated Design and Manufacturing in Mechanical Engineering (Dordrecth, Holland: Kluwer Academic Publishers), 11-18, (2002).
2. M. Grundstein, C. Rosenthal-Sabroux, A. Pachulski, *Reinforcing decision aid by capitalizing on company's knowledge: Future prospects*, European Journal of Operational Research, **145**(2), 256-272, (2003).
3. P. Serrafero, S. Gomes, D. Bonnivard, L. Jézéquel, *De la mémoire projet à la compétence métier : vers la synthèse de connaissances métier en ingénierie robuste des produits/process*, 6th International Conference on Integrated Design and Manufacturing in Mechanical Engineering (IDMME'06) (Grenoble, France, 2006).
4. C.B. Chapman, M. Pinfold, *The application of a knowledge based engineering approach to the rapid design and analysis of an automotive structure*, Advances in Engineering Software, **32**(12), 903-912, (2001).
5. K.P. Hew, N. Fisher, H.B. Awbi, *Towards an integrated set of design tools based on a common data format for building and services design,* Automation in Construction, **10**(4), 459-476, (2001).
6. C. Coppens, Les outils KBE : *Une approche chez PSA Peugeot Citroën*, 4th International Conference on Integrated Design and Manufacturing in Mechanical Engineering - IDMME 2002 (Clermont Ferrand, France, 2002).
7. J. Silva, K.H. Chang, *Design Parameterization for Concurrent Design and Manufacturing of Mechanical Systems,* Concurrent Engineering: Research and Applications, **10**(1), 3-14, (2002).
8. J. Noor, *A comprehensive approach to complex system product development: Operations management tools applied to automotive design*, Department of Mechanical Engineering, **142**, (Boston, USA: Massachusetts Institute of Technology, 2007)
9. N. Janthong, D. Brissaud, S. Butdee, *Combining axiomatic design and case-based reasoning in an innovative design methodology of mechatronics products*, CIRP Journal of Manufacturing Science and Technology In Press, Corrected Proof, (2010).
10. M. Callot, P. Quencez, C. Vargas, MOKA : *Projet de développement d'une méthode et des outils associés pour la réalisation d'applications à base de connaissances pour la CFAO*, in 18ème Conférence Internationale sur la CFAO, la Simulation et les Nouvelles Technologies de Conception et de Fabrication - MICAD'99 (Paris, France, 1999)
11. R. Hunter Alarcón, J. Ríos Chueco, J.M. Pérez García, A. Vizán Idoipe, *Fixture knowledge model development and implementation based on a functional design approach,* Robotics and Computer-Integrated Manufacturing, **26**(1), 56-66, (2010).

12. R. Roy, S. Hinduja, R. Teti, *Recent advances in engineering design optimisation: Challenges and future trends*, CIRP Annals - Manufacturing Technology, **57**(2), 697-715, (2008).
13. M. Schütz, H. Schwefel, *Evolutionary Approaches to Solve Three Challenging Engineering Tasks*, Computer Methods in Applied Mechanics and Engineering, **186**(2-4), 141-170, (2000).
14. A. Tiwari, *Evolutionary Computing Techniques for Handling Variable Interaction*, Engineering Design Optimisation (Cranfield, UK: Cranfield University, 2001).
15. C. Coello, *Theoretical and Numerical Constraitn-handling Techniques Used with Evolutionary Algorithms: A survey of the State of the Art*, Computer Methods in Applied Mechanics and Engineering, **191**(11-12), 1245-1287, (2002).
16. R. Landa Becerra, C. Coello, *Cultured Differential Evolution for Constrained Optimization*, Computer Methods in Applied Mechanics and Engineering, **195**(33-36), 4303-4322, (2007).
17. E. Shkvar, *Mathematical Modeling of Turbulent Flow Control by Using Wall Jets and Polymer Additives Poster Paper*, 2001 ASME Pressure Vessels and Piping Conference, 277-283, (New York, USA: American Society of Mechanical Engineers, 2001)
18. N. Lebaal, *Optimisation de la tête d'extrusion pour la fabrication de pièces thermoplastiques*, Centre de Recherche Outillage, Matériaux et Procédés, 219, (Nancy: Institut National Polytechnique de Lorraine, 2007)
19. T. Tomiyama, V. D'Amelio, J. Urbanic, W. ElMaraghy, *Complexity of Multi-Disciplinary Design*, CIRP Annals - Manufacturing Technology, **56**(1), 185-188, (2007).
20. H. Beyer, B. Sendhoff, *Robust Optimization - A Comprehensive Survey*, Computer Methods, Applied Mechanics and Engineering, 196(33-34), 3190-3218, (2007).
21. L. Toussaint, F. Demoly, N. Lebaal, S. Gomes, *PLM-based Approach for Design Verification and Validation using Manufacturing Process Knowledge*, Journal of Systemics, Cybernetics and Informatics, **8**(1), 1-7, (2010).
22. L. Toussaint, S. Gomes, D. Monticolo, N. Lebaal, *Knowledge Management and DFM - Future work on Design Optimization for Extrusion Blow Molding*, Workshop CoDeKF'09 – Collaborative Design and Knowledge Factory 2009 (Montbéliard, France, 2009).
23. N. Lebaal, F. Schmidt, S. Puissant, D. Schläfli, *Design of optimal extrusion die for a range of different materials*, Polymer Engineering & Science, **49**(3), 432-440, (2009).
24. H. Naceur, Y.Q. Guo, J.L. Batoz, C. Knopf-Lenoir, *Optimization of a drawbead restraining forces and drawbead design in sheet metal forming process*, International Journal of Mechanical Sciences, **43**(10), 2407-2434, (2001).
25. M. Rezayat, *Knowledge-based product development using XML and KCs*, Computer-Aided Design **32**, 299-309, (2000).

23

Structural Optimization of 3 MW Wind Turbine Blades Using a Two-Step Procedure

Kun-Nan Chen[1,a], Pin-Yung Chen[1]

[1] Department of Mechanical Engineering, Tungnan University, 22202, Taipei, Taiwan

Abstract – Modern large wind turbines, utilized to harness the kinetic energy of the wind, are rated at megawatts in output power. The design of large wind turbine blades must consider both their aerodynamic efficiency and structural robustness. This paper presents a two-step procedure for the optimum design of composite wind turbine blades. The results of the first step are the aerodynamically optimal cord lengths and twist angles of airfoils for the blade cross-sections along the blade spanwise direction. The second step yields optimal material distribution for the composite blade. A 3 MW wind turbine with blades having cross-sections of NREL S818, S825 and S826 airfoil types is demonstrated as the design example. Loaded by maximum forces and moments extracted from simulated time series, a parameterized finite element model of the aerodynamically optimized blade is created using the ANSYS software. The optimization results show that the initial blade model is an infeasible design due to a high level of the maximum stress, exceeding the upper limit of the stress constraint, but eventually the process converges to a feasible solution with the expense of increased total mass of the blade.

Key words: Wind turbine blade, Aerodynamic design, Structural optimization, Finite element analysis, Stress constraint

1 Introduction

Wind power has been one of the fastest growing renewable energy technologies throughout the world in recent years. Wind turbines, which are used to harness the kinetic energy of the wind, have two basic configurations: horizontal axis and vertical axis. Modern large wind turbines with output rated at megawatts (MW) predominantly have a horizontal axis. A horizontal-axis wind turbine equips a rotor (generally with two or three blades), a nacelle (housing the rotor shaft, gearbox, generator, electrical switch boxes and control systems), and a turbine tower. Based on the relative position of the rotor to the wind direction, horizontal-axis wind turbines can be further classified as upwind or downwind ones. A turbine rotor is made of a hub, a rotor shaft and blades that have good aerodynamic characteristics. For large wind turbines, turbine blades are usually made from composite materials to reduce the weight while attaining a reasonable strength to weight ratio. The design of large wind turbine blades must consider both their aerodynamic efficiency and structural robustness. Besides the circular shape at the blade root, the cross-sections along the spanwise direction of a blade have the shapes of airfoils. Early designs of wind turbine blades utilized airfoils intended originally for airplanes, such as the NACA series. Nowadays, except for some traditional shapes less sensitive to surface roughness, most blades use airfoils designed specifically for wind turbines, e.g., the NREL S series and DU series (Timmer [1]).

Maalawi and Badr [2] simplified the theoretical optimum values of airfoil cord lengths and twist angles for wind turbine blades, and suggested some practical shapes for the blades. Maalawi and Negm [3] proposed an objective function that was a composite function of several natural frequencies for a turbine blade, and maximized this function to achieve the goal of decreasing steady state and transient responses. Díaz Casás et al. [4, 5] investigated a turbine blade aerodynamic problem in a form of multi-disciplinary optimization, using an evolutionary-based procedure. Jureczko et al. [6] combined the finite element method and genetic algorithm to minimize the weight of a turbine blade, with stress and blade tip displacement as constraints. Vitale and Rossi [7] developed a blade design program, based on the blade element theory (BET), to calculate the optimal aerodynamic blade shape of a rotor that would generate the requested power output, with the blade number, airfoil curves and wind field mean speed as inputs. Several technical reports (Malcolm and Hansen [8], Bir and Migliore [9], Griffin [10]) provide valuable information for large scale composite blade design.

This paper proposes a two-step procedure to produce blade designs that are optimal both in aerodynamics and in structure. The result of the first step is the optimum cord lengths and twist angles of airfoils of the blade cross-sections along the blade spanwise direction. The second step provides optimal material distribution for the composite blade, while the stress is kept within preset design stresses and the natural frequencies of the blade well separated from the rotor's rated speed, and the mass of the blade minimized. To achieve the objectives, a wind field simulation program, TurbSim, and a wind turbine dynamics code, FAST, are utilized to perform simulation. The maximum loads on the turbine blade are extracted and applied to a parameterized finite element model of a blade created in the ANSYS environment, and then the composite blade model is optimized. The two-step

[a] Corresponding author: knchen@mail.tnu.edu.tw

procedure is demonstrated on a 3 MW, three-blade, horizontal-axis, upwind wind turbine, whose blades have cross-sections of NREL airfoil types: S818, S825 and S826.

2 The two-step procedure for wind turbine blade design

The first step of this two-step procedure follows the blade design scheme suggested by Spera [11]. Assume that the following parameters are known: radius of the rotor R, number of blades of the rotor N, designed lift coefficient C_{Ld} for a particular airfoil, and the designed angle of attack α_d of the airfoil. Define ω as the angular speed of the rotor and the tip speed ratio λ as the ratio of the blade tip speed of the rotor (ωR) to the mean wind speed in free stream (V_∞). For any given designed tip speed ratio λ_d, the cord length distribution of the airfoil along the blade spanwise has the form

$$c_r = \frac{8\pi r}{N C_{Ld}}(1 - \cos\phi_r) \tag{1}$$

where

$$\phi_r = \frac{2}{3}\tan^{-1}\frac{1}{\lambda_r} \quad \text{and} \quad \lambda_r = \lambda_d \frac{r}{R} \tag{2}$$

and λ_r is called the local tip speed ratio at position r, ϕ_r the local inflow angle. The local twist angle of the airfoil at position r is given as

$$\beta_r = \phi_r - \alpha_d \tag{3}$$

A rotor having blades with airfoils whose chord lengths and twist angles arranged according to Eqs. (1) and (3) will yield a maximum power output. Once the outer shape of the blade is determined, the material allocation of the composite blade can be decided in the second stage.

By setting the stress and frequency constraints and a minimum blade mass as the design objective, the structural optimization problem in the second phase can be defined as follows:

$$\textit{Minimize} \quad m_T \tag{4}$$

$$\textit{Subject to} \quad \sigma_t \le \sigma_{dt} \tag{5}$$

$$\sigma_{dc} \le \sigma_c \tag{6}$$

$$|f_i - f_r| \ge F_{ms}, \quad i = 1, 2, \ldots, s \tag{7}$$

$$X_{jL} \le x_j \le X_{jU}, \quad j = 1, 2, \ldots, l \tag{8}$$

where m_T is the total mass of one blade; σ_t and σ_c the maximum tensile and minimum compressive stresses in the spanwise direction, respectively; σ_{dt} the design tensile stress and σ_{dc} the design compressive stress; f_i, i=1, …, s the ith natural frequency of the blade and s the number of modes considered; f_r the wind turbine's rated rotor speed; F_{ms} the minimum frequency separation specified; x_j, j=1, …, l the design variables with l the number of design variables; and X_{jU} and X_{jL} the upper and lower bounds, respectively, of the design variables. Since the composite structure of the blade was treated macroscopically to simplify the problem, only tensile and compressive stresses were considered in the above formulation. The design stresses can be linked to the materials' ultimate strengths by $\sigma_{dt}=\sigma_{ut}/n_{fs}$ and $\sigma_{dc}=\sigma_{uc}/n_{fs}$, where σ_{ut} and σ_{uc} are the composite materials' ultimate tensile and compressive stresses, respectively, and n_{fs} is total factor of safety, accounting for the general effect and the effects from aging, temperature, resin infusion and post-cure (Germanischer Lloyd [12]).

3 Design example of a 3 MW wind turbine

A three-blade, horizontal-axis, upwind wind turbine with a rated power of 3 MW, which is a modified version of a 3 MW turbine proposed by Malcolm and Hansen [8] and uses a scale-up version of a 20.15 m long blade in Bir and Migliore [9], was chosen as the design example. The turbine has a rotor with a diameter of 93.3 m and rated speed of 14.5 rpm, and a tilted rotor shaft of 5°. Also, the height of the rotor hub is 119 m. Each rotor blade, which is 44.175 m long, has a circular cross-section from its root attaching the rotor hub to the 1.753-meter span location. Then the circular blade cross-sections gradually transition to airfoil sections that have NREL airfoil types S818 at the 9.648-meter span location, S825 at 32.667-meter and S826 at 41.873-meter and 44.175-meter (at the blade tip). Fig. 1 shows these NREL types of airfoils normalized by their cord lengths. Table 1 details the 14 cross-sections framing the blade. The section numbers 7, 8, 9, 10 and 12 in Table 1 are hybrid airfoils of the three basic types with different weighting factors to ensure proper transitions between two basic shapes.

For large-scaled wind turbines, two types of hollow rotor blades made of composite materials are commonly used: Type-A with web reinforcement as shown in Fig. 2 and Type-B with box-spar reinforcement as shown in Fig. 3. Although both types of blades were studied, only the Type-B's results are reported in this paper. Fig. 3 illustrates that a Type-A blade is composed of double-bias (DB), unidirectional, core and lining materials, and covered by an exterior coating of gelcoat with a layer of Nexus providing a smooth but absorbent surface in between for the painting of the gelcoat. Also shown in Fig. 3 are four different material models describing various parts of a blade cross-section. Table 2 lists the mechanical properties of the blade materials.

In this study, the wind turbine is undergone a turbulence with a mean wind speed of 25 m/s, which is assumed to be the maximum operation wind speed also known as the cut-out speed. TurbSim (Jonkman and Buhl [13]), a full-field stochastic simulation program, was used to simulate the turbulence. Fig. 4(a) displays the simulated wind at the center of the hub in the direction perpendicular to the plane of rotation of the rotor (V_x), using IEC normal turbulence model with the Kaimal spectrum. A wind turbine dynamics code, FAST (Jason and Marshall [14]), was utilized to perform wind turbine simulation. Fig. 4(b) shows the generator output power of the turbine. During operation, an active control was turned on to retain the rotor's rated speed and therefore the rated power. In Fig. 4 and thereafter, 600 seconds of time history were simulated, but the first 100 seconds were excluded to eliminate the initial effects and the rest 500 seconds of time series analyzed.

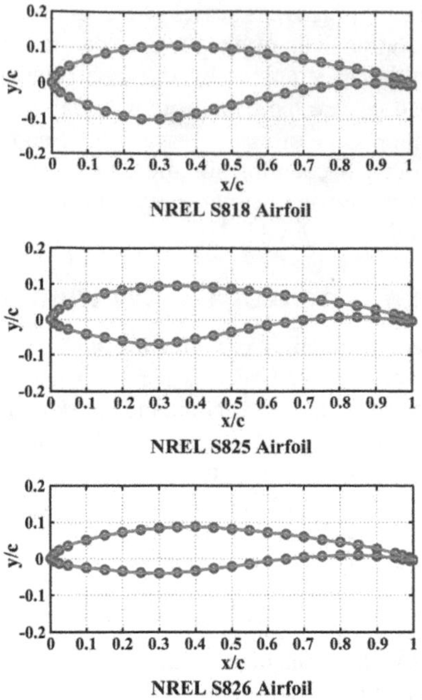

Fig. 1. NREL airfoil types: S818, S825 and S826

Table 1. Cross-sections of the blades

Section	1	2	3
Location (m)	0.0	1.051	1.206
Shape	Circular	Circular	Circular
Section	4	5	6
Location (m)	1.467	1.754	9.648
Shape	Circular	Circular	S818
Section	7	8	9
Location (m)	14.251	18.854	23.457
Shape	S818×0.8 + S825×0.2	S818×0.6 + S825×0.4	S818×0.4 + S825×0.6
Section	10	11	12
Location (m)	28.060	32.667	37.270
Shape	S818×0.2 + S825×0.8	S825	S825×0.5 + S826×0.5
Section	13	14	
Location (m)	41.873	44.175	
Shape	S826	S826	

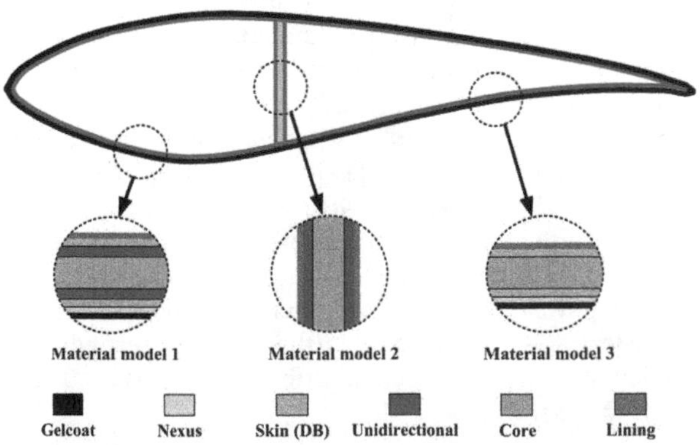

Fig. 2. Material layout of Type-A composite blade section

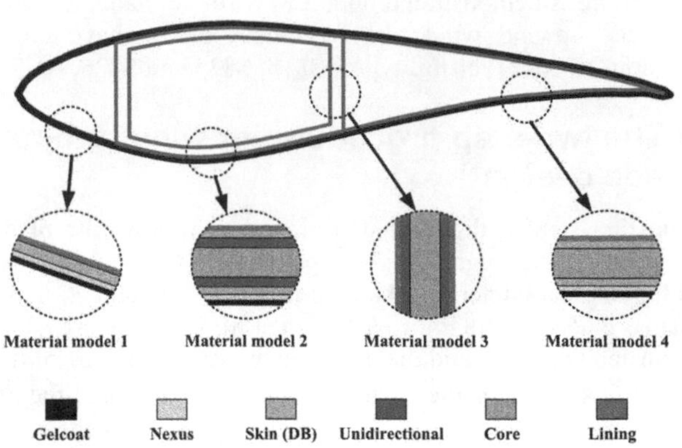

Fig. 3. Material layout of Type-B composite blade section

Table 2. Mechanical properties of the blade materials

Material	ρ (kg/m^3)	E (Pa)	G (Pa)	ν	σ_{ut} (Pa)	σ_{uc} (Pa)
Gelcoat	1664	--	--	--	--	--
Nexus	1830	--	--	--	--	--
Double-Bias	1830	10.3E+9	8.0E+9	0.3	151E+6	-174E+6
Lining	1830	10.3E+9	8.0E+9	0.3	151E+6	-174E+6
Unidirctional	1860	37.0E+9	4.1E+9	0.31	986E+6	-746E+6
Core	128.1	--	--	0.3	--	--

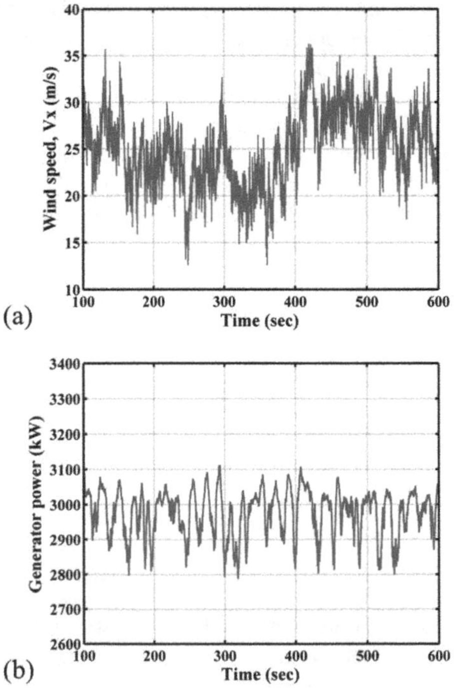

Fig. 4. (a) Simulated wind data at the center of the hub, and (b) generator output from the turbine

3.1 Result of optimization procedure step one

To achieve the optimum aerodynamic shape design for the blades using Eqs. (1) through (3), the designed lift coefficient C_{Ld} for a particular airfoil has to be established first.

The lift coefficient C_L of an airfoil is a function of the angle of attack, and so is the drag coefficient C_D. The coefficient C_{Ld} can be so determined that its corresponding angle of attack maximizes the ratio of C_L/C_D. An airfoil aerodynamics program, XFoil (Drela [15]), was employed to calculate the aerodynamic properties of the airfoils considered, and then a MATLAB script was coded to find the maximum ratio. The lift to drag ratios for the airfoil sections of the blade (sections 6 through 14 shown in Table 1) are plotted against the angles of attack as demonstrated in Fig. 5. Since the airfoil shapes for sections no. 13 and 14 are the same, i.e. S826, they share the plot as in Fig. 5(h). In executing the calculations using XFoil, a Reynolds number of 3×10^6 was assumed for all cases. The maximum lift to drag ratios C_{Ld}/C_D were found and are displayed in Table 3 along with their corresponding angles of attack α*, lift and drag coefficients.

Following the determination scheme for chord and twist angle distribution of the aerodynamically optimal blade, the local tip speed ratio λ_r, inflow angle ϕ_r, twist angle β_r and cord length c_r at difference sections are given in Table 4, with the designed tip speed ratio λ_d set to 8. Note that sections 1 through 5 have circular shapes with a diameter of 2.474 m and they assume the same twist angle as section 6 to facilitate the finite element modeling of the blade in the latter stage. The blade has larger chord lengths and twist angles for airfoil sections near the root and, except for section 12, sequentially diminishing chords and angles for sections approaching the blade tip.

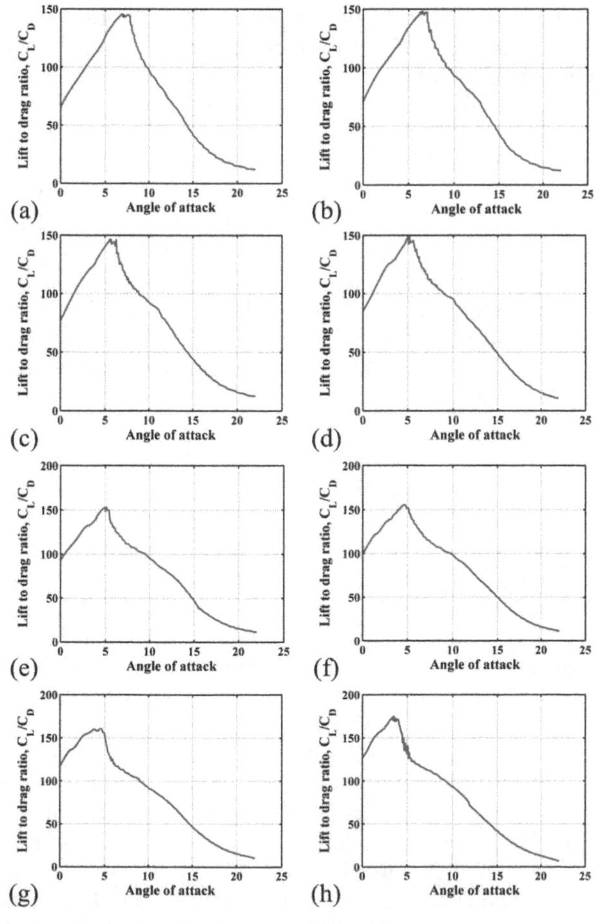

Fig. 5. Lift to drag ratios for airfoils at sections (a) 6, (b) 7, (c) 8, (d) 9, (e) 10, (f) 11, (g) 12, and (h) 13 and 14

Table 3. Optimal aerodynamic properties of the airfoil sections

Section	6	7	8	9
α_d (°)	7.00	6.45	5.65	5.15
C_{Ld}	1.2883	1.2601	1.2038	1.1774
C_D	0.0088	0.0085	0.0082	0.0079
C_{Ld}/C_D	146.398	148.247	146.805	149.038
Section	10	11	12	13 and 14
α_d (°)	4.90	4.65	4.55	3.50
C_{Ld}	1.1744	1.1708	1.1818	1.0975
C_D	0.0077	0.0076	0.0074	0.0063
C_{Ld}/C_D	152.519	154.053	159.703	174.206

Table 4. Chord and twist angle distribution of the aerodynamically optimal blade after design phase 1

Section	1 thru 5	6	7	8	9
λ_r	--	1.747	2.581	3.414	4.248
ϕ_r (°)	--	19.856	14.120	10.883	8.831
β_r (°)	12.856	12.856	7.670	5.233	3.681
c_r (m)	2.474	3.730	2.863	2.360	1.979
Section	10	11	12	13	14
λ_r	5.082	5.916	6.750	7.583	8.000
ϕ_r (°)	7.422	6.396	5.618	5.008	4.750
β_r (°)	2.522	1.746	1.068	1.508	1.250
c_r (m)	1.677	1.455	1.269	1.220	1.158

3.2 Result of optimization procedure step two

3.2.1 Simulation of the applied loads

Employing the full-field wind data with a mean speed of 25 m/s generated by TurbSim, the wind turbine simulation program FAST produced not only the generator output power shown in Fig. 4(b), but also accelerations of and moments and aerodynamic forces applied to the blade segments. There are 13 blade segments defined by those 14 cross-sections, and the moments, forces and accelerations were assumed to be applied to the centers of the segments. Time histories of 600 seconds of everything at all 13 segment centers were simulated. Fig. 6 depicts the time histories between the 100 and 200 seconds of three acceleration components (A_x, A_y and A_z) and three moments (M_x, M_y and M_z) acting on segment 1, which is defined as the portion between cross-sections 1 and 2, while Fig. 7 displays two aerodynamic forces (F_n and F_t). For the aerodynamic forces, the normal component F_n is in the direction normal to the plane of rotation and likewise for the tangential component F_t (Laino and Hansen [16]). Some quantities are apparently influenced by the rotor speed, which is 0.242 cps, as shown in Fig. 6(d), 6(e), 6(f) and 7(b). Multiplied by the mass of each segment, the accelerations lead to inertia forces acting on each segment. To simulate the extreme case that all the forces and moments at all 13 segments attain their maximum values at exactly the same time, the maximum values of the forces and moments were extracted from the histories, and then these forces and moments were simultaneously applied to the blade finite element model that will be described in the next subsection.

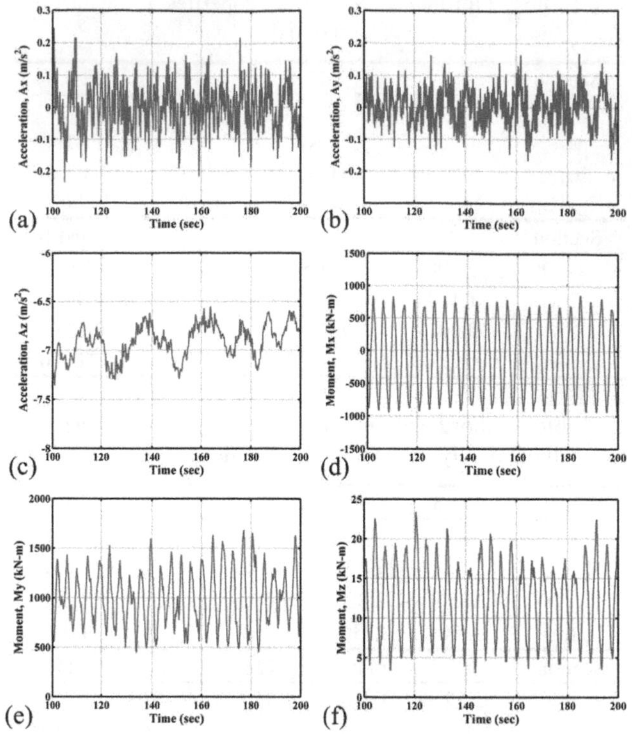

Fig. 6. Accelerations in (a) x, (b) y and (c) z directions, and moments in (d) x, (e) y and (f) z directions of segment 1

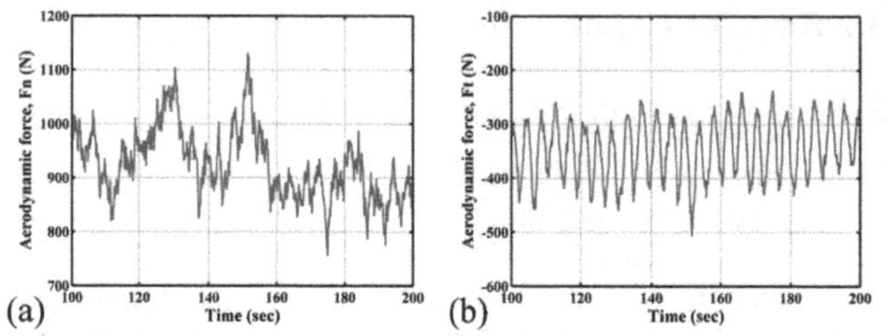

Fig. 7. Aerodynamic forces in (a) normal and (b) tangential directions, experienced by segment 1

3.2.2 Finite element modeling for the turbine blade

A parameterized finite element model of the aerodynamically optimized blade, with its circular-shaped blade root fixed as the boundary condition, was created using the ANSYS software. Fig. 8(a) shows the solid model of the blade and Fig. 8(b) displays more clearly from another viewing angle the airfoil sections with various chord lengths and twist angles. The finite element model composes of 8476 multilayer shell elements (SHELL99) for both the blade wall and box-spar reinforcement, and of 78 multipoint constraint elements (MPC184) for connecting the center nodes of the 13 segments to their respective cross-sectional perimeters. As for the material models used, since there are 4 material models for each blade segment (Fig. 3), 52 composite material models for the shell elements were defined overall. The maximum forces and moments were applied to those center nodes before a static finite element analysis was performed. In addition, modal analysis was also carried out to extract the blade's natural frequencies and mode shapes. In order to have a clear look inside the blade model, Fig. 8(c) illustrates the finite elements belonged to the lower half of the model.

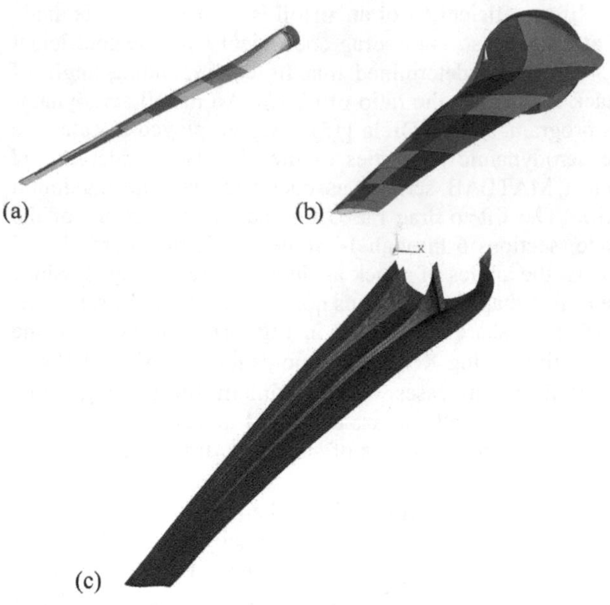

Fig. 8. (a) Solid model of the blade and (b) from another viewing angle, and (c) finite elements of the lower half of the blade model

3.2.3 Structural optimization for the turbine blade

The structural optimization problem, defined by Eqs. 4 through 8, was solved using ANSYS Parametric Design Language (APDL) with the first order optimization method under the ANSYS environment. When the first order optimization method is executed, the constrained optimization problem is transformed into an unconstrained one via penalty functions and derivatives are approximated using a forward difference approach. Exterior and extended interior penalty functions (Kirsch [17]) are applied, respectively, to the side constraints on the design variables and to the rest of the constraints. To form the search direction, the steepest descent method is used for the initial iteration, and conjugate directions are generated according to the Polak-Ribiere recursion formula (More and Wright [18]) for subsequent iterations. Moreover, the line search variable in the unconstrained optimization problem is solved by using a combination of a golden section algorithm and a local quadratic fitting technique.

The constants and limits in the optimization problem were set as follows: the total factor of safety n_{fs}=2.21 (Germanischer Lloyd [12]), σ_{ut}=151 MPa, $\sigma_{dt}=\sigma_{ut}/n_{fs}$=68.33 MPa, σ_{uc}= -174 MPa, $\sigma_{dc}=\sigma_{uc}/n_{fs}$= -78.73 MPa, f_r= 14.5 rpm (the turbine rotor's rated speed) = 0.242 Hz, F_{ms}= 0.25 Hz. The setting of the value of F_{ms} represents that the final optimized natural frequencies of the blade have to be more than twice as large as the rotor's rated speed, greatly reducing the possibility of resonance on the blades. Only the fundamental frequency (the first mode) is needed to achieve this goal, therefore the number of modes considered was set to 1.

Also, there are 5 design variables selected and the first 4 design variables are all about the thickness values of the double-bias materials in the 4 circular segments: the first design variable (x_1) is the thickness of the double-bias material in the first circular segment; the second (x_2) is defined as the thickness in the first segment minus that in the second segment, i.e. the thickness difference between the first and second segments; the third and fourth (x_3 and x_4) are the thickness difference between the second and third segments, and between the third and fourth segments, respectively. The rationale behind the definitions of x_2, x_3 and x_4 is to introduce a series of non-increasing thickness values for the double-bias materials. These circular segments have the thickest double-bias materials and account for a significantly large portion of the entire blade mass. The fifth design variable (x_5) is a proportional factor such that the new thickness values of the unidirectional materials in segments 5 to 13 are determined by multiplying this factor to their initial thickness values. The use of the proportional factor as a design variable can greatly reduce the number of design variables. The thickness values of the double-bias materials in the 4 circular segments of the initial finite element model are, starting from the blade root segment: 110.88 mm, 110.88 mm, 85.74 mm and 45.53 mm, which give the initial values of the design variables x_1, x_2, x_3 and x_4 as those shown in Table 5. Also shown in Table 5 are the initial values of x_5, constraints and the objective function.

After 30 iterations, the best feasible solution was chosen as the optimum solution, and the final optimal values of the design variables, constraints and the objective function are given in Table 5. Fig. 9(a) shows the iteration histories of the 5 design variables. During the structural optimization process, stress analysis and modal analysis of the blade model were repeated to acquire the maximum spanwise tensile and compressive stresses in the model and the natural frequencies of the blade. Fig. 9(b) demonstrates the iteration histories of the maximum tensile stress and the frequency difference between the first natural frequency of the blade and the rotor speed, and Fig. 9(c) depicts the iteration of the total mass of the blade, i.e. the objective function. Initially, the blade model was an infeasible design due to a high level of the maximum stress (127.88 MPa), exceeding the upper limit of the stress constraint (68.33 MPa). As the design variables were adjusting, especially the increasing design variable x_5, the total mass of the blade began to grow. After the process reaching the optimum, the mass had amplified from the initial 9773.9 kg to 15670 kg. The situation that the blade mass increased quite significantly should be alleviated if the design variable x_5 was split into two or more proportional factors, each linking fewer segments. However, this would inevitably cast more burdens on the already heavy computational cost. Fig. 10(a) displays the stress distribution of the optimal blade model, and Fig. 10(b) and 10(c) the first and second natural frequencies (0.584 Hz and 1.115 Hz) and their corresponding mode shapes.

Table 5. Initial and optimal values of the variables

Parameter		Initial value	Optimal value
Design variables	x_1 (mm)	110.88	96.02
	x_2 (mm)	0	16.98
	x_3 (mm)	25.1	25.83
	x_4 (mm)	40.21	39.77
	x_5	1.00	3.10
Constraints	σ_t (MPa)	127.88*	68.05
	σ_c (MPa)	-67.04	-59.23
	$\lvert f_1 - f_r \rvert$ (Hz)	0.256	0.343
Obj. function	m_T (kg)	9773.9	15670

*Infeasible

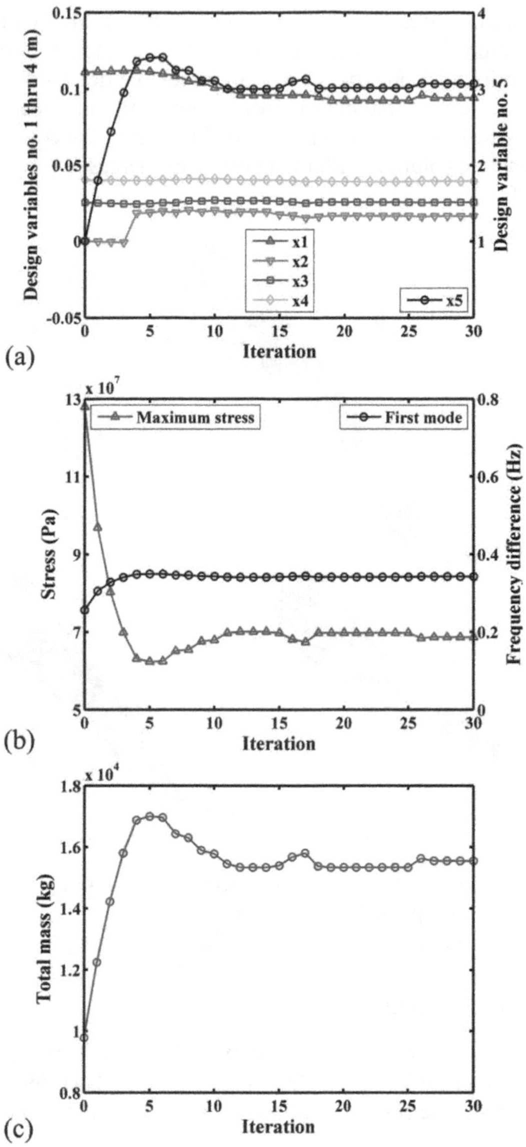

Fig. 9. Iteration histories of (a) the design variables, (b) maximum stress and frequency difference, and (c) total mass

3 Conclusions

This paper has presented a two-step procedure for the optimum design of composite wind turbine blades. A 3 MW, three-blade, horizontal-axis, upwind wind turbine with blades having cross-sections of NREL S818, S825 and S826 airfoil types was demonstrated as the design example. The result of the first step is the optimum cord lengths and twist angles of airfoils of the blade cross-sections along the blade spanwise direction. Generally, the aerodynamically optimized chord lengths and twist angles are larger near the blade root and sequentially diminish when approaching the blade tip. A parameterized finite element model of the aerodynamically optimized blade was created using the ANSYS software. A full-field turbulence with a mean speed of 25 m/s was simulated and applied to the wind turbine to produce time series of accelerations, moments and aerodynamic forces acting on the blade segments. Subsequently, the maximum values of the forces and moments were extracted and then simultaneously imposed to the blade finite element model to replicate the extreme case. The second step provides optimal material distribution for the composite blade. The results have shown that the initial blade model was an infeasible design due to a high level of the maximum stress, exceeding the upper limit of the stress constraint, but eventually the process converged to a feasible solution with the expense of increased total mass of the blade.

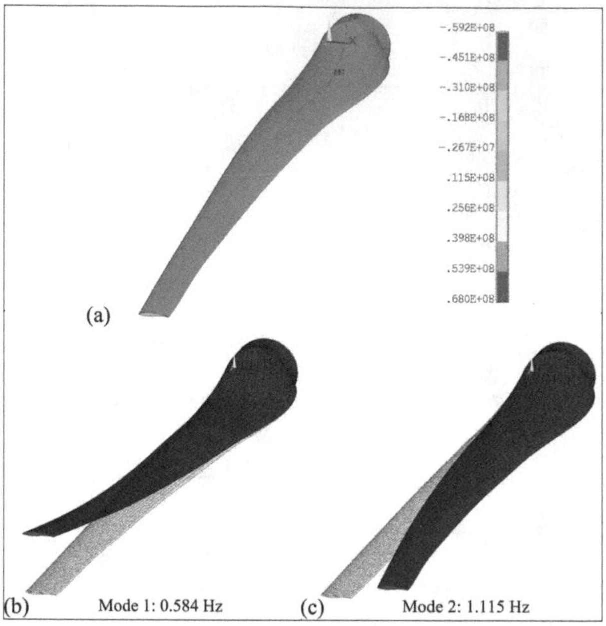

Fig. 10. (a) Stress distribution of the optimal model, (b) the first mode shape and its natural frequency, and (c) the second mode shape and its natural frequency

Acknowledgement

This research work has been supported by the National Science Council of Taiwan, ROC under grant no. NSC 99-2221-E-236-008. The financial support is gratefully appreciated.

References

1. W.A. Timmer, *An overview of NACA 6-digid airfoil series characteristics with reference to airfoils for large wind turbine blades*, in Proceedings of the 47th AIAA Aerospace Science Meeting Including the New Horizons Forum and Aerospace Exposition, Orlando, Florida, USA (2009).
2. K.Y. Maalawi, M.A. Badr, *A practical approach for selecting optimum wind rotors*. Renewable Energy. **28**, 803-822 (2003).
3. K.Y. Maalawi, H.M. Negm, *Optimal frequency design of wind turbine blades*. Journal of Wind Engineering and Industrial Aerodynamics. **90**, 961-286 (2000).
4. V. Díaz Casás, F. Lopez Peña, R.J. Duro, *Automatic design and optimization of wind turbine blades*, in Proceedings of International Conference on Computational Intelligence for Modeling Control and Automation, and International Conference on Intelligent Agents, Web Technologies and Internet Commerce, CIMCA-IAWTIC'06 (2006).
5. V. Díaz Casás, F. Lopez Peña, R.J. Duro, A. Lamas, *Automatic aerodynamic design of a wind turbine through evolutionary techniques*, in IEEE Workshop on Intelligent Data Acquisition and Computing System: Technology and Applications, Sofia, Bulgaria (2005).
6. M. Jureczko, M. Pawlak, A. Mężyk, *Optimization of wind turbine blades*. Journal of Material Processing Technology. **167**, 463-471 (2005).
7. A.J. Vitale, A.P. Rossi, *Computational method for the design of wind turbine blades*. International Journal of Hydrogen Energy. **33**, 3466-3470 (2008).
8. D.J. Malcolm, A.C. Hansen, *WindPACT Turbine Rotor Design Study*, Subcontract Report NREL/SR-500-32495, National Renewable Energy Laboratory, Golden, Colorado, USA, 2006.
9. G. Bir, P. Migliore, *Preliminary Structural Design of Composite Blades for Two- and Three-Blade Rotors*, Technical Report NREL/TP-500-31486, National Renewable Energy Laboratory, Golden, Colorado, USA, 2004.
10. D.A. Griffin, *WindPACT Turbine Design Scaling Studies Technical Area 1-Composite Blades for 80- to 120-Meter Rotor*, Subcontract Report NREL/SR-500-29492, National Renewable Energy Laboratory, Golden, Colorado, USA, 2001.
11. D.A. Spera, *Wind Turbine Technology: Fundamental Concepts of Wind Turbine Engineering* (ASME press, New York, 1994)
12. Germanischer Lloyd, *Rules and Guidelines IV–Industrial Services–Guideline for the Certification of Wind Turbine*, Germanischer Lloyd Industrial Services GmbH, Hamburg, Germany, 2003.
13. B.J. Jonkman, M.L. Buhl, *TurbSim User's Guide for Version 1.40*, National Renewable Energy Laboratory, Golden, Colorado, USA, 2008.
14. M.J. Jason, L.B. Marshall, Jr., *FAST User's Guide*, Technical Report NREL/EL-500-38230, National Renewable Energy Laboratory, Golden, Colorado, USA, 2005.
15. M. Drela, *XFOIL 6.9 User Primer* (MIT Press, Cambridge, MA, USA, 2001)
16. D.J. Laino, A.C. Hansen, *User's Guide to the Wind Turbine Dynamics Computer Software AeroDyn*, Windward Engineering, Salt Lake City, Utah, USA, 2001.
17. U. Kirsch, *Structural Optimization: Fundamentals and Applications* (Springer-Verlag, Berlin, 1993)
18. J.J. More, S.J. Wright, *Optimization Software Guide* (SIAM Publications, Philadelphia, 1993)

Localization of Radiating Sources by an Acoustical Array

Joseph Lardiès[a], Hua Ma, Marc Berthillier

DMA, Institute FEMTO-ST, UMR-CNRS 6174, Besançon, France

Abstract – Arrays of sensors are used in many fields to detect signals, to resolve closely spaced targets, to estimate the bearing, the position, the strength and other properties of radiating sources whose signals arrive from different positions. The purpose of the work is described in the paper is to provide estimators which are used to localize acoustical sources by an acoustical array of sensors. These estimators are based on acoustic processing algorithms: the conventional beamforming, the minimum variance and the constrained Capon algorithm. It is shown that these adaptive algorithms can detect radiating acoustical sources which are not detectable by classical weighted arrays of sensors.

Key words: Acoustical array, Directivity pattern, Minimum Variance algorithm, Source localization

1 Introduction

Arrays of receivers are used in many fields: in radio, radar, sonar, seismic exploration, chemical detection, ultrasonic diagnosis, and so forth, to detect weak signals, to resolve closely spaced targets and to estimate the bearing and other properties of a signal source. The receiving sensors may be any transducers that convert the receiving energy to electrical signals. The type of sensors used to detect these signals differ accordingly: microphones for the acoustic signals, electromagnetic antennas for radio waves, accelerometers/seismometers for the detection of earthquakes, ultrasonic probes and X-ray detectors in medical imaging, containers with membranes or biosensors for gas detection and so forth. In all these highly diverse applications of array signal processing, the sensors are designed with one basic objective in mind: to provide an interface between the environment in which the array is embedded and the signal processing part of the system and the physical manner in which this interface is established depends on the application of interest. In these applications, the goal is to determinate the distribution of the emitted energy in the medium (air, water, rock, etc) that surrounds the array. For example, in industrial environments to localize complex noise fields, in underwater surveillance with sonar systems, in communications to separate speakers, in seismology for the monitoring and analysis of global earthquakes, in all these cases signals received by sensor arrays are processed to obtain estimates of their strength and direction of arrival. In this communication we are concerned in industrial noise localization which has significant effects on labor's health and community living quality. It is highly desired to develop methods that are capable of locating noise sources in an accurate and systematic manner before any noise control measure can be applied. In all that follows, we consider only idealized arrays, those in which there are no cross-couplings between individual receivers. The receivers are assumed to sample the spatial field without distorting it. We further assume that the spatial field in the vicinity of the array is homogenous, an assumption that is often valid when all signal sources are distant from the array, and that all receivers have the same sensitivity.

In this paper we are concerned in industrial noise localization which has significant effects on labor's health and community living quality. It is highly desired to develop methods that are capable of locating noise sources in an accurate and systematic manner before any noise control measure can be applied. Conventional ways of noise source identifications include, for example, sound pressure measurement, sound intensity measurement and acoustic holography. These methods suffer from the drawbacks of being either inaccurate or being restrictive in only small areas or short distances when applied to complex noise fields in industrial environment. An alternative is the use of an array of sensors whose outputs are processed. The performances of these methods in the localization of closely spaced sources are presented. The approach taken here is to assume that the signal field at the array is comprised of K independent plane wave arrivals from unknown directions and the problem reduces to estimating the K directions in a background noise environment. One main of the work described in the paper is to provide estimators which are simple to implement on line. These estimators are based on acoustic processing algorithms: the conventional beamforming estimator, the Minimum Variance (MV) estimator and the robust Capon estimator.

2 Beamforming

2.1 Conventional beamformer

The principles of conventional beamforming were established many decades ago. Consider a linear array as shown in Fig.1. A plane wavefront arriving from a direction normal to the array (broadside array) arrives at all the receivers in phase, and so if summed the signal outputs from the receivers will add in phase and reinforce one another; signals from

[a] Corresponding author: joseph.lardies@univ-fcomte.fr

other directions will not be in phase, and so will not be reinforced. If it is desired to receive narrowband signals from some other direction than broadside, we simple shift the phases of the receiver outputs by appropriate amounts to bring all the receiver outputs into phase before summing. More generally, if the signals are broadband, we time delay the receiver outputs appropriately before summation. This process is called beamsteering. It can readily be seen that the same principles can be extended to arrays of arbitrary geometry in two or three dimensions: we simple insert the appropriate time delays.

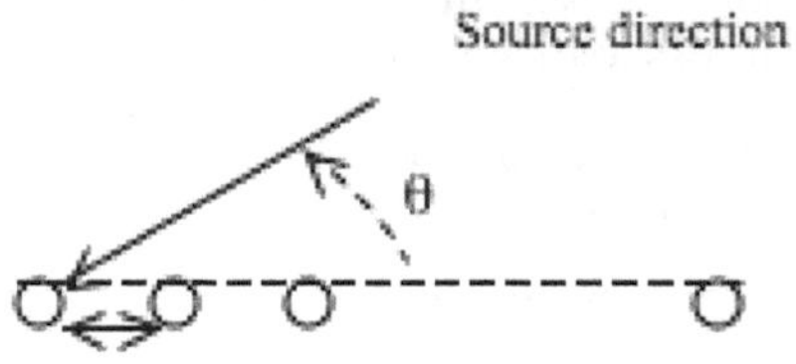

Fig. 1. A linear array of N elements

We consider a linear array of N equally spaced elements, located along the horizontal axis, with an element spacing of d. The beamformer output usually called the space or array factor is given by [1]:

$$y=\sum_{i=1}^{N} a_i\, v_i(k,\theta,\theta_0) = \sum_{i=1}^{N} a_i\, exp[j(i-1)kd(cos(\theta - cos\theta_0))] \quad (1)$$

where a_i are weighting coefficients used to control the shape of the directivity diagram, θ_0 determines the direction of the maximum output (the direction of main beam) and k the wavenumber of interest. Note a and v the columns vectors whose entries are $\{a_i\}$ and $\{v_i\}$. Equation (1) may be written as:

$$y = a^T v = v^T a \quad (2)$$

where T is the transpose vector.

In the case of a uniform weighting array we have $a_i = 1$, i=1, 2,…,N and it can be shown, that in order to avoid grating lobes, the condition for a scanned beam becomes :

$$d/\lambda \le \frac{1}{1+|cos(\theta_0)|} \quad (3)$$

If we plot the average power output as a function of signal direction, we obtain the polar diagram or polar response. By convention, the polar response is normalized so its response in the beamsteered direction θ_0 is unity. The beamwidth, that is the width of the main lobe, often defined as the angle between the points at which the power response falls by half, indicates the ability to resolve closely-spaced signal sources; the level of the sidelobes is a measure of susceptibility to interference by unwanted signals in directions away from the main beam. The directivity pattern, also known as the polar diagram is obtained by taking the normalized magnitude of y as a function of the polar angle θ for a given frequency. For a uniform weighting array we have the normalized magnitude:

$$D=\left|\frac{sin(N\Psi/2)}{N\, sin(\Psi/2)}\right| \quad (4)$$

where $\Psi = k\,d(cos\ \theta - cos\theta_0)$. For broadside arrays, where the beam maximum occurs in the direction perpendicular to the array axis, we have $\theta_0 = \pi/2$. For end-fire arrays where the beam maximum occurs in the direction of the array axis, we have $\theta_0 = 0$. Figures 2 (a) and 2(b) show the antenna directivity diagram with $N = 6$ and $d/\lambda = 0{,}4$ for broadside and end-fire arrays. In the case of broadside array, because of rotational symmetry, we are unable to distinguish between signals arriving from $+\pi/2$ or $-\pi/2$. We have two beam maximums. In the case of end-fire array we have only a beam maximum.

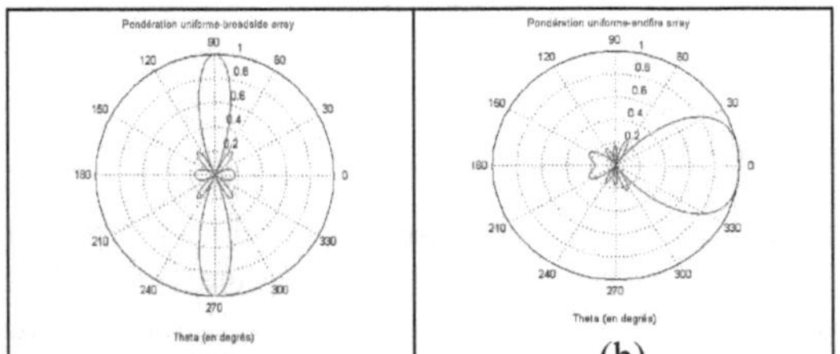

(a) (b)

Fig. 2. Directivity diagrams for broadside array (a) and end fire array (b)

It is instructive to examine the behaviour of the directivity diagram. In particular, it can be manipulated to yield information about locations of major maxima or beams, locations of nulls, angular widths of major maxima or beamwidths and locations of minor maxima or sidelobes.

2.2 Dolph-Tchebychev and binomial beamformer

Shading is a well-known technique used to modify the polar diagram of an array and low sidelobes are usually desirable to reduce the effect of interfering signals. Dolph [1] addressed that problem by noting the behaviour of the Tchebychev polynomials and devising suitable transformations of variables to link the behaviour of the polynomials to array side lobe levels. With the Dolph-Tchebychev shading the sidelobes all have the same peak level. For an even number of sensors the beamformer output is:

$$y = 2\sum_{i=1}^{N/2} a_i\, cos[(2i-1)\Psi/2] \quad (5)$$

We consider $t = cos(\Psi/2)$ and use the Moivre formula to write each $cos(p\Psi/2)$ function as a polynomial of degree p, called Tchebychev polynomial and noted $T_p(t)$. With this Tchebychev polynomial equation (5) becomes

$$y = 2\sum_{i=1}^{N/2} a_i\, T_{2i-1}(t) = T_{n-1}(t\,Z_0) \quad (6)$$

where Z_0 is associated to the sidelobes level. By identification we obtain the weighting coefficients a_i. Figure 3(a) shows the end-fire polar diagram of the Dolph-Tchebychev shading with six elements, $d/\lambda = 0{,}4$ and a constant sidelobe level of 20 dB. The sidelobes all have the same peak level which has been selected to be much lower than the levels for the conventional beamformer.

In order to suppress the sidelobes we use weighting coefficients C^{p}_{N-1} and we obtain for an even number of elements the beamformer output is:

$$y = \sum_{i=1}^{N/2} C^{N/2-i}_{N-1} \cos[(2i-1)\Psi/2] = 2^{N-1}\cos^{N-1}(\Psi/2) \quad (7)$$

The fundamental property of the binomial weighting concerns the absence of sidelobes in the polar diagram; this is because the directivity function has a general form in $\cos^{n-1}(\Psi/2)$ and this function does not oscillate between 0 and $\pi/2$. Figure 2(b) shows the directivity end-fire pattern of the binomial shading with six elements and $d/\lambda = 0{,}4$. The sidelobes are absent but the angular width of the main lobe has increased.

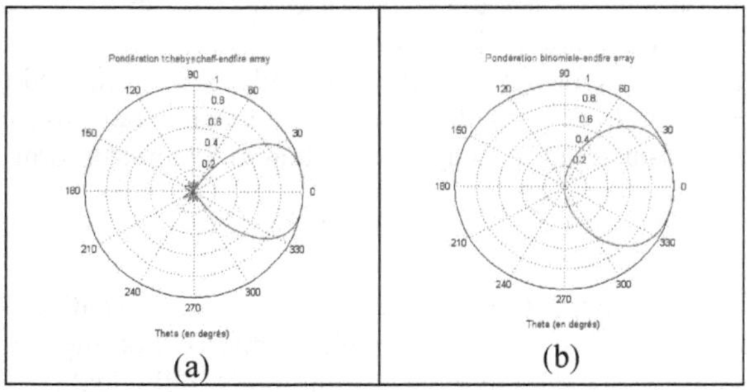

Fig. 3. Directivity diagrams for Dolph-Tchebychev (a) and binomial (b) weighting

2.3 Superdirectivity and optimal beamforming

It is sometimes desirable to use a given array at low frequencies. Conventional beamforming then yields a broad beam. However, by appropriate choice of the weight vector a, it is possible to generate narrow beamwidths and the array is called superdirective. But there is a penalty: as the frequency is reduced, the magnitude of the weight required becomes large, making the practical implementation of the superdirectivity difficult. Schelkunoff [2] showed that every linear array with commensurable separations between the elements can be represented by a polynomial and every polynomial can be interpreted as a linear array. The analytical representation of an output array is accomplished with the aid of the following transformation: $z=\exp(j\Psi)$ and we obtain :

$$y = \sum_{i=0}^{N-1} a_i z^i \quad (8)$$

This polynomial can be written in terms of its (n-1) roots ($z_1, z_2, \ldots, z_{N-1}$) and Schelkunoff has shown that if these roots are regularly spaced between 0 et $-kd(1+\cos\theta_0)$, the visible range of z, we have a superdirective array. Figure 4(a) shows the end-fire directivity pattern with a Schelkunoff distribution, six elements and $d/\lambda = 0{,}4$. The beamwidth, or angular space between the half-power points on each side of the main lobe, is narrower than that of a uniform, Dolph-Tchebychev or binomial weighted end-fire array.

We address now the problem of selecting a set of weights which maximize the directivity index of a passive acoustical array. The directivity index is defined as:

$$D(f) = \frac{|y(f,\Omega_0)|^2}{\frac{1}{4\pi}\int_{(\Omega)} |y(f,\Omega)|^2 d\Omega} = \frac{a^{*T} V(f,\Omega_0)\, a}{a^{*T} W(f)\, a} \quad (9)$$

where $|y(f,\Omega_0)|^2 = a^{*T} V(f,\Omega_0)\, a$ is the power out of the beamformer steered in direction implied by Ω_0, or in the direction of the main beam, and $\frac{1}{4\pi}\int_{(\Omega)} |y(f,\Omega)|^2 d\Omega = a^{*T} W a$ the average output power.

In these expressions we have : $V(f,\Omega_0) = v^*(f,\Omega_0)\, v^T(f,\Omega_0)$ and $W_{ij} = \frac{1}{4\pi}\int_{(\Omega)} v_i^* v_j \, d\Omega$. The denominator of (9) is the output power when the acoustical array is in a far field of plane waves arriving from all directions and having the same level. This is also the definition of the omnidirectional noise. In fact, the directivity index represents also the output signal-to-noise ratio which may be defined as the ratio of the power received per unit solid angle in the direction of the signal to the average noise power received per unit solid angle. The purpose is to determine an optimum set of weights $\{a_i\}$in amplitude and phase to yield the maximum directivity index with respect to a prespecified number of elements, spacing and frequency. The index directivity is expressed as the ration of two quadratic forms and it is shown [3] that maximisation of (9) is obtained when: $a = W^{-1} v$ and the directivity index is : $D_{Max}(f) = v^{*T} W^{-1} v$. Figure 4(b) shows the pattern of the six-element end-fire array with $d/\lambda = 0{,}4$ yielding maximum directivity index.

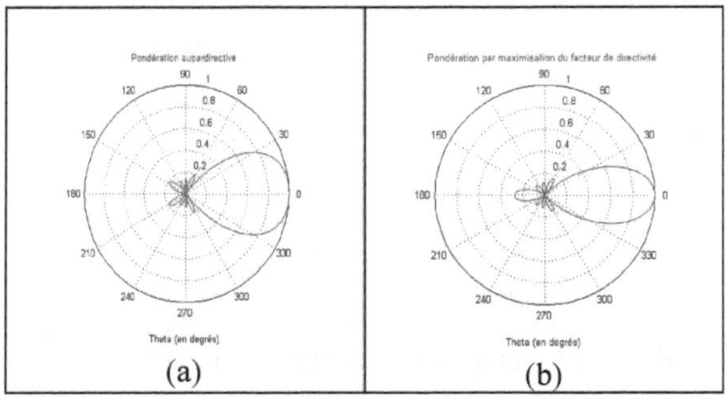

Figure 4. Directivity diagrams for superdirective (a) and optimal (b) weighting

A comparison of different weighting techniques developed in the communication are presented in table 1 for a linear end-fire array of six elements and a value of $d/\lambda = 0{,}4$.

Table 1. Comparison of weighting methods

weighting	Uniform	Dolph	Binomial	Schelk	optimal
beamwidth	84°	90°	126°	78°	58°
sidelobes	Important	low	absent	low	low

However, these weighted arrays have a fundamental resolution problem in the localization of different sources. Figure 5 shows the performances of the optimal end-fire array in the localisation of two sources at 10° and 19° relative to the antenna axis. An important beamwidth and important sidelobes are clearly present in this spectra and it is impossible to obtain the direction of arrival of these two sources.

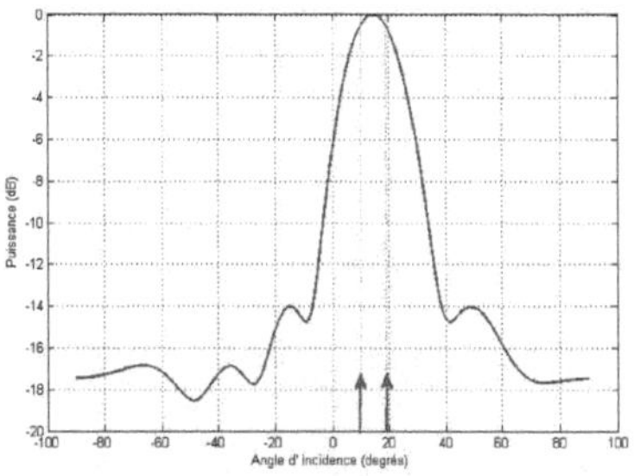

Fig. 5. Direction of arrival of two sources using the optimal beamforming

3 Adaptive array

3.1 Spatial correlation matrix

The receiving array has N omnidirectional sensors and is immersed in an acoustic noise field which consists of K independent discrete sources. Because of the geometric positions of the sensors, the total signal power incident on each sensor is the same, but the phase information is different on each receiver.

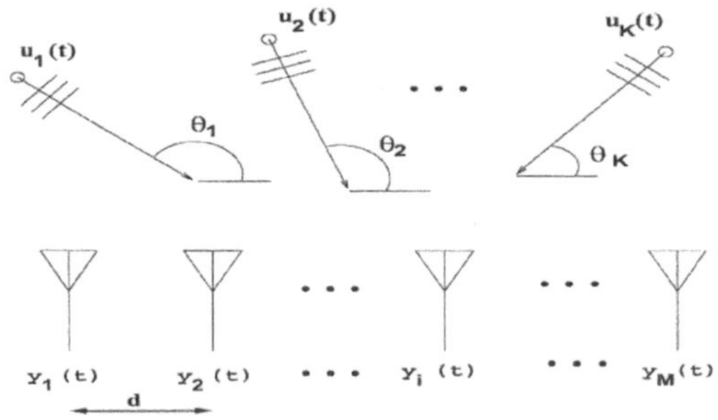

Fig.6. The setup of the source location problem

The purpose of any estimator is to use the phase information in some way to infer which signals reached the receiving array and the goal of sensor array source localization is to find the locations of sources of wavefields that impinge on the acoustical array. The available information is the geometry of the array, the parameters of the medium where wavefields propagate and the time measurements or outputs of the sensors. For purposes of exposition, we first focus on the narrowband scenario. For a set of K sources, the signals observed at the outputs of the N sensors array are represented by the N-dimensional vector [4-6]

$$x(t) = \sum_{i=1}^{K} b(\theta_i)\, s_i(t) + n(t) \qquad (10)$$

where $s_i(t)$ is the complex amplitude of the ith source. It is a zero-mean complex random variable : $E[s_i(t)] = 0$. The signal power p_i of the ith source which we wish to localize is represented by its variance $p_i = \mathrm{Var}[s_i(t)]=E[s_i(t)s_i(t)^*]$. Here E[ ] denotes an ensemble average and the superscript* represents the complex conjugate. The direction of arrival of the ith signal is represented by the N-dimensional vector $b(\theta_i) =[\, b_1(\theta_i)\ b_2(\theta_i) .... b_N(\theta_i)]^T$, often called the array manifold vector or the steering vector or the directional mode vector and $n(t)$ is the additive noise. The noise is assumed to be spatially white (independent or uncorrelated from sensor to sensor) and the same power level of noise is present in each receiver. With these assumptions, the cross-spectral matrix for the noise alone is $R_N = E[n(t)n(t)^H] = p_N I$ where p_N is the noise power, I is the (NxN) identity matrix and the superscript H denotes the complex-conjugate transpose operation. Equation (10) may be rewritten in the matrix form

$$x(t) = B\, s(t) + n(t) \quad t \in \{t_1, t_2, \ldots t_N\} \qquad (11)$$

The (NxK) matrix B where each column is a source direction vector, is the so-called array manifold matrix. For any single plane wave arrival, the outputs from the N individual receivers will differ in phase by an amount determined by the geometry of the array and the arrival direction. In other words, the elements B_{qr} of the matrix B are functions of the signal arrival angles and the array elements locations. Thus, one has $B_{qr} = \exp(j\,\phi_{qr})$ where ϕ_{qr} is the phase of the signal at the qth receiver from the rth source, measured relative to some arbitrary reference point. That is, B_{qr} depends on the qth array element, its position relative to the origin of the coordinate system, and its response to a signal incident from the direction of the rth source. $s(t)$ is the K-dimensional vector, the components of which are the complex amplitudes of the sources. It can readily be seen that the output signal from the qth sensor may be written as :

$$x_q(t) = \sum_{r=1}^{K} B_{qr}(\theta)\, s_r(t) + n_q(t) \qquad (12)$$

Since the K arrivals are by assumption independent, the correlation matrix between the different signal sources is

$$R_S = E[s(t)s(t)^H] = \mathrm{diag}(p_1, p_2, \ldots, p_K) \qquad (13)$$

and at the operating frequency, the spatial correlation matrix (or covariance matrix) of the receiver outputs may be expressed, for signals uncorrelated of each other and of noise, as

$$R = E[x(t)x(t)^H] = BR_SB^H + R_N \qquad (14)$$

In practice, the spatial correlation matrix is estimated by a finite number of time domain samples (snapshots) and the following estimated form is used :

$$\hat{R} = \frac{1}{M} \sum_{i=1}^{M} x(t_i)x(t_i)^H \qquad (15)$$

where $x(t_i)$ is the array signal vector sampled at time t_i and M is the number of such samples. The caret (^) denotes an estimated value.

We can now derive estimators for source localization using an acoustical array.

3.2 The minimum variance estimator

The minimum variance (MV) estimator was originally proposed by Capon who conducted a frequency wavenumber analysis on earthquake data analysis. The conventional beamformer can be considered as a kind of linear spatial filter with data-independent coefficients. In contrast, the minimum variance method (or Capon's method) can be considered as a kind of data-dependent spatial filter, in which the coefficients are chosen such that the filter has constant gain at a particular direction while its output power is minimized. The underlying principle of the method amounts to finding an optimal steering vector w_{opt} such that the array output power is minimized while maintaining the gain along the look direction to be constant, say unity [4]. That is,

$$\min \; w^H R\, w \qquad (16)$$

$$\text{subject} \quad w^H b(\theta) = 1 \qquad (17)$$

Minimizing the resulting beam energy reduces the contributions to this energy from sources and noise not propagating in the direction of look. The solution of this constrained optimization problem occurs often in the derivation of adaptive array processing algorithms. The solution technique is to use a Lagrange multiplier λ and a cost function

$$H(w) = w^H R\, w + 2\, \lambda\, (w^H b(\theta) - 1) \qquad (18)$$

The gradient with respect to w is

$$grad\, H(w) = 2\, R\, w + 2\, \lambda\, b(\theta) \qquad (19)$$

and the minimum of the cost function is obtained when

$$w_{opt} = -\, \lambda\, R^{-1}\, b(\theta) \qquad (20)$$

But w_{opt} must satisfy the constraint, one then has

$$\lambda = (-b^H(\theta)\, R^{-1}\, b(\theta))^{-1} \qquad (21)$$

$$w_{opt} = R^{-1}\, b(\theta)(b^H(\theta)\, R^{-1} b(\theta))^{-1} \qquad (22)$$

and the corresponding array output power is

$$p_{MV}(\theta) = E[\, |y(t)|^2\,] = (b^H(\theta)\, R^{-1}\, b(\theta))^{-1} \qquad (23)$$

The goal of the minimum variance estimator is that the contributions of the signals from directions other than θ to the array output are minimized while the signal at direction θ passes through without any distortion. Equation (23) is also known as the angular power spectrum of the minimum variance estimator and the signal directions are found by the locations of the spectrum peaks. The peaks level of the spectrum give a good estimate of the true targets power and the spectrum also has uniformly low sidelobes. Simulations have shown that this estimator gives satisfactory resolution if the number of snapshots is high. The algorithm does not require any knowledge of the number of sources present and can also be used with irregular arrays. It is expected that this estimator performs better than the classical beamforming and has super-resolution provided that the SNR is moderately high, the sources are not strongly correlated and the number of snapshots is sufficient.

The common advantage of this estimator is that it does not assume anything about the statistical properties of the data and, therefore, it can be used in situations where we lack information about these properties. Figure 7 shows the power spectral density of the adaptive array with six sensors and $d/\lambda = 0{,}4$. Two sources at 0° and 20° relative to the antenna axis are present are localized with this estimator.

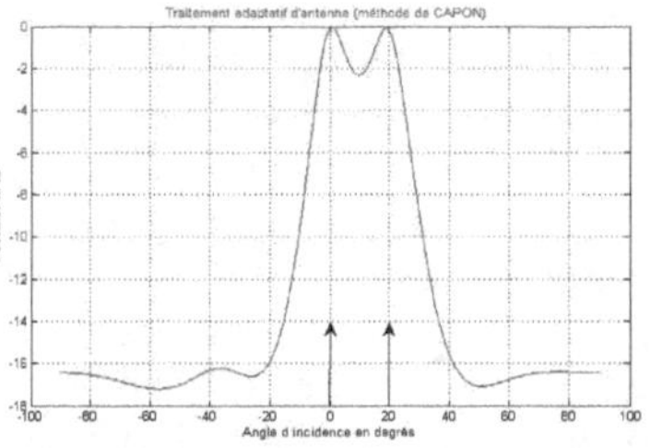

Fig. 7. Direction of arrival of two sources using the adaptive estimator

The resolution of the antenna array can be improved using a robust adaptive array.

3.3 The robust minimum variance estimator

The minimum variance estimator adaptively selects the weight vector to minimize the array output power subject to the linear constraint that the signal of interest does not suffer from any distortion. This beamformer has a better resolution and much better interference rejection capability than the standard beamformer, provided that the array steering vector corresponding to the signal of interest is accurately known. However, the knowledge of the signal of interest steering vector can be imprecise, which is often the case in practice due to the differences between the assumed signal arrival angle and the true arrival angle. Whenever this happens, the minimum variance estimator can give poor results. A robust minimum variance estimator is then proposed based on a diagonal loading [7] where a scaled identity matrix is added to the covariance matrix given in (14). The main idea of diagonal loading is to replace the covariance matrix R by the matrix $R+rI$ where the diagonal-loading factor r is a user-selected parameter. The weight vector so obtained is given by :

$$w = (R + rI)^{-1} b(\theta)[b^{*T}(\theta)(R+rI)^{-1} b(\theta)]^{-1} \qquad (24)$$

The robust minimum variance power estimate of array output is then :

$$P_{RMV} = [b^{*T}(R+rI)^{-1} R (R+rI)^{-1} b][\, b^{*T}(R+rI)^{-1} b]^{-2} \qquad (25)$$

Figure 8 shows the power spectral density of the robust adaptive array with six sensors and $d/\lambda = 0{,}4$. Two sources at 0° and 20° relative to the antenna axis are present are localized with this estimator which has a better resolution than the minimum variance estimator.

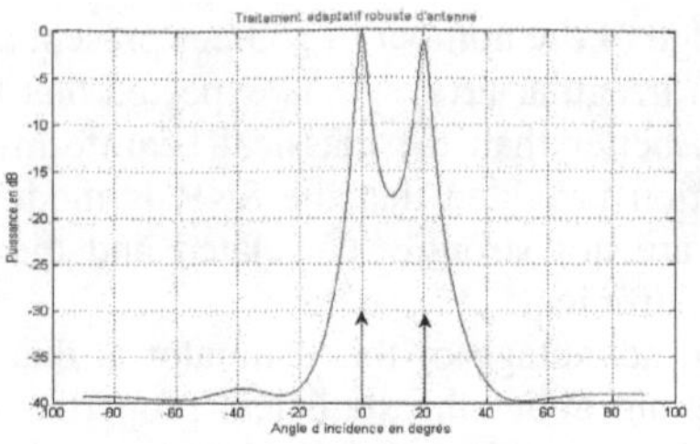

Fig. 8. Direction of arrival of two sources using the robust adaptive estimator

4 Conclusion

Beamforming techniques are useful for focusing sound waves but are not adapted for the localization of multiple sources. Two methods using adaptive arrays have been proposed and are based on the minimum variance and the robust minimum variance estimation. These algorithms have been tested by computer simulation studies and they perform satisfactory. In the future the resolution capability of these algorithms and their limitations in a broadband environment will be studied.

References

1. R. Elliot, *Antenna theory*, J. Wiley (2003)
2. S.A. Schelkunoff, *A mathematical theory of linear arrays*, Bell System Technology Journal, **22**, 80-107, (1943).
3. F.R. Gantmacher, *The theory of matrices*, Dunod (1966)
4. P. Stoica, R. Moses, *Introduction to spectral analysis*, Prentice Hall (1997)
5. J. Lardiès J., *Power estimation of multiple sources by an acoustical array*, Journal of Sound and Vibration, **145**, 309-320, (1991).
6. J. Lardiès, H. Ma, M. Berthillier, E. Foltête, *Performance of high-resolution sensor array processing algorithms in the localisation of acoustic sources*, Acoustics'08, Paris, June29-July 4, 2008.
7. J. Li, P. Stoica, Z. Wang, On robust Capon beamforming and diagonal loading, IEEE Trans. Signal Processing, **51**, 1702-1711, (2003).

Optimization of Unicondylar Knee Replacement according to Contact Pressure

Michal Ackermann[1A], Lukáš Čapek[1]

[1]Technical University of Liberec, Dept. of applied mechanics, Studentska 2, 461 17 Liberec 1, Czech Republic

Abstract – The project deals with contact pressure analysis on two constructional types of modern type of knee prosthesis - the unicompartmental knee replacement. In the first part of the project the contact pressure distribution on replacements is analyzed in two ways. The first method is experimental with using pressure sensitive Pressurex® films. Second approach is a numerical analysis with the support of finite element method (FEM) made in ANSYS Multiphysics 10.0 software package. Results from both approaches are compared at the end of the first part. In the second part the chosen type of replacements is optimized according to contact pressure. The goal was to reduce the contact pressure and to improve its distribution for taking its full advantages.

Key words: Biomechanics, Knee joint, Unicompartmental replacement, FEM, Contact pressure

1 Introduction

Nowadays we're able to increase the quality of life for those people who are disabled with knee joint failure thanks to research of artificial joints. These surgical interventions, which are replacing damaged joint surfaces of femoral, tibial bone and related soft tissues, belongs among today's standard orthopedic operations. The most common reasons for implantation of knee joint replacement are:

- Degenerative knee diseases (e.g. osteoarthritis);
- Destruction of the joint by the reason of rheumatic disease;
- Damage of the joint caused by an accident;
- And others.

Present experiences in the field of orthopedics and biomechanics lead to the progression of so-called mini-invasive operations. This means, that on specific cases, there's a possibility to use partial (unicondylar) knee replacements instead of total knee replacement. Quick process of operation, short term of convalescence and of course lower price of the implant are main reasons for further research of these modern replacements.

An unicondylar replacement generally consists of three parts: femoral component, tibial platform and between them inserted part made of an ultra-high molecular weight polyethylene (UHMWPE).

In this work, two constructional types of partial knee replacement were tested (Figure 1). These types differ by a movement ability of UHMWPE insert on tibial platform. The first of the two types is characterized by a possibility of free horizontal movement of insert on tibial platform, while in the second case the insert is fully fixed. Very important aspect is a shape of PE insert's contact area. If it's designed in a wrong way it could lead to fast failure. This is of course unacceptable so the question is which one of the mentioned constructional solutions is more suitable for use.

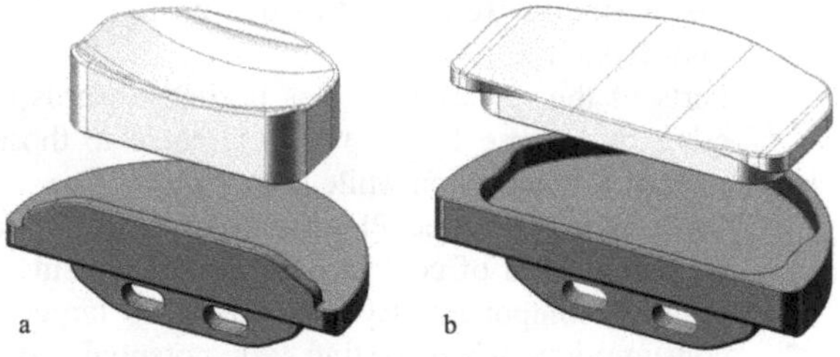

Fig.1. Two constructional options of partial knee replacement

Many works dealing with knee replacements indicate the value of contact pressure as one of the main signs of premature wear of PE insert (Lin, Y. [4], Shi, J. [7]). The aim of this article is to analyze distribution of contact pressure on tested replacements and to consider which of these two types is more suitable for use. Two methods were used: the experimental method, where contact pressure is measured by Pressurex films and by a numerical approach – finite element method (FEM).

1.1 Pressurex films

These films which react on load between contacting bodies are offering an easy way to find out contact pressure distribution and its value. Film itself is made of a material called Mylar (firm and highly durable polyester). It contains a layer of microcapsules filled with pigment. When a force is applied these microcapsules tear and pigment creates instantaneous and permanent topographical image of contact pressure distribution in contact area of bodies (Fig. 2).

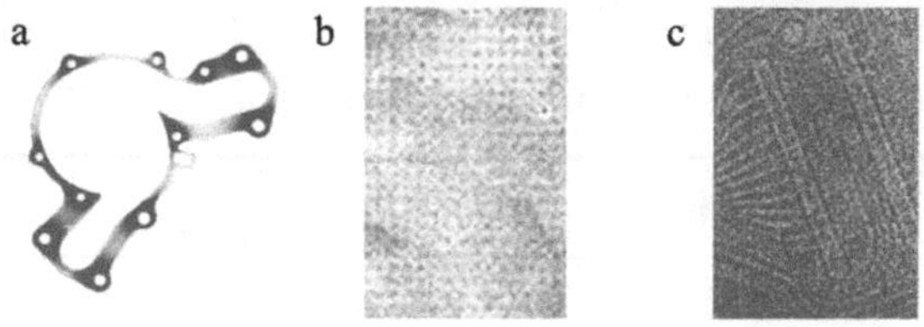

Fig.2. Examples of Pressurex film applications

[a] Corresponding author: michal.ackermann@gmail.com

1.2 Finite element method (FEM)

Solving the problem with defined contact belongs in FEM, considering nonlinearities which it brings, among one of its most computational and time consuming tasks. The contact definition is necessary in those cases, where it's impossible to replace it with some of the boundary conditions, for example:

- Dynamic impact simulation,
- Contact of bodies with defined coefficient of friction,
- Interaction of assembly components,
- Etc.

2 Materials and methods

Experiments and numerical analyzes were done in the same way:

- Replacements were tested in five positions of knee joint flexion;
- Parts of the replacement was pushed towards each other by a force 1270N which is equal to those in joint in full extension while standing;
- On a type with free PE insert there's difficult to choose an area of contact between PE housing and femoral component. By the reason of large time consumption when testing all potential contact points, only one of them was chosen.

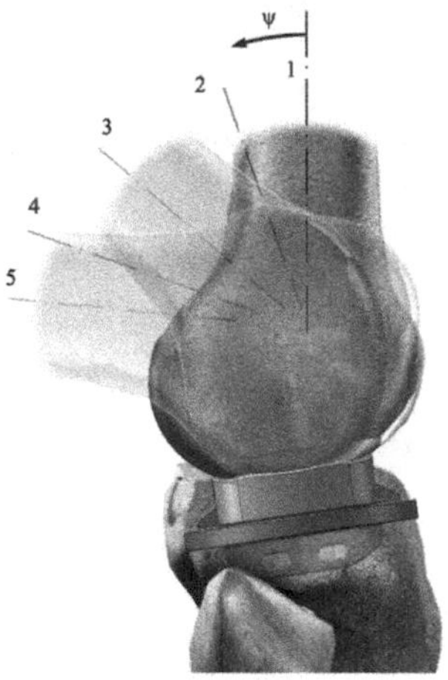

Fig.3. Five testing positions shown on knee joint

Table 1. Degrees of flexion

Position number	Flexion angle ψ [deg]
1	0
2	20
3	50
4	70
5	85

2.1 Experiments

Experiments were performed on uniaxial testing machine (TIRA test, Germany) on the Department of Applied Mechanics, Technical University of Liberec, Czech Republic. A device allowing variable positioning of the femoral component against tibial plate and PE insert simulating knee flexion/extension was built (Figure 3). The Pressurex® indicating film, cut into necessary size, was inserted between PE housing and femoral component and then pushed against each other to contact under the load of 1 270 N. The load was applied for over ten seconds so the topographical image of contact surface was developed on film. This process was repeated for five angles of flexion (Fig. 3). All obtained films were analyzed and distribution of contact pressure was reached.

In the case of partial knee replacement with free PE housing a LOW type (2,5 – 10 MPa) of Pressurex® film was used. By the reason of the presumption of higher contact pressures, MEDIUM type (10 – 50 MPa) was used for type with fixed PE insert.

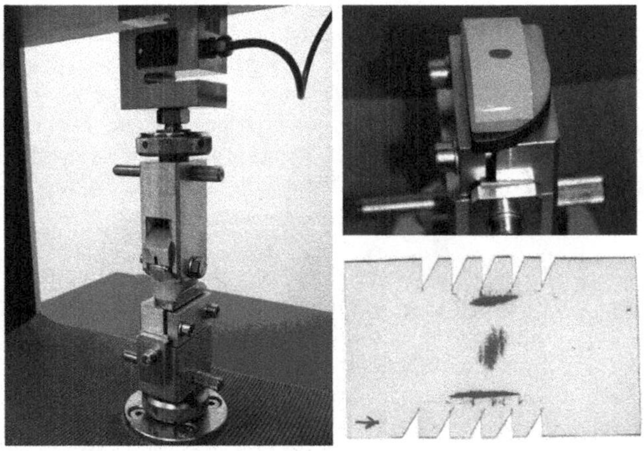

Fig.4. Snapshots of experiments

2.2 FEM analysis

After the experiments, FEM analyzes were proceeded too. The task was solved in ANSYS 10.0 software package. First of all, assemblies of the parts of tested replacements were crated in CAD/CAM software Pro/ENGINEER. Each assembly corresponded to a concrete angle of flexion. These entities were then exported directly into ANSYS software. Following premises were established:

- Material of the parts was considered as elastic and isotropic;
- In the case of fixed PE insert the contact of insert and tibial platform is replaced by boundary conditions, which fixes its movement in a more simple way;
- The force 1270 N was converted to pressure load and applied on top surfaces of femoral component.

Models were meshed by 10-noded tetrahedron shaped volume elements. Resultant mesh was locally refined in the area of contact to gain more accurate results of contact pressure.

Material models are characterized by constants, summarized in table 2.

Table 2. Material properties of tested components

Tibial plate and femoral component (Co-Cr-Mo alloy)		
Young's modulus	E [MPa]	228 000
Poisson's ratio	μ [-]	0,3
PE housing (ultra-high molecular weight polyethylene - UHMWPE)		
Young's modulus	E [MPa]	500
Poisson's ratio	μ [-]	0,3

In each defined contact, coefficient of friction f = 0.05 was used. This is essential in case of the type with free PE housing. It was impossible to set up the PE insert into proper position against femoral component in Pro/ENGINEER software. But thanks to defined friction there's a possibility for insert to move during the task evaluation and therefore gain the right position.

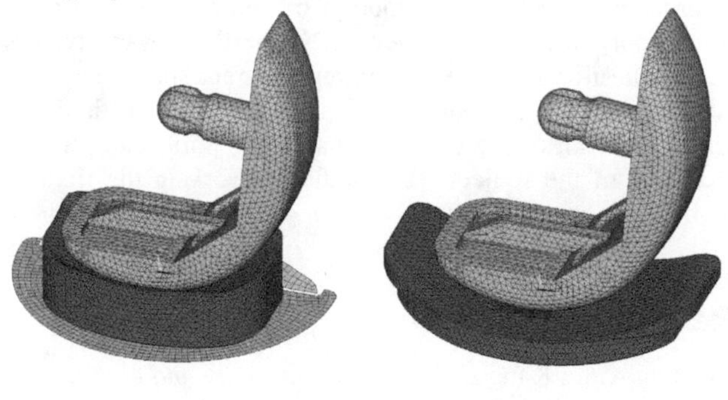

Fig.5. Meshed models of the both unicondylar knee replacement types

3 Results

The first set of results (Figure 6, 7) belongs to the partial knee replacement with fixed PE insert. On the left side can be seen result from FEM analysis, right side shows contact pressure distribution gained thanks to Pressurex films. Second set (Figure 7, 8) shows results of the free PE insert type.

The maximal values of contact pressure goes up to 36 MPa in case of free housing and 56 MPa in case of fixed housing. In case of free housing, we can see that results of contact pressure distribution are not, especially in position 5, in a good agreement. In case of fixed housing, results are more acceptable.

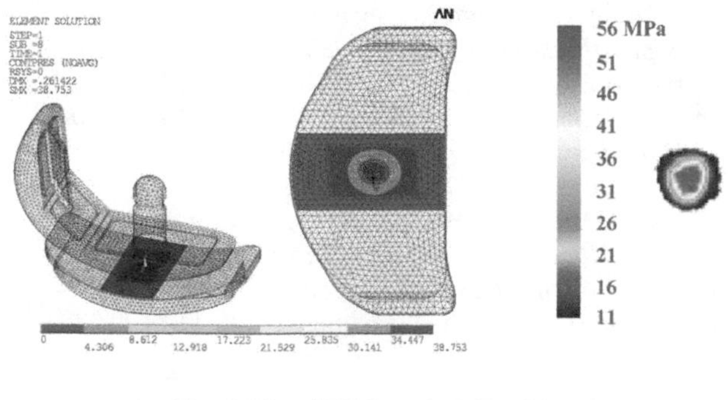

Fig.6. Fixed PE housing; Position 1

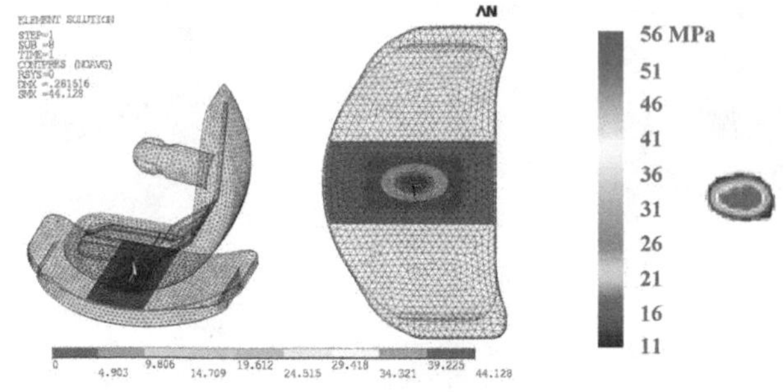

Fig.7. Fixed PE housing; Position 5

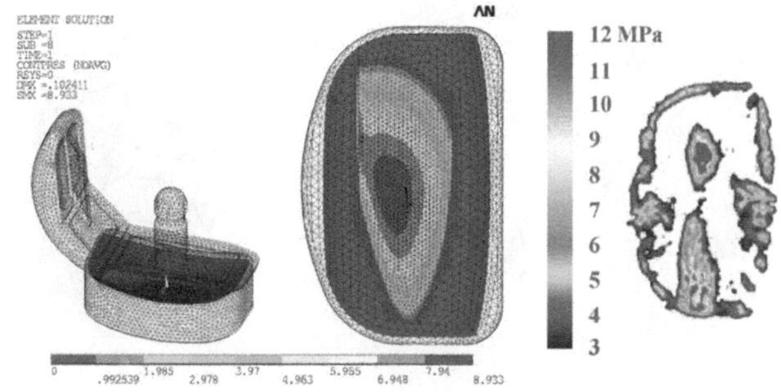

Fig.8. Free PE housing; Position 1

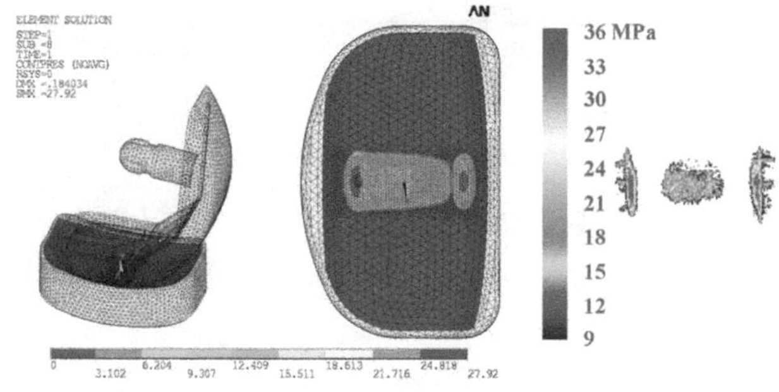

Fig.9. Free PE housing; Position 5

4 Optimization

According to previous results, the uni-compartmental knee replacement with free PE housing was chosen for the optimization process. Shape of contact surface, which follows convex shape of femoral component, guarantees more advantageous distribution of contact pressure and thereby reduction of its value. The shape of PE insert was modified only. Contact surface of the femoral part follows the shape of healthy condyle surface. Its modifications should therefore lead to changes in joint kinematical properties which isn't suitable.

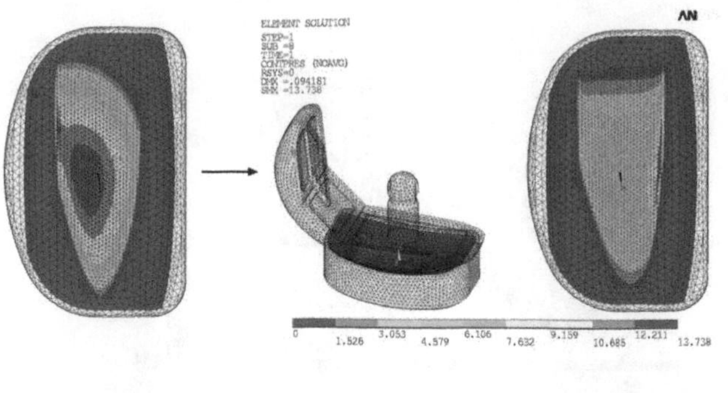

Fig.10 Result of optimization on a type with free PE insert in position 1

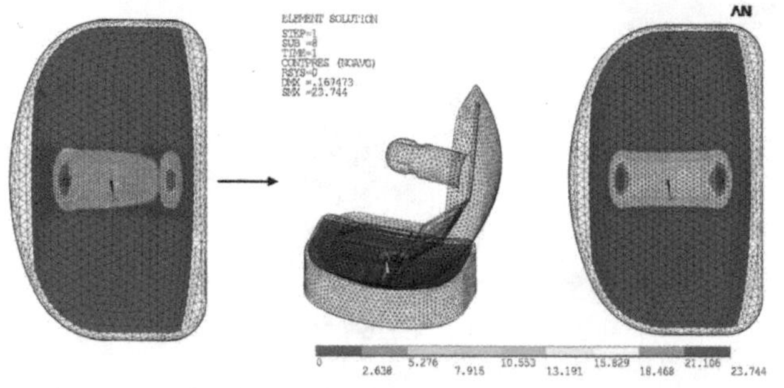

Fig.11 Result of optimization on a type with free PE insert in position 5

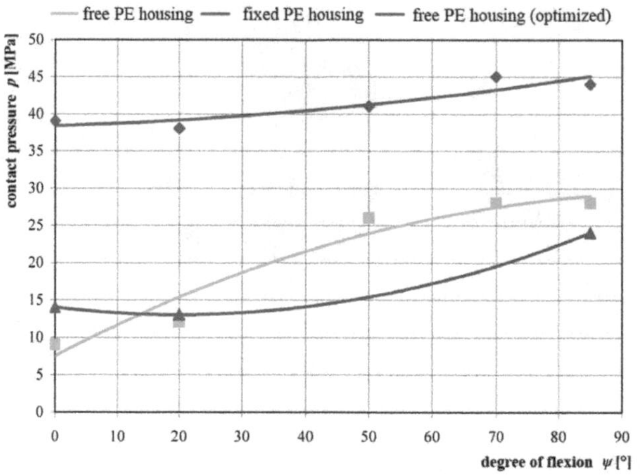

Fig.12 Results of contact pressure gained from FEM analyzes

5 Conclusions

An unicondylar knee replacement substitute only a half of the knee joint. This type of replacement is used when the damage is limited only to one side of the joint. This allows maintaining the healthy part of the knee, shortening the time and pricing. However, even with only half of the joint destroyed, many surgeons prefer doing a total knee replacement believing this is a better procedure than the half-knee (unicondylar) replacement. Nevertheless there are surgeons who believe it is more appropriate to perform a unicondylar knee replacement in the right circumstance.

In the article a contact pressure distribution on both tested types of partial knee replacement was performed. An experimental and a numerical approach were used for evaluation of contact pressures.

In general, performed experiments offered, comparing to FEM analyses, higher values of contact pressure. The highest difference between the two approaches was 18 MPa (32%). The type with a free housing seems to be more suitable for use thanks to its more effective contact pressure distribution. Graphical presentation of results gained from FEM analyzes can be seen on figure 12. Comparing of results with works of other authors (Guo, Y. et al. [1], Hopkins, A. R. et al. [2]) didn't show any major differences of values of contact pressures.

One of the main advantages of this work is that a new experimental approach was used compare to the usual numerical approach. FEM analysis is of course great apparatus but its results could be distorted by many factors. The most critical is the selection of boundary conditions, definition of contacts and finding a material model.

Testing of these modern knee replacements by static load in order to reveal the distribution of contact pressure is of course only one of many views to judge their usability. It's then a question how the chosen replacement should stand in other aspects (e.g. dynamic analyses, interaction with skeleton system, influence to biomechanics of joint, etc.). These are some of the subjects for our future work in the field of partial knee replacements.

References

1. Galvin A. L., Kang L., *Effect of conformity and contact stress on wear in fixed-bearing total knee prostheses*, Journal of Biomechanics, **42**(12), 1898-1902, (2009).
2. Guo Y., Zhang X., Chen W.: *Three-Dimensional Finite Element Simulation of Total Knee Joint in Gait Cycle*, Acta Mechanica Solida Sinica, **22**(4), 347-351, (2009).
3. Hopkins, Andrew R., New, Andrew M., Rodriguez-y-Baena F., Taylor M.: *Finite element analysis of unicompartmental knee arthroplasty*, Medical Engineering & Physics, **32**(1), 14-21, (2010).
4. Lin, Y.: *Experimental evaluation of a natural knee contact model using response surface optimization*, PhD thesis, University of Florida (2004)
5. Miyoshi, S., Takahashi, T., Ohtani M., Yamamoto H., Kameyama K.: *Analysis of the shape of the tibial tray in total knee arthroplasty using a three dimension finite element model*, Clinical Biomechanics, **17**(7), 521-525, (2002).
6. Rakotomanana, R.L., Leyvraz, P.F., Curnier, A., Heegaard, J.H., Rubin, P.J.: *A finite element model for evaluation of tibial prosthesis-bone interface in total knee replacement*, Journal of Biomechanics, **25**(12), 1413-1424, (1992).
7. Shi J.: *FEM of total knee replacement considering gait cycle load and malalignment*, PhD thesis, University of Wolverhampton, (2007)
8. Simpson, D.J., Gray, H., D'Lima, D., Murray D.W., Gill, H.S.: *The effect of bearing congruency, thickness and alignment on the stresses in unicompartmental knee replacements*, Clinical Biomechanics, **23**(9), 1148-1157, (2008).

26

Optimization of Source-Wire-Gas Systems for Efficient Robot Welding

Zdenek Hudec [1]

[1] Technical University of Liberec, KSP, Studentska 2, 46117 Liberec, Czech republic

Abstract – GMAW (Gas-Metal-Arc-Welding) as the last of main technologies, yet based for a most part on manual (semiautomatic) work, is gradually automated. But traditional advances of weld design, technology and quality assurance is not essentially changing. The result is non-efficient welding (overwelding). Especially T-joint (fillet weld), that is the most employed type of joint in welded structures, due to its geometry is often overwelded and twice or 3 times as much volume must be filled with metal as is needed for desired size. That increases not only direct costs and weight but also the shrinkage force and distortion that cause other added costs. This paper presents a new access to Design and Process optimization of T-joint and V-grooved Welding, based on fillet and butt weld performance efficiency optimizing of given source-wire-gas system with the help of set of experiments performance, proposed with DOE statistical method of central composite design. Moreover a new parametric field of stable metal transfer was discovered that markedly improves penetration and therefore performance efficiency.

Key words: GMAW, Fillet weld, T-joint, V-grooved joint, Optimization, Weld performance efficiency

1 Introduction

GMAW, used for joining of structural components, is widely employed as one of major fabrication process in industry and mostly plays a crucial role in determining the cost and quality of finished products and structures. Due to accompanying negative factors – stress and distortion, heat affected zone of base material, hydrogen absorption and defects emergence – using of welding technology is based on a very complex system of quality assurance. Design of weldments and welded structures has its own original multidisciplinary "production convenient" access, demonstrated on fig. 1.

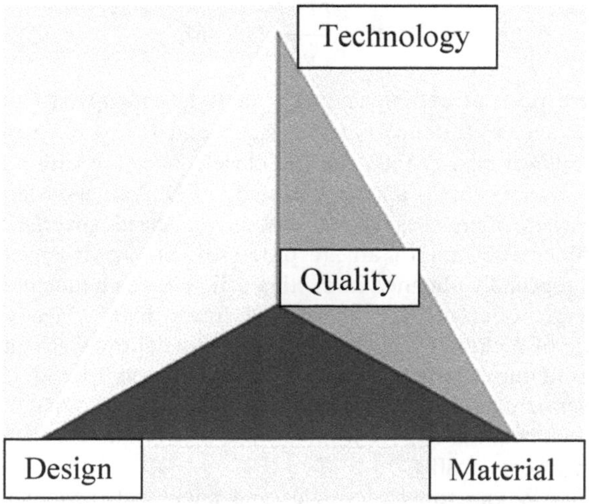

Fig. 1. Schema of welded structures design

Design must serve the purpose of structures, welded with chosen technology and material is chosen according to mechanical properties required in design, but the main factor of the whole design process there is join's property, connected with weldability that has changed from former material's factor to complex factor of quality assurance, defined (ISO) as keeping integrity of a material, manufactured with welding technology and preservation of joint properties, conform to design.

Quality assurance plays a crucial role in this system and due to fact, that quality of finished weldment cannot be evaluated by means of NDT control, another means of attests and various documents are used. Development from bureaucracy and paperwork to f.f.p. or f.f.s. (fitness for purpose or service) access is the main direction to welding productivity and efficiency increasing.

This access includes lightweight structures design with minimal share of additive weld metal that means assembled with minimum parts of minimal material's thickness and of course, as the base of it, joined with minimal number and volume of welds that is the object of this work. The following are GMAW "for and against" in this process.

1.1 General rule vs. overwelding and fit-up conditions

Even though all bead shapes are usable for various joint geometry and fit-up conditions in GMAW of structures and weldments, general rule of effective welding specifies that for stress-strain and metallurgical reasons in welding there is preferable to melt the minimum amount of material and melt the material with the minimum input energy because the energy, especially spent for melting of the consumable material significantly contributes to excessive welding costs and especially increases the shrinkage stress that affects distortion. Welded structure often includes many noise factors, such as poor fit-up. That makes difficult process automation. This is the reason why great portion of welding practice is still performed manually and therefore is based on welder skills that causes overwelding problem, especially for fillet welds (overwelding = laying down more weld metal than is structurally required).

1.2 GMAW metal transfer stability and melting rate

Replacing flux with shielding gas and GMAW (gas-metal-arc-welding) method developing has brought spatial freedom of arc that enabled robot application of arc, but at the costs of some process restriction. Process GMAW was the last of arc processes that was introduced to praxis. At 70-th, due to strong surface tension in low-current process stability field, only sources with improved dynamic condition and using thin wire, special short-arc metal transfer enabled welding with allowable spatter. Even now, welding pool dynamic behaviour during metal transfer causes that only several modes of metal transfer are useable inside of determined process variables fields. These fields vary each other with process intensity (power density), efficiency, productivity, certain material application and especially vary with source-wire-gas system used. Regarding to boundless development of GMAW method during last 40 years a lot of new source-wire–gas systems emerged and are performed for countless practical applications. Source with flat U-I characteristic with high speed feeding of thin wire and low penetrated short-arc process predicted this process for deposited (filled) welding. After first period, when only productivity and costs were concerned, special systems for special purposes begun to be developing during 90-th, when new inverter sources were developed. These sources opened new fields of stable metal transfer, especially non-spatter controlled droplet pulsed arc and two high productive processes – rapid short-arc and rotated arc. Both were high deposited but low penetrated. Revolutionary source improving was accompanied with 2 and 3 (or even 4) gases mixture shielding. Never-the-less this trend enabled only increasing of weld deposition rate = high productivity of bevel and gap filling that is not the same as welding.

Similar effect was reached with another way – using flux and metal cored wires with higher melting rates and better transfer stability than solid wires. All these methods of rapid filling the joint bevel with weld deposition suits well especially for manual (semiautomatic) welding and for variable and poor fit-up condition.

1.3 Manual and automatic manner of welding

Welder`s skills for filling any gap or bevel in any position with specified weld shape and size – that is the base of long and hard training in welding school. It is based on proper weaving of torch during slow forward movement. Some illustrated textbooks describe very closely this manner - Jeffus at al. [1], shown on fig. 3 and fig. 26. Current and therefore melting rate has to be low because of wire feed control assurance and than a penetration is shallow. On the contrary, automatic welding is mostly based on string bead with high travel speed and high current and therefore deep penetration.

The rate of automation in welding is increasing. Improved fit-up conditions due to precise details preparation and more accurate assembly, accompanied with CNC robot driving and laser sensing, supported with proper software, emulates real vision; all these factors together give the right conditions for replacing of manual welding methods with automation, costs reduction and productivity increasing.

1.4 GMAW power density, common criteria of process efficiency, conduction vs. convection

As mentioned above, due to base conception of GMAW, weld penetration depends on the net energy input, especially on the amperage value, so as the melting rate of the wire, therefore melting of the base metal and penetration is limited. Never-the-less due to complex action of various physical forces in heat and metal transfer and liquid flow in the weld pool, the resulted interval of dilution ranges from 30 to 60 % and the bead geometry varies in penetration from wide shallow to the narrow and deep finger-tip shape, very close to key-hole action.

Criteria used:

Dilution of weld metal with base metal $\boldsymbol{D}$ (1) is commonly used gauge for GMAW power density effect evaluation.

$$\boldsymbol{D} = (P_S - P_N)/P_S.100\ [\%], \qquad (1)$$

where $\boldsymbol{P_S}$ is weld bead etched cross-section area and $\boldsymbol{P_N}$ is deposited part of this area.

This purely geometrical criterion, even though it is accompanied with a current, has no connection with process variables and quality.

Melting efficiency η_m (2) is derived from the primary function performed by fusion welding heat sources that is to melt metal. The term efficiency denotes the fraction of the net energy input that actually melts base metal. Whereas the heat transfers (arc) efficiency is purely a heat source and used gas characteristic, the melting efficiency is a characteristic of both the heat source, gas and the process of heat transfer in the materials being joined. The melting efficiency under a given condition can be determined from post-weld knowledge of the cross-section area of the weld, the material welded, and the net energy input $\boldsymbol{Q_1}$ (3),

$$\eta_m = \frac{Q.(P_S - P_N)}{Q_1}, \qquad (2)$$

$$Q_1 = 0{,}06 \cdot \eta_a \cdot \frac{U \cdot I}{v_S}\ [\mathrm{kJ/cm}], \qquad (3)$$

where η_a is arc efficiency, **Q** is melting enthalpy, **I** (A) is amperage, $\mathbf{v_S}$ (m/min) is travel speed and **U** (V) is voltage. This power density indicator has close connection with process variables that is apparent in study of DuPont and Marder [2] where there was shown that travel speed governs the melting efficiency of all arc processes. Strong dependence was especially obtained in melting efficiency as a function of synergic effect of arc power and travel speed. Measured range of melting efficiency for various metal transfer conditions in our experiments was observed between 0.1 and 0.35. Nevertheless this factor is based on the model of radial conduction heat transfer (α/v_s factor) and also has no connection with process quality.

GMAW experimental studies and numerical modeling of heat transfer in weld pool during last ten years established that dominate mode of heat transfer during power density GMAW in the steel weld pool there is convection and the effect of various driving forces on liquid metal convection is highly complicated – as Wells [3] discussed. Advanced computational technique on the present enable creating more and more realistic model of heat and fluid flow during GMAW but the most realistic and easier access there is an experimental study.

2 New strategy for weld design and performance

Replacing manual welding with automation requires first of all changing common practice in design, performance, measuring and inspection of especially fillet welds.

2.1 Fillet weld design and performance optimization

2.1.1 Present state of design and performance for manual manner fillet welding

Fillet weld, especially in T-joint, is the most employed type of joint in welded structures. On the contrary of butt joint, the size of fillet is not limited with the thickness of material (except of lap joint on fig. 3) and therefore it inclines more to overwelding problems. It's ideal "filled" (fillet-deposited) cross-section area is throat size squared a^2 and every millimeter over its calculated size contributes with a great deal to area growing and in the same way to growing of costs and general shrinking force (fig. 2a). Common problem Fillet-Deposited Overwelding is simply a rate of measured (deposited) and ideal designed size squared.

Weld bead, created usually in PB position, slowly with torch weaving, directed 45^0 to the centre of the horizontal plate, is non-regular and has low penetration.

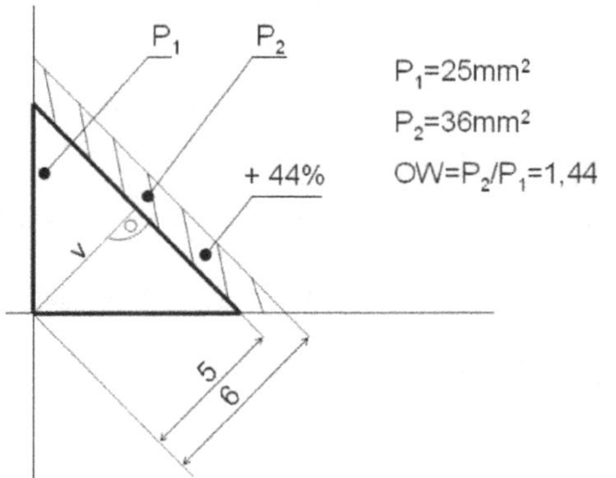

Fig. 2a. Fillet-deposited weld

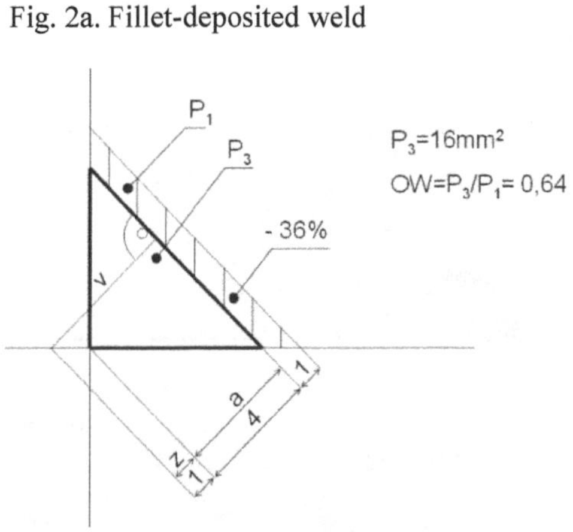

Fig. 2b. Fillet-penetrated weld

On the other hand, required deposited area dramatically decreases, when automatic welding in PA (ev. PG) position is used and penetration could be counted in computing the weld throat thickness **v** (fig. 2b). Manually led torch cannot turn profit this fact. More to the contrary, real weld mostly made in PB position has opposite no efficient unequal legs due to running a weld pool down, convex reinforcement and often root lack of penetration.

2.1.2 Fillet weld noise factors

A major problem with fillet welds is ensuring the gap between the components is within defined limits. Common sources of variability in fillet welding process include variations in part fit-up (root gap) and variation of the location of parts in the fixture (offset). These noise-factors have a great influence on real depth of penetration and thus weld size.

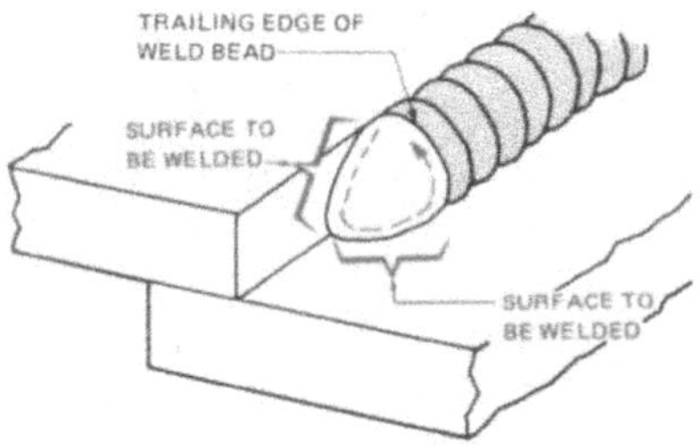

Fig. 3. Manual manner of fillet deposition [1]

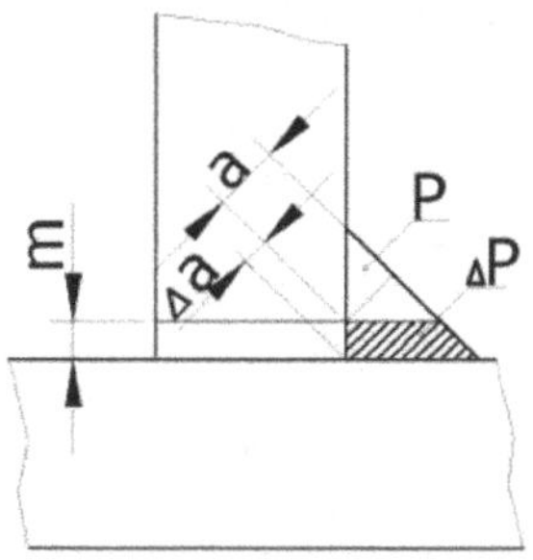

Fig. 4. Poor fit-up and wasted deposited area

Mostly a gap is not variable as codes assume but noise factor that represents sum of production and fit-up allowances and cannot be set. For fillet-deposited weld that grips two T-joined sheets every gap between them affects waste of weld-deposited area. Along the length of a T-joint, perfect fit is never possible, and some small gaps will exist. As illustrated on fig. 4, if the size of the gap between the two members increases, and if the fillet weld leg size is kept the same, the actual weld throat and its load capacity decreases. In poor fit-up fillet weld wasted area ΔP dramatically increases with growing gap dimension m as showed on fig. 4 and following equation (4):

$$\Delta P = m.(\sqrt{2}.a + m/2) \text{ [mm}^2\text{]} \quad (4)$$

E.g. weld sized 5 mm consume by 64% more material when 2 mm gap should be included.

2.1.3 Automatic and robotic fillet shape design and measuring

Essentially automatic welding process proposal must differ from manual. First of all string bead root penetration has to be directed to the gap (fig. 5) and special high power density regime has to be used. This regime was revealed during our experimenting with new inverter source [4]. Our experiments with GMAW confirmed existence and usability of deep penetrated arc process that researched Mendez at all for GTAW (Gas-Tungsten-Arc-Welding) [5].

Measuring and optimization of fillet-penetrated weld supposes to choose some base factor to compare. Maximal reachable penetration with acceptable reinforcement for given source-wire-gas condition, as a result of DOE based experimental research, was proposed as the base value and signed as Fillet Efficiency [4].

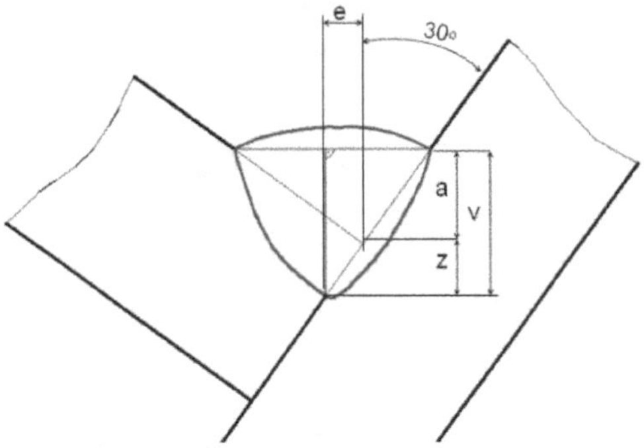

Fig. 5. Unequal-legged weld (deposit) with equal penetration

A value of max. weld penetration is the distance from the root of the fillet to the point at which fusion penetrates into the gap direction (**x** on fig. 12). This unequal-legged outer weld shape was legalized in latest edition of standard specifications [9], that enable to count penetration of fillet weld towards the effective throat size and this shape in etched weld cross-section should to be close to ideal isosceles triangle with its vertex on fillet joint gap (fig. 6). This was challenge for measurement producers enable to measure these unequal-legged welds [6], fig. 7.

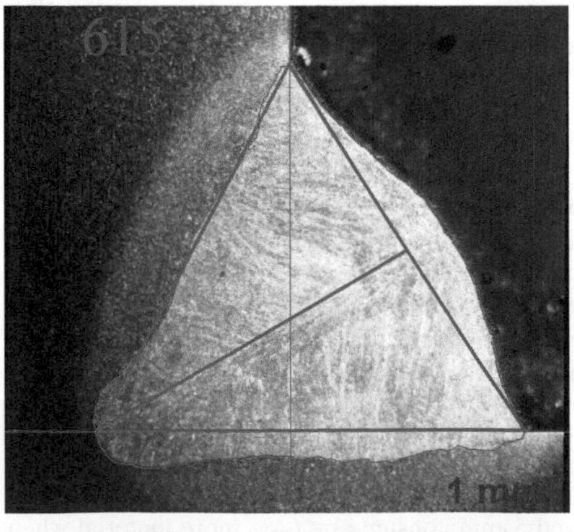

Fig. 6. Efficient shape of fillet-penetrated weld

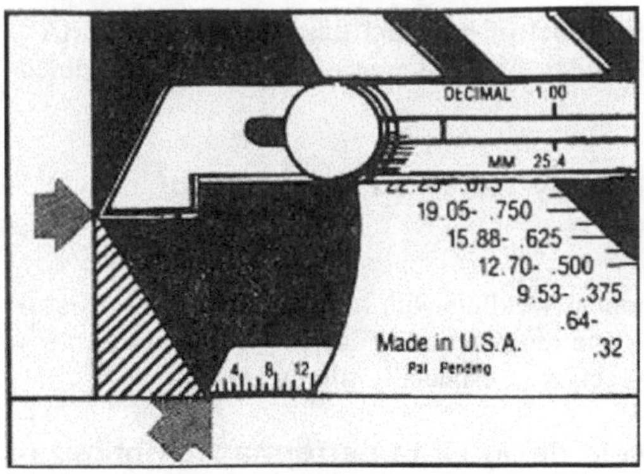

Fig. 7. Unequal-legged fillet gage [6]

2.2 Mathematical models of Fillet Efficiency (FE) evaluation

Two factors are principal for fillet efficiency evaluation – depth of penetration (x, z) and outer fillet deposited shape and area (**P**). Base of solved problem was to derive shape of ideal weld and evaluate rate of real and ideal shaped fillet weld. Three models were proposed and experienced during our several years' research:

1. $P = f(z), \quad v_t = const.$ (5)
2. $P = f(x), \quad v = const.$ (6)
3. $v_t = f(x), \quad P = const.$ (7)

where v, v_t, z is described on Fig. 10.

2.2.1 Model of penetration tailored weld geometry

The first model seems to be the most comprehensive. It introduces ideal welds shape compare that can be called as "depth of penetration tailored fillet weld geometry design". Weld deposited cross-section area **P**, for constant (ideal) throat size $\mathbf{v_t}$, is depended on reached depth of penetration **z**. Schema on fig. 8 and diagram on fig. 9 show that a curve of this relation starts with full-fillet weld with no penetration and ends with full-penetration joint without added consumable.

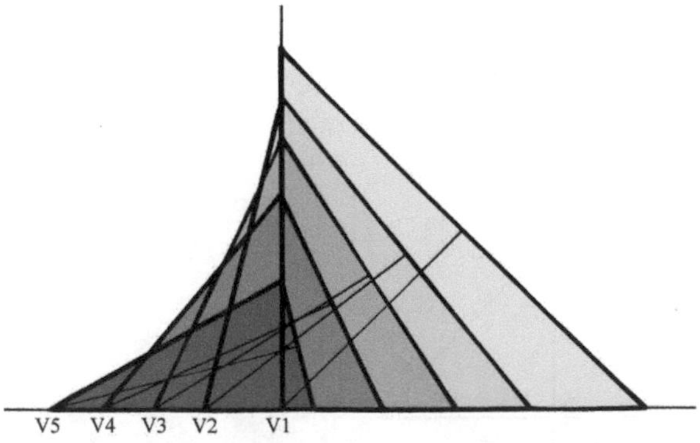

Fig. 8. Fillet deposited area **P** as a function of penetration **z** with constant throat size $\mathbf{v_t}$

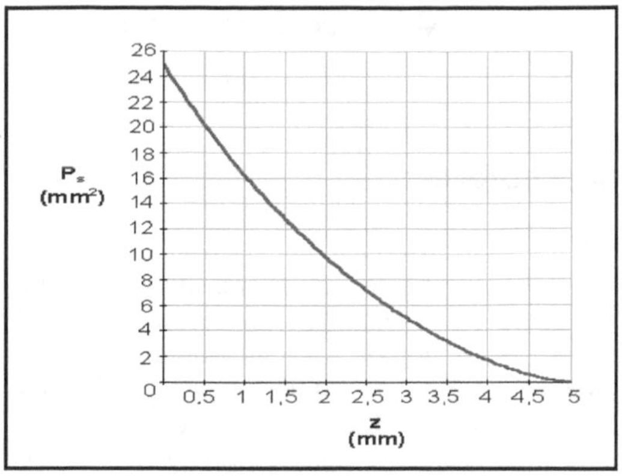

Fig. 9. Diagram P = f(z) for v_t = const.= 5 mm

Max. value of **Penetration Efficiency:**

$$\mathbf{PE = z/v_t} \quad (8)$$

of DOE optimized set of experiments there is characteristic value of every source-wire-gas system that intend variables field, deposition area and filet size included, where should be defined system effectively used. But this value is growing with amperage and travel speed growing, out of acceptable real fillet weld shape.

Real shape is concerned comparing of real fillet throat **v** to ideal $\mathbf{v_t}$, derived from ideal shape of deposited weld of the same, constant value of deposited area **P**.

Deposition Efficiency:

$$\mathbf{DE = v/v_t} \quad (9)$$

is correcting factor of **PE** that evaluates waste of reinforcement and a weld pool running down of real weld and therefore it is a factor of quality assurance. Considering that $\mathbf{v/v_t}$ ratio allows higher reinforcement, for the 1-st quality welds achieving can be used more restricted:

$$\mathbf{DE = a/a_t}. \quad (9a)$$

Fillet Efficiency:

$$\mathbf{FE = PE\ .\ DE} \quad (10)$$

considers both these factors and was chosen as response value for source-wire-gas system optimization.

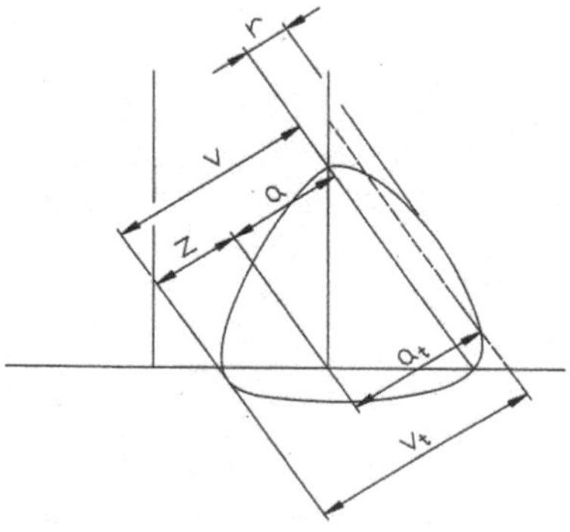

Fig. 10. Measured and calculated values

This model should be perfectly used for ideal or near ideal shaped and penetrated welds (fig. 6). Far from ideal shape, experiments are less valuable (fig. 11).

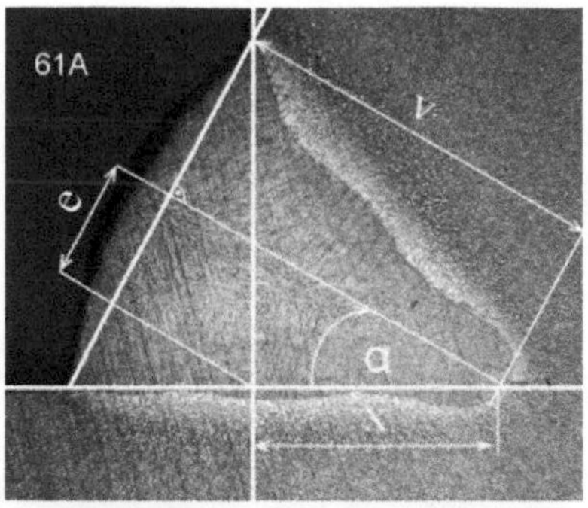

Fig. 11a

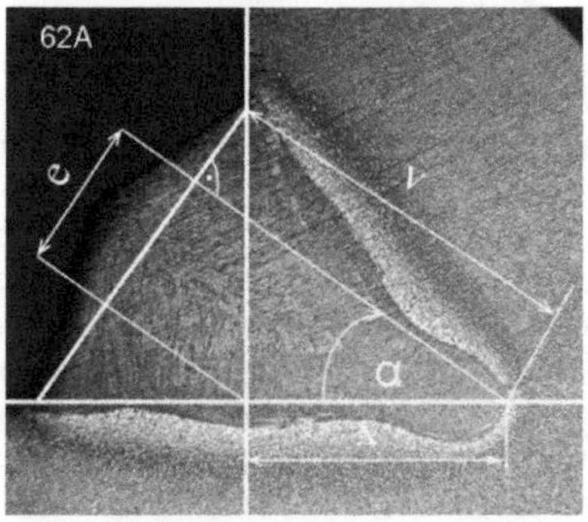

Fig. 11b

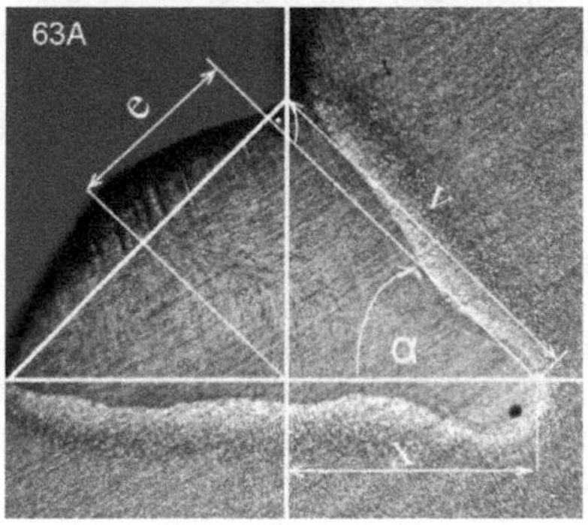

Fig. 11c

Fig. 11a,b,c. The same regime but different weld deposition shapes and different DE that evaluates waste of material

2.2.2 Overwelding measuring model

Second model was based on real fixed value of x-axis penetration **x** (replacing the changing value of weld-axis penetration **z** in 1-st model) but for constant value of real throat **v**, that is transforming to ideal shaped area $\mathbf{P_m}$ (min. area for given throat).

Penetration Efficiency $\mathbf{PE = x/v}$ (11)

is also corrected with

Deposition Efficiency $\mathbf{DE = P_m/P}$ (12)

when compared real and ideal value of **P** for resulted

Fillet Efficiency FE (10).

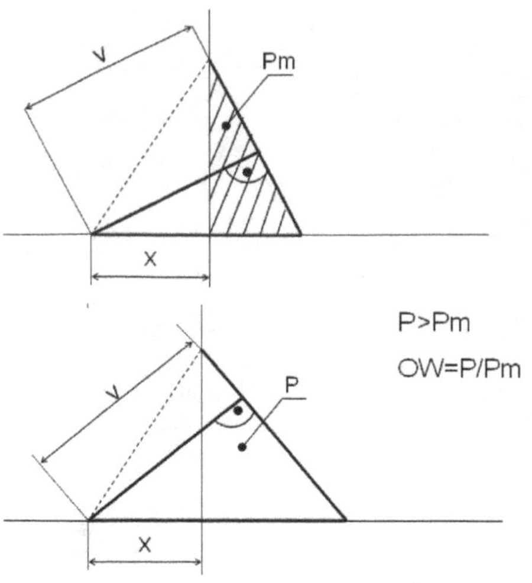

Fig. 12. Ideal and real weld with the same load-bearing throat

Real values - penetration **x** and throat **v** gives only one minimal triangle of deposition with area $\mathbf{P_m}$. Proposed methodology issues from fact that real and ideal fillet weld have the same depth of penetration and effective throat and differ only with cross-sectional area of deposited (filled) material. Simple dilution of area values $\mathbf{P/P_m}$ gives Fillet-Penetrated Overwelding value at % (fig. 12) that is inverse value of DE. This is the first attempt to express overwelding factor for deep penetrated fillet weld. This model can be used for good compare of deposition efficiency of any fillet weld shape.

2.2.3 Technological model of equal deposition

Third model is more close to real condition of GMAW process as mentioned above; penetration is matched to weld deposition because both are derived from amperage. Smaller deposition area cannot give the same penetration. Therefore **x** and **P** must be constant and **v** is changing (fig. 13) due to weld and torch geometry condition. Assumptions are similar to 1-st and 2-nd model.

Penetration Efficiency $\mathbf{PE = x/v_t}$, (13)

DE (9),, but now efficiency of real weld of any shape should be directly compared with ideal shaped weld of the same penetration **x** and weld deposition area **P**. This model with the most complex mathematical solution (quartic equation) seems to be the most practical solution of fillet-penetrated performance efficiency measuring and calculating.

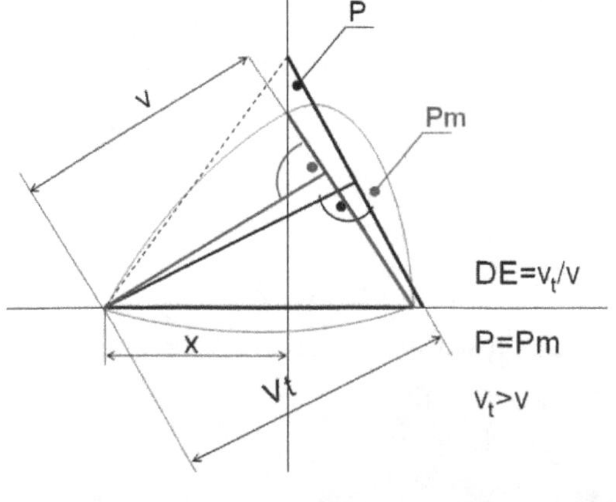

Fig. 13. Ultimate solution of FE measuring and calculating

3 Power density GMAW performance and its optimization

3.1 Short-spray process

In preliminary research all commonly used GMAW metal transfer regions were investigated (short arc, spray, rapid arc, pulsed arc) in synergic and out of synergy regimes, and all mentioned power density criteria were measured in addition to other geometrical parameters of an etched weld cross-section with the help of NIS-Elements software. The most interesting parametric field was found circa 6 V below standard spray process (fig.14). This field, throughout synergic lines, showed very deep penetration with high wire feed and travel speeds. Spray transfer was shortened and frequency of droplets was increased. An only excellent dynamic property of the used inverter power source enables this process. Several source-wire-gas systems were investigated and comprehensive diagrams of effective variables fields were obtained and published.

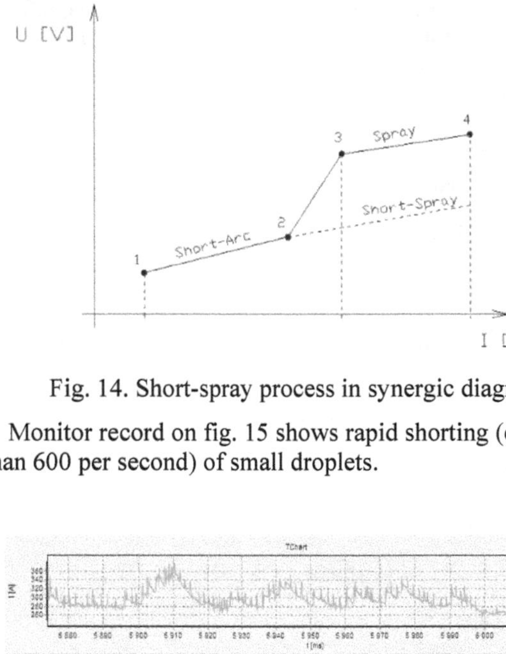

Fig. 14. Short-spray process in synergic diagram

Monitor record on fig. 15 shows rapid shorting (even more than 600 per second) of small droplets.

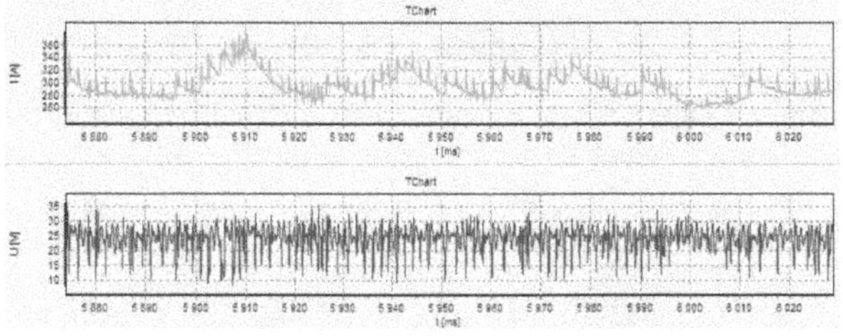

Fig.15. Short-spray process monitoring

3.2 Automatic fillet weld noise factors

The parts to be joined by fillet welds shall be brought into as close contact as practicable (AWS D1.1:2008). Special series of experiments were performed to study the effect of these noise factors on the fillet efficiency. The result seems to be quite promising to practical application because it was confirmed that root gap up to 0.5 mm has no or even beneficial influence to fillet efficiency (fig. 16) and also offset ranges +- 0.2 – 0.3 mm from the weld axis, depending on type of wire-gas composition, has also minimal influence on fillet efficiency.

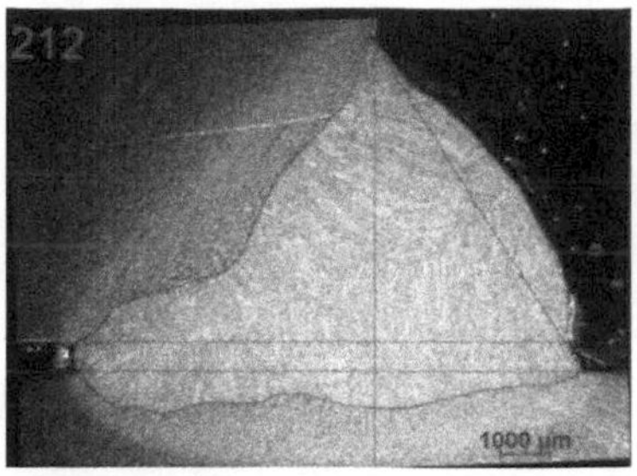

Fig. 16. Positive effect of small gap to penetration

3.3 Variables selection and optimization

Careful choice of variables is the basic necessity for successful results. Wire feed speed, travel speed, open arc voltage and contact tip-to-work distance are the main variables that can be set before welding. Amperage and voltage can be measured only during welding.

Our preliminary wide experimental research reduced all welding variables to 2 basic independent parameters – wire feed speed (WFS) $\mathbf{v_D}$ and travel speed (TS) $\mathbf{v_S}$. In respect to the defined goal, all remaining variables can be adjusted in a close dependence to these two main. Above mentioned research over an extensive parameters field allocated region of interest of near-optimum response conditions for given set of input conditions. Due to expected strong curvature in this region of FE response surface, statistical second order model "central composite design of experiments" was used – fig. 17 [7]. Choice of this model supposes a good knowledge of the process because the first step there is estimation of center (optimal) point and parameters levels range. Only solution, where point of maximum response is inside of field, is acceptable. Including minimum 3 center runs, design matrix consists of 11 sets of coded variables for experimental runs (tab. 1). For the case of two independent variables and their interactions the model is as follows:

$$y = b_0 + b_1x_1 + b_2x_2 + b_{11}x_1^2 + b_{22}x_2^2 + b_{12}x_1x_2 + \varepsilon \qquad (14)$$

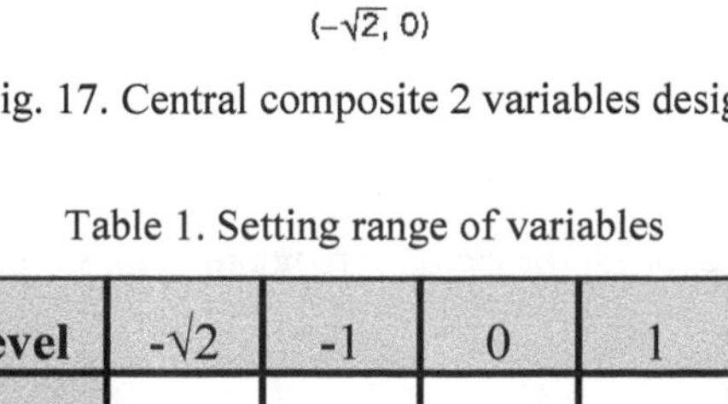

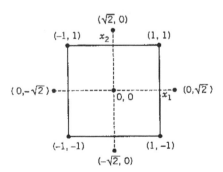

Fig. 17. Central composite 2 variables design

Table 1. Setting range of variables

var./level	-√2	-1	0	1	√2
v_D (m/min.)	11,6	12,3	13	13,7	14,4
P_M (mm^2)	10	13	16	19	22

Together with additional runs for stabilization and confirmation of FE response surface field, about 20 runs were performed for optimization of one set of input (material-source-wire-gas) conditions. Resulted two-dimensional contours plots of optimal variables operational windows on the base of v_D-v_S diagrams are shown in the next section. Number of experiments depends on a good estimation and is controlled with resulted statistical values.

3.4 Quality assurance during optimization

Several source-wire-gas systems were optimized as a foundation of potential database for implementation to robot control systems. Using 1.2 mm solid or cored wire, there was no case of optimized weld with non-acceptable outer shape according valid codes. The same can be said for 1.0 mm wire but without respect to quality level. The wire 0.8 mm was very difficult to optimize. Using high power density process for this diameter, narrow and reinforced welds were produced.

Except of outer weld shape requirements, no other defects were necessary followed. Small root pores were RTG evaluated as negligible and only very high power regime combined with "cold" gas mixture, improper weld geometry or great gap, effected hot crack (fig. 18) or tunnel porosity emergence.

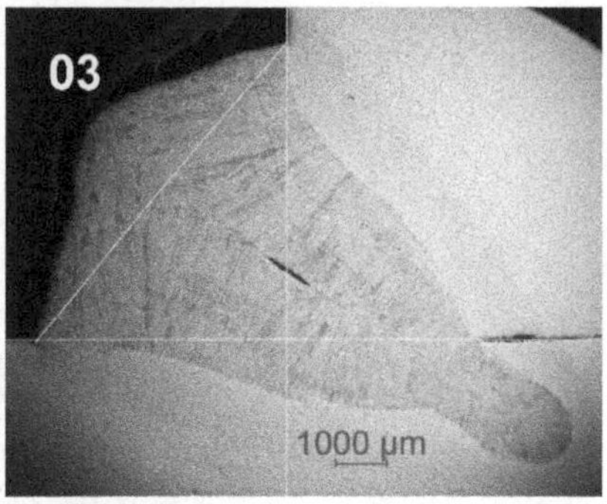

Fig. 18. Regime 448 A with Ar 92%/ CO_2 8% gas

Praxis realization of deep penetrated and unequal-fillet-outer-shaped welding needs employment of different quality assurance method. Precise solution would be with application of Laser scan as a measuring device for weld deposit geometry. Although every code permits to count penetration in computing the weld throat thickness, nobody in industry would realize it without attesting of real weld shape and depth of penetration. Contribution of penetration to fillet size should be measured only with non-destructive testing. Latest research of Noncontact Ultrasound "time of flight" weld penetration depth measuring [10] should be very promising for this purpose. Using RGLS TOF technique has proven to be accurate, precise and repeatable both off-line after welding and on-line during welding that enable closed loop control of weld penetration depth, analogical to other technological processes and can be incorporated into a robotic welding machine. Using closed loop control of weld penetration is associated with further lowering costs and improving quality.

4 Examples of source-wire-gas systems optimization (the same material)

4.1 System MIGATRONIC BDH 550 – ESAB Aristorod 1.2 mm – AirProducts Feromaxx Plus (Ar/He/CO_2)

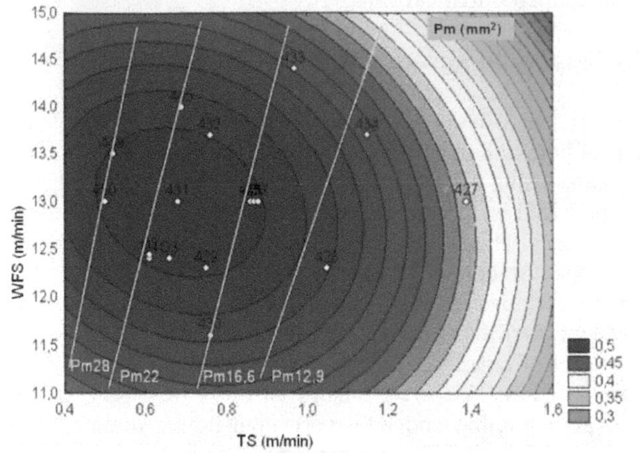

Fig. 19. FE optimized field

Fig. 19 shows the resulted diagram of system optimization, where there is evident optimal operational window of the main variables – wire feed speed and travel speed.
Near optimal weld no. 431 is on fig. 20.

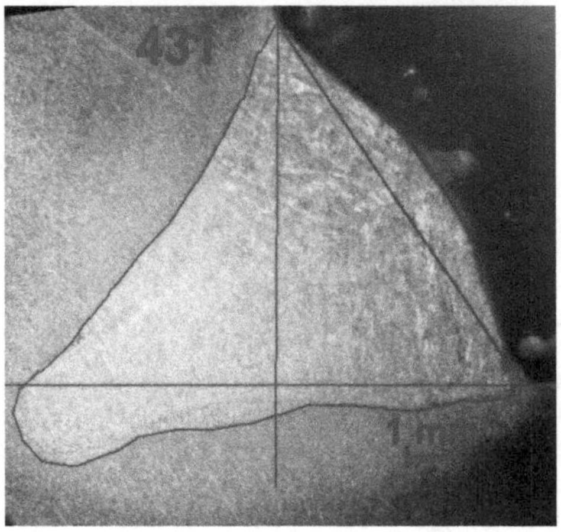

Fig. 20. The nearest weld to optimal peak

Due to He content in shielding gas mixture, efficiency of heat transfer is high that causes deep and regular penetration, without finger tip effect and gives more acceptable weld shape.

4.2 System MIGATRONIC BDH 550 – Filarc PZ 6102 1.2 mm - Ar/CO_2 82/18

Metal cored wire Filarc PZ 6102 has a higher deposition rate and wider and shallower penetration. Smoother surface with minimal reinforcement classify these welds as the best and of easier assured quality, but efficiency and productivity does not reach values of solid wires (figs. 21, 22).

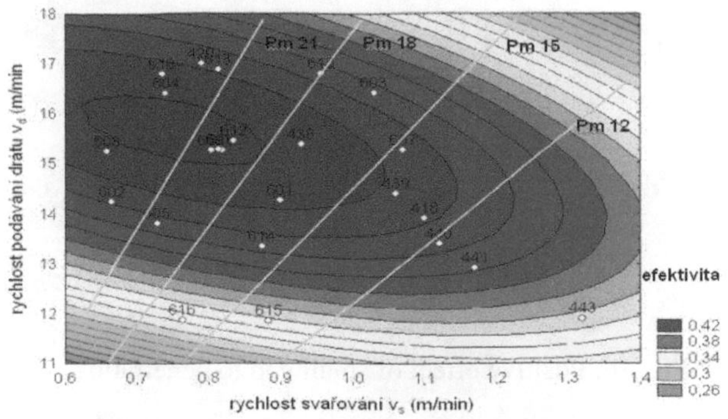

Fig. 21. FE optimized field

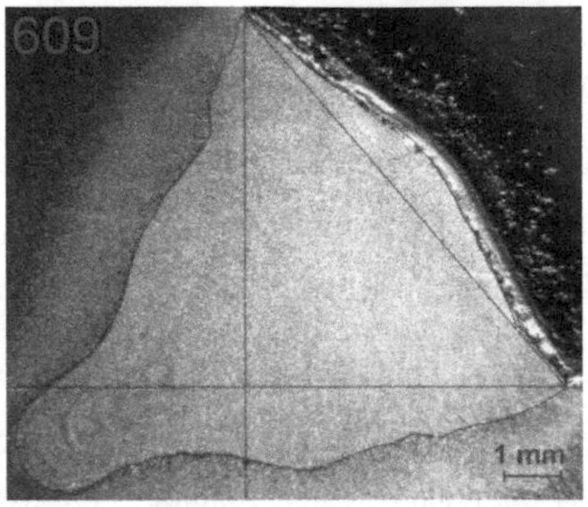

Fig. 22. The nearest weld to optimal peak

4.3 System MIGATRONIC SIGMA 500 – ESAB Aristorod 1.2 mm – AirProducts Feromaxx Plus (Ar/He/CO_2)

The same wire and gas as in first case was combined with new inverter source. After a few preliminary experiments that showed excellent stability of metal transfer, experimental field was moved to higher parameters field, but it turned out too optimistic and until second set of experiments (fig. 23) showed regular enclosed and statistically stable optimized field (fig. 24), evidently moved to higher travel speed.

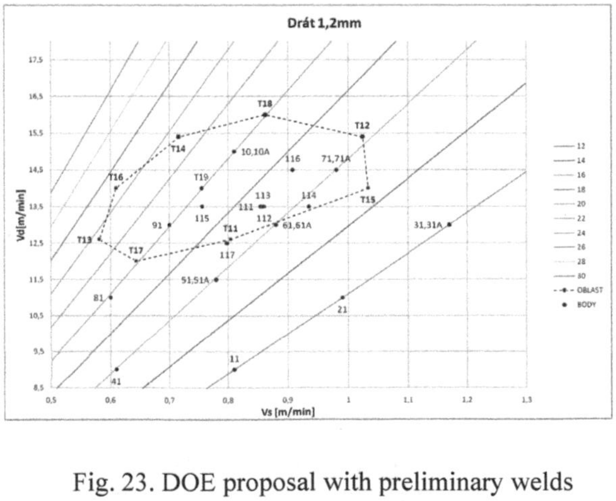

Fig. 23. DOE proposal with preliminary welds

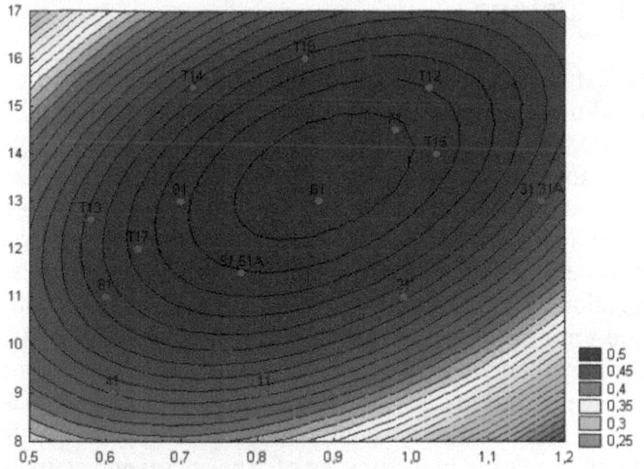

Fig. 24. Resulted FE optimized field

5 V-grooved Butt weld design and performance optimization

5.1 Present state of design and performance (manual manner, overwelding)

Poor fit-up for beveled weld (an excessive gap between the matching faces of the materials) is the most common imperfection caused with poor workshop practice or poor dimensioning and tolerance dimensions on drawings.

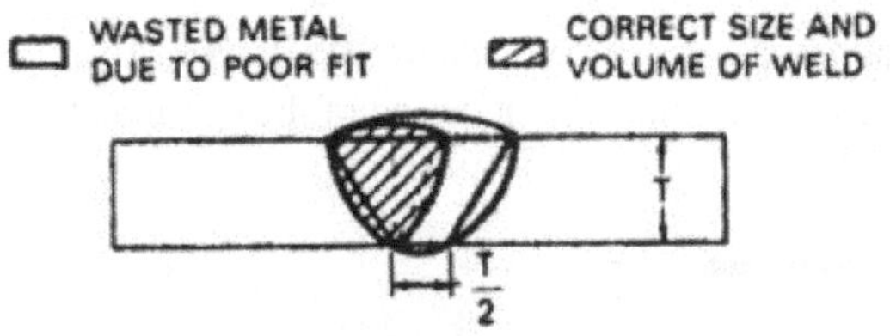

Fig. 25. Overwelding due to increased root opening of the groove [8]

In butt weld, cross section of wasted area = thickness of material x excessive width of gap as showed on fig. 25.

To the contrary of a fillet weld, butt weld is always designed as full-penetrated and in case of one side weld without backing (e.g. tube) for manually performed welding, that is showed on fig. 26, and minimum gap is prescribed for assurance of a perfect fusion of root back side. Welding to open root would be performed slowly with low parameters and therefore low penetration and productivity. Only experienced welders can provide this work out of position in RTG quality.

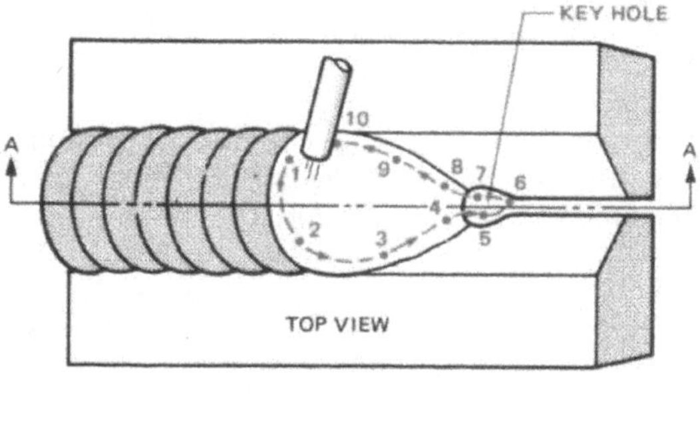

Fig. 26. Manual manner of butt weld deposition with back side root fusion assurance [1]

Root ceramic backing and if possible double-sided welding may replace this difficult, slow, quality-risk and wasteful method, but automation is really the only efficient solution.

5.2 Automated butt weld design shape and penetration

Automated string bead high power density weld has deep and uniform penetration and dilution. The shape of the groove should be tailored according to its experienced optimized shape. Great difference between design for manual and automated V-grooved weld is shown on fig. 27 [8]. Double-sided welding, when possible, needs half of the deposited area and ensures better root penetration (fig. 28) as it is known from literature [8].

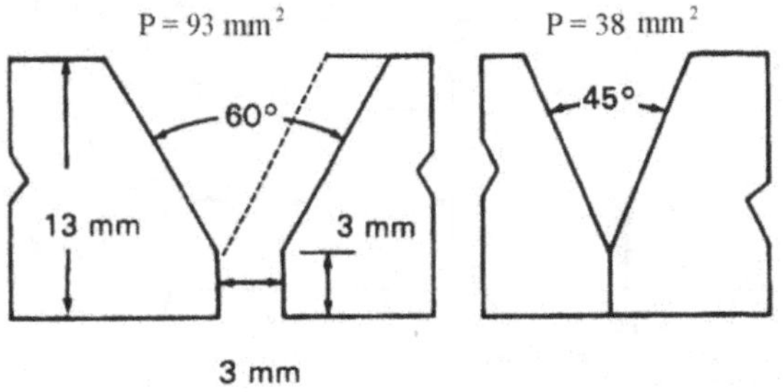

Fig. 27. Bevel design for manual and automated welding

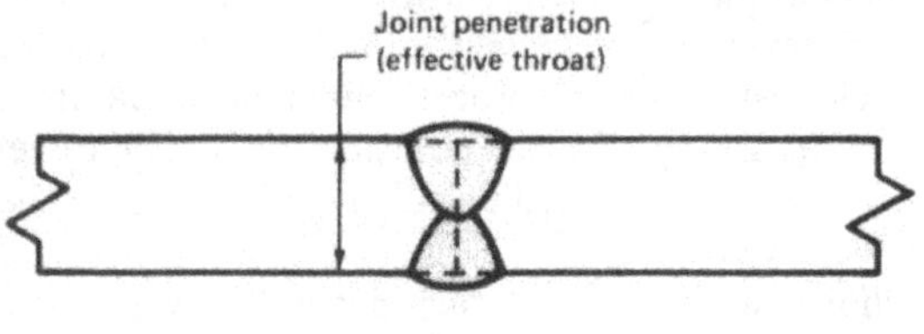

Fig. 28. Double-sided welding

5.3 Mathematical model of V-grooved weld shape efficiency

The objective of an efficient V-grooved weld is the same as in fillet weld – to reach maximal rate of penetration with minimal deposition, but now deposited part is defined by the V-groove area that is determined by the groove depth **a** and the groove angel **α** on fig. 28. Deposited area can be calculated with (15):

$$P = \sqrt{a^2 / \sin\alpha} \tag{15}$$

Compared to the fillet weld, mathematical model of the V-groove is very simple:

$$BE = v/P \tag{16}$$

Butt Efficiency BE = maximum rate of load-bearing dimension **v** for definite deposited area **P.**

Efficiency for butt weld with reinforcement is:

$$BE = v/P_n, \tag{16a}$$

where P_n is area of real weld deposition with reinforcement.

5.4 V-grooved weld shape efficiency optimization

DOE optimization of V-grooved welds has one parameter more than for fillet welds and minimal 3 variables field should be estimated for experimental program of design-process optimization. Fig. 29 shows preliminary DOE rough proposal for 2 dimensions of V-groove design optimization for deposition area, experienced in fillet weld research and with welding parameters, attested in fillet research. Results showed susceptibility to hot cracking and worse penetration accuracy for narrow bevels.

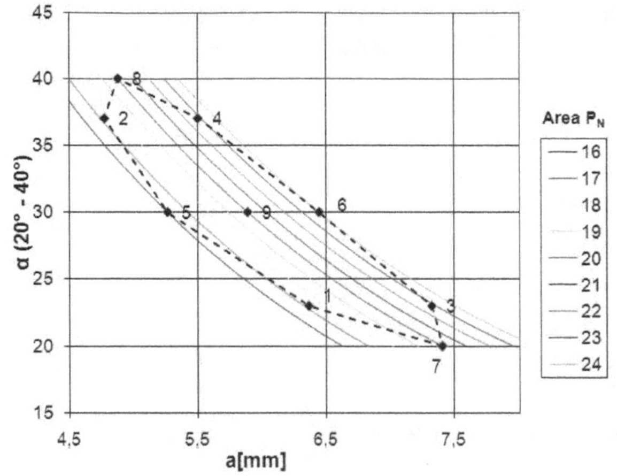

Fig. 29. DOE bevel edge proposal

With respect of these results, following 3 parameters DOE proposal used bevels range moved to higher values, out of hot cracks field, using resulted process parameters field from fillet weld optimization. Tunnel porosity for higher travel speeds showed as another quality risk in this case, on the contrary to fillet welds.

Fig. 30 shows an example of deep penetrated V-grooved weld, evaluated with geometric analysis, with a help of SW NIS-Elements.

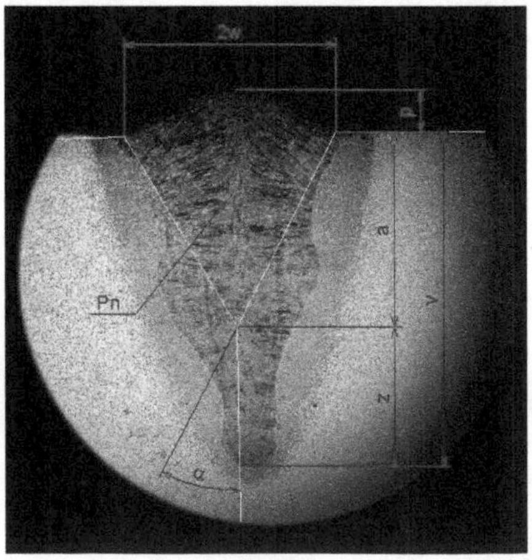

Fig. 30. Geometric analysis of V-grooved weld

6 Conclusions

Substantial differences in the technological characteristics and conditions between manual (semiautomatic) and automatic GMAW processes were discussed and original approach to the optimization of GMAW automatic process was proposed and demonstrated. GMAW process as the most employed and enhanced welding technology has a great variety in systems and conditions used. In a majority of cases, optimization of a particular application is still realized with trial-and-error approach that spends a lot of time and costs. Proposed method requires material and time for only about 20 to 30 weld designs, so the tests performance and evaluation could minimize costs and redundant procedure development and can save industry a lot of money. Several source-wire-gas systems were optimized as the start of potential database building for needs of designers and technologists as one of presented essential conditions for the especially real fillet throat size control welding process application.

Moreover a new parametric field of stable metal transfer was discovered that markedly improves penetration and therefore performance efficiency and brings no additional investments and is more versatile than new Hybrid Laser-MIG process that is solving the same problem.

Acknowledgement

Special thanks to MIGATRONIC CZ for technical support. This study is included in the frame of the research plan MSM 4674788501.

References

1. L. Jeffus, H.V. Johnson, *Welding: Principles and Applications, 2nd ed,* Delmar Pub., (1988)
2. J.N. DuPont, A.J. Marder, *Thermal Efficiency of Arc Welding Processes,* Welding Journal, 406 – 416, (1995).
3. A.A. Wells, *Heat Flow in Welding*, Welding Journal **31**(5), (1952)
4. Z. Hudec, *GMA Fillet Welds Design and Process Parameters Optimization,* Ph.D. thesis, Technical University of Liberec, (2005)
5. P.F. Mendez, T.W. Eagar, Penetration *and Defect Formation in High- Current Arc Welding,* Welding Journal **82**(10), 296 – 306 (2003*).*
6. *G.A.L. gage co. catalogue*
7. R.H. Myers, *Response Surface Methodology,* John Wiley & Sons Inc. N.Y., (1995)
8. *AWS Welding Handbook*
9. *EN ISO 5718*
10. A. Kita, I.C. Ume, *Measuring On-Line and Off-Line Non-contact Ultrasound Time of Flight Weld Penetration Depth,* Welding Journal Jan., 9 – 17 (2007).

Optimization of Baropodometric Device Instrumentation

Fany Chedevergne[1,a], Alain Burtheret[1], Marc Dahan[1], Bernard Parratte[2]

[1] FEMTO-ST Institute - Department of Applied Mechanics, University of Franche-Comte, 25 000 Besançon, France
[2] Laboratory of Physical Medicine and Rehabilitation, University of Franche-Comte, 25 000 Besançon, France

Abstract – This article presents the development of a baropodometric device. The aim is to record foot-to-ground force during natural gait. The device consists of an instrumented shoe equipped with force sensors wired to a backpack laptop. The instrumentation should be light, efficient, easy to use for clinical staff and adapted to fit most patients' gait. Thus, we looked to optimize sensor location under the foot and sensor dimensions inside the sole. Numerical simulation and tensile tests lead us to conceive CuBe2 tubular-shaped sensors and specifically-shaped contact aluminum plates. We chose weight/efficiency optimal acquisition system. And we developed a whole treatment process and following graph visualization, optimized over time running and easiness of results reading. Then, we realized dynamic calibration and dead loads weighting to validate our conception. Finally, clinical testing is performed. The gait of the four healthy subjects is presented through the innovating graph visualization.

Key words: Baropodometry; Plantar dynamics; Sensor dimension; Plantar force graph visualization

1 Introduction

Measurement of foot-to-ground force distribution is used for clinical evaluation of foot and gait pathologies. Baropodometric device provides a description of the foot dynamics and thus are clues to detect and predict musculo-skeletic traumas. The various areas of the foot are differently loaded depending on the pathology. For example, if the center of pressure rapidly leaves the heel area to the forefoot, this could indicate a short gastrocnemius muscle and consecutive metatarsal aches (Kowalski [1]).

Mats are ideal to record barefoot walking pressure whereas insoles are generally used for the contact between the foot and the shoe sole. They are both well-known easy-to-use and accurate devices (Allard [2], Cavanagh [3], Herzog [4], Meyring [5], Perry [6], Perttunen [7], Viel [8]). In both case, the number of sensors can reach four per square centimetre, which gives a high spatial precision of the measurement. Sensors are very slim and do not create discomfort. However, these high-technology tools are quite fragile and quite expensive. Moreover, such numerous sensors are not useful. The analysis process of the authors usually runs through a division of the footprint into very few areas, e.g. external and internal parts of the heel, mid-foot, metatarsal heads and toes regions. It wonders the clinical necessity of such numerous sensors.

Various instrumented shoes are also able to record plantar forces (Asphahani [9], Faivre [10], Gross [11], Kirtley [12], Miyazaki [13], Ranu [14], Spolek [15]). The sensor number is limited to one per area of interest. That reduced considerably the data processing duration. Unfortunately most of these authors focused strictly on heel and metatarsal heads. And some discomfort can occur as sensors are located either upon the sole or under the sole. That's why, Asphahani [9] and Faivre [10] proposed instrumented shoes with sole-incorporated sensors. The sensors are inside the sole and spread under the quite entire foot. Used sensors are metallic and based on strain gauge technology which ensures long life-expectancy and cheap price. However, those devices are still under development.

We are here continuing Faivre's work by improving the instrumentation and the data process. Faivre's prototype is covered by the European patent number EP 1 464 281 B1 (Faivre [16]). The mechanical process and the medical interest have been previously validated (Faivre [17]). This article presents the last evolution of these instrumented shoes. Design, treatment process, mechanical calibration and clinical tests are reported. An innovating visualization graph is used to draw the plantar force distribution along the stance phase.

2 Materials

2.1 Design of the baropodometric device

The new prototype (Fig. 1) is based on a pair of Pedar® wild-opening medical slippers. The thickness of the slipper soles has been pierced to incorporate force sensors. Sensors are thicker than the sole thickness so that they contact both foot and ground. The sole move freely around the sensors. During the stance phase, sensors are compressed with no alteration from the sole. The sensor strain is recorded and translated into force. During oscillation phase, the unstrained signal is recorded and used as the zero reference for next compression phase.

The number and locations of the sensors are in accordance with the usual mask used for insoles data analysis (Bertsch

[a] Corresponding author: fany.chedevergne@univ-fcomte.fr

[18], Hennig [19], Meyring [5]). Two sensors are located under the heel, four under the mid-foot, three under the metatarsal heads and two under the hallux and remaining toes. The number of sensors locations has thus been raised from eight to eleven in order to complete the entire sole. Previous prototype focussed on the healthy pathway of the foot stance, ignoring medial mid-foot and little toes. This new set of sensor covers the entire foot and will allow recording any healthy or pathological lay on the floor.

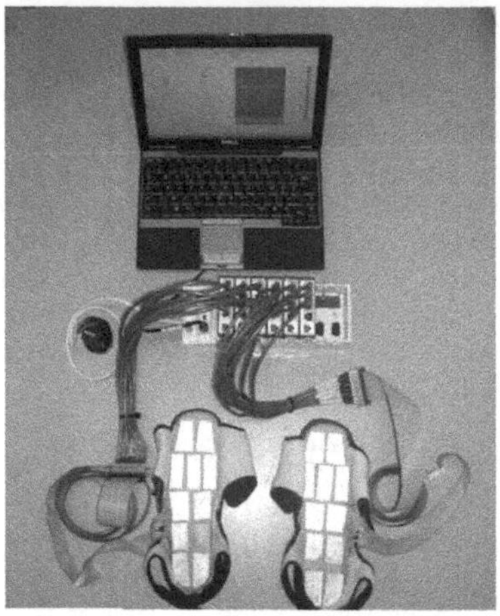

(a) Picture of the baropodometric device: a pair of instrumented slippers, a sensor conditioner and an acquisitioning laptop

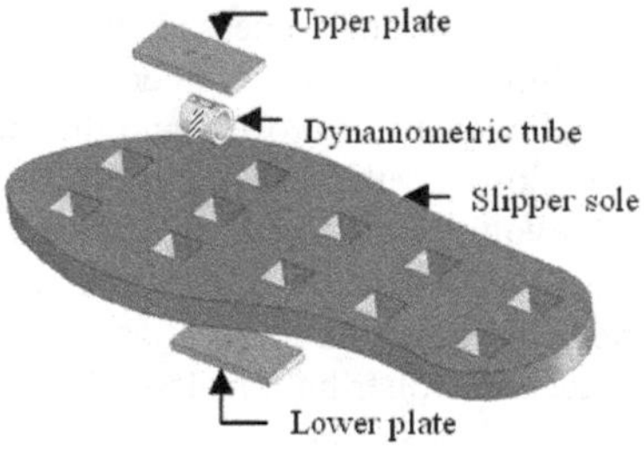

(b) Scheme of the sensors setup and distribution in the slipper
Fig. 1. The new prototype

Sensors are still CuBe2 dynamometric rings turned into dynamometric tubes by increased length from 8 to 16 mm. Nowadays, not only one but two precision strain gauges (resistance of 350 Ω) are pasted on each tube. The tube lies horizontally and from aft forward inside the sole. The main gauge is glued vertically along the medium perimeter. It gets the mechanical compression as well as the unavoidable thermal changes. The second gauge is glued longitudinally so it is negligibly affected by the mechanical compression but gets the same thermal changes. A Wheatstone half-bridge set up allows cutting the caloric effect and keeping out the single compression effect. A National Instrument® conditioner and a LabView® program acquire this output.

The previous metallic box welcoming the dynamometric was source of inconstant mechanical strain result for a same compression force. It is taken away and its role of vertical guideline for the compression is compensated by fixing the dynamometric tube in horizontal position. A bottom plane and an opposite upper plane cut from the tube surface determine the horizontal position. The tube external diameter (12.7 mm) remains at 12.3 mm between the plates in order to overpass the Pedar® slipper sole thickness (11 mm).

Both planes welcome an identical aluminum plate. The upper plate contacts the foot over the sole whereas the lower plate contacts the ground under the sole. During the stance phase, the foot pushes down the upper plate and compresses the tube vertically against the bottom plate lying on the ground. The slipper sole move freely between the two plates without altering the compression process. Each sensor provides the vertical compression force exerted by the foot on its own upper plate, i.e. the vertical reaction force exerted by the ground on its own bottom plate. The eleven upper plates, as well as the eleven bottom plates, cover 95% of the sole surface.

The tube internal diameter (9.7 mm) has been first determined by dimensional optimization through tensile simulation on COMSOL® software (Fig. 2) and then confirmed by reel crash tests on a tensile device (Fig. 3). The plastic threshold was set at 6000 N to ensure the elastic behavior of the tube during ambulation even if the foot hits the ground.

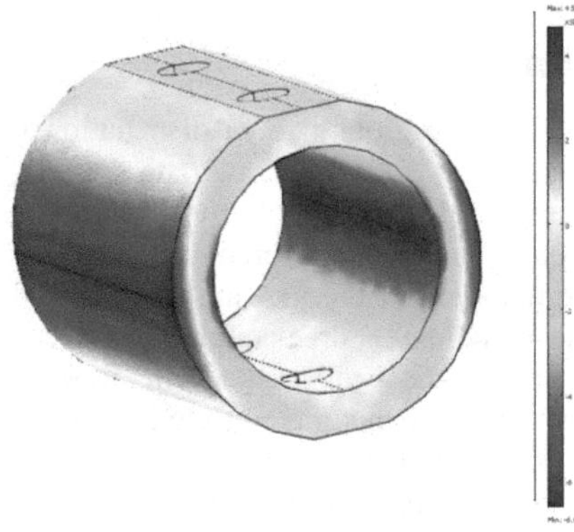

Fig. 2.Tensile simulation

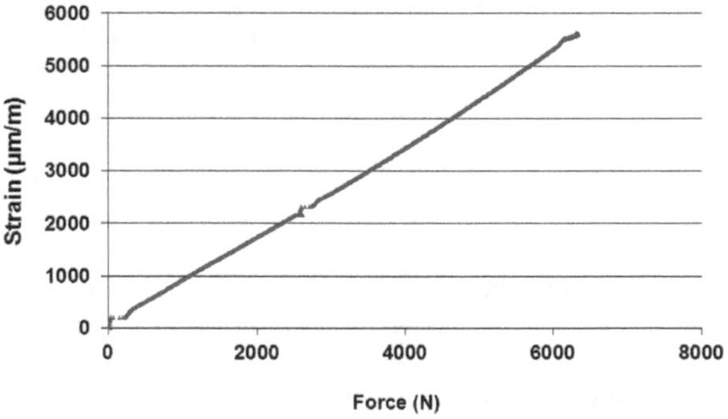

Fig. 3. Force/strain curve of the tensile test

The conditioning system and the acquisition laptop settled in a backpack. This 4 kg amount of mass does not affect the patient's natural kinematics as long as it is less than 10% of the individual's body mass (Grimmer [20]). Patient over 40 kg are free from added gait perturbation.

The treatment process indicates the force recorded by each sensor, the vertical ground reaction force deduced for the entire foot, the plantar pressure distribution under the foot and the center of pressure location, throughout the entire stance phase.

2.2 Treatment process

To translate the recorded strain into the plantar forces, we developed a complete Matlab® program. This program runs automatically and passes through offset and electronic drift correction, voltage to force translation, force to mass conversion, expression in percentage of body mass, stance phase detection, duration normalization, mean of values and graph plotting.

The offset and drift corrections are based on oscillation phase signals. When sensors are unloaded, each sensor residual signal is recorded and taken as reference. That induces needed initial and final lifted feet phase at the beginning and the end of the walking protocol. The correction started by the initial offset and then assesses a linear drift coefficient applied to the entire trial.

The translation into the exerted force (N) is deduced from previous sensor calibration. The force is then converted into mass (kg) and expressed in percentage of the experimental mass (i.e. body & backpack mass).

The stance phases of each foot are determined between the first moment a sensor yielded a value above 5% of the experimental mass and the last moment before all the sensors yielded a value under 5%. Each stance phase is then normalized over time and sensor signal are kept at every 10% of the stance duration (0%, 10%, 20%, …, 90% and 100%).

Then the mean value of each sensor at each of the 11 instants is processed over all the stance phases of the trial. That gives the evolution of each sensor signal during the mean stance at every 10% of the phase duration. These results are then used to obtain both the classical vertical ground reaction force and the innovating plantar force visualization graph.

2.3 Plantar forces visualization graph

An elaborate plotting function ends the Matlab® program. It draws a one-shot graph presenting the plantar forces distribution evolution throughout the stance phase for each foot.

The eleven instantaneous footprints of the mean stance phase are drawn for each foot. Each footprint is figured by the eleven sensors of the sole. The top row of footprints illustrated the left foot whereas the bottom one stands for the right foot. The stance phases runs from the left side ("0%" footprint) to the right ("100%" footprint), through footprints at every 10% of the phase duration.

The force magnitude exerted on each sensor is indicated in grey. The grey follows a shade scale going darker for every 10% of the experimental mass. White represents less than 10% of the experimental mass and black represents over 100%. This force magnitude scale is indicated at the very top of the graph. The force magnitude is expressed both in a percentage of the experimental mass and in an absolute value of the corresponding actual mass.

The center of pressure is illustrated by a little square on each footprint. This barycenter is assessed and plotted for each footprint provided the instantaneous mass undergone by each sensor.

3 Methods

3.1 Dynamic calibration

The sensors calibration aims to define the force/signal relationship of each sensor. Though apparently similar, each home-made dynamometric tube has its own inherent mechanical behavior.

The calibration used a 6025 Instron® electromechanical universal testing system. The device pushes down the upper plate while the bottom plate lies on a not deformable surface. The contact of the tensile machine was limited to one single sensor at once. Other sensors were not involved in the compression. A trial of five cycles of compression from 50 to 3000 N and back to 50 N has been chosen. Compression speed was set at 50 N/s and sample frequency at 10 Hz.

We first attested that calibration result was repeatable for a same sensor over 5 trials separated by unsetting and setting up of the sensor into the sole. Five random sensors were used and all presented excellent calibration repeatability.

Then, each of the 22 sensors has been calibrated. We observed the strain output of the compressed sensor along the entire test. We also observed the one of the other sensors, uncompressed, to ensure the absence of contact between the sensors.

3.2 Dead loads weighting

Dead loads weighting test consist in laying an inert known mass upon the sole over the eleven sensors at once.

Thanks to available masses, totals of 6 kg, 24 kg and 34 kg were loaded and unloaded until 0 kg, three times. The mean mass and force per sensor was so 0.6, 1.2 and 3.3 kg and 5, 11.6 and 32.4 N. The sample frequency was set at 100 Hz. The strain of each sensor was recorded for 2s. The offset and shift correction were proceeded for each cycle using the signal value of the unloaded phases (0 kg).

Recorded strains were converted into masses using the previous dynamic calibration results for each sensor. The sum of the mass measured by the eleven sensors of the slipper was assessed and compared to the loading masses. The comparison of the results across the cycle indicates the repeatability of the process.

3.3 Clinical testing

Two women and two men (Table 1) between 25 and 29 years old performed a standard return gait task of 10 meters. They had no residual locomotive deficiency from their past medical history. The subject mass was assessed using an eye-level mechanical physician scale.

Table 1. Characteristics of the four subjects

	Sex	Age	Height (cm)	Mass (kg)	BMI*
Subject A	F	29	169	76.5	26.8
Subject B	F	25	162	51	19.4
Subject C	M	27	183	83	24.8
Subject D	M	28	178	67	21.1

* Body Mass Index

	Past Medical History
Subject A	- right ankle: 1 fracture, 2 sprains - left ankle: 1 sprain
Subject B	- right ankle: 1 sprain - left ankle: 1 sprain - left knee: 1 sprain
Subject C	- beginning of scoliosis at adolescence
Subject D	- flat feet at adolescence

Subjects were equipped with the baropodometric device: the two instrumented slippers and the 4-kg backpack. The entire protocol was explained to each of the four subjects and one rehearsal was performed prior to recording three trials.

Subjects began in a seated position with both feet lifted for 3 seconds, stood up on both feet for 3 seconds, walked 10 meters forwards, returned back, stood on both feet for 3 seconds and resumed the seated position with feet lifted for 3 seconds. The sample frequency was set at 100 Hz.

Results were figured through the new plantar force visualization graph and comparison to the normal stance is established for each subject in two steps. Firstly, the evolution of the center of pressure location throughout the eleven footprints is observed. It defines the global dynamic of the foot. During normal stance, it usually shows a progressive headway along the medio-lateral axis, from the heel to the forefoot (Allard [2]). Other trajectories or headway paces could reveal pathology. Then, the shade of the eleven sensors is observed in each of the eleven footprints. During normal stance, a taligrade phase first appears for 20% of the stance phase time, then a mid-stance phase until 65% and finally a digital phase completing the 100% (Viel [8]). This normal dynamic of the foot compresses first the single heel sensors. Metatarsal heads join then for the mid stance phase. And finally, hallux and toes step on the floor before rearfoot lifts for the propulsive phase. Mid-foot areas are potentially participating in the mid-stance phase, depending on the dynamic shape of the foot: flat, normal or hollow foot as well as inversion. Any abnormal solicitation of sensor may alerts the clinician about current and/or consecutive pathologies.

4 Results

4.1 Dynamic calibration

The force/signal curves were obtained for each sensors of each slipper between 50 and 3000 N (Fig. 4). An elastic behavior was observed for every sensor as the compression phases and the release phases are perfectly superimposed. However each sensor has its own mechanical response which is not linear.

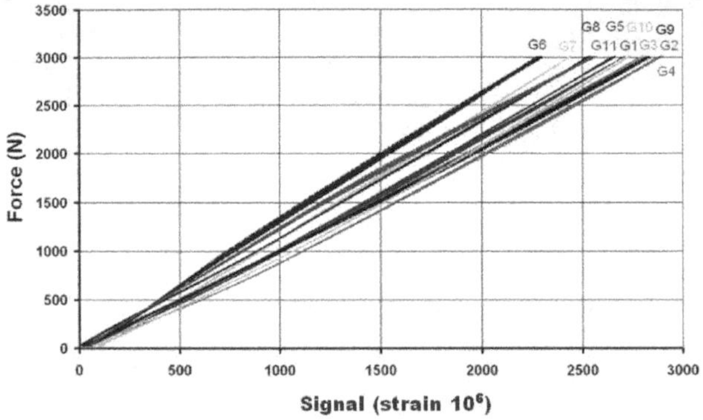

Fig. 4. Force/signal curves of the sensors of the left slipper

To best fit the sensor behavior, we approach each force/signal curve by a multi-degree equation, looking for the optimal degree to obtain minimal error. Six-degree equation appeared necessary to obtain less than 5 N of error throughout the 50-3000 N bandwidth.

The uncompressed sensors didn't show any signal variation during the calibration process whatever was the compressed sensor. That ensures the independence of each sensor and certifies that any signal variation means a direct solicitation of the sensor.

4.2 Dead load weighting

During the loading phase, the global mass measured by the sole was very similar across the 3 cycles (Fig. 5). However, measured masses were quite inaccurate: 5(±0.2) kg, 22(±0.5) kg, 31.1(±1) kg and 21.9(±0.7) kg and 5.2(±0.2) kg, instead of respectively 6, 24, 34, 24 and 6 kg. Those gaps were expected since the force/signal relationships can produce a maximal error of 5 N per sensor, according to the calibration, i.e. 55 N or 5.6 kg per slipper.

We conclude that static measurement can't be used for weighting the light loads but allow comparing two loads or the evolution of a same load.

4.3 Testing

The plantar forces visualization graph is obtained for each of the four subjects (Fig. 6).

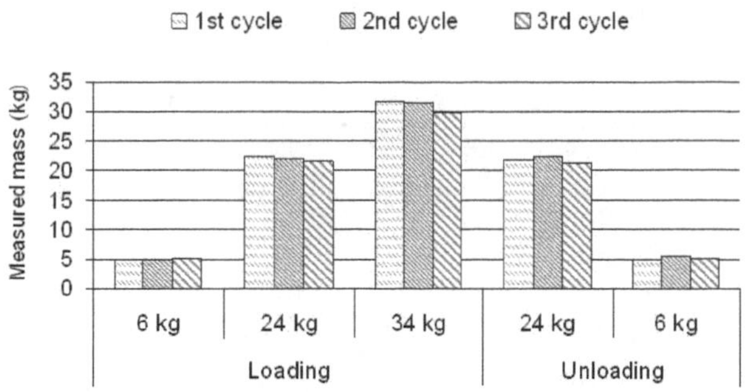

Fig. 5. Measured mass given by the slipper when loading and unloading at 6 kg, 24 kg, 34 kg, 24 kg and 6 kg, in three consecutive cycles, separated by total unloading and offset setup

The results of subject A show a difference between the feet. The left foot presents a rather normal dynamics. The center of pressure is located in the medio-lateral middle axis of the foot throughout the step and comes from the heel to the forefoot region progressively. The rearfoot contact phase takes up the first 20% of the duration of the stance phase. The full foot contact phase is spread over 50% of the stance phase, while the propulsion phase takes up the remaining 30%. However, during propulsion the third metatarsal head is more solicited (30% to 50% of the experimental mass) than the first and fifth metatarsal heads (10% to 20% of the experimental mass). This may indicate a sagging metatarsal head arch. The third metatarsal head could result in pain later in the future. The right foot shows a much abnormal dynamics. The center of pressure appears directly before the heel, which means that an isolated rearfoot contact phase does not exist. Moreover, none of the external sensors are solicited over 10% of the experimental mass. This may indicate pronation of the foot during the entire stance phase. This could be a consequence of the historic fracture and sprains of the right ankle.

The results of subject B reveal a rather normal dynamics for the right foot whereas the left foot presents a particularly long use of the rearfoot region. The medial heel still loads with 10% of the experimental mass at 80% of the stance phase duration. The very slow progression of the center of pressure confirms this phenomenon. This could be linked to the knee and ankle sprain subject B sustained in the left limb.

The results of subject C demonstrate a perfectly normal dynamics for left foot, starting at the medial heel before soliciting the lateral heel and ending with most of the force over the hallux. However, the first metatarsal head gets very little load and the hallux is bearing more than 10% of the mass as soon as 40% of the duration of the stance phase. This could lead to future hallux pain. For the right foot, the center of pressure describes a normal trajectory while, during the mid-stance phase, the forefoot is not solicited over 10% of the experimental mass and the rear part of the mid-foot is unusually constrained. This indicates a potential flatfoot behavior during the mid-stance phase. The global force can be spread over of a majority of sensors, with less than 10% of mass on most of them.

The results of subject D highlight healthy use of the left foot and possible flat foot behavior for the right foot like subject C. The right center of pressure indicates a normal roll but no sensor appeared to be more loaded than any other during the first 60% of the stance phase, except for the heel.

In all case, those results appeared thanks to the new graph and should be interpreted by competent clinicians.

5 Conclusion

Improved through a higher number of sensors and a new assembly system, instrumented slippers have ambitious baropodometric aims. Whereas the baropodometric insoles record the foot-to-sole pressure inside the shoe, the instrumented slippers acquire the foot-to-ground forces which are approaching the barefoot walking forces as the mechanical characteristics of the sole do not alter the foot contact.

As the eleven sensors cover 90% of the sole, any pathologic foot dynamics can be observed. Thanks innovating and user-friendly visualization graph, clinicians can check the evolution of the plantar force distribution throughout the entire stance phase. The instants of occurrence and duration of force exertion could be identified for every anatomic area. Symmetry of the feet can also be focused.

Calibration process ensures an error of measurement under 5 N for every of the 22 sensors solicited between 50 and 3000 N. For lighter loads, the inaccuracy increased but the measurement repeatability stays approved.

The clinical test underlined how informative the instrumented slippers coupled with the visualization graph could be. The dynamic behavior of the foot throughout the entire stance phase is easily recorded and observed at a glance. Clinician gets a new device to complete the gait diagnosis of their patients. While the subject walks, he can keep observing the global kinematics as the baropodometric device runs alone. Then, the entire treatment and the graph plotting process take less than fifteen minutes. Individual mass and trial acquired signal are the only required data. In conclusion, we improved and developed a new plantar force acquisition device and a visualization graph intended for everyday use in clinical lab.

Next step will be to miniaturize the gauge conditioner in order to insert it around the slipper and develop wireless record to quit the backpack holding.

Acknowledgments

Acknowledment goes to Arnaud Faivre who authorized this work. Fany Chedevergne received a research salary from the Ministry of National Education, Research and Technology of France to conduct this project.

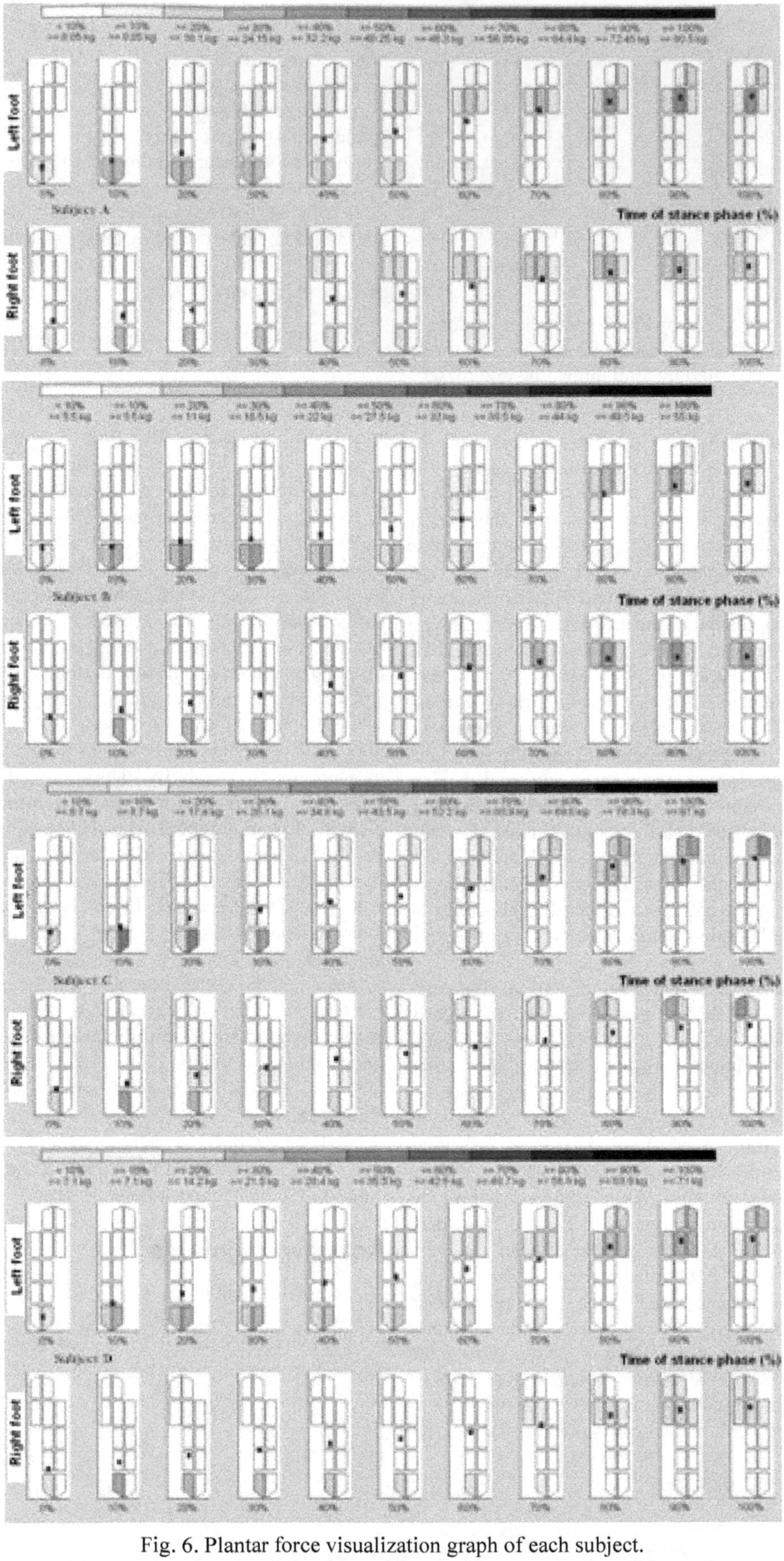

Fig. 6. Plantar force visualization graph of each subject.
Mean stance phase over the three trials of a 10-meters back walking task

References

1. C. Kowalski, *Conséquences pathologique de la brièveté des muscles gastrocnémiens*, Médecine et Chirurgie du Pied **22**(3), 159-180, (2006).
2. P. Allard, J. P. Blanchi, *La biomécanique* (Paris, France : PUF Collection Que sais-je ? 2000)
3. P.R.Cavanagh, F.G.Hewitt Jr., J.E. Perry, *In-shoe plantar pressure measurement: a review,* The Foot **2**(4), 185-194, (1992).
4. W.Herzog, B. Nigg, L.J. Read, E.Olsson, *Asymmetries in ground reaction force patterns in normal human gait,* Med. and Sci. Sport Exer. **21**, 110-114, (1989).
5. S.Meyring, R.R. Diehl, T.L.,Milani, E.M. Hennig, P. Berlit, *Dynamic plantar pressure distribution measurements in hemiparetic patient,* Clin. Biomech. **12**(1), 60-65, (1997).
6. J. Perry, *Gait Analysis. Normal and Pathological Gait* (Thorfare, USA : SLACK Incorporated, 1992)
7. J. Perttunen, *Foot loading in normal and pathological walking.* (University of Jyvaskyla, Finland : Ph.D. thesis, 2002)
8. E.Viel, *La marche humaine, la course et le saut.* (Paris, France : Masson, 2000)
9. F.A. Asphahani, H.C. Lee, *Portable system for analyzing human gait* (United States patent US6836744 B1, 2004)
10. A. Faivre, *Conception et validation d'un nouvel outil d'analyse clinique de la marche* (University of Franche-Comté , France : Ph. D. thesis, 2003)
11. T.S. Gross, R.P.Bunch, *Measurement of discrete vertical in-shoe stress with piezoelectric transducers,* J. Biomed. Eng. **10**(3), 261-265, (1988).
12. C.Kirtley, K.Tong, Insole gyro system for gait analysis, *Proceedings of the RESNA Annual Conference* (2000).
13. S.Miyazaki, H.Iwakura, *Foot-force measuring device for clinical assessment of pathological gait,* Medical and Biological Engineering and Computing **16**(4), 429-436, (1978).
14. H.S. Ranu, *Miniature load cells for the measurement of foot-ground reaction forces and centre of foot pressure during gait,* J. Biomed. Eng. **8**(2), 175-177, (1986).
15. G.A. Spolek, F.G. Lippert, *An instrumented shoe; a portable force measuring device,* Journal of Biomechanics, **9**(12), 779-783, (1976).
16. A.Faivre, M. Dahan, B.Parratte, *Instrumented shoe sole and shoe with instrumented sole.* (European patent EP1464281 B1, 2006).
17. A.Faivre, M. Dahan, B.Parratte, G. Monnier, *Instrumented shoe for pathological gait assessment,* Mechanics Research Communications **31**, 627-632, (2004).
18. C.Bertsch, H.Unger, W. Winkelmann, D. Rosenbaum, *Evaluation of early walking patterns from plantar pressure distribution measurements. First year results of 42 children,* Gait Posture **19**, 235-242, (2004).
19. E.M. Hennig, T.L. Milani, *In-shoe pressure distribution for running in various types of footwear,* J Appl Biomech, **11**(3), 299-310, (1995).
20. K.Grimmer, J. Williams, T.K. Gill, *The associations between adolescent head-on-neck posture, backpack mass, and anthropometric features,* Spine, **24**, 2262-2267, (1999).

Multidisciplinary design optimization of an accumulator for a large elasticity range of flexible webs

Dominique Knittel[1,2,a], David Kuhm[1,3], Jean Renaud[2]

[1]Centre d'Innovation et de Transfert Technologique (CITT), University of Strasbourg, 17 rue du Maréchal Lefebvre, 67100 Strasbourg
[2]Laboratoire de Génie de la Conception INSA Strasbourg, 24 boulevard de la Victoire, 67084 Strasbourg, France
[3]Laboratoire de Laboratoire de Physique et Mécanique Textiles, ENSISA, 11 rue Alfred Werner, 68093 Mulhouse, France

Abstract–This paper concerns the optimization of an accumulator used in an industrial elastic web processing plant (paper, fabric, polymer, metal …). A nonlinear model of an industrial accumulator is first detailed which enables to deduce a linear model. These models are derived from the physical laws describing web tension and velocity dynamics in each web span. The effects of time-varying rheological and mechanical parameters, such as web Young modulus, web length and rolls inertia, on accumulator dynamics and performances are analyzed. The second part presents several optimizations of industrial PI controllers using evolutionary algorithm for a realistic non-linear model, in conjunction with the controllers interpolation strategy. Finally, simulations made in the Matlab/Simulink software environment show performances improvements compared to hand tuned controllers.

Keywords: Industrial accumulator, Roll-to-roll, Dynamic modeling, PI controller optimization, Mono-objective optimization

1 Introduction

In many plants, accumulators (Fig. 1)are used to allow for rewind or unwind core change while the process continues at a constant velocity. Such systems store web during the regular phase of production. The web is then released during the wound roll change, in the case of an entry accumulator. Using an accumulator allows nonstop operation on the production line.

During the regular production phase, the accumulator carriage is placed at its nominal position. When the unwinder wound roll is almost empty, the accumulator carriage is moved up (vertically in our studied processing line)in order to maximize the web storage into the accumulator. However, during the unwinder roll change, the accumulator carriage is adequately moved downin order to release the web for having a constant web velocity. Finally, after the roll change, the accumulator carriage is moved to its initial position. The unwinder roll changing time will take place in very short time depending on the accumulated web length.

The web tensions inside the accumulator are easy to control in standard operating conditions (when the accumulator carriage is placed at its constant nominal position). Nevertheless, web tensions variations can often appear during the transition phases and generate web folds or breaks due to the inertia and friction of many free rollers.

Different works in web tension control of roll-to-roll systems have been published during the last years. For examplеZalhan et al. [23], Brandenburg [2], Benlatreche et al. [1], Knittel et al. [6] [8], Gassmann et al. [4] present the modeling and control of a continuous processing line composed only with tractors and free rollers, whereas Wolfermann [22], Gassmann[18], Knittel et al.[7] describe the unwinding and winding process. Only few papers present the modeling and control of industrial accumulators. Important results can be found in Koç et al. [11] [12], Pagilla et al. [19] [20], Kuhm et al. [13] [14] and Knittel et al. [15].

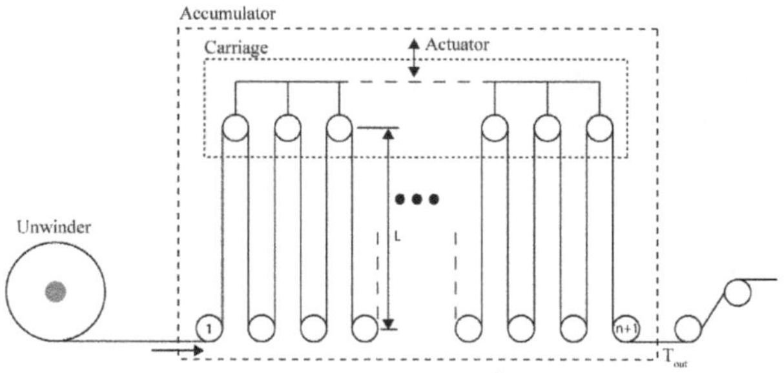

Fig. 1. Sketch of an industrial accumulator

In the second part of this paper, the accumulator model based on physical laws is described. This part also highlights the effect of mechanical parameters variations on the accumulator dynamic performances. The third part presents different accumulator optimization strategies. First, a mono-objective PI controller optimization is made. Then, controllers are optimized in conjunction with an interpolation strategy. The last PI controller optimization strategy, taking into account Young modulus variation, is performed. Finally simulation results obtained in the Matlab/Simulink software environment with a realistic accumulator model are presented.

2 Plant modeling

2.1 Nonlinear model of the accumulator

Web tension calculation:

Assuming there is no sliding between web and rollers, the equation of continuity applied to the web span between two consecutive rollers (Fig. 2) gives (Koç [9], Koç et al. [10]) :

[a] Corresponding author : knittel@unistra.fr

$$\frac{d}{dt}\left(\frac{L_k}{1+\varepsilon_k}\right) = -\frac{V_{k+1}}{1+\varepsilon_k} + \frac{V_k}{1+\varepsilon_{k-1}} \qquad (1)$$

where L_k is the variable web length between the kth and the $(k+1)^{th}$ rollers. This length can vary due to the accumulator carriage motion. V_k is the linear velocity of the kth roll and ε_k represents the strain of the kth web span. Web tension T_k is then deduced from relation (1) by applying the Hooke's law (see Koç [9] or Koç et al. [10]).

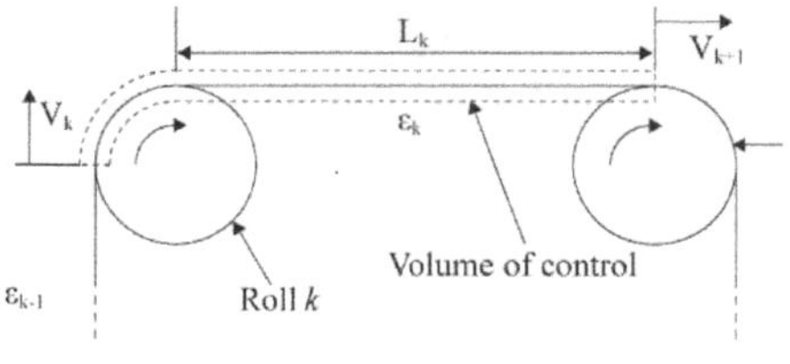

Fig. 2. Indices of web span between two consecutive rollers

Web velocity calculation:

The velocity dynamic of the kth roll is calculated by using the torque balance. Assuming there is no slippage between the web and the roll, the web velocity V_k is equal to the linear velocity of the roll. This velocity dynamic is given by equation 2:

$$\frac{d}{dt}(J_k.\Omega_k) = C_{mk} - C_{rk} - C_{fk} \qquad (2)$$

Where $\Omega_k = V_k/R_k$ is the angular velocity of the kth roll, J_k the roll inertia and R_k the roll radius. C_{mk} is the motor torque for a driven roll. C_{rk} and C_{fk} stand for the resistive torque introduced by the web and friction torque between the roll and its shaft respectively. The equations (1) and (2) are applied to each web span and roll of the studied accumulator and enable the construction of a non-linear longitudinal web dynamics simulator.

Accumulator representation:

The inputs/outputs block scheme of the studied accumulator is shown in Fig. 3. The system has three inputs: V_{inaccu} which is the web speed at the entrance of the accumulator, $V_{outaccu}$ the web speed at the exit and L that is the time-varying length between two consecutive rollers (depending on accumulator carriage position). The system output is the web span tension T_{out} just after the last roll in the accumulator, (see Fig. 1).

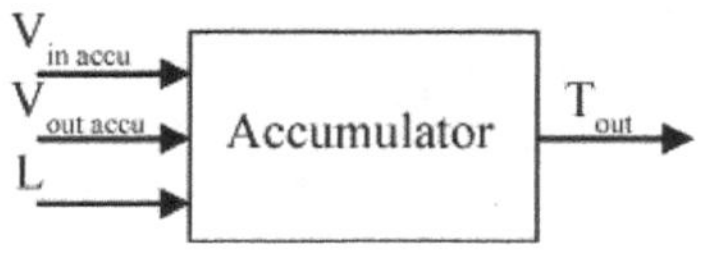

Fig. 3. Input / Output scheme of the accumulator

Accumulator carriage velocity reference:

In the phase of wound roll change, the accumulator output speed $V_{out\ accu}$ is maintained at the nominal speed V_{ref} whereas the input speed V_{inaccu} decreases to zero. In order to maintain the output web tension and speed constant during this change, it is necessary to move adequately the accumulator carriage. In our study, the accumulator is composed of $n+1$ rollers and therefore has n web spans. The accumulator carriage displacement speed reference is given by the following relation:

$$V_{accu} = \frac{1}{n}\left(V_{inaccu} - V_{out\_accu}\right) \qquad (3)$$

Unwinder speed reference during accumulation phase:

During the web storing phase, the unwinder speed reference has to be increased. This unwinding speed can be deduced from the equation (3):

$$V_{in\ accu} = nV_{accu} + V_{outaccu} \qquad (4)$$

2.2 Linear model of the accumulator

Linearization:

The linear model can be deduced from the nonlinear one around a working point. The web span dynamic linearization are detailed in Koç [9] and Kuhm et al. [13].

State space representation:

The linear model of the accumulator can be described by a state space representation given in (5). This linear model is useful for Bode diagrams calculation.

$$\begin{cases} \dot{x} = \left(A + \frac{A1}{L}\right)x + \frac{B}{L}u + B1\,v \\ Y = Cx + Du \end{cases} \qquad (5)$$

where

$$x = \begin{bmatrix} T_{in} \\ V_1 \\ T_1 \\ \vdots \\ V_{n+1} \\ T_{n+1} \end{bmatrix} \quad u = \frac{dL}{dt} \quad v = \begin{bmatrix} V_{inaccu} \\ V_{outaccu} \end{bmatrix}$$

Influence of the mechanical parameters

Two transfer functions have been studied in our accumulator (Fig. 3): one between the accumulator output tension T_{out} and the accumulator input velocity V_{inaccu} named W_1 and the other between T_{out} and the web span length L named W_2. In industrial accumulators, mainly two control strategies are applied: one using V_{inaccu} as control signal (controller output), the other using L. In this paper, we use a combination of the two strategies. In the following parts, the influences of some physical parameter variations around their nominal values are analysed on simulated Bode diagrams.

Influence of the elasticity modulus:

The web elasticity influences the web dynamics (tension and velocity) in the transient phases. One can observe on Fig. 4 that the static gain and the resonances (gains and frequencies) are depending on the web Young modulus. Similar observations have been made for transfer functions W_1. Very often in the industry, Young modulus changes occur during the manufacturing process and therefore the control performances are decreasing if the controllers synthesis do not take into account the web elasticity variations. Consequently, the controllers have to be adjusted for each range of web elasticity, or robust for a given (large) web elasticity range.

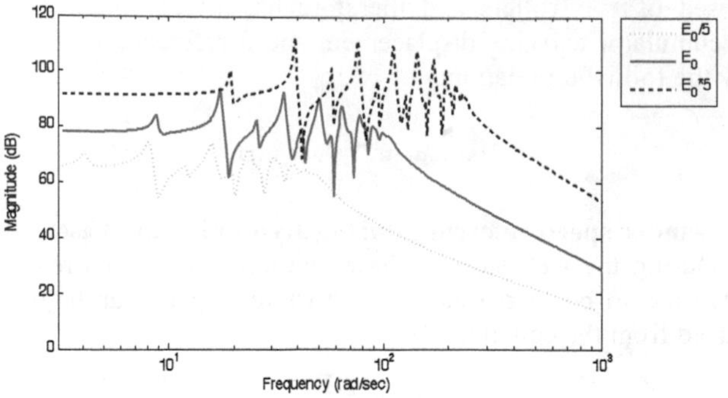

Fig. 4. Bode diagram of W_2 for different Young modulus

Variations of web span length:

Like the Young modulus, the web span length in the accumulator (related to the position of the carriage) has a significant influence on the web dynamic (Fig. 5).

A long web span will have a weaker resonance frequency and a lower gain. This observation has been made for both transfer functions W_1 and W_2. Therefore the dynamic sensitivity to the web length variations has to be taken into account in the controller synthesis because the web span length is varying each time a wound roll change occurs.

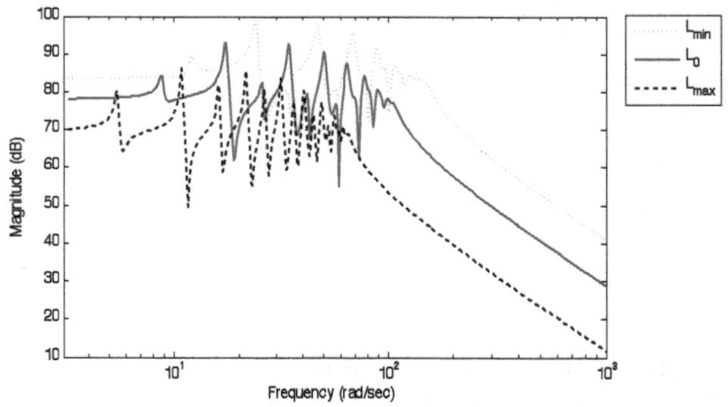

Fig. 5. Bode diagram of W_2 for different web span lengths

Study of the influence of roll inertia:

The free rollers inertia also influences the web dynamics. As we can observe on Fig. 6, these inertias should be as weak as possible. Indeed important inertias strongly decrease the bandwidth of the system; this low bandwidth will make it difficult to control the accumulator. On the contrary, the inertia has no effect on the static gain. This has been observed for both transfer functions W_1 and W_2.

Influence of other parameters

The shaft/roll frictions have low effect on the system bandwidth. A change of the friction value during the production will thus have a minor influence on the controller performances.

The nominal web velocity doesn't influence the system bandwidth. But a high speed reduces the resonance peaks. This effect doesn't depend on the web span length.

The nominal tension doesn't have any effect on the accumulator bandwidth and on the resonance peaks. This has been observed for both transfer functions W_1 and W_2. More detailed analysis can be found in Kuhm et al. [13].

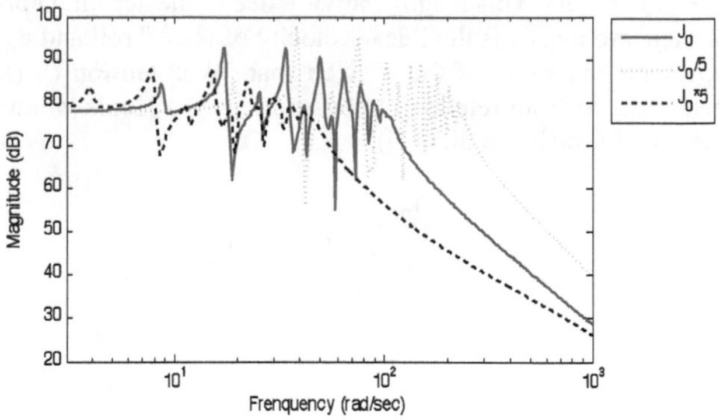

Fig. 6. Bode diagram of W_2 for different roll inertia

Remarks

This previous part shows that the most influent parameters in our studied industrial accumulator are the web Young modulus (which describes the web elasticity), the rollers inertias and the web span length.

3 Accumulator optimization

3.1 Accumulator control scheme

As indicated in the precedent part, the accumulator has two different entries used as control signals.

An output web tension controller can be synthesized by using the input velocity of the accumulator as control signal. The second control strategy needs the web length (by moving the accumulator carriage) as control signal. In industrial applications, both control schemes are programmed. This study combines the two strategies. During the regular production phase, we use the input velocity as actuator and during the wound roll change we use the web length as actuator. The switching strategy between the two controllers is performed by weighting the controllers output by a coefficient β varying between 0 and 1. The control scheme is illustrated on Fig. 7.

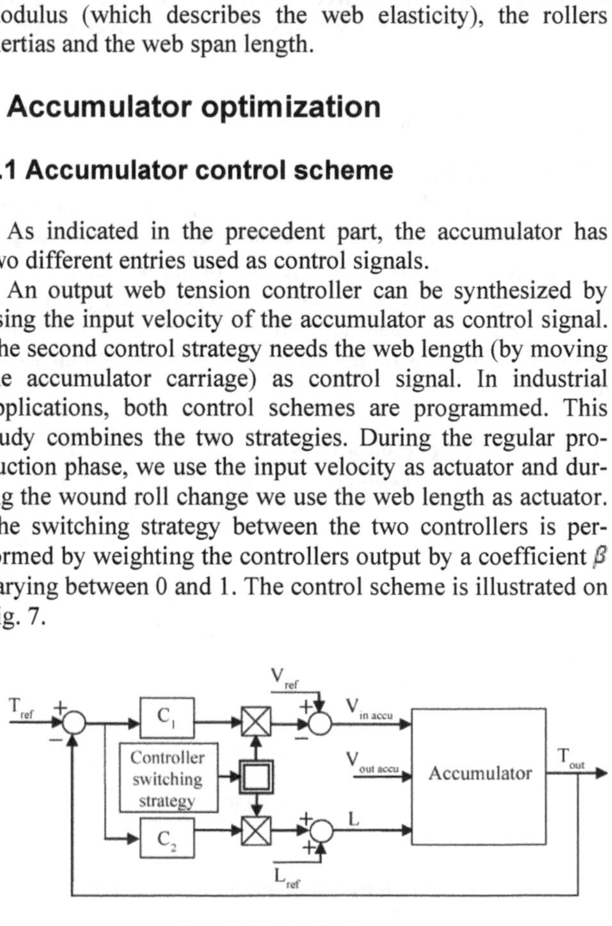

Fig. 7. Control scheme

These two PI controllers C_1 and C_2 have the following form:

$$C_i(s) = K_i \frac{1 + \tau_i . s}{s} \quad (6)$$

3.2 Optimization strategies

Mono-objective controllers optimization

The PI parameters K_1 and τ_1 for the first and K_2 and τ_2 for the second controller are determined with an optimization approach for our realistic non-linear model. Controller optimization approaches are presented for example in Frechard et al. [3], Lin et al. [17], Popov et al. [21] and Zielinski et al. [24]. Robust controller optimization can be found in Gassmann et al [5], Knittel et al. [16] and Kuhm et al. [14].

The PI parameters are optimized using an evolutionary algorithm minimizing a first cost function J given in (7). In this cost function, the parameter α is fixed at 10 in order to better minimize the tension peaks [15]. Another approach is to use the ITAE criterion as a cost function (see (8)). Using the ITAE criterion allows to minimize the static error.

$$J = \sqrt[\alpha]{\int_0^{t\,max} \left(T_{out} - T_{ref}\right)^{\alpha} \mathrm{d}t} \quad (7)$$

$$J_{ITAE} = \int_0^{tmax} t * abs\left(T_{out} - T_{ref}\right)dt \quad (8)$$

The optimization was performed with the mode FRONTIER optimization software (see Fig. 8),using the MOGA-II algorithm (130 generations and a probability of directional cross-over equal to 0,5), coupled with the Matlab/Simulink accumulator model .

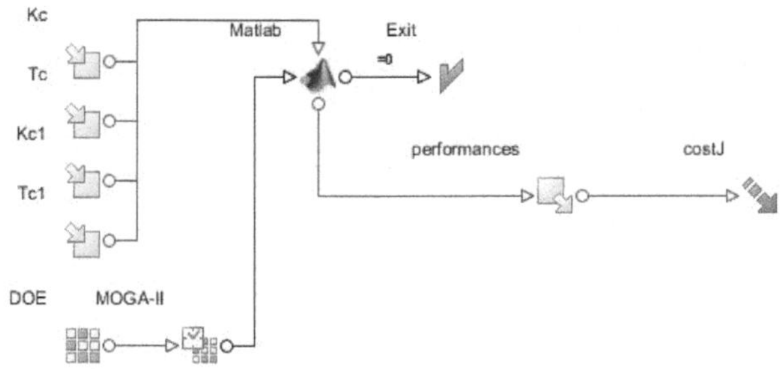

Fig. 8. Optimization scheme in mode FRONTIER

Controllers switching strategy optimization

The switching strategy function between each controller is optimized together with the controllers themselves. The chosen cost function is the ITEA criteria given in the previous part. Different mathematical interpolation laws can be applied between the two controllers. In this paper we tried to optimize controllers for four types of controller interpolation strategies given below. An optimal controller is found for each controller interpolation strategy.

The first one is a linear interpolation:

$$\beta_1 = \frac{V_{inaccu}}{V_0} \quad (9)$$

with V_{inaccu} the accumulator input velocity and V_0 the nominal accumulator velocity.

The second one is a parabolic interpolation:

$$\beta_2 = \frac{V_{inaccu}{}^2}{V_0{}^2} \quad (10)$$

The third on is an interpolation represented by a sigmoid function, the fourth interpolation method β_4 is a custom function.

$$\beta_3 = \left(\frac{1}{1 + \exp^{-5*V_{inaccu}}} - 0.5\right) * 2 \quad (11)$$

Mono-objective robust controllers optimization

As shown in part 2.2, the accumulator dynamic performances depend on the web elasticity. Consequently, our goal is to find the most robust controllers for a large of Young modulus variation. In order to obtain this robustness, the cost function has to take into account Young modulus changes. The cost function J_{ROB} , given in relation (12), is composed of the sum of the ITAE criterion calculated for each Young modulus value in the simulated accumulator. The selected interpolation strategy is β_3.

$$J_{ROB} = \sum_{E_{min}}^{E_{max}} \int_0^{tmax} t * abs\left(T_{out_E} - T_{ref}\right)dt \quad (12)$$

In this study three Young modulus values were used: E_0, E_0 multiplied by 5and E_0 divided by 5.

3.3 Optimization results

Mono-objective controllers optimization results

The evolution of the cost function J is shown on Fig. 9(a) and the evolution of the cost function J_{ITAE} is given in Fig. 9(b). The data have been sorted from the highest to the lowest value of each cost function. In reality, cost functions have more dissemination due to the use of a genetic algorithm. Fig. 10 shows the evolution of the controller C_1 parameters corresponding to cost function J. Fig. 11 gives the evolution of the controllerC_1 parameters corresponding to cost function J_{ITAE}.

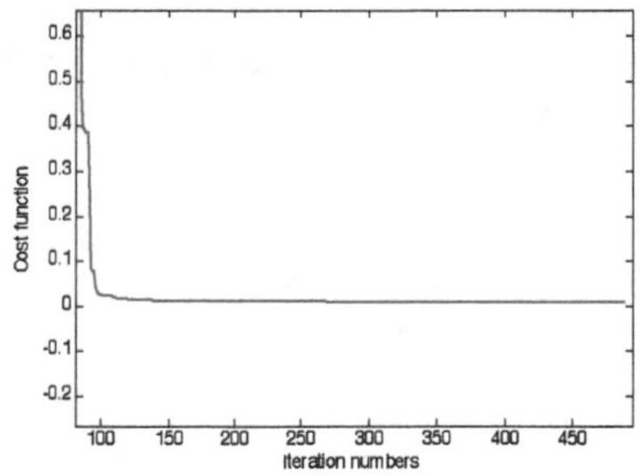

(a) Cost function J

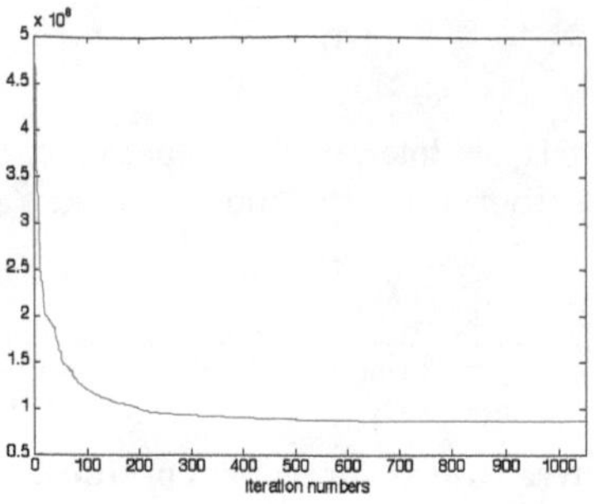

(b) Cost function J_{ITAE}

Fig. 9. Evolution of the cost function J and J_{ITAE}

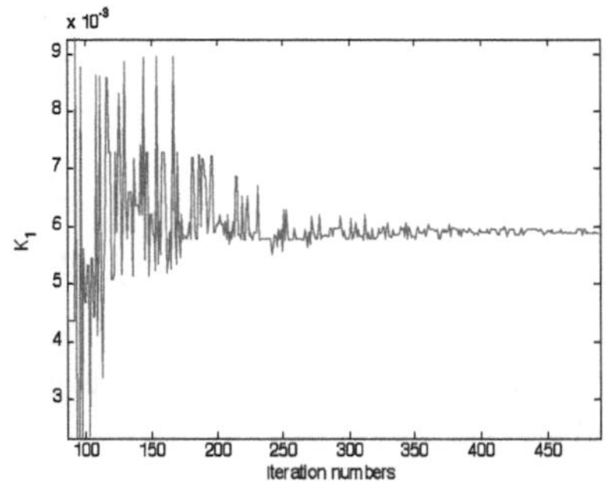

(a) Proportional gain K_1

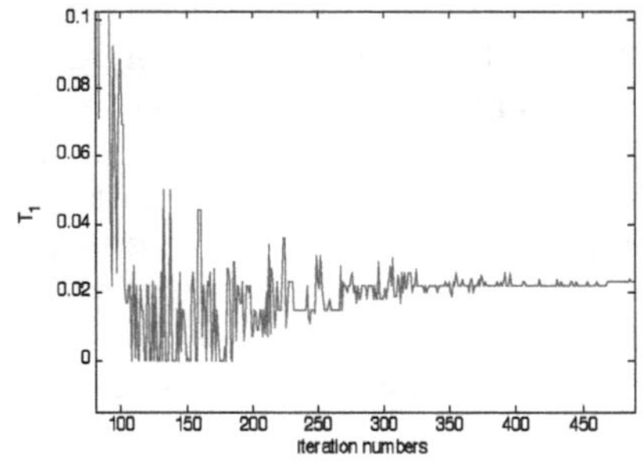

(b) Integral gain τ_1

Fig.10. Controller C_1 parameters for criterion J

As observed on Fig. 10, C_1 parameters using cost function J converge rapidly to an optimal value.

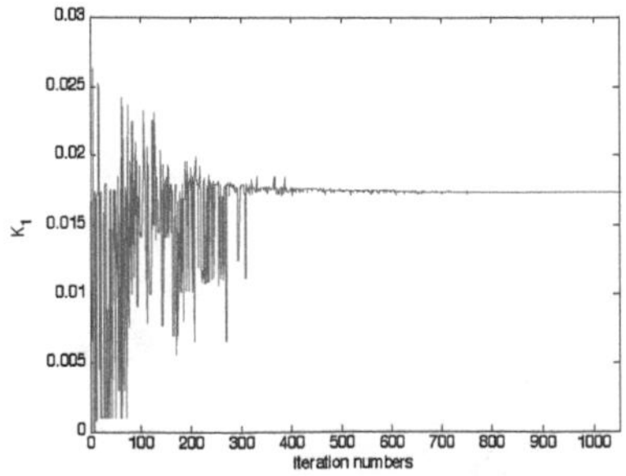

(a)Proportional gain K_1

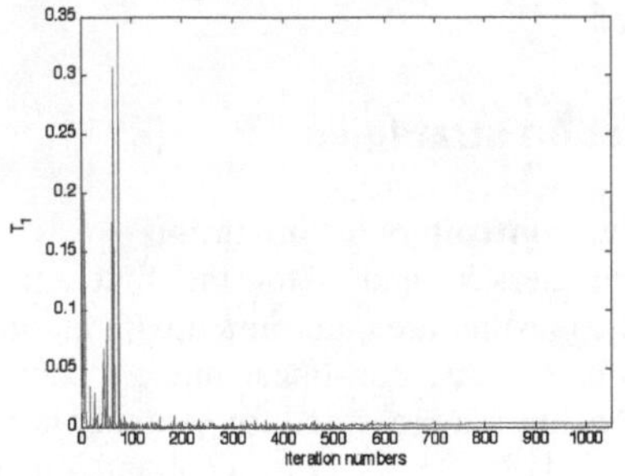

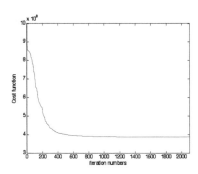

(b) Integral gain τ_1

Fig. 11. Controller C_1 parameters for criterion J_{ITAE}

Using cost junction J_{ITAE} does not really change the rapidity of the genetic algorithm convergence. But as seen on Fig. 11, J_{ITAE} leads to other controller values, as expected. This highlights that it's very important to adequately chose the cost function. The control strategy has also been optimized with the other switching strategies β_2, β_3 and β_4.

In this part, the controllers and switching strategies where optimized together.

A second optimization strategy consists to optimize sequentially the controllers. The simulation results are given in the part 3.4.

Robust controllers with mono-objective optimization

As observed on Fig. 12, the cost function J_{ROB} converges rapidly to an optimal value which is higher than J_{ITAE}. The algorithm has to find the best controllers for all the range of Young modulus, and therefore it is more robust but less performing. Nevertheless, the optimization algorithm needs more time for this controller synthesis strategy.

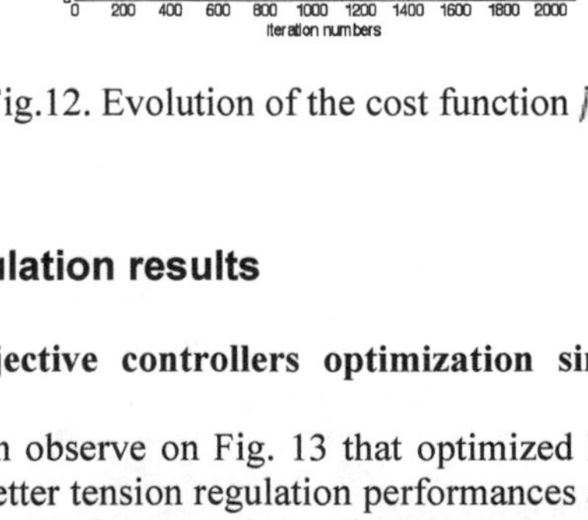

Fig.12. Evolution of the cost function J_{ROB}

3.4 Simulation results

Mono-objective controllers optimization simulation results

One can observe on Fig. 13 that optimized PI controllers leads to better tension regulation performances as hand tuned controllers. During a wound roll change phase which is the more critical production step (section d, e and f on Fig. 13), optimized controllers significantly reduce tensions variations while the input velocity is dropping to zero.

As expected, optimizing controllers together leads to better performances that sequentially optimizing. During the charging phase (section b), during the maximum web length phase (section c) and during the wound roll change phase, PI controllers optimized together gives the best results and reduce significantly web tensions variations.

Accumulator simulation sequence

a:The accumulator is at its nominal web length, velocity and tension.

b:The accumulator carriage is moved up to reach the maximum web length; the velocity is increased to maintain nominal web tension.

c:The accumulator is charged and maintained at maximum web length.

d:The input velocity decreases and the accumulator carriage is moved down to release web and maintain the nominal web tension.

e:The input velocity is equal to zero, the accumulator carriage is moved down to restore web and maintain the nominal web tension.

f: The input velocity increases to reach the nominal velocity, the accumulator carriage is moved down to restore web and maintain the nominal web tension.

g: The accumulator is maintained at a constant position to maintain a constant web length, web velocity and web tension in the accumulator.

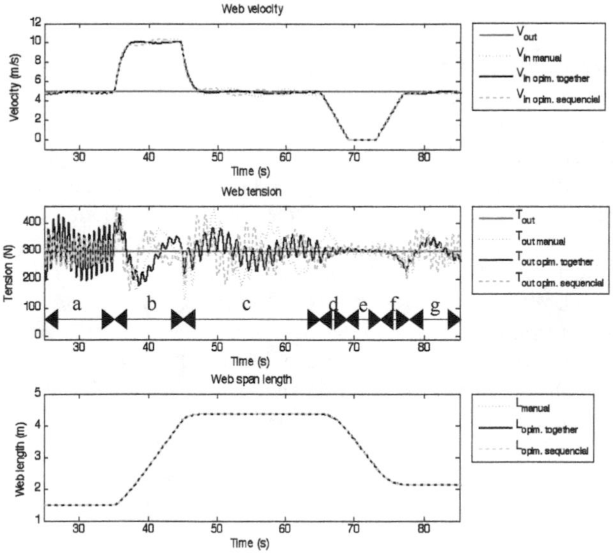

Fig.13. Optimized PI controllers simulation results using cost function J for switching strategy β_1

Controllers switching strategy optimization simulation results

As we can see on Fig. 14, using controllers interpolation strategies β_1, β_2 or β_3 leads to similar performances because controllers are optimized together with the switching function. Only the custom strategy β_4 seems to give better performances.

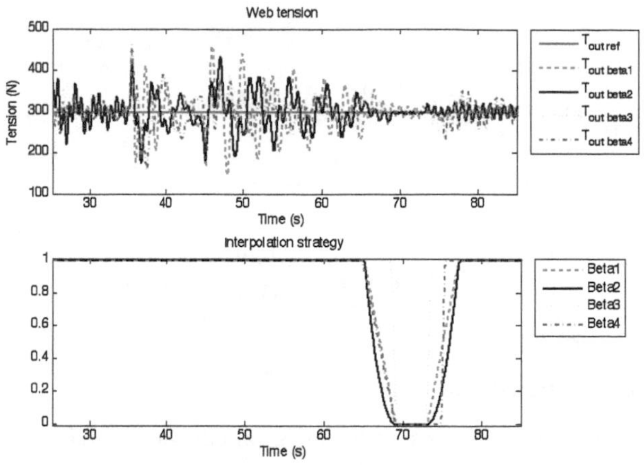

Fig. 14. Optimized PI controllers simulation results using cost function J_{ITAE} for different switching strategies

Simulation of robust controllers with mono-objective optimization

Fig. 15 to 17show the simulation results for three different Young modulus values. The obtained performances are maintained in acceptable range from E_0 divided by 5 to E_0 multiplied by 5, using J_{ROB} as cost function. Nevertheless, if we consider only the nominal pointE_0, the performances are better for the controller optimized for E_0 alone (cost function J_{ITAE}). This implies that we have to make a compromise between performances and robustness to web elasticity variations. Therefore a multi-objective optimization approach will be studied in the next future.

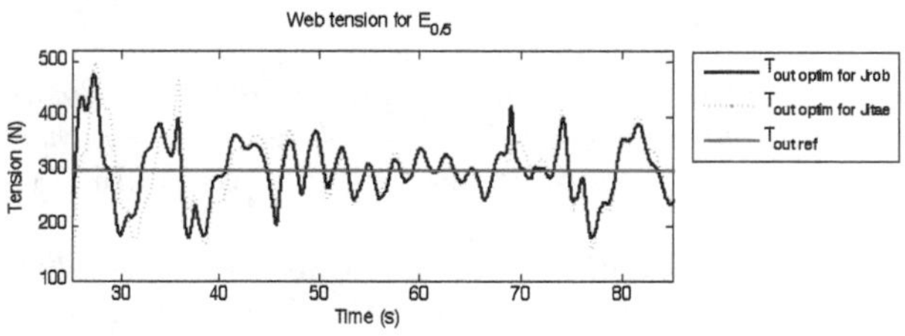

Fig. 15. Optimized PI controllers simulation results for J_{ROB} or J_{ITAE} using switching strategy β_2 (for $E_0/5$)

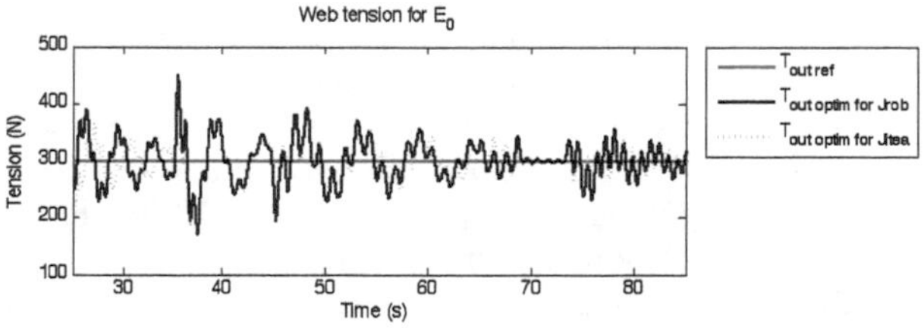

Fig. 16. Optimized PI controllers simulation results for J_{ROB} or J_{ITAE} using switching strategy β_2 (for E_0)

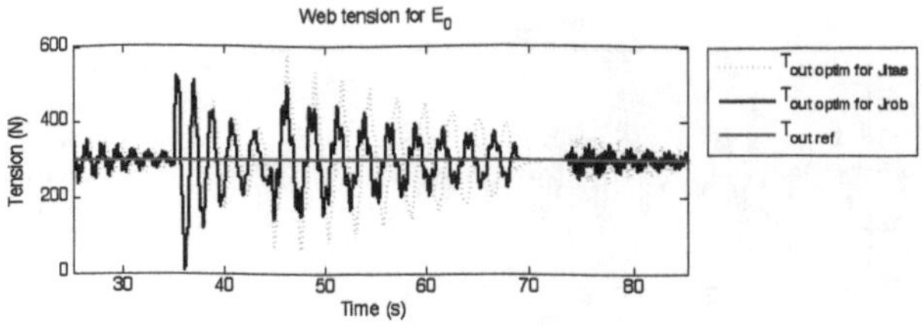

Fig. 17. Optimized PI controllers simulation results for J_{ROB} or J_{ITAE} using switching strategy β_3 (for $5*E_0$)

4 Conclusions

This study presents first the physical equations used in the modeling of an industrial accumulator. The nonlinear model, programmed in Matlab/Simulink software environment, enables a model based optimization of the controllers together with the controllers switching strategy. Several mono-objective controller optimization strategies are presented and simulation results are compared. Improved dynamic behaviours have been obtained using optimized controllers, in comparison to hand tuned controllers. Nevertheless, a compromise between web tension control performances and robustness against web elasticity variations has to be made. Therefore applying a multi-objective optimization approach will be the next step of our work.

Acknowledgement

The authors wish to thank Region Alsace for having partly funded this research and the Monomatic France company for their very helpful discussions.

References

1. A. Benlatreche, D.Knittel, and E.Ostertag, *"Robust decentralized control strategies for large-scale web handling systems"*, Control Engineering Practice, vol.16, 736-750(2008)
2. G. Brandenburg, *"Über das dynamische VerhaltendurchlafenderelasticherStoffbahnenbeiKraftübertragungdurchCoulomb'scheReibung in einem System angetriebener, umschlungenerWalzen"*, Doctoral Thesis, Technischen UniversitätMünchen (1971)
3. J. Frechard, D. Knittel, P. Dessagne, J.S. Pellé, G. Gaudiot, J.C. Caspar, G.Heitz, *"Modelling and fast position control of a new unwinding-winding mechanism design"*, Electrimacs 2011, Cergy-Pontoise, France (2011)
4. V.Gassmann, D.Knittel,P.R.Pagilla, M.-A.Bueno,*"H∞ unwinding web tension control of a strip processing plant using a pendulum dancer"* American Control Conference, ACC '09. , 901-906(10-12 June 2009)
5. V. Gassmann, D. Knittel, J. Frechard, *"Multi-Objective Robust Controller Optimization for Complex Mechatronic Systems Design: Application to Roll-to-Roll Systems"*, 12e congrès annuel de la Société Française de Recherche Opérationnelle et d'Aide à la Décision, ROADEF 2011, St Etienne, France, 2011.
6. D. Knittel, A. Arbogast, M. Vedrine, and P.R. Pagilla, *"Decentralized robust control strategies with model based feedforward for elastic web winding systems"*, in American Control Conferences, Minneapolis, Minnesota, USA (2006)
7. D. Knittel, L. Federlin, M. Boutaous, P. Bourgin, M. Loesh, and B. Muller, *"Modelling and tension control of an industrial winder with dancer mechanism"*, in IFAC Symposium on Automation in Mining, Mineral and Metal processing, MMM'2004, Nancy, France (2004)
8. D. Knittel, E. Laroche, D. Gigan, and H. Koc, *"Tension control for winding systems with two-degrees-of-freedom H∞ controllers"*, IEEE Transactions on Industrial Applications, vol. 39, 113-120 (2003)
9. H. Koc, *"Modélisation et commande robuste d'un système d'entrainement de bande flexible"* PhD Thesis, Louis Pasteur University, Strasbourg, France (2000)
10. H. Koc, D. Knittel, M. De Mathelin, and G. Abba, *"Modeling and robust control of winding systems for elastic webs"*, IEEE Transactions on Control Systems Technology, vol. 10, 197-206 (2002)
11. H. Koç, D. Knittel, M. de Mathelin, G. Abba, C. Gauthier, *"Web tension control in an industrial accumulator"*, Proceeding of the 5thInternational Conference on Web Handling, IWEB5, Stillwater (Oklahoma), USA (1999)
12. H. Koç, D. Knittel, G. Abba, M. de Mathelin, C. Gauthier, E. Ostertag, *"Modeling and control of an industrial accumulator in a web transport system"*, Proceeding of the European Control Conference ECC'99 (Sept. 1999)
13. D. Kuhm, D. Knittel, M-A. Bueno, *"Modelling and robust control of an industrial accumulator in roll to roll systems"*, Proceeding of the 35th Annual Conference of the IEEE Industrial Electronics Society, IECON09, Porto, Portugal (2009)
14. D. Kuhm, D. Knittel, *"New design of robust industrial accumulators for elastic webs"*, 18th World Congress of the International Federation of Automatic Control, IFAC, Milano, Italy (2011)
15. D. Knittel, D. Kuhm, *"Multidisciplinary design optimization of an accumulator for a large elasticity range of flexible webs"*, Proceeding of the Third International Conference on Multidisciplinary Design Optimization and Applications, 21-23 June 2010, Paris, France
16. D. Knittel, J. Frechard, M. Vedrines, *"Multi-objective optimization for manufacturing process design: application in roll-to-roll systems"*, Proceeding of the Third International Conference on Multidisciplinary Design Optimization and Applications, 21-23 June 2010, Paris, France
17. C. L. Lin, H. Y. Jan, *"Multi objective PID control for a linear brushless DC motor: an evolutionary approach"*, IEE Proceedings -Electric Power Applications, vol. 149, No 6(Nov 2002)
18. V. Gassmann,*"Commande décentralisée robuste de systemes d'entraînement de bandes à élasticité variable"*, PhD Thesis, University of Strasbourg, Strasbourg, France (2011)
19. P.R. Pagilla, S.S. Garimella, L.H. Dreinhoefer, E.O. King,*"Dynamics and Control of Accumulators in Continuous Strip Processing Lines"*, IEEE Transactions On Industry Applications, Vol. 37, No. 3 (May/June 2001)
20. P.R. Pagilla, I. Singh, R.V. Dwivedula, *"A study on control of accumulators in web processing lines"*, Proceeding of the American Control Conference (2003)
21. A. Popov, A. Farag, H. Werner, *"Tuning of a PID controller using a multi-objective optimization technique applied to a neutralization plant"*, European Control Conference 2005, Seville, Spain(2005)

22. W. Wolfermann, *"Tension control of webs - a review of the problems and solutions in the present and future"* Proceeding of the 3[rd]International Conference on Web Handling, IWEB3, Oklahoma, 198-229 (1995)
23. N. Zahlan, and D.P.Jones, *"Modeling web traction on rolls"*, Proceeding of the 3[rd]International Conference on Web Handling, IWEB3, Oklahoma, 156-171 (1995)
24. K. Zielinski, M. Joost, R. Laur, B. Orlik, *"Comparison of differential evolution and particle swarm optimisation for the optimisation of a PI cascade control"*, IEEE Congress on Evolutionary Computation (2008)

29

Multidisciplinary Design Optimization of Multi-Stage Launch Vehicle using Flight Phases Decomposition

Mathieu Balesdent[1,2,3,a], Nicolas Bérend[1], Philippe Dépincé[3], Abdelhamid Chriette[3]

[1] System Design and Performance Evaluation Department, Onera, 91120 Palaiseau, France
[2] CNES, Launchers Directorate, 91023 Evry, France
[3] Institut de Recherche en Communications et Cybernétique de Nantes, 44321 Nantes, France

Abstract – Optimal design of launch vehicles is a complex multidisciplinary problem. The traditional way to optimize such vehicles is to decompose the problem into the different disciplines and to combine specific solvers and a global optimizer. This paper presents a new MDO method to optimize the configuration of an expendable launch vehicle and describes the application of this method to the design optimization of a small liquid fueled multi-stage launch vehicle. The objective is the payload mass maximization. The proposed bi-level method splits up the original MDO problem into the flight phases and optimizes concurrently the different stages of the launch vehicle. This transversal decomposition allows to reduce the search domain at system-level because the optimization problem at this level is analog to a coordination one. Two formulations of the method are presented and the results are compared to the ones obtained by a standard MDO method.

Keywords: Multidisciplinary Design Optimization, MDO, Launch Vehicles Design, Optimal control, Multi-level optimization

1 Introduction

Optimal design of launch vehicles is a complex task which requires adapted tools to handle the numerous disciplines (*e.g.* propulsion, aerodynamics, structure, mass budget, sizing or trajectory optimization) present in the design problem. These disciplines (which can be coupled) may have antagonistic objectives (*e.g.* structure and mass budget) and the global optimal design might not correspond to the optimum in each discipline. Therefore, specific methods (called Multidisciplinary Design Optimization - MDO - methods) have to be employed in order to find the optimal launch vehicle design.

Optimal design of launch vehicle is a specific MDO problem because it combines optimizations of design and trajectory parameters. Indeed, trajectory optimization is responsible for the launch vehicle performance calculation and the optimal design is strongly dependent of the optimal trajectory found. The most used MDO method in literature to solve the launch vehicle design problem consists in combining disciplinary analyzers and a global optimizer (Multi Discipline Feasible method - MDF - [1], [3], [9]). In this method, the trajectory is considered as a standard discipline and is optimized in its whole. In this method, the global optimizer has to handle all of the design parameters and is subject to a great number of constraints that may induce several problems during the optimization (scaling, important dimension of search domain, lack of robustness with respect to trajectory parameters or initialization, *etc*).

In order to improve the optimization process behavior and to reduce the dimension of the search space, a new method, based on a transversal stage-wise decomposition of the launch vehicle design problem, is proposed. Each stage gathers all the disciplines and is optimized independently from the others. The trajectory is decomposed into elementary flight phases and each one of them is optimized during the different stages optimizations. The optimization method is composed of two levels of optimization. The subsystem-level is composed of the different stages optimizations and the system-level is responsible for the coordination of the optimization process. Each subsystem optimization is analog to the optimization of a single stage launch vehicle, which is easier to solve.

The decomposition into the flight phases has been applied to optimize the trajectory of reusable launch vehicles [6], [7], [8]. This process consists in optimizing separately the different flight phases (Ascent, Orbiter and Return To Launch Site phases) in order to split up the original optimization problem into small ones to improve the optimization process efficiency. In this paper, we propose an extension of this method to the complete multidisciplinary design optimization of expendable launch vehicles.

This paper is organized as follows: in Section 2, we describe the MDO formulations and we present the different MDO methods used in launch vehicle design. In Section 3, we present the application case. In this section, we define the objective, the parameters, the models and the MDO methods formulations. Two formulations of the proposed method will be explained. Section 4 presents the results obtained and compares the different methods described in the previous sections.

[a] Corresponding author : mathieu.balesdent@onera.fr

2 MDO formulations and design methods

A MDO problem can be resumed as follows:

$$\begin{array}{ll} \textbf{minimize} & f(y,z) \\ \textbf{with respect to} & z \\ \textbf{subject to} & g(y,z) \le 0 \quad (1) \\ & h(y,z) = 0 \quad (2) \end{array}$$

where :

- $f(y,z)$: objective function.
- z : design variables. They can be used in one or several subsystems $z = \{z_{sh}, \bar{z}_k\}$. The subscript $_{sh}$ stands for the variables which are shared between different subsystems (global variables) and $\bar{z}_k$ denotes the variables which are specific to one subsystem (local variables). Moreover, we use the notation z_k to describe the variables which refer to the kth subsystem.
- y : coupling variables. These variables are used to link the different subsystems and to evaluate the consistency of the design with regard to the coupling.
- g : inequality constraints.
- h : equality constraints.

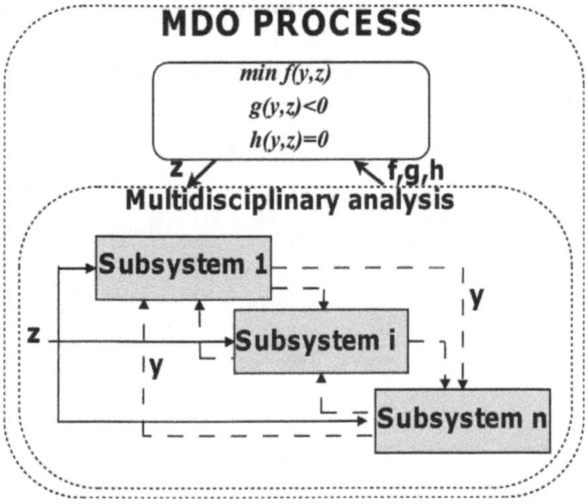

Fig. 1. MDO problem

2.1 Classical design methods

Launch vehicle design is a specific MDO problem because it combines the optimizations of design parameters and a control law. The classical engineering method to solve this problem consists in an interlacing of design parameters and trajectory optimizations. It generally ensues a loop between the design parameters optimization and the control law calculation (analogy with fixed point method). This process is very time consuming.

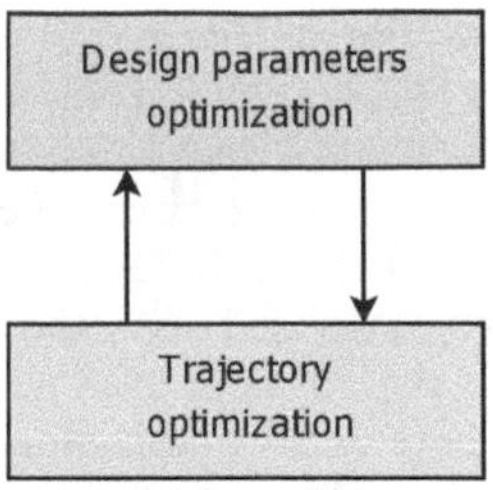

Fig. 2. Classical engineering method

The classical MDO method used in launch vehicle design consists in decomposing the process architecture into the different disciplines and using a MultiDiscipline Feasible (MDF) method. Several other methods (Collaborative Optimization, Bi-Level Systems Synthesis, All-At Once ...) have been tested in launch vehicle design but their use is sporadic. The MDF method consists in a MultiDisciplinary Analysis (MDA) and a global optimizer. The MDA is a process which calls disciplinary analyzers and ensures the consistency of the process with regard to the disciplinary feasibility and the coupling. A global optimizer is used to handle the optimization parameters and to satisfy the constraints. When the disciplines are coupled, the MDA generally consists in a loop between the disciplines. The MDA is performed at each iteration of the global optimizer.
In the MDF method, the optimizer has to handle a large number of variables, especially when trajectory parameters are considered at the same level as the design parameters [3].

Therefore, the important size of the optimizer search domain and the use of MDA at each iteration generate several drawbacks as an important calculation time, a well tuned initialization requirement, an accurate determination of design parameters variation domain (especially for the trajectory ones) or a particular sensitivity to multiple optima phenomena.

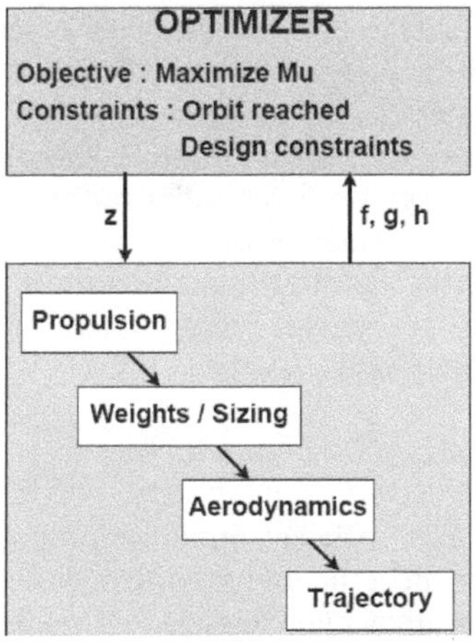

Fig. 3. MDF method

2.2 Stage-wise decomposition

Principle

Design problem decomposition
In order to have an efficient optimization process, a new decomposition of the design problem is proposed. The principle of this method consists in decomposing the initial

optimization problem into smaller ones which can be solved more easily. To this end, the optimization process considers each stage independently and transforms the initial optimization problem to a coordination of elementary ones.

The proposed method is a bi-level one in which the subsystem-level is composed of the different stages optimizations and the system-level is in charge of coordinating the subsystems optimizations (Fig. 4). In that way, each stage optimization is equivalent to the one of a single-stage launch vehicle for an elementary trajectory part, which is a less complex problem and can be quickly solved. Each stage optimization gathers all the different considered disciplines.

In this manner, for a n-stage launch vehicle, the stage-wise decomposition allows to split up the initial problem is into n coordinated smaller one.

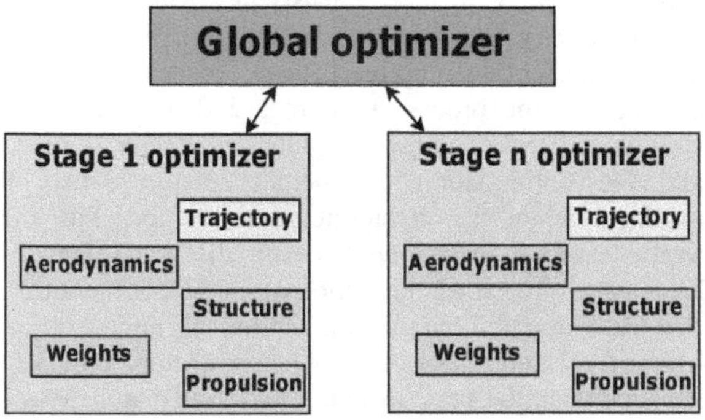

Fig. 4. Stage-wise decomposition

Trajectory handling

The global trajectory is decomposed into n elementary parts and the trajectory parameters corresponding to the different stages flight phases are optimized with the corresponding design parameters in the subsystems optimizations.

In order to take the couplings between the different stages into account, additional variables and constraints are introduced into the initial problem. These ones relate to the state vector at stages separations and the estimated mass of the intermediary and final stages. These variables are optimized by the system-level optimizer at the same time as the shared design parameters z_{sh}.

Thus, the trajectory optimization is performed at both system (state vectors at stages separations) and subsystem (elementary flight phases) levels.

Algorithms used

In order to have an efficient optimization process, we have chosen to implement an hybrid method which associates exploratory algorithm and local search method (Sequential Quadratic Programming) at system-level. First, the exploratory search is performed. The best found design (satisfying the constraints) is used to initialize the local SQP method. Thus, the optimization process takes advantage of the global search algorithm particularity to explore large solutions space and the local method one to efficiently converge to an optimum.

At subsystem-level, the same SQP algorithm is used at both phases I and II, because the optimization problems to solve have small dimension and can be correctly initialized.

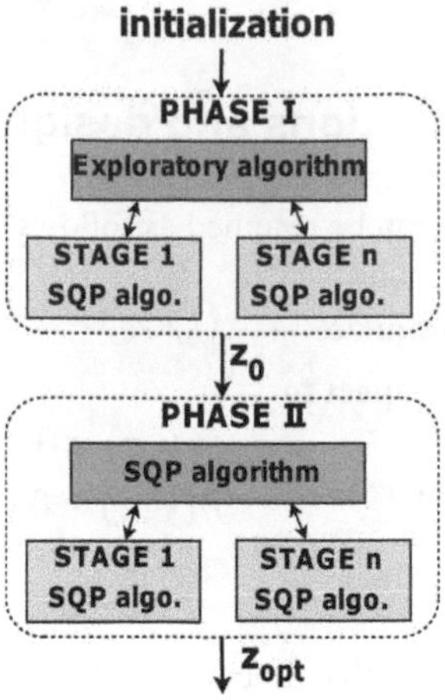

Fig. 5. Optimization process

3 Optimization of a micro liquid fueled launch vehicle

3.1 Presentation of the problem

The problem to solve consists in the optimization of a three-stage-to-orbit launch vehicle for the payload mass maximization. The Gross Lift-Off Weight (GLOW) is constrained to 10 tons. The orbit reached is a 250km altitude Low Earth Orbit. The disciplines considered are propulsion, aerodynamics, weights, and trajectory optimization. The launch vehicle is composed of three liquid fueled Liquid Oxygen/Kerosene (LOX/RP1) stages.

3.2 MDO formulation of the optimization problem

The design parameters used in the optimization process are resumed in Table 1.

Table 1. Design parameters

Disciplines	Stage 1	Stage 2	Stage 3	Payload fairing	Description
Weights	Mp_1	Mp_2	Mp_3		Propellant mass
				Mu	Payload mass
Propulsion	Rm_1	Rm_2	Rm_3		Mixture ratio
	Pc_1	Pc_2	Pc_3		Chamber pressure
	Pe_1	Pe_2	Pe_3		Nozzle exit pressure
	$\left(\frac{T}{W}\right)_1$	$\left(\frac{T}{W}\right)_2$	$\left(\frac{T}{W}\right)_3$		Thrust to weight ratio
Aerodynamics	D_1	D_2	D_3	D_c Al_c	Diameter, Length to diameter ratio
Trajectory	u_1	u_2	u_3		Control law parameter vector

Using the MDO formulation presented in the previous section, the launch vehicle optimization problem can be formulated as follows :

Maximize $f(z) = Mu$

With respect to $z = \{Me_i, \frac{T}{W_i}, Rm_i, Pc_i, Pe_i, D_i, D_c, Alc, u_i, Mu\}$

Subject to

$$g_1(z): Mu - Mu_{available\ under\ fairing} \le 0 \quad (3)$$

$$g_{2...4}(z): 0.4 - \frac{Pe_i}{Pa(r)} \le 0 \quad (4)$$

$$g_{5...7}(z): Dne_i - 0{,}8\ D_i \le 0 \quad (5)$$

$$h_1(z): GLOW - 10000 = 0 \quad (6)$$

$$h_2(z): r_f - r_{orbit} = 0 \quad (7)$$

$$h_4(z): \gamma_f - \gamma_{orbit} = 0 \quad (8)$$

$$h_3(z): v_f - v_{orbit} = 0 \quad (9)$$

where:

- Dne : nozzle exit diameter
- Pa : local atmospheric pressure
- r : radius
- v : velocity
- γ : flight path angle

The inequality constraint g_1 ensures the consistency of the fairing dimensions with regard to the payload, $g_{2...4}$ are flow separation constraints (Summerfield criterion), $g_{5...7}$ are geometry constraints which are introduced to avoid non-realistic designs despite the lack of structural calculation model. The equality constraint h_1 determines the total lift-off weight and $h_{2...4}$ ensure the satisfaction of the mission requirements.

3.3 Models

Propulsion

We have chosen to use liquid fueled stages LOX/RP1. The propulsion module aims to calculate the specific impulse (*Isp*) from *Pc*, *Pe* and *Rm*, by using standard propulsion equations [5].

Trajectory

The model chosen for the trajectory simulation is a bi-dimensional model with a non-rotating round Earth. The trajectory optimization is realized by using a direct method. The parametric control law (pitch angle) is composed of different waypoints θ_i which are optimized all along the trajectory. The pitch angle is calculated by piecewise linear function on θ_i.

$$\dot{r} = V.\sin\gamma \quad (10)$$

$$\dot{V} = -\frac{1}{2}\rho(r)\frac{S_{ref}.C_X(Mach)}{m}V^2 - g(r).\sin\gamma + \frac{F.\cos(\theta-\gamma)}{m} \quad (11)$$

$$\dot{\gamma} = \left(\frac{V}{r} - \frac{g(r)}{V}\right)\cos\gamma + \frac{F.\sin(\theta-\gamma)}{m.V} \quad (12)$$

$$\dot{\phi} = -\frac{V.\cos\gamma}{r} \quad (13)$$

$$\dot{m} = -q \quad (14)$$

with ρ : atmospheric density, S_{ref} : surface of reference, C_X : drag coefficient, $g(r)$: gravity acceleration, θ : pitch angle, m : launch vehicle mass, F : thrust ($F = q.g_0.Isp$) and q : mass flow rate (constant during the flight phase of each stage).

The axial load factor (n_f) is given by the following relationship:

$$n_f = \frac{g_0.q.Isp(r,Pc,Pe,Rm) - \frac{1}{2}\rho S_{ref}V^2 Cx\cos(\theta-\gamma)}{m.g_0} \quad (15)$$

Aerodynamics

We use a zero-lift aerodynamic. The drag coefficient is interpolated from the Mach during the trajectory evaluation. This model is generally sufficient in launch vehicles early phase studies.

Mass budget and geometry sizing

For simplification reasons, we do not perform a complete structural calculation but we use simplified models to determine the mass budget. For each stage, the different considered mass are:

- propellant mass
- dry mass

The upper composite mass is the sum of:

- payload mass
- adaptator mass
- fairing mass

From the propellant mass and the mixture ratio, the volumes and the surfaces of propellant and oxidizer tanks are defined. Then, we compute the dry mass (M_d) by the following simplified models:

$$M_d = (M_{tank} + M_{motor}).c_f \quad (16)$$

$$M_{tank} = kr.S_{tank} \quad (17)$$

$$M_{motor} = km.q \quad (18)$$

with $S_{tank} = S_{LOX} + S_{RP1}$: the total surface of the tanks and c_f : a coupling coefficient between mass budget estimation and trajectory. This coefficient is linearly dependent of the maximal load factor endured by the stage (Table 2). In order to compute the dry mass response surface, the coefficients k_r et k_m have been determined by least-squares estimation on small liquid-fueled stages registered in ESA launch vehicles catalog[4].

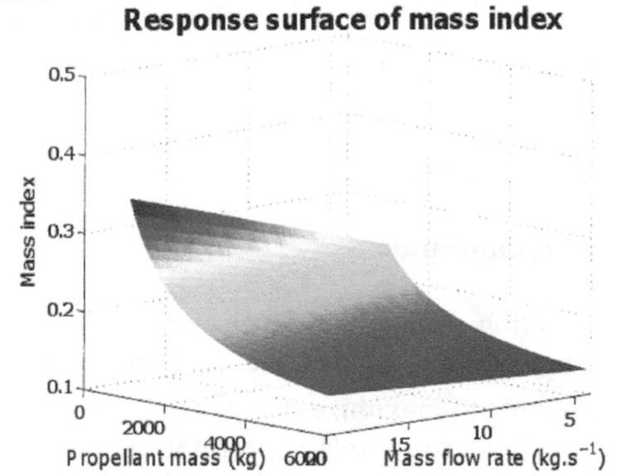

Fig. 6. Response surface of mass index (diameter and mixture ratio are fixed respectively to 1.4m and 2.4)

The GLOW is given by the formula:

$$GLOW = \sum_{i=1}^{3}(Mp_i + Md_i) + M_{fairing} + Mu + M_{adaptator} \quad (19)$$

Table 2. Variations of c_f with respect to the load factor

n_f	0	1	2	3	4	5
c_f	1	1.02	1.04	1.06	1.08	1.1

3.4 Optimization by MDF method

The optimization problem formulation of MDF method is the same as the original problem one. Indeed, a single optimizer has to handle all of the optimization variables and has to satisfy all of the constraints.

Maximize $f(z) = Mu$

With respect to $z = \{Me_i, \frac{T}{W}_i, Rm_i, Pc_i, Pe_i, D_i, D_c, Alc, u_i, n_{f_{max\ estimated}}, Mu\}$

Subject to

$$g_1(z): Mu - Mu_{available\ under\ fairing} \leq 0 \quad (20)$$

$$g_{2...4}(z): 0.4 - \frac{Pe_i}{Pa(r)} \leq 0 \quad (21)$$

$$g_{5...7}(z): Dne_i - 0,8\, D_i \leq 0 \quad (22)$$

$$h_1(z): GLOW - 10000 = 0 \quad (23)$$

$$h_2(z): r_f - r_{orbit} = 0 \quad (24)$$

$$h_3(z): v_f - v_{orbit} = 0 \quad (25)$$

$$h_4(z): \gamma_f - \gamma_{orbit} = 0 \quad (26)$$

$$h_5(z): n_{f_{max\ estimated}} - n_{f_{max\ calculated}} = 0 \quad (27)$$

In order to have a sequential MDA, an additional parameter $n_{f_{max\ estimated}}$ (and its equality constraint h_5) is introduced into the optimization problem. This parameter, used to compute the dry mass (Eq. 16), allows to decouple trajectory and mass budget and to avoid the use of a coupling loop between these disciplines during the MDA.

3.5 Optimization by decomposition into the flight phases

In this section, we present two formulations of the stage-wise decomposition method. The main difference between these two formulations concerns the state vector junction at stages separations.

First formulation

System-level optimization

In this formulation, the system-level optimizer handles the shared design variables z_{sh} and the coupling ones y. This optimizer attempts to maximize the payload mass Mu and to satisfy the junction constraints concerning the mass of second and third stages, which are respectively used by the first and second stages optimizers in order to optimize their configuration. These junction constraints have to be satisfied only at the convergence of phase II. In phase I, these equality constraints are replaced by inequality ones $Mu_{optimized} - Mu_{estimated} \leq 10kg$ in order to improve the exploratory search flexibility.

Maximize $f(z) = Mu$

With respect to $z_{sh} = \{D_1, D_2, D_3, D_c, Al_c\}$, $y = \{r_{f1}, v_{f1}, \gamma_{f1}, \theta_{f1}, r_{f2}, v_{f2}, \gamma_{f2}, \theta_{f2}, Mu_{stage\,1\ estimated}, Mu_{stage\,2\ estimated}, n_{f_{max\ estimated}}\}$

Subject to

$$h_1: Mu_{stage\,1\ estimated} - Mu_{stage\,1\ optimized} = 0 \quad (28)$$

$$h_2: Mu_{stage\,2\ estimated} - Mu_{stage\,2\ optimized} = 0 \quad (29)$$

Subsystem-level optimization

The optimizations at subsystem-level consist in optimizing the payload mass Mu_{stage_i} of the different stages, when the total mass of the stages are defined by the system-level optimizer and have to be satisfied at each iteration (h_{i5}). The payload mass of a stage is equivalent to the sum of the upper stages and the upper composite mass. In this formulation, at each iteration, the junction points at stages separations are consistent since the equality constraints $h_{i1...i5}$ are satisfied at subsystem-level.

Second formulation

Maximize $f_i(z_{sh}, \bar{z}_i, y) = Mu_{stage_i}$

With respect to $\bar{z}_i = \{Mp_i, \left(\frac{T}{W}\right)_i, Rm_i, Pc_i, Pe_i, \theta_i, Mu_{stage_i}\}$

Subject to

$$g_{i1}: n_{f_{max\ stage_i\ calculated}} - n_{f_{max}} \leq 0 \quad (30)$$

$$g_{i2}: 0,4 - \frac{Pe_i}{Pa(r)} \leq 0 \quad (31)$$

$$g_{i3}: Dne_i - 0,8.D_i \leq 0 \quad (32)$$

$$g_{i4}: Mu - Mu_{available\ under\ fairing} \leq 0 \ ^{(b)} \quad (33)$$

$$h_{i1}: r_{f_i} - r_{t=t_{f_i}} = 0 \quad (34)$$

$$h_{i2}: v_{f_i} - v_{t=t_{f_i}} = 0 \quad (35)$$

$$h_{i3}: \gamma_{f_i} - \gamma_{t=t_{f_i}} = 0 \quad (36)$$

$$h_{i4}: \theta_{f_i} - \theta_{t=t_{f_i}} = 0 \ ^{(c)} \quad (37)$$

$$h_{i5}: Mp_i + Md_i + Mu_{stage_i} - Mu_{stage_{i-1}\ estimated} = 0 \ ^{(d)} \quad (38)$$

System-level optimization

In this formulation, the system-level optimizer has to optimize the same objective as the first formulation. On the other hand, the two equality constraints handling the mass junction are replaced by three ones which characterize the convergence of the different subsystems. In comparison with the first formulation, an additional parameter Mu is introduced to the system-level and the inequality constraint relating to the fairing consistency is transferred from the 3rd stage optimizer to the system-level one. In the same way as the first

(b) only for stage 3

(c) only for stages 1 and 2

(d) $Mu_{stage_0\ estimated} = GLOW$

formulation, the equality constraints (40-42) are replaced by inequality ones $f_i \le 10^{-4}$ in phase I.

Maximize $f(z) = Mu$

With respect to $z_{sh} = \{D_1, D_2, D_3, D_c, Al_c\}$,

$y = \{r_{f1}, v_{f1}, \gamma_{f1}, \theta_{f1}, r_{f2}, v_{f2}, \gamma_{f2}, \theta_{f2}, Mu_1, Mu_2, Mu_3 n_{f_{max\ estimated}}\}$

Subject to

$$g_1 : Mu - Mu_{available\ under\ fairing} \le 0 \quad (39)$$

$$h_1 : f_1 = 0 \quad (40)$$

$$h_2 : f_2 = 0 \quad (41)$$

$$h_3 : f_3 = 0 \quad (42)$$

Subsystem-level optimization

The optimizers at subsystem-level aim to reach the instructions given by the system-level. Indeed, each subsystem has to minimize a quadratic sum of differences between the coupling variables y and the ones calculated in the subsystem. In comparison with the first formulation, all the equality constraints are removed and are included in the objective function.

Minimize

$$f_i(z_{sh},\bar{z}_i,y) = \left(\frac{r_{f_i}-r_{t=t_{f_i}}}{R}\right)^2 + \left(\frac{v_{f_i}-v_{t=t_{f_i}}}{V}\right)^2 + \left(\frac{\gamma_{f_i}-\gamma_{t=t_{f_i}}}{\Gamma}\right)^2 + \left(\frac{\theta_{f_i}-\theta_{t=t_{f_i}}}{\Theta}\right)^2 + \left(\frac{M_{stage_i}+Mu_i-Mu_{i-1}}{M}\right)^2 \quad ^{(e)}$$

With respect to $\bar{z}_i = \{Mp_i, \left(\frac{T}{W}\right)_i, Rm_i, Pc_i, Pe_i, \theta_i\}$

Subject to

$$g_{i1} : n_{f_{max\ stage_i\ calculated}} - n_{f_{max}} \le 0 \quad (43)$$

$$g_{i2} : 0{,}4 - \frac{Pe_i}{Pa(r)} \le 0 \quad (44)$$

$$g_{i3} : Dne_i - 0{,}8 . D_i \le 0 \quad (45)$$

where R, V, Γ, Θ and M are scaling coefficients.

4 Results and comparison

4.1 Results

With an appropriate adjustment of the system-level optimization, the MDF and the proposed methods converge to the same optimum (*Mu=60.9kg*). Indeed, in both methods, well tuned initializations and adapted settings have been found in order to allow the system-level optimizers to converge. Thus, the comparison between the two methods is not based on the optimal value of the objective but on the manner to reach it. The calculation volume to obtain the optimum is different for both methods:

- In MDF, the optimizer has to handle a 34-dimension search space, which is very time consuming with both exploratory and local search methods.
- In stage-wise decomposition method, the optimizer at system-level has to handle only 16 (17 for 2nd formulation) variables. The search space dimension of each subsystem optimizer is 10 (9 for 2nd formulation).

The optimal trajectory is given in figure 7. The maximum relative difference between the two optimized control laws is about 0.15°.

Table 3. Results obtained by using MDO and stage-wise decomposition methods

Parameters	MDF	Stage-wise decomposition
Mp_1 (kg)	5925	5929
Mp_2 (kg)	1949	1946
Mp_3 (kg)	266	266
Mu (kg)	60.9	60.9
Rm_1	2.26	2.26
Rm_2	2.35	2.35
Rm_3	2.38	2.38
Pc_1 (bar)	**60**(f)	**60**
Pc_2 (bar)	**50**	**50**
Pc_3 (bar)	**40**	**40**
Ps_1 (bar)	0.44	0.44
Ps_2 (bar)	**0.05**	**0.05**
Ps_3 (bar)	**0.05**	**0.05**
T/W_1(s)	1.94	1.94
T/W_2(s)	1.40	1.39
T/W_3(s)	0.63	0.63
D_1 (m)	1.41	1.41
D_2 (m)	1.41	1.41
D_3 (m)	1.41	1.41
Dc (m)	1.41	1.41
Al_c	2.50	2.51
n_f	4.63	4.64

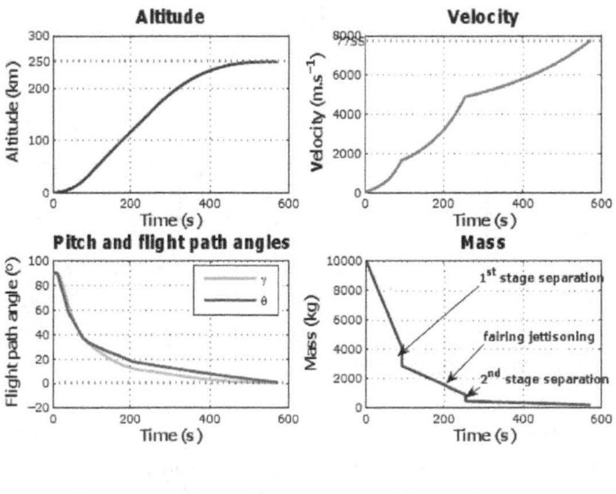

(a) State vector

(e) $\left(\frac{\theta_{f_i}-\theta_{t=t_{f_i}}}{\Theta}\right)^2$ only required for stages 1 and 2, $Mu_3 = Mu$ and $Mu_0 = GLOW$

(f) Bold characters indicate the parameters which reach upper or lower bounds

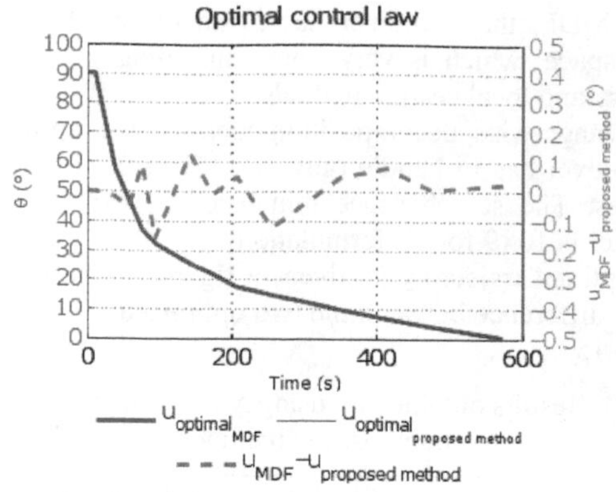

(b) Control law *(u)*

Fig. 7. Trajectory of the optimal design

4.2 Comparison of MDF and stage-wise decomposition formulations

Dimension of search spaces and numbers of constraints

By decomposing the optimization problem, the search domain of each optimization process at system and subsystem levels is considerably reduced, that makes the proposed method less sensitive to local optima phenomena than MDF method (in which the single optimizer has to handle a great number of variables).

Table 4 recapitulates the number of constraints and parameters handled by the MDF and stage-wise decomposition system-level optimizers. The stage-wise decomposition method allows to distribute constraints on system and subsystem levels.

Moreover, since the search domain at system-level is reduced, an exploratory algorithm can be used in order to initialize a local-search one. The joint use of these two kinds of algorithms avoids resorting to manual initialization. In the MDF method, the use of exploratory algorithm implies an important calculation time because the search domain is too large.

Table 4. Comparison of MDF and stage-wise decomposition formulations

	MDF	System-level, 1st formulation	System-level, 2nd formulation
Dimension of search space	34	16	17
Equality constraints	5	2	3
Inequality constraints	7	0	1

Numerical analysis of search space dimensions and number of constraints

In this section, we express the search space dimension and the number of constraints with respect to the problem characteristics, in order to compare the different formulations.

Dimension of search space

Let us consider:

- n_e : number of stages,
- n_x : dimension of the state vector,
- n_c : dimension of the control law parameters vector,
- n_{pp} : number of control law waypoints per stage,
- n_{psh} : number of design parameters per stage which play a part in the flight phases of several stages,
- $n_{fairing}$: number of parameters which are used to size the fairing,
- n_{pk} : number of design parameters per stage which only play a part in the kth stage flight phase.

The number of parameters n_{MDF} handled by the MDF optimizer can be expressed as follows:

$$n_{MDF} = n_e(n_{pk} + n_c.n_{pp} + n_{psh}) + n_{fairing} + 2 \quad (46)$$

where "2" stands for the payload mass and the estimated maximal axial load factor.

The numbers of parameters n_{f_1}, n_{f_2} handled by the system-level optimizers in case of the first and the second formulations of the proposed method are:

$$n_{f_1} = (n_e - 1).(n_x - 2) + (n_e - 1).n_c + n_e.n_{psh} + (n_e - 1) + n_{fairing} + 1 \quad (47)$$

$$n_{f_2} = (n_e - 1).(n_x - 2) + (n_e - 1).n_c + n_e.n_{psh} + n_e + n_{fairing} + 1 \quad (48)$$

where:

- $(n_e - 1).(n_x - 2)$: variables of state vector junctions (without mass and longitude)
- $(n_e - 1).n_c$: variables of control law junction (not required for the last stage)
- $n_e.n_{psh}$: design parameters which are shared at the system-level (stages diameters)
- $n_e - 1$ (g), n_e (h) : estimated payload mass of the different stages
- 1 : estimated maximal load factor

Dimension of search space

The number of constraints $n_{c_{MDF}}$ for the MDF problem is:

$$n_{c_{MDF}} = 2.n_e + (n_x - 1) + 2 \quad (49)$$

where:

- $2.n_e$: constraints about the pressures and the nozzle exit diameters (Eq. 21, 22)
- $(n_x - 1)$: sum of numbers of constraints about the state at the final time $(n_x - 2)$ (Eq. 24-26) and the GLOW (1) (Eq. 23)
- 2 : constraints about the consistency of the fairing and the load factor (Eq. 20, 27)

The numbers of constraints $n_{c_{f_1}}$, $n_{c_{f_2}}$ handled by the proposed method system-level optimizers are given by:

$$n_{c_{f_1}} = n_e - 1 \quad (50)$$

(g) 1st formulation

(h) 2nd formulation

$$n_{c_{f_2}} = n_e + 1 \quad (51)$$

The evolutions of the search spaces dimensions and the number of constraints with respect to the number of stages are given in figure 8. We can see that the proposed method is all the more beneficial as the number of stages grows.

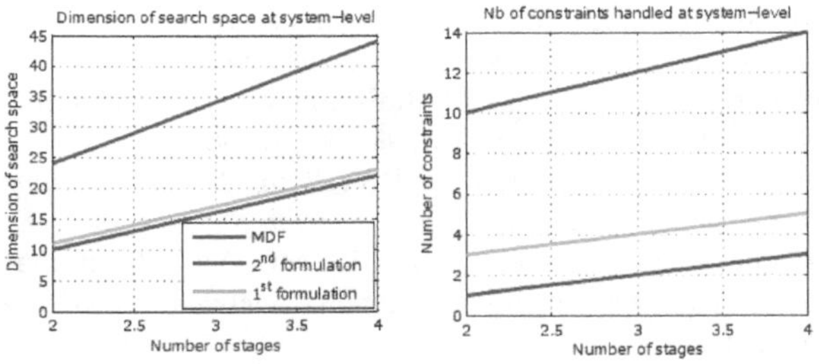

Fig. 8. Variations of search space dimension and number of constraints with respect to the number of stages

Modularity

The flight-phases decomposition method is very modular. Indeed, we can add or subtract a stage without modifying the design process architecture. Moreover, this architecture remains unchanged if the disciplinary codes are modified, which is not the case with the classical method.

Since the optimization problem is decomposed in two levels and the optimization problem at system-level is resumed to a coordination one, the proposed method allows to parallelize the optimizations of the different launch vehicle stages, in order to improve the efficiency of the optimization process.

Finally, the proposed method allows to freeze one or several stages while optimizing the others, which is useful when we want to reuse existing stages.

4.3 Comparison of first and second stage-wise decomposition formulations

The second formulation aims to improve convergence properties at the subsystem and system levels. Indeed, in this formulation, each stage does not optimize its payload Mu_{stage_i} and is not subject to equality constraints anymore, but minimizes a quadratic sum of differences with respect to system-level instructions. This formulation associates the proposed stage-wise decomposition and the Collaborative Optimization [2].

At the system-level, the two mass consistency constraints are replaced by three equality constraints, which ensure the convergence of each stage optimization. In comparison with the first formulation, the system-level design problem includes one parameter, one equality and one inequality constraint. The objective Mu is directly optimized by the system-level optimizer. The equality constraints at system-level consist in the objectives of the different subsystems. In that way, we can expect a better behavior of the optimization process by using the second formulation (particularly in phase I) because the subsystem-level objectives minimization aims to satisfy the system-level equality constraints.

At the subsystem-level, all the equality constraints are removed and each subproblem dimension is reduced by one (Table 5). The relaxation of the equality constraints in the objective function aims to improve the subsystem-level optimizers behaviors and the robustness with respect to the system-level parameters. Indeed, the strict satisfaction of the coupling constraints (particularly the continuity of the state vector at stages separations) has not to be satisfied at each iteration of the system-level, but only at the convergence (Eq. 40-42), which is not the case through the first formulation.

Table 5. Comparison of stage-wise decomposition formulations at system and subsystem levels

	System-level	Stage 1	Stage 2	Stage 3	Total
Dimension of search space					
First formulation	16	10	10	10	46
Second formulation	17	9	9	9	44
Equality constraints					
First formulation	2	5	5	4	16
Second formulation	3	0	0	0	3
Inequality constraints					
First formulation	0	3	3	4	10
Second formulation	1	3	3	3	10

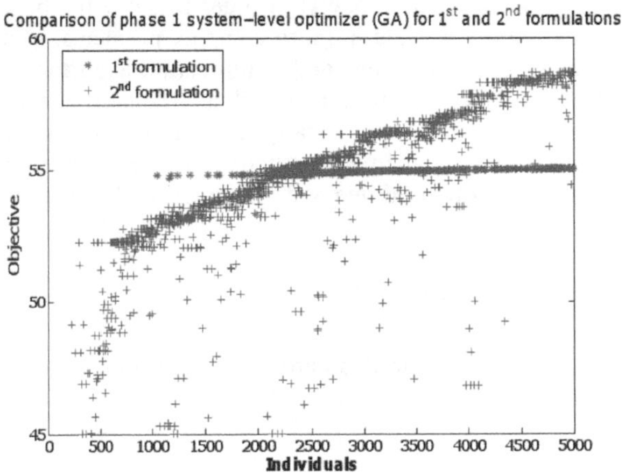

Fig. 9. Phase I optimization with first and second formulations (feasible points)

In order to quantify the improvements of the second formulation with respect to the first one, a comparative study has been realized. In this study, a genetic algorithm (100 generations of 50 individuals) with the same initialization and the same bounds of design parameters has been performed in case of both formulations. The results of the exploratory phase (Fig. 9) show that the second formulation is more adapted than the first one to the optimization problem and converges to the optimum while the first formulation limits the search around the first found design which satisfies the constraints. Study reveals than with the first formulation, 15% of the design points are non feasible (subsystem-level does not converge) but there are only 0.3% with the second formulation (Table 6). In that way, with the relaxation of the equality constraints to the objective function, the robustness of the subsystem-level with regard to the system-level parameters is improved and the 2nd formulation leads to a better efficiency of the design process in its whole.

Table 6. Summary of formulations tests

	1st formulation	2nd formulation
Nb. of individuals for which subsystems converge	4257	4987
Nb. of individuals for which subsystems do not converge	743	13
Total of individuals	5000	5000

5 Conclusion and future works

In this paper, we have presented a new MDO formulation adapted to the expendable launch vehicle design problem. The proposed bi-level method allows to turn the initial optimization problem into a coordination one which can be solved easier. By decomposing the problem, the search domain at system-level is considerably reduced and the behavior of the optimization process is improved. Two formulations of the method have been proposed and compared. Results show than the collaborative formulation of the method is more adapted to the design problem and allows to improve the robustness of the subsystem-level with respect to system-level parameters.
Future works will consist in improving the models (particularly the mass budget models) in order to study the benefits of the proposed method in more complex problems. Moreover, different formulations and optimization algorithms will be tested in order to determine which are the most adapted to the optimization problem. Finally, other trajectory optimization methods (*e.g.* indirect method) may be more efficient than the currently used one and are worth studying in future works.

Acknowledgement

The work presented in this paper is part of a PhD thesis cofunded by CNES and Onera.

References

1. D. Bayley, R. Hartfield, J. Burkhalter and R. Jenkins, *Design Optimization of a Space Launch Vehicle Using a Genetic Algorithm*, Journal of Spacecraft and Rockets, **45**(4), 733-740, (2008).
2. R. Braun and I. Kroo. *Development and application of the Collaborative Optimization architecture in a multidisciplinary design environment*, Multidisciplinary Design Optimization : State of the Art, SIAM, 98-116, (1996).
3. N. Duranté, A. Dufour and V. Pain. *Multidisciplinary Analysis and Optimisation Approach for the Design of Expendable Launchers*, 10th AIAA/ISSMO Multidisciplinary Analysis and Optimization Conference, Albany, New-York, USA (2004)
4. ESA Directorate of launchers, ESA Launch Vehicle Catalogue (2004)
5. R.W. Humble, G.N. Henry and W.J. Larson. *Space propulsion analysis and design*, The McGraw-Hill Companies, Inc. (1995)
6. L.A. Ledsinger and J.R. Olds *Optimized Solutions for Kistler K-1 Branching Trajectories Using Multidisciplinary Design Optimization Techniques*, Journal of Spacecraft and Rockets, **39**(3), 420-429, (2002).
7. L. Perrot. *Optimisation of reusable launchers by decomposition and coordination of trajectory optimization problems*, 5th International Conference on Launcher Technology, Space Launchers: Missions, Control and Avionics. Madrid, Spain (November 2003)
8. M. Rahn and U.M. Schöttle *Decomposition Algorithm for Flight Performance and System Optimization of an Airbreathing Launch Vehicle*, 45th Congress of International Astronautical Federation. Jerusalem, Israel, (October 1994)
9. T. Tsuchiya and T. Mori *Optimal Conceptual Design of Two-Stage Reusable Rocket Vehicles Including Trajectory Optimization*. Journal of Spacecraft and Rockets, **41**(5), 770-778, (2004).

30

A Procedure of Global Optimization and its Application to Estimate Parameters in Interaction Spatial Models

Edson Tadeu Bez[1], Mirian Buss Gonçalves[2], José Eduardo Souza de Cursi [3,a]

[1] Universidade do Vale do Itajaí – UNIVALI, Rodovia SC 407, Km 04, CEP 88122-000, São José/SC, Brazil
[2] Universidade Federal de Santa Catarina – UFSC, Depto de Engenharia de Produção e Sistemas, 88010-970, Florianópolis/SC, Brazil
[3] LMR – INSA – Rouen, Avenue de l'Université BP 8, Saint-Etienne du Rouvray, FR-76801, France

Abstract – This work concerns the calibration of trip distribution models issued from Transportation Planning. The optimal estimators are the global minima of a non-convex function. A mathematical result establishes that the solution is the limit of a sequence of means of convenient random variables. A population-based global optimization involving this representation and random perturbations of a local descent method is applied. Experiments are performed on classical test functions. In the application to the models of trip distribution, 4 sets of data, including real data are used. The results show that the use of the representation of the solution leads to a significant improvement and increases the robustness.

Key words: Global Optimization; Parameter Estimation; Calibration; Spatial Interaction Models

1 Introduction

Nowadays many studies focus on the development of robust mathematical methods that allow one to solve important problems in engineering. One carefully analyzes strategies for general solutions of the problems, instead of looking for particular solutions that would solve specific situations.

In Transport Planning, one of the problems that require the application of robust methods of optimization is the estimation of parameters of spatial interaction models. Beyond its utilization in transport planning, these models are also used in urban planning, in particular, in the planning of services as education and health. (Lowe[23], Soot[31], Almeida[1] and Almeida[2]).

Since its origin, in the middle of the past century, a good number of models of spatial interaction was developed and tested, mainly in the United States and the United Kingdom. Between them, the most popular and widely used is the gravitational model, conceived empirically from an analogy with the gravity law of Newton and which received, later, a more solid theoretical justification, based on the principle of the maximization of the entropy (Wilson[36] and Wilson[37]).

The gravitational models constitute the most common form of the models of trip distribution currently in use (Zhao[39]). They are aggregate models that are based on the hypothesis that the number of trips between two zones of traffic is directly proportional to the relative attractiveness of each zone and inversely proportional to some function of spatial separation between the zones.

Another important class of aggregate models is constituted by the models of opportunities, which are derived from postulates associated to the choice of destination. In this class of models, the models of intervening opportunities (Schneider[27]) and the models of competitive destinations can be cited (Fotheringham[12]).

From the amalgamation of the gravitational models and intervening opportunities models, the hybrid models appeared, also called of gravity-opportunity models (Baxter[3], Wills[35], Gonçalves[16] and Gonçalves[17]).

To incorporate, in a disaggregated manner, the behavior of the users in spatial interaction models, it has appeared, more recently, the models of choice of destination (Ben-Akiva[5] and Ortuzar[24]). These models have been accepted as a possible alternative to the aggregated models, especially, to the gravitational models. However, comparing these models with the gravitational ones, Zhao[39] affirm: "Aside from the disaggregate-versus-aggregate distinction, the two models actually share more similarities than differences. In terms of functional forms, the *logit* model, into which destination choice models are frequently formulated, actually belong to the gravity model family. A production-constrained gravity model with an exponential impedance function is identical, up to a constant multiplier, to a *logit* destination choice model with a utility function. The only difference is that disaggregate *logit* models of destination choice include attributes of the individual or household, and aggregate gravity models include zonal demographic and socioeconomic measures."

Another form to incorporate behavioral aspects in spatial interaction models was introduced by Almeida[2]. In their work, these authors present a methodology to incorporate behavioral aspects in the intervening opportunities models and/or hybrid models. For this, they use in the definition of intervening opportunities a function of utility, based on the Economic Theory of the Consumer and calibrated through

[a] Corresponding author: eduardo.souza@insa-rouen.fr

techniques of state preference. An advantage of the presented methodology is the incorporation of the disaggregated behavioral modeling in the aggregate models of trip distribution, which are more treatable in diverse practical situations.

We remark, in this context, that the aggregate models continue to have an important role in the planning of urban services and transports, both in the developed world (Zhao[39] and Horowitz[21]), and in developing countries (Wirasinghe[38]). So, the evolution of the aggregate models and/or the methodologies of calibration, aiming at making the operational procedures simple for the practitioners, is of great importance.

Although the calibration of the gravitational models is simple, this does not occur with the other aggregate models cited above. Until today, the model of intervening opportunities is cited as a model with calibration problems (Zhao[39]). The same occurs with the model of competitive destinations (Fotheringham[12] and Diplock[10]) and with the hybrid model of Gonçalves and Ulysséa-Neto (Gonçalves[17], Diplock[10] and Gonçalves[19]). All these models need robust methods of optimization for its calibration.

In the literature, we can find a great number of optimization methods that are adequate to solve problems characterized by convex functions, but that do not present good performance for more complex problems, involving non convex functions, finding the optimal in narrow and deep cracks or in extensive and plain regions, or local minimums with similar values, etc.

Many studies are centered in the determination of new procedures, more robust, that make possible the determination of the global optimal, independent of the problem to be solved. These methods combine, in the majority of the cases, already existing methods, generating hybrid procedures, with the objective to advantage what each one has of better. One of the ways mentioned in the literature combines evolutionary algorithms with classic descent methods, aiming at joining advantages of the evolutionary methods, as efficiency and flexibility, to the precision and speed of search of traditional descent methods.

In this paper, we present a hybrid procedure of representations of solutions in global optimization. This procedure uses an evolutionary version presented by Gonçalves[19], of an algorithm based on random perturbations of the gradient method and a formula of representation of the global optimal given by Souza de Cursi[32] and Souza de Cursi[33], on the improvement of the initial population. Also we introduce an optimal step in the gradient method, conveniently defined, in each iteration. Tests with classical functions show that the improvements introduced in the original algorithm made it sufficiently robust, with potential to resolve applied problems (Bez[6] and Bez[8]).

We present an evaluation of the potential of the developed algorithm to solve two relevant problems. The first one consists in calibrating the model of competitive destinations of Fotheringham[12], comparing its performance with the one of an evolutionary strategy used by Diplock[10]. The choice of this strategy is due to the empirical evidence of its good performance (Schwefel[29]), compared with eleven conventional optimization methods in the solving of 28 test problems.

The second problem consists in calibrating the hybrid model of Gonçalves[17]. This problem was object of previous study of two of the authors (Gonçalves[19]), and they used, in the tests, a real data set, corresponding to the intercities trips of bus passengers, in a region formed by 77 cities in the State of Santa Catarina, Brazil. Although in this work the calibration was successful, tests with other data bases showed a certain fragility of the algorithms presented in the initialization of its parameters. So, one looked for to develop a more robust algorithm, and to get a default set of parameters for its initialization, in order to make it simple of use for the professionals in the area of urban planning and transports.

The paper is organized as follows: In section 2, we present the models which will be studied, as well as the objective functions that must be minimized for the estimation of the model's parameters. In sections 3 and 4, we introduce the developed algorithm and we leave a proof of its convergence to the appendix. In section 5, we present some tests with classical functions. Next, in section 6, we present an application of the algorithm for the calibration of the model of competitive destinations of Fotheringham[12]. We also make a comparison between the results obtained with the use of the developed algorithm and with the use of and evolutionary strategy as done by Diplock[10]. In section 7, we show the results obtained in the calibration of the hybrid model of Gonçalves[17]. The goal of this application is the search of a set of default initialization parameters. Finally, in section 8, we present some conclusions.

2 Setting, calibrating and calibration criteria generalized gravitational model for spatial interactions

The flows observed between locations L_i and L_j are usually referred as *spatial interactions*. Their estimation is a crucial point in the evaluation or planning of transportation systems. An interesting – and popular – framework for this is furnished by the *gravity models*. These models are based on the empirical observation that spatial interactions decrease with the distance separating L_i and L_j. This observation has suggested to some authors that spatial interaction may be considered as being similar to gravitational one and that Newton's gravity model may be used in order to explain the empirical observations concerning flows between origins and destinations. In the pioneer works, a Newtonian-like law depending on the inverse of distance has been used and the expected flow T_{ij} going from L_i to L_j, separated by a distance d_{ij} has been estimated as $T_{ij} = M_i M_j / d_{ij}^{\gamma}$, where M_i and M_j are "masses" representing the importance of L_i and L_j, respectively, while γ is a parameter to be obtained from experimental evidence. In subsequent works, *generalized gravity models* have brought improvements to this basic model. For instance,

- the physical distance d_{ij} may be replaced by a more general quantity c_{ij} giving a measurement of the spatial separation of locations *i* e *j*. The matrix $c = \left[c_{ij}\right]_{1 \le i,j \le n}$ is referred as *spatial separation matrix*.
- the standard Newtonian-like law may be replaced by a decreasing function $g(\bullet)$. Usually, g is defined by

using a set of *parameters* **x**, which characterizes the attractiveness/generation of flows of the locations and the efficiency of the transport system.

- the "masses" M_i and M_j may be replaced by coefficients $M_{o,i}$ and $M_{d,j}$ representing the importance of L_i as origin and of L_j as destination of flows, respectively: a distinction is introduced in the importance as destination and the importance as origin of each location.

With these notations, the expected flows are given by

$$T_{ij} = M_{o,i} M_{d,j} g_{ij} \ , \ g_{ij} = g\left(\boldsymbol{x}, c_{ij}\right) \ .$$

A simple way to define the importance of each location as origin or destination of flows consists in using the global flows O_i originated at L_i and D_j destined to L_j:

$$D_j = T_{\bullet j} = \sum_i T_{ij} \ , \ O_i = T_{i\bullet} = \sum_j T_{ij} \ . \qquad (1)$$

O_i and D_j may be considered as measurements of such an importance and the coefficients $M_{o,i}$ and $M_{d,j}$ may be assumed to be proportional to these values:

$$M_{o,i} = A_i O_i \text{ and } M_{d,j} = B_j D_j ,$$

what leads to the expected flows

$$T_{ij} = A_i O_i B_j D_j g_{ij} \ . \qquad (2)$$

Eq. (1) implies that

$$A_i = \left(\sum_{j=1}^{n} B_j D_j g_{ij} \right)^{-1} \ , \ B_j = \left(\sum_{i=1}^{n} A_i O_i g_{ij} \right)^{-1} \qquad (3)$$

Eq. (3) shows that the coefficients $\boldsymbol{A} = \left(A_1, \ ..., \ A_n\right)$ and $\boldsymbol{B} = \left(B_1, \ ..., \ B_n\right)$ ensure that global coherence between inflows and outflows of the system: they are referred as *balancing factors*. For a given set of parameters $\boldsymbol{x}$ and a given spatial separation matrix **c**, the values of $\left[g_{ij}\right]_{1 \le i,j \le n}$ are known and Eqs. (1) – (3) form a nonlinear algebraical system for the unknowns A, B, $\boldsymbol{T} = \left[T_{ij}\right]_{1 \le i,j \le n}$, $\boldsymbol{O} = \left(O_1, \ ..., \ O_n\right)$, $\boldsymbol{D} = \left(D_1, \ ..., \ D_n\right)$. This feature is exploited in numerical calculations: for a given set of parameters $\boldsymbol{x}$, the solution of Eqs. (1) – (3) furnishes balancing factors $\boldsymbol{A}(x)$ and $\boldsymbol{B}(x)$, estimated fluxes $T(x) = \left[T_{ij}\left(\boldsymbol{x}\right)\right]_{1 \le i,j \le n}$, $\boldsymbol{O}\left(\boldsymbol{x}\right) = \left(O_1\left(\boldsymbol{x}\right), \ ..., \ O_n\left(\boldsymbol{x}\right)\right)$ and $D\left(\boldsymbol{x}\right) = \left(D_1\left(\boldsymbol{x}\right), \ ..., \ D_n\left(\boldsymbol{x}\right)\right)$.

In this work, we solve these equations by the classical iterative method of the equilibrium of the matrices, which is also called method of Furness. By limitation of the room, we do not give here the description of this classical method: the reader interested in these aspects may refer, for instance, to Gonçalves[19].

One of the main criticisms on the gravity models concerns the fact that other factors than the distance may influence the attractiveness of a destination: for instance, the same facility may be available in several possible destinations, but their attractiveness may be not directly connected to the distance. In such a situation, the destinations may be considered as being in competition in order to generate inflows and the probability of choosing a specific destination depends also of the opportunities offered in the region under analysis – referred as *intervening opportunities*.

This observation has led some authors to consider improvements of the generalized gravity model by the adjonction of supplementary parameters describing other spatial effects. This is generally performed by, on the one hand, the introduction in the model of a supplementary matrix $\boldsymbol{w} = \left[w_{ij}\right]_{1 \le i,j \le n}$ involving a measurement the supplementary effects to be considered and, on the other hand, a modification of the function g in order to take into account the supplementary variable $\boldsymbol{w}$:

$$g_{ij} = g\left(c_{ij}, w_{ij}\right). \qquad (4)$$

We consider in the sequel two classical models, which are used to illustrate the procedure proposed.

2.1 A model of competitive destinations

Sheppard[30] has considered that, for an individual from a given origin – for instance, L_i - the probability of a destination – for instance, L_j - depends on its relative accessibility when compared to the alternative destinations. For instance, this probability has not the same value if L_j is the only possible destination for a habitant of L_i or an individual from L_i may choose among several possible destinations, including L_j. These ideas have led to the model of *competitive destinations*, formulated by Fotheringham[12]. We consider here the version of this model proposed by Diplock[10], where **w** furnishes a measurement of the accessibility of the potential destinations (Gitlesen[15]). This version reads as:

$$\boldsymbol{B} = (1, \ ..., \ 1) \ , \ g(c_{ij}, w_{ij}) = w_{ij}^{-\delta} e^{-\beta c_{ij}}, \qquad (5)$$

where w_{ij} is a measurement of the perception by an individual from L_i of the relative accessibility of destination L_j when compared to the other possible destinations. Fotheringham[12], Fotheringham[13] and Fotheringham[14] has defined

$$w_{ij} = \sum_{\substack{k \\ k \ne i, k \ne j}} D_k e^{\sigma c_{jk}} \qquad (6)$$

For this model, $\boldsymbol{x} = (\delta, \ \beta, \ \sigma)$ which are impedance parameters connected to the accessibility, the spatial separation and the importance of the distance in the perception of the accessibility, respectively.

2.2 A model involving intervening opportunities

We consider also a second model, introduced by (Gonçalves[17]). This model takes into account intervening opportunities in the expected flows by using

$$g_{ij} = g\left(c_{ij}, w_{ij}\right) = e^{-(\beta c_{ij} + \lambda w_{ij})}. \quad (7)$$

Here, $w = \left[w_{ij}\right]_{1 \le i,j \le n}$ is a measurement of the intervening opportunities for a flow from location L_i to L_j. In this case, $x = (\beta, \lambda)$, which are impedance parameters for the spatial separation and the intervening opportunities, respectively.

2.3 Calibration of the models

An important step for the practical use of spatial interaction models is their calibration, i. e., the determination of the parameters x of the model and the associated balancing factors $A(x)$ and $B(x)$. These parameters are determined by comparing the estimations $T(x)$ of the model to empirical data T^*: the parameters must be set to values that furnish estimations which are as close as possible to the observed flows. In practice, the empirical data consists in

- The matrix of the measured flows $T^* = \left[T^*_{ij}\right]_{1 \le i,j \le n}$;
- The spatial separation matrix $c = \left[c_{ij}\right]_{1 \le i,j \le n}$;
- The supplementary matrix $w = \left[w_{ij}\right]_{1 \le i,j \le n}$.

The empirical vectors giving the generated and received flows at each location are denoted by $O^* = (O^*_1, O^*_2, \ldots O^*_n)$ and $D^* = (D^*_1, D^*_2, \ldots D^*_n)$, respectively, and are obtained from these data by using the relations (1):

$$D^*_j = T^*_{\bullet j} = \sum_i T^*_{ij} \;,\; O^*_j = T^*_{i\bullet} = \sum_j T^*_{ij} \;.$$

As previously observed, the goal is to determine a set of parameters and balancing factors such that the estimations furnished by the model are, on the one hand, consistent with the balance of inflow and outflow at each traffic zone and, on the other hand, as close as possible of the empirical data available.

Thus, the calibration involves,

- on the one hand, the choice of a *calibration criterion*, i. e., a measurement of the distance between empirical and estimated flows;
- on the other hand, a procedure for the determination of the parameters and balancing factors. This procedure is usually computational and involves optimization methods for the minimization of the calibration criterion.

Thus, the calibration consists in determining

$$x^* = Arg\,\underset{S}{Min}F \quad (8)$$

where $S \subset V = R^n$ is the admissible region for the parameters and F is the calibration criterium. The optimal value of F is $F^* = F(x^*)$.

Different choices of F may be considered for a given model, but in general, the calibration criterion is non convex and the determination of x^* is a difficult problem of global optimization. This work is mainly concerned by the resolution of this last difficulty and we shall illustrate the procedure proposed by using two choices of F.

2.4 Calibration criterion for the model of competitive destinations

For this model, we use the mean quadratic error introduced by Diplock[10]:

$$F(x) = \frac{1}{n^2} \sum_{i,j=1}^{n} (T^*_{ij} - T_{ij}(x))^2 \cdot \quad (9)$$

Although the parameters may take any non-negative value, it is more useful to look for the parameters in a box-bounded region:

$$S = \{x = (\delta, \beta, \sigma) \in V : 0 \le \delta \le \delta_{max},\; 0 \le \beta \le \beta_{max},\; 0 \le \sigma \le \sigma_{max}\}. \quad (10)$$

More general search regions may also be considered, such as, for instance, admissible regions defined by linear or nonlinear constraints (see, for instance, Bouhadi[9] or Souza de Cursi[34]).

2.5 Calibration criterion for the model involving intervening opportunities

By assuming that the flows T_{ij} are random variables multinomially distributed, the maximum likelihood estimations of x, A and B verify, in addition to Eqs. (1) – (4),

$$\frac{1}{T^*} \sum_{i,j=1}^{n} c_{ij} T^*_{ij} = \frac{1}{T(x)} \sum_{i,j=1}^{n} c_{ij} T_{ij}(x) \quad (11)$$

$$\frac{1}{T^*} \sum_{i,j=1}^{n} w_{ij} T^*_{ij} = \frac{1}{T(x)} \sum_{i,j=1}^{n} w_{ij} T_{ij}(x) \quad (12)$$

where T^* and $T(x)$ are the global flows:

$$T^* = \sum_{i,j=1}^{n} T^*_{ij} \;;\; T(x) = \sum_{i,j=1}^{n} T_{ij}(x) \quad . \quad (13)$$

In practice, these equations are not exactly satisfied and it is more convenient to look for approximate solutions, such as for instance, least squares ones by

$$E(x,a) = \frac{1}{T^*} \sum_{i,j=1}^{n} a_{ij} T^*_{ij} - \frac{1}{T(x)} \sum_{i,j=1}^{n} a_{ij} T_{ij}(x) \;, \quad (14)$$

an approximate solution is determined by minimizing $F : V \to R$ given by

$$F(x) = \left(E(x,c)\right)^2 + \left(E(x,w)\right)^2. \quad (15)$$

Here, we look for the parameters in the box-bounded region:

$$S = \{x = (\beta,\lambda) \in V : 0 \le \beta \le \beta_{\max}, 0 \le \lambda \le \delta_{\max}\}. \quad (16)$$

As previously remarked, more general search regions may be considered.

3 A population-based algorithm involving stochastic perturbations

When solving the general problem stated in Eq. (8), one of the main difficulties is connected to the non-convexity of the objective function F.

In order to fix the ideas, let us consider an iterative method generating a sequence $\{x_k\}_{k \in \mathbb{R}^*}$, recursively defined from a starting point:

$$\mathbf{x}_0 \in S \; ; \; \mathbf{x}_{k+1} = \mathbf{Q}_k(\mathbf{x}_k), \quad (17)$$

where Q_k is an iteration function, which may involve ns substeps of a standard descent method (for instance, steepest descent or Fletcher-Reeves):

$$Q_k(x) = Q^{ns}(x) = \underbrace{Q(Q(\ldots Q(x)))}_{ns\ times} \cdot \quad (18)$$

Here, Q is the iteration function associated to the descent method used for the substeps. It usually involves a descent direction d and a step $\alpha \ge 0$ to be determined. For instance, the classical gradient descent with a fixed step uses $d = -\nabla F(x)$ and a fixed parameter $\alpha_0 > 0$ in order to define $Q(x) = x - \alpha_0 \nabla F(x)$. In a more sophisticated approach, the step may be determined by one dimensional search involving a previously established maximal step α_{max} (for instance, we may consider the optimal step on the interval $[0, \alpha_{\max}]$).

Due to the lack of convexity, the convergence of these iterations to a global minimum x satisfying (10) is not ensured and may strongly depend on the parameters of the method, such as the initial point x_0, the descent method used in the substeps and their number ns, the maximum step α_{max} and the method used for the unidimensional search.

This difficulty makes that global optimization methods, such as stochastic or evolutionary algorithms are considered for the numerical solution of (8): for instance, we may use the random perturbation approach, where the iterations (17) are modified as

$$x_0 \in S \; ; \; x_{k+1} = Q_k(x_k) + P_k, \quad (19)$$

where P_k is a convenient random variable which ensures the convergence to a global minimum, such as, for instance, $P_k = \dfrac{\omega}{\sqrt{\log(k+1)}} Z$, where Z is a gaussian random vector following $N(0, \boldsymbol{Id})$ and $\omega > 0$ is fixed (see, for instance, Pogu[26] or Ellaia[11]). In practice, the implementation of random perturbations involve a finite sample $(P_k^1, \ldots, P_k^{nr})$ of nr variates from P_k: let $P_k^0 = 0$, $P_k = (P_k^0, P_k^1, \ldots, P_k^{nr})$, $q_k^0 = Q_k(x_k)$; $q_k^i = q_k^0 + P_k^i$, $1 \le i \le nr$; $q_k^{nr+1} = x_k$; $x_{k+1} = D(x_k, P_k) = Arg\ Min\{F(q_k^i) : 0 \le i \le nr+1\}$, i.e., x_{k+1} is the best point among the $nr+2$ available points q_k^i, $0 \le i \le nr+1$.

The random perturbations may be also used as part of a population-based algorithm. For instance, we may consider the following algorithm

<u>Population-based algorithm involving random perturbations:</u>

<u>Start:</u> let be given: $h > 0$; strictly non negative integers np, nc and nr; the initial population $\Pi_0 = \{x_0^1, \ldots, x_0^{np}\} \subset S$; the iteration function Q and the number of substeps $ns > 0$. k is initialized: $k = 0$.

<u>Step $k > 0$:</u> k is increased and Π_k is obtained from Π_{k-1} in three substeps:

1) We determine the set $C_k = \{u_k^i = \rho_k^i x_k^j + \kappa_k^i x_k^m + \eta_k^i : x_k^j, x_k^m \in \Pi_{k-1} : i = 1, \ldots, nc\}$ where $\rho_k^i, \kappa_k^i, \eta_k^i$ are random values from the uniform distribution on $[-h, h]$ and j, m are randomly chosen. Since C_k contains nc elements, $B_k = \Pi_{k-1} \cup C_k$ contains $nb = np + nc$ elements.
2) We determine the set $M_k = \{m_k^i = D(b_k^i, P_k^i) : b_k^i \in B_k : i = 1, \ldots, nb\}$, M_k has nb elements chosen among the $nb(nr+2)$ available points ($nr+2$ points for each element of B_k).
3) The elements of M_k are increasingly ordered according to the associated value of F. The population Π_k is formed by the first np elements of M_k, which correspond to the np best points of M_k.
4) Termination test: a stopping condition is tested and the iterations are terminated if it is verified.

At each iteration, the optimal point x^* and the optimal value F^* are approximated by

$$x^* \approx x_k^* = x_k^1 = Arg\ Min\{F(x_k^i), 1 \le i \le np\}, \; F^* \approx F_k^* = F(x_k^*)$$

The stopping conditions usually involve a maximum iteration number $kmax$, a minimal variation $\eta_{\min}$ of the optimal point and a minimal improvement ε_F of the objective function: the iterations are stopped when *one* among the following conditions is satisfied:

$$k = kmax \quad \text{OR} \quad \|x_k^* - x_{k-1}^*\| \le \eta_{\min} \quad \text{OR} \quad |F_k^* - F_{k-1}^*| \le \varepsilon_F$$

We denote by k_{stop} the iteration number where this condition is satisfied. Thus, our final estimation of the optimal point is $x_e^* = x_{k_{stop}}^*$ and the final estimation of the optimal value is $F_e^* = F\left(x_{k_{stop}}^*\right)$.

Each iteration performs *(np+nc)* × *ns* evaluations of Q and *(nr+2)* × *(nc+np)* evaluations of F. Thus, the computational cost corresponds to k_{stop} × *ns* × *(np+nc)* evaluations of Q and k_{stop} × *(nr+2)* × *(nc+np)* evaluations of F.

In a previous work we have presented a procedure of calibration by an analogous population-based strategy (Gonçalves[18] and Gonçalves[19]). The convergence of this method to the global minimum is ensured by a theorem, independently of the initial population, but the numerical behavior may be widely improved if a convenient initial population Π_0 is chosen: we present here a significant improvement based on the use of a representation of x. Our main result is a generalization of a pioneer result (Pincus[25]), which has been extended to a more numerically useful representation (Souza de Cursi[32] and Souza de Cursi[34]).

In our numerical experiments, we have considered different methods for the generation of the descent direction: gradient descent (GD), normalized gradient descent with (NGD); Fletcher-Reeves (FR), Polak-Ribière (PR), Davidon-Fletcher-Powell (DFP) and Broyden-Fletcher-Goldfarb-Shanno (BFGS). By reasons of limitation of the room, we do not present here these classical methods: the reader is invited to refer to the literature in continuous optimization, such as, for instance, Bazaraa[4].

4 A representation of the optimal point

In order to properly address the main theorem, we need some notations: let $\varepsilon > 0$ be a real number small enough. We denote by B_ε the open ball having center x and radius ε, while $S_\varepsilon = S - B_\varepsilon$ denotes its complement in S:

$$B_\varepsilon = \{y \in S : \|y - x\| < \varepsilon\};\ S_\varepsilon = \{y \in S : \|y - x\| \geq \varepsilon\}.$$

We denote by ψ_ε the characteristic function of S_ε:

$$\psi_\varepsilon(y) = 1, \text{ if } y \in S_\varepsilon \ ; \ \psi_\varepsilon(y) = 0, \text{ otherwise.}$$

Let us introduce a probability P defined on S. We assume that

$$\forall \eta > 0 : P(B_\eta) > 0 \ .$$

This assumption is verified by any probability defined by a strictly positive density. Let $\tau > 0$ be a real number large enough (in the sequel, we take $\tau \to +\infty$) and $g : R^2 \to R$ a continuous function such that $g \geq 0$ and $\xi \to g(\tau, \xi)$ is strictly decreasing for any $\tau > 0$. Let us denote by $E(\bullet)$ the meaning associated to the probability P. We assume that there exists a real number $\varepsilon_0 > 0$ and two functions $h_1, h_2 : R^2 \to R$ such that,

$$\forall \varepsilon \in (0, \varepsilon_0):$$
$$E(g(\tau, F(y))) \geq h_1(\tau, \varepsilon) > 0 \ ; \ E(\psi_\varepsilon(y) g(\tau, F(y))) \leq h_2(\tau, \varepsilon) \quad (20)$$

and

$$\forall \varepsilon \in (0, \varepsilon_0) : \frac{h_2(\tau, \varepsilon)}{h_1(\tau, \varepsilon)} \xrightarrow[\tau \to +\infty]{} 0 \ . \quad (21)$$

We have:

Theorem 4.1. Let $S \subset V$ be a non empty, closed, bounded set. Assume that $F : V \to R$ is continuous and that there is exactly one $x \in S$ satisfying (10). Assume also that (20) and (21) are satisfied. Then

$$x^* = \lim_{\tau \to +\infty} \frac{E(y g(\tau, F(y)))}{E(g(\tau, F(y)))} \quad (22)$$

Proof: Cf. Appendix 1.

The choice of the function g is guided by the following result:

Proposition 4.2. Let $h : R \to R$ be a continuous function such that $h > 0$, h is strictly decreasing on (0,+∞) and

$$\forall \xi, \delta > 0 \ : \ \lim_{\tau \to +\infty} \frac{h(\tau(\xi + \delta))}{h(\tau\xi)} = 0 \quad (23)$$

If $\mu : R \to R$ is continuous, strictly positive and strictly increasing on $(F(x), +\infty)$ then $g(\tau, \xi) = h(\tau\mu(\xi))$ satisfies (20) and (21). Consequently, we have (22).

Proof: Cf. Appendix 1.

A suitable choice, primarily suggested by (Pincus[25]) is

$$g(\tau, \xi) = \exp(-\tau\xi), \quad (24)$$

which corresponds to

$$h(\xi) = \exp(-\xi); \ \mu(\xi) = \xi. \quad (25)$$

The numerical experiments performed show that the representation (Eq. 22) furnishes good starting points for iterative descent methods (Souza de Cursi[32]). This suggests its use for the generation of the initial population S_0: it is expected an improvement, since the initial population is an approximate numerical representation of the solution. Recent experiments have shown a significant improvement by the use of a representation in the generation of the initial population, when compared to a purely random initial population (Shi[28], Souza de Cursi[33] and Bez[7]).

The representation (22) is numerically used as follows: a large fixed value of τ is selected and a finite sample $(x_1, \ldots, x_{ntirm})$ of admissible points is generated, according to the probability P. Then, the sample is used to generate an initial estimation of the optimal point:

$$x^* \approx x_0 = \frac{\sum_{i=1}^{ntirm} x_i g(\tau, F(x_i))}{\sum_{i=1}^{ntirm} g(\tau, F(x_i))} \quad (26)$$

Eq. (26) shows that Eq. (22) may be interpreted as a weighted mean of the values of the points of *S*. For conveniently chosen *g*, the weight of a point $\boldsymbol{y}$ decreases when $F(\boldsymbol{y})$ increases. The behaviour of *g* as function of τ must be such that the relative weight of points having values different of $F(\boldsymbol{x})$ vanishes when $\tau \rightarrow +\infty$.

The practical use of Eq. (26) (or Eq. (22)) requests the construction of a probability distribution on S. When the geometry of *S* is complex, this may be a hard point. In the sequel, we assume the existence of a projection operator *proj* transforming $\boldsymbol{x} \notin S$ into $\boldsymbol{x}_{proj} \in S$.

The use of (26) for the generation of the initial population Π_0 needs *np x ntirm* supplementary evaluations of *F*: the computational cost becomes k_{stop} *x ns x (np+nc)* evaluations of $\boldsymbol{Q}$ and *np x ntirm +* k_{stop} *x (nr+2) x (nc+np)* evaluations of *F*.

5 Numerical experiments

In this section, we present the results of some numerical experiments destined to validate the algorithm.

Extensive experimentation has been performed concerning the effects of the parameters: choice of the descent method used in the mutation phase and its internal parameters, size of population, standard deviation of the distributions used for generation, maximum step size etc. For each set of parameters, one hundred runs have been performed in order to estimate the probability of success of the method: a run is considered as successful when the relative error in the final evaluation $\boldsymbol{x}_e^*$ of the optimum $\boldsymbol{x}^*$ is inferior to 0.1%, *i.e.*, the distance between the final estimation $\boldsymbol{x}_e^*$ and the exact solution $\boldsymbol{x}^*$ ($\neq \boldsymbol{0}$ in all experiments) is inferior to 0.1% of the norm of the exact solution: $\left\| \boldsymbol{x}_e^* - \boldsymbol{x}^* \right\| \leq 10^{-3} \left\| \boldsymbol{x}^* \right\|$ (we have $\boldsymbol{x}^* \neq \boldsymbol{0}$ in all the experiments). The probability of success is estimated by the proportion of successful runs on a finite sample of 100 independent runs. We consider also the mean value and the standard deviation of k_{stop} in the sample, denoted by $m(k_{stop})$ and $s(k_{stop})$, respectively.

By reasons of limitation of the room, we present only the results concerning a few experiments, chosen in order to illustrate significant aspects.

We have considered different choices of the function *g*: (25) has been tested, but we have also considered the situations where $h(\xi) = \exp(-\xi)$ and

$$\mu(\xi) = \varphi \ln(\theta + \xi^{\gamma}) \Rightarrow g(\tau, \xi) = \left(\frac{1}{\theta + \xi^{\gamma}} \right)^{\nu\tau}, \quad \nu, \gamma, \theta > 0; \quad (27)$$

$$\mu(\xi) = \varphi \sqrt{\theta + \xi^{\gamma}} \Rightarrow g(\tau, \xi) = \exp\left(-\nu\tau\sqrt{\theta + \xi^{\gamma}}\right), \quad \nu, \gamma, \theta > 0; \quad (28)$$

In our experiments, the search region *S* has had a simple geometry:

- *disk:* $S = \{ y \in \mathbb{R}^n : \| y \| \leq r \}$, where *r* is the radius;

or

- *rectangular:* *S* is a product of intervals, $S = [x_{min}, x_{max}]^n$.

In order to apply the theorem 4.1, we need a probability P defined on *S*. In our experiments, we consider the restriction to S of a Gaussian distribution *N(0,ρ Id)*.

In practice, we generate points from *N(0, ρId)*. As previously observed, trial points lying outside *S* are projected by an operator *proj* in order to get an admissible point. We have considered two kinds of projection:

- The first one is the standard orthogonal projection (SOP) on *S*. This kind of projection brings the exterior point to the boundary of *S*. In our experiments, this projection reads as
- *disk:*

$proj(\mathbf{y}) = r\frac{\mathbf{y}}{\|\mathbf{y}\|}$, if $\|\mathbf{y}\| > r$; $proj(\mathbf{y}) = \mathbf{y}$, otherwise.

- *rectangular:* $proj(\mathbf{y}) = (p(y_1), \ldots, p(y_n))$,

where $p(y) = x_{min}$, if $y < x_{min}$; $p(y) = x_{max}$, if $y > x_{max}$; $p(y) = y$, otherwise.

- The second one is a randomly perturbed orthogonal projection (RPOP) where a random term is added to SOP in order to obtain an interior point whenever the trial point $\mathbf{y}$ lies outside from *S*. In our experiments, this projection is performed as follows:
- *disk:* $proj(\mathbf{y}) = (1-U)r\frac{\mathbf{y}}{\|\mathbf{y}\|}$, if $\|\mathbf{y}\| > r$ (*U* is a variable from the uniform distribution on *(0,1)*); $proj(\mathbf{y}) = \mathbf{y}$, otherwise.
- *rectangular:* let $\ell = (x_{max} - x_{min})$. $proj(\mathbf{y}) = (rp(y_1), \ldots, rp(y_n))$, where $rp(y) = x_{min} + \ell U$, if $y < x_{min}$; $rp(y) = x_{max} - \ell U$, if $y > x_{max}$; $rp(y) = y$, otherwise (*U* is a variable from the uniform distribution on *(0,1)*).

In order to investigate the effect of the projection, we have tested initial populations formed by purely boundary points and purely interior points, as well as mixed ones.

We recall that another distribution of probability is needed in order to generate the perturbations $\boldsymbol{P}_k$ (Eq. (19)). As previously observed, we use $\boldsymbol{P}_k = \frac{\omega}{\sqrt{\log(k+1)}}\boldsymbol{Z}$, where *Z* is a gaussian random vector following *N(0, Id)* and $\omega > 0$ is fixed.

5.1. Test functions

We have considered classical test functions existing in the literature. These functions are characterized by multimodal behaviour and difficulties in numerically obtaining the points of global optima. They are usually destined to the evaluation of the performance of global optimization algorithms.

In order to prevent bias introduced by the use of probability distributions having $\mathbf{0} = (0,0,0,...0) \in R^n$ as mean, we consider only situations where the theoretical solution is $x^* \neq \mathbf{0}$. The functions used are the following:

1) Davis' Function:

$$F(x) = 0.5 + \frac{\sin^2(\|x-\bar{x}\|_2) - 0.5}{(1+\|x-\bar{x}\|_2^2/1000)^2} \quad (29)$$

2) Rastringin's Function :

$$F(x) = 3n + \sum_{i=1}^{n} [(x_i - \bar{x}_i)^2 - 3\cos(2\pi(x_i - \bar{x}_i))] \quad (30)$$

3) Ackley's function:

$$F(x) = 20\left(1 - e^{-0.2\sqrt{\frac{\sum_{i=1}^{n}(x_i-\bar{x}_i)^2}{n}}}\right) + e - e^{\frac{\sum_{i=1}^{n}\cos(2\pi(x_i-\bar{x}_i))}{n}} \quad (31)$$

4) Griewank's function (Griewank[20]) :

$$F(x) = \frac{1}{200}\|x-\bar{x}\|_2^2 - \prod_{i=1}^{n}\cos\left(\frac{x_i-\bar{x}_i}{\sqrt{i}}\right), \quad (32)$$

5) Rosenbrock's function :

$$F(x) = 100\sum_{i=1}^{n}(x_i^2 - x_i)^2 + \sum_{i=1}^{n}(x_i-1)^2 \quad (33)$$

6) Schwefel's function :

$$F(x) = 418.9829\, n - \sum_{i=1}^{n} x_i \sin\left(\sqrt{|x_i|}\right) \quad (34)$$

The first four functions attain their global minima at $x^* = \bar{x}$ - our experiments use $\bar{x} = (1,2,3,...,n)$. We have $F(x^*) = 0$ for the 3 first ones (Davis, Rastringin, Ackley), while $F(x^*) = -1$ for the 4th one (Griewank). The 5th (Rosenbrock) has a global minimum $F(x^*) = 0$, attained at $x^* = (1,1,1,...,1) \in R^n$. The last one (Schwefel) has global minimum $F(x^*) = 0$, attained at $x^* = (420.96, 420.96, ..., 420.96) \in R^n$.

5.2. Numerical effect of the use of the representation

In order to evaluate the improvement furnished by the use of Eq. (26) for the generation of the initial population Π_0, the results have been compared to those furnished by a purely random one $\tilde{\Pi}_0$. In all the situations considered, Π_0 has furnished better results. The results have been analogous for all considered test functions: The results obtained for Rastringin's function are presented in Table 1. They concern the situation where *np* = 5, the search region is rectangular with x_{min} = *-500* and x_{max} = *500*; *ntirm* = *100*; ρ =*1*; ω = *0.5*; τ = *10*; *kmax* = *300*; *nr* = *5*; α_{max} = *0.5*; *ns*=*10*. When generating the initial population, we use the random projection RPOP.

Table 1 – Rastringin's function (n = 5, RPOP)

	GD	FR	DFP	BFGS	PR
Prob. of success	0.91	0.92	0.96	0.96	0.96
$m(k_{stop})$	53.98	55.72	47.56	67.25	68.75
$s(k_{stop})$	51.33	52.49	51.60	71.78	75.06
evaluations of Q	8098	8359	7134	10087	10312
evaluations of F	5668	5851	4994	7061	7218

a) Random Initial Population ($\tilde{\Pi}_0$)

Prob. of success	1	1	0.98	0.99	1
$m(k_{stop})$	23.38	25.56	33.97	35.69	24.75
$s(k_{stop})$	32.07	38.58	37.83	37.92	36.62
evaluations of Q	3597	3834	5095	5353	3712
evaluations of F	2954	3183	4066	4247	3098

b) Initial population generated by the representation(Π_0)

The method of projection has had no significant influence: standard projection has led to analogous results (see Table 2)

Table 2 – Rastringin's function (n = 5, SOP)

	GD	FR	DFP	BFGS	PR
Prob. of success	0.94	0.91	0.92	0.94	0.97
$m(k_{stop})$	79.02	66.28	65.19	71.24	62.93
$s(k_{stop})$	63.24	54.42	49.56	64.05	54.55
evaluations of Q	11853	9942	9779	10686	9440
evaluations of F	8297	6960	6845	7480	6608

a) Random Initial Population ($\tilde{\Pi}_0$)

Prob. of success	1	1	1	0.98	1
$m(k_{stop})$	25.70	26.22	34.24	35.43	26.22
$s(k_{stop})$	32.73	36.85	34.96	31.87	37.11
evaluations of Q	3855	3933	5136	5314	3933
evaluations of F	3198	3253	4095	4220	3253

b) Initial population generated by the representation(Π_0)

The Fig. 1 shows the probability of success for an increasing population size. The search region is a disk of radius *r* =*100;* the dimension is *n*=*6;* and the parameters are ρ =*1* ; *ntirm* = *50;* ω = *0.1;* τ = *10;* *kmax* = *30;* *nr* = *30;* *ns*=*10;* α_{max} = *1;* descent method: FR. We observe the improvement due to the use of the representation for the generation of the initial population.

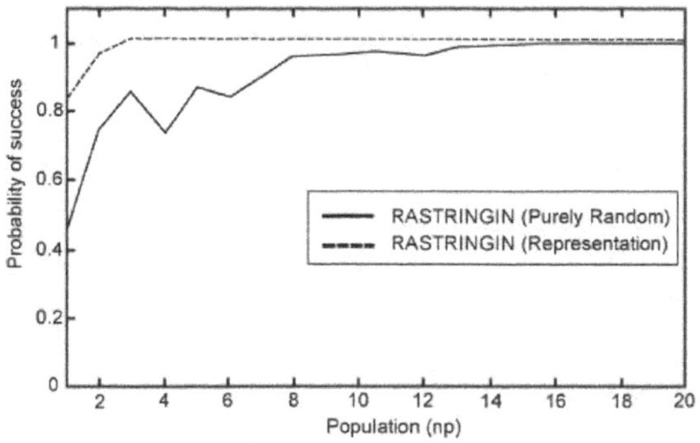

Fig. 1 – Results for an increasing population size (Rastringin's function)

In addition, the use of the representation formula may significantly reduce the number of random perturbations to be generated. This confirms that (22) furnishes good starting points. For instance, let us consider the situation above with $nr = 0$ (no random perturbation). The results are shown in Table 3. The projection method is RPOP.

Table 3 – Rastringin's function ($n = 5$, RPOP) – no random perturbation ($nr = 0$)

	GD	FR	DFP	BFGS	PR
Prob. of success	0.52	0.47	0.57	0.55	0.46
$m(k_{stop})$	114.67	114.14	123.29	122.6	138.54
$s(k_{stop})$	74.16	68.30	81.05	74.02	78.13
evaluations of Q	17200	17122	18494	18390	20781
evaluations of F	3440	3424	3698	3678	4156

a) Random Initial Population ($\tilde{\Pi}_0$)

Prob. of success	0.83	0.68	0.77	0.69	0.70
$m(k_{stop})$	62.33	75.65	64.93	64.04	76.92
$s(k_{stop})$	58.55	84.09	64.15	70.22	72.63
evaluations of Q	9350	11347	9739	9607	11538
evaluations of F	2370	2769	2447	2421	2807

b) Initial population generated by the representation(Π_0)

The results for the Ackley's function are given in Tables 4 and 5.

Table 4 – Ackley's function ($n = 20$, RPOP) – no random perturbation ($nr = 0$)

	GD	FR	DFP	BFGS	PR
Prob. success	1	1	1	1	1
$m(k_{stop})$	41.9	59.93	44.3	44.91	77.54
$s(k_{stop})$	18.88	31.74	19.42	18.66	46.40
evaluations of Q	3142	4494	3322	3368	5815
evaluations of F	1257	1797	1329	1347	2326

a) Random Initial Population ($\tilde{\Pi}_0$)

Prob. of success	1	1	1	1	1
$m(k_{stop})$	23.44	44.89	29.86	28.15	45.36
$s(k_{stop})$	9.88	20.77	14.63	15.70	22.62
evaluations of Q	1758	3366	2239	2111	3402
evaluations of F	953	1596	1145	1094	1610

b) Initial population generated by the representation(Π_0)

Table 5 – Ackley's function ($n = 10$, RPOP) – no random perturbation ($nr = 0$)

	GD	FR	DFP	BFGS	PR
Prob. of success	1	1	1	1	1
$m(k_{stop})$	18.59	29.76	19.42	20.84	24.7
$s(k_{stop})$	6.75	19.23	8.84	8.57	13.23
evaluations of Q	1394	2232	1456	1563	1852
evaluations of F	557	892	582	625	741

a) Random Initial Population ($\tilde{\Pi}_0$)

Prob. of success	1	1	1	1	1
$m(k_{stop})$	8.76	16.42	9.74	8.57	14.53
$s(k_{stop})$	7.98	10.27	8.33	7.01	11.30
evaluations of Q	675	1231	730	642	1089
evaluations of F	512	742	542	507	685

b) Initial population generated by the representation(Π_0)

5.3. Tuning of the main parameters

In order to verify the robustness of the algorithm and the simplicity of tuning, the effects of the variations of the main parameters np, α_{max}, ρ, ω and ns have been studied:

5.3.1. Size of the population

The tuning of the size of the population np was easy: good results have been obtained in all the situations for $np \geq 5$.

For instance, let us consider the situation where the search region is a disk of radius $r = 100$; $\rho = 100$; $ntirm = 150$; $\tau = 10$; $kmax = 50$; $ns = 5$; $nr = 50$; $\omega = 0.01$; $\alpha_{max} = 1$; the descent method is GD. The results obtained are given in Fig. 2 and confirm the observation.

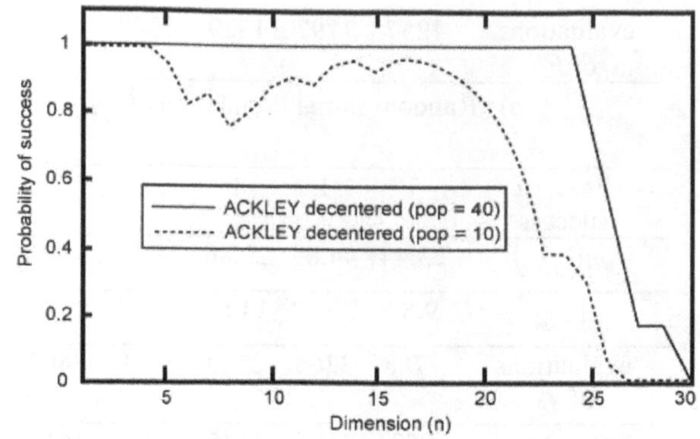

Fig. 2 – Influence of the population size (Ackley's function)

In Table 6, we present the results for different values of *np* and ρ. The search region is a disk of radius $r = 10$ and we use $ntirm = 100$; $\tau = 10$; $kmax = 50$; $ns = 10$; $nr = 30$; $\omega = 0.05$; $\alpha_{max} = 1$. The descent method is GD and the projection method is RPOP. As expected, increasing the size of population increases the probability of success.

Table 6 – Probability of succes for different values of *np* and ρ

P	0,1	0,5	1	5	10	100
$np = 5$	1	0,88	0,74	0,60	0,60	0,59
$np = 30$	1	1	1	1	1	1

5.3.2. Maximum step size α_{max}

The tuning of the step size α_{max} has shown to be easy: good results have been obtained in all the situations for $\alpha_{max} \geq 1$.

For instance, let us consider Davis's function decentered the situation where the search region is a disk of radius $r = 100$; $\rho = 1$; $np = 5$; $ntirm = 50$; $\tau = 10$; $kmax = 30$; $nr = 30$; $ns = 10$; $\omega = 0.01$; the descent method is GD. The results obtained are exhibited in Fig. 3 and confirm the observation. For ρ superior to 3.5, the probability of success is constant and it equals to 1.

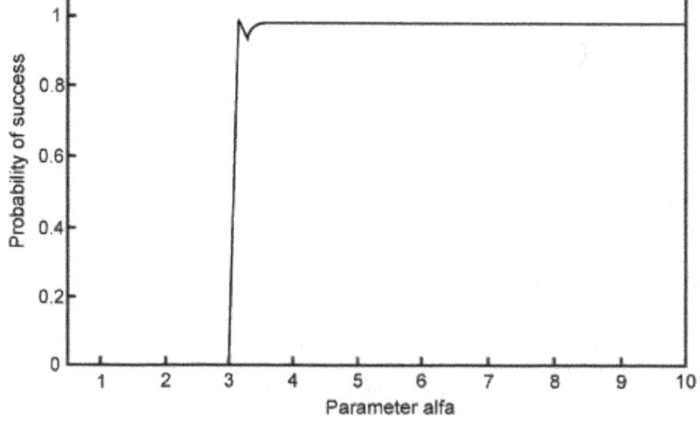

Fig. 3 – Influence of the parameters α_{max} (Davis)

5.3.3. Standard Deviation ω used in the random perturbations

We have analyzed the influence of the standard deviation ω, used in the random perturbations. For instance, Fig. 4 shows the results concerning the Schwefel's function in dimension $n = 5$ for an initial population formed of purely random points, without use of the Representation Formula (thus, $ntirm = 0$). The search region is rectangular with $x_{min} = -500$ and $x_{max} = 500$ and we use $np = 5$; $kmax = 30$; $\rho = 20$; $ns = 5$; $nr = 50$; $\alpha_{max} = 1$. The descent method is the GD and the projection method is SOP. We observe that the probability of success increases with the standard deviation.

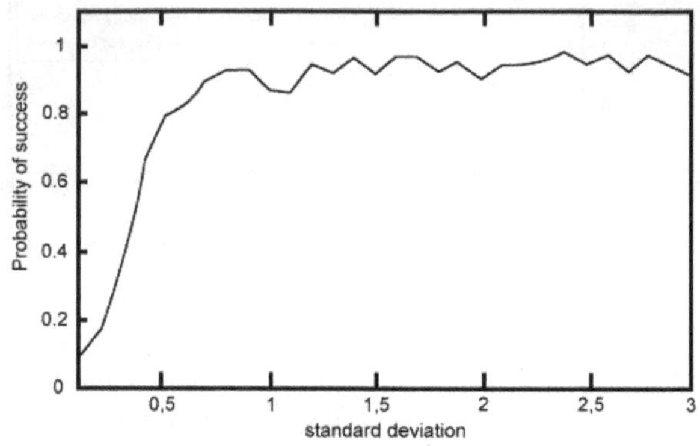

Fig. 4 – Influence of the standard deviation ω with $\tilde{\Pi}_0$ (Purely random)

The use of the Π_0 (Representation) has led to an improvement: the probability of success has been equal to one for all the values of ω. The speed of convergence has also increased with ω.

5.3.4. Number of substeps ns used in mutations

The tuning of *ns* has shown to be easy: good results have been obtained in all the situations for values superior to 2.

For instance, let us consider the situation where the search region is rectangular with $x_{min} = -500$ and $x_{max} = 500$; $n = 30$; $ntirm = 100$; $\rho = 1$; $\omega = 0.1$; $\tau = 10$; $kmax = 30$; $nr = 10$; $\alpha_{max} = 1$; the descent method is GD. The results obtained are exhibited in Table 7 and confirm the observation (Griewank's function).

Table 7 – Influence of the number of the substeps *ns* used in mutations

	$ns=1$	$ns=2$	$ns=3$	$ns=6$	$ns=13$	$ns=17$
Prob. of success	0	0,99	1	1	1	1
$m(k_{stop})$	-----	22,13	15,12	8,94	5,24	4,38
$s(k_{stop})$	-----	2,60	2,04	1,40	0,84	0,52
evaluations of Q		663	680	804	1021	1116
evaluations of F		4483	3221	2109	1443	1288

5.3.5. Standard deviation ρ

The tuning of the standard deviation ρ has shown to be easy: good results have been obtained in all the situations for $0.1 \leq \rho \leq 100$ (see Table 6 for examples of results).

5.4. Choice of *g*

The different choices of the function *g* have led to similar results, for a wide range of values of the parameters ν, γ, θ. In our experiments, ν, γ had varied in a interval mesh of 0.5 defined in a rectangle [0.5, 5] x [0.5, 5] and $\tau = 10$, $\theta = 5$ fixed.

Let us consider the situation where the search region is a disk of radius $r = 100$; $np = 5$; $ntirm = 100$; $kmax = 50$; $ns = 10$; $nr = 30$; $\alpha_{max} = 1$; $\omega = 0.1$. The descent method is GD. Table 8 shows the results furnished by the method for various functions *g*. The results for each choice of g are stable (small standard deviation) and Eq. (27) has been more performing, but its results are very close to those of Eq. (28).

Table 8 – Impact of g – (Griewank, $n = 10$)

	Eq. (25)	Eq. (27)	Eq. (28)
Probability of success	1	1	1
$m(k_{stop})$	2,92	2,05	2,09
$s(k_{stop})$	0,27	0,035	0,039
evaluations of Q	438	307	313
evaluations of F	1901	1484	1503

The results concerning the Rastringin's function are shown in Table 9. The results are analogous.

Table 9 – Impact of g – (Rastringin, $n = 5$)

	Eq. (25)	Eq. (27)	Eq. (28)
Probability of success	0,53	0,54	0,60
$m(k_{stop})$	35,33	34,15	34,20
$s(k_{stop})$	3,23	2,30	2,74
evaluations of Q	5299	5122	5130
evaluations of F	17458	16892	16916

6. Calibration of the model of competitive destinations

6.1. Set of initialization parameters and data

In order to evaluate the efficiency of the numeric methods in the calibration of the Fotheringham model, a set of hypothetical data presented by Kühlkamp[22] has been used. These data involve 30 traffic zones and has been often used to analyze the intervening opportunities model.

We compare the proposed numeric procedure ERPG-RF (Evolutionary version of the Random Perturbations of the Gradient – Representation Formula) to the evolutionary strategy of (Diplock[10]), denoted by EDO, where an evolutionary strategy involving a quasi-Newtonian method and a basic generic algorithm is used for the calibration of the Fotheringham model. The work (Diplock[10]) mentions that one of the reasons for the choice of the evolutionary strategy was the work developed by Schwefel[29] that verified, in an empiric way, the good performance of this strategy, when compared to eleven conventional optimization methods out of twenty eight test problems. According to Diplock[10], the same good performance of this method has been observed in the calibration, which motivates his use to get a comparison with the ERPG-RF approach.

The algorithm EDO reads as follows:

Evolutionary Strategy algorithm (Diplock[10]):

- ***Step 1:*** Identify initial parameter values and standard deviations for the parent.
- ***Step 2:*** Generate new parameter values for a descendant by mutation; this involves adding pseudo-random numbers drawn from a normal distribution centered on the parent values with a given standard deviation.
- ***Step 3:*** If the descendant performs better than the parent, then it becomes the parent for the next generation.
- ***Step 4:*** Repeat steps 2 and 3 for *n* mutations and count how many improved values have been found over the preceding *10n* mutations. If greater than *2n*, then reduce the standard deviations by *0,85*; else, increase them divide by *0,85*.
- ***Step 5:*** Return to step 2 until no change occurs over *10n* mutations on two consecutive occasions.

The tests using the ERPG-RF method involve as search region a disk of radius $r = 10$; $np = 5$; $\rho = 1$; $ntirm = 100$; $\tau = 10$; $kmax = 50$; $nr = 5$; $\alpha_{max} = 0.7$; $\omega = 0.1$; descent method: *GD*. The iterations have been stopped at the fixed maximal iteration number

For EDO, a random population of *100* elements is generated and $N(0,1)$ is used in the mutation phase.

An extensive set of tests for both methods has been executed, varying parameters, such as population size, standard deviation, among others.

6.2. Analysis of the obtained results

The executed tests verified, among other things, the number of evaluations of the function, the function value evolution, according to the applied numeric method and the influence of the Representation Formula in the performance of the ERPG-RF method.

Table 10 – Parameters estimated by minimizing F defined by Eq. (9)

	β	σ	δ	value of F
ERPG-RF	0,08	0.12	2.48	10679.30
EDO	0,04	0,12	2,29	10896,86

Table 10 presents the parameters obtained by minimizing the objective function given in Eq. (9). It is observed that the optimal values obtained by both methods are very close.

Nevertheless, the behavior of the methods is not the same, as shown in Fig. 5. We can notice that the ERPG-RF method presents a better performance, considering that the function optimal value is reached in a significantly smaller number of iterations. In addition, the ERPG-RF method uses a smaller population. It is known that a good initial population, linked to the method robustness, brings the necessity of a smaller number of evaluations of the function.

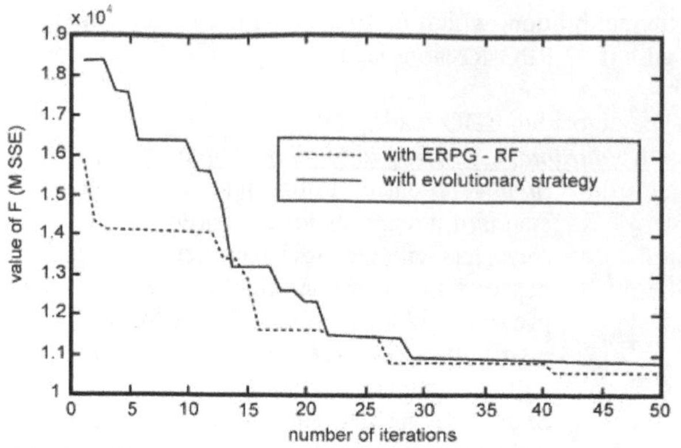

Fig. 5: Minimal value of the function at each interaction (Eq. 9)

The good performance of the ERPG-RF method in the calibration of the competitive destination models, presented in this study, was also verified in an application of the opportunities gravitational model (Bez[8]), according to what we'll see in the next section.

7. Calibration of the gravity-opportunity model

7.1. Set of initialization parameters and data

We have tested the method on 4 data sets: three sets of real data and one set of simulated data. The first set of real data comes from the region of Londrina, Brazil, which is divided into 12 traffic zones (Almeida[1]). The second one corresponds to a region that includes part of the State of Santa Catarina, Brazil, divided into 77 zones (Gonçalves[16]). The third ones is a subset of the previous region, corresponding to 44 zones of particular interest (Gonçalves[16]). The set of simulated data is defined on a region divided into 30 zones (Kühlkamp[22]).

All the experiments performed use the following set of parameters: $np = 2$; $ntirm = 100$; $nr = 5$; $\rho = 0.5$; $\omega = 0.02$; $\alpha_{max} = 0.7$. Furness iterations have been stopped when either the corresponding iteration number j has reached a prescribed maximum value $jmax = 100$ or the value of the objective function has attained 10^{-3}: $F(\beta,\lambda) < 10^{-3}$.

7.2. Analysis of the obtained results

The objective function under consideration is non-convex, as we can see in the Fig. 6 and 7.

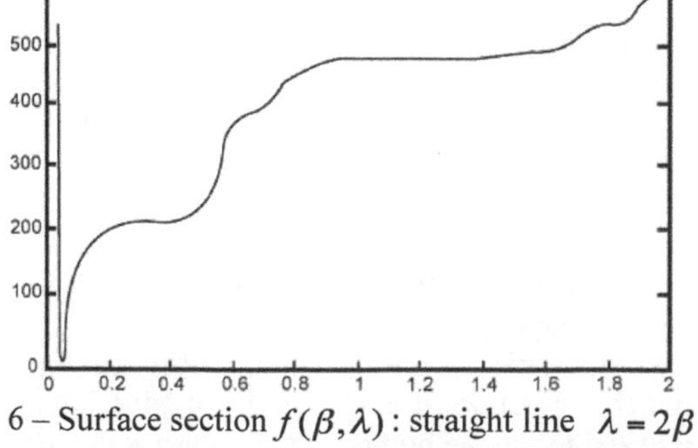

Fig. 6 – Surface section $f(\beta,\lambda)$: straight line $\lambda = 2\beta$ in the interval [0,009; 2] – 77 zones (Gonçalves[18])

In the Fig. 8, we can notice the difficulty in minimizing this function, by using the hypothetical data set generated by Kühlkamp[22], characterized by the large variations of its derivatives in a interval mesh of 0.001 defined in a rectangle [0, 0.07] x [0, 0.07].

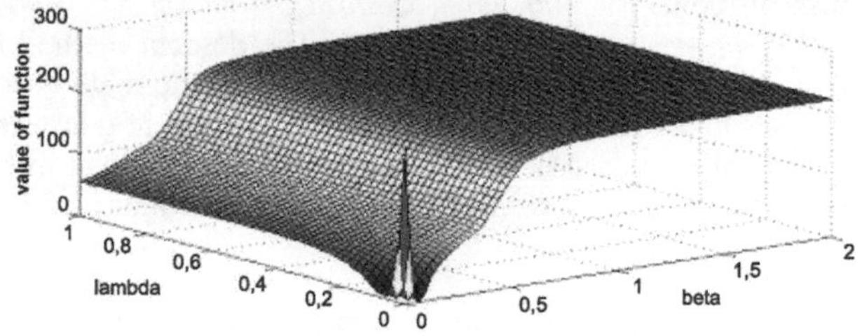

Fig. 7 – Function defined by the Maximum Likelihood criteria (Bez[6])

In the study developed by Gonçalves[19], the ERPG (*Evolutionary version of the random perturbations of the gradient*) algorithm was applied to the hybrid gravitational/intervening opportunities model (Gonçalves[16]). The variation of the parameters, such as the population size, random perturbations added to the gradient method, number of iterations, definition of the error (Gonçalves[19]) to be applied to the Furness method, among others, have been tested and evaluated. In practice, the Furness iterations are stopped at a given finite number of iterations (Gonçalves[19]). In this study, a maximum number of 100 iterations has been considered.

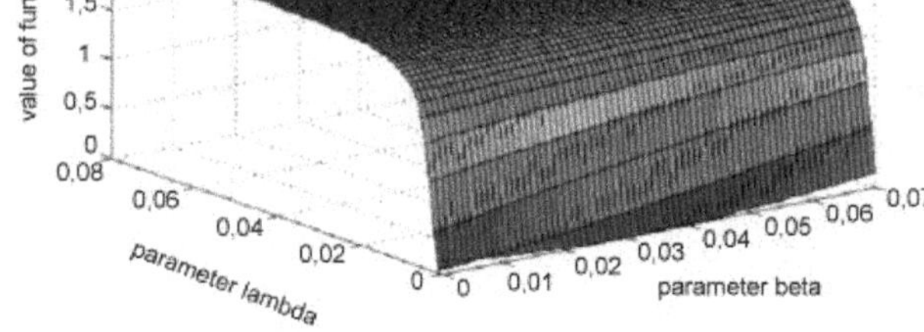

Fig. 8 – Function defined by the maximum verisimilitude criterion – 30 zones

In the application of the proposed method in this study, the same good performance, verified in the tests applied to the classic functions, was confirmed in the calibration of the gravity-opportunity model (Gonçalves[16]). The application of the Representation Formula in the improvement of the initial population has led to a better convergence speed. In the Table 11, we can observe the average value of the function, obtained after the execution of *100* runs, with or without the use of the Representation Formula. The Table 11 uses $\rho = 0.5$ and $ntirm = 100$. The results show the significant drop of these values obtained by the application of this Formula.

Table 11 – Mean optimal value of the objective function given by Eq. (15).

	Gonçalves[16] 77 zones	Gonçalves[16] 44 zones
without RF	70745.27	11178.77
with RF	22.94	7.96

	Almeida[1] 12 zones	Kühlkamp[22] 30 zones
without RF	257.27	52648.36
with RF	1.13	43.32

The use of the Representation Formula in the improvement of the initial population, contributed for the increase in the convergence speed, causing a less number of iterations and, as consequence, the reduction of the number of function evaluations, as we can verify in the results presented in the Table 12.

The values of the Table 12 were determined after the execution of *100* tests, performed with every data set.

Table 12 – Mean number of function evaluations given by Eq. (15).

	Gonçalves[16] 77 zones	Gonçalves[16] 44 zones
without RF	8800	6720
with RF	5960	2120

	Almeida[1] 12 zones	Kühlkamp[22] 30 zones
without RF	1960	3720
with RF	1160	2440

In the Fig. 9, we can observe the performance of the numeric procedure, with or without the use of the Representation Formula and, with or without the use of the optimal step. The best performance of the method is evidenced when we use the Representation Formula and the optimal step in the procedure. Then same tests were applied to all the data sets used and the obtained results presented the same tendency.

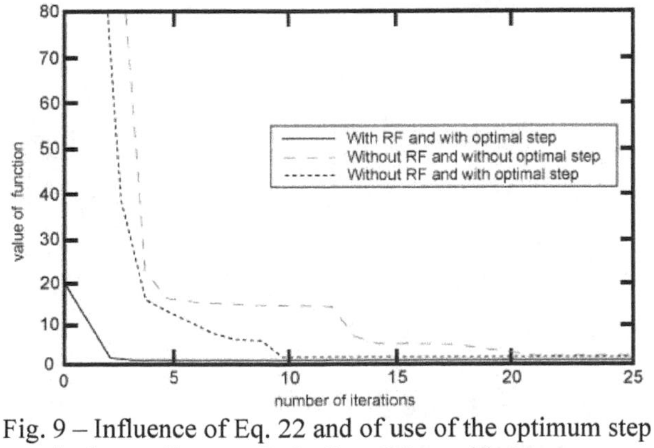

Fig. 9 – Influence of Eq. 22 and of use of the optimum step in the gradient method - Set of data with 44 zones

8. Conclusions

In this study, a stochastic global optimization procedure, of the evolutionary type, was presented, by using descent methods in the mutation phase and the Representation Formula of the global optimum in the determination of the initial population.

The initial population is one of the significant parameters for the performance of evolutionary methods and the use of the Representation Formula has shown to furnish an improvement. The random perturbations of the deterministic descent methods considered have shown to be effective in the mutation step, enhancing the speed of convergence and preventing from convergence local minima, excepted Newton's method.

The experiments have shown that different choices of g are possible, according to Souza de Cursi[33]: similar results have been obtained for the functions considered.

Another fact to be emphasized was that, in most of the cases, when the Representation Formula was used in the improvement of the initial population, there was no need to use a big number of individuals (points), this way avoiding an excessive number of function evaluations and, as a result, the increase of the processing time.

We verified that the proposed method showed itself as being efficient when compared to the evolutionary strategy presented by Diplock[10]. The use of the Representation Formula in the improvement of the initial population was one of the causes of this success.

In the process of calibration of the Gonçalves model, the use of the Representation Formula in the improvement of the initial population, caused the individuals to be positioned closer to the global optimal point location region and, thus, causing a reduction in the number of iterations and, as a consequence, a small number of functions evaluations.

With the results obtained in the tests executed in the calibration of the Gonçalves model, it was possible to determine, in an empiric way, a default set of parameters for the method, which makes it more attractive to be used by professionals of the transportation and planning areas.

Acknowledgement

This work has been partially financed by the project PRONEX "Núcleo de Pesquisa em Logística Integrada", from UFSC with funding from CNPq and FAPESC.

Appendix 1 – Proof of the main results.

Proof of the Theorem 4.1:

1. We have

$$\frac{E\left(yg(\tau,F(y))\right)}{E\left(g(\tau,F(y))\right)}=\frac{E\left(xg(\tau,F(y))\right)}{E\left(g(\tau,F(y))\right)}+\frac{E\left((y-x)g(\tau,F(y))\right)}{E\left(g(\tau,F(y))\right)}.$$

Thus,

$$\frac{E\left(yg(\tau,F(y))\right)}{E\left(g(\tau,F(y))\right)}=x+\frac{E\left((y-x)g(\tau,F(y))\right)}{E\left(g(\tau,F(y))\right)}. \quad \text{(A1)}$$

2. Let $\varepsilon\in(0,\varepsilon_0)$ and $\chi_\varepsilon(y)=1-\psi_\varepsilon(y)$. Then

$$E\left((y-x)g(\tau,F(y))\right)=$$
$$=E\left((y-x)(\chi_\varepsilon(y)+\psi_\varepsilon(y))g(\tau,F(y))\right)$$

and we have

$$E((y-x)g(\tau,F(y))) = E((y-x)\chi_\varepsilon(y)g(\tau,F(y))) + E((y-x)\psi_\varepsilon(y)g(\tau,F(y))) .$$

3. Moreover

$$|E((y-x)\chi_\varepsilon(y)g(\tau,F(y)))| \le \le E(|y-x|\chi_\varepsilon(y)g(\tau,F(y))) \le \varepsilon M$$

and, from Eq. (20) :

$$E(\psi_\varepsilon(y)g(\tau, F(y))) \le h_2(\tau, \varepsilon) .$$

Thus,

$$|E((y-x)g(\tau,F(y)))| \le \varepsilon E(\chi_\varepsilon(y)g(\tau,F(y))) + h_2(\tau,\varepsilon) .$$

and

$$\left|\frac{E((y-x)g(\tau,F(y)))}{E(g(\tau,F(y)))}\right| \le \frac{\varepsilon E(\chi_\varepsilon(y)g(\tau,F(y))) + h_2(\tau,\varepsilon)}{E(g(\tau,F(y)))} = \frac{\varepsilon E(\chi_\varepsilon(y)g(\tau,F(y)))}{E(g(\tau,F(y)))} + \frac{h_2(\tau,\varepsilon)}{E(g(\tau,F(y)))}.$$

4. Since

$$\frac{E(\chi_\varepsilon(y)g(\tau, F(y)))}{E(g(\tau, F(y)))} \le 1$$

and

$$\frac{h_2(\tau, \varepsilon)}{E(g(\tau, F(y)))} \le \frac{h_2(\tau, \varepsilon)}{h_1(\tau, \varepsilon)} ,$$

we have

$$\left|\frac{E((y-x)g(\tau, F(y)))}{E(g(\tau, F(y)))}\right| \le \varepsilon + \frac{h_2(\tau, \varepsilon)}{h_1(\tau, \varepsilon)}$$

5. This inequality combined to Eq. (21) yield that

$$\forall\, \varepsilon \in (0,\varepsilon_0): \lim_{\tau \longrightarrow +\infty} \left|\frac{E((y-x)g(\tau, F(y)))}{E(g(\tau, F(y)))}\right| \le \varepsilon .$$

Thus

$$\lim_{\tau \longrightarrow +\infty} \left|\frac{E((y-x)g(\tau, F(y)))}{E(g(\tau, F(y)))}\right| = 0$$

and we have

$$\lim_{\tau \longrightarrow +\infty} \frac{E((y-x)g(\tau, F(y)))}{E(g(\tau, F(y)))} = 0 ,$$

6. By taking the limit for $\tau \longrightarrow +\infty$ in Eq. (A1), we have

$$\lim_{\tau \longrightarrow +\infty} \frac{E(yg(\tau, F(y)))}{E(g(\tau, F(y)))} = x + \lim_{\tau \longrightarrow +\infty} \frac{E((y-x)g(\tau, F(y)))}{E(g(\tau, F(y)))} = x$$

and we have the result.

The proof of the proposition 4.2 needs the following auxiliary result:

Lemma A.1. *Let* $\varepsilon, \eta > 0$ *be such that* $B_\eta \ne \varnothing$ and $S_\varepsilon \ne \varnothing$. *Then*

$$\theta(\varepsilon) = \left(\min_{y \in S_\varepsilon} \mu(F(y))\right) - \mu(F(x)) > 0, \qquad (A2)$$

and

$$m(\eta) = \left(\max_{y \in B_\eta} \mu(F(y))\right) - \mu(F(x)) > 0 . \qquad (A3)$$

Moreover,

$$m(\eta) \xrightarrow[\eta \to 0+]{} 0 \ ; \ \theta(\varepsilon) \xrightarrow[\varepsilon \to 0+]{} 0 \ ; \qquad (A4)$$

If $g(\tau,\xi) = h(\tau\mu(\xi))$, *then* $\xi \to g(\tau,\xi)$ and $\tau \to g(\tau,\xi)$ *are strictly positive, decreasing, continuous. Moreover,*

$$\max_{S_\varepsilon} g(\tau, F(y)) \le h(\tau(\theta(\varepsilon) + \mu(F(x)))) ; \qquad (A5)$$

$$\min_{B_\eta} g(\tau, F(y)) \ge h(\tau(m(\eta) + \mu(F(x)))) . \qquad (A6)$$

Proof of the Lemma A.1:

1. Since $\xi \to \mu(\xi)$ is strictly increasing and x verifies (8), we have

$$\forall\, y \in S : \mu(F(y)) \ge \mu(F(x)). \qquad (A7)$$

2. (A5) shows that $\theta(\varepsilon) \ge 0$. Assume that $\theta(\varepsilon) = 0$: then there exists a sequence $\{x_n\}_{n \ge 0} \subset S_\varepsilon$ such that

$$\mu(F(x_n)) \xrightarrow[n \to +\infty]{} \mu(F(x)) .$$

Since S_ε is closed bounded, this sequence has a cluster point $\bar{x} \in S_\varepsilon$. We have $\bar{x} \ne x$, since $\|\bar{x} - x\| \ge \varepsilon$. Moreover, the continuity of μ implies that $\mu(F(\bar{x})) = \mu(F(x))$. Since $\xi \to \mu(\xi)$ is strictly increasing, we have $F(\bar{x}) = F(x)$, what is in contradiction with the uniqueness of x. Thus, $\theta(\varepsilon) \ge 0$ and $\theta(\varepsilon) \ne 0$, what establishes (A2).

3. (A6) implies also that $m(\eta) \ge 0$. Assume that $m(\eta) = 0$: then

$$\forall\, y \in B_\eta \ : \ \mu(F(y)) \le \mu(F(x)).$$

Since $\xi \to \mu(\xi)$ is strictly increasing, this implies that

$$\forall\, y \in B_\eta \ : \ F(y) \le F(x)$$

Thus, (8) implies that: $F(y) = F(x), \forall\, y \in B_\eta$, what is in contradiction with the uniqueness of x. Thus, we have (A3).

4. (A4) is a consequence of the continuity of μ.

5. $\xi \to g(\tau,\xi)$ and $\tau \to g(\tau,\xi)$ are strictly positive, decreasing, continuous, since h is continuous, strictly positive and strictly decreasing on $(0,+\infty)$, while μ is continuous, strictly positive and strictly increasing on *$(F(x), +\infty)$*.

6. Since, for $y \in S_\varepsilon$,

$$\tau\mu(F(y)) = \tau\mu(F(x)) + \tau(\mu(F(y)) - \mu(F(x))) \geq \tau\mu(F(x)) + \tau\theta(\varepsilon)$$

and h is strictly decreasing, we have

$$g(\tau, F(y)) = h(\tau\mu(F(y))) \leq h(\tau(\theta(\varepsilon) + \mu(F(x)))).$$

7. Analogously, for $y \in B_\eta$,

$$\tau\mu(F(y)) = \mu(F(x)) + \tau(\mu(F(y)) - \mu(F(x))) \leq$$
$$\leq \tau\mu(F(x)) + \tau m(\eta)$$

Thus, using that h is strictly decreasing, we have

$$g(\tau, F(y)) = h(\tau\mu(F(y))) \geq h(\tau(m(\eta) + \mu(F(x)))).$$

Proof of the Proposition 4.2:

1. Let $\varepsilon > 0$ be such that $S_\varepsilon \neq \varnothing$. From (A5):

$$E(\psi_\varepsilon(y)g(\tau, F(y))) \leq h(\tau(\theta(\varepsilon) + \mu(F(x))))E(\psi_\varepsilon(y)).$$

Since $E(\psi_\varepsilon(y)) = P(S_\varepsilon)$, we have

$$E(\psi_\varepsilon(y)g(\tau, F(y))) \leq h_2(\tau, \varepsilon) = h(\tau(\theta(\varepsilon) + \mu(F(x))))P(S_\varepsilon).$$

2. Let $\eta > 0$ be such that $B_\eta \neq \varnothing$. Since $g > 0$, we have

$$E(g(\tau, F(y))) \geq E(\chi_\eta(y)g(\tau, F(y))).$$

Thus, (A6) implies that

$$E(g(\tau, F(y))) \geq h(\tau(m(\eta) + \mu(F(x))))E(\chi_\eta(y)).$$

Since $E(\chi_\eta(y)) = P(B_\eta)$, we have

$$E(g(\tau, F(y))) \geq h_1(\tau, \varepsilon) = h(\tau(m(\eta) + \mu(F(x))))P(B_\eta) > 0$$

3. From (A2) and (A4), there exists $\eta > 0$ such that $0 < m(\eta) < \theta(\varepsilon)$. Thus, (23) applied to $\xi = m(\eta) + \mu(F(x))$ and $\delta = \theta(\varepsilon) - m(\eta)$ yields that

$$\frac{h_2(\tau, \varepsilon)}{h_1(\tau, \varepsilon)} = \frac{P(S_\eta)}{P(B_\eta)} \frac{h(\tau(\theta(\varepsilon) + \mu(F(x))))}{h(\tau(m(\eta) + \mu(F(x))))} \xrightarrow[\tau \to +\infty]{} 0.$$

4. Thus, we have (20) and (21) and all the requirements of the theorem 4.1 are fulfilled, what establishes the result.

References

1. L. M. W. Almeida, *Desenvolvimento de uma Metodologia para Análise Locacional de Sistemas Educacionais Usando Modelos de Interação Espacial e Indicadores de Acessibilidade.* Ph. D. Thesis (Doutorado em Engenharia de Produção) – Programa de Pós-Graduação em Engenharia de Produção, Universidade Federal de Santa Catarina, Florianópolis, Brazil, (1999).
2. L.M.W. Almeida, M.B. Gonçalves, *A methodology to incorporate behavioral aspects in trip distribution models with and application to estimate student flow,* Environment and Planning A, **33**(6), 1125-1138, (2001).
3. M. J. Baxter, G. O. Ewing, *Calibration of Production – Constrained Trip Distribution Models and The Effect of Intervening Opportunities.* Journal Regional Science; **19**(3), 319-330, (1979).
4. M. S. Bazaraa, H. D. Sherali, C. M. Shetty, *Nonlinear Programming – theory and algorithms.* 2. ed. New York: John Wiley & Sons (1993).
5. M. Ben-Akiva, S.R. Lerman. *Discrete Choice Analysis: Theory and Application to Travel Demand,* the MIT Press, Cambridge, Massachusetts (1985).
6. E. T. Bez, *Procedimento de representação de soluções em otimização global: aplicação em modelos de interação espacial.* Ph. D. Thesis (Doutorado em Engenharia de Produção) – Programa de Pós-Graduação em Engenharia de Produção, Universidade Federal de Santa Catarina, Florianópolis, Brazil (2005).
7. E. T.Bez, J. E. Souza de Cursi, M. B. Gonçalves, *Procedimento de Representação em Otimização Global.* In: XXVI Congresso Nacional de Matemática Aplicada e Computacional, 2003, São José do Rio Preto. Resumos das Comunicações do XXVI CNMAC. Rio de Janeiro: SBMAC **1**, 545-545, (2003).
8. E. T. Bez, J. E. Souza de Cursi, M.B. Gonçalves, *A Hybrid Method for Continuous Global Optimization Involving the Representation of the Solution.* 6th World Congress on Structural and Multidisciplinary Optimization – WCSMO6. Rio de Janeiro, RJ, Brazil (2005).
9. M. Bouhadi, R. Ellaia, J.E. Souza de Cursi, *Stochastic perturbation methods for affine restrictions,* Hadjisavvas, Nicolas (ed.) et al., Advances in convex analysis and global optimization. Honoring the memory of C. Caratheodory (1873-1950). Dordrecht: Kluwer Academic Publishers. Nonconvex Optim. Appl., **54**, 487-499, (2001).
10. G. Diplock, S. Openshaw, *Using Simple Genetic Algorithms to Calibrate Spatial Interaction Models.* Geographical Analysis, **28**(3), 262-279, (1996).
11. R. Ellaia, E. Elmouatasim, J.E. Souza de Cursi, *Random Perturbations of variable metric descent in unconstrained nonsmooth nonconvex perturbation,* International Journal of Applied Mathematics and Computer Science, **16**(4), (2006).
12. A.S. Fotheringham, *A new set of Spatial Interaction Models: The theory of competing destinations.* Environment and Planning A, **15**, 15-36, (1983).
13. A.S. Fotheringham, *Spatial Flows and Spatial Patterns.* Environment and Planning A, **16**, 529-543, (1984).
14. A.S. Fotheringham, *Spatial Competition and Agglomeration in Urban Modelling.* Environment and Planning A, **17**, 213-230, (1985).
15. J. P. Gitlesen, I. Thorsen, J. Ubøe, *Misspecifications due to aggregation of data in models for journeys-to-work.* Discussion Paper 13. NHH: Department of Finance and Management Science (2004).

16. M.B. Gonçalves, *Desenvolvimento e Teste de um Novo Modelo Gravitacional – de Oportunidades de Distribuição de Viagens.* Ph. D. Thesis (Doutorado em Engenharia de Produção) – Programa de Pós-Graduação em Engenharia de Produção, Universidade Federal de Santa Catarina, Florianópolis, Brazil (1992).
17. M.B. Gonçalves, I. Ulysséa Neto, *The Development of a new Gravity – Opportunity Model for Trip Distribution.* Environment and Planning, **25**, 817-826, (1993).
18. M.B. Gonçalves, J.E. Souza de Cursi, *Métodos Robustos para a Calibração de Modelos de Interação Espacial em Transportes.* Associação Nacional de Pesquisa e Ensino em Transportes, 11., 1997. Anais... 1997; **2**, 303-313, (1997).
19. M.B. Gonçalves, J.E. Souza de Cursi, *Parameter Estimation in a Trip Distribution Model by Random Perturbation of a Descent Method.* Transportation Research, **35B**, 137-161, (2001).
20. A.O. Griewank, *Generalized descent for global optimization*, Journal of optimization theory and applications, **34**(1), 11-39, (1981).
21. A.J. Horowitz, D.D. Farmer, *A Critical Review of Statewide Travel Forecasting Practice*, University of Wisconsin (http://my.execpc.com/~ajh/Statewid.pdf) (1998).
22. N. Kühlkamp, *Modelo de oportunidades intervenientes, de distribuição de viagens, com ponderação das posições espaciais relativas das oportunidades.* Ph. D. Thesis (Doutorado em Engenharia Civil) - Programa de Pós-Graduação em Engenharia Civil, Universidade Federal de Santa Catarina, Florianópolis, Brazil (2003).
23. J.M. Lowe, A. Sen, *Gravity model applications in health planning: Analysis of an urban hospital market.* Journal of Regional Science, **36**(3), 437-461, (1996).
24. J.D. Ortuzar, L.G. Willumsen, *Modelling Transport.* John Wiley & Sons, New York (1994).
25. M. Pincus, *A closed formula solution of certain programming problems*, Operations Research, **16**(3), 690-694, (1968).
26. M. Pogu, J.E. Souza de Cursi, *Global Optimization by Random Perturbation of the Gradient Method with a Fixed Parameter.* Journal of Global Optimization, **5**, 159-180, (1994).
27. M. Schneider, *Gravity models and trip distribution theory.* Papers and Proceedings of the Regional Science Association, **5**, 51-56, (1959).
28. Y.H. Shi, R.C. Eberhart, *Empirical study of particle swarm optimization,* Congress on Evolutionary Computation. Washington DC, USA, 1945-1950 (1999)
29. H.P. Schwefel, *Evolution and Optimization Seeking.* New York: Wiley (1995).
30. E. Sheppard, *Theoretical underpinnings of the gravity hypothesis*, Geographical Analysis, **10**(4), 386-402, (1978).
31. S. Soot, A. Sen, *A spatial employment and economic development model.* Papers in Regional Science, **70**(2), 149-166, (1991).
32. J.E. Souza de Cursi, *Une Formule de Représentation pour le point d'optimum global d'une fonctionnelle régulière en dimension finie.* Note de Recherche 061/02, LMR, Rouen, France (2002).
33. J.E. Souza de Cursi, *Representation and numerical determination of the global optimizer of a continuous function on a bounded domain*, Floudas, Christodoulos A. (ed.) et al., Frontiers in global optimization. Boston, MA: Kluwer Academic Publishers. Nonconvex Optim. Appl. 74, 517-539, (2004).
34. J.E. Souza de Cursi, R. Ellaia, M. Bouhadi, *Global Optimization under nonlinear restrictions by using stochastic perturbations of the projected gradient*, Floudas, Christodoulos A. (ed.) et al., Frontiers in global optimization. Boston, MA: Kluwer Academic Publishers. Nonconvex Optim. Appl. 74, 541-561, (2004).
35. M.J. Wills, A Flexible *Gravity-Opportunities Model for Trip Distribution.* Transportation Research, **20B**, 89-111, (1986).
36. A.G. Wilson, *A Statistical Theory of Spatial Distribution Models.* Transportation Research, **1**, 253-269, (1967).
37. A.G. Wilson *Entropy in Urban and Regional Modelling.* London: Pion (1970).
38. S.C. Wirasinghe, A.S. Kumarage, *An aggregate demand model for intercity passenger travel in Sri Lanka*, Transportation, **25**, 77-98, (1998).
39. F. Zhao, L.F. Chow, M.T. Li, A. Gan, *Refinement of Fsutms Trip Distribution Methodology.* Final Report, Prepared by Lehman Center for Transportation Research, Department of Civil & Environmental Engineering, Florida International University (2004).

Permissions

All chapters in this book were first published in IJSMDO, by EDP Sciences; hereby published with permission under the Creative Commons Attribution License or equivalent. Every chapter published in this book has been scrutinized by our experts. Their significance has been extensively debated. The topics covered herein carry significant findings which will fuel the growth of the discipline. They may even be implemented as practical applications or may be referred to as a beginning point for another development.

The contributors of this book come from diverse backgrounds, making this book a truly international effort. This book will bring forth new frontiers with its revolutionizing research information and detailed analysis of the nascent developments around the world.

We would like to thank all the contributing authors for lending their expertise to make the book truly unique. They have played a crucial role in the development of this book. Without their invaluable contributions this book wouldn't have been possible. They have made vital efforts to compile up to date information on the varied aspects of this subject to make this book a valuable addition to the collection of many professionals and students.

This book was conceptualized with the vision of imparting up-to-date information and advanced data in this field. To ensure the same, a matchless editorial board was set up. Every individual on the board went through rigorous rounds of assessment to prove their worth. After which they invested a large part of their time researching and compiling the most relevant data for our readers.

The editorial board has been involved in producing this book since its inception. They have spent rigorous hours researching and exploring the diverse topics which have resulted in the successful publishing of this book. They have passed on their knowledge of decades through this book. To expedite this challenging task, the publisher supported the team at every step. A small team of assistant editors was also appointed to further simplify the editing procedure and attain best results for the readers.

Apart from the editorial board, the designing team has also invested a significant amount of their time in understanding the subject and creating the most relevant covers. They scrutinized every image to scout for the most suitable representation of the subject and create an appropriate cover for the book.

The publishing team has been an ardent support to the editorial, designing and production team. Their endless efforts to recruit the best for this project, has resulted in the accomplishment of this book. They are a veteran in the field of academics and their pool of knowledge is as vast as their experience in printing. Their expertise and guidance has proved useful at every step. Their uncompromising quality standards have made this book an exceptional effort. Their encouragement from time to time has been an inspiration for everyone.

The publisher and the editorial board hope that this book will prove to be a valuable piece of knowledge for researchers, students, practitioners and scholars across the globe.

List of Contributors

P.Duysinx, L. Van Miegroet, E. Lemaire and O. Brüls
LTAS - Department of Aerospace and Mechanics, Institute of Mechanics and Civil Engineering, Université de Liège, 4000 Liege, Belgium

M. Bruyneel
Samtech S.A, Liege Science Park. 4031 Angleur, Belgium

Fabiano Maggio
EnginSoft S.p.A., Via Giambellino 7, 35129, Padova, Italy

Y. H. Yang, M. Wan and W.H. Zhang
The Key Laboratory of Contemporary Design & Integrated Manufacturing Technology, Ministry of Education, Northwestern Polytechnical University, P.O. Box 552, 710072 Xi'An, Shaanxi, China

Ke-peng Qiu, Wei-hong Zhanga and Ji-hong Zhu
The Key Laboratory of Contemporary Design & Integrated Manufacturing Technology, Northwestern Polytechnical University, 710072, Xi'an, Shaanxi, China

Begoña González, Gabriel Winter, José Maria Emperador and Blas Galván
Institute of Intelligent Systems and Numerical Applications in Engineering (SIANI), Laboratory of Evolutionary Computation and Applications (CEANI), University of Las Palmas de Gran Canaria, 35.017 Las Palmas de Gran Canaria, Spain

Bendali Salhi , Joseph Lardiès and Marc Berthillier
Institute FEMTO-ST; UMR-CNRS 6174-Department LMARC, 25000, Besancon, France

Sofiane Guessasma
INRA, Reserach Unit Biopolymers Interactions and Assemblies (BIA), rue de la géraudière, 44316 Nantes, France

Kun Marhadi
Computational Science Research Center, San Diego State University, San Diego, United States

Satchi Venkataraman
Department of Aerospace Engineering and Engineering Mechanics, San Diego State University, San Diego, United States

Álvaro Noriega, Ricardo Vijande, Jose Luis Cortizo, Eduardo Rodríguez and Jose Manuel Sierra
Department of Mechanical Engineering, University of Oviedo. Campus de Viesques, 33204 Gijón, Asturias, Spain

Q.Q. Chen, A. Saouab, C.H. Park and J. Bréard
Laboratoire Ondes et Milieux Complexes, FRE 3102, CNRS, Université du Havre, France

P. Boisse
Laboratoire de Mécanique des Contacts et des Structures, UMR 5259, CNRS, INSA Lyon, France

Jun Yan, Geng-dong Cheng and Ling Liu
State Key Lab of Structural Analysis for Industrial Equipment and Department of Engineering Mechanics, Dalian University of Technology, Dalian, 116024, P.R.China

S. Grihon
AIRBUS, Toulouse, France

L. Krog
AIRBUS, Filton, United Kingdom

D. Bassir
TUDelft, Delft, The Netherlands

Gabriel Bugeda
Escola Universitària d'Enginyeria Tècnica Industrial de Barcelona (EUETIB), Universitat Politècnica de Catalunya (UPC), C/ Comte d'Urgell, 187, 08036, Barcelona, Spain
International Center for Numerical Methods in Engineering (CIMNE), Universitat Politècnica de Catalunya (UPC), C/ Gran Capitán s/n, Campus Nord UPC, Módulo C1, 08034, Barcelona, Spain

Juan José Ródenas and José Albelda
Centro de Investigación de Tecnología de Vehículos (CITV), Universidad Politécnica de Valencia (UPV), Camino de Vera s/n, 46022, Valencia, Spain

Eugenio Oñate
International Center for Numerical Methods in Engineering (CIMNE), Universitat Politècnica de Catalunya (UPC), C/ Gran Capitán s/n, Campus Nord UPC, Módulo C1, 08034, Barcelona, Spain

V. Argod and A.D. Belegundu
Mechanical & Nuclear Engineering, Pennsylvania State University, University Park, PA 16802, USA

A. Aziz and V. Agrawala
Research Computing & Cyberinfrastructure, Pennsylvania State University, University Park, PA 16802, USA

R. Jain and and S. D. Rajan
Civil, Environmental and Sustainable Engineering, Arizona State University, Tempe, AZ 85287, USA

Thabet Assem, Hamdaoui Rim and Abdelkrim M.N
Unit Modeling, Analyzes and Control of Systems (MACS), Street Omar Iben Elkhattab Zrig-6029-Gabés (Tunisia)
National School of Engineers of Gabés, Omar Iben Elkhattab Zrig-6029-Gabés (Tunisia)

Michael Bruyneel, Benoît Colson, Philippe Jetteur, Caroline Raick and Alain Remouchamps
SAMTECH s.a., Liège Science Park, 8 Rue des chasseurs-ardennais, 4031, Angleur, Belgium

Stéphane Grihon
Airbus France, 316 Route de Bayonne, 31060, Toulouse, France

Yingjie Xu and Weihong Zhang
Key Laboratory of Contemporary Design & Integrated Manufacturing Technology, Northwestern Polytechnical University, 710072, Xi'an, Shaanxi, China

M. Rezoug,A, R.El Meouche, R. Hamzaoui, J.F Khreim and D. Bassir
FIT / ESTP/ Constructibility Research Institute. 28, avenue du Président Wilson - 94234 Cachan cedex, France

Z.Q Feng
EVRY Laboratory LME-Evry. Evry University, 40 rue du Pelvoux, 91020 Evry, France

Mohamed Sahli, Thierry Barrière and Jean-Claude Gelin
Femto-st Institute, Applied Mechanics dept., CNRS UMR 6174, ENSMM, 25030 Besancon, France

Fatemeh Farhatnia
Islamic Azad University-Branch of Khomeinishahr,Mechanical Engineering Faculty, Boulvard Manzarie, Khomeinishahr, Isfahan, Iran

Arash Golshah
Iran Aircraft Manufacturing (HESA), Moallem Highway, Isfahan, Iran

Pavel Vik, Dias Luís, Pereira Guilherme and José Oliveira
University of Minho, Centro ALGORITMI, Campus de Gualtar, Braga, 4710 - 057, Portugal

Luis Toussaint
Mark IV Systèmes Moteurs, ZA Les grands près N°6, 68370 Orbey, France
M3M Laboratory, Université de Technologie de Belfort-Montbéliard, 90010 Belfort Cedex, France

Nadhir Lebaal, Daniel Schlegel and Samuel Gomes
M3M Laboratory, Université de Technologie de Belfort-Montbéliard, 90010 Belfort Cedex, France

Kun-Nan Chen and Pin-Yung Chen
Department of Mechanical Engineering, Tungnan University, 22202, Taipei, Taiwan

Joseph Lardièsa, Hua Ma and Marc Berthillier
DMA, Institute FEMTO-ST, UMR-CNRS 6174, Besançon, France

Michal Ackermann and Lukáš Čapek
Technical University of Liberec, Dept. of applied mechanics, Studentska 2, 461 17 Liberec 1, Czech Republic

Zdenek Hudec
Technical University of Liberec, KSP, Studentska 2, 46117 Liberec, Czech republic

Fany Chedevergne, Alain Burtheret and Marc Dahan
FEMTO-ST Institute - Department of Applied Mechanics, University of Franche-Comte, 25 000 Besançon, France

Bernard Parratte
Laboratory of Physical Medicine and Rehabilitation, University of Franche-Comte, 25 000 Besançon, France

Dominique Knittel
Centre d'Innovation et de Transfert Technologique (CITT), University of Strasbourg, 17 rue du Maréchal Lefebvre, 67100 Strasbourg
Laboratoire de Génie de la Conception INSA Strasbourg, boulevard de la Victoire, 67084 Strasbourg, France

David Kuhm
Centre d'Innovation et de Transfert Technologique (CITT), University of Strasbourg, 17 rue du Maréchal Lefebvre, 67100 Strasbourg
Laboratoire de Laboratoire de Physique et Mécanique Textiles, ENSISA, 11 rue Alfred Werner, 68093 Mulhouse, France

Jean Renaud
Laboratoire de Génie de la Conception INSA Strasbourg, boulevard de la Victoire, 67084 Strasbourg, France

Nicolas Bérend
System Design and Performance Evaluation Department, Onera, 91120 Palaiseau, France

Philippe Dépincé and Abdelhamid Chriette
Institut de Recherche en Communications et Cybernétique de Nantes, 44321 Nantes, France

Mathieu Balesdent
System Design and Performance Evaluation Department, Onera, 91120 Palaiseau, France CNES, Launchers Directorate, 91023 Evry, France
Institut de Recherche en Communications et Cybernétique de Nantes, 44321 Nantes, France

Edson Tadeu Bez
Universidade do Vale do Itajaí - UNIVALI, Rodovia SC 407, Km 04, CEP 88122-000, São José/SC, Brazil

Mirian Buss Gonçalves
Universidade Federal de Santa Catarina - UFSC, Depto de Engenharia de Produção e Sistemas, 88010-970, Florianópolis/SC, Brazil

José Eduardo Souza de Cursi
LMR - INSA - Rouen, Avenue de l'Université BP 8, Saint-Etienne du Rouvray, FR-76801, France

Index

Printed in the USA
CPSIA information can be obtained
at www.ICGtesting.com
JSHW051430221024
72173JS00006B/1426